Control of the
Onset of Puberty

CONTROL OF THE ONSET OF PUBERTY

Proceedings of a Conference Sponsored by the Growth and Development Branch of the National Institute of Child Health and Human Development held at Airlie, Virginia, October 8–11, 1972

Edited by

MELVIN M. GRUMBACH, M.D.

Department of Pediatrics
University of California-San Francisco
San Francisco, California

GILMAN D. GRAVE, M.D.

Growth and Development Branch
National Institute of Child Health and Human Development
Bethesda, Maryland

FLORENCE E. MAYER, M.D.

Growth and Development Branch
National Institute of Child Health and Human Development
Bethesda, Maryland

A WILEY BIOMEDICAL-HEALTH PUBLICATION

JOHN WILEY & SONS, New York • London • Sydney • Toronto

Library of Congress Cataloging in Publication Data

Main entry under title:

The control of the onset of puberty.

(Clinical pediatrics, maternal, and child health) (A Wiley Biomedical-Health publication)
"Proceedings of a conference sponsored by the Growth and Development Branch of the National Institute of Child Health and Human Development, held at Airlie, Virginia, October 8-11, 1972."
1. Puberty—Congresses. I. Grumbach, Melvin M., ed. II. Grave, Gilman D., ed. III. Mayer, Florence E., ed. IV. United States. National Institute of Child Health and Human Development. Growth and Development Branch. [DNLM: 1. Puberty—Congresses. WS450 C764 1972]

QP84.4.C66   612.6'61   73-18091

ISBN 0-471-32265-2

Printed in the United States of America

10 9 8 7 6 5 4 3 2 1

Organizing Committee

Charles A. Barraclough

Robert M. Blizzard

Frank T. Falkner

Gilman D. Grave

Mortimer B. Lipsett

Florence E. Mayer

Griff T. Ross

Melvin M. Grumbach, Chairman

Contributors

Dr. Max Amoss
Salk Institute for Biological Studies
P.O. Box 1809
San Diego, California 92112

Dr. Robert M. Blizzard
Department of Pediatrics
University of Virginia School of Medicine
Charlottesville, Virginia 22901

Dr. Donald B. Cheek
Royal Children's Hospital Research Foundation
Flemington Road
Parkville, Victoria, 3052. Australia

Dr. Julian M. Davidson
Department of Physiology
Stanford University School of Medicine
Stanford, California 94305

Dr. Donald J. Dierschke
Regional Primate Center
University of Wisconsin
1223 Capitol Court
Madison, Wisconsin 53706

Dr. Bernard Donovan
Department of Physiology
Institute of Psychiatry
De Crespigny Park
London SE 5, England

Dr. Arnold Eisenfeld
Department of Pharmacology and Internal Medicine
Yale University School of Medicine
333 Cedar Street
New Haven, Connecticut 06510

Dr. Charles Faiman
Department of Physiology
University of Manitoba Faculty of Medicine
770 Bannatyne Avenue
Winnipeg, 3, Canada

Dr. Rose E. Frisch
Center for Population Studies, Harvard University
9 Bow Street
Cambridge, Massachusetts 02138

Dr. Roger Gorski
Department of Anatomy
University of California School of Medicine
Los Angeles, California 90024

Dr. Melvin M. Grumbach
Department of Pediatrics
University of California-San Francisco School of Medicine
San Francisco, California 94122

Dr. Alvin E. Hayles
Department of Pediatrics
The Mayo Clinic
Rochester, Minnesota 55901

Dr. Howard E. Kulin
Department of Pediatrics
Milton S. Hershey Medical Center
Hershey, Pennsylvania 17022

Dr. Samuel M. McCann
Department of Physiology
University of Texas Southwest Medical School
5323 Harry Hines Boulevard
Dallas, Texas 75235

Dr. William D. Odell
Division of Endocrinology, Department of Medicine
Harbor General Hospital
1000 West Carson Street
Torrance, California 90509

Dr. Neena B. Schwartz
The Medical School
Northwestern University
Chicago, Illinois 60611

Dr. Emil Steinberger
Program in Reproductive Biology and Endocrinology
University of Texas Medical School
Houston, Texas 77025

Dr. James M. Tanner
Institute of Child Health
University of London
30 Guilford Street
London, WC1, England

Series Preface

The series in Clinical Pediatrics is intended to be a broad consideration of the field.

One area of concern covers modern methodologies, therapies, and advances important in the care of infants and children. Another concern relates to the importance of pediatrics in the whole of human development. As a field it intertwines with obstetrics in the consideration of prenatal and perinatal phenomena and then extends through to problems of adolescence. The full comprehension of the vastness of human developmental biology depends on continued scholarly input from the sciences of biochemistry, physiology, anatomy, psychology, and sociology.

Thus the individual volumes in this series, though seemingly unrelated, will all contribute to our general knowledge of pediatrics and human development.

NORMAN KRETCHMER, M.D., PH.D.
Series Editor

Preface

The physiology of puberty has been a challenging area of research since the beginning of the modern era of endocrinology. The advent of the technology of radioimmunoassay of hormones, the availability of highly purified gonadotropic hormones and synthetic hypothalamic hypophysiotropic hormones, developments in the regulation of endocrine function by the central nervous system, and fresh insights into the action of hormones on cells have provided a deeper understanding of the complex mechanisms involved in the control of puberty. This conference was organized to provide an opportunity for the exchange of ideas in this field by specialists in a variety of disciplines. After considerable discussion the Organizing Committee decided to limit the scope of the conference to aspects of the control of the onset of puberty. The contributors were asked to provide a comprehensive overview of their subjects and were encouraged to include not only published data but the results of their current research when pertinent. The program was designed to gather the available information on control mechanisms at the level of the central nervous system, pituitary gland, gonads, and peripheral tissues, hormonal interactions, and the hormonal, metabolic, and somatic changes affecting or associated with the transition into puberty. A major aim was to provide a forum for animal experimentalists and clinical investigators to compare, contrast, and reconcile, when possible, species variations as well as similarities.

This book records the proceedings of the Conference entitled "The Control of the Onset of Puberty," which was sponsored by the Growth and Development Branch of the National Institute of Child Health and Human Development. The lively exchange of ideas, definition of areas of controversy, and the highlighting of deficient knowledge generated by the presentations and discussions reflect the interest of the participants and the diverse areas of scientific competence they represent.

The Organizing Committee is especially indebted to Dr. Merrill S. Read and the members of the Growth and Development Program, National Institute of Child Health and Development, for their crucial support. The editors gratefully acknowledge the outstanding editorial assistance of Mrs. Anne M. Schmid and Mrs. Lynette M. Helfstein.

MELVIN M. GRUMBACH

San Francisco, California
September 1973

Participants

Dr. Max Amoss
Salk Institute for Biological Studies
San Diego, California 92112

Dr. Conwell Anderson
University of Illinois Medical Center
Chicago, Illinois 60680

Dr. Akira Arimura
Tulane University School of Medicine
New Orleans, Louisiana 70112

Dr. Gilbert August
Children's Hospital
Washington, D.C. 20009

Dr. Nicholas Barnes
The Mayo Clinic
Rochester, Minnesota 55901

Dr. Charles A. Barraclough
University of Maryland
Baltimore, Maryland 21201

Dr. Rafael L. Bejar
Coral Gables, Florida 33146

Dr. Jennifer Bell
Columbia University
New York, New York 10032

Dr. Robert Blizzard
Johns Hopkins University
Baltimore, Maryland 21205

Dr. George J. Bloch
University of California
San Francisco, California 94122

Dr. Emanuel M. Bogdanove
Medical College of Virginia
Richmond, Virginia 23219

Dr. Robert M. Boyar
Montefiore Hospital and
    Medical Center
Bronx, New York 10467

Dr. Donald B. Cheek
Royal Children's Hospital
    Research Foundation
Parkville, Victoria, 3052
Australia

Dr. James Coffey
The University of North Carolina
Chapel Hill, North Carolina 27514

Dr. John F. Crigler, Jr.
The Children's Hospital
    Medical Center
Boston, Massachusetts 02115

Dr. Julian M. Davidson
Stanford University
Stanford, California 94305

Dr. Delbert H. Dayton
National Institute of Child Health
    and Human Development
Bethesda, Maryland 20014

Dr. Donald J. Dierschke
University of Wisconsin
Madison, Wisconsin 53706

Dr. Bernard Donovan
Institute of Psychiatry
London SE 5, England

Dr. Arnold Eisenfeld
Yale University
New Haven, Connecticut 06510

Dr. John Everett
Duke University Medical Center
Durham, North Carolina 27710

Dr. Charles Faiman
University of Manitoba
Winnipeg 3, Canada

Dr. Jordan W. Finkelstein
Montefiore Hospital and
   Medical Center
Bronx, New York 10467

Dr. Delbert A. Fisher
Harbor General Hospital
Torrance, California 90509

Dr. Gilbert Forbes
University of Rochester
Rochester, New York 14620

Dr. Douglas L. Foster
University of Michigan
   Medical Center
Ann Arbor, Michigan 48104

Dr. S. Douglas Frasier
University of Southern California
   Medical Center
Los Angeles, California 90033

Dr. Rose E. Frisch
Harvard University
Cambridge, Massachusetts 02138

Dr. Hortense M. Gandy
Cornell Medical Center
New York, New York 10021

Dr. William F. Ganong
University of California
San Francisco, California 94122

Dr. Vernon L. Gay
University of Pittsburgh
Pittsburgh, Pennsylvania 15213

Dr. Irving I. Geschwind
University of California
Davis, California 95616

Dr. Bruce Goldman
University of Connecticut
Storrs, Connecticut 06268

Dr. Roger Gorski
University of California
Los Angeles, California 90024

Dr. Gilman D. Grave
National Institute of Child Health
   and Human Development
Bethesda, Maryland 20014

Dr. Melvin M. Grumbach
University of California
San Francisco, California 94122

Dr. Peter Hamill
National Center for Health Statistics
Rockville, Maryland 20852

Dr. Sherrel Hammar
Kauikeolani Children's Hospital
Honolulu, Hawaii 96812

Dr. Alvin E. Hayles
The Mayo Clinic
Rochester, Minnesota 55901

Dr. Felix Heald
University of Maryland
Baltimore, Maryland 21205

Dr. Peter Hill
American Health Foundation
New York, New York 10021

Dr. William H. Hoffman
Baltimore, Maryland 21206

Dr. Herbert Jacobson
The Albany Medical College
Albany, New York 12208

Dr. Robert B. Jaffee
University of Michigan
Ann Arbor, Michigan 48104

Dr. J. C. Job
Hôpital Saint Vincent de Paul
Paris, (14e) France

Dr. Ann Johanson
University of Virginia School of
  Medicine
Charlottesville, Virginia 22901

Dr. Donald Johnson
University of Kansas Medical Center
Kansas City, Kansas 66103

Dr. Lois B. Johnson
Cincinnati General Hospital
Cincinnati, Ohio 45229

Dr. Roger Johnsonbaugh
Naval Hospital
Bethesda, Maryland 20014

Dr. Selna L. Kaplan
University of California
San Francisco, California 94122

Dr. Robert P. Kelch
University of Michigan
Ann Arbor, Michigan 48104

Dr. Frederic M. Kenny
University of Pittsburgh
Pittsburgh, Pennsylvania 15213

Dr. Howard E. Kulin
Milton S. Hershey Medical Center
Hershey, Pennsylvania 17022

Dr. Peter Lee
Johns Hopkins Hospital
Baltimore, Maryland 21205

Dr. Margaret MacGillivray
The Children's Hospital of Buffalo
Buffalo, New York 14222

Dr. Samuel M. McCann
The University of Texas
Dallas, Texas 75235

Dr. Charles E. McCormack
Chicago Medical School
Chicago, Illinois 60612

Dr. Bruce S. McEwen
Rockefeller University
New York, New York 10021

Dr. John McKigney
National Institute of Child Health
  and Human Development

Bethesda, Maryland 20014

Dr. Florence E. Mayer
National Heart and Lung Institute
Bethesda, Maryland 20014

Dr. James C. Mittler
Coney Island Hospital
Brooklyn, New York 11235

Dr. John Money
Johns Hopkins University
Baltimore, Maryland 21205

Dr. Thomas Moshang
The Children's Hospital of
  Philadelphia
Philadelphia, Pennsylvania 19146

Dr. William D. Odell
Harbor General Hospital
Torrance, California 90509

Dr. Sergio Ojeda
The University of Texas
Dallas, Texas 75235

Dr. Albert F. Parlow
Harbor General Hospital
Torrance, California 90509

Dr. C. Alvin Paulsen
University of Washington School
  of Medicine
Seattle, Washington 98105

Dr. Leslie Plotnick
Johns Hopkins Hospital
Baltimore, Maryland 21205

Dr. John C. Porter
Southwest Medical School
Dallas, Texas 75235

Dr. Salvatore Raiti
University of Maryland
Baltimore, Maryland 21201

Dr. Judith A. Ramaley
University of Nebraska
  Medical Center
Omaha, Nebraska 68105

Dr. V. Domingo Ramirez
University of California
Los Angeles, California 90024

Dr. Merrill S. Read
National Institute of Child Health
   and Human Development
Bethesda, Maryland 20014

Dr. Russell J. Reiter
The University of Texas
   Medical School
San Antonio, Texas 78229

Dr. John A. Resko
Oregon Regional Primate
   Research Center
Beaverton, Oregon 97005

Dr. Charles H. Rodgers
University of Illinois
Chicago, Illinois 60680

Dr. Allan W. Root
Albert Einstein Medical Center
Philadelphia, Pennsylvania 19141

Dr. Robert Rosenfield
University of Chicago
Chicago, Illinois 60637

Dr. Griff T. Ross
National Institute of Child Health
   and Human Development
Bethesda, Maryland 20014

Dr. Jeffery Roth
University of California
San Francisco, California 94122

Dr. Neena B. Schwartz
University of Illinois Medical Center
Chicago, Illinois 60680

Dr. P. C. Sizonenko
Hôpital Cantonal
Geneva, Switzerland

Dr. Charles A. Snipes
The Hahnemann Medical College and
   Hospital
Philadelphia, Pennsylvania 19102

Dr. R. Steele
Johns Hopkins Hospital
Baltimore, Maryland 21205

Dr. Emil Steinberger
University of Texas Medical School
Houston, Texas 77025

Dr. Marcia L. Storch
The Roosevelt Hospital
New York, New York 10019

Dr. Ronald S. Swerdloff
Harbor General Hospital
Torrance, California 90509

Dr. James M. Tanner
University of London
London, WCIN IEH, England

Dr. Robert Thompson
Johns Hopkins Hospital
Baltimore, Maryland 21205

Dr. Judson J. Van Wyk
University of North Carolina
Chapel Hill, North Carolina 27514

Dr. Michelle P. Warren
Columbia University
New York, New York 10032

Dr. Judith Weisz
Hershey Medical Center
Hershey, Pennsylvania 17033

Dr. Norman Wettenhall
Melbourne, Australia

Dr. Jeremy S. Winter
The Children's Hospital of Winnipeg
Winnipeg 3, Manitoba
Canada

Dr. Samuel S. Yen
University of California, San Diego
La Jolla, California 92037

Contents

Chapter 9.   Delayed Sexual Maturation, with Special Emphasis on the Occurrence of the Syndrome in the Male   238

H. E. KULIN AND E. O. REITER

Discussion   258

BOYAR, FAIMAN, GANONG, GRUMBACH, JOB, MONEY, MOSHANG, OJEDA, SIZONENKO, ROSENFIELD, ROSS, STEINBERGER, SWERDLOFF, TANNER, AND WINTER

Chapter 10.   Ontogeny of Estrogen and Androgen Receptors   271

A. J. EISENFELD

Discussion   307

ARIMURA, BOGDANOVE, DAVIDSON, JACOBSEN, JAFFE, KULIN, RAMALEY, RAMIREZ, RODGERS, SNIPES, AND WEISZ

Chapter 11.   The Role of the Gonads in Sexual Maturation   313

W. D. ODELL AND R. S. SWERDLOFF

Discussion   333

BLOCH, DAVIDSON, GAY, JOHNSON, KULIN, SCHWARTZ, SIZONENKO, SNIPES, STEINBERGER, VAN WYK, WEISZ, AND WINTER

Chapter 12.   The Interrelationship of Steroids, Growth Hormone, and Other Hormones in Pubertal Growth   342

R. M. BLIZZARD, R. G. THOMPSON, A. BAGHDASSARIAN, A. KOWARSKI, C. MIGEON, AND A. RODRIGUEZ

Discussion   360

CHEEK, FAIMAN, FINKELSTEIN, FRASIER, GRUMBACH, MACGILLIVRAY, RAMALEY, ROOT, ROSENFIELD, AND TANNER

Chapter 13.   Follicular Maturation   367

N. B. SCHWARTZ, C. H. ANDERSON, L. G. NEQUIN, AND C. A. ELY

Discussion   382

FISHER, GANONG, GESCHWIND, PAULSEN, RAMIREZ, RODGERS, STEINBERGER, AND WEISZ

Introduction

Puberty, next to birth itself, is the most dramatic change we experience in life, but, unlike birth, we are acutely aware of the exciting transitions through which we pass. Within the space of a few years high-pitched little boys become husky, potent men, and skinny little girls become curvaceous, ovulating women. What triggers these profound metamorphoses? We know a good deal about the hormonal events that accompany puberty but very little about the control of its onset. For too long we have accepted concomitance as causality. The discovery of the hormones of the hypothalamus has made us look at the brain itself as a master endocrine organ which has afferent nervous stimulation, neurohumoral production, and venous effluent drainage and affects target organs at a distance.

The need for a conference on puberty was first identified by Drs. Florence E. Mayer and Merrill S. Read in the Fall of 1971. Dr. Mayer then approached Dr. Melvin M. Grumbach, who suggested holding a seminar on the control of its onset. In addition to classical endocrinologists, the program committee invited neuroanatomists, organic chemists, clinicians, statisticians, nutritionists, and biochemists, 100 in all, to participate.

The program was divided into six sessions: (1) hormonal patterns in pubescence, (2) hypothalamic-pituitary regulation of puberty, (3) central nervous system and puberty, (4) steroid receptors and target organs during puberty, (5) somatic growth patterns and puberty, and (6) gonadal maturation. Concluding comments were delivered by Dr. Bernard Donovan, whose summary appears as the last section of this book. The Organizing Committee is greatly indebted to the chairmen of the sessions, C. A. Barraclough, R. M. Blizzard, W. F. Ganong, M. M. Grumbach, G. T. Ross, and J. J. Van Wyk. They contributed much to stimulate and promote the lively interactions during the discussions of the formal presentations.

The mixture of scientists generated many lively discussions, during which the concept of pubertal control was viewed from different points of view. A resetting of the level of sensitivity to steroid hormones by the hypothalamic gonadostat was the theory of the control of pubertal onset to which most participants adhered; the role of a change in target organ sensitivity was discussed also. A number of participants indicated that there is a hierarchy of levels of control, each of which receives input from elsewhere; even the hypothalamus receives messages from the hippocampus and the cerebral cortex. Ultimate control of pubertal onset may reside in a clock mechanism in the brain, one that senses the diurnal and seasonal cycles of the environment; the onset of puberty is temporal, after all, and may somehow be linked to timed events in nature in a manner similar to mammalian hibernation and avian migration.

The contents of this book represent a thorough compilation of the state of the art today at both the theoretical and the practical level. If few of the key questions received definitive answers at the conference, at least most of them were asked. They are now gathered in this volume in which they will, we hope, stimulate more research on the control of the onset of puberty.

GILMAN D. GRAVE

Bethesda, Maryland

Control of the
Onset of Puberty

1.

Sex Steroid, Pituitary and Hypothalamic Hormones During Puberty in Experimental Animals

S. M. McCANN, S. OJEDA, & A. NEGRO-VILAR

A symposium dedicated to an understanding of the mechanism of induction of puberty should begin with a consideration of the hormone levels found during development. Their interaction with target glands and tissues is undoubtedly responsible for the onset of puberty. The principal problem involved in probing the mystery of puberty is to determine what comes first: changes in hormone levels or changes in target tissue responsiveness to these levels. We stress data obtained in the rat, which has been used more than any other species as a model for this investigation. We discuss the available data from other species as well but exclude data from man.

Abbreviations

FSH	Follicle stimulating hormone
LH	Luteinizing hormone
LH-RH	Luteinizing hormone-releasing hormone
LRF	Luteinizing releasing factor
RF	Releasing factor
RIA	Radioimmunoassay

Analysis of the levels of gonadal steroids, pituitary and plasma gonadotropins, and stored hypothalamic releasing factors are followed by a brief consideration of target tissue responsiveness to releasing factors (RF), pituitary hormones, and gonadal steroids. An attempt has been made to integrate this information into a hypothesis to explain the induction of puberty in the two sexes separately, and to compare and contrast them. We consider the male first because the hormonal control mechanisms are simpler in this sex.

HORMONAL LEVELS DURING DEVELOPMENT IN THE MALE

Plasma Levels of Gonadal Steroids

Because target tissues are exposed to plasma concentrations of hormone, we emphasize these levels. It has been inferred since the classical studies of Pfeiffer (1935) that the infantile male gonad can produce androgens. This concept has been validated by actual measurements of plasma and testicular androgens in fetal animals. Levels of plasma testosterone in the rat are extremely low after birth and gradually rise to adult levels at about the time of puberty (Resko, Feder, & Goy, 1968). A similar pattern for plasma testosterone reported in the bull (Rawlings, Hafs, & Swanson, 1972) rises from undetectable levels at birth to 3.7 ng/ml at 11 months. Puberty, as determined by the presence of sperm, appears to take place between 5 and 8 months. In the rhesus monkey the fetal testis can convert ^{14}C-pregnenolone to testosterone and androstenedione (Resko, 1970). The relatively high levels of testosterone in peripheral blood of the fetus decrease rapidly after birth and remain undetectable until approximately 3 years of age, a time when the monkeys are still in the prepubertal state (Resko, 1967). Testosterone appears at the same time as granular Leydig cells in the testis. Similarly, testosterone in the infant chimpanzee is not detectable in plasma but increases with age (McCormack, 1971). In all species examined so far levels of androstenedione in testes and peripheral blood appears to be relatively higher in neonatal animals than later, and the ratio of testosterone to androstenedione increases with age. Testosterone or its metabolite dihydrotestosterone, rather than androstenedione, is almost certainly responsible for the androgenic actions of testicular secretions, because the androgenic potency of androstenedione is only one-tenth that of testosterone.

The important point, in terms of the induction of puberty, is the level of hormones to which the target tissues are exposed. Because steroid hormones are largely protein-bound, this is undoubtedly the free rather than the total steroid hormone level. Consequently it is of interest to examine steroid binding by plasma proteins at various ages. To our knowledge there has been only one study on this subject. Some complex changes have been observed with development in the rat, but none was clearly related to puberty (Ramaley, 1971). Therefore we can consider that protein binding is approximately constant and that tissue levels of steroids are related directly to the total plasma concentration.

The $t_{1/2}$ disappearance of trace quantities of injected labeled testosterone was similar in immature and adult rats, which suggests that the metabolism of testosterone is not markedly altered at puberty (Ulrich & Kent, 1968). The increase in body size which takes place during development and is accentuated at the time of puberty means that the volume of distribution of testosterone must increase and that hormonal output must increase also to maintain constant levels. The rising plasma testosterone at puberty must be associated with marked increases in testicular hormone output.

Plasma and Pituitary Levels of FSH, LH, and Prolactin

At least 2 factors determine the levels of steroid hormones: (1) the responsiveness of the testes to pituitary hormones and (2) the plasma levels of pituitary hormones that circulate through the gonads. The advent of radio-immunossays (RIA) for the measurement of pituitary hormones has made it possible to quantitate the levels of gonadotropins and prolactin in plasma of developing animals. Serum FSH was not only detectable but somewhat elevated in the neonatal period in male rats (Goldman, Grazia, Kamberi, & Porter, 1971; Ojeda & Ramirez, 1972), and declined by 10 to 15 days before a rise to peak levels at 30 and 35 days (Fig. 1). Thereafter the levels fell to a minimum at 70 days but no higher than those observed at 15 days (Negro-Vilar, unpublished data; Swerdloff, Walsh, Jacobs, & Odell, 1971).

The rise in plasma FSH preceded an acceleration in absolute growth rate of the testes, the growth rate of which became maximal at 25 days, just before the peak of plasma FSH (Fig. 2). The growth rate of sex accessory structures became maximal later, at 35 to 60 days. The decline in plasma FSH, which sets in at 30 to 35 days, was associated with the appearance of mature spermatozoa. Values of plasma FSH had approached a minimum at a time when spermatogenesis had reached normal adult levels, which suggests that a product associated with spermatogenesis is involved in producing this reduction in FSH levels (Swerdloff et al, 1971). This supposition is supported by the fact that plasma levels of FSH did not decline in animals rendered cryptorchid and in which spermatogenesis did not develop normally. These data are consistent with the notion that testicular development is causally related to previous increases in plasma FSH levels.

Plasma luteinizing hormone (LH) was similarly somewhat elevated in

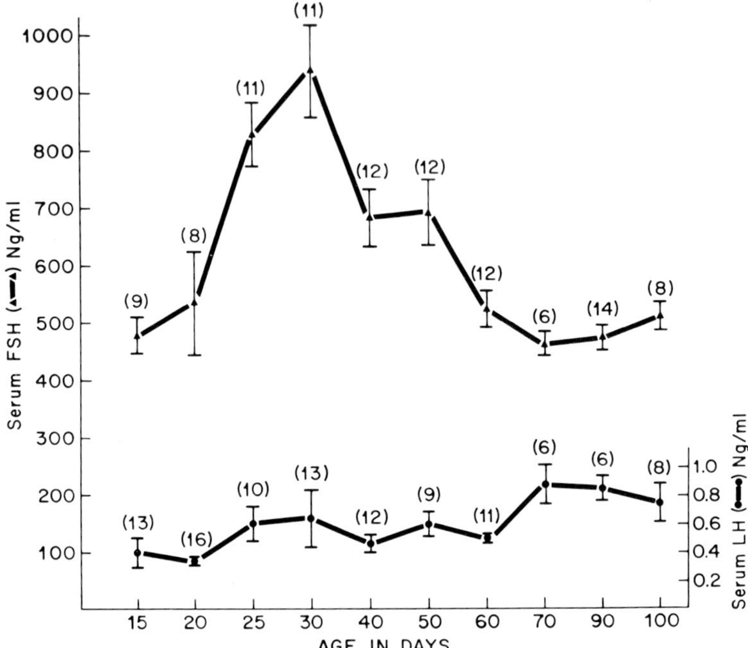

FIG. 1. Serum FSH and LH during development in male rats. Each point is the mean; the vertical bars give the SE. Numbers in parenthesis are the numbers of animals used. Values are given in terms of the NIH-LH-S-1 after conversion from a rat pituitary LH standard. Assay by the Niswender, Midgley, Monroe, and Reichert method (1968). FSH was assayed by the NIAMD kit and values are expressed in terms of the FSH-RP-1 standard.

neonatal male rats and declined to minimum values from day 12 to 15 (Ojeda & Ramirez, 1972). From this minimum value levels of plasma LH rose gradually to reach a maximum at about 70 days (Fig. 1) (Negro-Vilar, unpublished data; Swerdloff et al, 1971). The rise in plasma LH, which accompanies development, although significant statistically is clearly much less pronounced than that of FSH, and there is no secondary decline associated with the onset of spermatogenesis.

Several studies have indicated that prolactin also may play a role in development of sex accessory organs in the male (Hafiez, Philpott, & Bartke, 1971). Consequently an evaluation of the developmental changes in plasma prolactin in males was of interest (Negro-Vilar & Saad, 1972). Plasma prolactin was detectable at all ages studied and rose from low values at 15 and 20 days to an initial peak at 25 days of age (Fig. 3). These elevated levels were maintained until 50 days of age; they then rose

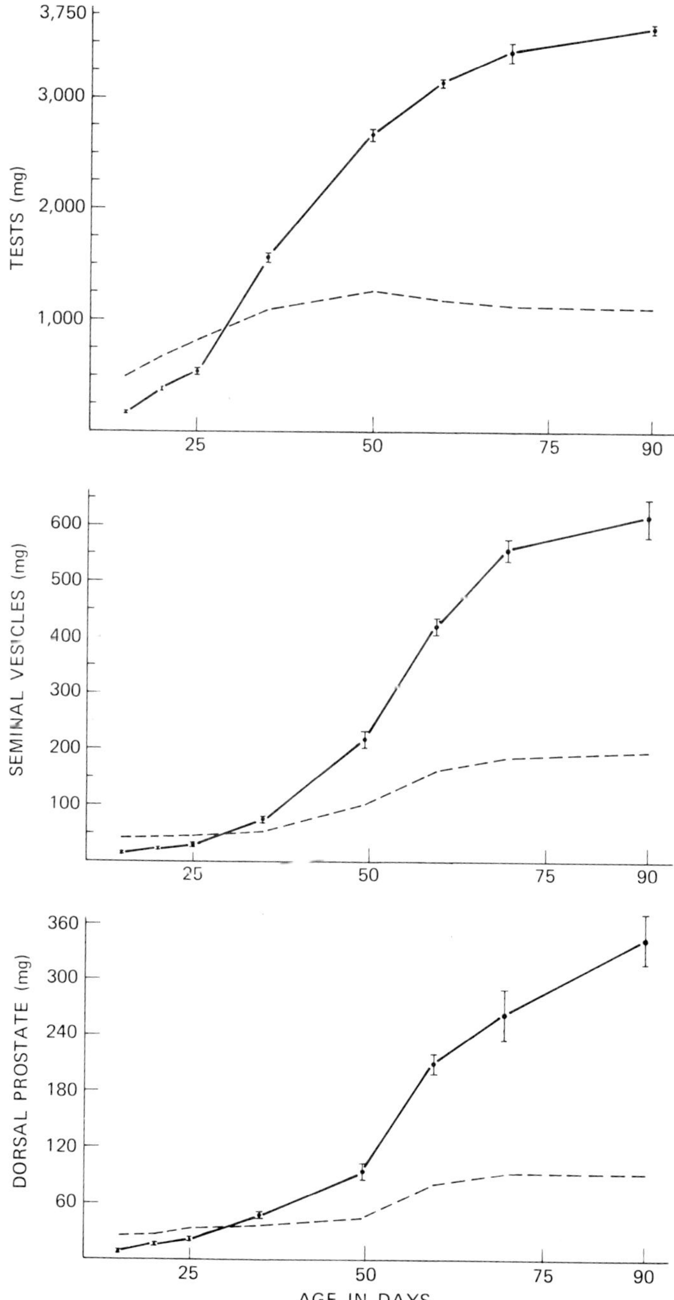

FIG. 2. Absolute (mg) _________ and relative (mg/100 g) _________ weights of testes and accessory organs during development in male rats.

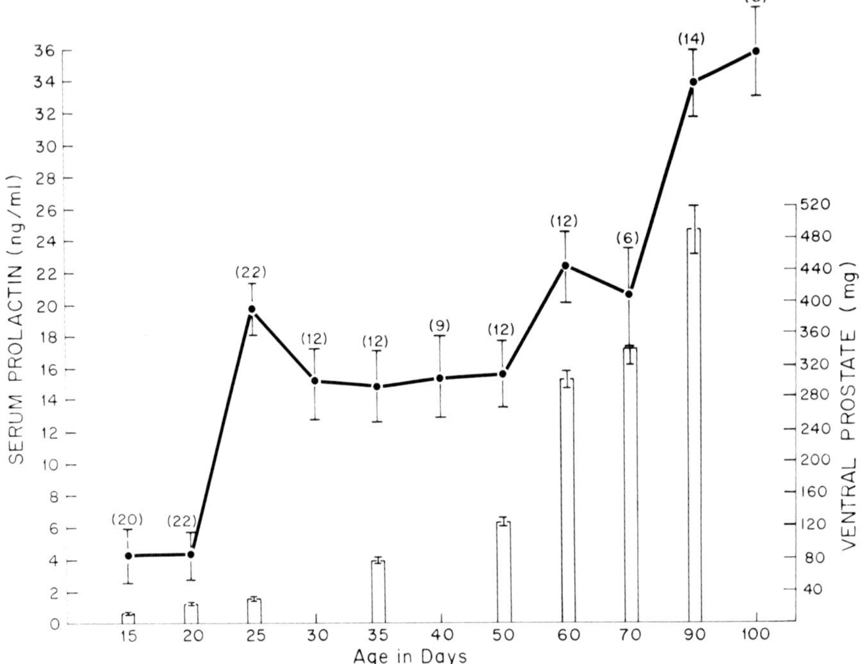

FIG. 3.   Plasma prolactin during development in male rats. The NIAMD kit was used, and values are expressed in terms of the prolactin-RP-1 standard.

significantly between 50 and 100 days. The initial elevation in prolactin at day 25 was associated with beginning growth of sex accessory organs as typified by ventral prostate weight; further accessory organ growth was associated with the second rise in plasma prolactin. We therefore hypothesize that plasma prolactin may synergize with testicular androgens to bring about growth of the testes and sex accessory organs. It has been shown that hypophyseal grafts under the kidney capsule can bring about increased accessory organ weight in immature, intact, hypophysectomized, or adrenalectomized, gonadectomized rats. This would indicate that the hypophysis can secrete sufficient prolactin under certain circumstances to augment growth of accessory organs, even in the absence of androgens (Negro-Vilar & Saad, 1972).

In males it appears that pituitary hormone content roughly parallels the plasma levels of the hormones; for example, pituitary hormone levels of FSH rise to a peak at about 35 days and then fall off to lower levels at puberty (Kragt & Ganong, 1968b; Labhsetwar, 1970). LH rises to a peak at about 60 days, then also falls (Dupon & Schwartz, 1971). To our knowledge no data exist on levels of pituitary prolactin in males during development. These changes in pituitary hormone content suggest that increases in release of the hormones are associated with parallel changes in rates of synthesis during development in male rats.

Few studies of the developmental changes in plasma and pituitary gonadotropins have been carried out in other species. Plasma LH in the bull appears to increase up to 4 months and again between 6 and 10 months. In other words, the increase precedes puberty in this species and is associated with an increase in pituitary LH content up to 6 months (Mac-Millan & Hafs, 1968). Similarly, pituitary FSH content reaches a maximum at 5 to 6 months and then declines.

Response of Gonadotropins to Castration

Castration is followed by elevated levels of plasma gonadotropins at all ages studied from birth to maturity (Ramirez & McCann, 1965; Yamamoto, Dicbcl, & Bogdanove, 1970; Amatayakul, Ryan, Uojumi, & Albert, 1971; Goldman et al, 1971; Swerdloff et al, 1971; Negro-Vilar & Ojeda, unpublished). LH response in the male rat was minimal at days 15 and 28, rose to a peak at day 58 (a time close to puberty), and declined to an intermediate value by day 88 (Fig. 4) (Negro-Vilar & Ojeda, unpublished). These results are consistent with the notion that testicular steroids feed back at the hypothalamic or pituitary level to inhibit gonadotropin secretion even in neonatal male rats. The responsiveness of the hypothalamic-pituitary unit to androgen deprivation appears to be maximal around the time of puberty, at day 58.

Early work suggested that the sensitivity of the hypothalamic-pituitary unit to the negative feedback of androgens declined at the time of puberty and was probably responsible for initiation of increased release of gona-

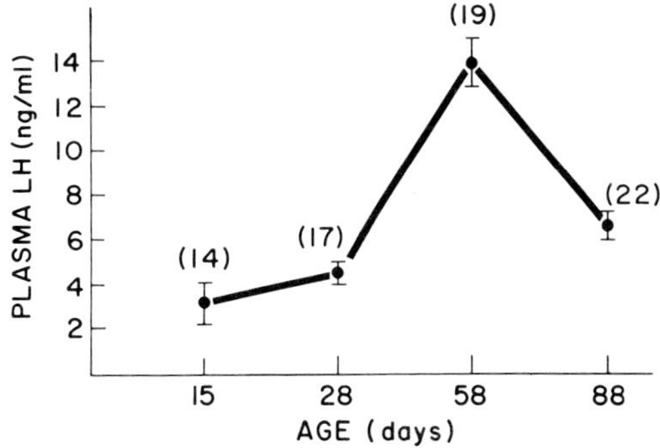

FIG. 4.   Plasma LH 48 hours after castration in male rats of various ages.

dotropin and the induction of puberty. Ramirez and McCann (1965) showed that smaller doses of testosterone replacement therapy (expressed on a body-weight basis) were more capable of inhibiting LH release in prepubertal than in adult rats; this observation supported the concept of a change in the set point of the hypothalamic gonadostat. Because they had measured LH by the ovarian ascorbic acid depletion bioassay, they repeated these studies with the more precise and specific RIA for gonadotropins which also permitted an extension of the study to FSH. In the meantime Jacobs, Swerdloff, and Odell, (1972), who used this technique, observed no change in sensitivity to testosterone feedback.

In our study animals were castrated, then injected subcutaneously once daily for 2 days, either with oil or with various doses of testosterone propionate expressed as μg/100 g body weight to correct for the disparity in weight of the animals during development. Whereas 10 and possibly even 5 μg/100 g body weight of testosterone propionate were sufficient to prevent the rise in plasma LH which occurred 2 days after castration in 15-day-old animals, the suppressibility of plasma LH decreased with age; by 58 days the 10 μg/100 g body-weight dose was no longer effective (Fig. 5). Similarly, the 10 μg/100 g body-weight dose suppressed FSH in 28-day-old animals but no longer did so at 58 days; 25 μg/100 g body weight of testosterone propionate was effective at all times studied.

The difference between the present results and those obtained by Jacobs et al (1972) might have occurred because they did not begin replacement therapy until 5 days after castration, which could have led to a change in the set point of the feedback mechanism. Consequently we repeated the Jacobs experiment. In agreement with their results, when replacement therapy was delayed for 5 days, there was no significant difference in the response of 15- and 58-day-old animals to the 10 μg/100 g body-weight dose of testosterone propionate (Fig. 5). We speculated that removal of the gonads induces an alteration in the set point of the feedback system and sets it to the higher level of androgens encountered in the mature animal. This fits with the early work of Greep and Chester-Jones (1950) in which removal of the gonads of infantile animals followed by their transplantation to the neck resulted in the development of precocious puberty. These animals would have been similarly subjected, for a period, to very low levels of gonadal steroids which could produce an elevation of the set point and result in enhanced release of gonadotropin and induction of puberty.

Hypothalamic Content of Gonadotropin-Releasing Factors

Gonadotropin-releasing factor activity appears in the hypothalamus very early in life; it has even been known to occur in the hypothalamus of fetal

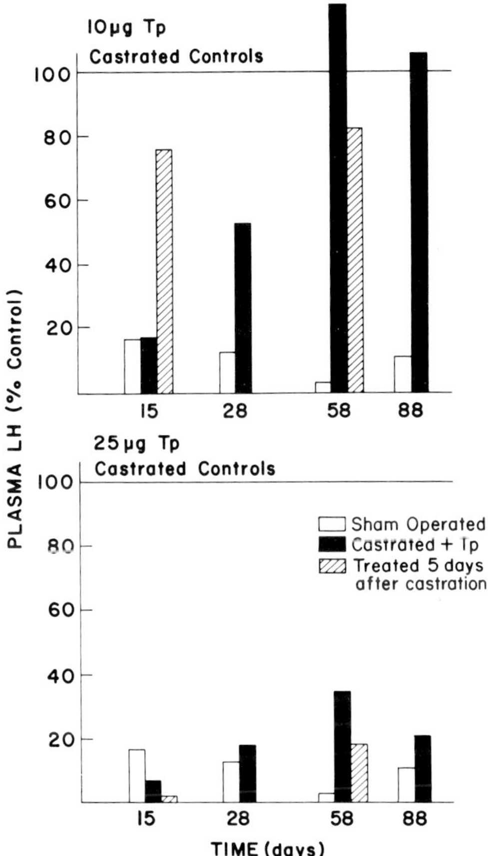

FIG. 5.   Plasma LH (per cent control) 2 days after castration in animals castrated at various ages and treated with daily subcutaneous injections of either testosterone propionate (T_p) or oil (controls). Treatment was started in some rats at 5 days postcastration (hatched bars).

rabbits (Campbell & Gallardo, 1966). Ramirez (1972) followed the LRF activity in boiled hypothalamic extracts of male rats at various ages and found a sharp decline just before the onset of puberty. LRF activity was assayed by measurement of ovarian ascorbic acid depletion induced by the extracts. In maturing bulls LRF was not detected before 5 months of age but increased between 6 and 10 months (MacMillan & Hafs, 1968) in association with an increase in plasma LH as the bulls approached puberty at 5 to 8 months. To our knowledge no studies of the developmental changes in FSH-releasing potency of hypothalamic extracts have been reported in males.

RESPONSES OF TARGET GLANDS TO TROPIC HORMONES

Response of Male Pituitary to LRF

In the only report on the developmental changes in responsiveness to releasing factors in male animals purified LRF was administered to male rats of various ages (Debeljuk, Arimura, & Schally, 1972a). Significant release of LH occurred at all ages studied, beginning at 15 days. The maximal response was observed at 35 and 45 days, the minimal responses at 15 and 40 days. The heightened responsiveness to LRF at 35 and 45 days appears to indicate an increased pituitary sensitivity to the hypo-thalamic hormone before puberty. It is not clear, however, when puberty actually occurred in these animals, for neither organ weights nor the status of spermatogenesis were reported.

Effect of Age on Responsiveness of the Testes to Gonadotropin and of Target Tissues to Androgens

One hypothesis, advanced by Hooker (1942), holds that puberty is caused by an increase in end-organ responsiveness to constant levels of androgens. A correlate to this hypothesis is that the phenomenon might also be related to an enhanced sensitivity of the testes to constant doses of gonadotropins from birth to maturity. On the other hand, Hooker (1942) reported a definitely enhanced responsiveness of sex accessory organs to androgens at the time of puberty. This has been confirmed in the rat by Ojeda and Ramirez (1972), who found a decrease in the minimal effective dose of testosterone needed to increase the weight of seminal vesicles between 46 and 66 days, i.e., when puberty is taking place.

HORMONAL LEVELS DURING DEVELOPMENT IN THE FEMALE

Plasma Levels of Gonadal Steroids

The infantile ovary also produces estrogenic steroids long before puberty, for the removal of the gonads results in uterine atrophy when the animal is operated on at 2 days of age and killed after 12, but not after 6 (Price, 1947). In the experiments of Price and Ortiz (1944) gonadotropins failed to increase uterine weight when administered during the first 6 days of life but were effective when the treatment was started at 4 days. From these data it can be inferred that the output of estrogen in the neonatal period is almost nonexistent and cannot be stimulated by gonadotropins but that it certainly begins at about 5 days. In the only report of levels of plasma estrogen during development a fluorometric method was used to deter-mine estrogens after preliminary purification (Presl, Herzmann, & Horsky, 1969). At 5 days the levels were similar to those observed in adult ovariectomized, adrenalectomized rats, which led to the conclusion that there was no detectable estrogen at this time. After day 5, up to and including 55 days, detectable levels were observed which, surprisingly enough, did not change and were similar whether the vagina was open or closed. There was a later rise in plasma estrogen at 65 to 70 days, the first appearance of which could be correlated with ovarian 3β-hydroxysteroid dehydrogenase and follicular cavitation. The second rise, beginning at 65 to 70 days, was associated with an increase in the levels of 3β-hydroxysteroid dehydrogenase.

In the male there was little evidence to support the view that the metabolism of testosterone changed at the time of puberty. In the female it is considerably different. On the basis of experiments in which hemi-ovaries were grafted to the spleen Donovan and O'Keefe (1966) concluded that the liver developed an increasing capacity to inactivate estrogens near the time of puberty. In a subsequent experiment Donovan, O'Keefe, and O'Keefe (1967) implanted pellets of estradiol of a constant size in the spleen at different ages in developing females and did observe inactivation by the liver at all ages, an inactivation that increased with age. Because a constant-sized pellet was used in rats of increasing size, it is hard to draw quantitative conclusions from these data. The initial short, but not the later long, $t_{1/2}$ of labeled estradiol was greater in adult than in immature female rats (Ulrich & Kent, 1968). de Hertogh, Ekka, Vanderheyden, and Hoet (1970) studied the metabolic clearance rates of estrone and estradiol in immature and adult female rats and found an increase in the metabolic clearance rate of both steroids in the adult compared with the immature animals. When corrected for differences in body size, the clearance rates for estradiol were quite similar to those observed in man. These data indicate an increase in metabolism of estrogen, probably largely by the liver, in adult compared with immature females; however, such an alteration has not yet been demonstrated experimentally (Brown & Meyer, 1958). If estrogen inactivation increases with age, then rates of estrogen production by the gonads must increase to maintain the apparently constant levels of hormone observed during development. Because the volume of distribution would also be increasing with enlarging size, the estrogen production by the mature ovary must be much greater than that of the immature organ.

Plasma and Pituitary Levels of FSH, LH, and Prolactin

Recent measurements by RIA have clarified the levels of these hormones during development. The pattern of levels of release of FSH is unlike that described previously in the male. In the female plasma FSH rises from already elevated levels at 5 days to a peak at 15 days; it then declines to minimal levels at about the time of puberty and is maintained even after vaginal opening (Fig. 6). This contrasts with the pattern previously described in the male in which the high levels observed at 5 days were followed by a decline at 10 to 15 days, a time when peak levels were observed in the females. A second peak at 25 to 30 days in the males was not observed in females. Thus ovarian development follows an initial peak in the face of relatively low levels of FSH (Ojeda & Ramirez, 1972; Negro-Vilar, unpublished data, 1972).

Patterns of LH (Fig. 6) are quite similar for male and female in that the initial high levels begin to decline to minimal values at approximately 15 days and remain low until the time of puberty (Ojeda & Ramirez, 1972; Negro-Vilar, unpublished data, 1972). The first ovulation, which coincides with vaginal opening, is preceded by a preovulatory peak of LH, as in adult animals (Ramirez & Sawyer, 1965; Ojeda & Ramirez, 1972). Thus, as with FSH, the female gonads develop after exposure to relatively high levels of LH only in the very early days of life.

Voogt, Chen, & Meites (1970) observed low levels of plasma prolactin

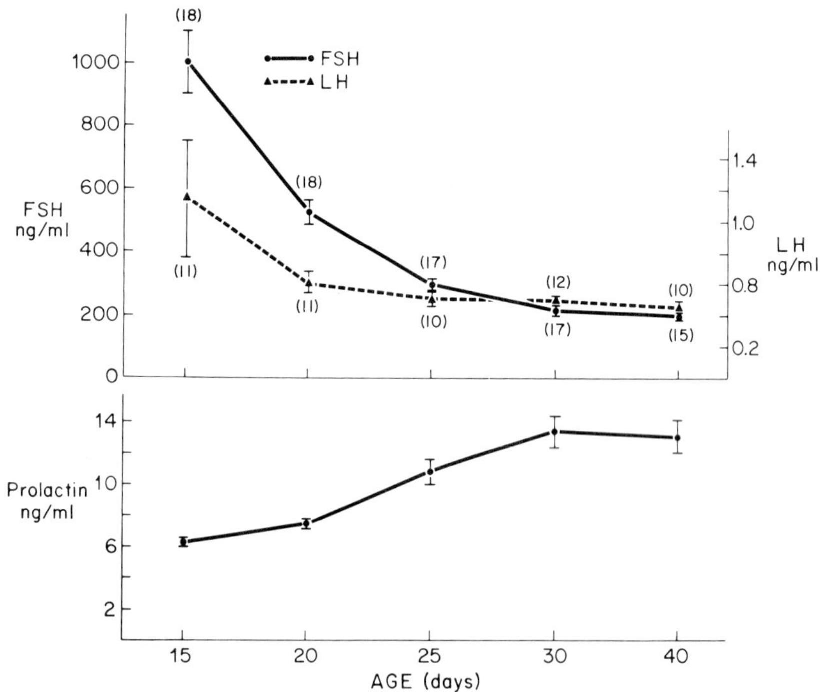

FIG. 6.   Plasma gonadotropins and prolactin during development in female rats.

during development until the day before vaginal opening, at which time plasma levels rose; they remained high at the first estrus after vaginal opening. The elevation in plasma gonadotropins and prolactin observed just before vaginal opening is probably brought about by estrogen, just as it is before ovulation in the adult rat (McCann, 1972). When plasma prolactin was measured at more frequent intervals during development (Negro-Vilar, unpublished data, 1972; Fig. 6), it was found to be low at 15 and 20 days; it then rose at 25 days to higher levels which were maintained after puberty.

In the only study of plasma levels of these hormones during development in a species other than rat Swanson, Hafs, and Morrow (1972) found increasing LH levels in plasma at the time of approaching first estrus in heifers; this was followed by an estrous peak and lower values were observed between subsequent estrous periods. Prolactin was similarly elevated before the first estrus and then decreased; subsequent elevations took place just before each estrus. This pattern is quite similar to that described in the rat.

In studies of the developmental changes in pituitary LH content, determined by the Parlow assay, Dupon and Schwartz (1971) observed a gradual rise in pituitary LH, followed by a decline near puberty. This confirms the earlier observation of Ramirez and Sawyer (1965) that a decline in pituitary LH occurs at the time of vaginal opening in the rat. A number of workers (Kragt & Ganong, 1968a; Watanabe & McCann, 1969; Labhsetwar, 1970; Kragt & Dahlgren, 1972) have observed that pituitary FSH content is high in immature females and declines as puberty approaches. There is little correlation between the rates of LH release in females, as indicated by plasma levels and pituitary content, except at the time of the preovulatory release when high plasma levels are followed by a decline in LH content. There is an excellent correlation, however, between plasma and pituitary levels of FSH, both of which fall slowly as puberty approaches. An acute drop in pituitary FSH presumably follows an elevation of plasma FSH just before ovulation. Voogt et al (1970) found that levels of pituitary prolactin correlate with plasma levels; they are low initially and rise after puberty. These changes in pituitary prolactin content were attributed to estrogen.

Response of Gonadotropins to Castration

Castration in males is followed by elevated levels of plasma gonadotropins at all ages from birth to maturity. This is in contrast to the situation in females in which no rises in FSH and LH have been observed in the neonatal period (Goldman et al, 1971; Ojeda & Ramirez, 1972). If the infantile ovary is producing no steroids, then no effect from castration would be expected. An alternate explanation for the failure of gonadotropins to rise after ovariectomy is the possibility that estrogen receptors may not be present in the hypothalamus at this time (Kato, Atsumi, & Inaba, 1971; Ramirez, 1972).

At later times an increase in the release of LH follows removal of the ovaries; for example, in the early work of Ramirez and McCann (1963) ovariectomy on day 10 was followed by high levels of LH in plasma by day 25, indistinguishable from levels found in adult castrates. They also used replacement therapy with varying doses of estradiol benzoate and found, as in the male, that a larger dose of estradiol benzoate (expressed in terms of body weight of the animal) was required in adult than in immature animals to inhibit the LH rise after ovariectomy. They postulated that, as in males, a resetting of the hypothalamic gonadostat might be responsible for the induction of puberty in the female. In view of the altered metabolism of estrogen, which appears to take place during development, it is more difficult to be sure of this conclusion. In fact, to establish this hypothesis, it would be necessary to monitor estrogen levels in plasma after replacement therapy to determine whether higher plasma levels must be achieved in adult than in immature animals to inhibit gonadotropin secretion.

Hypothalamic Content of Gonadotropin Releasing Factors

As we have indicated, gonadotropin releasing factors are present in the hypothalamus even in fetal life, and the pituitary can respond to them. This has been re-emphasized in a study by Foster et al (1972) in fetal and neonatal lambs. Ramirez and Sawyer (1966) observed a decline in stored LRF at the time of natural or estrogen-induced puberty in the rat. Similarly, Corbin and Daniels (1967) observed a decline in activity of FSH releasing factor (FSH-RF) at the time of puberty in females, and a lesser but significant decline was observed by Watanabe and McCann (1969) and Kragt and Dahlgren (1972). From these studies it would appear that the surge of gonadotropins just before vaginal opening and first ovulation in the rat is brought about by a discharge of gonadotropin releasing factors.

RESPONSES OF TARGET GLANDS TO TROPIC HORMONES

Response of the Female Pituitary to LRF

Debeljuk, Arimura, and Schally (1972b), who tested pituitary responsiveness to synthetic LRF at various ages, found that the maximal increase in plasma LH occurred when the first tests were performed at day 15. The sensitivity to LRF declined to a minimum at day 35, i.e., at the time of puberty; it then increased somewhat to a constant level between 45 and

210 days. The high responsiveness at 15 days fits with the elevated levels of plasma LH found at this time by other workers; in this particular study, however, no detectable LH was observed before injection of LRF. These workers observed a pattern of FSH release in response to synthetic LRF similar to that previously described for LH; they found that it declined from a maximum at 15 days to an undetectable response at 35 or more days. Because no effort was made to determine the actual time of puberty in these studies, the results are difficult to interpret, but if we assume that puberty took place at about 35 days, it would be associated, if anything, with a reduction in sensitivity to LRF.

Effect of Age on the Responsiveness of the Ovaries to Gonadotropins and the Sensitivity of Target Tissues to Estrogen

It could be postulated that puberty is due, as in the male, to increased end-organ responsiveness to constant levels of hormones. Without reviewing the extensive literature on ovarian responsiveness to gonadotropins (for references, see Ramirez, 1972; Greenwald & Peppler, 1968), we can say that an early period during which there may be no response to gonadotropins is followed by a period of responsiveness without ovulation. After the development of antral follicles ovulation can be induced long before puberty. Zarrow and Wilson (1961) and Ramirez (1971) have even reported a period of decreased responsiveness to gonadotropins before the onset of puberty. It appears likely that an increase in ovarian responsiveness to gonadotropins is not responsible for puberty in the female. There seems to be a change in the sensitivity of the uterus to stimulation by estradiol in the female rat. Uterine growth induced by a given dose of estradiol reaches a maximum at the time of puberty (Ojeda & Ramirez, cited by Ramirez, 1972).

DISCUSSION AND CONCLUSIONS

With the wealth of new data on hormone levels during development is it now possible to develop a coherent theory for the induction of puberty? Certain facts are clear. First of all, the hypothalamic-pituitary machinery is essentially intact at birth, as indicated by the presence of stored gonadotropin releasing factors in the hypothalamus and relatively high levels of gonadotropins in plasma. In the male the gonad is already producing small quantities of androgens and therefore is susceptible to gonadotropic stimulation. In the female, on the other hand, it is doubtful whether the ovary has the capacity to respond to gonadotropins until around day 5 in the rat. In the male the feedback of testicular androgens is sufficient initially to hold the secretion of FSH in check, but later, around day 30, plasma FSH rises to a peak. FSH levels then decline, perhaps because of the feedback action of a hormonal product secreted by the testes as spermatogenesis commences. The high levels of FSH accompanied by relatively low levels of LH (probably kept low by testicular androgen) are sufficient to bring about testicular development with consequent secretion of androgen and stimulation of male accessory organs. The rising levels of prolactin from day 25 may also be involved in the stimulation of testicular growth, androgen secretion and further development of sex accessory organs. The cause of the enhanced secretion of prolactin which begins at about day 25 is unknown. Because testosterone levels rise with the onset of puberty, accompanied by a slight further elevation of LH and relatively constant levels of FSH, it is probable that a change occurs in the set point for control of gonadotropins in the male; recent studies with replacement therapy in castrates support the reset hypothesis. Clearly this is not the only factor involved in male puberty, and an additional element may enhance end-organ sensitivity to hormones. This has been demonstrated in the male accessory organs.

In the female the situation is somewhat different in that high levels of gonadotropins are present at an early age, perhaps because of failure of the ovary to produce steroids and/or a lack of estrogen receptors in the hypothalamic-pituitary unit to mediate negative feedback. Gonadotropin levels fall progressively thereafter until the first ovulation. Consequently one could postulate that the initial high levels of gonadotropins are sufficient to initiate ovarian development, which continues in the presence of relatively low levels of gonadotropins. Levels of prolactin rise gradually during development, but its function at this stage in the female is speculative. It is not clear whether a change in set point for negative feedback takes place in the female because the levels of gonadotropins are falling and are associated with rising or constant levels of estrogen. No change in estrogen levels was observed in the only study available (Presl et al, 1969). It appears that the metabolic clearance of estrogen increases with development; this is indicative of increased release of hormones by the ovary. It is possible to induce ovulation in the immature rat by treatment with gonadotropins or with estrogen, which would seem to indicate that the site for positive feedback of estrogen in the hypothalamic-pituitary unit is developed long before puberty (McCormack & Meyer, 1962). Therefore we postulate that the cyclic timing mechanism operative in adult animals interacts with these levels of estrogen to induce an ovulatory discharge of gonadotropins and prolactin after estrogen levels from preovulatory follicles reach a sufficient level. Under the influence of the discharge of gonadotropins a new crop of follicles matures, and the adult pattern of cyclic activity is assumed gradually. There may be alterations in sensitivity of end organs to gonadotropins and sex steroids in females, as also postulated in the male.

In conclusion puberty appears to be brought about in both male and female by a complex series of events that takes place at all levels of the reproductive tract. It consists of changes in sensitivity of sex accessory organs and gonads and alterations in secretion of gonadotropins brought about by altered rates of release and possibly by altered sensitivity to gonadotropin releasing factors which are probably caused by changes in the negative feedback of gonadal steroids.

REFERENCES

Amatayakul, K., Ryan, R., Uozumi, T., & Albert, A. (1971). A reinvestigation of testicular-anterior pituitary relationships in the rat. *Endocrinology* **88**, 872–880.

Brown, F. U. & Meyer, R. K. (1958). *In vitro* inactivation of three naturally occurring estrogens by liver from fetal, newborn, day-old and adult rats. *Am. J. Physiol.* **195**, 179–184.

Campbell, H. J. & Gallardo, E. (1966). Gonadotropin-releasing activity of the median eminence at different ages. *J. Physiol.* **186**, 689–697.

Corbin, A. & Daniels, E. L. (1967). Changes in concentration of female rat pituitary FSH and stalk-median eminence follicle stimulating hormone releasing factor with age. *Neuroendocrinology* **2**, 304–314.

Debeljuk, L., Arimura, A., & Schally, A. V. (1972a). Studies on the pituitary responsiveness to luteinizing hormone-releasing hormone (LH-RH) in intact male rats of different ages. *Endocrinology* **90**, 585–588.

Debeljuk, L., Arimura, A., & Schally, A. V. (1972b). Pituitary responsiveness to LH-releasing hormone in intact female rats of different ages. *Endocrinology* **90**, 1499–1502.

deHertogh, R., Ekka, E., Vanderheyden, I., & Hoet, J. J. (1970). Metabolic clearance rates and the interconversion factors of estrone and estradiol-17β in the immature and adult female rat. *Endocrinology* **87**, 874–880.

Donovan, B. T. & O'Keefe, M. C. (1966). The liver and the feedback action of ovarian hormones in the immature rat. *J. Endocrinol.* **34**, 469–478.

Donovan, B. T., O'Keefe, M. C., & O'Keefe, H. T. (1967). Intrasplenic implants of estradiol and uterine growth in infantile and pubertal rats. *J. Endocrinol.* **37**, 93–98.

Dupon, C. & Schwartz, N. B. (1971). Pituitary LH patterns in prepubertal normal and testosterone-sterilized rats. *Neuroendocrinology* **7**, 236–248.

Foster, D. L., Roach, J. F., Karsch, F. J., Norton, H. W., Cook, B., & Nalbandov, A. V. (1972). Regulation of LH in the fetal and neonatal lamb. I. LH in blood and pituitary. *Endocrinology* **90**, 102–111.

Goldman, B., Grazia, Y. R., Kamberi, I. A., & Porter, J. C. (1971). Serum gonadotropin concentrations in intact and castrated neonatal rats. *Endocrinology* **88**, 771–776.

Greenwald, G. S. & Peppler, R. D. (1968). Prepubertal and pubertal changes in the hamster ovary. *Anat. Record* **161**, 447–458.

Greep, R. O. & Chester-Jones, I. (1950). Steroid control of pituitary function. *Rec. Progr. Hormone Res.* **5**, 197–261.

Hafiez, A. A., Philpott, J. E., & Bartke, A. (1971). Role of prolactin in regulation of testicular function. *J. Endocrinol.* **50**, 619–623.

Hooker, C. W. (1942). Pubertal increase in responsiveness to androgen in the male rat. *Endocrinology* **30**, 77–84.

Jacobs, H. S., Swerdloff, R. S., & Odell, W. D. (1972). Personal communication.

Kato, J., Atsumi, Y., & Inaba, M. (1971). Development of estrogen receptors in the rat hypothalamus. *J. Biochem.* **70**, 1051–1053.

Kragt, C. L. & Dahlgren, J. (1972). Development of neural regulation of follicle stimulating hormone (FSH) secretion. *Neuroendocrinology* **9**, 30–40.

Kragt, C. L. & Ganong, W. F. (1968a). Pituitary FSH content in female rats at various ages. *Endocrinology* **82**, 1241–1244.

Kragt, C. L. & Ganong, W. F. (1968b). Pituitary FSH content in male rats at various ages. *Proc. Soc. Exptl. Biol. Med.* **128**, 965–967.

Labhsetwar, A. P. (1969). Age-dependent changes in pituitary gonadal relationship. II. A study of pituitary FSH and LH content in the female rat. *J. Reprod. Fertil.* **20**, 21–28.

Labhsetwar, A. P. (1970). Age-dependent changes in pituitary gonadal relationship. III. Changes in pituitary LH and FSH levels in the male rat. *J. Reprod. Fertil.* **21**, 407–415.

McCann, S. M. (1972). Regulation of the secretion of follicle stimulating hormone and luteinizing hormone. In *Handbook of Physiology* (E. Knobil, Ed.). In press.

McCormack, C. E. & Meyer, R. K. (1962). Ovulating hormone release in gonadotropin-treated immature rats. *Proc. Soc. Exptl. Biol. Med.* **110**, 343–346.

McCormack, S. A. (1971). Plasma testosterone concentration and binding in the chimpanzee; effect of age. *Endocrinology* **89**, 1171–1177.

MacMillan, K. L. & Hafs, H. D. (1968). Pituitary and hypothalamic endocrine changes associated with reproductive development of Holstein bulls. *J. Anim. Sci.* **27**, 1614–1620.

Negro-Vilar, A. & Saad, W. A. (1972). Influence of prolactin-secreting pituitary homografts on male sex accessory organs. *Proc. IV Intl. Congr. Endocrinology* **73** (abstract).

Niswender, G. D., Midgley, Jr., A. R., Monroe, S. E., & Reichert, Jr., L. E. (1968). Radioimmunoassay for rat luteinizing hormone with antiovine LH serum and ovine LH[131]I. *Proc. Soc. Exptl. Biol. Med.* **128**, 807–811.

Ojeda, S. R. & Ramirez, V. D. (1972). Plasma LH and FSH in maturing rats: response to hemigonadectomy. *Endocrinology* **90**, 466–472.

Pfeiffer, C. A. (1935). Origin of functional differences between male and female hypophyses. *Proc. Soc. Exptl. Biol. Med.* **32**, 603–605.

Presl, J., Herzmann, J., & Horsky, J. (1969). Oestrogen concentration in blood of developing rats. *J. Endocrinol.* **45**, 611–612.

Price, D. (1947). The influence of maternal hormones on the reproductive organs of suckling rats. *Anat. Record* **97**, 519–549.

Price, D. & Ortiz, E. (1944). The relation of age to reactivity in the reproductive system of the rat. *Endocrinology* **34**, 215–239.

Ramaley, J. A. (1971). Steroid binding to serum proteins in maturing male and female rats. *Endocrinology* **89**, 545–552.

Ramirez, V. D. (1971). Sex and brain-pituitary function at puberty. In *Steroid Hormones and Brain Function* (C. H. Sawyer & R. A. Gorski, Eds.), UCLA Forum in Medical Sciences, Los Angeles, California, pp. 301–310.

Ramirez, V. D. & McCann, S. M. (1963). A comparison of the regulation of luteinizing hormone (LH) secretion in immature and adult rats. *Endocrinology* **72**, 452–464.

Ramirez, V. D. & McCann, S. M. (1965). Inhibitory effect of testosterone on luteinizing hormone secretion in immature and adult rats. *Endocrinology* **76**, 412–417.

Ramirez, V. D. & Sawyer, C. H. (1965) Advancement of puberty in the female rat by estrogen. *Endocrinology* **76**, 1158–1168.

Ramirez, V. D. (1972). Endocrinology of puberty. In *Handbook of Physiology* (R. O. Greep, Ed.). In press.

Ramirez, V. D. & Sawyer, C. H. (1966). Changes in hypothalamic luteinizing hormone releasing factor (LH-RF) in the female rat during puberty. *Endocrinology* **78**, 958–964.

Rawlings, W. C., Hafs, H. D., & Swanson, L. V. (1972). Testicular and blood plasma androgens in Holstein bulls from birth through puberty. *J. Anim. Sci.* **34**, 435–440.

Resko, J. A. (1967). Plasma androgen levels of the Rhesus monkey, effects of age and season. *Endocrinology* **81**, 1203–1212.

Resko, J. A. (1970). Androgen secretion by fetal and neonatal Rhesus monkey. *Endocrinology* **87**, 680–687.

Resko, J. A., Feder, H. H., & Goy, R. W. (1968). Androgen concentrations in plasma and testis of developing rats. *J. Endocrinol.* **40**, 485–491.

Swanson, L. V., Hafs, H. D., & Morrow, D. A. (1972). Ovarian characteristics and serum LH, prolactin, progesterone and glucocorticoid from first estrus to breeding size in Holstein heifers. *J. Anim. Sci.* **34**, 284–293.

Swerdloff, R. S., Walsh, P. C., Jacobs, H. S., & Odell, W. D. (1971). Serum LH and FSH during sexual maturation in the male rat; effect of castration and cryptorchidism. *Endocrinology* **88**, 120–128.

Ulrich, R. S. & Kent, J. R. (1968). The disappearance rates of sex steroids in immature and mature rats. *Proc. Soc. Exptl. Biol. Med.* **128**, 1093–1096.

Voogt, J. L., Chen, C. L., & Meites, J. (1970). Serum and pituitary prolactin levels before, during and after puberty in female rats. *Am. J. Physiol.* **218**, 396–399.

Watanabe, S. & McCann, S. M. (1969). Alterations in pituitary follicle-stimulating hormone (FSH) and hypothalamic FSH-releasing factor (FSH-RF) during puberty. *Proc. Soc. Exptl. Biol. Med.* **132**, 195–201.

Yamamoto, M., Diebel, N. D., & Bogdanove, E. M. (1970). Analysis of initial and delayed effects of orchidectomy and ovariectomy on pituitary and serum LH levels in adult and immature rats. *Endocrinology* **86**, 1102–1111.

Zarrow, M. X. & Wilson, E. D. (1961). The influence of age on superovulation in the immature rat and mouse. *Endocrinology* **69**, 851–855.

DISCUSSION

DR. ODELL. You indicated that the high testosterone levels in the male rat near birth, which fall as the animal ages, might be due to gonadotropins produced by the placenta. Do you know of any evidence that the rat placenta produces gonadotropins?

DR. McCANN. The pituitary is required in the early stages of pregnancy in the rat. But after day 12, if one hypophysectomizes the animal, pregnancy continues, presumably because a gonadotropin of placental origin continues to stimulate the corpora lutea. The rat data are from Resko, Feder, and Goy (1968) who did the analyses by gas chromatography and then quantified them by electron capture. The results obtained by Resko in the rhesus monkey were similar; again there were initially high values in the newborn. They also measured testosterone in the fetal monkey. After birth the levels went down and practically disappeared but began to rise in the prepubertal stage. The values obtained by Hafs' group in the bull are similar, as are McCormack's results in the chimpanzee.

DR. SNIPES. Our data agree with Dr. Resko's group (Rivarola, Forest, & Migeon, 1968; Snipes, Forest, & Migeon, 1969).

DR. ODELL. Gonadotropins are produced by the elephant placenta, the pregnant mare's cusps, and the primate placenta, but not by other mammals.

DR McCANN. Perhaps the placental prolactin-like hormone maintains the corpora in late pregnancy in the rat.

DR. FOSTER. It was shown by Linkie and Niswender that there is a placental gonadotropin or gonadotropin of pregnancy in the rat .

DR. GANONG. On the question of whether or not gonadotropins from the placenta are involved, Mel Grumbach pointed out that in rabbits hypophysectomized in utero there is no early rise in testosterone. So the rise in the rabbit is clearly dependent on the pituitary.

DR. ARIMURA. Dr. McCann, I understand you to say that in male rats the effect of castration on LH release was most striking at the age of 58 days, which may be due to the change in the sensitivity of the pituitary to luteinizing-hormone releasing hormone (LH-RH). Our experimental data indicate that the most sensitive time for LH-RH is 25 to 30 days of age, and at 58 days of age the pituitary responsiveness starts decreasing. You also mentioned that in female rats the effect of ovariectomy on the release of LH is most striking at the age of 25 to 30 days, which correlates well with the time when estrogen receptors in the hypothalamus are formed.

DR. McCANN.   With respect to your first comment, we do not know the reason why we get a greater rise in LH following castration at 58 days than at any other time. We were quite surprised to find this. In relating our results to yours on age-related changes in sensitivity to LRF, do not forget we are dealing with different laboratories and strains of rats. I do not know what the time of peak responsiveness to LRF would be under our conditions. So that is one possible cause for the difference. Perhaps the hypothalamic drive is stronger at that time than at any other time; this could be another possible cause.

With respect to the question about ovariectomy in females at different ages, the failure to respond early may be due to the fact that the gonad is not putting out estrogens. Also, there may not be any steroid receptors present at that time. Drs. Kato and Ramirez and others have also looked for the receptors.

DR. STEELE.   The ages during which the immature rat fails to respond to ovariectomy with a demonstrable increase in gonadotropins correspond to those in which Raynaud, Mercier-Uclaf, and Baulieu (1971) noted high serum levels of estradiol-binding plasma protein. Might the presence of serum-binding proteins also contribute to the delay in the rise in gonadotropins in immature female rats following ovariectomy?

DR. McCANN.   The work to which you refer was done in the male. Estrogen-binding protein presumably would have a role in the female rat. Actually, Baulieu's group found a very high affinity estrogen-binding protein in female rats which disappears about the time of weaning.

If this is true, and if it plays a significant role in estrogen binding in the female, then its disappearance would mean that the amount of free hormone would increase if everything else remained constant. I don't know if it has any function in the male, do you?

DR. STEELE.   It does not bind testosterone. The delay following gonadectomy in the female may be due to the fact that the estradiol was being bound, whereas, in the male, gonadotropin secretion is under the control of testosterone which is not bound by the binding protein. Therefore, following gonadectomy in the male, plasma testosterone decreases readily, and the plasma gonadotropins increase.

DR. McCANN.   If, indeed, there is estrogen production by the ovary during the infantile period, and if, in spite of the existence of the presumed estrogen-binding protein, minute levels of free estrogen are high enough to exert feedback suppression of gonadotropins, then the bound estrogen may serve as a reservoir for free estrogen after ovariectomy and thus might account for the observed delay in rise of levels of gonadotropins in the female. The trouble with the binding protein story is that if the feedback mechanisms are intact and responding to free hormone then (except for transient changes) the level of binding protein will not affect the steady-state level of estrogens. That is my concept. There would be transient changes if you suddenly get a rise in levels of binding protein, but the gonadotropin mechanism would respond and bring the estrogen concentration back to control levels. That may be very naïve; but the binding proteins are not really key points in puberty, even though I do think that this subject is a weak link in the chain of evidence. We need much more data on it.

Dr. Ross.   In your superb review I was disappointed that you did not refer to the interaction of steroid hormones and gonadotropins in the gonad per se. Drs. Reiter and Goldenberg, working in my laboratory, have treated female rats with anti-estradiol serum daily for 4 days beginning on the first postnatal day. They demonstrated that ovarian weight and uterine weight increments are inhibited in animals of all ages from 1 to 25 days. These data suggest that even at this early age estrogens and gonadotropins interact in stimulating maturation of the gonad. If you treat an intact sexually immature rat with anti-estradiol serum, that animal's ovaries do not enlarge at the same rate as the ovaries of a littermate treated with normal rabbit serum. This phenomenon can be demonstrated in rats at all ages from the first through the twenty-fifth postnatal day.

Dr. McCann.   So, with your anti-estrogen serum, you will decrease plasma levels of estrogens, which should give you an increase in gonadotropins. But the gonad cannot respond to it in the absence of the effects of the estrogen presumably secreted as the result of the gonadotropins.

Dr. Ross.   That is correct, but we do not know where the estrogen came from. Specifically, we could not show that the hormone was being produced in the ovary.

Dr. McCann.   It probably means the estrogen is interacting at the ovarian level with gonadotropins.

Dr. Rosenfield.   The data of Mizuna, Lobotsky, Lloyd, Kobayashi, and Murasawa (1968), Rivarola et al (1968), and August, Tkachuck, and Grumbach (1969) indicate that in the newborn human the male and female testosterone levels are equal and above those of the normal adult. They are in the range of the hirsute female. In the human it appears that hCG crosses the placenta in appreciable amounts (Faiman, Ryan, Zwirek, & Rubin, 1968). Apparently, however, the well-developed Leydig cells of the newborn do not respond to hCG stimulation by secreting testosterone; something about the pregnant state inhibits testicular testosterone production.

Dr. Steinberger.   I should like to comment on testosterone. We found that the individual plasma values in the rat varied tremendously at each sampling; in other words, if you sample every half-hour, you get different results. If you measure the testicular levels, you find the highest testicular concentration per milligram wet weight just before birth and at birth. This is much higher than at any other time during the life of the rat. But calculation per gonad is quite a different matter, since the mass of the testis increases tremendously from about 1 mg at birth to about 3 g in the adult. Yet, per testis, the highest concentration of testosterone per milligram of testicular weight is found right at birth. And this is very important for those of us who are interested in the effect of testosterone on spermatogenesis (which must be a local effect, e.g., per milligram of testis).

DR. SWERDLOFF.   I want to make a comment about the levels of gonadotropins that occur after ovariectomy in animals of different ages. Dr. McCann, in his excellent review, described data which suggest that the immature female rat demonstrates a sluggish response of serum LH and FSH after castration. Actually, our studies suggest the opposite: in the immature rat oophorectomy results in a significantly greater increase in serum LH levels than in the mature animal. In Fig. 7 you can see that the rise in serum LH after oophorectomy in 75-day-old animals is considerably more sluggish than in the 10- and 21-day-old animals, in contrast to the data on serum FSH levels where there is not nearly the difference between age groups. So, our experience is different from that quoted by Dr. McCann, in that the immature animals seem to be more responsive to gonadectomy in regard to elevations of serum LH.

DR. McCANN.   We have not made the measurements; I am only quoting other people. There may well be this unresponsive period initially; then, as the female gonad begins to put out estrogen, you might have a response to castration. I would further predict that the response would come on quicker in this period than in the adult because you are dealing with less steroid and, therefore, the biological half-time of the estrogen would be shorter in this earlier period than in the adult animal in which you must get rid of more estrogen.

DR. BOGDANOVE.   In Fig. 7, Dr. Swerdloff, you showed differences in the intensity of the castration response of the female rat at various ages. How do these differences compare quantitatively with those between males and females noted some years ago? We found that although the immature female has a more marked LH secretory response to castration than the adult female, she still has a very much weaker castration response than the immature. Do your observations confirm this?

DR. SWERDLOFF.   Yes. The mature male has a much brisker rise than the mature female with regard to LH (Fig. 8). The magnitude of increase for the male and female in the immature period is approximately the same in our experience.

DR. GAY.   What is the interval of castration?

DR. SWERDLOFF.   Five days.

DR. BLIZZARD.   Would anyone care to comment on target organ sensitivity?

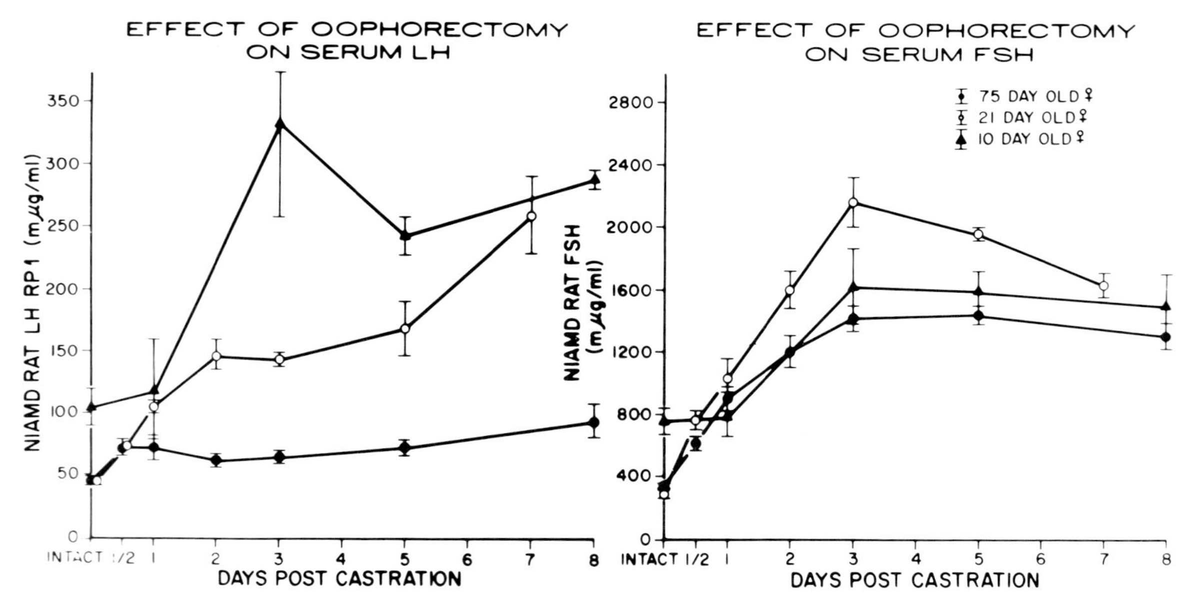

FIG. 7.   Effect of oophorectomy on levels of gonadotropins in sera of rats of different ages.

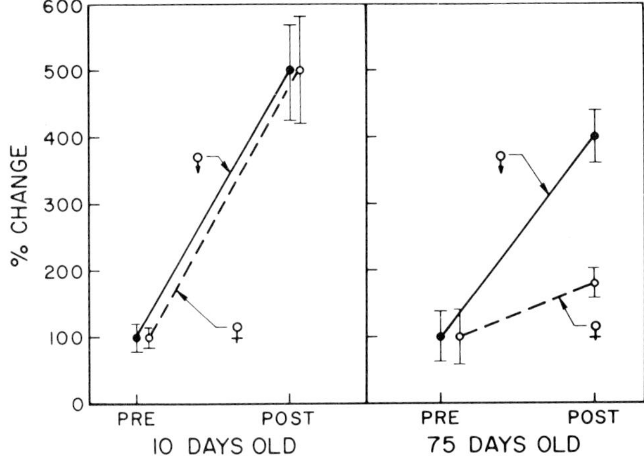

FIG. 8.   Effect of castration on serum LH concentration in 10- and 75-day-old rats of both sexes.

Dr. Moshang.   The increase of target organ sensitivity to gonadal steroids after puberty is probably not due to any innate change in the target organ itself. We have looked at the effect of increasing substrate (testosterone) concentration on the ability of the rat prostate in vitro to utilize testosterone (T) or to form the active metabolite, dihydrotestosterone (DHT). There is no difference between the prepubertal and postpubertal intact rat in the disappearance rate of T or the rate of formation of DHT at different concentrations of substrate. However, if the immature rat is hypophysectomized, increasing substrate concentrations will inhibit the rate of formation of DHT by the rat prostate in vitro. The increase in target organ sensitivity is probably related to changes in pituitary hormonal factors.

Dr. Grumbach.   Studies of the effect of unilateral castration on compensatory ovarian hypertrophy in the young prepubertal rat suggest that this does not occur before about age 25 days. This observation, the data summarized by Dr. McCann on the high gonadotropin levels before 15 days of age, and the comments of Dr. Swerdloff are all consistent with the notion that, in the rat, the prepubertal ovary is relatively unresponsive to gonadotropins. In contrast, in the unilaterally orchiectomized male rat, compensatory testicular hypertrophy can be demonstrated by 1 week of age.

Dr. Blizzard.   Would anyone comment on prolactin in animals or in man?

Dr. Grumbach.   The role of prolactin in puberty appears to differ in man and in the rat. Dr. Michel Aubert, Dr. Selna Kaplan, and I have determined recently the concentration of serum prolactin in prepubertal and pubertal children and in normal adult males and females in blood samples obtained during the day. No differences were noted in the serum values for male and female subjects between 1 year of age and puberty. The levels did not differ in *pre-adolescent* and adolescent males and females, including menarchial girls, or in adult males. However, adult females had higher mean values than adult males. In females, sometime between the onset of menarche and adulthood, the mean concentration of serum prolactin rises. These results differ from those reported in the rat.

DR. JOHNSON.   One of the points not brought up in the discussion of gonado-tropins is the periodic release of LH and FSH and probably of prolactin. The sensitivity to these hormones would depend upon the sequence of their release; steroids may play some role in determining this sequence. In regard to the effect of prolactin on sex accessory organs, for example, time is very vital. If prolac-tin is given before LH it may not work so well as when given after LH. If prolactin and LH are given in the evening, they work much better than when given in the morning. So, it seems that the sensitivity of the target is involved somehow with these periodicities of gonadotropin.

DR. WINTER.   In studies of human puberty we have learned the importance of nocturnal gonadotropin secretion. In studies in the rat are you studying serum gonadotropin levels at night as well as during the daytime?

DR. McCANN.   We are studying at night, but we have not worked down to the prepubertal animal yet.

DR. FOSTER.   I would like to make a few comments about the sheep and the secretion of gonadotropins prior to and during puberty. We have published data recently (Foster et al, 1972 a,b) which show that a sex difference in concentration of serum LH exists at least during the first 14 days of life; i.e., serum LH in the male is at very low basal levels (< 1.0 mg/ml) during this period, about that of the adult. In the female lamb serum LH is very high. Shortly after birth it is elevated, at times to levels almost as high as those observed in the castrated adult ewe (Roche, Foster, Karsch, Cook, & Dziuk, 1970). These high levels, when monitored on a daily basis during the first 45 days after birth, appear to be very sporadic in that they appear to go up and down in an apparently unpredictable manner. When one looks again at the fluctuating concentrations of circulating LH at 20-minute intervals for about a 6½ hour period within the same day, it becomes apparent that some sort of episodic secretion is taking place which allows levels of LH to be elevated at times; so the high and low concentrations of peripheral LH observed on a daily basis are just apparently due to infrequent sampling. The important point is that serum LH in the female sheep, when monitored frequently (20-minute intervals), is high before puberty.

We have obtained about 6000 samples in groups of 20 samplings from 12 or 14 lambs during development in a longitudinal study of gonadotropins. Our preliminary data suggest that LH secretion in the female during the peripuber-tal period undergoes a change in frequency. A greater frequency in the pulsatile release of LH becomes evident around the time of first ovulation. During the second and subsequent ovulations there is also more frequent release of LH, but during midcycle (between the estrus periods) spikes of LH tend to decrease in frequency. We do not really know what is going on, but we do know it is not as it has been reported classically in the rat and possibly in the human.

DR. BLIZZARD.   Are you sure that it is not an assay difference with respect to the LH?

DR. FOSTER.   No, it is not. For instance, in the assays performed to obtain these data, we calculated the intra-assay error to be about 5 per cent and the inter-assay variation to be about 10 per cent. However, during a single 6½ hour sampling period the coefficient of variability for concentrations of serum LH in the 20 samples obtained ranged anywhere from 60 to 300 per cent. So we feel it is not an assay error but, instead, reflects a true biologic phenomenon.

DR. BLIZZARD.   What happens to LH if you gonadectomize?

DR. FOSTER.   In the male lamb castrated at birth serum LH increased within 8 days following orchiectomy. In the female lamb it is difficult to distinguish the difference in concentrations of circulating LH between the intact and the gonadectomized female in samples of serum obtained daily until 1 or 2 months after gonadectomy because of the periodically high levels found in the intact female lamb. However, if one observes the pattern of LH secretion obtained from samples collected at frequent intervals (20 minute), one finds a uniform increase in both the frequency and amplitude of the LH release over a 3-to-4-week period following neonatal ovariectomy.

DR. GESCHWIND.   Dr. Foster spoke of some of his work in the fetal and the perinatal period of the lamb and has shown changes in gonadotropin levels and in the ability of the fetal lamb in the early perinatal period to respond to LRF injections. This same type of research was undertaken on somewhat older ram lambs (Crim & Geschwind, 1972). Generally, in the male animal, there is a period of lack of responsivity somewhere around 5 to 10 days of age, when LH levels are quite low, and when one does not see responses to LRF. In the female there is a period of time during which the animal does not respond to estrogen injection by means of an LH surge. Land, Thimonier, and Pelletier (1970) found 13-day-old ewe lambs unresponsive, while 38-day-old lambs were fully responsive. One should also be aware of some findings of Courot, Thimonier, and Pelletier, who have shown that in rams of 3 different breeds of sheep there is a progressive increase in circulating LH levels between about 25 and 75 days of age. This is before the period of puberty in this animal; thereafter, the levels fluctuate quite widely, but the peak is reached somewhere around 70 days. One would see beginning formation of spermatozoa, for example, when the ram is between 4 and 5 months of age. I am not convinced entirely that the sheep is a woolly rat; I think there are definite differences. The female sheep, the ewe, is a seasonally estrus animal, which may prove to be a good model to use in studies of the onset of puberty, because this is an animal which, during the period from about December to July, does not cycle. In July she starts coming into heat the first time for that year and then has repeated cycles which last about 17 days. What happens each year so that the ovaries become active again? Is this is a question of rebirth during the spring and early summer? Is this a question of a repubertizing of the animal each time? We know that the ovaries are quiescent during the anestrus period but can be stimulated by injections of gonadotropin. The pituitary also appears to be quiescent during this period but can be stimulated by injections of LRF, as Gay, Niswender, and Midgley (1970) and Reeves et al (1970) have shown, and also by estrogen administration as reported by Goding, Catt, Brown, Kaltenbach, Cumming, and Mole (1969). If one hemicastrates the animal, there is a compensatory ovarian hypertrophy during this period (Dufour, Ginther, & Casida, 1971); finally, if one castrates the animal, there is an increase in the circulating LH (Roche et al, 1970). Quite obviously that very quiescent ovary is doing something during this time which is depressing hypothalamic or pituitary function. We seem to have here a very nice case of extreme depression with low circulating LH levels and very low steroid levels. In other words, there is an extreme sensitivity of the hypothalamus to steroid levels. Then the animal takes certain cues from the environment, cues of light, temperature, and olfactory cues from a male which is present which help to initiate the onset of estrus again, and the whole new period of estrus begins for a period of about 6 months. All these things will help to reset the hypothalamus in terms of its sensitivity to steroids and other factors.

DR. FOSTER.   I would like to mention some studies that indicate that there are a number of parameters that are known about the developmental endocrinology of the lamb. Some of the high points are that, in the sheep, gestation is 150 days, gonadal sexual differentiation occurs between 20 and 30 days of gestation, and increased testicular activity (Attal, 1969) as well as first spontaneous cortical activity becomes apparent early in the second trimester (Bernhard, Kaiser, & Kolmodin, 1959). This may be the period of sexual differentiation of the hypothalamus, if this phenomenon actually exists in higher mammals other than the rat, the hamster, and guinea pig. There is a sex difference in levels of both pituitary and serum LH during fetal life (Foster, Roche Karsch, Norton, Cook, & Nalbandov, 1972). LH in the fetal circulation of the lamb is of fetal pituitary origin, since LH does not cross the placenta of the sheep, as shown experimentally by Foster, Karsch, and Nalbandov (1972). The pituitary of the fetal sheep can respond repeatedly to injections of exogenous LRF in a manner comparable to that of the adult; however, the response to LRF shortly after birth is much less than that during fetal life (Foster, Cruz, Jackson, Cook, & Nalbandov, 1972). Assay of the endogenous gonadotropin releasing factors in the hypothalamus shows that they are present after birth, but not before birth (Foster, Jackson, Cook, & Nalbandov, 1972). Postnatally, a sex difference in circulating concentration of gonadotropins exists. Gonadotropins are low in the male, which strongly suggests that the testes are probably functioning in a negative feedback manner (Foster, Cook, & Nalbandov, 1972). However, in the female, gonadotropins, LH and FSH, are markedly increased at times prior to pubescence, which would indicate either that the ovaries are not producing sufficient steroids for negative feedback or that the hypothalamic-hypophyseal axis cannot recognize such a negative feedback if it is present. In the immature female levels of gonadotropins are unpredictable from day to day, but on multiple short-interval samplings within the same day (such as 20 collections at 20-minute intervals for a period of 6½ hours) a very rhythmic secretion of LH, and to some extent FSH, occurs. Regarding feedback of ovarian steroids, the anterior pituitary and/or the hypothalamus of the lamb can respond to negative feedback at birth because estradiol-17β, when administered continuously to either intact or ovariectomized lambs during the first 45 days of life, suppresses the high levels of serum LH observed during this period (Liefer, Foster, & Dziuk, 1972). However, only after 4 to 6 weeks after birth is enough estrogen produced to inhibit partially the secretion of gonadotropins. Positive feedback has been shown by Land et al (1970) to be firmly established by 5 weeks of age in the lamb. Finally, the ovary can be induced to ovulate by administration of exogenous gonadotropins as early as 4 to 8 weeks of age (Mansour, 1959), and I must remind you that puberty does not occur until 7 to 10 months of age. The main point is that many of the mechanisms influencing reproductive endocrine events appear, at least experimentally, to be operative at a very early age in the female sheep.

REFERENCES

Attal, J. (1969). Levels of testosterone, androstenedione, estrone and estradiol-17β in the testes of fetal sheep. *J. Endocrinol.* **85**, 280–290.

August, G. P., Tkachuck, M., & Grumbach, M. M. (1969). Plasma testosterone-binding affinity and testosterone in umbilical cord plasma, late pregnancy, pre-pubertal children, and adults. *J. Clin. Endocrinol.* **29**, 891–899.

Bernhard, C. G., Kaiser, I. H., & Kolmodin, G. M. (1959). On the development of cortical activity in fetal sheep. *Acta physiol. Scand.* **47**, 333–349.

Crim, L. W. & Geschwind, I. I. (1972). Patterns of FSH and LH secretion in the developing ram: the influence of castration and replacement therapy with testosterone propionate. *Biol. Reprod.* **1**, 47–54.

Dufour, J., Ginther, O. J., & Casida, L. E. (1971). Compensatory hypertrophy after unilateral ovariectomy and destruction of follicles in the anestrous ewe. *Proc. Soc. Exp. Biol. Med.* **138**, 1068–1073.

Faiman, C., Ryan, R. J., Zwirek, S. J., & Rubin, M. E. (1968). Serum FSH and HCG during human pregnancy and puerperium. *J. Clin. Endocrinol.* **28**, 1323–1330.

Foster, D. L., Cook, B., & Nalbandov, A. V. (1972). Regulation of luteinizing hormone (LH) in the fetal and neonatal lamb. Effect of castration during the early postnatal period on levels of LH in sera and pituitaries of neonatal lambs. *Biol. Reprod.* **6**, 253–257.

Foster, D. L., Cruz, T. A., Jackson, G. L., Cook, B., & Nalbandov, A. V. (1972b).

Regulation of luteinizing hormone in the fetal and neonatal lamb: III. Release of LH by the pituitary in vivo in response to crude ovine hypothalamic extract or purified porcine gonadotropin releasing factor. *Endocrinology* **90**, 673–684.

Foster, D. L., Jackson, G. L., Cook, B., & Nalbandov, A. V. (1972). Regulation of luteinizing hormone (LH) in the fetal and neonatal lamb: IV. Levels of LH releasing activity in the hypothalamus. *Endocrinology* **90**, 684–690.

Foster, D. L., Karsch, F. J., & Nalbandov, A. V. (1972). Regulation of luteinizing hormone in the fetal and neonatal lamb: II. Study of placental transfer of LH in sheep. *Endocrinology* **90**, 589–595.

Foster, D. L., Roche, J. F., Karsch, F. J., Norton, H. W., Cook, B., & Nalbandov, A. V. (1972). Regulation of luteinizing hormone in the fetal and neonatal lamb: I. LH concentrations in blood and pituitary. *Endocrinology* **90**, 102–112.

Gay, V. L., Niswender, G. D., & Midgley, A. R. (1970). Response of individual rats and sheep to one or more injections of hypothalamic extract as determined by radioimmunoassay of plasma LH. *Endocrinology* **86**, 1305–1313.

Goding, J. R., Catt, K. J., Brown, J. M., Kaltenbach, C. C., Cumming, I. A., & Mole, B. J. (1969). Radioimmunoassay for ovine luteinizing hormone. Secretion of luteinizing hormone during estrus and following. *Endocrinology* **85**, 133–143.

Land, R. B., Thimonier, J., & Pelletier, J. (1970). Possibilité d'induction d'une décharge de LH par une injection d'oestrogene chez l'agneau femelle en fonction de l'age. *C. R. Acad. Sci. (Paris)* **Ser. D 271**, 1549–1551.

Liefer, R. W., Foster, D. L., & Dziuk, P. J. (1972). Levels of LH in the sera and pituitaries of female lambs following ovariectomy and administration of estrogen. *Endocrinology* **90**, 981–986.

Mansour, A. M. (1959). Hormonal control of ovulation in the immature lamb. *J. Agric. Sci. (Cambridge)* **52**, 87–94.

Mizuno, M., Lobotsky, J., Lloyd, C. W., Kobayashi, T., & Murasawa, Y. (1968). Plasma androstenedione and testosterone during pregnancy and in newborn. *J. Clin. Endocrinol.* **28**, 1133–1143.

Raynaud, J. P., Mercier-Uclaf, C., & Baulieu, E. E. (1971). Rat estradiol binding plasma protein (EBP). *Steroids* **18**, 767–769.

Reeves, J. J., Arimura, A., & Schally, A. V. (1970). Serum levels of prolactin and luteinizing hormone (LH) in the ewe at various stages of estrous cycle. *Proc. Soc. Exp. Biol. Med.* **134**, 938–942.

Resko, J. A., Feder, H. H., & Goy, R. W. (1968). Androgen concentrations in plasma and testis of developing rats. *J. Endocrinol.* **40**, 485–491.

Rivarola, M. A., Forest, M. G., & Migeon, C. J. (1968). Testosterone, androstenedione and dehydroepiandrosterone in plasma during pregnancy and at delivery: concentration and protein binding. *J. Clin. Endocrinol.* **28**, 34–40.

Rivarola, M. A., Snipes, C. A., & Migeon, C. J. (1968). Concentration of androgens in systemic plasma of rats, guinea pigs, salamanders and pigeons. *Endocrinology* **82**, 115–122.

Roche, J. F., Foster, D. L., Karsch, F. J., Cook, B., & Dziuk, P. J. (1970). Levels of luteinizing hormone in sera and pituitaries of ewes during the estrous cycle and anestrus. *Endocrinology* **86**, 568.

Roche, J. F., Foster, D. L., Karsch, F. J., & Dziuk, P. J. (1970). Effect of castration and infusion of melatonin on levels of luteinizing hormone in sera and pituitaries of ewes. *Endocrinology* **87**, 1205–1211.

Salle, B., Hedinger, C., & Nicole, R. (1968). Significance of testicular biopsies in cryptorchidism in children. *Acta Endocrinol.* **58**, 67–76.

Snipes, C. A., Forest, M. G., & Migeon, C. J. (1969). Plasma androgen concentrations in several species of old and new world monkeys. *Endocrinology* **85**, 941–946.

Yamamoto, M., Diebel, N. B., & Bogdanove, E. M. (1970). Analysis of initial and delayed effects of orchidectomy and ovariectomy on pituitary and serum LH level in adult and immature rat. *Endocrinology* **86**, 1102–1112.

2.

Gonadotropins and Sex Hormone Patterns in Puberty: Clinical Data

C. FAIMAN and J. S. D. WINTER

More sensitive and specific techniques have been used in recent years to describe the hormonal events of puberty, but to date reports have been limited to cross-sectional surveys of levels of serum or urinary hormones during adolescence. These surveys have included studies of immunoassayable gonadotropin levels in serum (August, Grumbach, & Kaplan, 1972; Burr, Sizonenko, Kaplan, & Grumbach, 1970; Johanson, Guyda, Light, Migeon, & Blizzard, 1969; Jenner, Kelch, Kaplan, & Grumbach, 1972; Lee, Midgley, & Jaffe, 1970; Penny, Guyda, Baghdassarian, Johanson, & Blizzard, 1970; Raiti, Light, & Blizzard, 1969; Root, Moshang, Bongiovanni, & Eberlein, 1970; Sizonenko, Burr, Kaplan, & Grumbach, 1970; Winter & Faiman, 1971, 1972a; Yen, Vičic, & Kearchner, 1969; Yen & Vičic. 1970) and urine (Buckler & Clayton, 1970; Baghdassarian, Guyda, Johanson, Migeon, & Blizzard, 1970; Raiti et al, 1969; Rifkind, Kulin, &

Abbreviations

FSH	Follicle stimulating hormone
hCG	Human chorionic gonadotropin
LH	Luteinizing hormone
RIA	Radioimmunoassay

Ross, 1967; Sciarra & Leone, 1970) and of circulating levels of estradiol in females (Jenner et al, 1972; Winter & Faiman, 1971).

Most of the studies agree that gonadotropin and sex steroid levels rise during puberty in both sexes. Differences in the time of onset of this rise are apparent, however, in the data from different investigators and from different groups of subjects (Blizzard, Penny, Foley, Baghdassarian, Johanson, & Yen, 1972). Aside from a few short-term studies in small numbers of perimenarchial girls (Beardwood & Russell, 1970; Hayes & Johanson, 1972; Keller, 1971; Nathanson, Towne, & Aub, 1941; and Pennington & Dewhurst, 1969), no longitudinal studies of circulating levels of gonadotropins and sex steroids during puberty have been reported. It is the purpose of this chapter to describe both cross-sectional and longitudinal studies of puberty in both sexes, to relate the findings to recent developments, and to point out areas that merit further study.

PROCEDURE AND RESULTS

All hormone assays were performed in duplicate. Serum specimens were obtained between the hours of 0900 and 1400 and kept at $-20°C$ until analyzed. FSH* (Faiman & Ryan, 1967a), LH* (Faiman & Ryan, 1967b), and estradiol (Winter, Taraska, & Faiman, 1972) were determined by RIA. A new FSH antiserum was used during the last 2 years of the male longitudinal study, and values obtained with this assay system were indistinguishable from those in which the previously described antiserum was used (Faiman & Shome, 1971). Progesterone (Reyes, Winter, & Faiman, 1972) and testosterone (Winter & Grant, 1971) were determined by competitive protein-binding methods except for the last 2 years of the male longitudinal study, when a RIA method for testosterone (in preparation) was used. Values obtained with this RIA were virtually the same as those obtained by competitive binding for normal adult male samples, but for female samples the values were lower (e.g., the normal adult female testosterone range <65 ng/100 ml by RIA and <80 ng/100 ml by competitive protein binding).

MALE PUBERTY

The cross-sectional study of 253 healthy subjects who ranged in age from 0.2 to 25 years has been reported (Winter & Faiman, 1972a). Some of the data are shown in Figs. 1 to 4.

---

* Values for FSH and LH are reported as μg LER-907 standard/100 ml. To convert to mIU 2nd IRP-HMG/ml multiply the FSH value by 0.5 and the LH value by 4.5.

The Preadolescent Years

Below age 10 all the boys were considered clinically prepubertal (stage P1). From age 6 to 10 there was a gradual increase in mean testis length (Fig. 1) ($r=0.48$, $P<0.001$), but no significant change in plasma testosterone concentration (Fig. 2) occurred during childhood ($r=0.18$, $P>0.1$), and all values were below 40 ng/100 ml. Serum LH (Fig. 3) and serum FSH (Fig. 4) concentrations did not change before age 6; between 6 and 10 years, however, there was a gradual but significant rise in the mean levels of both ($r=0.55$ and 0.53, respectively; $P<0.001$). This pattern closely resembled that seen for testis growth in late childhood.

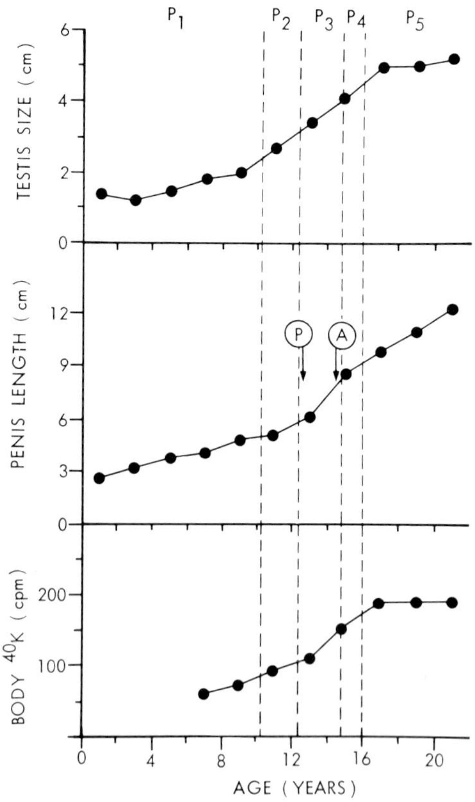

FIG. 1. Mean values for testis size (mean of longest diameters), penis length, and whole body ^{40}K (cpm) in 253 males as a function of age. Ⓟ and Ⓐ refer to the 50th percentile for the age of development of pubic and axillary hair, respectively. P₁ to P₅ refer to pubertal stages modified from Tanner (1962). Data in this figure were derived from Winter & Faiman (1972a).

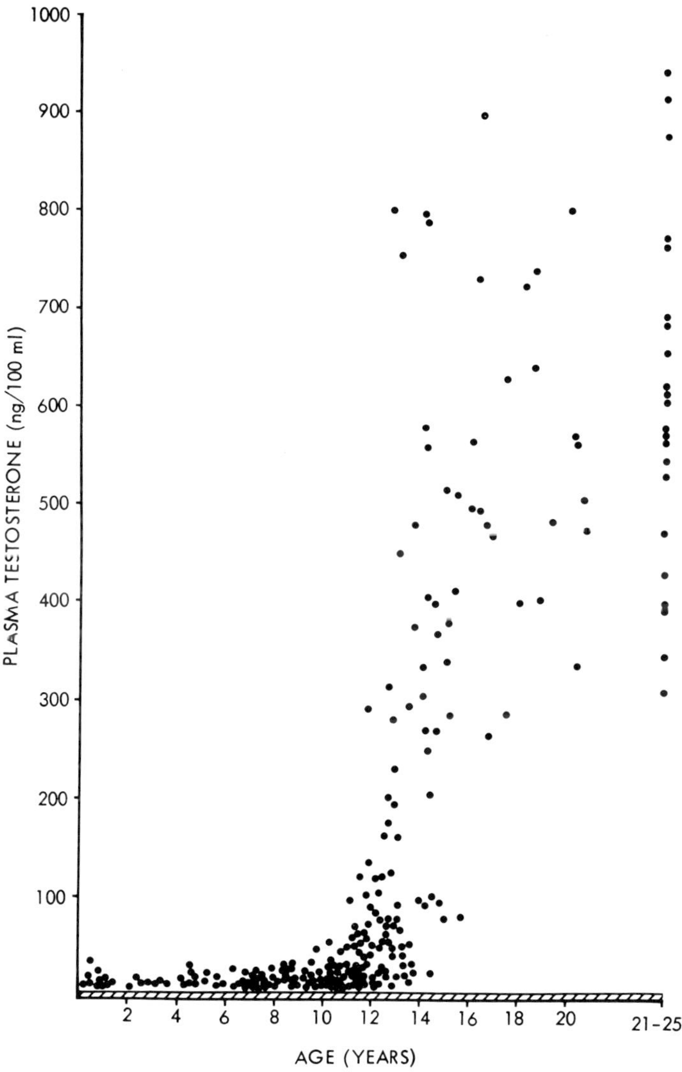

FIG. 2. Plasma testosterone concentrations in males at different ages. The shaded area represents the limit of sensitivity of the assay. Reproduced with permission from Winter & Faiman (1972a).

Puberty

The earliest recognizable sign of puberty was a more rapid rate of testicular enlargement which usually preceded any signs of androgen effect (identi-

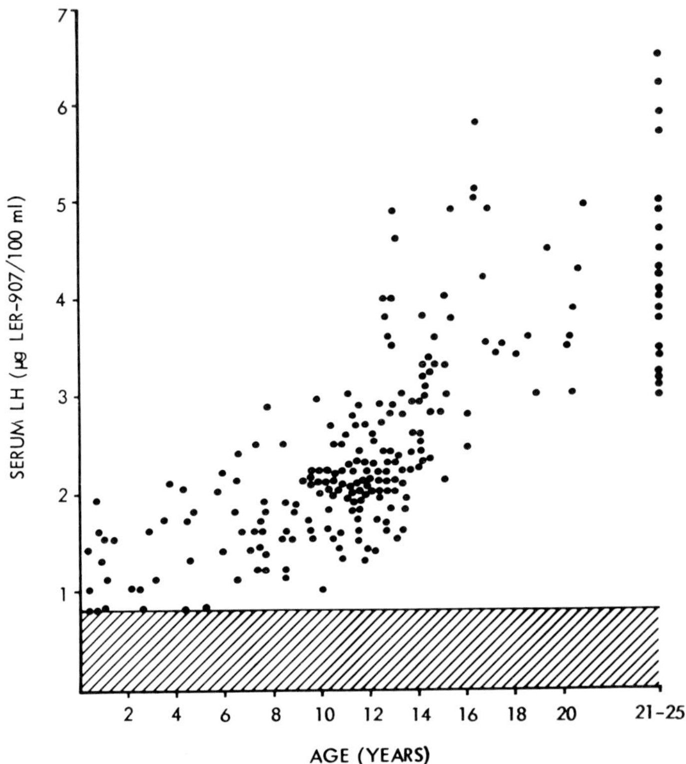

FIG. 3. Serum LH concentrations in males at different ages. The shaded area represents the limit of sensitivity of the assay. Reproduced with permission from Winter & Faiman (1972a).

fied as Stage P2). The mean chronologic age during this stage was 11.8 years (range 9.6-15.1) and the mean bone age 11.9 years (range 10.5-13.5). Boys in this stage showed significantly higher FSH, LH, and testosterone levels than the prepubertal subjects. Between 10 and 17 years of age there was approximately a twentyfold increase in plasma testosterone, accompanied by more rapid phallic growth and the appearance of pubic and axillary hair (Fig. 1). The anabolic action of testosterone was reflected in the rising whole body ^{40}K content after age 12. The mean serum FSH concentration continued to rise during this period, but the slope of this rise was not significantly greater than that observed during the preadolescent years ($t=1.15$, $P>0.1$). On the other hand, a significant increment appeared in the slope of the serum LH rise after age 12 ($t=4.76$, P

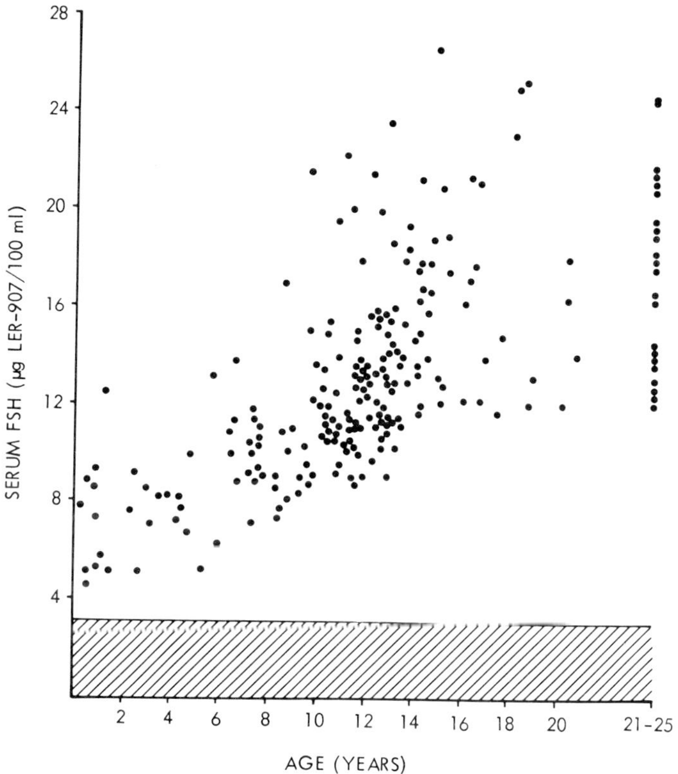

FIG. 4. Serum FSH concentrations in males at different ages. The shaded area represents the limit of sensitivity of the assay. Reproduced with permission from Winter & Faiman (1972a).

<0.001). Note that mean levels into the adult range were achieved by age 10 for FSH and by age 13 for LH.

The Young Adult

Mean serum FSH and LH levels ceased to rise after about ages 15 and 17, respectively. Similarly, no further change occurred in mean testis size, secondary sexual characteristics, or plasma testosterone concentration after age 17. Bone maturation was almost complete by age 17, and there was no further increase in mean whole body ^{40}K content; hence the period of rapid bone and muscle growth was completed. The mean adult serum FSH level was approximately twice the mean prepubertal level, whereas the mean adult LH concentration was 3 times that in children. Although there was a significant correlation between plasma testosterone, serum LH ($r=0.77$, $P<0.001$), and FSH ($r=0.57$, $P<0.001$) when all age groups were considered together, there was no correlation between testosterone and either gonadotropin in the adult subjects.

Longitudinal Study

As pointed out by Tanner (1962), the major shortcoming of a cross-sectional study is that rapid incremental changes during growth and development tend to be obscured, mainly because of variability in time of onset. Accordingly, we performed a longitudinal study in order to document whether this approach would prove more meaningful. We were aware that certain other factors, such as the variability of assay performance with time and biologic variability due to diurnal changes (Faiman & Winter, 1971a), or more frequent changes due to the pulsatile nature of hormonal release (Nankin & Troen, 1971), might militate against the usefulness of this approach.

Fifty-six healthy males (aged 6 to 14 years) were studied at 4 successive yearly examinations. Mean trends in hormone concentrations were calculated according to the method of Tanner and Gupta (1968). Values for mean serum testosterone, FSH, and LH as functions of chronologic age are shown in Fig. 5. Note that the most marked testosterone increments occurred between ages 12 and 14. Values for both FSH and LH increased in an apparently parallel fashion from age 10 to age 15 to attain the adult range.

Mean values for serum testosterone, FSH, and LH in each stage of pubertal development are shown in Fig. 6. The most rapid change in serum testosterone levels occurred between stages 2 and 4. In contrast to the preceding data plotted by age (Fig. 5), the rise in serum FSH levels occurred *before* any appreciable change in serum testosterone concentration or in testicular size (stage 2). The changes in LH did not begin until stage 2 had appeared and roughly paralleled (but with a lower relative increment) the changes in testosterone.

The data shown in the longitudinal study and in the earlier cross-sectional study indicate that levels of FSH begin to rise in male puberty earlier than those of LH and reach the adult range earlier than LH levels. This early FSH rise occurs at a time when the only pubertal change is a small degree of testicular enlargement. This is followed (after age 12) by increments of LH and testosterone which herald the onset of secondary sexual development. This pattern supports a model in which FSH plays a primary role in testicular growth and tubular development and in which Leydig cell function is primarily LH-dependent.

Although this general pattern of gonadotropin levels during male

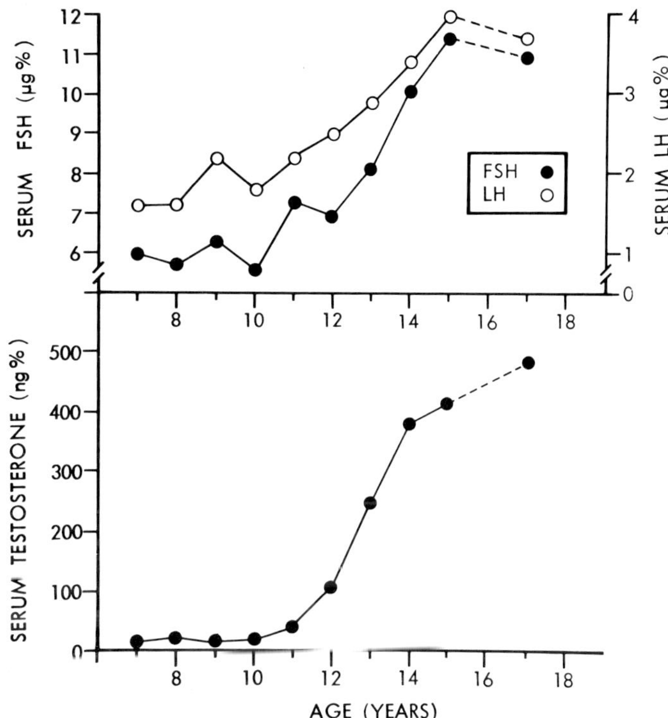

FIG. 5. Mean trends by age for serum concentrations of FSH, LH, and testosterone derived by the method of Tanner and Gupta (1968) from the longitudinal study of 56 male subjects. Individual increments in hormone levels were calculated for each yearly period and the mean increments successively added or subtracted from the mean value at age 10. The value of the 17-year-olds represents the mean for 11 subjects between ages 16 and 18.

puberty is in general agreement with FSH and LH levels reported by Yen and Vičic (1970) and Yen et al (1969) and noted by Blizzard et al (1972), differences in patterns as well as in absolute levels have been reported by different investigators. These discrepancies may be explained by differences in population sampling and in assay technique (Cargille, Rodbard, & Ross, 1968; Taymor & Miyata, 1969); or compare the LH data of Burr et al (1970) with those of August et al (1972). In addition, statistical approaches that compare levels in successive 1- to 2-year age groups, in which small numbers of observations are utilized, might be expected to lead to discrepant results in the time of the earliest significant increments.

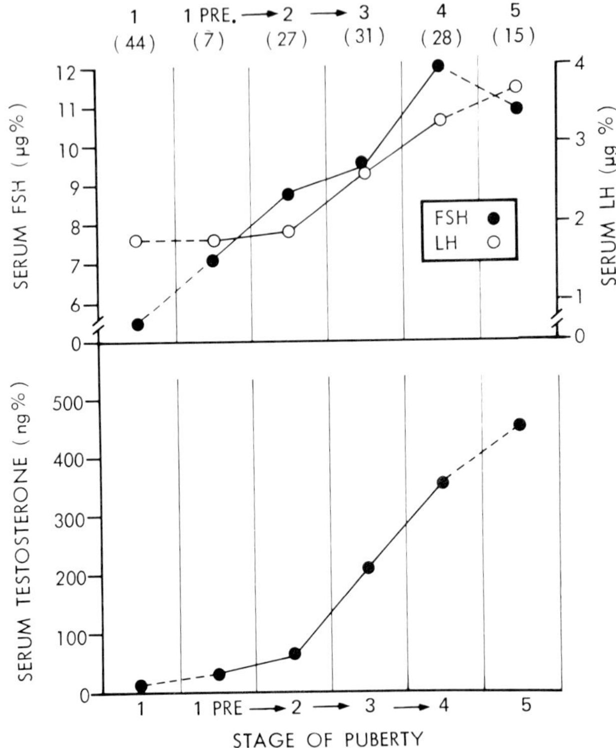

FIG. 6.   Mean trends by pubertal stage for serum concentrations of FSH, LH, and testosterone derived from the longitudinal study of 56 male subjects by the method described for Fig. 5; pubertal stages are defined in the legend to Fig. 1; stage 1-pre refers to subjects who advanced to stage 2 in the following year. The stage 5 level represents the mean values of 15 subjects who were sexually mature on entering the study. The bracketed numbers below each stage number represent the number of observations from which each mean level is derived.

FEMALE PUBERTY

A cross-sectional study was made of a group of healthy females ranging in age from 0.5 to 25 years (Fig. 7).

Preadolescence (pubertal stage 1)

Estradiol was undetectable in the serum of most of the prepubertal girls (Fig. 8); levels of 1.0 to 1.7 ng/100 ml were seen in a few of the older ones before the onset of breast development. Serum LH concentrations (Fig. 9) were low (<3.5 µg/100 ml) throughout childhood, with no increment until after signs of puberty had already appeared. In contrast,

FEMALE PUBERTY

STAGE	CRITERIA	AGE (YRS)*	MENSES
1	PREADOLESCENT	7.0 (0.5 – 12.5)	0/82
2	BREAST BUD AND/OR SPARSE LABIAL HAIR	10.7 (8.4 – 12.0)	0/23
3	BREAST 2 – 11 cm; PUBIC HAIR	11.8 (9.2 – 16.0)	7/28
4/5	ADULT BREAST AND PUBIC HAIR; AXILLARY HAIR	16.0 (11.9 – 25.0)	50/52

FIG. 7. Characteristics of 185 female subjects in a cross-sectional study of puberty (staging according to Tanner, 1962;* represents the median range); note that stages 4 and 5 have been combined.

levels of serum FSH (Fig. 10) showed a biphasic pattern, with high levels in some infants, a decline through childhood to a nadir at age 8, and another rise coincident with the onset of puberty.

Early Midadolescence (pubertal stages 2 and 3)

The appearance of labial hair or of a subareolar breast bud was the first physical sign of puberty, each occurring first in an equal number of girls. This transition was accompanied by rises in the mean plasma concentrations of FSH, estradiol, and testosterone (Fig. 11); levels of serum LH rose later, becoming significantly higher than prepubertal values only in pubertal stage 3, when secondary sexual characteristics were well developed.

Menarche and Beyond (pubertal stages 4 and 5)

In this group of girls menarche occurred 12 to 30 months (by history) after the onset of breast enlargement, usually toward the end of stage 3 or early in stage 4. After menarche serum estradiol concentrations (Fig. 8) were in the adult range. The wide range of estradiol values 0–25.0 ng/ 100 ml) in these healthy young women reflected their menstrual cycle, and the highest estradiol concentrations occurred near midcycle. As with estradiol, mean levels of serum LH and FSH were higher after menarche and showed a wide range of values, primarily as a reflection of the gonadotropin surge in midcycle.

In the longitudinal study 58 healthy girls (aged 6 to 16 years) were observed in 3 successive yearly examinations. Data for mean trends for serum FSH, LH, and estradiol with age are shown in Fig. 12. Levels of

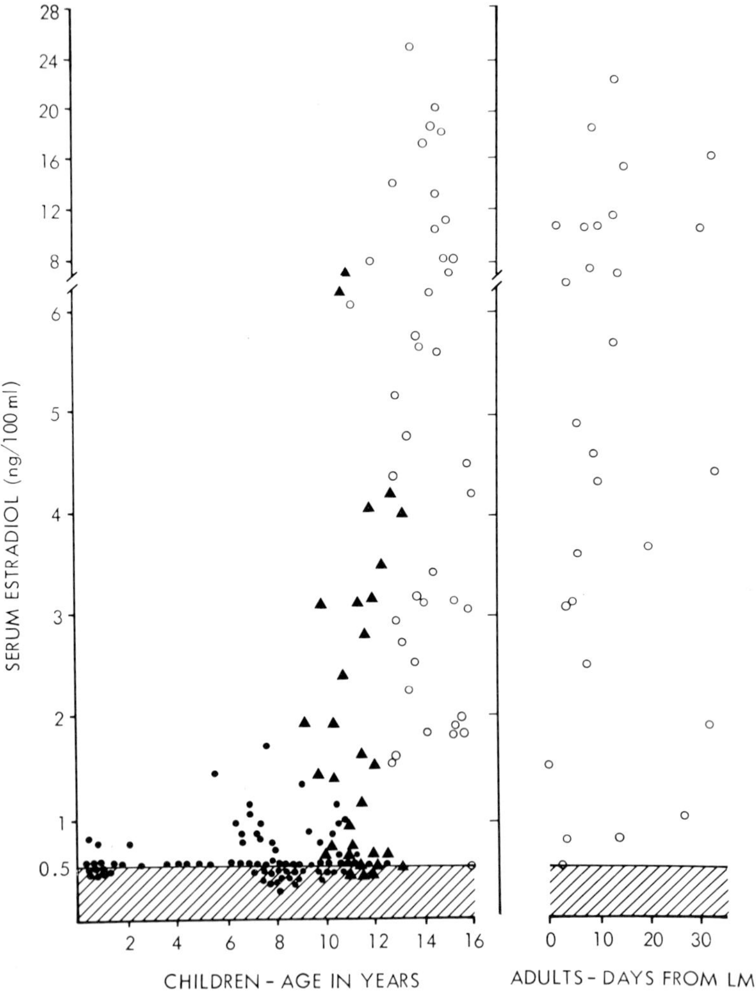

FIG. 8. Serum estradiol concentrations in females of different ages. The shaded area represents the limit of sensitivity of the assay: ○ prepubertal; ▲ premenarchial with breast development; ● postmenarchial. Values for the 16- to 25-year-old subjects are plotted on the right by days from the last menstrual period (LMP).

estradiol did not change appreciably before age 10, whereas both FSH and LH showed small increments; estradiol increased after age 10 to reach a plateau by age 14 and was accompanied by further increments in levels of FSH and LH.

The pattern in levels of gonadotropin during early female puberty

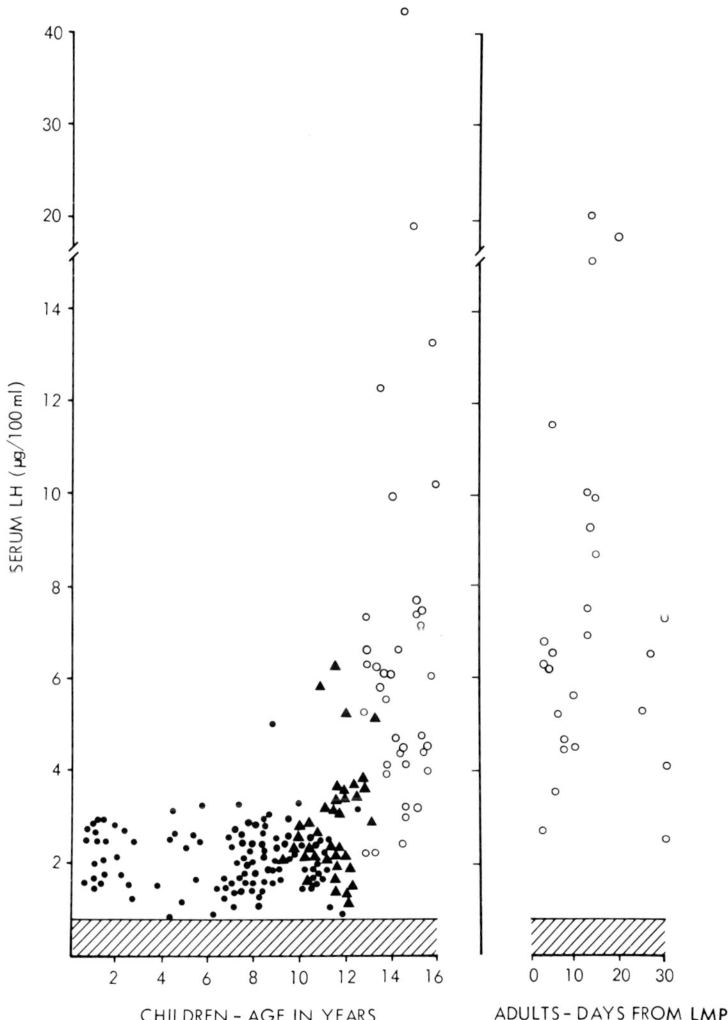

FIG. 9. Serum LH concentration (micrograms LER-907/100 ml) in females at different ages and by days from last menstrual period (LMP) for adults. The shaded area and symbols are those for Fig. 8.

resembles that in males; the FSH increment tends to precede that for LH and reaches the adult range earlier during pubertal development. This is in general agreement with the data of Jenner et al (1972); Penny et al (1970); Sizonenko et al (1970); Yen and Vičic (1970); and Yen et al (1969). A similar increment in levels of serum estradiol during female

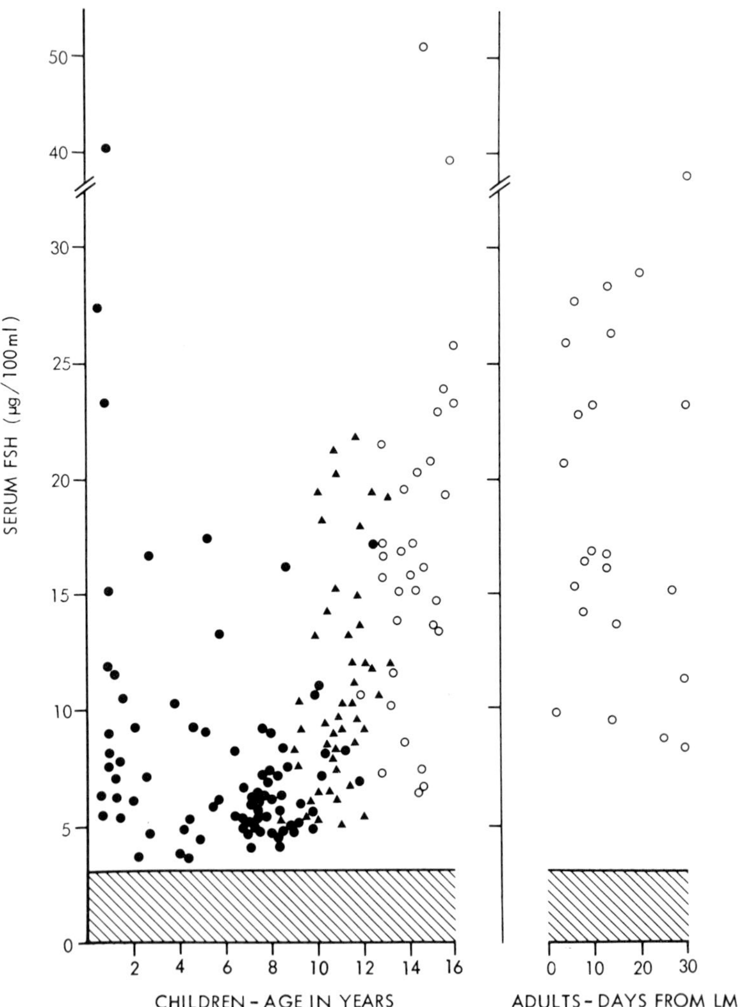

FIG. 10. Serum FSH concentrations (micrograms LER-907/100 ml) in females at different ages and by days from last menstrual period (LMP) for adults. The shaded area and symbols are those for Fig. 8.

puberty has been described by Jenner et al (1972). A rise in levels of plasma testosterone during puberty in the female has not been reported previously.

There were 2 prominent differences from the gonadotropin patterns in males: (1) the marked scatter of data in mature female subjects and (2) the elevated levels of FSH in some female infants (compare Figs. 4 and

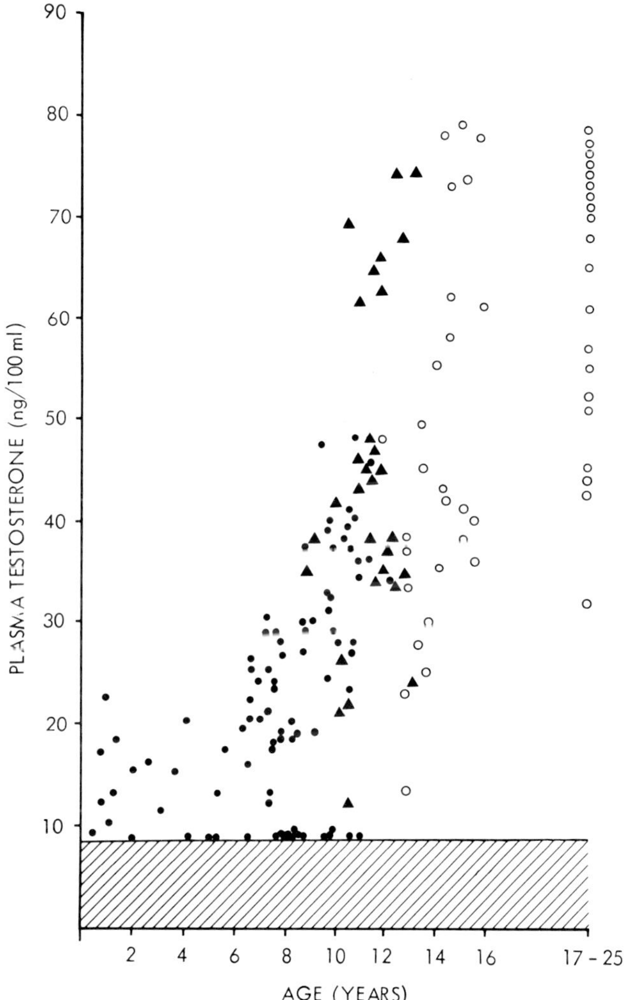

FIG. 11.   Plasma testosterone concentrations in females of different ages. The shaded area represents the limit of sensitivity of the assay: ● prepubertal; ▲ premenarchial with labial hair; ○ postmenarchial.

10). The wide scatter in values of the older girls is a reflection of a super-imposed menstrual rhythm. There is a possibility that the scatter observed in infants also reflects rhythmic FSH secretion.

Because data remain sparse on the first appearance of a rhythmic change in gonadotropins and sex steroids in females and because longitudinal data would be of less value if large day-to-day (or more frequent) fluctuations

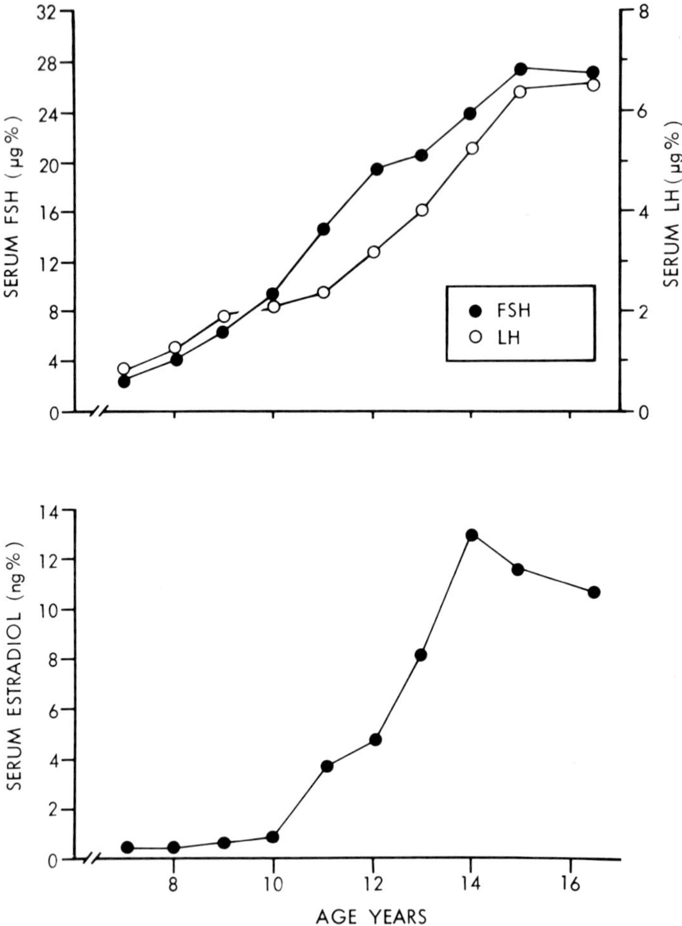

FIG. 12.   Mean trends by age for serum concentrations of FSH, LH, and estradiol derived from the longitudinal study of 58 female subjects by the method described in legend to Fig. 5.

occurred early in pubertal development, a small group of perimenarchial subjects was studied. Serum samples were obtained at 1- to 2-day intervals for one month from 7 healthy girls (ages 8 to 14).

FSH and LH (Fig. 13).   Levels of FSH were low, with little fluctuation in the preadolescent subject (K). In early puberty values were higher, and more marked variation in FSH levels was noted, eg., both the premenarchical subjects (S and W) and L, who was studied from the onset of her menarche. Levels of LH tended to rise with development in these 5 sub-

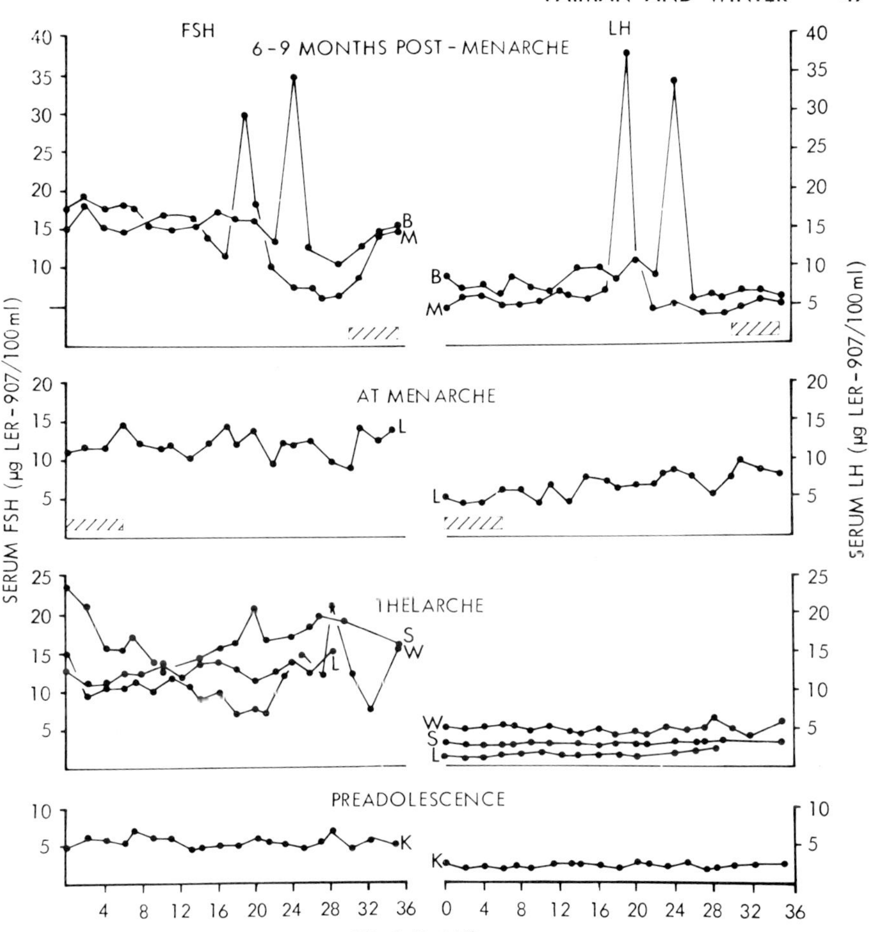

FIG. 13.   Serial serum concentrations of FSH and LH in 7 perimenarchial girls. The hatched bars denote menses.

jects, and some random variability in levels was seen in the menarchial subject. In the two 6- to 9-month postmenarchial subjects LH peaks of ovulatory magnitude were accompanied by FSH peaks and menstrual FSH patterns. Note, however, the short LH peak-menstrual interval in one patient (B), which suggests inadequate corpus luteum function; in subject M a luteal phase of normal duration was observed.

Estradiol and Progesterone.   The patterns of secretion of ovarian hormone in these same subjects are shown in Fig. 14. In early puberty (subjects W

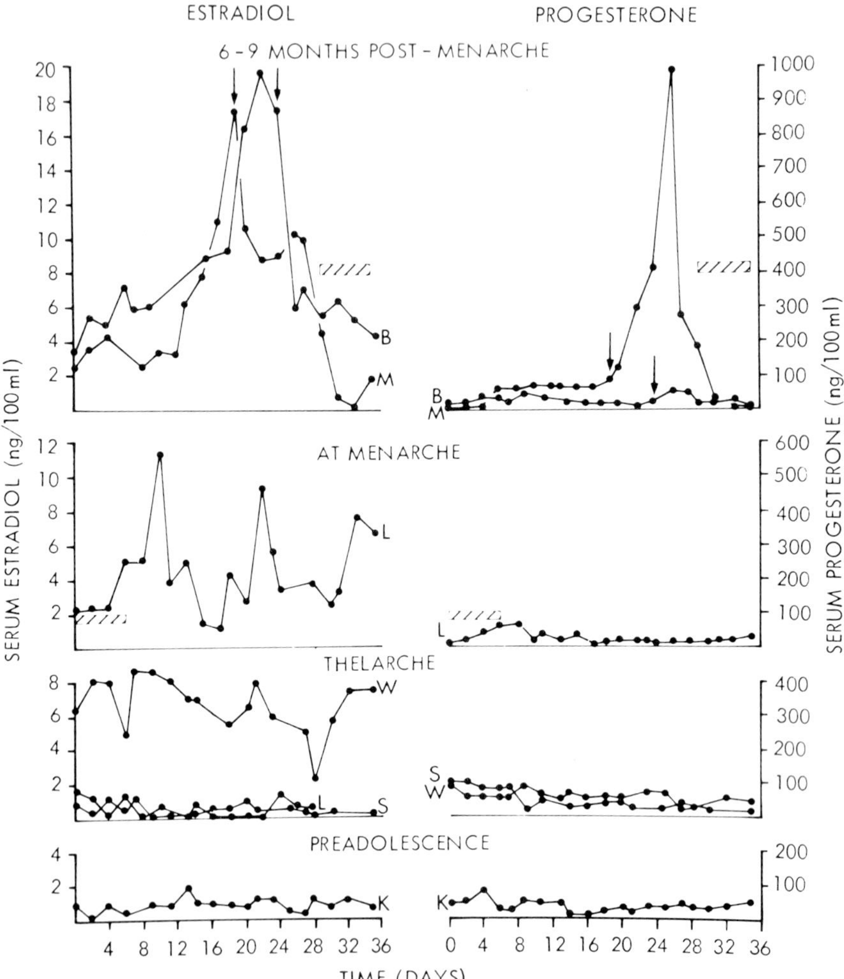

FIG. 14.   Serial serum concentrations of estradiol and progesterone in the 7 peri-menarchial girls in Fig. 13. The hatched bars denote menses; the arrows indicate the time of serum LH/FSH peaks.

and L) levels of estradiol were elevated with marked day-to-day variability but with no change in serum progesterone levels. By 6 to 9 months postmenarche an adult menstrual rhythm in levels of estradiol appeared. These cycles may be anovulatory, as shown in patient B by the lack of any progesterone rise, or ovulatory, as shown in patient M by a normal luteal rise in serum progesterone levels (Ross, Cargille, Lipsett, Rayford, Marshall, Strott, & Rodbard, 1970).

These findings confirm the observations of day-to-day fluctuations in the urinary FSH and LH excretion in perimenarchial girls (Hayes & Johanson, 1972) and suggest fluctuations in ovarian estrogen production as well.

Similar fluctuations in urinary estrogen excretion were reported by Nathanson et al (1941). The demonstration of adult menstrual patterns in levels of gonadotropin and sex steroids within a year after menarche indicates that ovulatory cycles can occur earlier than thought and that the relative infertility of adolescent girls may be due to other factors. Thus among the thirty girls in our cross-sectional study who were within 3 years of menarche (aged 12 to 17 years) 11 had serum progesterone concentrations between 200 to 1300 ng/100 ml, which suggests that ovulation had occurred. Of the 4 girls who had had their menarche less than a year earlier and their last menses 14 to 28 days before the sampling 2 had serum progesterone levels in the luteal phase range.

GONADOTROPIN LEVELS DURING INFANCY

Sex Differences

Serum FSH and LH concentrations in males and females during early childhood are shown in Fig. 15. Note especially the significantly higher mean FSH values and the considerable scatter seen in infant females below the age of 2 years which suggest the possibility of rhythmic FSH secretion.

Day-to-Day Cyclicity of FSH in Infant Females

Because serial sampling of blood from healthy human infants is unethical, we chose the infant chimpanzee (in which species puberty begins at 7 to 9 years of age) as a suitable model with which to study cyclicity (Faiman et al, 1972). Figure 16 shows serial levels of FSH and LH in four 2-year-old chimpanzees. Note the significantly higher levels of FSH in the 2 female infants; their levels show greater variability than those of the males. The presence of day-to-day sine-wave cyclicity was assessed by computer curve fitting and showed a significant cycle in FSH levels, with an 8-day period for one female (No. 709) and a 17-day period for the other (No. 710).

Cyclic FSH secretion begins in early infancy in the female and is damped during childhood (Fig. 10), although the nature of the damping signal (possibly an ovarian secretory product) is not clear. This sex difference in hypothalamic-pituitary function may reflect the prenatal sex difference in gonadal function (Jost, 1970; Reyes et al, 1973).

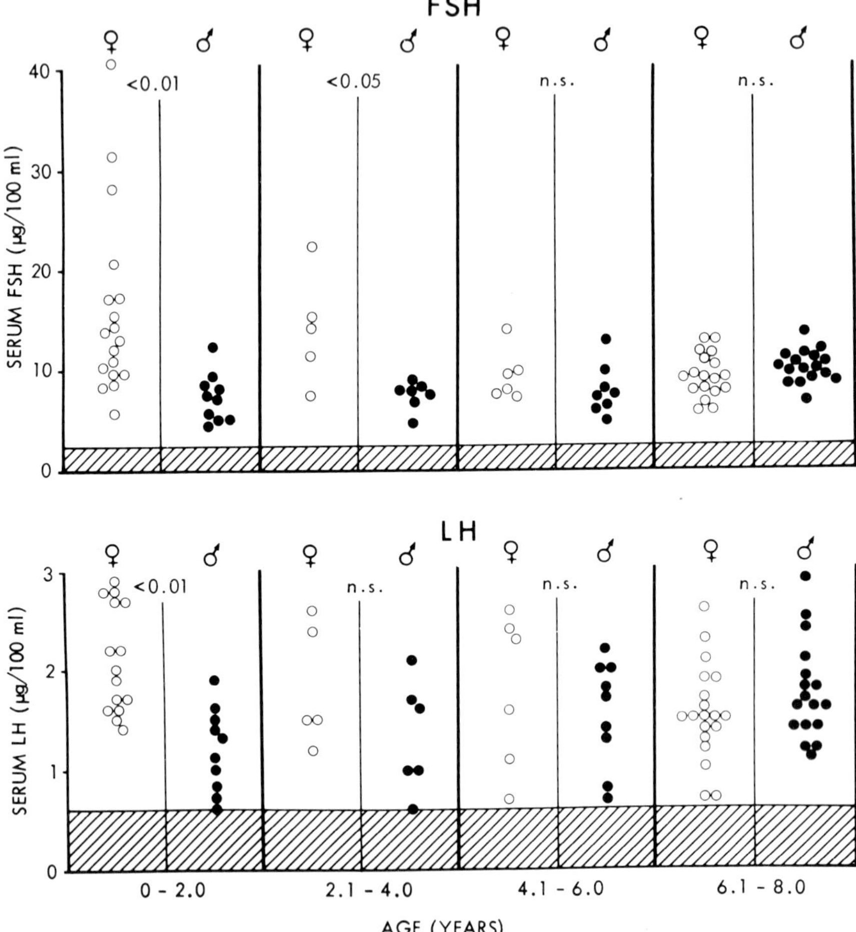

FIG. 15. Serum FSH and LH levels in boys and girls in early childhood. The
shaded areas represent the limit of sensitivity of each assay. *P* values for sex differences are indicated above each pair of observations (ns = *P* > 0.1). Reproduced with
permission from Faiman & Winter (1971b).

FUTURE RESEARCH

Methodologic Problems

Can a single serum value adequately describe glandular hormone secretion patterns? Interassay variability for most RIA and competitive-binding
assays ranges from 10 to 20 per cent. Perhaps more important is the biological variability resulting from day-to-day, diurnal or minute-to-minute

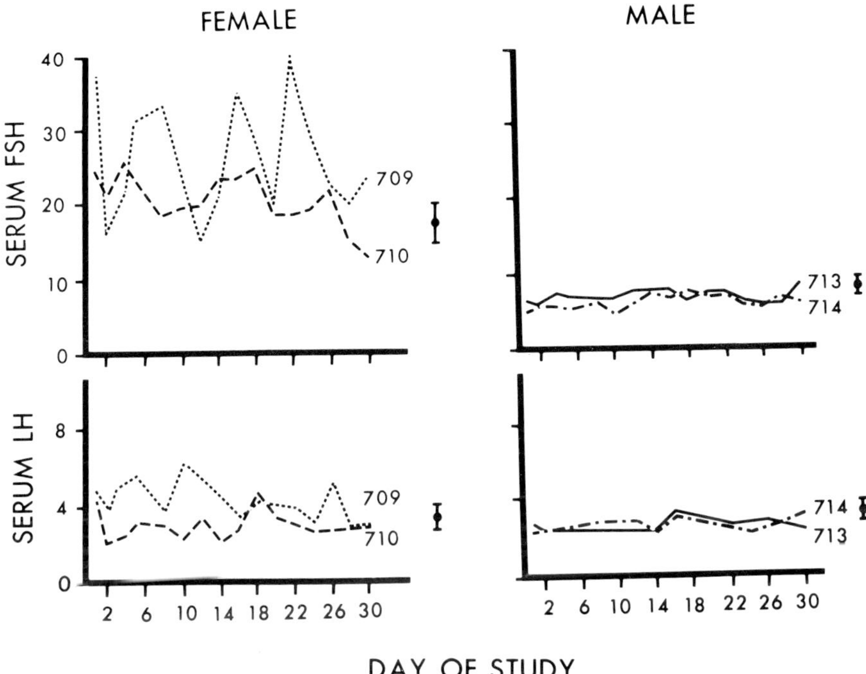

FIG. 16.   Serial levels of serum FSH and LH (in micrograms LER-907/100 ml) in 4 infant chimpanzees: ● represents the 95 per cent confidence limits about any individual measurement. Reproduced with permission from Faiman et al (1972).

variation in hormonal secretion. Biological variability appears to be especially important in studies of gonadotropin patterns since the recent report of pulsatile nocturnal LH secretion during early puberty in boys (Boyar, Finkelstein, Roffwarg, & Hellman, 1972).

Serum Versus Urine

Estimations of 24-hour urinary excretion offer the theoretical advantage of smoothing out or integrating short-term fluctuations in hormone secretion. Data qualitatively similar to ours have been reported in which the urinary excretion of FSH and LH was estimated; increments observed during puberty appear to be larger (Raiti, Light, & Blizzard, 1969); Baghdassarian et al, 1970). Values obtained by immunoassay of unextracted or acetone- (or ethanol-) extracted urine are higher, especially for LH, than those obtained by bioassay (Rifkind et al, 1967); few data are available to determine whether the renal clearance of gonadotropins varies as a function of the serum level and/or age. Correlations of FSH (Raiti et al, 1969a,b) and LH (Baghdassarian et al, 1970) in both serum and urine suggest that at low serum levels relatively large elevations may not be reflected in any noticeable urinary increments.

Onset of Fertility

Few data concerning the development of complete spermatogenesis in man are available. Similarly, although it is widely claimed that the early postmenarchial girl is relatively infertile, exact information on ovulation, corpus luteum function, and sperm capacitation is not yet available.

Pituitary and Gonadal Function Before Birth and During Childhood

This area appears to be fruitful for further investigation because variations in prenatal gonadal hormone levels and in "sexing" of neural tissues may result in early or late puberty, abnormalities in menstrual cyclicity, relative infertility, or even abnormal behavior patterns. The observation that prepubertal castration results in elevated FSH levels (Winter & Faiman, 1972b) demonstrates that the prepubertal gonad secretes products, the nature and exact function of which are unclear.

Adrenarche in the Female

Whether the observed increments in levels of serum testosterone during female puberty reflect increases in ovarian or adrenal androgen secretion has not been clearly established; nor, if these increments do represent increased adrenal secretion, has the tropic regulating hormone been identified.

Neurohumoral Basis of Puberty

Two main theories have been postulated to explain the increased gonadotropin secretion that initiates puberty: (1) this increase reflects maturation of the central nervous system which results either in increased secretion of stimulatory neurohumoral products or in reduced production of inhibitory products, and (2) (not mutually exclusive) a progressive reduction in hypothalamic sensitivity to the negative feedback effect of some gonadal secretion product results in increasing gonadotropin production, related to which is the question whether FSH and LH are under separate neurohumoral control.

ACKNOWLEDGMENTS

We wish to thank Mrs. R. Poturnak, Miss E. Sarna, and Mr. I. Riyaz for technical assistance and Mrs. J. A. McDougall for typing the manuscript. This work was supported by Medical Research Council of Canada Grant No. MA-2997, and the Children's Hospital Research Foundation, Winnipeg, Manitoba.

REFERENCES

August, G. P., Grumbach, M. M., & Kaplan, S. (1972). Hormonal changes in puberty: III. Correlation of plasma testosterone, LH, FSH, testicular size, and bone age with male pubertal development. *J. Clin. Endocrinol.* **34**, 319–326.

Baghdassarian, A., Guyda, H., Johanson, A., Migeon, C. J., & Blizzard, R. M. (1970). Urinary excretion of radioimmunoassayable luteinizing hormone (LH) in normal male children and adults, according to age and stage of sexual development. *J. Clin. Endocrinol.* **31**, 428–435.

Bearwood, C. J. & Russell, G. F. M. (1970). Gonadotrophin excretion at puberty. *J. Endocrinol.* **48**, 469–470.

Blizzard, R. M., Penny, R., Foley Jr., T. P., Baghdassarian, A., Johanson, A., & Yen, S. C. C. (1972). In *Gonadotropins* (B. B. Saxena, C. G. Beling, and H. Gandy, Eds.), Wiley, New York, pp. 502–523.

Boon, D. A., Keenan, R. E., Slaunwhite, Jr., W. R., & Aceto, Jr., T. (1972). Conjugated and unconjugated plasma androgens in normal children. *Pediat. Res.* 6, 111–118.

Boyar, R. M., Finkelstein, J., Roffwarg, H., & Hellman, L. (1972). Identification of puberty by synchronization of luteinizing hormone release with sleep. *J. Clin. Invest.* **51**, 13a.

Buckler, J. M. H. & Clayton, B. E. (1970). Output of luteinizing hormone in the urine of normal children and those with advanced sexual development. *Arch. Dis. Childh.* **45**, 478–481.

Burr, I. M., Sizonenko, P. C., Kaplan, S. L., & Grumbach, M. M. (1970). Hormonal changes in puberty: I. Correlation of serum luteinizing hormone and follicle stimulating hormone with stages of puberty, testicular size, and bone age in normal boys. *Pediat. Res.* **4**, 25–35.

Cargille, C. M., Rodbard, D., & Ross, G. T. (1968). Radioimmunoassay of human follicle stimulating hormone: bias due to antisera. *J. Clin. Endocrinol.* **18**, 1276–1280.

Faiman, C. & Ryan, R. J. (1967a). Radioimmunassay for human follicle stimulating hormone. *J. Clin. Endocrinol.* **27**, 444–447.

Faiman, C. & Ryan, R. J. (1967b). Radioimmunoassay for human luteinizing hormone. *Proc. Soc. Exptl. Biol. Med.* **125**, 1130–1133.

Faiman, C. & Shome, B. (1971). Report of the Medical Research Council Committee on Human Pituitary Hormones: radioimmunoassay kits for human follicle stimulating hormone and luteinizing hormone. *Canad. J. Physiol. Pharmacol.* **44**, 685–687.

Faiman, C. & Winter, J. S. D. (1971a). Diurnal cycles in plasma FSH, testosterone and cortisol in men. *J. Clin. Endocrinol.* **33**, 186–192.

Faiman, C. & Winter, J. S. D. (1971b). Sex differences in gonadotrophin concentrations in infancy. *Nature* **232**, 130–131.

Faiman, C., Winter, J. S. D., Chebib, F. S., & Butler, T. M. (1972). Sex differences in gonadotropins in the infant chimpanzee. *J. Clin. Endocrinol.* **34**, 601–604.

Frasier, S. D., Gafford, F., & Horton, R. (1969). Plasma androgens in childhood and adolescence. *J. Clin. Endocrinol.* **29**, 1404–1408.

Hayes, A. & Johanson, A. (1972). Excretion of follicle-stimulating hormone (FSH) and luteinizing hormone (LH) in urine by pubertal girls. *Pediat. Res.* **6**, 18–25.

Jenner, M. R., Kelch, R. P., Kaplan, S. L., & Grumbach, M. M. (1972). Hormonal changes in puberty: IV. Plasma estradiol, LH, and FSH in prepubertal children, pubertal females, and in precocious puberty, premature thelarche, hypogonadism, and in a child with a feminizing ovarian tumor. *J. Clin. Endocrinol.* **34**, 521–530.

Johanson, A. J., Guyda, H., Light, C., Migeon, C. J., & Blizzard, R. M. (1969). Serum luteinizing hormone by radioimmunoassay in normal children. *J. Pediat.* **74**, 416–424.

Jost, A. (1970). Hormonal factors in the development of the male genital system. In *The Human Testis* (E. Rosenberg, & C. A. Paulsen, Eds.), Plenum, New York/London, pp. 11–18.

Keller, P. J. (1971). Die gonadotrope steuerung der weiblichen sexualfunktion. *J. Neuro-Visceral Rel.* **Suppl. 10**, 430–435.

Lee, P. A., Midgley, Jr., A. R., & Jaffe, R. B. (1970). Regulations of human gonadotropins: VI. Serum follicle stimulating and luteinizing hormone determinations in children. *J. Clin. Endocrinol.* **31**, 248–253.

Nankin, H. H. & Troen, P. (1971). Repetitive luteinizing hormone elevations in serum of normal men. *J. Clin. Endocrinol.* **33**, 558–560.

Nathanson, I. T., Towne, L. E., & Aub, J. C. (1941). Normal excretion of sex hormones in childhood. *Endocrinology* **28**, 851–865.

Pennington, G. W. & Dewhurst, C. J. (1969). Hormone excretion in premenarcheal girls. *Arch. Dis. Childh.* **44**, 629–636.

Penny, R., Guyda, H. J., Baghdassarian, A., Johanson, A., & Blizzard, R. M. (1970). Correlation of serum follicle stimulating hormone (FSH) and luteinizing hormone (LH) as measured by radioimmunoassay in disorders of sexual development. *J. Clin. Invest.* **49**, 1847–1852.

Raiti, S., Johanson, A., Light, C., Migeon, C. J., & Blizzard, R. M. (1969a). Measurement of immunologically reactive follicle-stimulating hormone in serum of normal male children and adults. *Metabolism* **18**, 234–240.

Raiti, S. M. B., Light, C., & Blizzard, R. M. (1969b). Urinary follicle-stimulating hormone excretion in boys and adult males as measured by radioimmunoassay. *J. Clin. Endocrinol.* **29**, 884–890.

Reyes, F. I., Winter, J. S. D., & Faiman, C. (1972). Pituitary-ovarian interrelationships during the puerperium. *Amer. J. Ob. Gyn.* **114**, 589–594.

Reyes, F. I., Winter, J. S. D., & Faiman, C. (1973). Studies on human sexual development: I. Fetal gonadal and adrenal sex steroids. *J. Clin. Endocrinol.* In press.

Rifkind, A. B., Kulin, H. E., & Ross, G. T. (1967). Follicle-stimulating hormone (FSH) and luteinizing hormone (LH) in the urine of prepubertal children. *J. Clin. Invest.* **46**, 1925–1931.

Rifkind, A. B., Kulin, H. E., Rayford, P. L., Cargille, C. M., & Ross, G. T. (1970). 24-hour urinary luteinizing hormone (LH) and follicle stimulating hormone (FSH) excretion in normal children. *J. Clin. Endocrinol.* **31**, 517–525.

Root, A. W., Moshang, T., Jr., Bongiovanni, A. M., & Eberlein, W. R. (1970). Concentration of plasma luteinizing hormone in infants, children, and adolescents with normal and abnormal gonadal function. *Pediat. Res.* **4**, 175–186.

Ross, G. T., Cargille, C. M., Lipsett, M. B., Rayford, P. L., Marshall, J. R., Strott, C. A., & Rodbard, D. (1970). Pituitary and gonadal hormones in women during spontaneous and induced ovulatory cycles. *Rec. Progr. Hormone Res.* **26**, 1–62.

Sciarra, N. & Leone, U. (1970). Urinary excretion of luteinizing hormone in boys and adult men. *J. Endocrinol.* **46**, 229–236.

Sizonenko, P. C., Burr, I. M., Kaplan, S. L., & Grumbach, M. M. (1970). Hormonal changes in puberty: II. Correlation of serum luteinizing hormone and follicle stimulating hormone with stages of puberty and bone age in normal girls. *Pediat. Res.* **4**, 36–45.

Tanner, J. M. (1962). *Growth in Adolescence* (2nd ed.). Blackwell, Oxford.

Tanner, J. M. & Gupta, D. (1968). A longitudinal study of the urinary excretion of individual steroids in children from 8 to 12 years old. *J. Endocrinol.* **41**, 139–156.

Taymor, M. L. & Miyata, J. (1969). Discrepancies and similarities of serum FSH and LH patterns as evaluated by different assay methods. *Acta Endocrinol. (Kbh) Suppl.* **142**, 324–337.

Wieland, R. G., Yen, S. C. C., & Pohlman, C. (1970). Serum testosterone levels and testosterone binding affinity in prepubertal and adolescent males; correlation with gonadotropins. *Amer. J. Med. Sci.* **259**, 358–360.

Winter, J. S. D. & Faiman, C. (1971). Changes in the pituitary-gonadal axis during childhood and adolescence. *Proc. XIIIth Intl. Cong. Pediatrics. Wiener Med. Akad.* **8**, 271–275.

Winter, J. S. D. & Faiman, C. (1972a). Pituitary-gonadal relations in male children and adolescents. *Pediat. Res.* **6**, 126–135.

Winter, J. S. D. & Faiman, C. (1972b). Serum gonadotropin concentrations in agonadal children and adults. *J. Clin. Endocrinol.* **35**. In press.

Winter, J. S. D. & Grant, D. R. (1971). A rapid and sensitive assay for plasma testosterone in adults and children. *Analyt. Biochem.* **40**, 440–449.

Winter, J. S. D., Taraska, S., & Faiman, C. (1972). The hormonal response to HCG stimulation in male children and adolescents. *J. Clin. Endocrinol.* **34**, 348–353.

Yen, S. S. C. & Vičic, J. J. (1970). Serum follicle-stimulating hormone levels in puberty. *Amer. J. Ob. Gyn.* **106**, 134–137.

Yen, S. S. C., Vičic, W. J., & Kearchner, D. V. (1969). Gonadotropin levels in puberty: I. Serum luteinizing hormone. *J. Clin. Endocrinol.* **29**, 382–385.

DISCUSSION

Dr. Blizzard. Did you find any age difference between males and females in the onset of gonadotropin elevation? Also, which attained adult values first?

Dr. Faiman. We have not looked at this in a statistical sense. The female may enter puberty and show FSH increments perhaps a little earlier. The LH increment appears to occur somewhat earlier in the male. The attainment of "adult" values for FSH and LH probably occurs a bit earlier in the female than in the male, on the average.

Dr. Blizzard. Earlier data would suggest that the FSH and LH in the male and female go up at the same age but that the female reaches adult values several years before the male (Blizzard, Penny, Foley, Baghdassarian, Johanson, & Yen, 1972).

Dr. Faiman. These comparisons are not very meaningful, especially when one considers the large day-to-day variability in the perimenarchial female. Some investigators have, in fact, removed the very high values, suggestive of ovulatory peaks, from such comparisons.

Dr. Steinberger. Am I correct in interpreting your composite study in which the FSH was higher than LH throughout the development, all the way up to adulthood?

Dr. Faiman. If you mean comparison of FSH to LH in micrograms per cent, we should recognize that the standard is a crude pituitary material and, therefore, values do not represent amounts of pure material. For what it is worth, the LER-907 standard contains somewhere around 1 unit to 1½ units of NIH-FSH-S1, per milligram of FSH, being 1 per cent pure FSH. The LH potency is roughly 0.1 U (NIH-LH-S1) per milligram. Comparing that to 4 U perhaps for pure LH, it thus contains about 2.5 per cent pure LH. After these mental gymnastics are performed, you can see how many moles of pure material there are, since FSH and LH are of similar molecular weight.

Dr. Ross. In man, the evidence is quite clear that FSH and LH in pituitary extracts are different from FSH and LH in serum; both, in turn, are different from FSH and LH in urine. These 3 species are antigenically distinct and therefore any consideration of relative numbers of molecules of FSH and LH is meaningless when serum concentrations are measured relative to a pituitary or a urinary extract. If we ever get around to producing a serum reference preparation and antisera, generated against serum immunogens, then perhaps we will be in a position to compare these numbers. For the present, however, it is useless to attempt to draw conclusions about colligative properties from data generated by these assays.

DR. FAIMAN.   I agree, and perhaps we should include some of the other hormones that are measured in serum.

DR. RAMIREZ.   Dr. Faiman, what are your thoughts on comparing the values of FSH in infant girls and boys in the 0- to 2-year age group; how many girls were 6 months, 1 year, or 2 years?

DR. FAIMAN.   There were no neonates. There was a total of about 30 infants fairly evenly distributed in both sexes between 6 months and 2 years of age. The 4 chimpanzees (2 of each sex) were all 2 years of age. We have now studied another 3 females and 2 males, ranging from 6 to 18 months of age, and the same differences apply. The male levels are low or undetectable. The female levels are easily detectable, fluctuate widely, and, in fact, on occasion reach adult peak values.

DR. FRASIER.   Dr. Robert Penny has measured FSH and LH in the cord blood of 25 female and 26 male newborns. The same sex differences in FSH concentration are observed. Female newborns have significantly higher FSH concentrations than males.

DR. FRISCH.   Are the girls you studied from a middle-class population? If they are, the age at which your data show a rapid hormonal change is close to the mean age of the initiation of the adolescent growth spurt, 9.6 years, found by us for middle-class girls. The rise of estradiol at age 10 would be in accord. Also, we found that initiation of the spurt and peak velocity each takes place in boys 2 years later than in girls. We, therefore, predicted that boys would reach a stage comparable to menarche at about 14.9 to 15 years, since the mean age of menarche of girls in our study was 12.9 years. Your data level off at about 15 years, which are also in accord.

DR. FAIMAN.   Actually, the girls all reached their menarche by age 13 in this group. They were middle-class girls, by and large.

DR. FRISCH.   It sounds like a very comparable group, in which case the endocrinological findings fit well with our findings on the ages of attainment of the critical weights at initiation of the adolescent spurt and at peak velocity.

DR. TANNER.   Drs. Faiman and Winter are providing data for which all those dealing with the human have been waiting. We also in the last 2 or 3 years have been studying the concentrations of LH and FSH, but in 24-hour urine specimens in a longitudinal study comprising 50 to 60 boys and 50 to 60 girls. We started them all off at age 9, so we do not yet have many results. It is, however, perfectly clear that the LH rise in the urine begins in girls before it does in boys.

DR. GRUMBACH. I would like to emphasize the usefulness of determining urinary FSH and LH in prepubertal and pubertal children, and here I disagree with Dr. Faiman. There are striking differences in the excretion of urinary FSH and LH during puberty. As shown by Rifkind, Kulin, and Ross (1967) and confirmed by Dr. Blizzard's and our group, the excretion of FSH increases about fourfold during puberty, whereas LH increases about twelvefold. The large increase in LH during puberty is not reflected in the serum values obtained during the day. With the onset of puberty, episodic secretion of LH is first clearly demonstrable. Further, Boyar, Finkelstein, Roffwarg, Kapen, Weitzman, and Hillman (1972) have shown that during puberty, but not before its onset or after sexual maturation, there is an augmentation of LH secretion during sleep. For these reasons serum LH values have serious limitations in assessing the changes in secretion of LH which occur during puberty, although the overall pattern is of interest. Your data on the relationship between the increase in serum LH and testosterone levels in boys during puberty show an additional association. With Drs. August and Kaplan, we reported (1972) that a sharp rise in serum LH in early puberty (P2) preceded the major increment in serum testosterone which occurred at a later stage of puberty (P3 according to our modified criteria of Tanner). This sequential relationship also appeared to be present in your cross-sectional and longitudinal study. An additional problem, on which I would be interested to have your comments, is the significantly higher mean serum FSH and LH values in girls under 2 years of age than in boys. The question arises whether this reflects a difference at this early age in the sex steroid secretion of the testis and ovary and, thus, in negative feedback. We find a similar sex difference in the pituitary content and concentration of FSH and LH and the concentration of serum FSH in the human fetus. Is, for example, the concentration of serum testosterone higher in male than in female infants? We have an opportunity to examine this possibility in small samples of blood by utilizing the great sensitivity provided by the RIA methods for testosterone and related steroids.

DR. FAIMAN. More sensitive methods are now available for measuring testosterone. The observation that prepubertal castration results in FSH and LH increments in the human has now been documented by our group, yours, and, of course, earlier by Dr. Blizzard's group. It would be of much interest to be able to measure a decrement in the serum level of some feedback inhibitory product in the agonadal subject, and also, perhaps, a difference in some steroid level between the two sexes in the first couple of years of life as well. Although the increments in urine are somewhat larger than in serum from pre- to postpubertal years, one still has to document whether or not the renal clearance of gonadotropins is changing during this time.

DR. RAITI. I wanted to make a comment about early infancy. Buckler (1970) looked at urinary excretion of LH within the first 6 months of life and showed a sex difference.

DR. FAIMAN. I think the differences were only seen in neonates, and they were probably measuring hCG levels. They happened to have more males than females at the early ages and claimed that LH levels were higher in male infants.

Dr. Lee.   I have some data on LH and FSH levels in the first 2 years of life which confirm those of Dr. Faiman. When the LH data are analyzed, males versus females by the Student t test, there is no significant difference. However, when the males from 1 month to 2 years of age are compared with males between 2 and 6 years of age, the males in the younger group have higher LH levels. Similar comparison with data from girls shows no difference. The concentrations in the first 3 months of life appear to be higher than later. However, the females in the first 12 months of life have significantly higher FSH values than the males.

Dr. MacGillivray.   From your human studies it is apparent that plasma FSH is high in early life; however, the animal work suggests that the pituitary content of gonadotropins is low in the early postnatal period. I would like to ask two questions: (1) Is there any evidence that the material we are measuring early in life is of equal biological activity to the material measured later in life? (2) Is there any evidence that the gonadotropin values which are high early in life may be, in themselves, suppressing gonadotropin production by the pituitary?

Dr. Faiman.   I really cannot answer those questions.

Dr. Rosenfield.   We have studied the response to 5 days of hCG stimulation in a few prepubertal children, 1 week to 16 years of age. Plasma testosterone levels consistently increased more than those of androstenedione or dehydro-epiandrosterone (unpublished).

Dr. Ramirez.   There is some evidence from a physiological point of view that what we are measuring in the plasma with RIA means something, although the plasma gonadotropins measured by RIA are not the complete story; e.g., immature male and female rats have different responses to castration. Besides, using the same RIA, the infantile male rat has very low plasma FSH values compared to infantile female rats, and the changing plasma FSH levels as a function of age showed completely different curves in both sexes. So there is some evidence from a physiological point of view that the high FSH level detected in the infantile female rat, compared to the male, has some physiological meaning.

Dr. Faiman. The question raised is whether or not the FSH level in prepubertal individuals represents the same biologically active molecule as in the post-pubertal adult. It is a good question, but one which has not been examined.

Dr. Paulsen.   With respect to your noted testosterone increment in relation to serum FSH changes and chronological age, it appears that your data are in contrast to Bryan Hudson's. Although he did not specifically measure serum FSH levels, he noted a significant rise in plasma testosterone levels about 6 months before pubertal changes were observed somatically. You tend to minimize early testosterone increases.

DR. FAIMAN.   In the cross-sectional data there was no change in testosterone until the age of 10. Hudson has data suggesting that there is. Is that what you are saying?

DR. PAULSEN.   The fundamental point which requires clarification is whether the FSH increase by itself accounts for testicular growth or whether increased testosterone secretion is important in this regard.

DR. FAIMAN.   Testosterone did not show any change until the age of 10, whereas increments in both FSH and LH began at about the age of 6.

DR. GANDY.   We also have shown that plasma testosterone begins to rise at about age 8 in a limited number of children in a cross-sectional study in a mixed population in New York and also that there is a rise in plasma levels of dehydroepiandrosterone and its sulfate about age 8. These adrenal steroids reach maximal levels by age 20 and begin to decline at about age 35 or 40. There is little information about the role of dehydroepiandrosterone and/or its sulfate in sexual maturation and in the control of FSH and LH secretion prepubertally.

DR. GRUMBACH.   Dr. Faiman raised a number of questions in his discussion. We recognize that preceding the somatic changes of puberty in man there is a sequence of hormonal changes. In studying normal children classified as prepubertal by physical signs, some who are close to puberty may be expected to have serum FSH, LH, and especially sex steroid values which fall into the pubertal range. So it is important to make a distinction between the chronology of the hormonal and somatic changes of puberty; for example, 3 prepubertal males and 3 prepubertal females in a group of over 60 prepubertal children who were given LRF had a pubertal LH response to LRF; all 6 had serum testosterone or estradiol values which were in the early pubertal range, despite their lack of physical signs of puberty.

DR. SIZONENKO. I would like to remind you of a steroid, estrone, which is probably secreted by the adrenal glands before you can observe any clinical signs of puberty. This was reported partly at the International Congress of Endocrinology and at the European Society of Pediatric Endocrinology meeting in Louvain (1972) by Saez, Morera, and Bertrand, who showed that there was an inhibition of secretion of estrone with administration of dexamethasone in children. They stimulated estrone secretion when they gave ACTH, thus suggesting an adrenal origin of estrone.

REFERENCES

August, G. P., Grumbach, M. M., & Kaplan, S. L. (1972). Hormonal changes in puberty: III. Correlation of plasma testosterone, L.H., F.S.H., testicular size and bone age with male pubertal development. *J. Clin. Endocrinol.* **34**, 319–326.

Blizzard, R. M., Penny, R., Foley, Jr., T. P., Baghdassarian, A., Johanson, A., & Yen, S. S. C. (1972). Pituitary gonadal interrelationships in relation to puberty, In *Gonadotropins,* (S. Saxena, C. G. Beling, & H. M. Gandy, Eds.), Wiley, New York.

Boyar, R., Finkelstein, F., Roffwarg, H., Kapen, S., Weitzman, E., & Hellman, L. (1972). Synchronization of augmented luteinizing hormone secretion with sleep during puberty. *New Eng. J. Med.* **287**, 582–586.

Buckler, J. M. H. & Clayton, B. E. (1970). Output of luteinizing hormone in urine of normal children and those with advanced sexual development. *Arch. Dis. Child.* **45**, 478–484.

Rifkind, A. B., Kulin, H. J., & Ross, G. T. (1967). Follicle stimulating hormone (FSH) and luteinizing hormone (LH) in the urine of prepubertal children. *J. Clin. Invest.* **46**, 1925–1931.

Saez, J. M., Morera, A. M., & Bertrand, J. (1972). Mesure de la concentration plasmatique de la dihydro-testosterone. *Rev. Eur. Etude Clin. Biol.* **16**, 284–287.

3.

Chemistry and Function of Hypophysiotropic Factors in Relation to Puberty

M. S. AMOSS, JR., and R. GUILLEMIN

We have undertaken the study of the various hypophysiotropic factors of hypothalamic origin by utilizing biochemical and molecular biological

---

Abbreviations

ACTH	Adrenocorticotropic hormone
CMC	Carboxymethyl cellulose
CRF	Adrenocorticotropic hormone releasing factor
FSH	Follicle stimulating hormone
GH	Growth hormone
LH	Luteinizing hormone
LFR	Luteinizing hormone releasing factor
PCA	Pyroglutamic acid
PIF	Prolactin inhibiting factor
PRF	Prolactin releasing factor
PTH	Phenyl-thiohydantoin
PTU	Propylthiouracil
RF	Releasing factor
RIA	Radioimmunoassay
SRF	Somatotropin releasing factor
TRF	Thyroid releasing factor

approaches. This presentation concerns itself with the chemistry of LRF, its analogues, and the relation of its chemistry to biological activity.

Many studies have led to the concept that the juvenile gonads are capable of responding to gonadotropins at a very early age; many more have shown that the pituitary gland will respond to the signals received from the hypothalamus, regardless of the sex of the pituitary donor. This has led us to investigations concerning the development of the hypothalamus, the possible modifying factors, the role of the releasing factors, and those factors that modify their secretion and synthesis.

Two groups have reported the sequence of porcine and ovine LRF, its synthesis, evaluation in experimental animals, clinical studies, and the synthesis of many analogues, two of which are said to be antagonistic to LRF. Now 8 additional peptides which have the ability to antagonize the effect of LRF are available.

Although this presentation centers on LRF, some attention must be paid to TRF (thyroid releasing factor) and to those factors that modify GH and ACTH secretions. The ultimate influence of the other hypothalamic-hypophysial-target organ axes must also be studied in relation to their possible roles in pubescence.

Two laboratories have now published purification sequences that yield highly pure LRF of porcine (Schally, Arimura, Baba, Nair, Matsuo, Redding, Debeljuk, & White, 1971a) and ovine origins (Amoss, Burgus, Blackwell, Vale, Fellows, & Guillemin, 1971). Although both use similar methods, the initial extractions are quite different, and the sequence of the purification methods is not the same. The purification of porcine LRF reported by Schally, Baba, Nair, and Bennett (1971c) is a 12-step process in which the initial step is a 2N acetic acid extraction. Gel filtration on Sephadex G-25 is followed by phenol extraction and then by ion exchange chromatography on carboxymethyl cellulose (CMC). The biologically active fractions of several columns are combined and rechromatographed under the same conditions and followed by purification by free-flow electrophoresis. The next 3 steps utilize partition chromatography in 3 different solvent systems. Countercurrent distribution of 500 transfers in the 11:5:3 system (0.1 per cent acetic acid, *n*-butanol, and pyridine) is followed by column partition chromatography with Sephadex G-25 as the solid support in the system 4:1:5:.33 (*n*-butanol, acetic acid, water, and benzene), after which the material is rechromatographed in a 25:7:30:2:1:10 system (*n*-butanol, ethanol, water, acetic acid, pyridine, and benzene). The final stage of purification consists of zone electrophoresis.

The initial extraction of the ovine hypothalami (Amoss et al, 1971) consists of an alcohol-chloroform extraction, which is followed by an ether-petroleum ether separation; the extract is then leached with glacial acetic acid. Ultrafiltration of this material is accomplished on a Diaflo

UM-05 membrane. Gel filtration on Sephadex-25 of the entire batch of hypothalami results in the separation of TRF and LRF activity. Ion exchange chromatography on CMC with step gradients of molarity and pH of ammonium acetate buffer is used. At this stage a 0.2 μg aliquot of ^{125}I-LRF is added and used as a marker. The material for iodination was of the same degree of purity as that used for N-terminal identification (Amoss, Burgus, Ward, Fellows, & Guillemin, 1970). The LRF fractions are then subjected to column electrophoresis with Sephadex G-25 as the support in 0.05M pyride acetate, followed by partition chromatography on a Sephadex G-25 matrix in the system 0.1 per cent acetic acid, n-butanol, pyridine (11:5:3). The final step is partition chromatography in n-butanol, acetic acid, water (4:1:5). This material is 56 per cent peptide, of which 94 per cent of the amino acids present are those of LRF.

It is interesting to note that, unlike TRF, LRF was not completely isolated (see Burgus, Dunn, Desiderio, & Guillemin, 1969); however, the contaminating material was not peptidic in nature nor related to LRF and posed no problem in the sequencing of the decapeptide.

Both laboratories reported the same amino acid composition after 6N HCl hydrolysis (His 1, Arg 1, Ser 1, Glu 1, Pro 1, Gly 2, Leu 1, and Tyr 1). The existence of a tryptophan moiety was reported subsequently by Matsuo, Baba, Nair, Arimura, and Schally (1971) with the use of alkaline and acid hydrolysis in the presence of thioglycolic acid. Burgus, Butcher, Ling, Monahan, Rivier, Fellows, Amoss, Blackwell, Vale, and Guillemin (1971) were able to show the presence of tryptophan by analysis of the hydrolyzed ^{14}C-dansylated amino acids and a combination of gas chromatography-mass spectroscopy of the trimethylsilylated-phenyl-thiohydantoin derivatives after Edman degradation.

In the determination of the structure of porcine LRF and ovine LRF completely different approaches to the problem were utilized. Matsuo et al (1971) subjected aliquots of LRF to enzymatic degradation by chymotrypsin and thermolysin. N-terminal residues resulting from the enzyme degradation were determined by dansylation, and the C-terminal analyses were determined by selective tritiation. Amino acid sequences of the fragments resulting from the enzyme treatments were determined by the Edman degradation and by using the dansyl reaction to identify the N-termini. Although they could not draw unambiguous conclusions about the structure, only the sequence pGlu-His-Trp-Ser-Tyr-Gly-Leu-Arg-Pro-Gly-NH$_2$ was consistent with all the data. In a later publication (Baba, Matsuo, & Schally, 1971) the N-terminal pyro-Glu was removed by a pyrrolidone carboxylyl peptidase, followed by a stepwise Edman-dansyl degradation that confirmed the structure of LRF.

The first step in the structural analysis of ovine LRF was the determination of the N-terminal pyroglutamic acid (PCA) by the use of pyrrolidone carboxylyl peptidase (Amoss et al, 1970), which was confirmed (Burgus et al, 1971) by partial hydrolysis, followed by dansylation and mass spectrometry which revealed peaks of $m/e = 84$ and 129, characteristic of PCA-amides. The final sequencing of the ovine LRF was reported by Burgus et al (1971, 1972). Chymotryptic digests yielded 4 major peptide fragments with smaller amounts of 2 other fragments. C-termini were determined by hydrazinolysis-dansylation. The use of ^{14}C-labeled dansyl chloride allowed accurate quantitation of the N-termini, and the Edman degradation of the peptide fragments was used to determine the sequence of each moiety. Analysis of these data does not allow the unambiguous positioning of the Ser-4 and Gly-6 residues which could be interchanged. Treatment with pyrrolidone carboxylyl peptidase followed by the Edman-dansylation analysis produced the data necessary to confirm the correct sequence of ovine LRF. Mass spectroscopy of the trimethylsilylated PTH derivatives was used to confirm cleaved amino acid residues after the Edman degradation. In both approaches the simultaneous analysis of synthetic LRF produced identical results. The structure of ovine LRF was shown to be identical to porcine LRF, i.e., pGlu-His-Trp-Ser-Tyr-Gly-Leu-Arg-Pro-Gly-NH$_2$.

Total solid phase synthesis of LRF on a benzhydrylamine resin was originally reported by Monahan, Rivier, Burgus, Amoss, Blackwell, Vale, and Guillemin (1971). Since then several laboratories have reported the synthesis, classical synthesis, and combinations of the two. Purification of synthetic LRF after cleavage from the resin and determination of the homogeneity of the product are of utmost importance. Ion-exchange chromatography on CMC followed by partition chromatography in the system n-butanol, acetic acid, water (4:1:5) has yielded essentially homogeneous LRF peptide and the many analogues of LRF that have been synthesized in this laboratory. To date we have synthesized approximately 10 g of LRF in 5 different batches, all obtained in maximal purity and maximal biological activity. More than 1 g of this pure synthetic LRF (for which an IND number was obtained) has been distributed for clinical studies.

Although early reports that LH-releasing activity could be separated from FSH-releasing activity (Dhariwal, Watanabe, Antunes-Rodrigues, & McCann, 1967; Schally, Arimura, Bowers, Kastin, Sawano, & Redding, 1968), the proposal has been made that LRF is the sole mediator of gonadotropin release (Schally et al 1971a,b). The synthetic decapeptide LRF and highly purified native ovine LRF elicit the release of LH and FSH (Amoss et al, 1971; Blackwell, Amoss, Vale, Burgus, Rivier, Monahan, Ling, Burgus, & Guillemin, 1972, in press (Table 1). Several

TABLE 1.   Release (ng) of FSH and LH in vivo by synthetic LRF

Treatment (ng)	N	FSH/ml±SE	p	LH/ml±SE	p
Saline		1753±129		856±188	
1	5	1863±131	—	2376±187	*
5	5	2072±130	—	3424±187	*
25	5	2606±129	*	4608±188	*
125	5	2581±130	*	4834±192	*
625	5	2818±130	*	5461±188	*
3125	5	2744±137	*	5471±189	*

p=level of statistical significance of the difference from control, determined by the one-sided multiple comparison test of Dunnett: —=non significant; *=99%

lines of research, one of which involves the very divergent slopes of the responses of LH and FSH to injections of LRF, have led us to view the concept of a single releasing factor with considerable caution. The release of LH induced by LRF is appreciably greater than FSH in all the in vivo rat preparations we have utilized to date. This is also true when the decapeptide is tested in vitro by using either hemipituitaries or the cell culture technique reported by Vale, Grant, Amoss, Blackwell, and Guillemin (1972a). Injection of LRF into chronically ovariectomized rats blocked with estrogen produces a statistically significant increase in LH with as little as 1 to 2 ng; the response then plateaus at about 80 ng in most preparations. FSH concentration in the plasma reaches significant levels at doses of LRF approximately 5 times higher than those required for LH. Arimura, Debeljuk, and Schally (1972) reported that maximal LH and FSH levels in plasma could be obtained by infusing relatively large amounts of LRF (0.2, 1, and 3 μg LRF) over a 4-hour period, in contrast to rapid intravenous injections.

Clinical investigations reported by Yen et al (1972a) indicate that significant LH responses induced by LRF are not always accompanied by significant FSH responses (Fig. 1). There are also instances in which there is a differential release of LH and FSH. Rubin, Kales, Adler, Fagan, and Odell, (1971) have shown that plasma LH (but not FSH) is increased during rapid eye movement in sleep. Stevens (1969) has reported that FSH secretory peaks occur 2 or 3 times during the normal menstrual cycle, whereas LH peaks only once. The report by Cargille, Ross, and Yoshimi (1969) of a surge of FSH during the early follicular phase of the menstrual cycle with no apparent change in the secretion of LH is an additional piece of evidence. In a study investigating pulsatile patterns of gonadotropin release Yen, Tsai, Naftolin, VandenBerg, and Ajabor (1972b) were able to show that LH is released as a series of pulses, whereas a definite

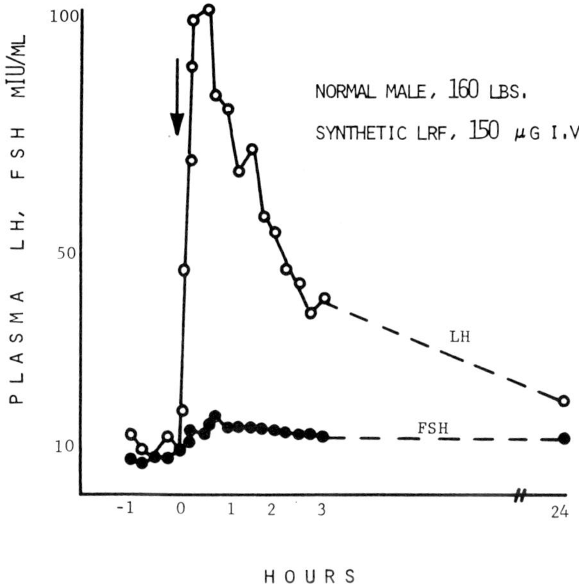

FIG. 1. Typical LH and FSH response of a normal adult male subject to a rapid intravenous injection of synthetic LRF: ○=LH; ●=FSH. Time of injection indicated by arrow.

pulsatile pattern of FSH secretion was not found during the normal menstrual cycle. In postmenopausal women both gonadotropins showed distinct pulsatile patterns; however, the peaks were not completely synchronous, although this apparent lack of synchrony might be caused by the difference in the biological half-life of the two gonadotropins.

There is still some evidence supporting the hypothesis that a separate hypothalamic hormone may control the release of FSH. There is no doubt that the decapeptide LRF is capable of eliciting both LH and FSH release. We are of the opinion that the extraction, purification, and subsequent isolation of hypothalami must be done by sensitive assay techniques for the assessment of FSH-releasing activity throughout the stages of purification. The claim that LRF is the sole mediator of gonadotropin secretion may be a bit premature, although it may eventually prove to be correct. This question remains one of the important problems in neuroendocrinology and must respond to all the accumulated data.

LRF ANALOGUES

Our laboratory and several others have initiated an extensive program concerning the structure-activity relationships of the two known hypothalamic factors TRF and LRF. To date more than 60 LRF analogues have been synthesized and tested, or are being tested, in the in vitro cell culture system or in the ovariectomized rat blocked with steroids. The synthesis and purification of these peptides, all of which were obtained as primary amides, have been similar to those described by Monahan et al (1971) for LRF. Two series of analogues have been tested completely for agonist as well as antagonist activities in vitro and in vivo.

In the first series, referred to as the Gly substitutes of LRF, 8 decapeptides were prepared with the sequence of LRF, each residue normally different from Gly being replaced with Gly. In Gly^1 LRF blocking of the N-terminal residue was achieved by preparing the protected decapeptide propionyl-$[Gly^1]$ LRF. In that series Gly^4 LRF had the highest potency when compared with the LRF standard (1.5 per cent). The $[Gly^{1,7,9}]$ LRF analogues had 0.2 per cent activity and the $[Gly^{2,3,5 \text{ and } 8}]$ LRF peptides had 0.1 per cent or less of the activity of the synthetic LRF standard when tested in both the in vitro and in vivo systems described. In vitro experiments with $[Gly^2]$ LRF and $[Gly^3]$ LRF yielded results that indicated that the slope of the function relating biological response (release of LH) to $\log_{10}$ of the dose of the peptide administered were statistically different from those of LRF in the same system. Because this precludes the use of the classical calculations of potency in terms of LRF activity, the figures given here are approximations based primarily on the dose necessary to achieve a response.

In the second series (Rivier, Monahan, Vale, Grant, Amoss, Blackwell, Guillemin, & Burgus, 1972), the des-LRF, 7 peptides corresponding to the primary sequence of LRF from which one residue starting at the C-terminus was subtracted were synthesized. All the peptides of this series, when tested both in vivo and in vitro, yielded potencies of less than 0.11 per cent that of LRF, the exception being des-Gly^{10} LRF which had a potency of 10 per cent that of LRF.

Since the 3-methyl-histidine derivative of TRF was more active than TRF itself in the release of TSH by a factor of 10 (Vale, Rivier, & Burgus, 1971), methyl-histidine derivatives of LRF were tested. Both the 1- and 3-methyl-histidine derivatives were synthesized and had 2 and 6 per cent, respectively, of the activity of LRF.

All the analogues were tested for their ability to release LH and FSH by the in vitro cell-culture method and the in vivo test in which chronically ovariectomized rats were injected with estrogens and progestagens. The changes in the levels of the gonadotropins, either in the culture medium or in plasma, were determined by RIA. All the relative potencies expressed here are in terms of LH release. The FSH potency values were quite similar; however, the usually flat dose-response curve obtained from FSH assays makes a precise assignment of potency quite hazardous. Although

Arimura, A., Debeljuk, L., & Schally, A. V. (1972). Stimulation of FSH release *in vivo* by prolonged infusion of synthetic LH-RH. *Endocrinology* 91, 529–532.

Baba, Y., Matsuo, H., & Schally, A. V. (1971). Structure of the porcine LH- and FSH-releasing hormone. II. Confirmation of the proposed structure by conventional sequential analyses. *Biochem. Biophys. Res. Commun.* 44, 459–463.

Bala, R. M., Burgus, R., Ferguson, K. A., Guillemin, R., Kudo, C., Olivier, G. C., Rodger, N. W., & Beck, J. C. (1970). Control of growth hormone secretion. In *The Hypothalamus* (L. Martini, M. Motta, E. Fraschini, Eds.), Academic, New York, pp. 401–448.

Blackwell, R., Amoss, M., Vale, W., Burgus, K. A., Rivier, J., Monahan, M., Ling, N., Burgus, R., & Guillemin, R. (1972). Concomitant release of LH and FSH induced by native or synthetic LRF. *Amer. J. Physiol.* 224, 170–175.

Bowers, C. Y., Chang, J-K, Sievertsson, H., Bogentoft, C., Currie, B. L., & Folkers, K. (1971a). Activity of a new synthetic tetrapeptide in hypothalamic luteinizing and follicle stimulating releasing hormone assay systems. *Biochem. Biophys. Res. Commun.* 44, 414–421.

Bowers, C. Y., Friesen, H., Hwang, P., Guyda, H. T., & Folkers, K. (1971b). Prolactin and thyrotropin release in man by synthetic pyroglutamyl-histidyl-prolineamide. *Biochem. Biophys. Res. Commun.* 45, 1033–1039.

Burgus, R., Butcher, M., Amoss, M., Ling, N., Monahan, M., Rivier, J., Fellows, R., Blackwell, R., Vale, W., & Guillemin, R. (1972). Primary structure of the hypothalamic luteinizing hormone releasing factor (LRF) of ovine origin. *Proc. Natl. Acad. Sci.* 69, 278–281.

Burgus, R., Butcher, M., Ling, N., Monahan, M., Rivier, J., Fellows, R., Amoss, M., Blackwell, R., Vale, W., & Guillemin, R. (1971). Structure moléculaire du facteur hypothalamique (LRF) d'origine ovine contrôlant la sécretion de l'hormone gonadotrope hypophysaire de lutéinisation (LH). *C.R. Acad. Sci. (Paris)* 273, 1611–1614.

Burgus, R., Dunn, T. F., Desiderio, D., & Guillemin, R. (1969). Structure moléculaire du facteur hypothalamique hypophysiotrope TRF d'origine ovine: evidence par spectrométrie de masse de la séquence PCA-His-Pro-NH$_2$. *C.R. Acad. Sci. (Paris)* 269, 1870–1873.

Cargille, C. M., Ross, G. T., & Yoshimi, T. (1969). Daily variations in plasma follicle stimulating hormone, luteinizing hormones and progesterone in the normal menstrual cycle. *J. Clin. Endocrinol.* 29, 12–19.

Dhariwal, A. P. S., Watanabe, S., Antunes-Rodrigues, A., & McCann, S. (1967). Chromatographic behavior of follicle stimulating hormone-releasing factor in Sephadex and carboxymethyl cellulose. *Neuroendocrinology* 2, 294–303.

Frohman, L. A. & Bernardis, L. L. (1970). Growth hormone secretion in the rat; metabolic clearance and secretion rates. *Endocrinology* 86, 305–308.

Grant, G., Vale, W., & Guillemin, R. (1972). Interaction of thyrotropin releasing factor with membrane receptors of pituitary cells. *Biochem. Biophys. Res. Commun.* 46, 28–32.

Guillemin, R. (1971). Biosynthesis of the hypothalamic tripeptide-amide TRF. *Society for Neurosciences Meeting*, Washington, D.C., October, 1971, (abstract).

Guillemin, R., Amoss, M., Blackwell, R., Rivier, J., Ling, N., & Vale, W. (1972).

On the biological activities of the synthetic tetrapeptide pyro-glutamyl-tyrosyl-arginyl-tryptophanyl-amide. *Biochem. Biophys. Res. Commun.* **48**, 1093–1099.

Jacobs, L., Snyder, P., Wilber, J. F., Utiger, R., & Daughaday, W. H. (1971). Increased serum prolactin after administration of synthetic thyrotropin releasing hormone (TRH) in man. *J. Clin. Endocrinol.* **33**, 996–1002.

Kastin, A. J., Schally, A. V., Gual, C., Glick, S., & Arimura, A. (1972). Clinical evaluation in men of a substance with growth-hormone releasing activity in rats. *J. Clin. Endocrinol.* **35**, 326–329.

Labrie, F., Borden, N., Poirier, G., & DeLean, A. (1972). Binding of TRF to plasma membranes of bovine anterior pituitary gland. *Proc. Natl. Acad. Sci.* **69**, 283–286.

Malacara, J. M. & Reichlin, S. (1971). Elevation of radioimmunoassayable plasma growth hormone (RIA-GH) in the rat induced by porcine hypothalamic extract. *Fed. Proc.* **30**, 198 (abstract).

Matsuo, H., Baba, Y., Nair, R. M. G., Arimura, A., & Schally, A. V. (1971). Structure of the porcine LH- and FSH-releasing hormone. I. Proposed amino acid sequence. *Biochem. Biophys. Res. Commun.* **43**, 1334–1339.

Mitnick, M. & Reichlin, S. (1971). Thyrotropin releasing hormone: biosynthesis by hypothalamic fragments. *Science* **172**, 1241–1244.

Monahan, M., Rivier, J., Burgus, R., Amoss, M., Blackwell, R., Vale, W., & Guillemin, R. (1971). Synthése totale par phase solide d'un décapeptide qui stimule la sécrétion des gonadotropines hypophysaires LH et FSH. *C.R. Acad. Sci. (Paris)* **273**, 508–512.

Monahan, M., Rivier, J., Vale, W., Guillemin, R., & Burgus, R. (1972). Gly^2 LRF and des-His^2 LRF. The synthesis, purification and characteristics of two LRF analogues antagonistic to LRF. *Biochem. Biophys. Res. Commun.* **47**, 551–554.

Nair, R. M. G., Barrett, J., Bowers, C. Y., & Schally, A. V. (1970). Structure of porcine thyrotropin releasing hormone. *Biochem.* **9**, 1103–1106.

Rivier, J., Monahan, M., Vale, W., Grant, G., Amoss, M., Blackwell, R., Guillemin, R., & Burgus, R. (1972). Solid phase peptide synthesis on a benzhydrylamine resin of LRF (luteinizing hormone releasing factor) and analogues including antagonists. *Chimia* **26**, 300–303.

Rodger, N. W., Beck, J. C., Burgus, R., & Guillemin, R. (1969). Variability of response in the bioassay for a hypothalamic somatotrophin releasing factor based on rat pituitary growth hormone content. *Endocrinology* **84**, 1373–1383.

Rubin, R. T., Kales, A., Adler, R., Fagan, T., & Odell, W. (1971). Gonadotropin secretion during sleep in normal adult men. *Science* **175**, 196–198.

Schally, A. V., Arimura, A., Bowers, C. Y., Kastin, A., Sawano, S., & Redding, T. W. (1968). Hypothalamic neurohormones regulating anterior pituitary function. *Rec. Progr. Hormone Res.* **24**, 497–580.

Schally, A. V., Arimura, A., Baba, Y., Nair, R. M. G., Matsuo, H., Redding, T. W., Debeljuk, L., & White, W. F. (1971a). Isolation and properties of the FSH and LH releasing hormone. *Biochem. Biophys. Res. Commun.* **43**, 393–399.

Schally, A. V., Baba, Y., Arimura, A., Redding, T. W., & White, W. F. (1971b). Evidence for peptide nature of LH and FSH releasing hormones. *Biochem. Biophys. Res. Commun.* **42**, 50–56.

Schally, A. V., Baba, Y., Nair, R. M. G., & Bennett, C. D. (1971c). The amino acid sequence of a peptide with growth hormone-releasing activity isolated from porcine hypothalamus. *J. Biol. Chem.* **246**, 6647–6650.

Stevens, V. C. (1969). Comparison of FSH and LH patterns in plasma, urine and urinary extracts during the menstrual cycle. *J. Clin. Endocrinol.* **29**, 904–910.

Tashjian, Jr., A. H., Barowsky, N. J., & Jenson, D. K. (1971). Thyrotropin releasing hormone: direct evidence for stimulation of prolactin production by pituitary cells in culture. *Biochem. Biophys. Res. Commun.* **43**, 516–523.

Vale, W., Rivier, J., & Burgus, R. (1971). Synthetic TRF (thyrotropin releasing factor) analogues: II. pGlu-N^3imME-His-Pro-NH_2: A synthetic analogue with specific activity greater than that of TRF. *Endocrinology* **89**, 1485–1488.

Vale, W., Grant, G., Amoss, M., Blackwell, R., & Guillemin, R. (1972a). Culture of enzymatically dispersed anterior pituitary cells: functional validation of a method. *Endocrinology* **91**, 562–572.

Vale, W., Grant, G., Rivier, J., Monahan, M., Amoss, M., Blackwell, R., Burgus, R., & Guillemin, R. (1972b). Synthetic polypeptide antagonists of the hypothalamic luteinizing hormone releasing factor. *Science* **176**, 933–942.

Wilber, J., Nagel, T., & White, W. F. (1971). Hypothalamic growth hormone releasing activity (GRA); characterization by the *in vitro* rat pituitary and radioimmunoassay. *Endocrinology* **89**, 1419–1424.

Yen, S. S. C., Rebar, R., VandenBerg, G., Naftolin, F., Ehara, Y., Engblom, S., Ryan, K. J., Benirschke, K., Rivier, J., Amoss, M., & Guillemin, R. (1972a). Synthetic luteinizing hormone-releasing factor: a potent stimulator of gonadotropin release in man. *J. Clin. Endocrinol.* **34**, 1108–1111.

Yen, S. S. C., Tsai, C. C., Naftolin, F., VandenBerg, G., & Ajabor, L. (1972b). Pulsatile patterns of gonadotropin release in subjects with and without ovarian function. *J. Clin. Endocrinol.* **34**, 671–675.

DISCUSSION

DR. WEISZ.   One thing that puzzles me is that the pattern of response obtained with synthetic LRF seems to differ from that obtained with the native releasing factors. The discrepancy is observed both in vivo and in vitro. Specifically, with the native substances, crude or highly purified hypothalamic extracts, or in the experiments of Dr. Porter in which blood collected from pituitary portal vessels was used the response is characterized by a rapid rise in gonadotropin output followed by a rapid fall. The response obtained with the synthetic substance, on the other hand, tends to be flatter and more prolonged. It is also easier to obtain straight dose-response relationships with the native than with the synthetic material. Therefore, when testing substances, we should find out not only if there is a response but also look at the pattern and the time course of the response.

DR. PORTER.   I, too, am confused. If one looks at the pulsatile release of LH in vivo, one sees that the decay of the pulse corresponds closely to the half-life of LH in plasma, i.e., about 30 minutes, which suggests that LH release may be an off-on sort of thing. When synthetic LRF is infused directly into a portal vessel of the rat, an increase in release of LH occurs; but, when the infusion is stopped, the release of LH persists at a reasonably high rate for as long as 1½ hours. I agree with Dr. Weisz that the response of the pituitary to synthetic LRF appears to be different from that with "naturally occurring" LRF.

DR. AMOSS.   It has been reported by Yen, Rebar, VandenBerg, Naftolin, Ehara, Engblom, Ryan, and Benirschke (1972) that the half-life of LH and FSH after LRF stimulation appears to be about 3 times longer than observed after hypophysectomy.

DR. GRUMBACH.   I wish to point out a technical detail that may be of use in studies on the dose response to LRF, especially when attempting to determine the minimal effect in raising plasma LH and FH. Since LRF may adsorb to glass and plastic surfaces, we add 0.5 g/100 ml of human serum albumin to the diluent.

DR. GAY.   There might be a more prolonged LH release in response to the synthetic LH-RH decapeptide compared with the response to hypothalamic extracts. However, we have given the synthetic material to steroid-blocked castrated rats, which is the only preparation that allows a valid comparison with the response to crude extracts. So long as the animal is unanesthetized, we get exactly the same response with the decapeptide as with the crude LRF, i.e., a very rapid increase and a rapid decrease that approximates the disappearance rate for LH in the rat. Anesthesia (in this case pentobarbital) causes the animals to be more responsive to both crude and purified LRF, i.e., it augments the initial response. After this we observe a somewhat prolonged response pattern in which high levels of serum LH are seen as much as 1 hour later. However, I am convinced that the dynamics of LH release in an unanesthetized rat are similar following injections of crude extracts and the decapeptide.

DR. AMOSS.   In the data presented by Dr. Yen the patients were not anesthetized, and yet they exhibited this prolonged half-life.

DR. MCCANN.   Dr. Guillemin and his group have some reservations about whether there is a single gonadotropin-RF and feel that there might still be an FSH-RF hidden somewhere in these extracts. The reason I am coming back to this is because I like his position on this point and wish to mention a little more evidence to suggest the possibility that there is more than one gonadotropin RF. In the early days, using bioassay, a number of laboratories actually claimed to have separated these two activities, i.e., the FSH and LH releasing activities. We obtained such separations. Dr. Schally actually reported the isolation of a separate FSH-RF. Dr. Kobayshi's group in Japan and Dr. Jutisz in France also claimed such separation. Now, with the use of immunoassay, no group has reported a separation, and that would include the groups of Drs. Guillemin, Schally, and Fawcett in our own laboratory. Nearly all of this recent isolation work has used the in vitro assay which, as Dr. Amoss points out maximizes response with respect to FSH. We agree that there are much smaller responses in terms of FSH to acute injections of either highly purified or synthetic LRF. In addition, there is some physiological evidence in the rat that is hard to reconcile with the existence of only one factor. For example, it is possible to stimulate in the preoptic region and provoke a very nice release of LH in the absence of any FSH release. If stimulated further caudally, one gets the release of both hormones in most cases. However, in 2 cases, Kalra, Ajika, Krulich, Fawcett, Quijada, and McCann (1971) were able to obtain a release of FSH in the absence of LH release. This is very hard to reconcile with one factor. Conversely, with hypothalamic lesions we were able to abolish the stimulation of LH by progesterone, whereas the response of FSH persisted. This is again almost impossible to explain on the basis of one releasing factor. I would like to re-emphasize the point that Dr. Amoss made; we have to look very carefully now for a separate FSH-RF. We should probably use in vivo assays which do not get us into the problems that we may have with in vitro assay in this situation.

DR. AMOSS. Faced with the physiological data which argues in favor of the existence of a distinct chemical entity controlling the release of FSH, it may become a very real problem to prove the nonexistence of FSH-RF from negative data if, in fact, this is the case.

DR. RESKO.   Does the decapeptide LRF have any reactivity in the radioimmunoassay for LH?

DR. AMOSS.   No, neither the decapeptide nor purified hypothalamic extract cross-react in our radioimmunoassay system for LH which utilizes chicken anti-ovine LH antibody. I do not know whether others have actually checked this out in their systems, but I know of no similar peptide sequences present in both LRF and LH.

DR. RAMALEY.   Drs. Beck, Bogdanove, and I at various times and in various combinations have used an in vitro setup to study the synthetic LRF of Schally, and also a median eminence extract, using continuous in vitro infusion of materials. We get the same result as Dr. Weisz, i.e., a smeary response to the LRF and a very prolonged secretion. Although anesthesia may be important, as Dr. Gay suggests, it would not be significant in this setup. There seem to be some other differences. Perhaps the inactivation of the material occurs elsewhere in the animal and accounts for the sharper response in vivo.

DR. BLIZZARD.   We know that TRF is inactivated quickly in plasma at room temperature. Presumably the same is true for LRF. Have we any studies on the half-life of LRF from the hypothalamic extracts versus synthetic LRF? If there is a difference, could it account for the difference in response?

DR. AMOSS.   I have been unable to show a decrease consistently in the biological activity of LRF after incubation with plasma. However, there is a recent abstract in the literature (Sandow, Enzmann, Schröder, & Vogel, 1972) which claims that LRF was inactivated in 20 to 30 minutes by rat, dog, guinea pig, and human plasma. To my knowledge no one has published the comparative half-life of synthetic LRF versus crude hypothalamic extract, but one might surmise that binding or adsorption of the releasing factor to other molecules in the crude extract might, in fact, alter its apparent half-life.

REFERENCES

Kalra, S. P., Ajika, K., Krulich, L., Fawcett, C. P., Quijada, M., & McCann, S. M. (1971). Effects of hypothalamic and preoptic electrochemical stimulation on gonadotropin and prolactin release in proestrous rats. *Endocrinology* **88**, 1150–1159.

Sandow, J., Enzmann, F., Schröder, H. G., & Vogel, H. G. (1972). Inactivation of LH-RH by the plasma of various species, *Naunyn-Schmiedeberg Arch. Pharmakol.* **274** suppl:R95 xii (abstract).

Yen, S. S. C., Rebar, R., VandenBerg, G., Naftolin, F., Ehara, Y., Engblom, S., Ryan, K. J., & Benirschke, K. (1972). Synthetic luteinizing hormone-releasing factor: a potent stimulator of gonadotropin release in man. *J. Clin. Endocrinol.* **34**, 1108–1111.

4.

Hypothalamic-Pituitary Regulation of Puberty, Evidence from Animal Experimentation

J. M. DAVIDSON

This chapter is concerned with the current status of conceptualization about mechanisms involved in the onset of puberty, particularly as they relate to the central role of the hypothalamic-pituitary system. The excellent reviews of Critchlow and Bar-Sela (1967) and Donovan and van der Werff ten Bosch (1965) provide a convenient starting point, although

Abbreviations

CNS	Central nervous system
FSH	Follicle stimulating hormone
FSH-RH	Follicle stimulating hormone-releasing hormone
GH	Growth hormone
LH	Luteinizing hormone
LRF	Luteinizing hormone releasing factor
OAAD	Ovarian ascorbic acid depletion (assay)
RF	Releasing factor
RIA	Radioimmunoassay

they were written before the methodology of saturation analysis had made any impact on this field of research. Now that reliable measurements of gonadotropin and gonadal steroid levels in the blood of immature individuals are possible, the way is open for the quantitative evaluation of concepts. This methodological revolution is just beginning to bear fruit in the field of experimental puberty.

In this chapter we examine several prominent concepts related to hypothalamic-pituitary involvement in the onset of puberty and evaluate briefly their present status and interrelations. The main emphasis is on female rats and reflects the (possibly unfortunate) bias of most workers in the field.

THE CONCEPT OF CEREBRAL DOMINANCE

The dominant change that triggers puberty is believed to occur in the hypothalamus. This does not imply that the hypothalamus is an independent system that functions in a physiological vacuum in response to a genetic command. It is clear that several classes of factors, including extrahypothalamic brain influences from the limbic system and perhaps the pineal body, modulate hypothalamic function. Presumably these central nervous pathways mediate certain influences on puberty which originate in the external environment. Internal environmental factors also influence the hypothalamus; among them gonadal steroids are particularly relevant to our discussion.

Why then speak of hypothalamic control of puberty if this segment of the brain is only a link in a chain of causality, a way-station on a circular tour, incessantly sending and receiving its messages to and from the gonads? The hypothalamus is singled out to define a hypothetical crucial period in development, the time before the onset of reproductive maturity. At that time the peripheral target tissues of steroids, the gonads, and the pituitary are all competent and ready to respond to their respective tropic hormones, but none is released in sufficient quantity to trigger puberty until some event occurs in the hypothalamus.

Historically, the concept of a "sexual centrum" in the diencephalon related to puberty had been prophetically postulated by Hohlweg and Junkmann (1932), although adequate experimental evidence was lacking at that time. Two experiments are now linked with the concept of hypothalamic dominance and are largely responsible for its widespread acceptance. The first is that of Harris and Jacobsohn (1952). Pituitary tissue removed from 1- to 10-day-old male and female rats was grafted under the median eminences of their hypophysectomized mothers. These grafts, but not others placed under the temporal lobe or in the emptied pituitary capsules, reinitiated full reproductive function in the mothers at a time when the donor pituitaries were well below the age of normal puberty (in several cases between 12 and 16 days). This classic experiment showed that the prepubertal pituitary was capable of maintaining normal adult gonadal function. Since it had already been established that the prepubertal gonad could be stimulated to full function by gonadotropins, it suggested, but did not prove, that the "signal" which initiates puberty emanates from the hypothalamus.

Hypothalamic Changes at Puberty

Evidence of the nature of that signal is now available. Several authors have noted decreases in the content of bioassayable FSH-RF (Kragt & Dahlgren, 1972; Watanabe & McCann, 1969; Corbin & Daniels, 1969; Baker & Kragt, 1969) and LRF (Ramirez & Sawyer, 1966) in the hypothalamus around the time of vaginal opening in the rat. Changes in hypothalamic content need not, however, reflect release; furthermore, the changes noted may be the result rather than the cause of non-hypothalamic puberty-initiating events.

Because certain biogenic amines have been implicated in controlling the production of gonadotropin RF, changes in the content or the turnover of amines in the hypothalamus could herald the onset of puberty. This point has not yet been clarified. Coppola (1969) as well as Weiner and Ganong (1972) could find no changes in hypothalamic content or turnover of norepinephrine at the time of vaginal opening.

In the male it is more difficult to correlate hypothalamic events with the onset of puberty because of his slower maturation. Investigation of possible hypothalamic changes which occur around the age of 60 days in the male rat might be illuminating. At that time, shortly after sexual maturation, there is a rather dramatic switch in LH content of the pituitary (Dupon & Schwartz, 1971) and in plasma testosterone (Grota, 1971; Knorr, Vanha-Pertulla, & Lipsett, 1970), both of which rise precipitously before and fall precipitously after 60 days.

Adequate evaluation of inferred changes in RF secretion depends on a knowledge of the sensitivity of the pituitary to these factors. The relationship between LRF responsiveness and maturation has been studied by Debeljuk, Arimura, and Schally (1972a,b), who found only small and possibly unimportant changes in relation to age in male rats and that LRF sensitivity is highest around the time of puberty. A considerable amount of work still needs to be done, however, by using different doses of RFs and by correlating possible changes with other key peripubertal events. In humans, increased sensitivity to LRF has been reported for pubertal groups of both sexes (Job, Garnier, Chaussain, Binet, Rivaille, & Milhaud, 1972; see also Chapter 6).

That changes in pituitary sensitivity may be a critical factor in reproductive events is indicated by various experiments, including several in our laboratory. When ovulation was advanced in adult cycling rats by exposure of the pituitary to estradiol benzoate in the form of crystalline implants, this apparently direct effect of estrogen on the pituitary could be blocked by pentobarbital and restored by administration of hypothalamic extract (Weick, Smith, Dominguez, Dhariwal, & Davidson, 1971). This suggests that conditions that seem to precipitate a dramatic change in pituitary function independent of hypothalamic influences in fact may operate via alteration in sensitivity to continuing hypothalamic input.

The hypothalamic-pituitary-gonadal axis is a system so dominated by dynamic interplay that slight perturbation of one element may profoundly affect the others, thereby altering the function of the whole system. In attempting to isolate hypothalamic influences, physiologists are victims of inadequate methodology. That the peripubertal organism is in a state of delicate equilibrium is suggested by the large array of factors that can alter the timing of puberty (Donovan & van der Werff ten Bosch, 1965; Chapter 2). This should be borne in mind, particularly when considering experiments that involve the introduction of large amounts of electricity, steel tubes, and blobs of crystalline steroid into the delicate brains of infantile rodents.

Hypothalamic Lesions

The second major experiment that laid the basis for the concept of hypothalamic dominance of puberty was that of Donovan and van der Werff ten Bosch (1956; 1959). Working in the laboratory of G. W. Harris, these investigators demonstrated that electrolytic lesions in the anterior hypothalamus of 14- or 15-day-old rats precipitated early vaginal opening (about a week early) and accelerated development of ovaries and uterus. Vaginal opening can be a rather misleading index of puberty in a variety of circumstances, but hypothalamic lesions frequently result in true precocious puberty in that many of the animals ovulate, cycle, and generally seem to show precocious reproductive function.

The period of "adolescent sterility" (non-ovulatory cycles) that seems to be common in the human (Montagu, 1957) and the cow (Donaldson, Bassett, & Thorburn, 1970) is not prominent in the rat (Critchlow & Bar-Sela, 1967), although in the Long Evans strain there is frequently a period of irregular cycling following vaginal opening (unpublished observations). In the hamster the period of noncycling is reported to last 9 days (Diamond & Yanagimachi, 1970).

Despite the great influence of these experiments and their frequent replication in other laboratories (Critchlow & Bar-Sela, 1967), they are considerably more difficult to interpret than the pituitary transplantation experiment discussed. The puberty-inducing lesion is generally assumed to remove inhibitory mechanisms for gonadotropin secretion. Unfortunately, as pointed out by Donovan and van der Werff ten Bosch (1965), puberty is most often induced by damage to structures which are those known to maintain gonadotropic function in the adult. Even if a dramatic reversal in the function of the hypothalamus following puberty is postulated, the maintenance of normal reproductive function would be difficult to explain if the lesion had destroyed a significant portion of the hypophysiotropic area. The same reasoning applies to the view that the effects of the lesions are due to interference with normal feedback relationships.

The problem of understanding the effect of puberty-inducing neural lesions is compounded by the fact that subsequent research has shown a considerable lack of anatomic specificity in the hypothalamic area which has to be destroyed (Critchlow & Bar-Sela, 1967). Recent research has again confirmed that advanced vaginal opening can result from both anterior and mid- to posterior hypothalamic lesions (Meijs-Roelofs & Moll, 1972). Although most animal experimenters stress the anterior hypothalamus, this localization does not correspond to clinical experience. In humans small lesions around the posterior hypothalamus are those most closely related to precocious puberty (Critchlow & Bar-Sela, 1967, pp. 1–4).

In view of this apparent neuroanatomic nonspecificity, is it possible that the effect of electrolytic lesions in immature animals is due not to destruction of tissue but rather to stimulation of tissue on the periphery of the lesion? Donovan and van der Werff ten Bosch (1965) answered this question in the negative, albeit their evidence was indirect. Their early attempts to advance the onset of seasonal reproductive capacity in the ferret by chronic electrical stimulation failed, whereas lesions in the same locations did advance the breeding season. Such negative evidence is only of limited value, however. A more serious criticism of the idea of a chronic irritative effect of the lesion is the finding of Bar-Sela and Critchlow (1966) that stimulation of the amygdala daily, from 25 days of age, delayed puberty in female rats. They explain the effect of hypothalamic lesions as due to the interruption of inhibitory stria terminalis connections from the amygdala. If their puberty-delaying effect could be reproduced, it would give important support to this idea. Consistent with the concept of afferent inhibitory influences feeding into the hypophysiotropic area to retard puberty is the observation that rats with mediobasal hypothalamic islands show advanced vaginal opening (Ramaley & Gorski, 1967).

Horowitz and van der Werff ten Bosch (1962) showed that even when hypothalamic lesions were placed very early in life (3 to 4 days) the advancement of puberty did not exceed that obtained with the later lesions.

This, too, is difficult to interpret. It suggests, vaguely, that the treatment disrupts some programming mechanism that determines the time of puberty, but it is difficult to imagine such a specific effect resulting from anatomically diverse lesions. It might be postulated that the lesion removes elements of a network of pathways which inhibit gonadotropin secretion, but their effect is not manifest until about 1 week before normal vaginal opening because other components are not yet quite mature. All the inhibitory influences may not be removed by any particular lesion so that the full advancement of puberty achievable within the limits of pituitary and gonadal readiness cannot be obtained. This possibility could be evaluated by investigating RF and gonadotropin levels following lesion production, although very sensitive assays might be necessary to demonstrate these changes.

Other Experiments

Since the pattern of postpubertal gonadotropin production is presumably determined by the type of steroid exposure in the perinatal environment (Gorski, 1971), it is apropos to inquire about the effect of manipulation of that environment on the onset of puberty. The most relevant finding in this respect is that administration of androgen to the neonatal female rat may advance vaginal opening, often to an extreme degree (Tramezzani, Voloschin, & Nallar, 1963; Justo, Colillas, & Tramezzani, 1970), although it may not occur with lower doses (Brown-Grant, Munck, Naftolin, & Sherwood, 1971). The early vaginal opening is presumably caused by changes in gonadotropin secretion attendant on neonatal androgen administration; it is known that the prepubertal pattern of pituitary and serum gonadotropins is altered in these animals (Brown, 1971; Weisz & Ferin, 1970). It has been proposed that the neonatal androgen treatment has the effect of causing an early maturation of feedback mechanisms (van der Werff ten Bosch, Tuinebreijer, & Vreeburg, 1971). If so, precocious puberty would be predictable.

On the other hand, there are reasons for believing that this early vaginal opening is not related to normal puberty. Both in the rat (unpublished observations) and in the hamster the introitus is abnormally small; in the hamster a common urethro-vaginal cleft develops (Alleva, Alleva, & Umberger, 1969). Normal cycling does not, of course, follow the opening. Furthermore, in 2 species in which the "critical period" for androgenization is before birth [the rhesus monkey (Goy & Resko, 1972) and the guinea pig (Brown-Grant & Sherwood, 1971)] androgen treatment of pregnant mothers actually resulted in delay of puberty.

Another experimental manipulation that advances vaginal opening, presumably by hypothalamic, pituitary and/or pineal changes, is constant illumination (Fiske, 1941). This observation has been used as a basis for speculation that the earlier menarche found in recent years in the western world may be due to the increase in artificial illumination (Jafarey, Khan, & Jafarey, 1970). One possible mechanism for the advanced vaginal opening with constant illumination is the increase in plasma prolactin levels that we have found in similarly exposed adults (Davidson, Smith, & Bowers, unpublished). This hormone is capable of producing precocious puberty (Clemens, Minaguchi, Storey, Voogt, & Meites, 1969).

The concept of cerebral dominance of puberty is a clear outcome of the experiments of Harris and Jacobsohn (1952), which were confirmed in mice by Martinez and Bittner (1956). These studies indicate that puberty is not the result of independent processes of pituitary maturation but depends on the milieu of the mature organism and presumably on the influence of the hypothalamus. The role of the hypothalamus is reinforced by observations on peripubertal RF changes and by lesion experiments, the interpretation of which is still obscure. Thus, although the concept of cerebral dominance remains secure, evidence of the details of the dynamic interaction between hypothalamus and pituitary which apparently results in final reproductive maturation is still sketchy.

DIFFERENTIAL FEEDBACK SENSITIVITY

A key concept in current thinking is one that we call the hypothesis of differential sensitivity. In this concept the major event that precipitates puberty is an increase in the threshold (or set point) of the inhibitory ("negative") feedback receptors which respond to changes in circulating steroid levels by inducing reciprocal changes in gonadotropin output. As a result the circulating levels of gonadotropins typical of adulthood are not attained, despite the low levels of circulating gonadal steroid in the immature individual. This hypothesis has the virtue of explaining a variety of phenomena without resorting to unattractive concepts like the reversal of hypothalamic function from inhibitory to facilitatory at puberty. Its origins go back to the early period shortly after the gonadotropic function of the pituitary was discovered. We now ask how it looks today, considering first the experimental facts and then their theoretical significance.

The first point to be established is whether inhibitory feedback exists appreciably before puberty. The ample early evidence that it does has been reviewed by Donovan and van der Werff ten Bosch (1965, pp. 59–64). It includes the observation that castration in infancy increases pituitary and blood gonadotropins, measured by bioassay and parabiosis. Castration cells appear in the pituitary of prepubertal castrates, and these cytological changes can be prevented by steroid administration. Hemiovariectomy or hemiorchiectomy before puberty is followed by compensatory hypertrophy, an effect that can also be inhibited by concurrent administration of steroids.

The pattern of development of feedback sensitivity is not yet entirely known, but it certainly exists in female rats by 20 days. It is also clear that it develops earlier in the male. Yaginuma, Matsuda, Murasawa, Kobayashi, and Kobayashi (1969) found that hemicastration of rats on the day of birth resulted in compensatory testicular hypertrophy at 3 days. In a similar experiment on females compensatory ovarian hypertrophy was not detected until 25 days (Baker & Kragt, 1969). Recent work of Ojeda and Ramirez (1972) showed that hemigonadectomy of 10-day-old male rats resulted in increased plasma FSH on day 12, although females on which similar operations were performed showed an increase over controls only after 20 days of age. In the experiments of Bloch, Kragt, and Masken (1971) plasma LH was elevated at 17 days in male rats that had been castrated at 7 days. Goldman, Grazia, Kamberi, and Porter (1971) studied serum gonadotropins in neonatal rats 1 day after castration and found increases in FSH and LH in males, with responses greater from 5 to 10 days of age than earlier. Neonatal females, whose levels were higher than those of males in the intact state, showed no significant response to castration. Castration in neonatal lambs has likewise been found to have greater or more rapid effects in the male (Foster, Cook, & Nalbandov, 1972).

Experiments that indicated that castration-induced pituitary changes could be inhibited by smaller doses of gonadal steroids in pre- than in postpubertal rats were reported as early as 1931, when Dohrn and Hohlweg found that estrogen was particularly effective in preventing castration cell formation and elevated gonadotropin content in rats before puberty. These findings were confirmed in further experiments by them and other workers. In 1951 Byrnes and Meyer showed that immature female rats joined in parabiosis manifested gonadotropic inhibition with doses of estrogen lower than those required to stimulate the growth of the uterus. More recently Smith and Davidson (1967; 1968) found that crystalline testosterone and estradiol implants in the hypothalamus of 30-day-old male or female rats respectively were considerably more effective in suppressing the reproductive system than in adults. The overall dimensions of the basal hypothalamus did not appear to differ at the 2 age periods.

When the introduction of the ovarian ascorbic acid depletion (OAAD) assay made measurements of circulating LH activity feasible, Ramirez and McCann (1963; 1965) conducted important studies that showed that gonadectomy-induced increases in this activity could be inhibited by lower doses of estrogen in the female and of testosterone in the male than were required in adult rats. In both sexes and at both age periods, however, more steroid was required to inhibit plasma OAAD activity than to maintain normal growth of the reproductive tract. They explained this apparent anomaly by suggesting that more than one steroid was involved in normal feedback inhibition in each sex. The discrepancy with the findings of Byrnes and Meyer (1951) could, however, be due either to the inadequacies of the OAAD method of measuring plasma LH or to artifacts of the parabiosis experiment.

Is it possible that the greater effectiveness of administered steroids before puberty is a function of the immaturity of disposal mechanisms for steroids, i.e., could the steroid injections actually result in higher and/or more sustained circulating titers of steroids than the same treatment in adults? Such a possibility is suggested by observations that, following the administration of ^{3}H estradiol to very young rats, much higher levels of blood radioactivity were found than in adults (Woolley, Holinka & Timi ras, 1969).

Experiments on the effects of intrasplenic ovary grafts on uterine growth, which suggest relatively slow inactivation of estrogens by the livers of young female rats (Donovan, 1969), support this idea, but more direct measurements of gonadal steroid metabolism do not. Thus studies comparing clearance of testosterone and estradiol in rats before and after puberty show that any differences that may exist are not enough to constitute an important factor in the onset of puberty (Ulrich & Kent, 1968; De Hertogh, Ekka, Vanderheyden, & Hoet, 1970; Ramaley, 1971). This issue, however, should be settled when such experiments include frequent monitoring of steroid levels, which is now both feasible and highly desirable.

Recent Tests of the Hypothesis

The concept of differential sensitivity is essentially a qualitative statement, and only RIA measurements of circulating gonadotropins (and steroids) are capable of providing a sufficiently precise quantitative evaluation of its validity. Such a comprehensive evaluation is not presently available, but several studies, which employed RIA, have been published. Odell, Hescox, and Kiddy (1970) could find no relation between age at castration and blood LH in cattle of both sexes. Bloch castrated male rats at various ages, from 7 to 80 days, and plasma LH was elevated in all cases 10 days after (Bloch et al, 1971). Increases of more than 100 per cent were found in 7 of the 8 groups studied, and the magnitude of increase was again not clearly related to age (Bloch, Kragt, Masken, & Ganong, unpublished manuscript). Administration of testosterone propionate for 10 days after castration at 10, 40, and 70 days of age showed that prepubertal males required least androgen to suppress LH back to normal (i.e., intact) levels (Bloch et al, 1971).

Consistent with the concept of differential sensitivity are the recent results of Ramirez (1972). In the female rat he found that after the first 2 weeks of life, during which time rising FSH titers are unaffected by spaying or by estrogen treatment, there is a period of great sensitivity to the FSH inhibitory effects of estrogen that is lost again as puberty approaches.

Seemingly contradictory data were presented by Swerdloff, Jacobs, and Odell (1972), who could find no evidence that the doses of testosterone or ethinyl estradiol required to return FSH and LH titers to those of intact control male or female rats differed, whether castration was performed at 21 or 75 days. Gonadotropin changes were expressed as per cent of controls, without description of absolute levels, and 5 daily steroid treatments were begun 5 days after castration.

The differential sensitivity to inhibitory feedback effects of exogenous steroids has, however, been observed so often with different methods that the protocols of investigations purporting to deny it should be carefully scrutinized in terms of such factors as dose regimen, route of administration, ages at castration, and injection. Results might be difficult to interpret if feedback suppression is compared between animals in which the initial gonadotropin levels differ significantly (probably not the case in the study of Bloch et al, 1971).

The effects of prepubertal castration on feedback sensitivity have not yet been elucidated, but work on adult rats in this laboratory has demonstrated certain changes in gonadotropic responses several weeks after castration. In a study of spayed females larger doses of estradiol benzoate (administered daily for 2 weeks) were necessary to suppress plasma LH when replacement therapy began 6 weeks postoperatively ("restoration") than when it began at the time of ovariectomy ("maintenance"), although the starting level was higher in the restoration groups (Damassa & Davidson, unpublished). This is reminiscent of the large decreases in sensitivity of behavioral and reproductive tract responses that follow castration in the adult male (Davidson, 1972) and female (Damassa & Davidson, unpublished) rats. In the male testosterone propionate was administered from the day of castration or 8 weeks thereafter to age mates (Davidson & Smith, unpublished). No large or clearcut differences in feedback sensitivity were demonstrated, possibly because no doses of testosterone were given between 25 and 100 μg/100 g body weight. When treatment was terminated, however, there was a surprisingly long lag, greater than 1 week, before plasma LH returned to the castrate control level, with the 100 μg/100 g dose in the maintenance situation (Fig. 1). It is interesting to note that when the restoration paradigm was studied the return to normal was more rapid, even though LH secretion had to rise further to reach the vehicle-injected, castrate control level (Fig. 2). Furthermore, a "rebound" over control levels was found with 12.5 and 25 μg doses on day 5 after cessation of treatment. Although the precise interpretation of these data is not yet clear, they indicate that in feedback experiments of this type the history of the animal may be of crucial importance in determining the dynamic response. They also supply one of the few existing examples of stimulatory ("positive") feedback in the male, albeit in rather peculiar circumstances. Another example in rats in which immunoassay was used is the study of Bloch et al (1971) in which treatment with 6 μg testosterone propionate/(100 g) (day) stimulated LH secretion in pubertal or adult male castrates but not in immature castrates.

Finally, given the reality of differential sensitivity, its mechanism is still a mystery. One explanation may be a change in receptor characteristics, but another would be a change in the capacity of tissues to execute metabolic conversion of steroids. An example of this kind of change is found in studies by Eckstein, Mechoulam, and Burstein (1970), Springer and Eckstein (1971), and Eckstein and Springer (1971), who reported that 5α-androstane-3α-17β-diol is the major metabolite of pregnenolone at the

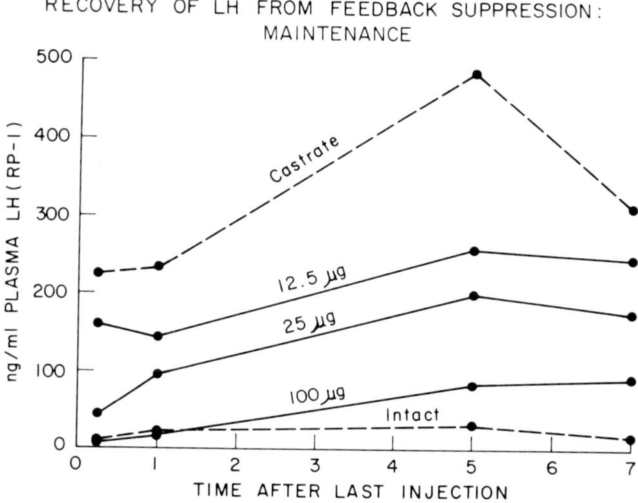

FIG. 1. Plasma LH in adult male castrate Long-Evans rats at various times after the last of 7 daily subcutaneous injections of testosterone propionate, commencing on the day of castration. Radioimmunoassays in this and subsequent figures by the method of Niswender, Midgley, Monroe, and Reichert (1968).

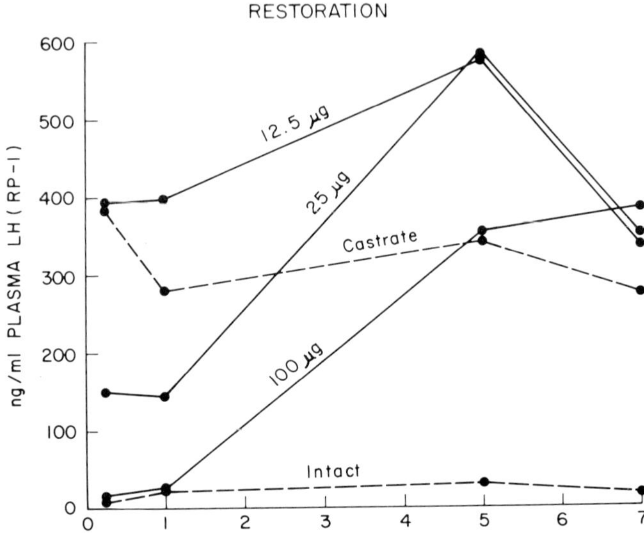

FIG. 2. As in Fig. 1, except that testosterone treatment began 8 weeks after castration.

onset of puberty in the female rat and becomes insignificant 2 days later. Although this compound had no biological effects, its 3β epimer was effective (albeit in high doses) in precipitating vaginal opening and cycling and was catalyzed by FSH. It was postulated that FSH-activated epimerization of the androstanediol was a key event in precipitating puberty. Any definite conclusions about the physiological significance of this steroid must presumably await its determination in the circulation. This work, however, serves to illuminate the general question whether steroids that precipitate or influence pubertal events may act via conversion to active metabolites. Age-related changes in such conversions would be a potential mechanism for changing feedback sensitivity.

Can Differential Sensitivity Explain the Onset of Puberty?

Now we must inquire about the relevance of differential sensitivity to the physiological situation in the developing organism. Can these observations really serve as the basis for a theory of the control of puberty?

First let us examine some assumptions that will lead, if accepted, to the suggestion that the experiments described should not be necessary to demonstrate the reality of differential sensitivity. If, indeed, steroid feedback is the major factor in determining gonadotropin secretion, the existence of low circulating gonadotropin titers in the presence of low blood steroid concentrations proves that the feedback threshold is lower in prepuberty. Thus the statement about differential sensitivity would be a tautology. If, on the other hand, gonadotropin secretion is not normally determined by steroid levels, one may well forget the whole business. In other words, differential sensitivity is either obvious or irrelevant.

We must query two basic assumptions of the differential sensitivity concept: that gonadotropin titers are lower before than after puberty and that negative feedback is a principal determinant of gonadotropin secretion. As to the former assumption, recent studies show that blood levels of FSH and LH do not necessarily follow a steadily rising course throughout prepubertal development. This is dramatically illustrated in the exceedingly high plasma FSH levels found in very young female rats, before feedback and gonadal sensitivity are developed (Kragt & Dahlgren, 1972; Ojeda & Ramirez, 1972). It would be interesting to know if this immunoreactive FSH is also bioactive. In male rats, as well, plasma FSH was higher before than after puberty (Swerdloff, Walsh, Jacobs, & Odell, 1971). LH levels are higher in prepubertal females than in diestrous adults (Weisz & Ferin, 1970; Goldman et al, 1971; Ojeda & Ramirez, 1972); in the male rat increases in plasma LH values before puberty have also been reported (Ojeda & Ramirez, 1972; Block et al, 1971). In these reports, however, the absolute (non-castrate) levels are much higher than those reported by other laboratories, including our own (Fig. 3), in which a slight rise in plasma LH from an early age to after puberty has been observed (Davidson and Smith, unpublished; Swerdloff et al, 1972).

The meaning of these large discrepancies in basal LH values of prepubertal and adult rats reported in different laboratories is not clear. In several studies in which the lower values are reported, often with the same standards (although usually with different antisera), postpubertal declines were not obtained. Yamamoto, Diebel, and Bogdanove (1970), however, reported low basal serum LH and values for 25-day-old male and female rats which were probably significantly higher than those for adults. This situation is more in line with observations on humans.

Even if resting gonadotropin levels are relatively high shortly before puberty, they could be explained without discarding the differential sensitivity concept by postulating a slight change in gain at the level of the gonadal steroid-producing cells. These data raise a variety of questions. Is puberty in the male really due to increased gonadotropin levels in the circulation? If so, which gonadotropin, and at what time does the crucial increase occur? Has prolactin a role, as suggested by Dowd and Bartke (1972)? We do not yet know precisely what conditions of gonadotropic stimulation are required for the development and maintenance of normal

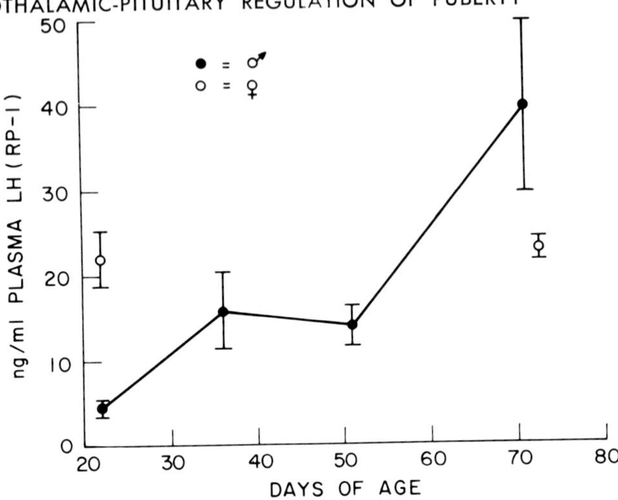

FIG. 3. Plasma LH levels in Long-Evans rats at various ages. The actual ages of the adult females varied, but all were proved to have regular 4- or 5-day cycles and were sampled on the morning of proestrus.

testicular function. As for the female, normal function depends on a complicated alternation of FSH, LH, and prolactin secretion. We shall return to the difficult question of which aspect of this complex pattern of pituitary activity is absent before puberty and which may be the crucial one.

As to the second assumption, just what is the physiological role of inhibitory feedback in the maintenance of normal gonadal function under physiological conditions? We still do not know if it is involved in minute-to-minute regulation of hormone secretion, or if it comes into play only when extreme fluctuations occur, which may be seldom in the (non-seasonal) male. In females the positive or stimulatory effect of estrogen in producing the LH surge is an essential feature of normal cycling and ovulation (Brown-Grant, 1972). Is it possible, therefore, at least as far as this sex is concerned, that the differential sensitivity hypothesis concerns itself with the wrong type of feedback?

We must then ask whether the ability to respond with an ovulatory gonadotropin surge to the stimulus of increased estrogen levels is found only in the pubertal and postpubertal female. Clearly, this is not so. The Hohlweg effect (i.e., estrogen-induced ovulation in immature rats) was discovered during the 1930s (Hohlweg, 1934). Recent measurements have shown that estrogen can induce large surges of FSH and LH in the immature rat (Ying, Fang, & Greep, 1971). Petrusz and Flerko (1965) suggested that cyclic gonadotropin release is dependent on negative feedback.

Recent work has shown that estrogen induction of LH surges in spayed rhesus monkeys and rats is preceded by suppression of the LH level (Knobil, Dierschke, Yamaji, Karsch, Hotchkiss, & Weick, 1972; Caligaris, Astrada, & Taleisnik, 1971). The ability to respond to estrogen with an LH surge does not appear to be present in the male (Taleisnik, Caligaris, & Astrada, 1972); Petrusz and Flerko (1965) suggested that this was due to greater sensitivity to negative feedback. Boyd and Johnson (1968) point out that this is not necessarily so. They found that the male rat is not less sensitive to LH suppression by testosterone than the female and that neonatally-androgenized rats showed even greater sensitivity to testosterone feedback. Although early evidence from pituitary cytology and parabiotic studies showed that immature females require less estrogen for suppression than immature males, the responses measured could have been the result of FSH and not LH stimulation. The relation between negative and positive stimulation according to age requires further clarification.

Another rather mystifying problem, when ovulation is initiated by a variety of short-term measures such as brief estrogen administration or lesion, is why normal cycling follows thereafter. This phenomenon may be related to the finding of Johnson and Naqvi (1969) that a single dose of estradiol or, better still, testosterone, resulted in cyclic release of FSH in female rats for several days.

Finally, this discussion has not addressed itself to the still controversial phenomenon of short-loop feedback. Ojeda and Ramirez (1969), on the basis of experiments on intracranial implantation of FSH, have proposed a stimulatory feedback effect of FSH on its own secretion which could help to explain the early FSH peak in immature females.

LOCALIZATION OF FEEDBACK RECEPTORS

So far, we have considered CNS regulation of puberty without regard to feedback mechanisms, and feedback mechanisms without regard to the location of the receptors. Now we must ask for evidence of the sites of steroid feedback action in relation to pubertal mechanisms; this question applies to both inhibitory and stimulatory feedback mechanisms. Are the two types of responses mediated by different areas of brain or pituitary, or do the same steroid-sensitive cells respond differently, depending on conditions? Most of the relevant evidence is based on intracranial implantation of crystalline steroids. Because this method, at best, involves exposure of all cells in the vicinity of the implant to the steroid, it could not discriminate if "positive" and "negative" cells were intermingled in one anatomic region.

As far as inhibitory feedback is concerned, most of the evidence points to the medial basal hypothalamus (median eminence region). This evidence includes results with intracranial implantation of crystalline steroids (references in Davidson, 1969) and observations on effects of gonadal steroids on levels of releasing factors (references in Meites, 1970). Steroid implants in this location are considerably more effective in prepubertal than postpubertal rats: this has been demonstrated for testosterone (Smith & Davidson, 1967); estradiol (Smith & Davidson, 1968); progesterone (Smith, Weick, & Davidson, 1969); and cortisol, which is an effective inhibitor of the reproductive system when implanted in the median eminence region in immature male or female rats (Smith, Johnson, Weick, Levine, & Davidson, 1971).

The problems that arise in distinguishing between pituitary and hypothalamic sites of inhibitory feedback, due to possible diffusion of hormone implanted in the hypothalamus through the portal vessels to the pituitary, are difficult to circumvent; they have been discussed elsewhere (Davidson, 1969; Bogdanove, 1964). Additional evidence suggests that testosterone can act at the hypothalamic level. Acute testosterone implants lower plasma LH levels in castrated male rats before any decrease in pituitary responsiveness to LH occurs (Davidson, Cheung, Smith, Damassa, & Johnston, 1973). These findings, if substantiated, seem more relevant than other recent experiments that show effects of intrapituitary testosterone implants in pituitary cytology and gonadotropin content (Bogdanove, 1972) and comparing single (ineffective) hypothalamic implants with bilateral (effective) pituitary implants (Kamberi & McCann, 1972).

Although steroid implantation experiments at least point clearly to the median eminence-pituitary unit as the location of inhibitory feedback receptors, the situation is less clear for the stimulatory feedback effect. The Hohlweg effect (induction of corpora lutea by estrogen in prepubertal rats) was best duplicated by Döcke and Dörner (1965) by intrapituitary implantation of estradiol benzoate in doses well below those effective systemically. Larger doses were required when the implants were in the anterior hypothalamus. The effects of intrapituitary implantation were prevented, however, by anterior hypothalamic lesions, which suggests some kind of dependence of the steroid effect on that region. Smith and Davidson (1968), on the other hand, found that anterior hypothalamic implants of estradiol benzoate were effective in inducing precocious puberty in female rats, whereas implants in the region of the median eminence were less effective, although the pituitary was not eliminated as a possible additional site of action in that study. Döcke and Dörner (1972), who used the same procedure as Smith and Davidson (implantation for 48 hours at 26 days of age with subsequent removal of the implant), were unable to distinguish between medial basal hypothalamus, anterior hypothalamus, and pituitary. In experiments by Motta, Fraschini, Giuliani, and Martini (1968) stimulatory effects were found from median eminence region implants, i.e., early vaginal opening and pituitary LH release. Pituitary implants were ineffective and anterior hypothalamic implants were not attempted.

Indirect evidence for an involvement of hypothalamic estrogen receptors in puberty comes from findings by Kato (1971) that differential binding by hypothalamic tissue of estradiol, which became apparent at 25 days of age, reached the adult pattern at 45 days in the female rat, i.e., close to the time of the first cycle. Furthermore, by using autoradiographic methods MacKinnon (1970) noted increased protein synthesis in the medial preoptic area at this period.

Although findings in our laboratory support an anterior hypothalamic site for the puberty-advancing effects of estrogen, different results were obtained when stimulatory feedback was studied in the adult. Advancement of ovulation by 1 day in 5-day cycling rats followed intrapituitary implantation of estradiol benzoate, but hypothalamic implants were not effective (Weick & Davidson, 1970; Weick, Smith, Dominguez, Dhariwal, & Davidson, 1971). Similar results were recently obtained when ovulation was blocked by injection of the anti-estrogen ICI[46474] on diestrus and restored by intrapituitary estradiol benzoate (Aiyer & Davidson, unpublished).

In our hands chronic progesterone implantation inhibited development of the reproductive system when the implants were in the medial basal hypothalamus but not the pituitary or anterior hypothalamus (Smith et al, 1969), but Döcke and Dörner (1972) found that among the three sites ovulation was delayed most effectively when the implant was in the pituitary. The stimulatory effect of progesterone, on the other hand, was found by these same authors (Döcke & Dörner, 1969) to follow medial basal hypothalamic implantation more often than when the implant was in the anterior hypothalamic region.

No attempt will be made to reconcile the differences between different laboratories or even in the same laboratory. At this juncture implantation experiments on feedback sites must be very sophisticated to be worth performing, particularly in reference to methods of testing for spread and systemic absorption of the hormone. Alternatively, other new approaches should be sought to study the question if the proliferation of contradictory and perhaps meaningless results is to be prevented. An approach now being used increasingly is the study of the effects of steroids on pituitary responsiveness to synthetic RFs. Though these effects unquestionably exist in vivo (Weick, et al, 1971; Debeljuk et al, 1972a,b), their relevance to the question of localization depends on whether observed changes in pituitary sensitivity are secondary to previous changes in hypothalamic RF secretion.

CONCLUDING REMARKS

What emerges from this assessment is that past work only sets the stage for a more precise and definitive evaluation of the hypothalamic-pituitary regulation of puberty. Acquisition of new data from discriminating experiments by RIA of steroid and peptide hormones will lead to the formulation of new concepts.

The hypothesis of cerebral dominance of puberty, though still without serious challenge, remains vague. Among other things, more definitive data are required on the peripubertal output of RFs and their relation to pituitary-gonadal changes. In this area methodology is not yet securely developed because appropriate assays are available only for assessing the hypothalamic concentration but not the production of RFs.

In regard to the differential sensitivity hypothesis differences in the gonadotropin-inhibiting effectiveness of steroid injections can be demonstrated in relation to puberty. This does not, however, prove that these differences are ultimately *responsible* for transforming the sterility of immaturity into the fertility of adulthood. Attractive as the differential sensitivity hypothesis is, we have to admit that it is a gross oversimplification as presently formulated. Nevertheless, the questions to which it addresses itself are amenable to experimental solution and have been answered in part. They can be phrased as follows:

1. During that prepubertal period in which the organism has the capacity to proceed to full reproductive development, if given exogenous hormones, what are the precise blood levels of FSH, LH, and prolactin?

2. What are the critical levels and ratios of circulating FSH, LH, and prolactin necessary for the adult female to cycle and ovulate and for the adult male to maintain adequate spermatogenesis and testicular steroidogenesis?

3. Are the differences between the answers to (1) and (2) explicable on the basis of changing thresholds to stimulatory ("positive") and inhibitory ("negative") feedback?

In re-evaluating this hypothesis, a number of important concerns should be borne in mind. First, among methodological considerations, we might suggest that when steroids are administered at different ages, it would be helpful to monitor the circulating levels of steroids produced by the injections. Hypothalamic implantation experiments of Smith and Davidson

(1967; 1968) suggest that the apparent difference in feedback sensitivity is not merely due to different distribution, binding, or metabolism in peripheral tissues. Nevertheless, a quantitative evaluation of differential sensitivity still requires precise information on the actual titers of steroids.

Second, we should determine whether measurements of immunoreactive material always reflect the presence of bioreactive gonadotropins.

Third, the validity of determinations of resting levels of gonadotropins has to be carefully scrutinized, for crucial peripubertal changes may be quite small, and assay error is high at the lower values.

In studying the mechanisms of puberty, we are concerned with a hierarchy of levels of control: environment-brain-pituitary-gonads-peripheral tissues. The impact of a hormonal change at one level is only as great as the sensitivity of its target, and multiple changes of responsiveness may occur at different levels of the organism. This is particularly relevant to experiments on the rat, whose telescoped development, while making it a convenient species for studies on puberty, may also limit its usefulness as a model for species that develop more slowly.

As for the male rat, it is unlikely that any experimental procedure could lead to precocious maturation of spermatozoa because the spermatogenic cycle in the rat has a duration about as long as the period of puberty. Regardless of species, however, there is a lack of definitive knowledge of the hormonal control of spermatogenesis. These disadvantages do not apply to the maturation of androgenogenesis, and the central control of this still neglected aspect of puberty provides excellent opportunities for animal investigation.

In the female it is crucial to find out whether positive feedback sensitivity changes in relation to puberty. If so, this information must be fitted into our overall scheme of differential sensitivity, together with changes in negative feedback reactivity. If not, there must be concentration on the conditions that allow the follicle to mature to the point at which an estrogen surge can take over. We must then look precisely at negative feedback sensitivity in relation to whatever FSH and LH stimuli are required to produce the first pre-ovulatory follicle.

If it can be established that differential feedback sensitivity is the mechanism that precipitates puberty, we must ask whether the crucial change occurs in hypothalamic or pituitary receptors. Cerebral dominance does not necessarily imply the former because the hypothalamus may conceivably exert a chronic "permissive" action on pituitary function, whereas the main steroid action (positive or negative) may be on pituitary responsiveness. Research on the location of feedback receptors has not been emphasized in this review because of the existing lack of agreement among different laboratories. Further experiments on intracranial implantation of steroids in relation to puberty would be helpful if they were discriminating and if they included a variety of needed controls. Additionally, however, important information on this question will develop from careful analysis of pituitary sensitivity to gonadotropin RF at different stages of development.

ACKNOWLEDGMENT

This research was supported by USPHS Grant HD-778. Radioimmunoassay materials were kindly supplied by Dr. G. D. Niswender, Dr. L. Reichert, and the NIAMD.

REFERENCES

Alleva, F. R., Alleva, J. J., & Umberger, E. J. (1969). Effect of a single prepubertal injection of testosterone propionate on later reproductive functions of the female golden hamster. *Endocrinology* **85**, 312–318.

Baker, F. S. & Kragt, C. L. (1969). Maturation of the hypothalamic-pituitary-gonadal negative feedback system. *Endocrinology* **85**, 522–527.

Bar-Sela, M. E. & Critchlow, V. (1966). Delayed puberty following electrical stimulation of amygdala in female rats. *Amer. J. Physiol.* **211**, 1103–1107.

Bloch, G. J., Kragt, C. L., & Masken, J. F. (1971). Plasma LH levels in male rats of various ages: effects of castration and treatment with testosterone propionate (TP). *Fed. Proc.* **30**, 475a.

Bogdanove, E. M. (1964). Role of the brain in the regulation of pituitary gonadotropin secretion. *Vitamins & Hormones* **22**, 205–260.

Bogdanove, E. M. (1972). Hypothalamic-hypophyseal interrelationships: basic aspects. In *Reproductive Biology*, H. Balin & S. Glasser, Eds., *Excerpta Medica*, Amsterdam, pp. 1–70.

Boyd, R. & Johnson, D. C. (1968). Gonadotrophin patterns in male and female rats: Inhibition of LH release by testosterone propionate in animals gonadectomized at puberty. *Acta Endocrinol.* **58**, 600–612.

Brown, P. S. (1971). Pituitary follicle-stimulating hormone in immature guinea-pigs and hamsters and in female rats after neonatal treatment with testosterone. *J. Reprod. Fertil.* **27**, 187–192.

Brown-Grant, K. (1972). Role of steroid hormones in the control of gonadotropin secretion in adult female mammals. In *Steroid Hormones and Brain Function*, C. H. Sawyer & R. A. Gorski, Eds., University of California Press, Los Angeles, pp. 269–288.

Brown-Grant, K., Munck, A., Naftolin, F., & Sherwood, M. R. (1971). The effects of the administration of testosterone propionate alone or with phenobarbitone and of testosterone metabolites to neonatal female rats. *Hormones & Behavior* **2**, 173–182.

Brown-Grant, K. & Sherwood, M. R. (1971). "Early androgen syndrome" in the guinea-pig. *J. Endocrinol.* **49**, 277–291.

Byrnes, W. W. & Meyer, R. K. (1951). Effect of physiological amounts of estrogen on secretion of follicle stimulating and luteinizing hormones. *Endocrinology* **49**, 449–460.

Caligaris, L., Astrada, J. J., & Taleisnik, S. (1971). Release of luteinizing hormone induced by estrogen injection into ovariectomized rats. *Endocrinology* **88**, 810–815.

Clemens, J. A., Minaguchi, H., Storey, R., Voogt, J. L., & Meites, J. (1969). Induction of precocious puberty in female rats by prolactin. *Neuroendocrinology* **4**, 150–156.

Coppola, J. A. (1969). Turnover of hypothalamic catecholamines during various states of gonadotrophin secretion. *Neuroendocrinology* **4**, 75–80.

Corbin, A. & Daniels, E. L. (1969). Induction of puberty in immature female rat: Effect of estrogen on pituitary FSH and stalk-median-eminence FSH-releasing factor. *Neuroendocrinology* **4**, 65–74.

Critchlow, V. & Bar-Sela, M. E. (1967). Control of onset of puberty, *Neuroendocrinology* **2**, 101–147.

Davidson, J. M. (1969). Feedback regulation of gonadotropin secretion. In *Frontiers in Neuroendocrinology, 1969,* W. F. Ganong & L. Martini, Eds. Academic, Chicago, pp. 343–388.

Davidson, J. M. (1972). Hormones and reproductive behavior. In *Reproductive Biology,* H. Balin & S. Glasser, Eds., Excerpta Medica, Amsterdam, pp. 877–918.

Davidson, J. M., Cheung, C., Smith, E. R., Damassa, D., & Johnston, P. (1973). Feedback mechanisms in relation to reproduction. *Proc. IV Intl. Congr. Endocrinol.* In press.

Debeljuk, L., Arimura, A., & Schally, A. (1972a). Studies on the pituitary responsiveness to luteinizing hormone-releasing hormone (LH-RH) in intact male rats of different ages. *Endocrinology* **90**, 585–588.

Debeljuk, L., Arimura, A., & Schally, A. W. (1972b). Effect of estradiol and progesterone on the LH release induced by LH-releasing hormone (LH-RH) in intact diestrous rats and anestrous ewes. *Proc. Soc. Exptl. Biol. Med.* **139**, 774–777.

de Hertogh, R., Ekka, E., Vanderheyden, I., & Hoet, J. J. (1970). Metabolic clearance rates and the interconversion factors of estrone and estradiol-17β in the immature and adult female rat. *Endocrinology* **87**, 874–880.

Diamond, M. & Yanagimachi, R. (1970). Reproductive development in the female golden hamster in relation to spontaneous estrus. *Biol. Reprod.* **2**, 223–229.

Döcke, F. & Dörner, G. (1965). Mechanism of the induction of ovulation by oestrogens. *J. Endocrinol.* **3**, 491–499.

Döcke, R. & Dörner, G. (1969). A possible mechanism by which progesterone facilitates ovulation in the rat. *Neuroendocrinology* **4**, 139–149.

Döcke, F. & Dörner, G. (1972). Mechanisms of estrogen action in female puberty. In press.

Dohrn, M. & Hohlweg, W. (1931). Hormonale Beziehungen Zwischen Hypophysenvorderlappen und Keimdrüsen. In *Proc. 2nd Intl. Congr. Sex Res.,* Oliver & Boyd, Edinburgh, pp. 436–442.

Donaldson, L. E., Bassett, J. M., & Thorburn, G. D. (1970). Peripheral plasma progesterone concentration of cows during puberty, oestrous cycles, pregnancy and lactation, and the effects of under-nutrition or exogenous oxytocin on progesterone concentration. *J. Endocrinol.* **48**, 599–614.

Donovan, B. T. (1969). Control of synthesis and release of anterior pituitary hormones in vivo. *Adv. Biosci.* **1**, 187–200.

Donovan, B. T. & van der Werff ten Bosch, J. J. (1956). Precocious puberty in rats with hypothalamic lesions. *Nature* **178**, 745.

Donovan, B. T. & van der Werff ten Bosch, J. J. (1959). The hypothalamus and sexual maturation in the rat. *J. Physiol. (Lond.)* **147**, 78–92.

Donovan, B. T. & van der Werff ten Bosch, J. J. (1965). *Physiology of Puberty*, Williams & Wilkins, Baltimore.

Dowd, A. J. & Bartke, A. (1972). Serum levels of prolactin, LH and FSH, and testis cholesterol content in rats from one to ten weeks of age. *Biol. Reprod.* **7**, 115.

Dupon, C. & Schwartz, N. B. (1971). Pituitary LH patterns in prepubertal normal and testosterone-sterilized rats. *Neuroendocrinology* **7**, 236–248.

Eckstein, B., Mechoulam, R., & Burstein, S. H. (1970). Identification of 5α-androstane-3α, 17β-diol as a principal metabolite of pregnenolone in rat ovary at the onset of puberty. *Nature* **228**, 866–868.

Eckstein, B. & Springer, C. (1971). Induction of an ovarian epimerase system catalyzing the transformation of 6-alpha-androstane-3-alpha, 17-beta-diol to 5-alpha-androstane-3-beta, 17-beta-diol after treatment of immature rats with gonadotrophins exhibiting FSH-like activity. *Endocrinology* **89**, 347–352.

Fiske, V. M. (1941). Effect of light on sexual maturation, estrous cycle, and anterior pituitary of the rat. *Endocrinology* **29**, 187–196.

Foster, D. L., Cook, B., & Nalbandov, A. V. (1972). Regulation of luteinizing hormone (LH) in the fetal and neonatal lamb: Effect of castration during the early postnatal period on levels of LH in sera and pituitaries of neonatal lambs. *Biol. Reprod.* **6**, 253–257.

Goldman, B. D., Grazia, Y. R., Kamberi, I. A., & Porter, J. C. (1971). Serum gonadotropin concentration in intact and castrated neonatal rats. *Endocrinology* **88**, 771–776.

Gorski, R. A. (1971). Gonadal hormones and the perinatal development of neuroendocrine function. In *Frontiers in Neuroendocrinology*, L. Martini & W. F. Ganong, Eds., Oxford University Press, New York, pp. 237–290.

Goy, R. W. & Resko, J. A. (1972). Gonadal hormones and behavior of normal and pseudohermaphroditic female primates. *Rec. Progr. Horm. Res.* **28**, 707–733.

Grota, L. J. (1971). Effects of age and experience on plasma testosterone. *Neuroendocrinology* **8**, 136–143.

Harris, G. W. & Jacobsohn, D. (1952). Functional grafts of the anterior pituitary gland. *Proc. Roy. Soc.* **(B) 139**, 263–276.

Hohlweg, W. (1934). Veränderungen des Hypophysenvorderlappens und des Ovariums nach Behandlung mit grossen Dosen von Follikelhormon. *Klin. Wschr.* **13**, 92–95.

Hohlweg, W. & Junkmann, K. (1932). Die Hormonal-Nervose Regulierung der Funktion des Hypophysenvordenlappens. *Klin. Wschr.* **11**, 321–323.

Horowitz, S. & van der Werff ten Bosch, J. J. (1972). Hypothalamic sexual precocity in female rats operated shortly after birth. *Acta Endocrinol.* **41**, 301–313.

Jafarey, N. A., Khan, M. Y., & Jafarey, S. N. (1970). Role of artificial lighting in decreasing the age of menarche. *Lancet* **2**, 471.

Job, J. C., Garnier, P. E., Chausain, J. L., Binet, E., Rivaille, P., & Milhaud, G. (1972). Effects of synthetic luteinizing hormone-releasing hormone (LH-RH) on serum gonadotropins (LH and FSH) in normal children and adults. *Rev. Europ. Etud. Clin. Biol.* **17**, 411–414.

Johnson, D. C. & Naqvi, R. H. (1969). Positive feedback action of androgen on pituitary follicle stimulating hormone: Induction of a cyclic phenomenon. *Endocrinology* **85**, 881–885.

Justo, S. N., Colillas, O. J., & Tramezzani, J. H. (1970). The influence of prepubertal ovariectomy, and subsequent hormone treatment, on vaginal opening in the rat. *J. Endocrinol.* **46**, 543–544.

Kamberi, I. A. & McCann, S. M. (1972). Effects of implants of testosterone in the median eminence and pituitary on FSH secretion. *Neuroendocrinology* **9**, 20–29.

Kato, J. (1971). Estrogen receptors in the hypothalamus and hypophysis in relation to reproduction. In *Proc. 3rd Steroid Hormone Conf. 1970,* Intl. Congr. Series #219, pp. 764–773.

Knobil, E., Dierschke, D. J., Yamaji, T., Karsch, F. J., Hotchkiss, J., & Weick, R. F. (1972). Role of estrogen in the positive and negative feedback control of LH secretion during the menstrual cycle of the Rhesus monkey. In *Gonadotropins,* B. B. Saxena, C. G. Beling, & H. M. Gandy, Eds., Wiley, New York, pp. 72–86.

Knorr, D. W., Vanha-Pertulla, T., & Lipsett, M. B. (1970). Structure and function of rat testis through pubescence. *Endocrinology* **86**, 1298–1304.

Kragt, C. L. & Dahlgren, J. (1972). Development of neural regulation of follicle stimulating hormone (FSH) secretion. *Neuroendocrinology* **9**, 30–40.

MacKinnon, P. C. (1970). Some observations of protein synthesis in the medial preoptic area of mice before and after puberty and of female rats at different phases of the oestrus cycle. *J. Endocrinol.* **48**, xliv.

Martinez, C. & Bittner, J. J. (1956). A non-hypophyseal sex difference in estrous behavior of mice bearing pituitary grafts. *Proc. Soc. Exptl. Biol. Med.* **91**, 506–509.

Meijs-Roelofs, H. M. A. & Moll, J. (1972). Differential effects of anterior and middle hypothalamic lesions on vaginal opening and cyclicity. *Neuroendocrinology* **9**, 297–303.

Meites, J. (1970). Direct studies of the secretion of the hypothalamic hypophysiotropic hormones (HHH). In *Hypophysiotropic Hormones of the Hypothalamus: Assay and Chemistry,* J. Meites, Ed., Williams & Wilkins, Baltimore, pp. 261–281.

Montagu, M. F. A. (1957). *Reproductive Development of the Female.* Julian, New York.

Motta, M., Fraschini, F., Giuliani, G., & Martini, L. (1968). Central nervous system, estrogen and puberty. *Endocrinology* **83**, 1101–1107.

Niswender, G. D., Midgley, Jr., A. R., Monroe, S. E., & Reichert, Jr., L. E. (1968). Radioimmunoassay for rat luteinizing hormone with antiovine LH serum and ovine LH-^{131}I, *Proc. Soc. Exptl. Biol. Med.* **128**, 807–811.

Odell, W. D., Hescox, M. A., & Kiddy, C. A. (1970). Studies of hypothalamic-pituitary-gonadal interrelations in prepubertal cattle. In *Gonadotrophins and Ovarian Development*, W. R. Butt, A. C. Crooke & M. Ryle, Eds., E. & S. Livingstone, Edinburgh, pp. 371–385.

Ojeda, S. R. & Ramirez, V. D. (1969). Automatic control of LH and FSH secretion by short feedback circuits in immature rats. *Endocrinology* **84**, 786–797.

Ojeda, S. R. & Ramirez, V. D. (1972). Plasma level of LH and FSH in maturing rats: response to hemigonadectomy. *Endocrinology* **90**, 466–472.

Petrusz, B. & Flerko, B. (1965). On the mechanism of sexual differentiation of the hypothalamus. *Acta Biol. Hung.* **16**, 169–173.

Ramaley, J. A. (1971). Steroid binding to serum proteins in maturing male and female rats. *Endocrinology* **89**, 545–552.

Ramaley, J. A. & Gorski, R. A. (1967). Effect on hypothalamic deafferentation upon puberty in the female rat. *Acta Endocrinol.* **56**, 661–674.

Ramirez, V. D. (1972). Maturation of the gonadotrophin control system. In *The Use of Non-Human Primates in Research on Human Reproduction*, WHO Symposium, F. Diczfalusy and E. E. Stanley, Eds., Sukhumi, pp. 170–176.

Ramirez, V. D. & McCann, S. M. (1963). Comparison of the regulation of luteinizing hormone (LH) secretion in immature and adult rats. *Endocrinology* **72**, 452–464.

Ramirez, V. D. & McCann, S. M. (1965). Inhibitory effect of testosterone on luteinizing hormone secretion in immature and adult rats. *Endocrinology* **76**, 412–417.

Ramirez, V. D. & Sawyer, C. H. (1966). Changes in hypothalamic luteinizing hormone releasing factor (LHRF) in the female rat during puberty. *Endocrinology* **78**, 958–964.

Roth, J. C., Kelch, R. P., Kaplan, S. L. & Grumbach, M. M. (1972) FSH and LH response to luteinizing hormone-releasing factor in prepubertal and pubertal children, adult males and patients with hypogonadotropic and hypergonadotropic hypogonadism. *J. Clin. Endocrinol.* **35**, 926–930.

Smith, E. R. & Davidson, J. M. (1967). Differential responses to hypothalamic testosterone in relation to male puberty. *Amer. J. Physiol.* **212**, 1385–1390.

Smith, E. R. & Davidson, J. M. (1968). Role of estrogen in the cerebral control of puberty in female rats. *Endocrinology* **82**, 100–108.

Smith, E. R., Johnson, J., Weick, R. F., Levine, S., & Davidson, J. M. (1971). Inhibition of the reproductive system in immature rats by intracerebral implantation of cortisol. *Neuroendocrinology* **8**, 94–106.

Smith, E. R., Weick, R. F., & Davidson, J. M. (1969). Influence of intracerebral progesterone on the reproductive system of female rats. *Endocrinology* **85**, 1129–1136.

Springer, C. & Eckstein, B. (1971). Regulation of production in vitro of 5-alpha-androstane-3-alpha, 17-beta-diol in the immature rat ovary. *J. Endocrinol.* **50**, 431–439.

Swerdloff, R. S., Jacobs, H. S., & Odell, W. D. (1972). Hypothalamic-pituitary-gonadal interrelationships in the rat during sexual maturation. In *Gonadotropins*, B. B. Saxena, C. G. Beling & H. M. Gandy, Eds., Wiley, New York, pp. 546–561.

Swerdloff, R. S., Walsh, P. C., Jacobs, H. S., & Odell, W. D. (1971). Serum LH and FSH during sexual maturation in the male rat. Effect of castration and cryptorchidism. *Endocrinology* **88**, 120–128.

Taleisnik, S., Caligaris, L., & Astrada, J. J. (1972). Sex differences in hypothalamo-hypophysial function. In *Steroid Hormones and Brain Function,* C. H. Sawyer & R. A. Gorski, Eds., University of California Press, Los Angeles, pp. 171–184.

Tramezzani, J. H., Voloschin, L. M., & Nallar, R. (1963). Effect of a single dose of testosterone propionate on vaginal opening in the rat. *Acta Anat.* **52**, 244–251.

Ulrich, R. S. & Kent, J. R. (1968). Disappearance rates of sex steroids in immature and mature rats. *Proc. Soc. Exptl. Biol. Med.* **128**, 1093–1096.

van der Werff ten Bosch, J. J., Tuinebreijer, W. E., & Vreeburg, J. Th. M. (1971). Incomplete or delayed early-androgen syndrome. In *Hormones in Development,* M. Hamburgh & E. J. W. Barrington, Eds., Appleton-Century-Crofts, New York, pp. 669–676.

Watanabe, S. & McCann, S. M. (1969). Alterations in pituitary follicle-stimulating hormone (FSH) and hypothalamic FSH-releasing factor (FSH-RF) during puberty. *Proc. Soc. Exptl. Biol. Med.* **132**, 195–201.

Weick, R. F. & Davidson, J. M. (1970). Localization of the stimulatory feedback effect of estrogen on ovulation in the rat. *Endocrinology* **87**, 693–700.

Weick, R. F., Smith, E. R., Dominguez, R., Dhariwal, A. P. S., & Davidson, J. M. (1971). Mechanism of stimulatory feedback effect of estradiol benzoate on the pituitary. *Endocrinology* **88**, 293–301.

Weiner, R. I. & Ganong, W. F. (1972). Norepinephrine concentration in the hypothalamus, amygdala, hippocampus and cerebral cortex during postnatal development and vaginal opening. *Neuroendocrinology* **9**, 65–71.

Weisz, J. & Ferin, M. (1970). Pituitary gonadotrophins and circulating LH in immature rats—a comparison between normal females and males and females treated with testosterone in neonatal life. In *Gonadotrophins and Ovarian Development,* W. R. Butt, A. C. Crooke, & M. Ryle, Eds., E. & S. Livingstone, Edinburgh, pp. 339–350.

Woolley, D. E., Holinka, C. F., & Timiras, P. S. (1969). Changes in ^{3}H-estradiol distribution with development in the rat. *Endocrinology* **84**, 157–164.

Yaginuma, T., Matsuda, A., Murasawa, Y., Kobayashi, T., & Kobayashi, T. (1969). Presence of hypothalamo-pituitary-testicular axis in the early postnatal period. *Endocrinol. Jap.* **16**, 5–10.

Yamamoto, M., Diebel, N. D., & Bogdanove, E. M. (1970). Analysis of initial and delayed effects of orchidectomy and ovariectomy on pituitary and serum LH levels in adult and immature rats. *Endocrinology* **86**, 1102–1111.

Ying, S-Y, Fang, V. S., & Greep, R. O. (1971). Estradiol benzoate (EB)-induced changes in serum-luteinizing hormone (LH) and follicle-stimulating hormone (FSH) in immature female rats. *Fertil. Steril.* **22**, 799–801.

5.

Hypothalamic-Pituitary Regulation of Puberty: Feedback Control of Gonadotropin Secretion in the Rhesus Monkey

D. J. DIERSCHKE, F. J. KARSCH, R. F. WEICK, G. WEISS, J. HOTCHKISS and E. KNOBIL

In primates, as in the rat, LH is secreted in both the tonic and cyclic modes. Tonic LH secretion is under negative feedback control by estrogen, presumably exerted at the hypothalamic level, and is reflected in a low, relatively constant, circulating level throughout most of the menstrual cycle. This is interrupted once every 28 days on the average by an LH surge which is triggered by a positive feedback action of estrogen on the hypothalamo-hypophysial unit (Knobil, Dierschke, Yamaji, Karsch, Hotchkiss, & Weick, 1972).

Abbreviations

CNS	Central nervous system
FSH	Follicle stimulating hormone
LH	Luteinizing hormone
LRF	Luteinizing releasing factor

THE NEGATIVE FEEDBACK SYSTEM

In adult monkeys interruption of the negative feedback loop by gonadectomy in either sex is followed within a day or two by an increase in circulating levels of LH. This rise continues until a plateau of about 10 times the initial basal concentration is reached about 15 to 20 days later (Atkinson, Bhattacharya, Monroe, Dierschke & Knobil, 1970).

In sharp contrast to the dynamics of the negative feedback loop in adults the elevation in plasma gonadotropin concentrations following bilateral ovariectomy in premenarchial rhesus females was delayed for as long as 3 months (Fig. 1).

The concentrations in plasma were determined by radioimmunoassays described by Monroe, Peckham, Neil, and Knobil (1970) for LH; and by Yamaji, Peckham, Atkinson, Dierschke, and Knobil (1973) for FSH. In 4 of the 5 animals the postovariectomy levels of FSH rose before those of

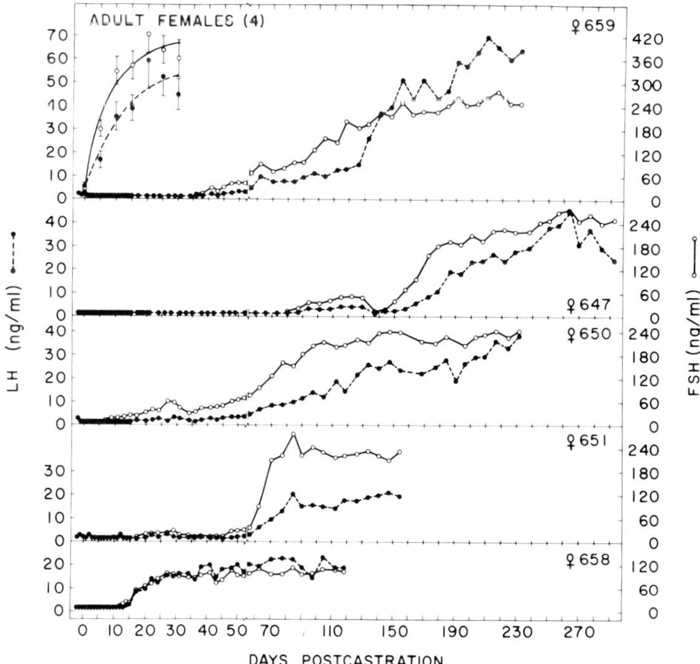

FIG. 1. Effects of bilateral ovariectomy on circulating levels of LH and FSH in 5 sexually immature rhesus females. Upper left corner shows group means ±SE of plasma LH and FSH concentrations in 4 representative adult females ovariectomized on day 0. Blood samples were obtained daily before and during the first 15 days after castration, then 3 times a week until 50 days postcastration, and weekly thereafter.

TABLE 1. Indices of maturational development in premenarchial rhesus females at ovariectomy and estimated bone age at postcastration increase in concentration of gonadotropin in plasma

Animal number (Fig. 1)	659	647	650	651	658
Body weight (kg)	2.5	2.3	2.3	2.6	2.7
Bone age (months)[a]	17	11	17	25	19
Plasma estradiol (pg/ml)[b]	9.5±0.9	...	9.9±0.6	6.5±1.4	16.4±1.5
Ovarian histology[c]	Many vesicular (~1 mm diameter) and primordial follicles	Many primordial and polyovular (no vesicular) follicles	Many vesicular (~1 mm diameter) and primordial follicles	Many primordial, few polyovular and few vesicular (~0.5 mm diameter) follicles	Many primordial and few vesicular (~1 mm diameter) follicles
Bone age (months) at first sustained elevation in plasma concentrations of LH and FSH	18	16	17.5	27	19.5

[a] Estimated by the method of van Wagenen and Asling (1958) 5 months after ovariectomy. The chronological ages of these animals are not known.

[b] Mean ±SE of 5 observations. The radioimmunoassay of Hotchkiss, Atkinson, and Knobil (1971) was used with the substitution of Sephadex LH-20 columns for thin layer chromatography in the isolation of estradiol. Postcastration samples from immature females were used as plasma blanks. Minimal level of sensitivity was 5 pg of estradiol, and 1 ml plasma aliquots were used for each extraction.

[c] To be compared with the maturational description by van Wagenen and Simpson (1965).

LH. Some indices of maturation in the prepubertal females are listed in Table 1. The initiation of a sustained rise in concentrations of plasma gonadotropins occurred, with one exception (#651), at similar ages, regardless of the age at castration.

Before castration the levels of LH and FSH, as determined in 200 μl aliquots of plasma, were below the sensitivity of the methods utilized (1.5 ng/ml for LH and 10 ng/ml for FSH of our respective laboratory standards), despite the fact that vesicular follicles were present in the ovaries of all except 1 of these females (Table 1). Plasma concentrations of estradiol (Table 1) were clearly detectable, albeit low relative to the basal levels of 50 to 75 pg/ml in adult cyclic females (Hotchkiss, Atkinson, & Knobil, 1971).

Four prepubertal rhesus males were studied in a similar manner (Fig. 2,

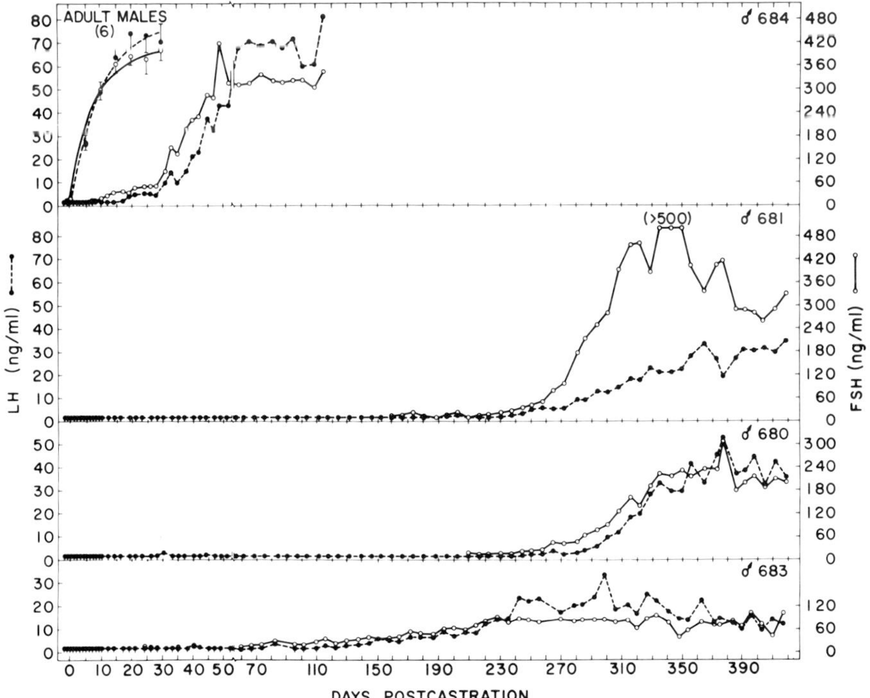

FIG. 2.   Effects of bilateral orchiectomy on circulating levels of LH and FSH in 4 sexually immature rhesus males. These data are compared with a group of 6 adult males (upper left corner) in which the group means (+SE) are shown. Blood samples were obtained daily before and during the first 10 days after castration, then 3 times a week until 50 days postcastration, and weekly thereafter.

Table 2). In 3 no evidence of a functional negative feedback system was observed until about 200 or more days after the operation, when the plasma levels of both LH and FSH began to increase gradually. In the fourth and oldest male (#684) a similar pattern in peripheral levels of gonadotropin obtained after a delay of only 30 days. The plasma concentrations of testosterone before castration were low (Table 2) in relation to an average level of 5000 pg/ml in adult intact males and were not greatly reduced after castration. The residual circulating testosterone is presumably of adrenal origin (Resko & Phoenix, 1972).

These findings in the monkey differ from those reported in prepubertal rats (Yamamoto, Diebel, & Bogdanove, 1970; Goldman, Grazia, Kamberi, & Porter, 1971; Swerdloff, Jacobs, & Odell, 1972); sheep (Foster, Cook, & Nalbandov, 1972; Crim & Geschwind, 1972); and cattle (Odell, Hescox, & Kiddy, 1970). In these species the time course of the postcastration increase in concentration of plasma gonadotropin in sexually immature animals does not differ markedly from that found in adults.

The observation by Foster, Lemons, and Jaffe (1972) that peripheral levels of LH in newborn male and female monkeys are elevated above those of adults in both sexes suggests that the open loop secretion of gonadotropic hormones *may* exist in early neonatal life. Our own findings as well as theirs indicate, however, that later in development the production or secretion of these hormones is very low, but not because of a negative feedback action by the gonadal steroids, for gonadectomy does not result in a prompt increase in gonadotropin secretion.

Once gonadotropin secretion occurs in the open loop mode it is responsive, perhaps more than in adults, to the negative feedback action of estrogen. Eighteen months after castration of the prepubertal females, when they had attained bone ages equivalent to young adults, elevation of their circulating estradiol levels to 41 ± 3 pg/ml ($n=22$) for 8 to 19 days by the use of subcutaneously implanted silastic capsules containing 17β-estradiol (Karsch, Dierschke, Weick, Yamaji, Hotchkiss, & Knobil, 1973) resulted in a decline of the elevated plasma gonadotropin concentrations to undetectable levels. In contrast, higher concentrations of plasma estradiol (71 ± 4 pg/ml), administered in the same way to females gonadectomized when adult, although effecting a reduction in plasma LH concentrations to levels characteristic of adult intact animals during the follicular phase of the menstrual cycle, did not suppress them further (Karsch et al, 1973); lower estradiol concentrations were usually ineffective in reducing the elevated gonadotropin levels, (to be published).

TABLE 2. Indices of maturational development in juvenile rhesus males at orchiectomy and estimated age at post-castration increase in concentration of gonadotropin in plasma

Animal number (Fig. 2)	684	681	680	683
Body weight (kg)	2.5	2.7	2.7	3.0
Bone age (months)[a]	33	22	21	—
Plasma testosterone (pg/ml)[b]				
Precastration	310±29 (2)	160±1 (2)	82±10 (2)	112± 8 (2)
30 days postcastration	122± 1 (4)	36±8 (4)	66± 2 (4)	133±10 (4)
Weight of both testes (mg)	1100	461	722	800
Testicular histology[c]	Beginning differentiation (no spermatozoa)	Undifferentiated	Undifferentiated	Undifferentiated
Bone age months first sustained elevation in plasma concentrations of LH and FSH	34	28	27	—

[a] Estimated by the method of van Wagenen and Asling (1958) 3 months after orchiectomy. The chronological ages of these animals are not known.

[b] Mean ±SE of number of observations in parentheses. A radioimmunoassay with minimal sensitivity of 10 pg of testosterone (unpublished) was used and a 0.5 ml plasma aliquot was extracted for each observation.

[c] To be compared with the maturational description by van Wagenen and Simpson (1954).

THE POSITIVE FEEDBACK SYSTEM

The surge of LH and FSH that initiates ovulation during the menstrual cycle in adult females is preceded by a rise in circulating estrogen levels (Hotchkiss et al, 1971). That this increase is the primary stimulus for the preovulatory discharge of gonadotropic hormone was suggested by the demonstration that the subcutaneous injection of estradiol benzoate in oil during the early follicular phase of the menstrual cycle (Yamaji, Dierschke, Hotchkiss, Bhattacharya, Surve, & Knobil, 1971) resulted in premature surges of LH and FSH which were indistinguishable from those occurring spontaneously (Fig. 3e). The identical regimen of estradiol ben-

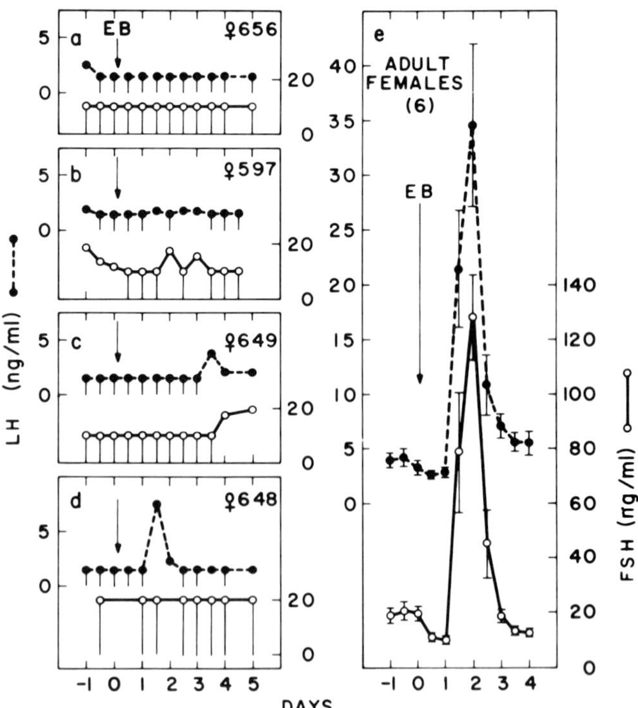

FIG. 3.   The influence of estradiol benzoate (EB) administered as a single injection (42 μg/kg in oil, subcutaneously) on the morning of day 0 (↓) on gonadotropin secretion in sexually immature (a-d) and adult (e) female rhesus moneys. Results in adult animals are presented as a composite of the means (±SE) of 6 experiments. Blood samples were obtained twice daily (0900 and 1700 to 2100). The vertical lines between data points and baseline (a-d) indicate values below the sensitivity of the radioimmunoassay system.

zoate, when given to 6 premenarchial females having bone ages of 10 to 25 months and body weights of 2.2 to 3.9 kg, failed to elicit evidence for a positive feedback action of estrogen on gonadotropin release like that seen in adults. The results of 4 representative experiments are shown in Fig. 3a-d. One of these animals (#597) started to menstruate, albeit at irregular intervals, about 3 months later. The occasional small and short-lived increases in concentration of plasma gonadotropin could not always be related to the steroid injections and in any case could not be described as gonadotropic surges. The injection of larger (694 μg/kg) or smaller (7 μg/kg) quantities of estradiol benzoate were similarly ineffective in eliciting gonadotropic surges.

The failure to demonstrate a positive feedback action of estrogen on LH and FSH secretion in young female primates that were chronologically near menarche was surprising, since immature 38-day-old female lambs (Land, Thimonier, & Pelletier, 1970) and 26- to 30-day-old female rats (Ramirez & Sawyer, 1965; Ying, Fang, & Greep, 1971) have shown clear surges following administration of estrogen. These observations suggested that the positive feedback control of the release of gonadotropin by estrogen in primates develops later in the maturational process than in sub primate forms and may not become fully competent until well after the advent of menarche. Recent findings in our laboratory have shown that although the positive feedback system is definitely not operational in most monkeys during the first few months of the postmenarchial period, usually it can be demonstrated shortly before spontaneous ovulatory cycles are detected. The latter event generally does not occur until about a year after menarche (to be published).

Attempts to Induce Maturation of the Positive Feedback System

As reviewed in the previous chapter by Dr. Davidson, it has been known for 40 years that the administration of estrogen induces precocious puberty in the rat, and the efficacy of 5α-androstane-3β, 17β-diol in this regard has been reported recently. To determine the effectiveness of similar steroids in advancing the maturation of the positive feedback control of secretion of gonadotropin in monkeys the following treatments were imposed in premenarchial females that weighed 1.1 to 2.8 kg and had estimated bone ages of 8 to 25 months:

1.   Circulating levels of estrogen were raised from about 10 to 15 pg/ml to averages of 75 to 150 pg/ml for 4 months in 4 animals by inserting silastic capsules containing 17β-estradiol (Karsch et al, 1973) and leaving them in place throughout the period of treatment. Single subcutaneous injections of estradiol benzoate in oil (42 μg/kg) were administered 3

times at intervals of 4 to 5 weeks during the 4 months. An identical injection of estradiol benzoate was given 3 months after removal of the implants.

2.   Plasma progesterone concentrations in 6 females were raised from undetectable to levels averaging 10 to 20 ng/ml for 7 weeks by the use of subcutaneous silastic capsules containing crystalline progesterone. Estradiol benzoate was then injected, as above, 2 weeks after the implants were removed.

3. 5α-androstane-3β, 17β-diol was injected in peanut oil subcutaneously into 6 females at a dosage of 5 mg/kg (day) for 6 weeks and followed 2 weeks later by a single injection of 42 μg/kg estradiol benzoate.

Parenthetically, an attempt was made to induce the positive feedback response to estrogen in 4 juvenile males with body weights of 2.3 to 2.6 kg by giving them subcutaneous insertions of estradiol-containing silastic capsules. This elevated and maintained their concentrations of plasma estrogen at averages of 50 to 75 pg/ml for 7 months. Six weeks after insertion of the implants the animals were bilaterally orchiectomized. Single injections of estradiol benzoate were then administered, as above, on 3 occasions at intervals of 6 weeks, beginning 2 months after castration. These and all of the above efforts yielded negative results.

On the basis of these studies a new operational definition of puberty may be formulated for the rhesus monkey: the time when the hypothalamo-hypophysial unit is competent to respond to an effective increment in circulating estrogens by a preovulatory surge of LH and FSH. Before that time reproduction cannot occur.

In the normal course of events puberty, so defined, does not occur until many months after menarche. The menstrual episodes that occur before that time are usually irregular and seem to be akin to "breakthrough bleeding" which appears during continuous stimulation by estrogen at low levels.

ACKNOWLEDGMENT

This research was supported by grants HD-03969 and RR-00298, HD-19799 (D. J. Dierschke, Special Research Fellow), HD-52172 (F. J. Karsch, Postdoctoral Research Fellow), and the Ford Foundation (R. F. Weick, Postdoctoral Fellow).

REFERENCES

Atkinson, L. E., Bhattacharya, A. N., Monroe, S. E., Dierschke, D. J., & Knobil, E. (1970). Effects of gonadectomy on plasma LH concentration in the rhesus monkey. *Endocrinology* **87**, 847–849.

Crim, L. W. & Geschwind, I. I. (1972). Patterns of FSH and LH secretion in the developing ram: The influence of castration and replacement therapy with testosterone propionate. *Biol. Reprod.* **7**, 47–54.

Foster, D. L., Cook, B., & Nalbandov, A. V. (1972). Regulation of LH in the fetal and neonatal lamb: effect of castration during the early post-natal period on levels of LH in sera and pituitaries of neonatal lambs. *Biol. Reprod.* **6**, 253–257.

Foster, D. L., Lemons, J. A., & Jaffe, R. B. (1972). Pituitary-gonadal relationships in the immature rhesus monkey. *Biol. Reprod.* **7**, 134 (abstract).

Goldman, B. D., Grazia, Y. R., Kamberi, I. A., & Porter, J. C. (1971). Serum gonadotropin concentrations in intact and castrated neonatal rats. *Endocrinology* **88**, 771–776.

Hotchkiss, J., Atkinson, L. E., & Knobil, E. (1971). Time course of serum estrogen and LH concentrations during the menstrual cycle of the rhesus monkey. *Endocrinology* **89**, 177–183.

Karsch, F. J., Dierschke, D. J., Weick, R. F., Yamaji, T., Hotchkiss, J., & Knobil, E. (1973). Positive and negative feedback control, by estrogen, of leuteinizing hormone secretion in the rhesus monkey. *Endocrinology,* **92**: 799–804.

Knobil E., Dierschke, D. J., Yamaji, T., Karsch, F. J., Hotchkiss, J., & Weick, R. F. (1972). Role of estrogen in the positive and negative feedback control of LH secretion during the menstrual cycle of the rhesus monkey. In *Gonadotropins,* B. B. Saxena, C. G. Beling & H. M. Gandy, Eds., Wiley, New York, pp. 72–86.

Land, R. B., Thimonier, J., & Pelletier, J. (1970). Possibilité d'induction d'une décharge de LH par une injection d'oestrogène chez l'agneau femelle en fonction de l'âge. *C.R. Acad. Sci. (Paris)* **271**, 1549–1551.

Monroe, S. E., Peckham, W. D., Neill, J. D., & Knobil, E. (1970). A radioimmunoassay for rhesus monkey LH. *Endocrinology* **86**, 1012–1018.

Odell, W. D., Hescox, M. A., & Kiddy, C. A. (1970). Studies of hypothalamic-pituitary-gonadal interrelations in prepubertal cattle, in *Gonadotropins and Ovarian Development,* W. R. Butt, A. C. Crooke, & M. Ryle, Eds., E & S Livingstone, Edinburgh, pp. 371–385.

Ramirez, V. D. & Sawyer, C. H. (1965). Advancement of puberty in the female rat by estrogen. *Endocrinology* **76**, 1158–1168.

Resko, J. A. & Phoenix, C. H. (1972). Sexual behavior and testosterone concentrations in the plasma of the rhesus monkey before and after castration. *Endocrinology* **91**, 499–503.

Swerdloff, R. S., Jacobs, H. S., & Odell, W. D. (1972). Hypothalamic-pituitary-gonadal interrelationships in the rat during maturation. In *Gonadotropins,* B. B. Saxena, C. G. Beling & H. M. Gandy, Eds., Wiley, New York, pp. 546–561.

van Wagenen, G. & Asling, C. W. (1958). Roentgenographic estimation of bone age in the rhesus monkey. *Amer. J. Anat.* **103**, 163–185.

van Wagenen, G. & Simpson, M. E. (1954). Testicular development in the rhesus monkey. *Anat. Rec.* **118**, 231–243.

van Wagenen, G. & Simpson, M. E. (1965). Embryology of the ovary and testis, *Homo sapiens* and *Macaca mulatta.* Yale University Press, New Haven.

Yamaji, T., Dierschke, D. J., Hotchkiss, J., Bhattacharya, A. N., Surve, A. H., & Knobil, E. (1971). Estrogen induction of LH release in the rhesus monkey. *Endocrinology* **89**, 1034–1041.

Yamaji, T., Peckham, W. D., Atkinson, L. E., Dierschke, D. J., & Knobil, E. (1973). Radioimmunoassay of rhesus monkey follicle-stimulating hormone. *Endocrinology.* 92: 1652–1659.

Yamamoto, M., Diebel, N. D., & Bogdanove, E. M. (1970). Analysis of initial and delayed effects of orchidectomy and ovariectomy on pituitary and serum LH levels in adult and immature rats. *Endocrinology* **86**, 1102–1111.

Ying, S-Y., Fang, V. S., & Greep, R. O. (1971). Estradiol benzoate-induced changes in serum LH and FSH in immature female rats. *Fertil. Steril.* **22**, 799–801.

6.

Hypothalamic-Pituitary Regulation of Puberty In Man: Evidence and Concepts Derived from Clinical Research

M. M. GRUMBACH, J. C. ROTH, S. L. KAPLAN, and R. P. KELCH

The onset of puberty in man is associated with a complex sequence of maturational changes that is imperfectly understood. For many years, however, it has been appreciated that certain central nervous system (CNS) lesions involving the hypothalamus and its neighboring structures may advance or retard the onset of human puberty. Considerable evidence supports the concept that the CNS, and not the pituitary gland or gonads, inhibits or restrains activation of the hypothalamic-pituitary gonadotropin-gonadal system. Studies in experimental animals (summarized by Donovan

---

Abbreviations

CNS	Central nervous system
LRF	Luteinizing hormone releasing factor
LH	Luteinizing hormone
FSH	Follicle stimulating hormone
LH-hCG	Luteinizing hormone-human chorionic gonadotropin

& van der Werff ten Bosch, 1965; Critchlow & Bar-Sela, 1967), many initiated by pioneers in neuroendocrinology, have provided a hypothesis of the control of puberty that is now susceptible to test in the human being.

We present indirect evidence that this inhibiting effect is mediated via the hypothalamus and its neurosecretory neurons which synthesize and release the gonadotropin releasing factor LRF (luteinizing hormone releasing factor). Suppression of LRF secretion, and quite likely its synthesis, appears to be the limiting hormonal factor that restricts the pituitary secretion of gonadotropin and maturation of the gonads. The secretion of LRF is affected by biogenic amines. Dopaminergic neurons within the hypothalamus are thought to stimulate LRF release by an alpha-adrenergic receptor mechanism (Coppola, 1971; McCann, 1971; Knobil, Dierschke, Yamaji, Karsch, Hotchkiss, & Weick, 1972; Bhattacharya, Dierschke, Yamaji, & Knobil, 1972; Schwartz & McCormack, 1972). Extrahypothalamic structures in the CNS, including the limbic system, influence gonadotropic secretion through neural pathways that connect with the hypothalamus. The dopaminergic neurons are a link in the conduit for information transfer from the limbic system (hippocampus and amygdala) to the hypothalamic neurosecretory cells which secrete LRF (Everett, 1964; 1969; Gorski, 1970). Hence the hypothalamic regulation of gonadotropin is not influenced solely by sex steroids but by complex neural influences that integrate a variety of intrinsic and extrinsic stimuli.

There are 3 patterns of secretion of gonadotropins: tonic, cyclic, and pulsatile or episodic. *Tonic* secretion is regulated by the classic negative or inhibitory feedback mechanism by which changes in the concentration of circulating sex steroids result in reciprocal changes in the secretion of pituitary gonadotropins. This is the pattern of secretion in the male and one of the control mechanisms in the female. *Cyclic* secretion involves a positive or stimulatory feedback mechanism in which an increment in circulating estrogens, to a critical level and of sufficient duration, initiates a synchronous release of LH and FSH (the preovulatory LH surge). This cyclic secretion of gonadotropin with its preovulatory LH and FSH surge is characteristic of the pattern in the normal adult female before menopause. Finally, intrinsic CNS influences, not dependent on the sex steroid levels, are thought to mediate episodic or *pulsatile* secretion of gonadotropins in the male and female. All these mechanisms have a different and independent sequence of maturation.

We have selected 6 aspects of the CNS and related mechanisms that are involved in the control of the onset of puberty in man: (1) the presence of negative feedback control of the secretion of FSH and LH before puberty which exhibits a change in sensitivity or set point with the onset of puberty; (2) the hypothesis that the hypothalamic-pituitary-gonadal negative feedback mechanism becomes operative in late fetal life; (3) the change in pituitary sensitivity to LRF at puberty and the qualitative change in the LH response; (4) the sequential maturation of the hypothalamic-pituitary-gonadal circuit; (5) the maturation and activation of the positive feedback mechanism in mid-puberty; (6) the development of episodic secretion of gonadotropins.

There are 2 broad aspects to the neural control of puberty, e.g., mechanisms in the control of the onset of puberty and factors that influence the time of its onset. We limit our discussion to the former. With regard to the latter, the time of onset of puberty and its course are affected by inheritance and genotype and a variety of environmental factors acting through the CNS, such as geography, altitude, chronic disease, light perception, and socioeconomic conditions, especially as the socioeconomic factors influence nutrition and general well-being (Zacharias & Wurtman, 1969; Marshall & Tanner, 1968). The onset of puberty is correlated with skeletal maturation (which reflects general somatic maturity) and with "critical weight" (Frisch & Revelle, 1969; 1971). These considerations are beyond the scope of this presentation.

Neither the pituitary gland nor the gonads are major factors in limiting or restraining the onset of puberty. Children with true precocious puberty, either idiopathic or secondary to a CNS mass or a destructive lesion that involves the hypothalamus, provide evidence that the hypothalamic-pituitary gonadotropin-gonadal axis can be awakened prematurely (Weinberger & Grant, 1941; Bauer, 1954; Liu, Grumbach, de Napoli, & Morishima, 1965; Wilkins, 1965). A dramatic example of the activation of ovarian function in a 15-year-old sexually infantile hypopituitary female who had an hypophysectomy and irradiation of the pituitary area at 8 years of age for craniopharyngioma is shown in Fig. 1. Evidence of ovulation was obtained after a single 34-day course of human menopausal gonadotropin during which human chorionic gonadotropin (hCG) was administered concurrently for the last 5 days (Abrams, Grumbach, Dyrenfurth, & Vande Wiele, 1967). Hence the clinical investigator as well as the animal experimentalist has focused attention on the role of the CNS in seeking to gain insight into the mechanism of the onset of puberty.*

* LER-869 was used as the standard for plasma and pituitary FSH (1 ng is equivalent to 100 ng LER-907) and LER-960 for plasma and pituitary LH (1 ng is equivalent to 40 ng LER-907). The second IRP-HMG was the assay standard for urinary FSH and LH. The methods utilized in the studies reported herein and their precision and sensitivity have been described: for plasma FSH and LH (Burr et al, 1970; Sizonenko et al, 1970); for urine FSH and LH (Kulin et al, 1972); for plasma testosterone (August et al, 1972; Roth et al, 1973b); for plasma estradiol (Jenner et al, 1972); and for plasma estrone (Kelch et al, 1973a).

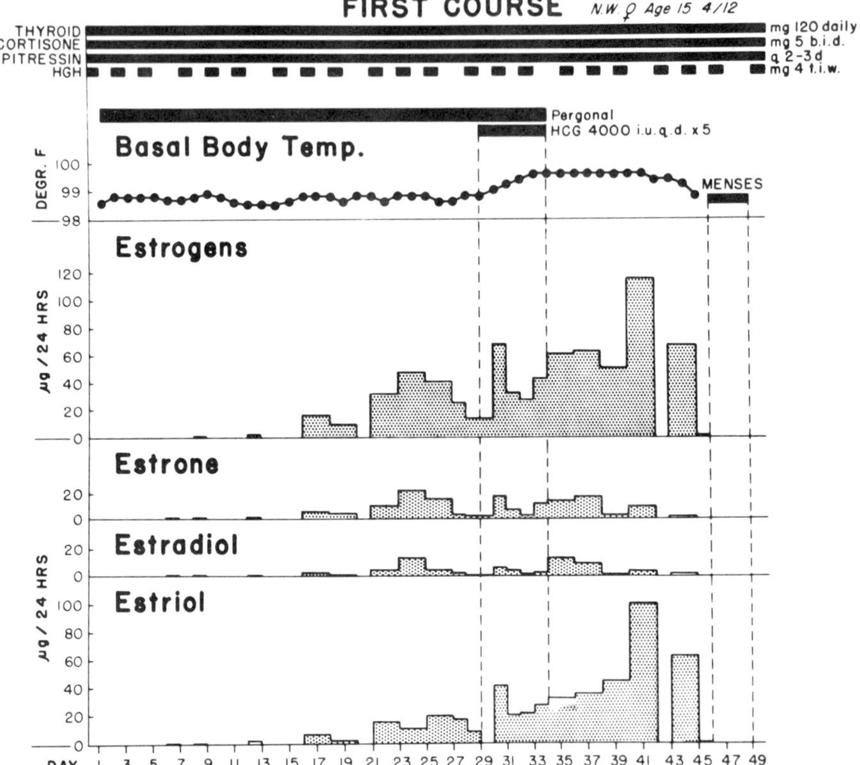

FIG. 1. Evidence of increased estrogen secretion, ovulation, and menses in a 15-year-old sexually infantile hypophysectomized female following the initial course of daily administration of human menopausal gonadotropin (Pergonal) alone for 29 days and with hCG for an additional 5 days. From Abrams et al, 1967.

EVIDENCE FOR AN OPERATIVE NEGATIVE FEEDBACK MECHANISM BEFORE PUBERTY

In now numerous reports it has been clearly established, by bioassay and radioimmunoassay, that FSH and LH are detectable in the blood and urine of prepubertal children (Fitschen & Clayton, 1965; Rifkind, Kulin, & Ross, 1967; Blizzard, Johanson, Guyda, Baghdassarian, Raiti, & Migeon, 1970; Blizzard, Penny, Foley, Baghdassarian, Johanson & Yen, 1972; Buckler & Clayton, 1970; Burr, Sizonenko, Kaplan, & Grumbach, 1970; Lee, Midgley, & Jaffe, 1970; Rifkind, Kulin, Rayford, Cargille & Ross, 1970; Sizonenko, Burr, Kaplan, & Grumbach, 1970; Yen & Vičic, 1970; Maffezzoli, Kaplan, & Chrambach, 1972). At that time the concentrations of plasma testosterone in boys (Frasier, Gafford, & Horton, 1969; August, Grumbach, & Kaplan, 1972; Roth, Grumbach & Kaplan 1973a; Winter & Faiman, 1972) of plasma estradiol and estrone in girls (Jenner, Kelch, Kaplan, & Grumbach, 1972; Kelch, Kaplan & Grumbach, 1973a) are low. Noteworthy is the small increment in urinary FSH and LH during childhood and the striking increase during puberty. Adults excrete about 10 to 16 times as much immunoreactive LH as prepubertal children and about 4 to 6 times as much FSH; differences in the plasma concentration are less marked and there is significant overlap. These studies support the concept that the hypothalamic-pituitary gonadotropin-gonadal circuit is functional in prepubertal children but at a low level of activity.

Additional evidence for a functional negative feedback system prepubertally is the occurrence of "compensatory hypertrophy" in the descended testes of unilateral cryptorchid prepubertal boys (Laron & Zilka, 1969), the suppression by exogenous sex steroids of plasma and urinary gonadotropins in prepubertal children (Kulin, Grumbach, & Kaplan, 1969, 1972; Kelch, Grumbach, & Kaplan, 1973b), and the presence of elevated gonadotropin levels in prepubertal children with the syndrome of gonadal dysgenesis (Penny, Guyda, Baghdassarian, Johanson, & Blizzard, 1970; Kelch, Grumbach, & Kaplan, 1972a; Conte, Grumbach, & Kaplan, 1972).

Gonadotropin Secretion in Agonadal Infants and Children

We have studied plasma immunoreactive gonadotropins in 32 patients with 45, XO gonadal dysgenesis, age 2 days to 16 years (Fig. 2a,b); (Conte et al, 1972; Kelch et al, 1972a). In patients aged 2 days to 3 years the mean concentration of plasma FSH was 45 ± 9 ng/ml SE; all but the 2-day-old infant had elevated values, the highest being 200 ng/ml. On the other hand, the mean LH level was 2.4 ± 0.43 ng/ml, and in 2 of 11 patients the concentration of LH was within the normal range for age. In the 6- to 10-year-old group the mean concentration of plasma FSH was strikingly lower (4.4 ± 1.7 ng/ml, $p < .02$), but the mean LH level was comparable to the younger group (1.3 ± 0.25 ng/ml). After 10 years of age the mean concentration of FSH was 54 ± 6 ng/ml, similar to the mean value for the 2-day to 3-year-old group; the mean LH level, however, was also elevated to 6.9 ± 0.9 ng/ml.

In the absence of functional gonads in the prepubertal individual the secretion of FSH, and to a lesser extent LH, is increased. This observation provides evidence that CNS regulation of gonadotropin secretion through the negative feedback mechanism (hypothalamic gonadostat) is operative by early infancy and that its development is not dependent on the presence of functional gonads. Indeed, this mechanism appears to undergo maturation and become functional in late fetal life.

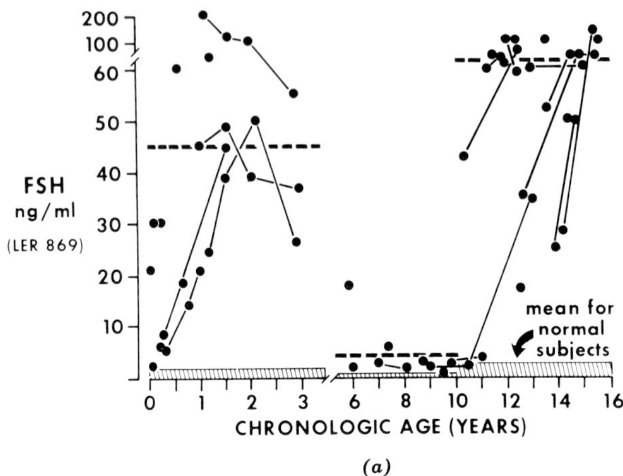

FIG. 2a.   The concentration of plasma FSH for patients with XO gonadal dysgenesis at chronologic ages of 1 day to 15 years. Connecting lines denote serial studies in the same patients and interrupted horizontal lines, the mean values for 3 different age groups. These are compared with mean levels of FSH in normal children in 3 different age groups, indicated by solid horizontal bars. In one patient, at 2 days of age, the plasma FSH level was comparable to that in a normal infant. Note the diphasic pattern of plasma FSH with elevated levels present in infants 5 days to 6 months of age with gonadal dysgenesis; in the age group between 6 to 10 years the mean level of plasma FSH was slightly above normal levels for age. After 10 years of age the concentration of plasma FSH in patients with XO gonadal dysgenesis was comparable to that of postmenopausal women.

Two other aspects are of interest. The mean FSH/LH ratio in the 10- to 16-year-old patients with XO gonadal dysgenesis is considerably higher than in adult castrates and postmenopausal women, because of the lower concentration of plasma LH in the patients with gonadal dysgenesis. The fall in mean value for plasma FSH and, to a lesser degree, LH in the 6- to 10-year-old patients with XO gonadal dysgenesis seems an exaggeration of the normal diphasic pattern of gonadotropic secretion that occurs in normal females between infancy and adolescence. It may be a consequence of the negative feedback action of sex steroids secreted by the adrenal cortex in the 6- to 10-year old group on a highly sensitive hypothalamic gonadostat or to an inherent change in its set point or to both factors.

Maturation of Negative Feedback Mechanism

Synthesis of gonadotropins by the human fetal pituitary gland occurs as early as 68 days, and secretion of FSH and "LH-hCG" is detectable by 84 days, the earliest fetus studied (Kaplan, Grumbach, & Shepard, 1969;

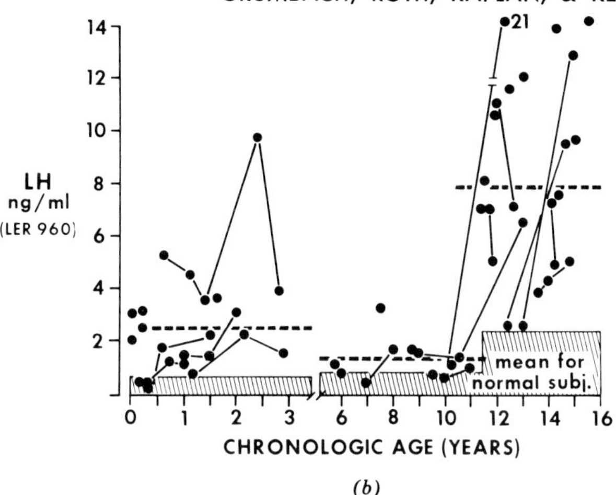

(b)

FIG. 2b. The concentration of LH for patients with XO gonadal dysgenesis at different chronologic ages of 1 day to 15 years. Connecting lines denote serial studies in the same patient and horizontal interrupted lines the mean levels in 3 different age groups. This is compared with the mean levels of LH at different ages in normal children indicated by solid horizontal bars. In children with gonadal dysgenesis less than 3 years of age the mean concentration of plasma LH is slightly higher than in normal children of a similar age. Between 6 and 10 years of age the mean concentration of plasma LH in patients with gonadal dysgenesis is similar to those of normal children at that age and lower than that seen in younger (< 3 years) or older patients (> 10 years) with gonadal dysgenesis. Note the consistently high concentrations of LH in all the older untreated patients.

Grumbach & Kaplan, 1973). The mean content of immunoreactive pituitary LH rose from 82 ng at 10 to 14 weeks gestational age to 1906 ng at 25 to 29 weeks; the mean immunoreactive FSH content increased from 9 to 1532 ng during the same period of gestation (Fig. 3a,b). At 25 to 29 weeks the mean value for LH content was about twice that of the newborn infant; the FSH content was about fivefold greater in the 25 to 29 week pituitary glands than in newborn infants. In addition, the pituitary glands of female fetuses had a higher content and concentration of FSH and LH than of male fetal pituitary glands of comparable gestational age (Fig. 3c,d). On the other hand, the pituitary gland from an anencephalic fetus born at term contained only about 2 per cent of the LH and FSH as of newborn infants.

Beginning at 84 days of gestation the pattern of serum FSH was one of increasing concentration to about 150 days (most of the values exceeded 15 ng/ml, which is in the castrate range). From about 150 days of gestation there is a striking fall in serum levels to term; at term umbilical venous

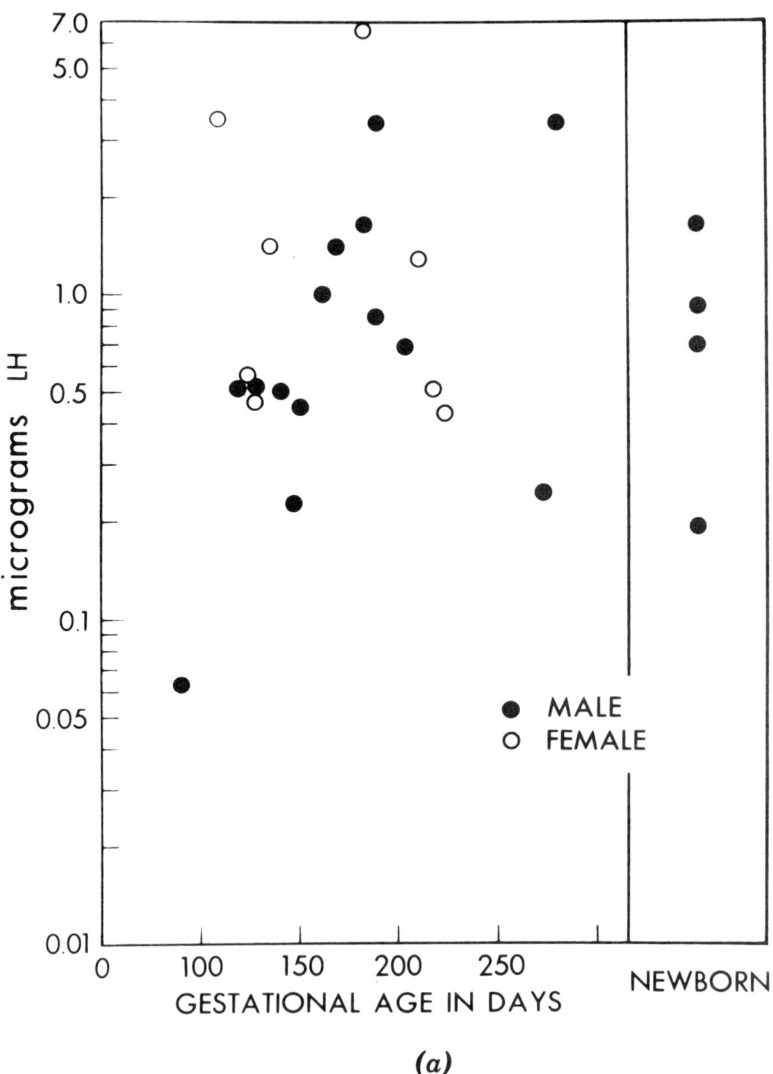

(a)

FIG. 3a. The content of LH in the pituitary gland of the human fetus is plotted as μg LH on the ordinate against gestational age in days on the abscissa. This is compared with the content in the pituitary gland of 4 newborn infants. Solid dots indicate male fetuses and open dots female fetuses. The content of LH was 0.06 μg in a 90-day-old fetus with a rise to peak levels of 5 to 7 μg between 120 to 180 days of gestation. In late gestation and in the newborn period the content of LH decreased to levels of 0.3 μg. From Grumbach & Kaplan, 1973.

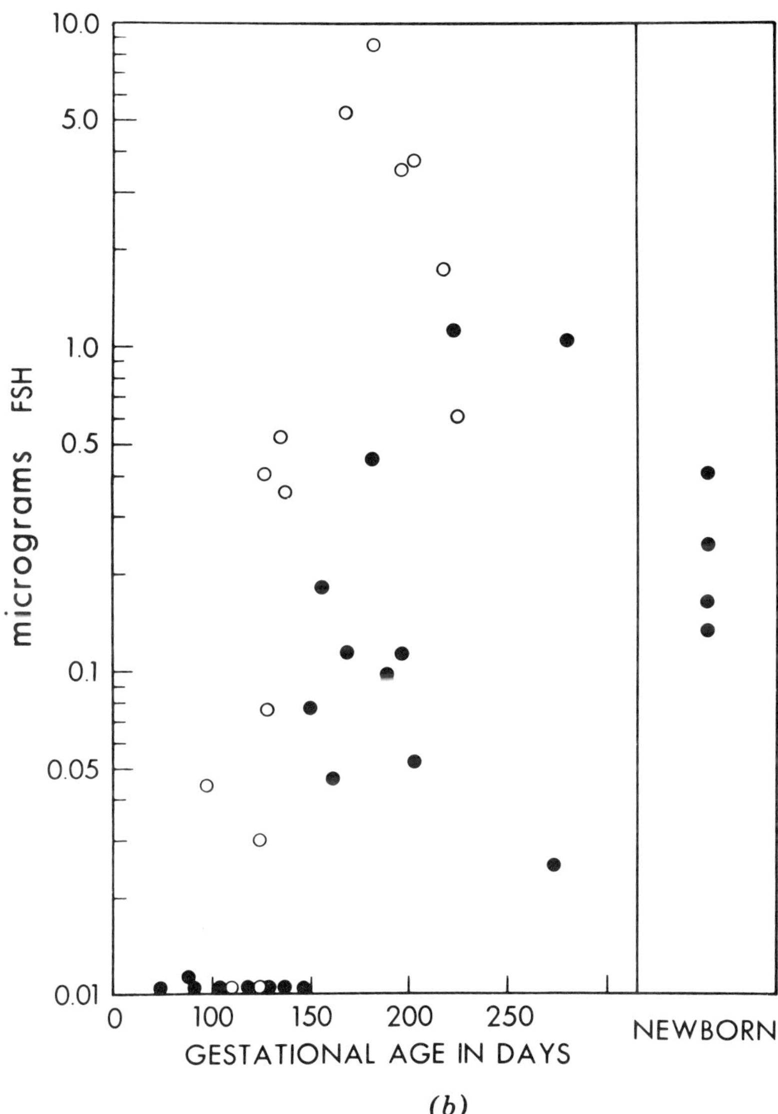

(b)

FIG. 3b. The content of FSH in the human fetal pituitary gland plotted on a log scale in micrograms on the ordinate against gestational age in days on the abscissa. These values are compared with those in the pituitary gland of the newborn in the panel on the right. Male fetuses are indicated by solid dots and female fetuses by open dots. FSH is present by 88 days of gestation. A sharp rise is noted by 120 days, with peak content by 180 days of gestation. By late gestation and at term the pituitary content of FSH is less than at mid-gestation. In female fetuses the content of pituitary FSH in mid-gestation is generally higher than that in pituitary glands of male fetuses. From Grumbach & Kaplan, 1973.

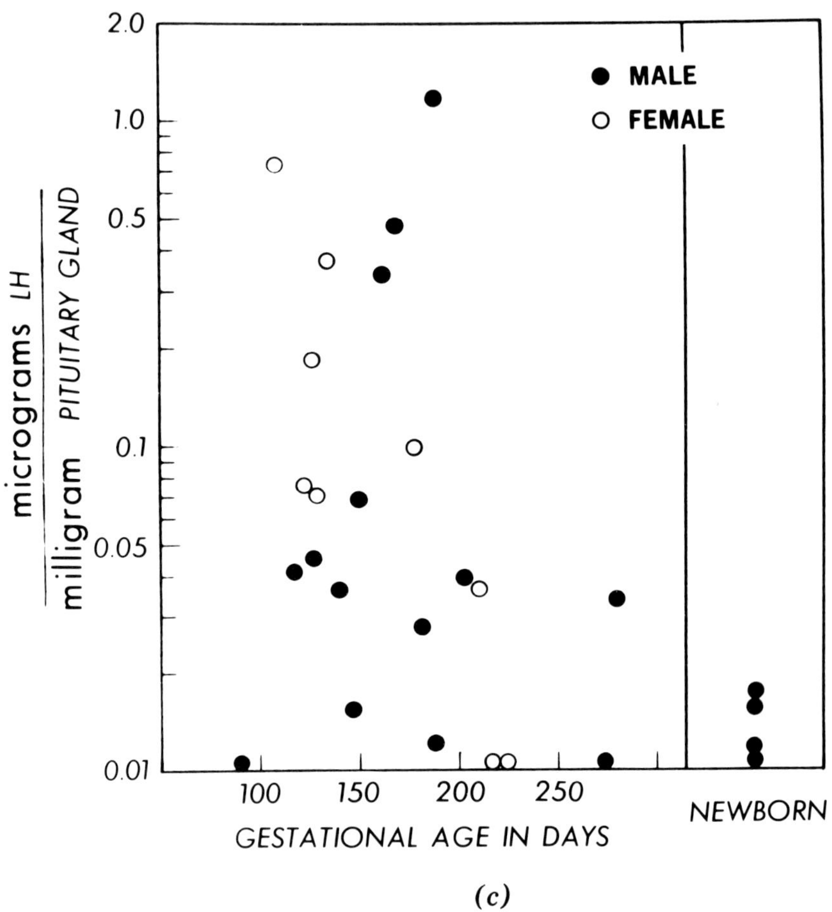

(c)

FIG. 3c. Scattergram of the concentration (μg/mg) of LH in pituitary glands of human fetuses plotted on a log scale on the ordinate against gestational days on the abscissa. This is compared with the concentration in the pituitary glands of newborns. Solid dots indicate male fetuses and open dots, female fetuses. Detectable levels of pituitary LH are present at 90 days of gestation, with peak levels between 120 to 180 days of gestation. A significant decrease in concentration is noted in late gestation and in the newborn. From Grumbach & Kaplan, 1973.

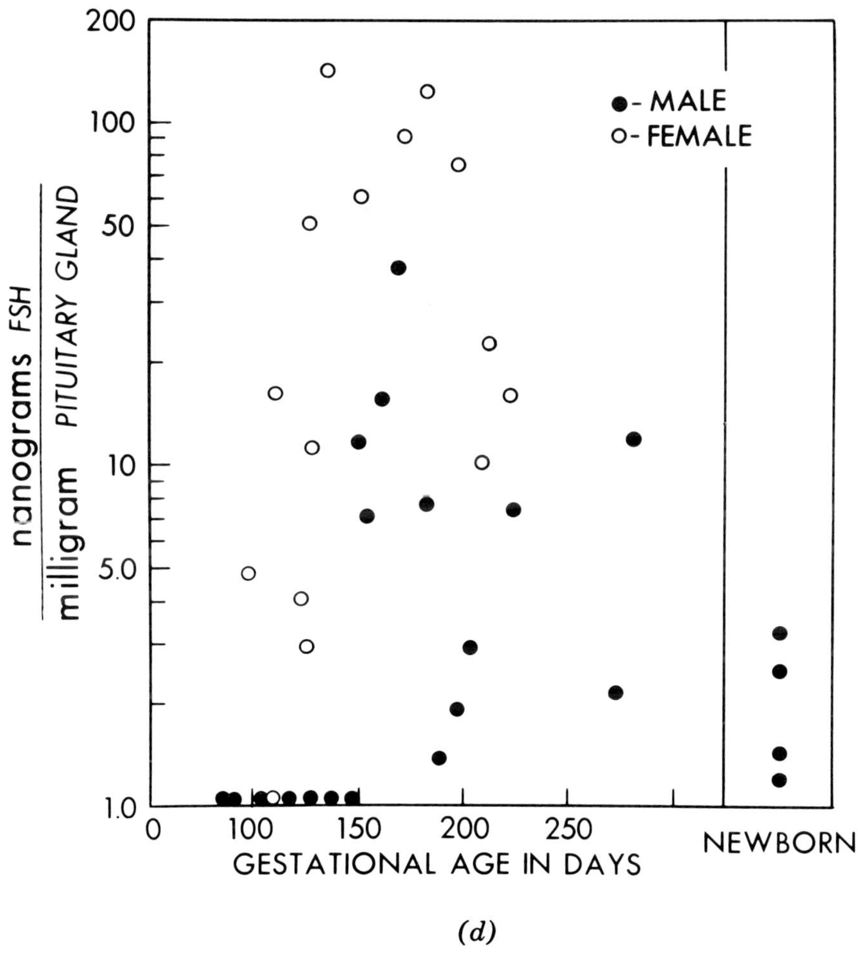

(d)

Fig. 3d.   The concentration of FSH (ng/mg) in the pituitary gland of human fetuses is plotted on a log scale on the ordinate against gestational age in days on the abscissa. The concentration of FSH in the pituitary glands of 4 newborns is plotted in the right panel. Male fetuses are indicated by solid dots and female fetuses by open dots. FSH is present by 88 days of gestational age with peak levels by 120 to 180 days. During the late gestational and newborn period the pituitary concentration of FSH decreases. Note the higher concentration of FSH in the pituitary glands of the female fetuses than in the male fetuses. From Grumbach & Kaplan, 1973.

serum contains 1 ng/ml or less of serum FSH. As for pituitary content, the data suggest that the concentration of serum FSH between 110 and 140 days of gestation is higher in female than male fetuses. The pattern for serum "LH-hCG" showed a similar trend. The highest values were between 84 and 140 days, after which LH-hCG tended to fall to levels below 10 ng/ml by term. The data are described elsewhere (Grumbach & Kaplan, 1973).

Two aspects of the ontogenesis of FSH and LH secretion in the human fetus are pertinent to the control of the onset of puberty: the development of the negative hypothalamic gonadal feedback mechanism and the sex difference in the pituitary content of FSH and LH and in serum FSH.

The pattern of change in the concentration of immunoreactive pituitary FSH and LH and serum FSH, and possibly LH, in the fetus suggests a sequence of increasing synthesis and secretion in which peak serum values reach castrate levels between 14 and 24 weeks, followed by a decline that persists through the remainder of gestation. The high serum FSH (and perhaps LH) values may be attributed to autonomous secretion of FSH and LH or of the relatively unrestrained secretion of the hypothalamic gonado-tropin releasing factor LRF. There is some evidence to support the latter hypothesis; Levina (1970) detected FSH and LH releasing activity in the hypothalamus of human fetuses. Quantitative studies of the ontogenesis of hypothalamic gonadotropin releasing factor(s) are not yet available, however. Later in fetal development the inhibitory feedback mechanism matures and becomes operative. The increasing sensitivity of the hypothalamic gonadostat to circulating sex steroids in the fetus leads to suppression of LRF release and to decreased synthesis and secretion of FSH and LH. Thus it appears that the hypothalamic gonadal negative feedback mechanism is functional in the human fetus by the third trimester of gestation. In this context the concentration of serum FSH in the 2-day-old patient with XO gonadal dysgenesis (streak gonads were identified at laparotomy) was within the normal range for age, but in a 5-day old XO patient the level of serum FSH was strikingly elevated.

The higher mean pituitary content and concentration of FSH and LH in the female fetus is of interest. It is the first evidence in man that in the male fetus the secretion of androgens by the fetal Leydig cells, the only clearly established difference in the sex steroid hormone milieu between the male and female fetus (Reyes, Winter, & Faiman, 1973), may advance the maturation of the negative feedback mechanism in the male fetus (Grumbach & Kaplan, 1973). Recently, Ryan, Naftolin, Reddy, Flores, and Petro (1972) demonstrated the aromatization of androgens to estrogens by the anterior hypothalamus and hippocampus (limbic system) of the first trimester human fetus. This suggests that at an early fetal stage these neural structures can bind and metabolize sex steroids. Of interest is the higher concentration of serum FSH in human and chimpanzee female infants (Faiman & Winter, 1971; Faiman, Winter, Chehib, & Butler, 1972; Lee et al, 1970) which is not present in prepubertal children after about 2 years of age. It is not known whether this finding is explicable by a sex difference in prenatal maturation of the gonadostat or in the sex steroid output of the ovary and testis during infancy.

Change in Set Point of Negative Feedback Mechanism

It is now 40 years since Hohlweg and Dohrn (1932; Hohlweg, 1936) from experiments in the rat, advanced the concept of a change at puberty in sensitivity to circulating sex steroids of a CNS *Sexualzentrum* that regulates gonadotropin secretion. A substantial body of data in experimental animals, mainly the rat, has been generated to support the hypothesis in its present form, i.e., that the hypothalamic gonadotropin regulating mechanism of the prepubertal individual is much more sensitive to the negative feedback effects of circulating androgens and estrogens than in the adult. As a consequence, the low levels of sex steroids in the prepubertal individual suppress the release of LRF and thus the secretion of FSH and LH. With the approach of puberty there is a progressive decrease in sensitivity (higher set point) of the hypothalamic negative feedback receptors to sex steroids, which results in increased secretion of pituitary gonadotropins, stimulation of sex steroid output, and the development of secondary sex characteristics (Donovan & van der Werff ten Bosch, 1965; Ramirez & McCann, 1963; Critchlow & Bar-Sela, 1967; Smith & Davidson, 1967; 1968; Davidson, 1969; 1972; Ramirez, 1971).

The concept of decreasing sensitivity of the hypothalamus to gonadal steroid feedback as a critical occurrence in the initiation of human puberty is illustrated in Fig. 4. According to this hypothesis, LRF, gonadotropins, and sex steroids interact at low levels on a highly sensitive negative feedback. The initiation of puberty is associated with an increase in the set point of the hypothalamic negative feedback receptors; as a consequence, the low concentrations of sex steroids are no longer effective in suppressing the secretion of FSH and LH. This results in increased release of LRF, FSH, and LH, increased stimulation of the gonads, and finally the attainment of an adult set point of the gonadostat. The change in sensitivity is probably a gradual rather than acute event. It may exhibit narrow fluctuations in childhood before pubertal increase in set point is well established. As mentioned earlier, it seems to correlate with the attainment of a critical level of the CNS and general somatic maturation that correlates with skeletal age.

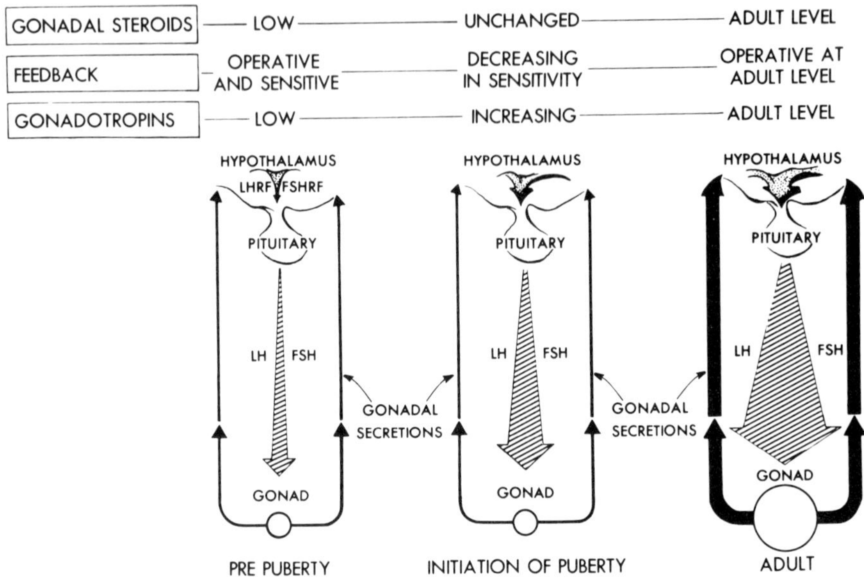

FIG. 4. A schematic diagram of the changes in sensitivity of the hypothalamic gonadostat. In the prepubertal state the concentration of sex steroids and gonadotropins is low; the hypothalamic "gonadostat" is functional but highly sensitive to low levels of sex steroids. With the onset of puberty there is decreased sensitivity of the hypothalamus to negative feedback by sex steroids, increased release of LRF, and enhanced secretion of gonadotropins. In the negative feedback mechanism the hypothalamus is less sensitive to feedback by sex steroids (adult set point) and adult levels of gonadotropins and sex steroids are present.

In an attempt to test the change in the set-point hypothesis in the human being 2 types of experiment were carried out in our laboratory. In the first a wide dose-range of clomiphene citrate was administered orally to prepubertal children and to pubertal individuals in various stages of puberty. The effect was assessed on the urinary excretion of immunoreactive FSH and LH. Serum testosterone also was determined in boys.

Clomiphene citrate (Clomid), an anti-estrogen with weak estrogenic properties, at doses ranging between 25 and 200 mg/day stimulates gonadotropic secretion and excretion in the adult (Roy, Greenblatt, Mahesh, & Jungck, 1963; Bardin, Ross, & Lipsett, 1967; Jacobsen, Marshall, Ross, & Cargille, 1968; Peterson, Midgley, & Jaffe, 1968) apparently by competitively inhibiting estradiol binding by tissue receptors, including those in the hypothalamus and pituitary gland (Wood, Wrenn, & Bitman, 1968; Korenman, 1970; Kahwango, Heinrichs, & Herrmann, 1970). If the effect in the prepubertal child was similar to that in adult males and females, we postulated that the anti-estrogen action of clomiphene citrate would block the negative feedback effect of the low level of circulating sex steroids and evoke a rise in plasma and urinary gonadotropin. No such stimulatory effect on gonadotropins was detected, even when the dosage was decreased from 100 to 0.001 mg/day for 7 days (Kulin et al, 1969; 1972). Instead there was suppression of urinary FSH and LH and serum testosterone, which we attribute to the weak estrogenic properties of clomiphene citrate (Wood et al, 1968).

As little as 0.1 mg/day for 1 week suppressed the urinary excretion of FSH to undetectable levels in prepubertal children (Table 1). Children in early puberty (P2) exhibited suppression of urinary gonadotropins (and testosterone in boys) when given 100 mg/day but not 1.0 or 0.01 mg/day. A boy tested over a 16-month period (from 15–2/12 to 16–6/12 years) with 100 mg/day of clomiphene for 1 week showed a change from decreased excretion of gonadotropins in very early puberty to no effect, neither a decrease nor increase, when puberty was more advanced. A rise in the urinary excretion of FSH and LH was elicited with 100 mg/day for 7 days in 2 mid-pubertal females but not at an earlier stage. A normal adult male, in whom stimulation of gonadotropic secretion was obtained with doses of 25 to 200 mg/day, had decreased gonadotropic output on 500 mg/day for 1 week (Kulin et al, 1972). If the inhibitory effect of clomiphene citrate is mediated by its weak anti-estrogenic properties, the results are consistent with a change in sensitivity of the negative feedback mechanism in prepubertal and pubertal children, as shown in Fig. 4.

TABLE 1.   The effect of clomiphene citrate on urinary FSH, LH, and plasma testosterone in prepubertal and pubertal children[a]

Pubertal stage	No.	Dose (mg/day×7 d)	Significant suppression
P1 (prepubertal)	3	100	3/3
	6	10	5/6
	3	1.0	3/3
	5	0.1	2/5
	6	0.01	0/6
	3	0.001	0/3
P2 (early puberty)	3	100	3/3
	4	10	2/4[b]
	4	1.0	1/4[b]
	4	0.1	0/4

[a] Kulin, Grumbach, & Kaplan (1969; 1972)
[b] Questionable suppression. See original reports for experimental details.

To test this hypothesis further and more directly we administered, orally, varying doses of a potent estrogen, ethinyl estradiol, to children in different stages of sexual maturation (Kelch et al, 1972b; 1973b). As shown in of urinary gonadotropins to undetectable levels ($<$0.1 IU/day) on a dose of 5 μg/day or more of ethinyl estradiol for 4 to 7 days, and 3 of 6 children suppressed gonadotropic output on 2 μg/day (Fig. 5). In the early to mid-pubertal males 10 μg/m^2/day produced slight or no suppression and had no significant suppressive effect on the patients in an advanced stage of puberty (Fig. 6, Table 2).

These studies indicate that the hypothalamic-pituitary gonadotropin-gonadal negative feedback mechanism in the human being (1) is operative and highly sensitive to sex steroids in prepubertal children, (2) exhibits decreased sensitivity to sex steroid feedback with the onset and progression of puberty, and (3) provides support for the concept that decreased

TABLE 2.   Suppression of urinary FSH by ethinyl estradiol[a]

Pubertal stage	No.	Dose (μg/day$\times$5 d)	Significant suppression of urine FSH
P1 (prepubertal)	6	2	3/6
P1 (prepubertal)	5	5	5/5
P1 (prepubertal)	3	10	3/3
Total			11/14
P2 (early puberty)	2	2	0/2
P3 (mid-puberty)	2	10	1/2[b]
P4 (advanced puberty, premenarche)	2	10	0/2
Adult males[c]	4	8[d]	0/4[e]
	2	16	0/2
	2	20	0/2
	2	30	0/2
	4	40	3/4
	2	50	2/2

[a] Kelch, Grumbach, & Kaplan, 1972b; 1973b.
[b] Questionable suppression.
[c] Data of Kulin & Reiter (1972).
[d] Administered daily for 7 days.
[e] Significant suppression of LH was not demonstrated. See original reports for experimental details.

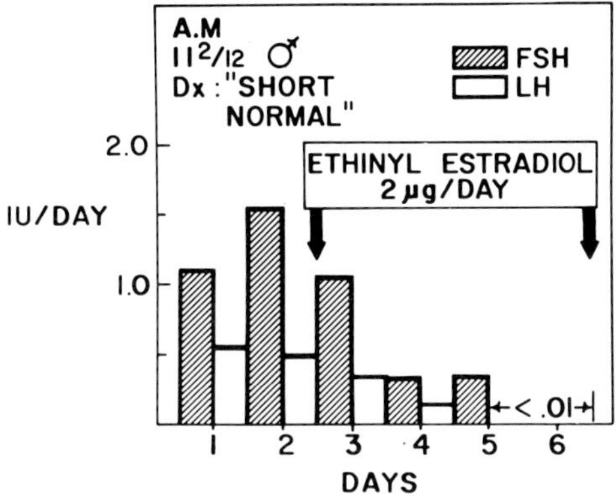

FIG. 5.   The effect of administration of ethinyl estradiol (2 µg/day) to a prepubertal normal male on the urinary excretion of LH and FSH. Note the rapid and significant decrease in LH and FSH by the third day following treatment with estradiol. Kelch et al, 1972.

sensitivity is a major determinant of the increased gonadotropin secretion at puberty. Recently, in a study of similar design which utilized ethinyl estradiol, Kulin and Reiter (1972) demonstrated that significant suppression of urinary FSH output occurred in normal adult men at a dose of 32 µg/day; the concentration of plasma FSH was decreased by 42 µg/day (Table 2). LH secretion was not diminished at these dosages. In none of the men was urinary or plasma gonadotropin suppressed to undetectable levels. An estimate of the differential sensitivity of the prepubertal and adult set point to estrogen feedback can be approximated from these data; the results suggest that the prepubertal hypothalamic gonadostat is about 6 to 15 times more sensitive than the adult negative feedback mechanism if the metabolic clearance rate of estrogen is within the same range in children and adult men.

We have obtained some evidence that suggests that sexually infantile adolescent patients with hypergonadotropic hypogonadism (syndrome of gonadal dysgenesis) develop decreased sensitivity to sex steroid feedback in the absence of functional gonads; indeed, larger doses of ethinyl estradiol were required to decrease gonadotropins to within the normal range than to suppress gonadotropic secretion in normal adolescent individuals (Fig. 7a,b). In this respect the relatively "unrestrained gonadostat" is less sensitive to negative feedback (Kelch, Conte, Kaplan, & Grumbach, 1972a).

It is unlikely that the differential sensitivity to estrogen in man is attributable to differences between prepubertal and adult individuals in

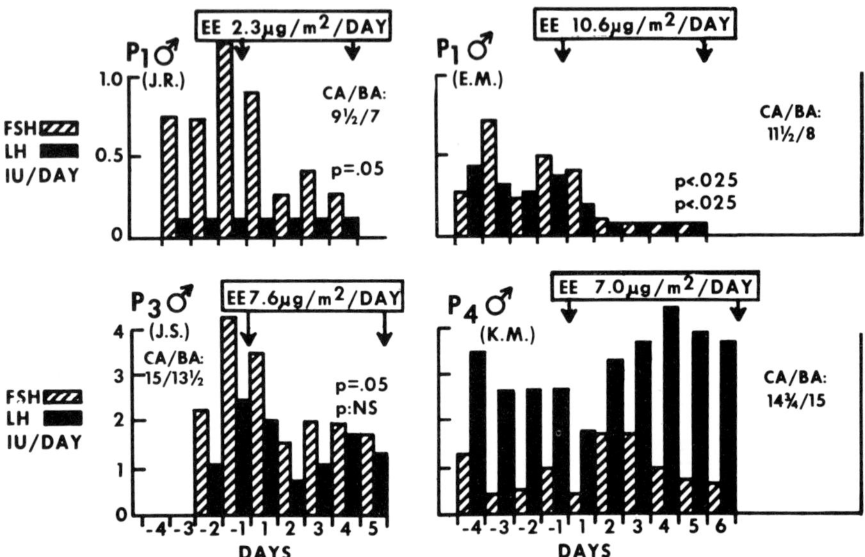

FIG. 6. The effect of oral ethinyl estradiol on the excretion of urinary LH and FSH in 2 prepubertal and 2 pubertal males. Both prepubertal (P1) males exhibited suppression of urinary FSH excretion. Urinary LH was suppressed in one prepubertal male (E.M.); in the other (J.R.) the levels of urinary LH were too low to assess suppressive effects of estradiol. In the male at mid-puberty (J.S.) urinary FSH excretion was significantly less following estradiol treatment [7.6 μg/m² (day)] but urinary LH was unaffected. In the male at late puberty (K.M.) neither urinary LH nor FSH was affected by estradiol treatment [7.0 μg/m² (day)]. From Kelch et al, 1973b.

the metabolic clearance rate of gonadotropins or sex steroids; data on this point are meager, however, and the possibility that these factors may have a contributory role merits further study.

PITUITARY GONADOTROPIC RESERVE AND PITUITARY AND GONADAL SENSITIVITY TO TROPIC STIMULI

Puberty appears to encompass orderly maturational changes that involve, sequentially, the suprahypothalamic CNS, the hypothalamus, the pituitary gland, the gonads and the target end organs for sex steroids. At each level the target structure may exhibit differences in responsiveness to neural or tropic stimuli, dependent on its sensitivity or a particular hormonal milieu. If we postulate that the increased secretion of gonadotropin with the approach of puberty is a consequence of a change in the neural and hor-

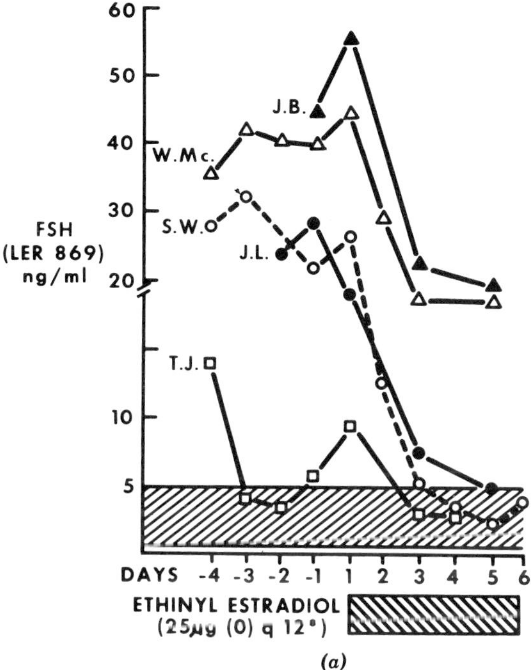

FIG. 7a. Suppression of plasma FSH in patients with the syndrome of gonadal dysgenesis.

monal restraints on synthesis and secretion of LRF, the decreased sensitivity of the gonadostat should lead, initially, to increased release of LRF, followed by increased gonadotropic secretion by the pituitary, and, finally, to augmented output of sex steroid by the gonads (Fig. 8).

The recent availability of LRF (Schally, Arimura, Baba, Nair, Matsuo, Redding, & Debeljuk, 1971; Baba, Arimura, & Schally, 1971; Amoss, Burgus, Blackwell, Vale, Fellows, & Guillemin, 1971; Matsuo, Baba, Nair, Arimura, & Schally 1971; Monahan, Rivier, Burgus, Amoss, Vale, & Guillemin, 1971) has made it possible to compare and contrast its effect on secretion of FSH and LH at different stages of sexual maturation and in disorders involving the hypothalamic-pituitary-gonadal system. Although it has been suggested that LRF is the gonadotropic releasing factor (RF) (Schally et al, 1971a), the possibility has not been excluded that more than one hypophysiotropic hormone is involved in the secretion of FSH and LH. Further, it remains uncertain whether FSH and LH are secreted by the same pituitary cell or by more than one type of pituitary gonadotrope.

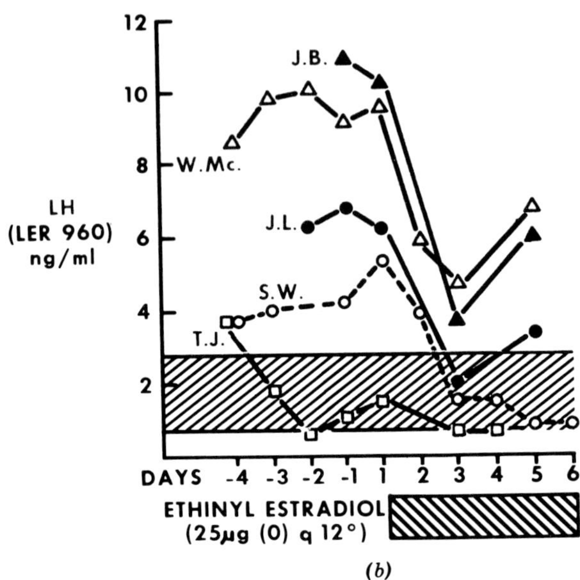

FIG. 7b. Suppression of plasma LH in patients with the syndrome of gonadal dysgenesis.

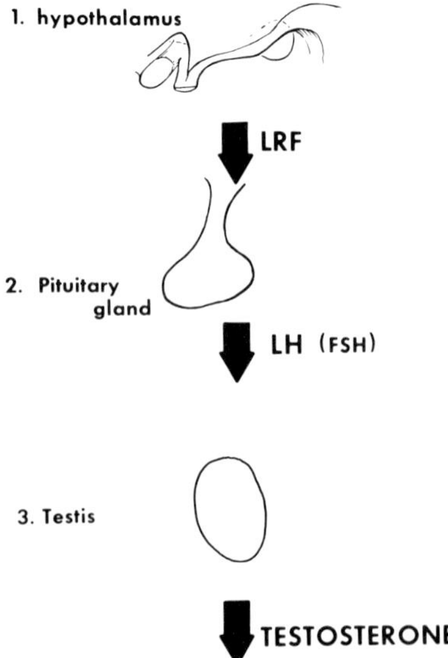

FIG. 8. Schematic representation of the sequential events in the maturation of the hypothalamic-pituitary-gonadal system in the male. At puberty increased secretion of LRF leads to increased stimulation of the pituitary gland and increased responsiveness to LRF; both factors lead to enhanced release of pituitary LH. The increased secretion of LH (in the presence of FSH) stimulates the Leydig cells of the testes, which results in increased synthesis and release of testosterone.

Response to LRF at Different Stages of Sexual Maturation

Studies in our laboratory (Roth, Kelch, Kaplan, & Grumbach, 1972a;b) and by Job, Garnier, Chaussain, and Milhaud (1972) have demonstrated a clear difference in pituitary responsiveness to LRF in prepubertal and pubertal children. We have studied the effects of different doses of synthetic LRF (1 μg/m^2 to 100 μg) by rapid intravenous infusion (in distilled water containing 5 mg/ml of human serum albumin) to 60 prepubertal boys and girls, 29 pubertal males and females, and 19 adult males (Roth, Grumbach, & Kaplan, 1973b). The LRF, synthesized by Dr. J. Rivier and generously provided by Dr. Roger Guillemin of the Salk Institute, was characterized and prepared especially for clinical studies (Monahan et al, 1971; Amoss et al, 1971). As already reported (Job et al, 1972; Roth et al, 1972a;b), there was a striking increase in LH responsiveness to LRF with the onset of puberty; a comparable increase in FSH release was not found. Plasma FSH and LH were increased by 5 minutes. Peak values, however, were attained at different times; for plasma FSH the modal time was 60 to 120 minutes and for plasma LH, 30 minutes. The readily releasable FSH and LH (which we regard as an indicator of pituitary gonadotropic reserve) was assessed by a variety of methods, including the peak value and maximal increment of plasma FSH and LH, and by the area circumscribed by a 4-hour curve of the concentrations of plasma FSH and LH after subtraction of basal values. The latter method, which utilizes a computer program, was the most sensitive indicator of the response of FSH and LH to graded doses of LRF. The results are shown in Fig. 9.

Because a significant difference in the increase in plasma LH was not observed for 10 μg/m^2 and 100 μg LRF in prepubertal and pubertal males and females and for 5 μg/m^2 and 100 μg LRF in adult males, the results for each of these dosages were pooled. Plasma FSH showed a different dose-response pattern, however; only the response to 100 μg LRF is illustrated (Fig. 9). For plasma LH there was a threefold increase in peak LH values, a fourfold increase in the mean maximal increment and area units between prepubertal and pubertal males and females, a fourfold increase in peak values, and a sixfold increase in the mean maximal increment and area units between prepubertal males and females and adult males. For plasma FSH the response to LRF was comparable in prepubertal, pubertal, and adult males to 100 μg of LRF, but the response in prepubertal girls was greater than in all the male groups (Fig. 9). Job et al (1972) have reported a similar sex difference in release of FSH in prepubertal children.

These results indicate that release of LH following the administration of an acute dose of LRF is minimal in prepubertal children, increases strikingly at puberty ($p < .001$), and is even greater in adult males. There is a sex difference in the rise of serum FSH: prepubertal and pubertal females

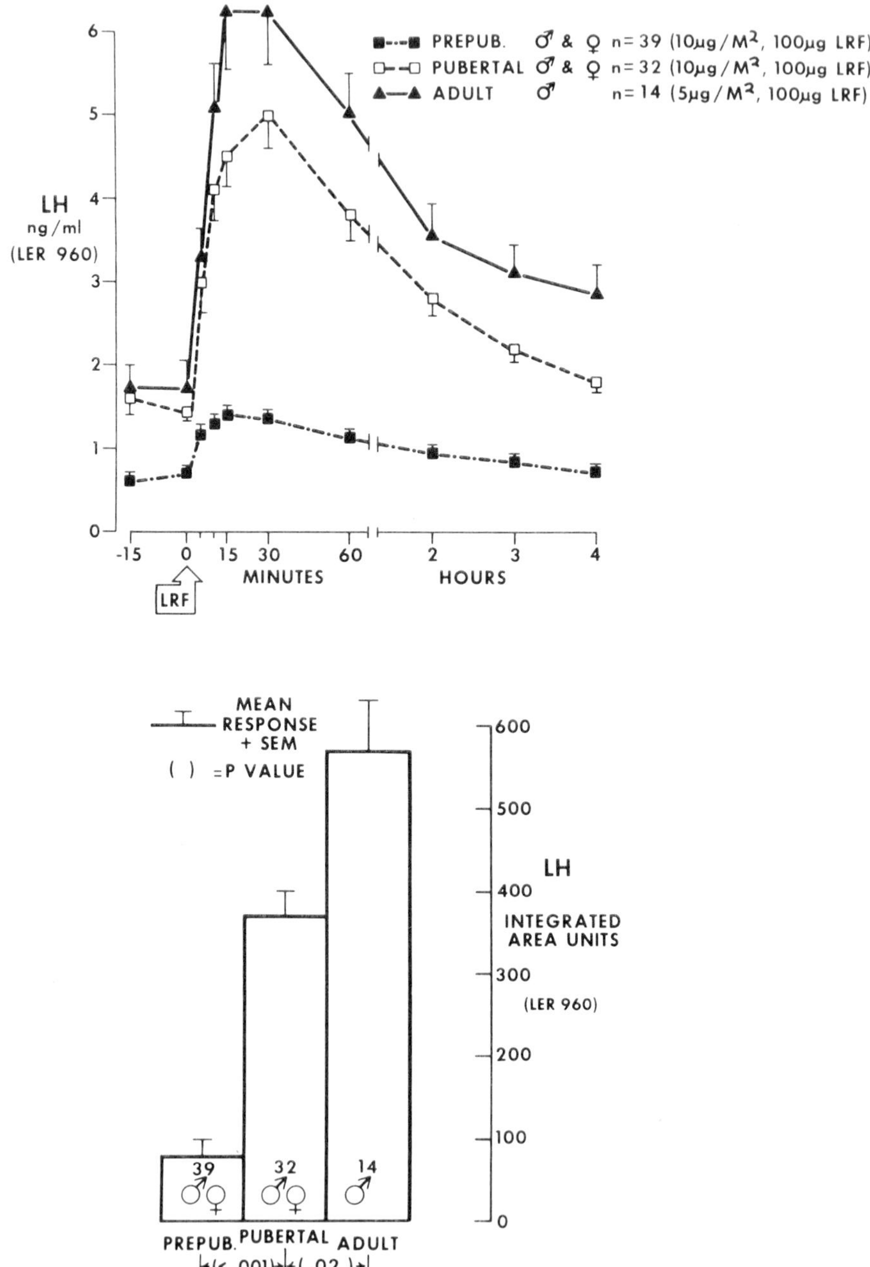

FIG. 9. The change in plasma LH and FSH in response to intravenous LRF in pre-pubertal, pubertal, and adult subjects (*upper panels*). The area circumscribed by a 4-hour curve of plasma LH or FSH concentrations following LRF after subtraction of the basal gonadotropin value is designated as integrated area units and compared for each group (*lower panels*). Note the limited LH response in prepubertal children

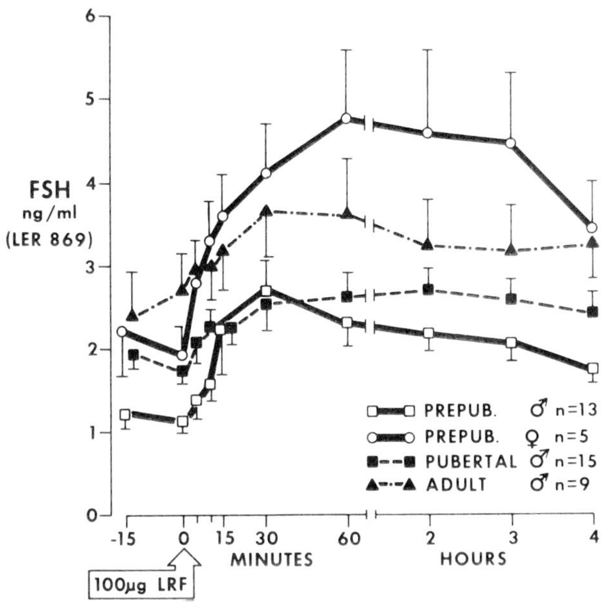

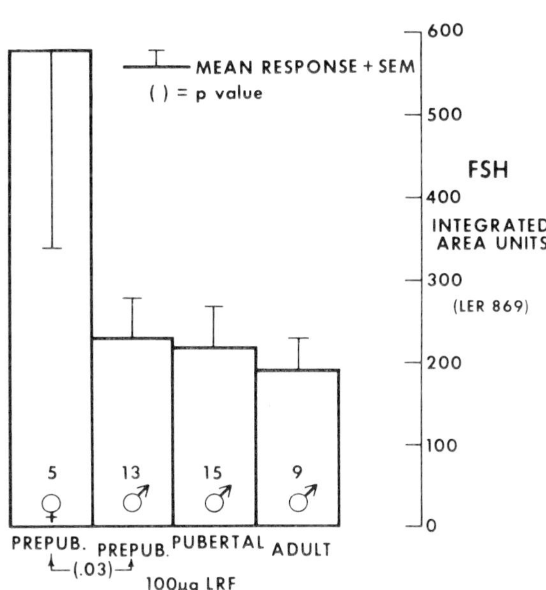

when compared with that of pubertal and adult subjects (*upper left panel*). Significant differences in LH integrated area units are shown for prepubertal and pubertal subjects and between pubertal and adult subjects (*lower left panel*). The FSH response to LRF is similar in prepubertal, pubertal, and adult males (*upper and lower right panels*). In females the FSH response is significantly greater than that of prepubertal, pubertal, or adult males.

release significantly more ($p<.02$) FSH than males at all stages of sexual maturation. Hence there is a striking discordance between the pituitary "reserve" of FSH and LH in prepubertal and pubertal individuals as well as a sex difference in readily releasable pituitary FSH.

When we explored the dose-response to LRF at various stages of sexual maturation (Table 3), we found that prepubertal males had a greater rise in plasma LH after 10 μg/m^2 and 100 μg of LRF than 1 and 5 μg/m^2 (Fig. 10a). A significant difference was not detected between 10 μg/m^2 and 100 μg of LRF in pubertal males or between 5 μg/m^2 and a total dose of 100 μg in adult males. FSH release was greater after 100 μg than 1 to 10 μg/m^2 in prepubertal males. There was no difference in the FSH response to 10 μg/m^2 and to 100 μg of LRF in pubertal males. Adult males had a comparable release of FSH to 5 μg/m^2 and to 100 μg of LRF but a lesser response to a dose of 1 μg/m^2.

Prepubertal females, in contrast to males, did not exhibit a difference in release of LH over a dosage range that varied from 1 μg/m^2 to 100 μg of LRF, nor was a difference observed in pubertal females tested at doses of

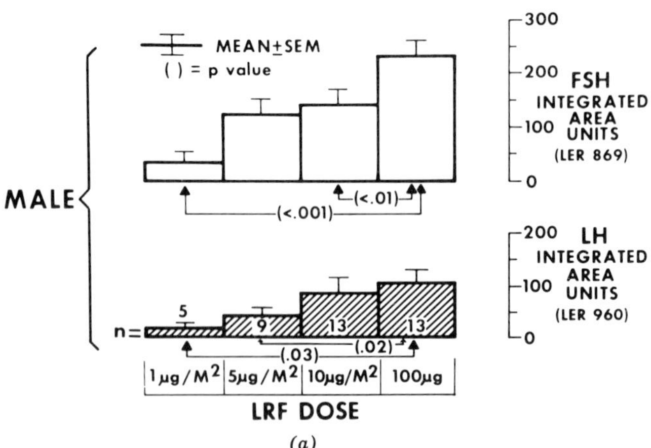

(*a*)

FIG. 10*a*. The mean LH and FSH responses to different doses of LRF (1 μg/m^2, 5 μg/m^2, 10 μg/m^2, and 100 μg) in prepubertal males are expressed as integrated area units. This value represents the area circumscribed by a 4-hour curve of plasma LH or FSH concentrations following LRF after subtraction of the basal gonadotropin value. The mean FSH response at 1 μg/m^2 is significantly different from that at 100 μg ($p < .001$). At 10 μg/m^2 the LH response is significantly different from that following a 100 μg dose ($p < .03$) and between 5 μg/m^2 and the 100 μg dose ($p < .02$). No significant difference in the LH response is noted between the 10 μg/m^2 and 100 μg.

10 $\mu g/m^2$ and 100 μg. Release of FSH was significantly greater in girls than boys at all doses of LRF administered and, like release of LH, did not exhibit a significant dose-response over the dosage range utilized (Fig. 10b).

The sex difference in the response to LRF suggests that the pituitary gonadotropes of prepubertal females are more sensitive to LRF than those of prepubertal males, even though there is no apparent difference in the concentration of circulating sex steroids at this stage of maturation, as exhibited by the apparent maximal response at the lowest dose tested (1 $\mu g/m^2$) over the dosage range examined. Further, prepubertal girls have a larger readily releasable pool of pituitary FSH than prepubertal or pubertal males. This sex difference in sensitivity to LRF and releasable FSH may be a factor in the higher frequency of idiopathic precocious puberty in girls and the higher prevalence of constitutional delayed adolescence in boys. The data, including the sex difference in the dose-response to LRF, are consistent with the hypothesis that less LRF is required for FSH than LH synthesis and its storage in a readily releasable form. This difference could be explained as well by the secretion of an FSH-RF, although the existence

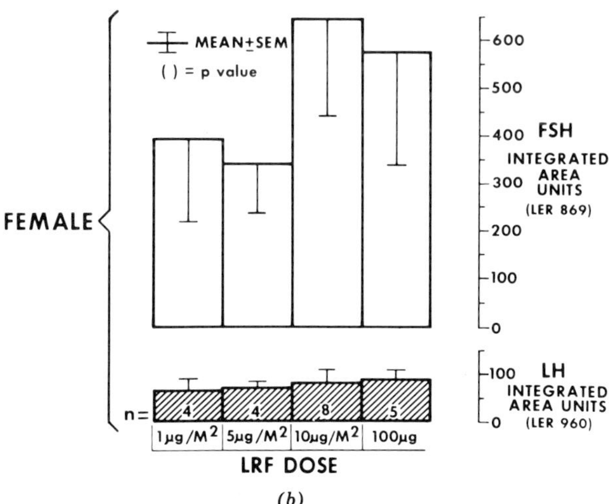

FIG. 10b. The mean LH and FSH responses to different doses of LRF (1 $\mu g/m^2$, 5 $\mu g/m^2$, 10 $\mu g/m^2$, and 100 μg) in perpubertal females are expressed as integrated area units. This value represents the area circumscribed by a 4-hour curve of plasma LRF after subtraction of the basal gonadotropin value. The mean LH or FSH response is not significantly different at any dose tested in the prepubertal females. Note again the significantly greater FSH response at all doses in the prepubertal female compared with that seen in the prepubertal male.

TABLE 3.   LRF dose-response in prepubertal, pubertal, and adult subjects

LRF dose $\mu g/m^2$	p^b	Males (N) area U±SE	p^b	Females (N) area U±SE	p^b	Male+female area U±SE	p
				Prepubertal—LH			
0^a		2± 11 (7)		−9± 20 (3)		4.6±12	
1		21± 7 (4)		65± 22 (5)	.04	45±14	
5	.03	47± 12 (9)		65± 14 (4)		51±10	.03
10		0.2 94± 23 (13)		81± 24 (8)		89±16	
100^c		107± 19 (13)		84± 25 (5)	.01	101±15	
				Prepubertal—FSH			
0	.01^d	−6± 7 (7)		11± 17 (3)	.001^d		
1		38± 15 (4)		397±174 (5)			
5	<.001	128± 25 (9)	<.01	343±103 (4)			
10	.005	144± 22 (13)	<.01	649±205 (8)			
100	<.01	235± 23 (13)	.03	579±241 (5)			
				Pubertal—LH			
0	<.001	−26± 18 (7)					
10		340± 60 (11)				340±60	
100		448± 45 (15)		411±114 (6)		479±42	

Pubertal—FSH

0	−11± 12 (7)
	.01
10	156± 49 (11)
100	208± 43 (15) —— .01 −434± 81 (6)

Adult—LH

1	126± 19 (5)
	.02 <.001
5	516±138 (5)
100	596± 71 (9)

Adult—FSH

1	16± 9 (5)
	.01 <.01
5	172± 46 (5)
100	194± 37 (9)

[a] Sham test.
[b] p values are indicated only when significant differences occur. Data without p values are not significantly different.
[c] 100 μg total dose LRF.
[d] Male and female response at 0 μg/m^2 are combined.

of such a factor is, at present, hypothetical. It also emphasizes the distinction between pituitary FSH reserve and basal FSH secretion.

Increased Responsiveness to LRF in "Late" Prepubertal Children

If an increased pituitary responsiveness to LRF is a major factor in the increased gonadotropic secretion (especially LH) at puberty, a change that may be mediated by increased endogenous secretion of LRF, we might expect to observe a pubertal response to LRF in prepubertal children in whom LRF secretion has already increased but who are still at a prepubertal stage of sexual development. During our studies we identified a group of 6 prepubertal children among the 60 tested who exhibited a comparable increase in LH release to that observed in pubertal children following administration of LRF (Table 4). The 3 boys were 11–10/12 to 12–6/12 years of age and the girls were 11–4/12 to 14–7/12 years old. The basal levels of plasma testosterone and estradiol, respectively, were slightly but significantly higher than normal values for prepubertal children. Thus, increased LH release in response to LRF can be elicited before the development of secondary sex characteristics in both boys and girls. This observation supports the hypothesis that this change in pituitary responsiveness is an early and striking feature of puberty.

Spontaneous maturation of increased pituitary responsiveness to LRF was observed in a patient who had an LRF test at age 11–9/12 years and a second test 10 months later at age 12–7/12 (Fig. 11). During this period his LH response to LRF had changed from prepubertal to pubertal. In the interval between the two tests there had been an increase in testicular diameter and the basal level of plasma testosterone.

Effect of LRF on Plasma Testosterone

The effect of LRF on the concentration of plasma testosterone was studied in prepubertal, pubertal, and adult males (Roth et al, 1973a). The increment in plasma testosterone and LH for each group is compared in Fig. 12. The pubertal and adult testis is more responsive to LRF than the prepubertal testis. A significant increase in the concentration of plasma testosterone was elicited only in the patients who had signs of puberty; the peak value for testosterone occurred 3 to 4 hours after LRF and 2½ to 3½ hours after the maximal rise in plasma LH. The failure to evoke an increase in plasma testosterone following an acute intravenous dose of LRF in prepubertal boys is quite likely attributable to the meager LH release following LRF in prepubertal boys (in contrast to pubertal and adult males), and to the diminished responsiveness of the prepubertal testis to LH as manifested by secretion of testosterone in comparison with the pubertal and adult testis (Saez & Bertrand, 1968; Frasier et al, 1969; Rivarola, Bergada, & Cullen, 1970; Winter, Tarasaka, & Faiman, 1972.) These data are con-

TABLE 4. Late prepubertal children with pubertal LRF responses

Sex	Age (years)	Bone age (years)	Weight (kg)	Plasma estradiol (pg/ml)	Plasma testosterone (ng/dl)	LH area U	FSH area U	Diagnosis
M[a]	12-6/12	8	26.5		35	368	187	Normal
M[a]	12-6/12	8	27.2		33	304	221	Normal
M	11-10/12	11	27.7		71	263	173	Normal
F	11-4/12	8	27.5	10		338	516	GH-deficient[b]
F	14-7/12	10	41.2	22		281	770	Normal
F	13-8/12	10	24.5	15		274	459	Normal
Normal values mean±SE — Prepubertal — Male						107±19	235±23	
Normal values mean±SE — Prepubertal — Female						84±25	579±241	
Normal values mean±SE — Pubertal — Male						448±45	208±43	
Normal values mean±SE — Pubertal — Female						411±114	434±81	

[a] Twins.
[b] On hGH replacement therapy (isolated growth hormone deficiency).

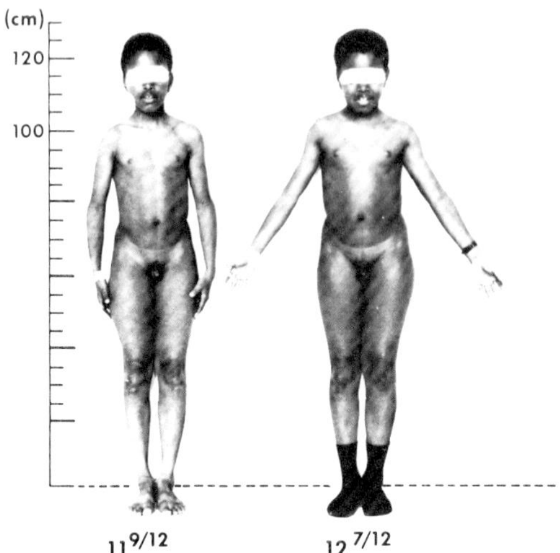

PHYSIOLOGICAL MATURATION OF LH
RESPONSE TO LRF

AGE YEARS	BONE AGE YEARS	WT. (kg)	MAX. Incr. LH (ng/ml)	MAX. Incr.FSH (ng/ml)	PLASMA TESTOST. ng/100ml		TESTIC. DIAM. (cm)
					Basal	Peak	
11 9/12	9 6/12	22.2	1.2	3.6	21	13	1.7
12 7/12	11	26.4	4.6	2.0	33	38	2.0

FIG. 11. The spontaneous maturation of an increased LH response to LRF in a prepubertal male. At 11–9/12 years the LH and testosterone response were consistent with a prepubertal state. Ten months later, with no advancement in physical signs of puberty, a pubertal LH response to LRF was present in association with an advancement in bone age and an increase in testosterone secretion. Roth et al, 1937a.

sistent with the proposal that (1) the magnitude of LH release induced by LRF increases markedly at puberty and appears to be conditioned by the degree of previous stimulation of the anterior hypophysis by LFR; (2) the caliber of testosterone release following LRF increases at puberty and appears to be affected by the extent of previous stimulation of the Leydig cells by LH (in the presence of FSH) (Odell, Swerdloff, Jacobs & Hescox, 1973); (3) there is hierarchal maturation of the hypothalamic→ pituitary→ gonadal circuit in human puberty.

We have already adduced that the degree of previous exposure of gona-

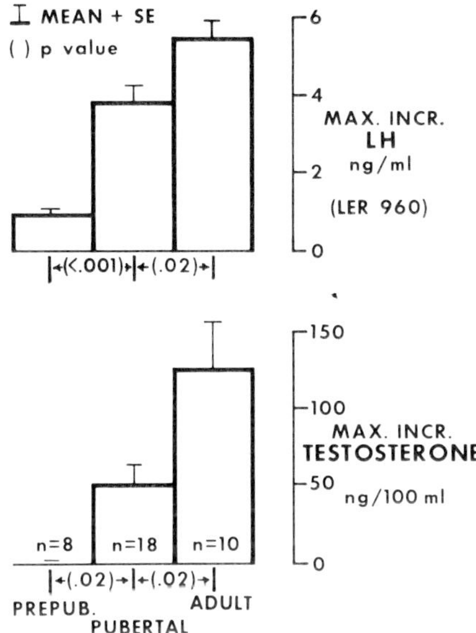

FIG. 12. The mean maximal increment in plasma LH (*upper section*) and plasma testosterone (*lower section*) following intravenous LRF compared in prepubertal, pubertal, and adult males. The magnitude of the increment in plasma LH and testosterone was significantly different between prepubertal and pubertal males and between pubertal and adult males. From Roth et al, 1973a.

dotropes appears to effect both the magnitude and the quality of the FSH and LH responses to a single intravenous dose of LRF (Roth et al, 1972a,b). Let us examine this notion and the evidence, in addition to that already described, that supports it. Studies in hypergonadotropic hypogonadism, hypogonadotropic hypogonadism, constitutional delayed adolescence, and idiopathic precocious puberty have provided substantiating data.

Response to LRF in Hypergonadotropic Hypogonadism

In 10 patients with documented hypergonadotropic hypogonadism, including a 3–3/12-year-old patient with XO gonadal dysgenesis, LRF evoked a striking augmentation of FSH and LH release (Table 5). This observation implies that chronic increased stimulation of the gonadotropes by endogenous LRF results in increased pituitary stores of readily releasable FSH and LH. Note the discordance between the basal concentration of plasma LH in the 3-year-old patient and the very high LH reserve. Comparable responses have been described by Kastin, Gual, Schally, and Arimura (1972) in adult patients and by Reeves, Arimura and Schally (1970) in sheep.

TABLE 5.   Effect of acute intravenous dose of LRF in hypergonadotropic hypogonadism

Chronologic age (years)	Diagnosis or karyotype	LRF dose (μg)	LH (ng/ml)		FSH (ng/ml)	
			Basal	Maximal increment	Basal	Maximal increment
3-3/12	XO	100	1.6	14.7	23.0	($>$39.0)
10-9/12	Oophorectomy	1/m²	5.6	34.6	46.0	49.0
11-1/12	XO/XXX	10/m²	3.5	11.2	22.0	9.5
13-10/12	XO	10/m²	9.6	37.5	108.0	82.0
16	XO/XX_r	100	7.5	21.5	7.7	11.0
16-10/12	XO	100	13.0	34.0	41.0	32.0
16-10/12	XXY	100	6.0	13.2	28.0	11.0
17	XO	100	6.6	55.9	23.0	13.0
18-2/12	Pure G.D. XX	10/m²	5.9	13.1	40.0	32.0
18-6/12	XO/XYY	100	13.0	($>$13.4)	38.0	24.0

Response to LRF in Hypogonadotropic Hypogonadism and Constitutional Delayed Adolescence

The diagnosis of hypogonadotropic hypogonadism usually is not considered until the age of adolescence, when signs of puberty fail to appear, although it may be suspected at an earlier age in children with multiple pituitary hormone deficiencies, anosmia, other affected siblings, or in males with small external genitalia usually accompanied by cryptorchidism. A variable pattern of LH release has been reported in patients with hypogonadotropic hypogonadism (Naftolin, Harris, Bobrow, 1971; Roth et al, 1972a,b; Schally et al, 1972). Those patients who have a normal response to LRF provide evidence that the primary hormonal defect is a deficiency of hypothalamic gonadotropin releasing factor(s).

We have now studied the effect of LRF on the release of FSH and LH in 18 patients with documented idiopathic hypothalamic hypophysiotropic hormone deficiencies (age 1 to 24 years); 7 patients (age 15 to 20 years) with isolated gonadotropin deficiency, of whom 5 had Kallmann's syndrome (anosmia or hyposmia and gonadotropin deficiency), 11 boys with constitutional delayed adolescence (age 14 to 17 years), and 3 patients who had been hypophysectomized (Savage, de Groppa, Kaplan, & Grumbach, 1973). The last group had no increase in plasma FSH or LH. In our experience no LH response was detected in less than 2 per cent of the normal subjects, and no rise in SH in about 5 per cent of the normal males.

Among 18 patients with idiopathic multiple pituitary hormone deficiencies 14 had no increase in LH release. None of the 14 patients exhibited any signs of pubertal maturation. The 4 others (3 with clinical evidence of arrested puberty) had an impaired response inappropriate for their stage of sexual development; only 2 of these 4 patients exhibited a rise in FSH (Fig. 13a,b).

Among 7 patients with isolated hypogonadotropic hypogonadism 5 had Kallmann's syndrome (Fig. 14a,b). Two of the 5 patients were sexually infantile; in one there was neither a rise in plasma LH nor FSH and in the other the LH response was indistinguishable from that of a normal prepubertal male. Three other patients with Kallmann's syndrome had arrested pubertal development; 2 had a prepubertal and the other a pubertal pattern of response to LRF. Of the 2 patients with normal olfaction the patient with sexual infantilism failed to respond to LRF, whereas in the other, who had minimal signs of sexual maturation, the pattern of FSH and LH release was characteristic of a normal prepubertal male.

The 11 male patients with *delayed adolescence* had some signs of pubertal development, but they were minimal. In contrast to the hypogonadotropic individuals, all exhibited a rise in LH and FSH indistinguish-

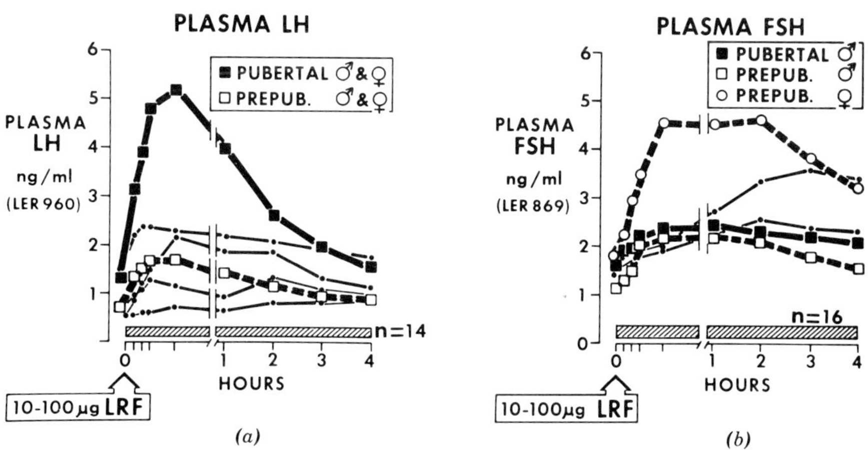

FIG. 13. The LH (*a*) and FSH response (*b*) to LRF in 18 patients with idiopathic hypopituitarism is compared with that of normal prepubertal (*open squares*) and pubertal individuals (*closed squares*): 14 had no LH response to LRF and 4 had an LH response comparable to that of prepubertal individuals; 16 had no FSH response to LRF and the other 2 had an appropriate FSH response. Savage et al, 1973.

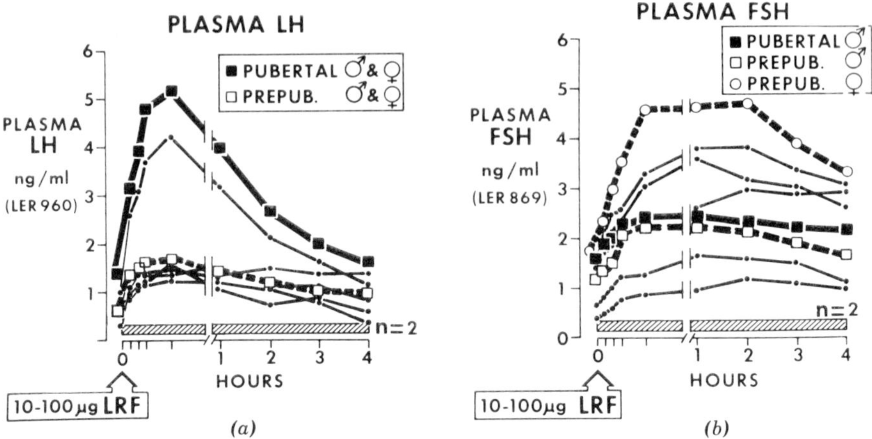

FIG. 14. The LH (*a*) and FSH response (*b*) to LRF in 7 patients with isolated hypogonadotropic hypogonadism is compared with that of normal prepubertal (*open squares*) and pubertal individuals (*closed squares*). In 2 patients with hypogonadotropic hypogonadism neither a LH nor FSH rise was observed; 4 of the remaining 5 patients had an LH response comparable to that of pubertal individuals. The FSH rise was similar to that seen in normal prepubertal children and adolescents. Savage et al, 1973.

able from that of normal pubertal males and in each instance consistent with their level of sexual maturation (Fig. 15a,b). Hence in this group of males with delayed adolescence LRF evoked a response similar to that elicited in "late prepubertal" and pubertal individuals. The LRF test in many instances may provide a useful means of distinguishing between patients with constitutional delayed adolescence and hypogonadotropic hypogonadism when interpreted in the light of the clinical findings.

In sum, FSH and LH response to LRF in hypogonadotropic hypogonadism was highly heterogeneous. The variable response suggests differences in the readily releasable pool of FSH and LH in these patients that are related to the degree of endogenous LRF deficiency and the severity and duration of the hypothalamic understimulation of the gonadotropes, especially those that secrete LH. Again, there appears to be a difference in the capacity to store gonadotropins and to release gonadotropins into the circulation.

The diminished LH reserve in prepubertal children and the changes in response to LRF with the onset of puberty may be interpreted similarly. Before puberty the low set point of the gonadostat to the inhibitory feedback effect of low concentrations of plasma sex steroids suppresses secretion of LRF; as a consequence, the prepubertal pituitary gland has a sig-

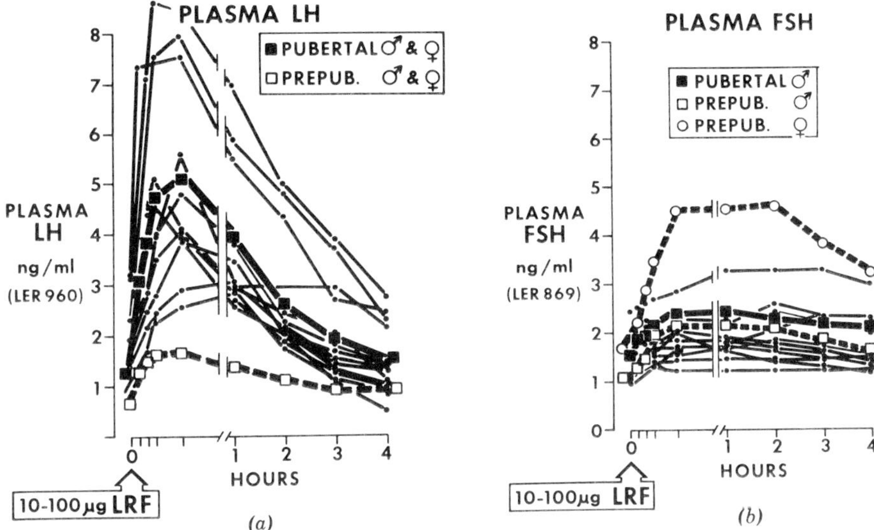

FIG. 15. The rise in plasma LH (*a*) and FSH (*b*) following intravenous LRF for 11 patients with delayed adolescence and minimal physical signs of puberty. The LH and FSH responses were comparable to those of the pubertal subjects who are indicated by thick lines and open squares (*see text*). From Savage et al, 1973.

nificantly smaller pool of releasable LH and exhibits decreased responsiveness to the acute administration of synthetic LRF. With the approach of puberty, increased release of RF augments pituitary responsiveness to LRF and enlarges the reserve of LH. The explanation for the discordance in FSH and LH released prepubertally is not clear. It seems possible that the greater FSH release is related to a more autonomous basal secretion, the greater FSH reserve, an FSH synthesizing mechanism which is more sensitive to LRF, or even the action of an FSH-RF. If this concept has substance, then prolonged administration of LRF to prepubertal individuals should induce a pubertal type of LH response.

Response to Prolonged Administration of LRF in Hypogonadotropic Hypogonadism

The effect of repeated doses of LRF was assessed in patients with hypogonadotropic hypogonadism in an attempt to test the hypothesis that the diminished release of gonadotropins in some patients with hypogonadotropic hypogonadism and the meager secretion of LH in prepubertal individuals elicited by an acute dose of LRF is a consequence of decreased sensitivity of the pituitary gonadotropes (owing to insufficient pituitary

stimulation by endogenous LRF). Figure 16 illustrates the peak concentrations of plasma LH and FSH evoked by an acute injection of LRF before
and after 14 injections of 100 μg LRF administered subcutaneously over
a 3-day period in 6 patients (3 with isolated hypogonadotropic hypogonadism and 3 with multiple hypophysiotropic hormone deficiencies).
There was a significant increase in the peak concentration of plasma LH
and FSH from day 1 to 3.

Two of these patients, a 16-year-old male with isolated hypogonadotropic
hypogonadism and a 24-year-old female with idiopathic multiple hypothalamic hypophysiotropic hormone deficiencies, were given daily subcutaneous injections of 100 μg LRF for 14 days. FSH and LH release to an
acute intravenous dose of 100 μg LRF was studied before and at the end
of the 14-day course. Both patients showed a significant increase in LH
release, and the 24-year-old patient with multiple pituitary hormone deficiencies released more FSH (Fig. 17a,b).

There is still no practical method of reproducing the physiologic pattern
of endogenous secretion of LRF, including the more sustained tonic stimulation of the gonadotrope(s) and, quite likely, superimposed periodic pulses
of LRF. However, the increased gonadotropin secretion evoked by repeated
doses of LRF administered for 3 to 14 days supports the concept that the
primary hormonal defect in most patients with hypogonadotropic hypogonadism is a variable deficiency of gonadotropin releasing factor(s),
which results in inadequate secretion of LH and FSH. The contrast between
the effect of thyrotropin releasing factor (TRF) deficiency on the responsiveness of the thyrotrope and lactotrope to TRF and of LRF deficiency on
the responsiveness of the gonadotrope has been pointed out (Roth et al,
1972a,b). Further, these results are compatible with the hypothesis of

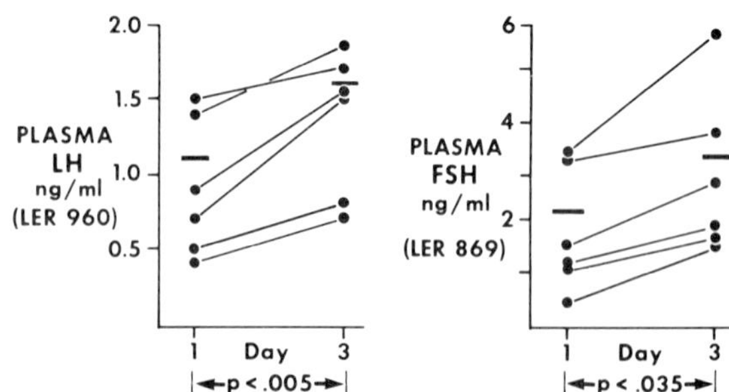

FIG. 16. The peak LH and FSH values following intravenous administration of
LRF in 6 patients with isolated hypogonadotropic hypogonadism before (day 1) and
after (day 3) 14 subcutaneous injections of LRF over a 3-day period. A significantly
increased response was observed after this short-term treatment with LRF. The
horizontal bars denote the mean peak value for each test.

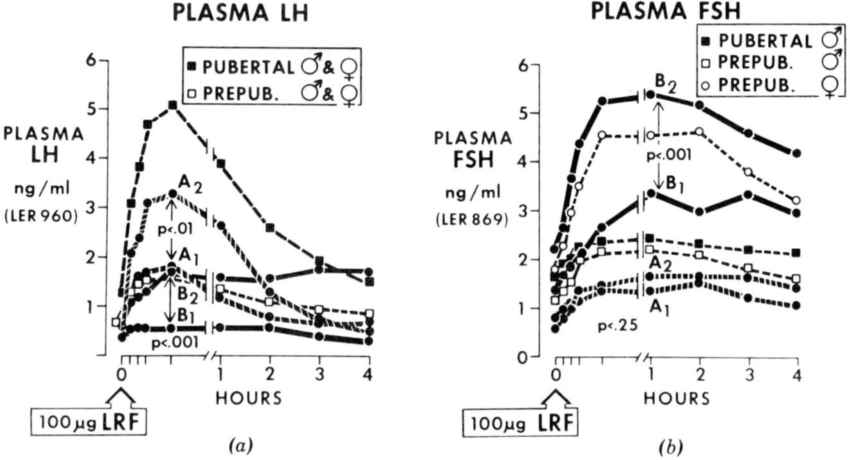

FIG. 17. The change in plasma LH (a) and FSH (b) in one male (A) and 1 female (B) with hypogonadotropic hypogonadism before and after 14 daily subcutaneous injections of 100 µg of LRF. In both a significantly higher LH response to 100 µg intravenous LRF was observed after prolonged LRF therapy (A₂, B₂) than before (A₁, B₁). The FSH response increased after prolonged therapy only in the female patient.

insufficient endogenous secretion of LRF as a major factor in the diminished LH release in response to exogenous LRF in prepubertal children with LRF promoting synthesis as well as release of pituitary gonadotropins (Schally et al, 1972; Redding, Schally, Arimura, & Matsuo, 1972). Prepubertal children appear to have insufficient release of LRF to maintain a readily releasable store of LH comparable to pubertal individuals. In the absence of functioning gonads, however, there is a striking increase in releasable gonadotropins, even in prepubertal children (Table 5). The availability in the future of repository forms of synthetic LRF and of long-acting analogues should make it possible to explore this matter in more detail.

Effect of LRF in Sexual Precocity

A pubertal-to-adult pattern of pituitary responsiveness to LRF was found in 6 patients with idiopathic true precocious puberty (Table 6). Indeed, in 3 patients there was evidence of augmented gonadotropin reserve. These results indicate that idiopathic precocious puberty is associated, even by 13 months of age, with a mature pattern of LH release presumably secondary to the premature increase in endogenous secretion of LRF.

Of interest is the 4-year-old boy with congenital virilizing adrenal hyperplasia and sexual precocity due to a defect in 21-hydroxylation. When

TABLE 6. Response to LRF in patients with idiopathic true precocious puberty and congenital virilizing adrenal hyperplasia

Sex	Chronological age (years)	Bone age (years)	LRF (μg)	LH (ng/ml)		FSH (ng/ml)	
				Basal	Maximal increment	Basal	Maximal increment
Idiopathic precocious puberty							
M	1-1/12	2	100	1.9	6.5	1.3	0.5
F	4-10/12	6-10/12	100	0.7	21.9	3.5	14.9
F	5-11/12	8-4/12	100	0.6	4.0	4.4	3.1
F	7-8/12	7-10/12	100	2.1	11.4	0.6	9.2
F	8	10-6/12	100	1.7	13.1	1.1	2.4
F	8-7/12	13	10	2.7	3.1	2.4	0.8
Congenital virilizing adrenal hyperplasia (21-hydroxylase deficiency)							
M	4-3/12	11	100	0.7	6.0	3.2	4.8

tested with LRF he had a bone age of 11 years; he exhibited an FSH and LH response indistinguishable from normal adult males. We interpret this observation as evidence that the increased circulating sex steroids of adrenal origin secondary to the deficiency of 21-hydroxylase induced maturation of the central nervous system and precociously decreased the sensitivity of the negative feedback mechanism to sex steroids. As a result the release of endogenous LRF was increased, which led to an increase in gonadotropin reserve. Whether the high levels of sex steroids had a direct effect on the synthesis of pituitary gonadotropins remains to be determined.

Effect of Sex Steroids on the Response to LRF

Studies of the effects of sex steroids on release of LRF and on pituitary responsiveness to LRF are at a preliminary stage, but there is already evidence of sex and species differences and of complex interactions. Estrogens increase pituitary responsiveness to LRF in several species (Schally et al, 1972). Yen, VandenBerg, Rebar, and Ehara (1972) reported augmented responses to LRF in women at midcycle. Roth et al (1972a) studied the effect of a single intramuscular injection of estradiol benzoate (10 μg/kg) on the response to LRF before and 48 hours after administration of the estrogen in 3 prepubertal and 2 pubertal individuals and 2 patients with hypergonadotropic hypogonadism. No augmentation of FSH and LH release was found. In the prepubertal and pubertal subjects there was suppression of the peak FSH response. Similarly, Kastin, Schally, Gual, and Arimura (1972) failed to demonstrate an increase in pituitary responsiveness to LRF after administration of estrogen to adults. These discrepant responses may be related to species differences and to differences in hormonal milieu.

Malacara, Selyer, and Reichlin (1972) have demonstrated that estrogens also stimulate LRF release in the human female, as suggested by the increase in the LRF activity of plasma at midcycle in women, coincident with the LH surge. Kerdelhué and Jutisz (1972) reported a rise in immunoreactive plasma LRF on the day of ovulation in sheep, and there is increased gonadotropin releasing factor activity in the hypothalamus of female sheep at estrus (Jackson, Roche, Foster, & Dziuk, 1971). Clearly, the availability of a sensitive radioimmunoassay for plasma LRF may clarify many aspects of LRF secretion before and during puberty.

MATURATION OF THE POSITIVE FEEDBACK MECHANISM

It has been known for many years that estrogen has the capacity to induce ovulation in the rat (Holweg, 1934; Everett, 1964; 1969; Schwartz & McCormack, 1972). In man and subhuman primates there is much evidence to indicate that in the adult female the midcycle surge in LH and FSH is initiated by a preceding critical increase in the concentration of plasma estrogens during the latter part of the follicular phase of the menstrual cycle (Vande Wiele, Bogumil, Dyrenfurth, Ferin, Jewelewicz, Warren, Rizkallah & Mikhail, 1970; Harris & Naftolin, 1970; Knobil, Dierschke, Yamaji, Karsch, Hotchkiss & Weick, 1972). Estrogen administered to adult females, if sufficient to sustain a critical increment in the plasma level for at least 12 hours, triggers an LH and FSH surge.

This positive feedback action of estrogen is not demonstrable in prepubertal and early pubertal children (Fig. 18). No evidence of increased release of gonadotropin was observed, even though we were able to reproduce the late follicular phase concentration of plasma estradiol by parenteral administration of estradiol benzoate (Kelch et al, 1973b). However, among 6 patients with the syndrome of gonadal dysgenesis (age 10 to 20 years) who were given 50 μg per day of ethinyl estradiol for 5 days, a diphasic pattern of plasma LH concentrations was observed in the 3 oldest (age 16 to 20 years); initial suppression was followed by a rise after 4 days of treatment (Fig. 7b). We suggest that the late increase in plasma LH may be a result of the positive feedback effect of estrogen. If so, it indicates that

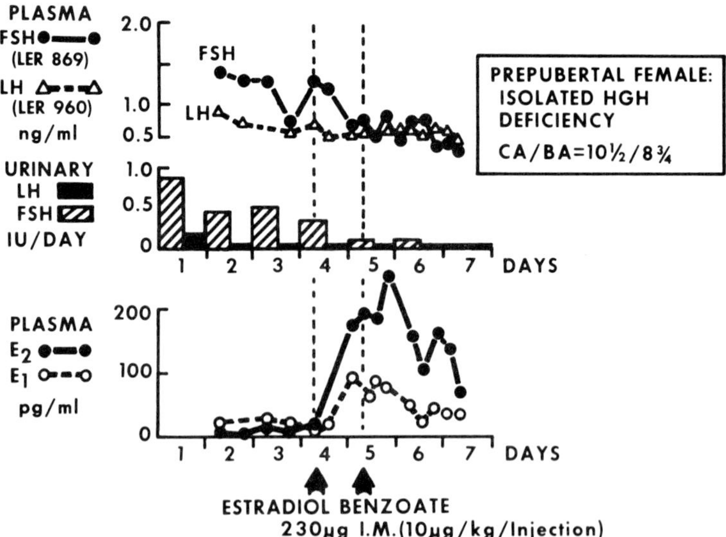

FIG. 18.   The effect of estradiol benzoate (10 μg/kg IM) on plasma and urinary FSH in a prepubertal female. Suppression of plasma and urinary FSH occurred coincident with the rise in plasma estradiol (E_2) and estrone (E_1). The basal levels of plasma and urinary LH were too low to assess significant suppressive effects of estradiol benzoate. Even though the concentration of plasma estradiol and estrone rose to the range reported at midcycle in the adult female an LH surge was not found. From Kelch et al, 1973a.

the positive feedback mechanism can mature in the absence of functional gonads. Yen and Tsai (1971) described a similar diphasic pattern in the concentration of serum FSH and LH in postmenopausal women treated with ethinyl estradiol. Indeed, Yamaji, Dierschke, Hotchkiss, Bhattacharya, Surve, and Knobil (1971) have reported data consistent with a functional positive feedback system in castrated adult male monkeys and observed a diphasic pattern. Preliminary studies by Kulin (personal communication) and in our own laboratory also suggest that the positive feedback action of estrogen is not sex-specific.

Among the factors necessary for a positive feedback effect of estrogen at puberty are ovarian follicles capable of secreting the requisite amount of estrogen in response to FSH, an operative positive feedback mechanism in the CNS capable of inducing an acute release of LRF, and a pituitary gland which is already sensitive to LRF and contains a large enough pool of releasable LH to provide an LH surge. Because the LH-secreting gonad-otropes are relatively insensitive to LRF before puberty, one would not expect to demonstrate a positive feedback action in the prepubertal individual, even though the neural component might be functional.

We have obtained indirect evidence that the potential for exhibiting a positive feedback response to estrogen does not appear until mid- to late puberty. Clomiphene citrate, 100 mg daily for 1 week, elicited a stimulatory LH response in two midpubertal females (Fig. 19), and both had the onset of menarche 17 to 24 days after the onset of treatment (Kulin et al, 1972). This dose of clomiphene decreased urinary gonadotropins in pre-pubertal and early pubertal individuals. Because increased pituitary sensitivity to LRF and an enhanced LH reserve are present by early puberty, the apparent inability to elicit positive feedback before midpuberty suggests that this mechanism is not operational before this stage. Further, that Knobil et al (1972) failed to demonstrate a positive feedback action of estrogen in sexually immature female monkeys suggested that this mech-anism does not become functional in the monkey before menarche. More definitive studies are needed to document the pubertal stage at which the positive feedback mechanism becomes operative.

In boys a stimulatory effect of clomiphene citrate on gonadotropin secretion has not been demonstrated before advanced puberty (Kulin et al, 1972; Kulin, Reiter & Bridson, 1971; Nankin, Yanaihara, & Troen, 1971).

EPISODIC SECRETION OF GONADOTROPINS AND THE ONSET OF PUBERTY

Superimposed on the negative feedback control of gonadotropin secretion are episodic or pulsatile discharges of LH, and quite likely FSH, from the

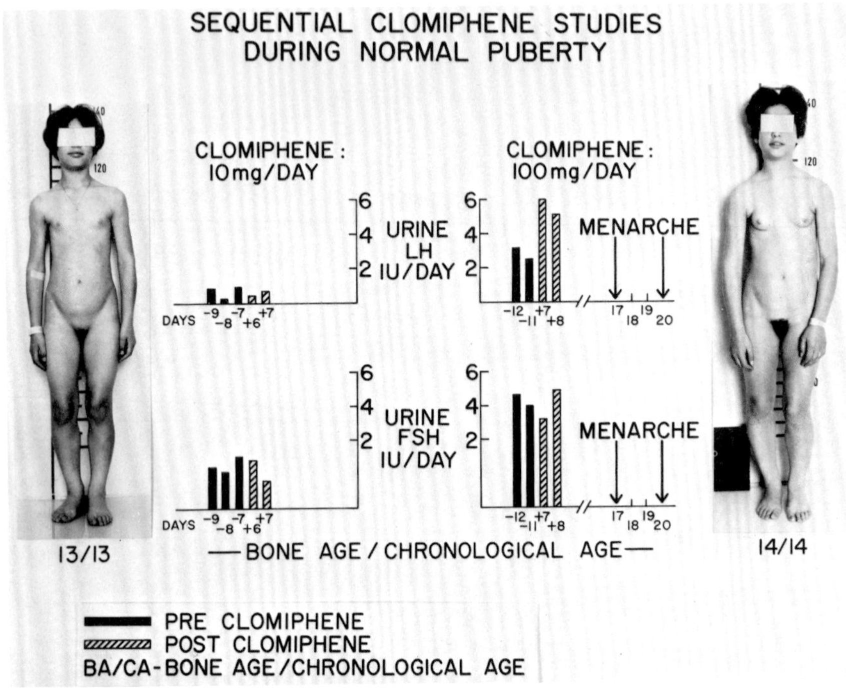

FIG. 19. Sequential study of the effect of clomiphene citrate on urinary LH and FSH in a pubertal female at age 13 and at 14 years. At 13 years of age, when in early puberty, 10 mg/day of clomiphene were administered for 1 week; no effect on the excretion of gonadotropins was detected. One year later, when secondary sex characteristics had advanced to a midpubertal stage, she was given 100 mg/day of clomiphene for 1 week and had a sharp increase in LH output; menstruation occurred 17 days after the onset of treatment. There was no increase in excretion of urinary FSH during the second clomiphene test, despite the rise in FSH output between 13 and 14 years of age. From Kulin et al, 1972.

pituitary gland in normal men, both awake and asleep (Nankin et al, 1971; Rubin, Kales, Adler, Fagan, & Odell, 1972), in pre- and postmenopausal women (Midgley & Jaffe, 1971; Njen, Tsai, Naftolin, VandenBerg, & Ajabor, 1972), in adolescent patients with the syndrome of gonadal dysgenesis (Kelch, Conte, Kaplan, & Grumbach, 1973a), and in gonadectomized rhesus monkeys (Dierschke, Bhattacharya, Atkinson, & Knobil, 1970). Dierschke et al (1970) have applied the term "circhoral pulsatile discharge" to this phenomenon.

Boyar, Finkelstein, Roffwarg, Kapen, Weitzman, and Hellman (1972) recently demonstrated a striking difference in sleep-associated release of LH in prepubertal, pubertal, and adult individuals. Beginning in early puberty, augmented LH secretion was observed only during sleep, characterized by widely fluctuating plasma LH concentrations. A difference in LH release associated with sleep was not detected in prepubertal or adult male subjects or in women studied during menstruation. Episodic secretion was noted throughout the 24-hour period in adult individuals but without an increase in the amplitude of the pulsatile discharge of LH that occurred during sleep.

We have not detected evidence of episodic circhoral secretion of FSH and LH before the age of puberty, either in normal individuals or in children with hypergonadotropic hypogonadism (Kelch et al, 1973a). Figure 20a,b illustrates the secretory pattern of LH and FSH in 7 patients with the syndrome of gonadal dysgenesis. The 3 youngest patients, age 10 to 13 years (S.W., T.J., C.W.) did not exhibit significant pulsatile episodes of FSH release, whereas they were seen in the 4 older subjects, age 13–10/12 to 20 years. Episodic secretion of LH was noted in 5 of 7 (all but the 10- and 13-year-old patients).

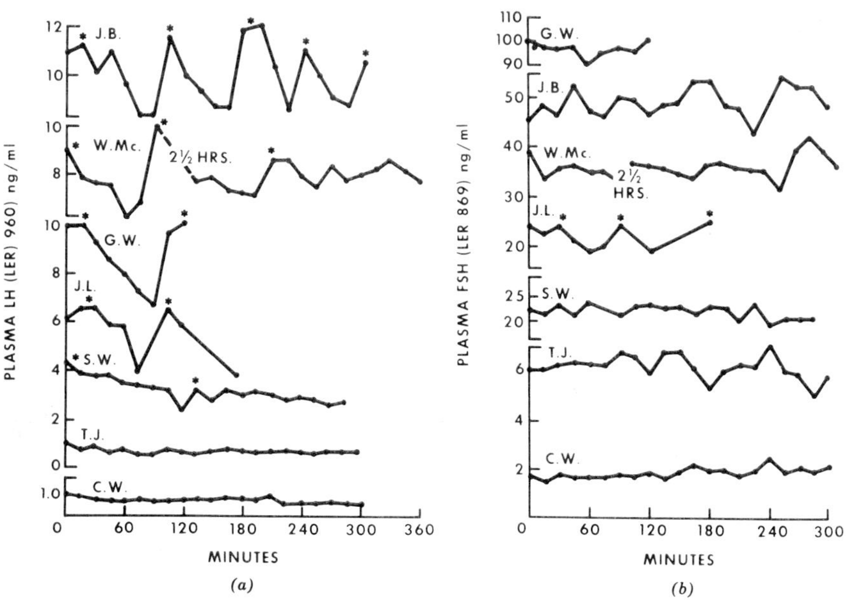

FIG. 20a.   The secretory pattern of LH in 7 patients with gonadal dysgenesis. In 2 of the youngest patients (10 and 13 years) no pulsatile changes in plasma LH were detected. Significant oscillations (*) were noted in all the older patients (13 to 20 years) who had elevated levels of plasma LH. From Kelch et al, 1973b.

FIG. 20b.   The secretory pattern of FSH in 7 patients with gonadal dysgenesis. Episodic secretion of FSH was noted in only 1 (J. L.) of the 7 patients. From Kelch et al, 1973b.

These observations support the notion that episodic secretion of gonadotropins is a maturational phenomenon related to changes in the CNS that effect pulsatile release of LRF and quite likely participates in the peripubertal increase in pituitary responsiveness to LRF. In any event, a pubertal-type pattern of LH release in response to LRF seems necessary before episodic secretion of LH, especially the augmented release of LH during sleep, can be demonstrated. Thus episodic secretion of LH is another maturational change that occurs at the onset of puberty.

Fluctuations in the daily output of gonadotropins and in the concentration of plasma FSH and LH occur in prepubertal individuals (Kulin et al, 1969; Kelch et al, 1973b). These variations, which may even be rhythmic, must, however, be distinguished from the episodic circhoral pattern of discharge discussed above. Intra-assay variability for low values of plasma FSH and LH restricts the ability to detect small pulsatile bursts of gonadotropin secretions in prepubertal individuals.

CONCLUDING COMMENT

Our present concept of the ontogeny of the hypothalamic-pituitary gonadotropin-gonadal circuit in relation to the control of the onset of puberty in the human being is summarized in Table 7 and illustrated in Fig. 21. There are large gaps in our knowledge of many of the aspects of the physi-

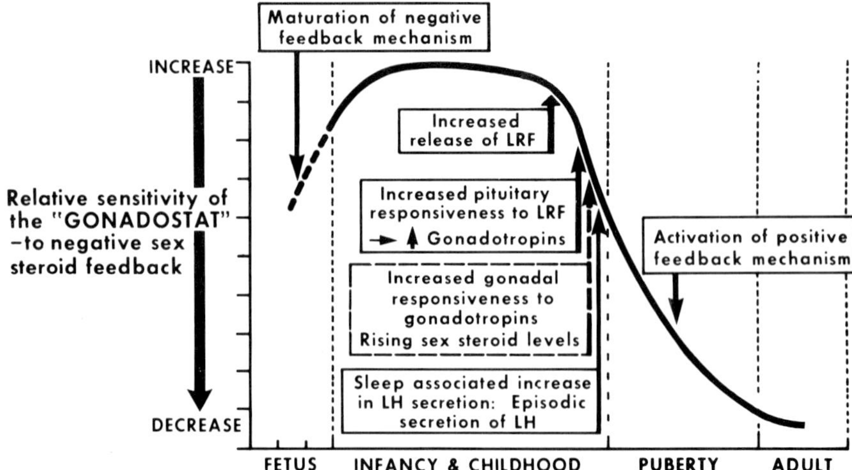

FIG. 21. Schematic illustration of the change in set point of the hypothalamic gonadostat (denoted by the dashed and solid lines) and the maturation of the negative and positive feedback mechanism from fetal life to adulthood in relation to the hormonal changes of puberty.

TABLE 8. Postulated ontogeny of hypothalamic-pituitary gonadotropin-gonadal circuit

---

Fetus
(a) Secretion of pituitary FSH and LH by 80 days gestation
(b) "Unrestrained" secretion of LRF (100 to 150 days)
(c) Maturation of negative sex steroid feedback mechanism after 150 days gestation—sex difference
(d) Low level of LRF secretion at term

Infancy
(a) Negative feedback control of FSH and LH secretion highly sensitive to sex steroids (low set point)
(b) Higher mean serum FSH and LH levels in females

Late Prepubertal Period
(a) Decreasing sensitivity of hypothalamic gonadostat to sex steroids (increased set point)
(b) Increased secretion of LRF
(c) Increased responsiveness of gonadotropes to LRF
(d) Increased secretion of FSH and LH
(e) Increased responsiveness of gonad to FSH and LH
(f) Increased secretion of gonadal hormones

Puberty
(a) Further decrease in sensitivity of negative feedback mechanism to sex steroids
(b) Sleep-associated increase in episodic secretion of LH
(c) Progressive development of secondary sex characteristics
(d) Mid- to late puberty—maturation of *positive* feedback mechanism and capacity to exhibit an estrogen-induced LH surge
(e) Spermatogenesis in male; ovulation in female

---

ology of puberty. The hypotheses set forth within the framework of data accumulated express our assessment and conceptualization of the present status of this complex maturational event.

ACKNOWLEDGMENTS

This work was supported in part by grants from the National Institute of Child Health and Human Development and the National Institute of Arthritis, Metabolism, and Digestive Diseases, NIH, and by the Pediatric Clinical Research Center, sponsored by the Division of Research Resources, NIH. Drs. J. C. Roth and R. P. Kelch have been trainees in Pediatric Endocrinology under the program sponsored by the National Institute of

Arthritis, Metabolism, and Digestive Diseases, NIH. We thank Drs. M. de Groppa and D. C. L. Savage for their generous assistance.

REFERENCES

Abrams, C. A. L., Grumbach, M. M., Dyrenfurth, I., & Vande Wiele, R. L. (1967). Ovarian stimulation with human menopausal and chorionic gonadotropins in a prepubertal hypophysectomized female. *J. Clin. Endocrinol.* **27**, 467–472.

Amoss, M., Burgus, R., Blackwell, R., Vale, W., Fellows, R., & Guillemin, R. (1971). Purification, amino acid composition and N-terminus of the hypothalamic luteinizing hormone releasing factor (LRF) of ovine origin. *Biochem. Biophys. Res. Comm.* **44**, 205–210.

August, G. P., Grumbach, M. M., & Kaplan, S. L. (1972). Hormonal changes in puberty. III. Correlation of plasma testosterone, LH, FSH, testicular size, and bone age with male pubertal development. *J. Clin. Endocrinol.* **34**, 319–326.

August, G. P., Tkachuk, M., & Grumbach, M. M. (1969). Plasma testosterone binding affinity and testosterone in umbilical cord plasma, late pregnancy, prepubertal children, and adults. *J. Clin. Endocrinol.* **29**, 891–899.

Baba, Y., Arimura, A., & Schally, A. V. (1971). On the tryptophan residue in porcine LH and FSH-releasing hormone. *Biochem. Biophys. Res. Comm.* **45**, 483–487.

Bardin, C. W., Ross, G. T., & Lipsett, M. B. (1967). Site of action of clomiphene citrate in men: a study of the pituitary-Leydig cell axis. *J. Clin. Endocrinol.* **27**, 1558–1564.

Bauer, H. G. (1954). Endocrine and other clinical manifestations of hypothalamic disease. *J. Clin. Endocrinol.* **14**, 13–31.

Bhattacharya, A. N., Dierschke, D. J., Yamaji, T., & Knobil, E. (1972). The pharmacologic blockade of the circhoral mode of LH secretion in the ovariectomized rhesus monkey. *Endocrinology* **90**, 778–786.

Blizzard, R. M., Johanson, A. J., Guyda, H., Baghdassarian, A., Raiti, S., & Migeon, C. J. (1970). Recent developments in the study of gonadotropin secretion in adolescence. In *Adolescent Endocrinology*, R. M. Blizzard, F. P. Heald, & W. Hung, Eds., Appleton-Century Crofts, New York, p. 1.

Blizzard, R. M., Penny, R., Foley, Jr., T. P., Baghdassarian, A., Johanson, A., & Yen, S. S. C. (1972). Pituitary-gonadal interrelationships in relation to puberty. In *Gonadotropins*, B. B. Saxena, C. G. Beling, & H. M. Gandy, Eds., Wiley, New York, pp. 502–523.

Boyar, R., Finkelstein, J., Roffwarg, H., Kapen, S., Weitzman, E., & Hellman, L. (1972). Synchronization of augmented luteinizing hormone secretion with sleep during puberty. *New Eng. J. Med.* **287**, 582–586.

Buckler, J. M. H. & Clayton, B. E. (1970). Output of luteinizing hormone in the urine of normal children and those with advanced sexual development. *Arch. Dis. Childh.* **45**, 478–484.

Burr, I. M., Sizonenko, P. C., Kaplan, S. L., & Grumbach, M. M. (1970). Hormonal changes in puberty. I. Correlation of serum luteinizing hormone and follicle stimulating hormone with stages of puberty, testicular size, and bone age in normal boys. *Ped. Res.* **4**, 25–35.

Conte, F., Grumbach, M. M., & Kaplan, S. L. (1972). Variations in plasma LH and FSH with age in 35 patients with XO gonadal dysgenesis. *Ped. Res.* **6**, 353.

Coppola, J. A. (1971). Brain catecholamines and gonadotropin secretion. In *Frontiers in Neuroendocrinology*, L. Martini & W. F. Ganong, Eds., Oxford University Press, Oxford, pp. 129–143.

Critchlow, V. & Bar-Sela, M. E. (1967). Control of the onset of puberty. In *Neuroendocrinology*, Vol. II, L. Martini & W. F. Ganong, Eds., Academic, New York, pp. 101–162.

Davidson, J. M. (1969). Feedback regulation of gonadotropin secretion. In *Frontiers in Neuroendocrinology*, L. Martini & W. F. Ganong, Eds., Academic, New York, pp. 343–388.

Davidson, J. M. (1972). Hormones and reproductive behavior. In *Reproductive Biology*, H. Balin & S. Glasser, Eds., Excerpta Medica, Amsterdam, pp. 877–918.

Dierschke, D. J., Bhattacharya, A. N., Atkinson, L. E., & Knobil, E. (1970). Circhoral oscillations of plasma LH levels in the ovariectomized rhesus monkey, Endocrinology 87, 850–853.

Donovan, B.T. & van der Werff ten Bosch, J. J. (1965). *Physiology of Puberty*, Williams & Wilkins, Baltimore.

Everett, J. W. (1964). Central neural control of reproductive functions of the adenohypophysis. *Physiol. Rev.* **44**, 373–431.

Everett, J. W. (1969). Neuroendocrine aspects of mammalian reproduction. *Ann. Rev. Physiol.* **31**, 383–416.

Faiman, C. & Winter, J. S. D. (1971). Sex differences in gonadotrophin concentrations in infancy. *Nature* **232**, 130–131.

Faiman, C., Winter, J. S. D., Chehib, F. S., & Butler, T. M. (1972). Sex differences in gonadotrophins in the infant chimpanzee. *J. Clin. Endocrinol.* **34**, 601–604.

Fitschen, W. & Clayton, B. E. (1965). Urinary excretion of gonadotrophins with particular reference to children. *Arch. Dis. Childh.* **40**, 16–26.

Frasier, S. D., Gafford, F., & Horton, R. (1969). Plasma androgens in childhood and adolescence. *J. Clin. Endocrinol.* **29**, 1404–1408.

Frisch, R. & Revelle, R. (1969). Variation in body weights and the age of the adolescent growth spurt among Latin American and Asian populations, in relation to calorie supplies. *Human Biol.* **41**, 185–212.

Frisch, R. & Revelle, R. (1971). Height and weight at menarche and a hypothesis of menarche. *Arch. Dis. Childh.* **46**, 695–701.

Gorski, R. A. (1970). Localization of hypothalamic regulation of anterior pituitary function. *Amer. J. Anat.* **129**, 219–223.

Grumbach, M. M. & Kaplan, S. L. (1973). Ontogenesis of growth hormone, insulin, prolactin, and gonadotropin secretion in the human foetus. In *Foetal and Neonatal Physiology, Proc. Sir Joseph Barcroft Centenary Symposium,* Cambridge University Press, Cambridge, pp. 462–487.

Harris, G. W. & Naftolin, F. (1970). The hypothalamus and control of ovulation. *Brit. Med. Bull.* **26**, 3–9.

Hohlweg, W. (1934). Veränderungen des Hypophysenvorderlappens und des Ovariums nach Behandlung mit grossen Dosen von Follikelhormon. *Klin. Wschr.* **13**, 92–95.

Hohlweg, W. (1936). Der Mechanismus der Wirkung von gonadotropen Substanzen auf das Ovar der infantilen Ratte. *Klin. Wschr.* **15**, 1832–1835.

Hohlweg, W. & Dohrn, M. (1932), Uber die Beziehungen zwischen Hypophysen'vorderlappen und Keimdrüsen. *Klin. Wschr.* **11**, 233–235.

Jackson, G. L., Roche, J. F., Foster, D. L., & Dziuk, P. J. (1971). Luteinizing hormone releasing activity in the hypothalamus of anestrous and cyclic ewes. *Biol. Reprod.* **5**, 5–12.

Jacobsen, A. R., Marshall, J. R., Ross, G. T., & Cargille, C. M. (1968). Plasma gonadotrophins during clomiphene-induced ovulatory cycles. *Amer. J. Ob. Gyn.* **102**, 284–290.

Jenner, M. R., Kelch, R. P., Kaplan, S. L., & Grumbach, M. M. (1972). Hormonal changes in puberty. IV Plasma estradiol, LH, and FSH in prepubertal children, pubertal females, and in precocious puberty, premature thelarche, hypogonadism, and in a child with a feminizing ovarian tumor. *J. Clin. Endocrinol.* **34**, 521–530.

Job, J. C., Garnier, P. E., Chaussain, J. L., & Milhaud, G. (1972). Elevation of serum gonadotropins (LH and FSH) after releasing hormone (LH-RH) injection in normal children and in paitents with disorders of puberty. *J. Clin. Endocrinol.* **35**. 475–476.

Kahwango, I., Heinrichs, W. L., & Herrmann, W. L. (1970). Estradiol "receptors" in hypothalamus and anterior pituitary gland: inhibition of estradiol binding by SH-group blocking agents and clomiphene citrate. *Endocrinology* **86**, 1319–1326.

Kaplan, S. L., Grumbach, M. M., & Shepard, R. H. (1969). Gonadotropins in serum and pituitary of human fetuses and infants. *Ped. Res.* **3**, 512–513.

Kastin, A. J., Gual, C., Schally, A. V., & Arimura (1972). Clinical experience with hypothalamic releasing hormones. Part 2. Luteinizing hormone-releasing hormone and other hyphysiotropic releasing hormones. *Rec. Progr. Hormone Res.* **28**, 201–217.

Kelch, R. P., Conte, F. A., Kaplan, S. L., Grumbach, M. M. (1972a). Evidence for the episodic secretion of LH and decreasing sensitivity of the hypothalamic-pituitary "gonadostat" in adolescent patients with gonadal dysgenesis. *Ped. Res.* **6**, 349.

Kelch, R. P., Grumbach, M. M., & Kaplan, S. L. (1972b). Studies on the mechanism of puberty in man. In *Gonadotropins*, B. B. Saxena, C. G. Beling, & H. M. Gandy, Eds., Wiley, New York, pp. 524–534.

Kelch, R. P., Conte, F. A., Kaplan, S. L., & Grumbach, M. M. (1973a). Episodic secretion of luteinizing hormone (LH) in adolescent patients with the syndrome of gonadal dysgenesis. *J. Clin. Endocrinol.* **36**, 424–427.

Kelch, R. P., Kaplan, S. L., & Grumbach, M. M. (1973b). Suppression of urinary and plasma follicle-stimulating hormone by exogenous estrogens in prepubertal and pubertal children. *J. Clin. Invest.* **52**, 1122–1128.

Kerdelhué, B. & Jutisz, M. (1972). Development of a radioimmunoassay of a hypothalamic hormone which stimulates the release of pituitary LH and FSH (LH-RH) using a synthetic decapeptide as antigen. IV. International Congress of Endocrinology, *Excerpta Medica Intl. Congr.* **Series #256**, p. 141.

Knobil, E., Dierschke, D. J., Yamaji, T., Karsch, F. J., Hotchkiss, J., & Weick, R. F. (1972). Role of estrogen in the positive and negative feedback control of LH secretion during the menstrual cycle of the rhesus monkey. In *Gonadotropins*,

B. B. Saxena, C. G. Beling, & H. M. Gandy, Eds., Wiley, New York, p. 72–86.

Korenman, S. G. (1970). Relation between estrogen inhibitory activity and binding to cytosol of rabbit and human uterus. *Endocrinology* **87**, 1119–1123.

Kulin, H. E., Grumbach, M. M., & Kaplan, S. L. (1969). Changing sensitivity of the pubertal gonadal hypothalamic feedback mechanism in man. *Science* **166**, 1012–1013.

Kulin, H. E., Grumbach, M. M., & Kaplan, S. L. (1972). Gonadal-hypothalamic interaction in prepubertal and pubertal man: Effect of clomiphene citrate on urinary follicle-stimulating hormone and luteinizing hormone and plasma testosterone. *Ped. Res.* **6**, 162–171.

Kulin, H. E. & Reiter, E. O. (1972). Gonadotropin suppression by low dose estrogen in men: Evidence for differential effects upon FSH and LH. *J. Clin. Endocrinol.* **35**, 836–839.

Kulin, H. E., Reiter, E. O., & Bridson, E. W. (1971). Pubertal maturation of the gonadotropin stimulatory response to clomiphene: case report. *J. Clin. Endocrinol.* **33**, 551–553.

Laron, Z. & Zilka, E. (1969). Compensatory hypertrophy of testicle in unilateral cryptorchidism. *J. Clin. Endocrinol.* **29**, 1410–1413.

Lee, P. A., Midgley, Jr., A. R. & Jaffe, R. B. (1970). Regulation of human gonadotropins. VI. Serum follicle stimulating and luteinizing hormone determinations in children. *J. Clin. Endocrinol.* **31**, 248–253.

Levina, S. E. (1970). Regulation of secretion of hypophyseal gonadotropins in human embryogenesis, *Probl. Endokrinol. (Mosk.)* **16**, 53–59.

Liu, M., Grumbach, M. M., de Napoli, R. A., & Morishima, A. (1965). Prevalence of electroencephalographic abnormalities in idiopathic precocious puberty and premature pubarche: Bearing on pathogenesis and neuroendocrine regulation of puberty. *J. Clin. Endocrinol.* **25**, 1296–1308.

McCann, S. M. (1971). Mechanism of action of hypothalamic-hypophyseal stimulating and inhibiting hormones. In *Frontiers of Neuroendocrinology,* L. Martini & W. F. Ganong, Eds., Oxford University Press, New York, pp. 209–235.

Maffezzoli, R. D., Kaplan, G. N., & Chrambach, A. (1972). Physical characterization by polyacrylamide gel electrophoresis of human follicle stimulating hormone from urinary extracts of children, men, and pre- and postmenopausal women. *J. Clin. Endocrinol.* **34**, 375–379.

Malacara, J. M., Selyer, Jr., L. E., & Reichlin, S. (1972). Luteinizing hormone releasing factor activity in peripheral blood from women during the midcycle luteinizing hormone ovulatory surge. *J. Clin. Endocrinol.* **34**, 271–278.

Marshall, W. A. & Tanner, J. M. (1968). Growth and physiological development during adolescence. *Ann. Rev. Med.* **19**, 283–300.

Matsuo, H., Baba, Y., Nair, R. M. G., Arimura, A., & Schally, A. V. (1971). Structure of the porcine LH- and FSH-releasing hormone. I. The proposed amino acid sequence, *Biochem. Biophys. Res. Comm.* **43**, 1334–1339.

Midgley, Jr., A. R. and Jaffe, R. B. (1971) Regulation of human gonadotropins. X Episodic fluctuations of LH during the menstrual cycle. *J. Clin. Endocrinol.* **33**, 962–969.

Monahan, M., Rivier, J., Burgus, R., Amoss, M., Vale, W., & Guillemin R. (1971).

Synthèse totale par phase solide d'un décapeptide qui stimule la hypophysaires LH et FSH. *C. R. Acad. Sci. Paris* (D) **273**, 508–510.

Naftolin, F., Haris, G. W., & Bobrow, M. (1971). Effect of purified luteinizing hormone releasing factor on normal and hypogonadotrophic anosmic men. *Nature* **232**, 496–497.

Nankin, H. R., Yanaihara, T., and Troen, P. (1971). Response of gonadotropins and testosterone to clomiphene stimulation in a pubertal boy. *J. Clin. Endocrin.* **33**, 360–363.

Odell, W. D., Swerdloff, R. S., Jacobs, H. S., & Hescox, M. A. (1973). FSH induction of sensitivity to LH: one cause of sexual maturation in the male rat. *Endocrinology* **92**, 160–165.

Penny, R., Guyda, H. J., Baghdassarian, A., Johanson, A. J., & Blizzard, R. M. (1970). Correlation of serum follicular stimulating hormone (FSH) and luteinizing hormone (LH) as measured by radioimmunoassay in disorders of sexual development. *J. Clin. Invest.* **49**, 1847–1852.

Peterson, Jr., N. T., Midgley, Jr., A. R., & Jaffe, R. B. (1968). Regulation of human gonadotropins. III. Luteinizing hormone and follicle stimulating hormone in sera from adult males. *J. Clin. Endocrinol.* **28**, 1473–1478.

Ramirez, V. D. (1971). Sex and brain-pituitary function at puberty. In *Steroid Hormones and Brain Function* (C. H. Sawyer & R. A. Gorski, eds.), University of California Press, Los Angeles, California, pp. 301–310.

Ramirez, V. D. & McCann, S. M. (1963). A highly sensitive test for LH-releasing activity: the ovariectomized, estrogen-progesterone-blocked rat. *Endocrinology* **73**, 193–198.

Ramirez, V.D. & McCann, S. M. (1965) Inhibitory effects of testosterone on luteinizing hormone secretion in immature and adult rats. Endocrinology **76**, 412–417.

Redding, T. W., Schally, A. V., Arimura, A., & Matsuo, H. (1972). Stimulation of release and synthesis of luteinizing hormone (LH) and follicle stimulating hormone (FSH) in tissue cultures of rat pituitaries in response to natural and synthetic LH and FSH releasing hormone. *Endocrinology* **90**, 764–770.

Reeves, J. J., Arimura, A., & Schally, A. V. (1970). Serum levels of prolactin and luteinizing hormone (LH) in the ewe at various stages of the estrous cycle. *Proc. Soc. Exp. Biol. Med.* **134**, 938–942.

Reyes, F. I., Winter, J. S. D., & Faiman, C. (1973). Studies on human sexual development. 1. Fetal gonadal and adrenal sex steroids. *J. Clin. Endocrinol.* In press,

Rifkind, A. B., Kulin, H. E., Rayford, P. L., Cargille, C. M., & Ross, G. T. (1970). 24-hour urinary luteinizing hormone (LH) and follicle-stimulating hormone (FSH) excretion in normal children. *J. Clin. Endocrinol.* **31**, 517–525.

Rifkind, A. B., Kulin, H. E., & Ross, G. T. (1967). Follicle-stimulating hormone (FSH) and luteinizing hormone (LH) in the urine of prepubertal children. *J. Clin. Invest.* **46**, 1925–1931.

Rivarola, M. A., Bergada, C., & Cullen, M. (1970). HCG stimulation test in prepubertal boys with cryptorchidism, in bilateral anorchia and in male pseudohermaphroditism. *J. Clin. Endocrinol.* **31**, 526–530.

Roth, J. C., Grumbach, M. M., & Kaplan, S. L. (1973a). Effect of synthetic luteinizing hormone releasing factor on serum testosterone and gonadotropins in prepubertal, pubertal, and adult males. *J. Clin. Endocrinol.* In press.

Roth, J. C., Grumbach, M. M., & Kaplan, S. L. (1973b). Hormonal changes in puberty. I. Patterns of LH and FSH release evoked by synthetic luteinizing hormone releasing factor in prepubertal, and pubertal children, and adult males (to be published).

Roth, J. C., Kelch, R. P., Kaplan, S. L., & Grumbach, M. M. (1972a). Patterns of LH, FSH and testosterone release stimulated by synthetic LRF in prepubertal, pubertal, and adult subjects, and in patients with gonadotropin deficiency and XO gonadal dysgenesis. In *Hypothalamic Hypophysiotropic Hormones: Clinical and Physiological Studies, Proc. Serano Foundation Conference,* Acapulco, Mexico, June 1972, G. Gual & E. Rosenberg, Eds., Excerpta Medica, Amsterdam. In press.

Roth, J. C., Kelch, R. P., Kaplan, S. L., & Grumbach, M. M. (1972b). FSH and LH response to luteinizing hormone-releasing factor in prepubertal and pubertal children, adult males and patients with hypogonadotropic and hypergonadotropic hypogonadism. *J. Clin. Endocrinol.* **35,** 926–930.

Roy, S., Greenblatt, R. B., Mahesh, V. B., & Jungck, E. C. (1963). Clomiphene citrate-further observations on its use in induction of ovulation in the human and on its mode of action. *Fertil. Steril.* **14,** 575–595.

Rubin, R. T., Kales, A., Adler, R., Fagin, T., and Odell, W (1972). Gonadotropin secretion during sleep in normal adult men. *Science* 175, 196–198.

Ryan, K. J., Naftolin, F., Reddy, V., Flores, F., & Petro, Z. (1972). Estrogen formation in the brain. *Amer. J. Ob. Gyn.* **114,** 454–460.

Saez, J. M. & Bertrand, J. (1968). Studies on testicular function in children: plasma concentrations of testosterone, dehydroepiandrosterone and its sulfate before and after stimulation with human chorionic gonadotrophin. *Steroids* **12,** 749–762.

Savage, D. L., de Groppa, M. I., Kaplan, S. L., & Grumbach, M. M. (1973). Response to synthetic luteinizing hormone releasing factor (LRF) in idiopathic hypopituitarism, isolated gonadotropin deficiency, and constitutional delayed adolescence. (Submitted for publication.)

Schally, A. V., Arimura, A., Baba, Y., Nair, R. M. G., Matsuo, H., Redding, I. W., & Debeljuk, L. (1971). Isolation and properties of the FSH and LH-releasing hormone. *Biochem. Biophys. Res. Comm.* **43,** 393–399.

Schally, A. V., Kastin, A. J., & Arimura, A. (1972). The hypothalamus and reproduction. *Amer. J. Ob. Gym.* **114,**423–442.

Schwartz, N. B. & McCormack, C. E. (1972). Reproduction: Gonadal function and its regulation. *Ann. Rev. Physiol.* **34,** 425–472.

Sizonenko, P. C., Burr, I. M., Kaplan, S. L., & Grumbach, M. M. (1970). Hormonal changes in puberty. II. Correlation of serum luteinizing hormone and follicle stimulating hormone with stages of puberty and bone age in normal girls. *Ped. Res.* **4,** 36–45.

Smith, E. R. & Davidson, J. M. (1967). Differential response to hypothalamic testosterone in relation to male puberty. *Amer. J. Physiol.* **212,** 1385–1390.

Smith, E. R. & Davidson, J. M. (1968). Role of estrogen in the cerebral control of puberty in female rats. *Endocrinology* **82,** 100–108.

Vande Wiele, R. L., Bogumil, J., Dyrenfurth, I., Ferin, M., Jewelewicz, R., Warren, M., Rizkallah, T., & Mikhail, G. (1970). Mechanisms regulating the menstrual cycle in women. *Rec. Progr. Hormone Res.* **26**, 63–95.

Weinberger, L. M. & Grant, F. C. (1941). Precocious puberty and tumors of the hypothalamus. *Arch. Int. Med.* **67**, 762–792.

Wilkins, L. (1965). *The Diagnosis and Treatment of Endocrine Disorders in Childhood and Adolescence,* 3rd ed., Thomas, Springfield, Ill.

Winter, J. S. D. & Faiman, C. (1972). Pituitary-gonadal relations in male children and adolescents. *Ped. Res.* **6**, 126–135.

Winter, J. S. D., Tarasaka, S., & Faiman, C. (1972). The hormonal response to HCG stimulation in male children and adolescents. *J. Clin. Endocrinol.* **34**, 348–353.

Wood, J. R., Wrenn, T. R., & Bitman, J. (1968). Estrogenic and anti-estrogenic effects of clomiphene, MER-25 and CN-55, 945-27 on the rat uterus and vagina. *Endocrinology* **82**, 69–74.

Yamaji, T., Dierschke, D. J., Hotchkiss, J., Bhattacharya, A. N., Surve, A. H., & Knobil, E. (1971). Estrogen induction of LH release in the rhesus monkey. *Endocrinology* **89**, 1034–1041.

Yen, S. S. C. & Tsai, C. C. (1971). The biphasic pattern in the feedback action of ethinyl estradiol on the release of pituitary FSH and LH. *J. Clin. Endocrinol.* **33**, 882–887.

Yen, S. C. C., VandenBerg, G., Rebar, R., & Ehara, Y. (1972). Variation of pituitary responsiveness to synthetic LRF during different phases of the menstrual cycle. *J. Clin. Endocrinol.* **33**, 882–887.

Yen, S. S. C. & Vičic, W. J. (1970). Serum follicle-stimulating hormone levels in puberty. *Amer. J. Ob. Gyn.* **106**, 134–137.

Zacharias, L. & Wurtman, R. J. (1969). Age at menarche. Genetic and environmental influences. *New Eng. J. Med.* **280**, 868–875.

DISCUSSION

Dr. Ganong. I would like to ask for further comment on the fact that hypothalamic lesions cause precocious puberty. In the rat one can explain this in terms of the negative feedback hypothesis, on the assumption that one destroys some of the negative feedback elements. But, in the monkey and also in the human, if you postulate that puberty occurs only when the positive feedback mechanism matures, how can you explain the occurrence of puberty in a 2-year-old girl with hypothalamic disease? It seems to me you have to postulate that a lesion accelerates the maturation of the positive feedback. This is a disturbing point, in terms of explaining the mechanisms included in the onset of puberty.

Dr. Grumbach. We have observed the onset of true precocious puberty by 3 months of age in a male and female infant; the female exhibited menarche by 5 months of age (Liu, Grumbach, de Napoli, & Morishima, 1965). The normal pattern of sexual maturation may be telescoped in time in idiopathic or organic forms of neurogenic precocious puberty. In these patients there is a functional or organic disturbance in the inhibitory mechanisms which normally restrain the premature onset of puberty or an activiation of stimulatory neural influences. Similarly, the positive feedback mechanism also develops precociously. Whether this is a direct effect of the CNS lesion or merely the consequence of attaining more rapidly a critical and sustained level of circulating estradiol, which both activates and triggers the stimulatory feedback mechanism, remains to be determined; but I favor the latter possibility.

Dr. Kulin. We have some clinical data bearing on this point. In order to study the ontogeny of positive feedback in the human female, we gave a variety of doses of 17-β estradiol intramuscularly to adult females, pre- and early-pubertal girls. Not until sexual maturation was moderately advanced did exogenous estrogen induce a rise in LH, while the steroid hormone levels remained elevated. We also administered 17-β estradiol to a 7-year-old girl with moderately advanced sexual precocity who had not yet experienced menarche. She displayed an LH surge during the estrogen injections. Her precocious development was due to a large hypothalamic cyst, which apparently started the whole pubertal process, including changes in both negative and positive feedback.

Dr. Grumbach. Patients with true precocious puberty exhibit a pubertal

FSH and LH response to the administration of LRF. This was true, as well, for the 3-year-old boy with congenital virilizing adrenal hyperplasia who had a skeletal age of 11 years, an observation which suggests that sex steroids lead to premature maturation of the hypothalamus as well as accelerated somatic development.

DR. JOB.   The data from our group are similar to those of Dr. Grumbach. Synthetic LH-RH 0.1 mg was injected intravenously in 19 prepubertal control children, 11 boys and 8 girls. Figure 22 shows the LH and FSH mean values. As these values are expressed as ng of standard pituitary extract LER-907 per ml, apparently high levels of FSH can be attributed to the fact that LER-907 has more LH than FSH radioimmunological activity, so that no comparison can be drawn between levels of FSH and LH. For each individual gonadotropin mean peak levels of LH are higher in boys and mean peak levels of FSH higher in girls. In Fig. 23 the basal and peak levels of each gonadotropin are compared in prepubertal and pubertal controls of both sexes. Peak levels of both gonadotropins increase with puberty. The relative rise, i.e., the ratio of mean peak level after LH-RH injection to mean basal level, increases for LH before puberty from 3.6- to 5.9-fold after the beginning of puberty in boys and similarly from 3.1- to 6.2-fold in girls. But for FSH it decreases with puberty, from 2.8- to 1.9-fold in boys and from 7.8- to 2.1-fold in girls, so that this relative decrease is much more important in females than in males. These preliminary data would have to be extended to more control subjects to permit interpretation. They indicate, however, that puberty induces a different trend of regulation of the mobilizable pituitary reserve for each gonadotropin and, as regards FSH, for each sex. These facts lead us to ask what really happens at puberty. Does the pituitary content of FSH increase less than the

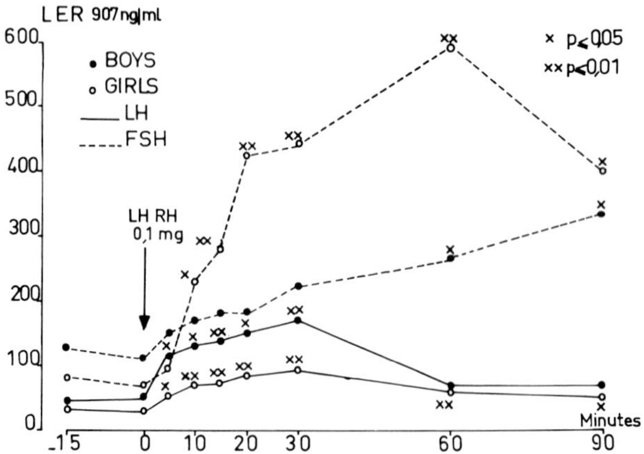

FIG. 22.   Mean values of LH and FSH after intravenous injection of 0.1 mg synthetic LH-RH in prepubertal controls (11 boys and 8 girls).

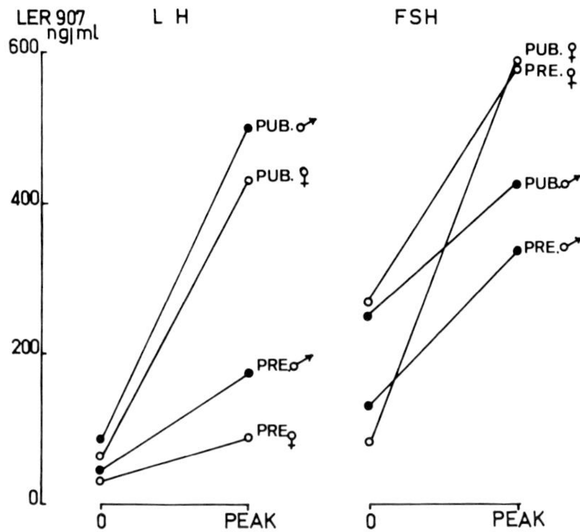

FIG. 23.   Mean basal and peak levels of LH and FSH after 0.1 mg LH-RH in normal subjects (prepubertal: 11 boys and 8 girls; pubertal: 7 males and 5 females).

content of LH? Or, does it seem so because LH-RH is not FSH-RH? Or, does the pubertal elevation of gonadotropin secretion caused by endogenous secretion of releasing hormone or hormones deplete FSH pituitary reserve more than LH reserve? Moreover, an LH-RH test may demonstrate a higher pituitary gonadotropic reserve in infants than in children. The size of our control groups did not allow us to study this point in normal subjects. But it is clearly evidenced in agonadal patients. Figure 24 shows data obtained with LH-RH in 5 agonadal children (3 with complete gonadal dysgenesis and 2 with accidental castration). The scale for gonadotropins is tenfold less than on the previous 2 figures. Patient #1 was 2 months old; #2 and #3 were 10 years old; #4 and #5 were 12 and 13 years old, respectively. The mobilizable pituitary reserve of gonadotropins was very high in the baby, less in the 10-year-old children, and very high in the older patients. These facts agree with data reported by Grumbach on serum levels of gonadotropins in patients of different ages with gonadal dysgenesis and must be related to those reported by Faiman and Winter on FSH serum levels in girls before 2 years. So, we have two questions: Why does the sensitivity of the feedback mechanism decrease at puberty? And why does it increase in the first months of life?

DR. GESCHWIND.   At the International Congress of Endocrinology in Washington in June, 1972, Dr. Jutisz's group reported for the first time a RIA for LRF, and the broad picture that he observed for LRF in the peripheral circulation was exactly what we would have anticipated on the basis of LH levels. However, he did see an earlier peak, about 3 days before one would have anticipated a peak for an LH surge. I wonder whether anybody has values for circulating LRF by RIA, particularly as they relate to the onset of puberty.

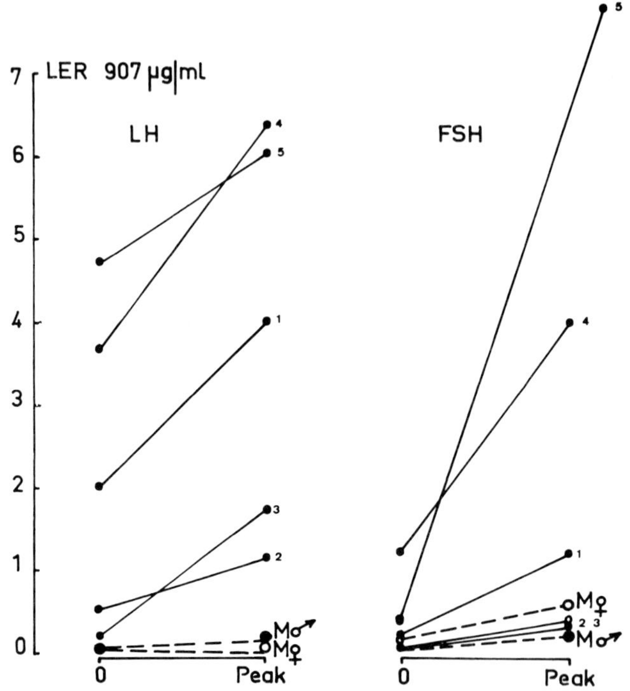

FIG. 24. Mean basal levels and peak levels of LH and FSH after 0.1 mg LH-RH in agonadal patients (#1, 2, 5: gonadal dysgenesis; #3, 4: accidental castration; M = mean of prepubertal controls).

Dr. Arimura. We are still working to validate the RIA method for LH-RH using our antiserum to LH-RH which was generated in the rabbit. Our antiserum seems to be different from that obtained by Dr. Jutisz. Ours exhibits paradoxical binding with the antigen at very low dose ranges of LH-RH. As discussed by Dr. Weintraub in Washington this summer, this kind of serum may be highly specific and also sensitive, as it can detect 4 pg LH-RH or less. It is possible to determine LH-RH in the peripheral blood when the release of LH-RH is increased. But we have not yet measured LH-RH in the blood of animals or human beings at the onset of puberty.

Dr. Foster. We have looked at circulating LH in 30 infant monkeys and in their mothers through the first 24 weeks of life. LH levels are extremely high during the first 10 to 15 weeks, after which they taper toward maternal values by 6 months of age. This is about where Dr. Dierschke's study of gonadotropin levels in the immature monkey takes over.

Dr. McCann. As a corollary to that, I wonder if the failure of the young monkey to respond to castration may be due to what Dr. Grumbach pointed out in man; i.e., perhaps some adrenal secretion comes in here at this stage in the monkey's life which acts as a suppressant. It may be important, before drawing a final conclusion, to study ovariectomized-adrenalectomized monkeys just to see whether or not they might show elevated LH levels following that operation.

DR. ODELL. I would like to ask a question about one of Dr. Grumbach's slides on the comparison of responses in mature and immature animals. If one looks at bioassay responses, such as the prostatic response to testosterone or the uterine response to estradiol, the responsive tissue in the immature animal does not obtain (in absolute weight) a value as large as the adult even with maximal stimulation. The tissues start out at a different baseline, and one does not expect them to increase to the same absolute value. Perhaps the comparison of absolutes with very different baselines is not appropriate; relative changes may be more appropriate. In Fig. 9 the LH response to LRF in the immature goes from about 0.4 up to about 1.2 ng/ml, a 300 percent increase. The adult increased from about 1.6 to 6 ng/ml, perhaps a 400 per cent response. Do the adults and immatures actually differ in incremental responses?

DR. GRUMBACH. The maximal increment in serum LH (ΔLH) after LRF, whether expressed as an absolute increment or in percentage change, is strikingly different in prepubertal and pubertal individuals, as is the integrated area of the plasma concentrations × minutes.

DR. ODELL. Dr. Job, you showed almost a twofold difference between the immature and mature, when based on per cent increases. Are those numbers significantly different or were the populations so small that you could not tell?

DR. JOB. The difference was significant if you consider that people from pubertal stages 2 to 5 are the same group. It is not, if you consider they are 4 different groups.

DR. JAFFE. Dr. Foster mentioned that he and Dr. Lemons had found elevated levels of immunoassayable gonadotropins of the 35 immature monkeys they studied in the first 6 months of life. They then asked: What is the capacity of the immature monkey ovary to aromatize androgen, i.e., to convert androgen during this stage, and how does it compare with the adult? They found no difference, essentially, in the capacity of the immature ovary to aromatize androstenedione and convert it to estrogen when compared with the adult. Based on these observations, I should like to ask Dr. Dierschke whether he quantified estradiol during this time of life. We have not as yet, although we are very anxious to do so. Is this just a manifestation of the capacity of the ovary to aromatize, or, indeed, is some of this estrogen in the circulation at this age; if so, might it be having an effect on the hypothalamic-pituitary axis?

DR. DIERSCHKE. The plasma concentrations of estradiol in these young females are very low but measurable. They average about 10 to 15 pg/ml. However, this circulating estrogen is apparently not exerting a negative feed-back effect on gonadotropin concentrations following its removal.

DR. JAFFE.   At what age do you see these levels?

DR. DIERSCHKE.   The youngest animals we sampled were 4 to 5 months old.

DR. BOGDANOVE.   In considering the hypersecretion of gonadotropins in very early stages in gestation, Dr. Grumbach, you implied that this hypersecretion is due to an unrestrained secretion of LRF. This is certainly a possibility, of course, but it is only one possibility, one for which there is, as yet, no evidence. Would it not be equally logical to postulate that the pituitary may be functioning autonomously, particularly if phylogeny and ontogeny are parallel? After all, there are animals in which the thyroids and gonads function without any leadership or support from a pituitary. There are also animals in which there is a pituitary but no portal system. Why, therefore, do we have to suppose that the pituitary in early fetal or embryonic life is under the control of the brain, even though we all recognize the importance of the central nervous system for pituitary function in adult life?

DR. GRUMBACH.   Dr. Bognadove raises an important issue: What is the evidence in the human fetus to support CNS regulation of pituitary hormone secretion, as opposed to the autonomous release of pituitary hormones? The evidence for the hypothesis we put forth for the role of hypothalamic hypophysiotropic hormones in the human fetus is entirely indirect. We have not yet assayed any of the hypophysiotropic hormones in the human fetal hypothalamus. In a recent report of the ontogenesis of human growth hormone, Dr. Kaplan, Dr. Shepard, and I (1972) summarized the evidence supporting, at least by midgestation, the role of the hypothalamus in the release of fetal pituitary growth hormone. For GH, FSH, and LH it is related to the change in fetal serum levels during gestation: an initial rise in serum GH and serum FSH, with peak levels between 15 to 24 weeks, is followed by a fall to significantly lower serum concentrations. In addition, sex-specific differences were found in the concentration of serum FSH and the pituitary content and concentration of FSH and LH. These observations were evaluated with the findings in anencephalic fetuses and the limited information on the morphogenesis of the human hypothalamus and portal system and other CNS functions. Our observations in the anencephalic fetus provide evidence of the role of hypophysiotropic hormone in the release of GH and the gonadotropins. On the other hand, prolactin secretion in the human fetus appears to be autonomous. In any case, we postulate that relatively unrestrained secretion of certain hypophysiotropic hormones is a primitive regulatory system in the human fetus, quite possibly preceded by a period of autonomous pituitary secretion, which is followed by the maturation of inhibitory CNS influences on the secretion of GH-RF and LRF. As Dr. Bogdanove well knows, there are important species differences in the ontogenesis of the endocrine system; in contrast to the human neonate, CNS regulation of pituitary function in the rat is much less mature.

DR. RAMIREZ.   I would like to show 3 slides. One is in relation to the ontogeny of the negative feedback action of estrogen on plasma FSH in the rat, and relates to what has been said here this morning. I would also like to show you data that could explain the sex difference in plasma FSH values between male and female rats and to postulate a different mechanism of action of FSH in both sexes. We castrated our animals (Fig. 25) at intervals of 5 days, e.g., animals were castrated at birth and killed at 5 days of age; castrated at 5 days and killed at 10 days of age, etc. Estradiol benzoate (given, 0.05 μg $\times$ 100 g/b.w. $\times$ 4 days) is effective only starting at 20 days of age. This estrogen dose is close to what we think is the daily physiological release of estrogen in the rat. At puberty, which started in our group of animals between 35 and 40 days, there is again a loss of the negative action of estrogen on plasma FSH. This is interesting in relation to the finding in humans and emphasizes the idea that when we talk about the negative feedback action of estrogen we are probably referring mainly to the control of FSH secretion. In this second experiment (Fig. 26) we demonstrated, in the prepubertal female rat, that FSH implanted in the medial basal hypothalamus has a positive feedback action on the release of endogenous FSH. This is not true in the male. This could be one of the explanations for the sex difference we have been hearing about.

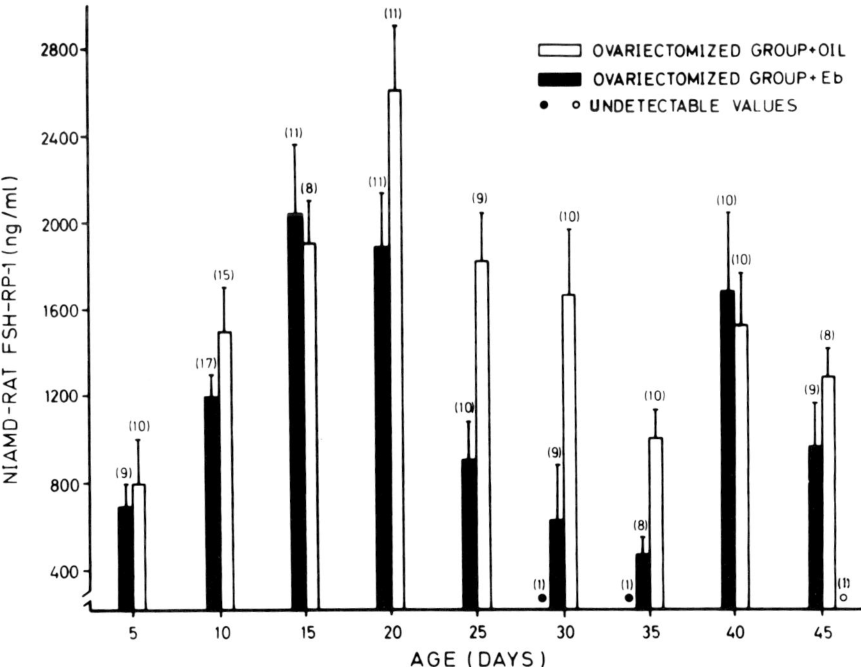

FIG. 25.   Plasma FSH values as a function of maturation in 5-day castrated rats treated with estradiol benzoate. The rats were castrated at intervals of 5 days, from day 1 to 40. Columns are mean values ±SE. Numbers in parenthesis indicate animals used. From Ojeda & Ramirez, unpublished.

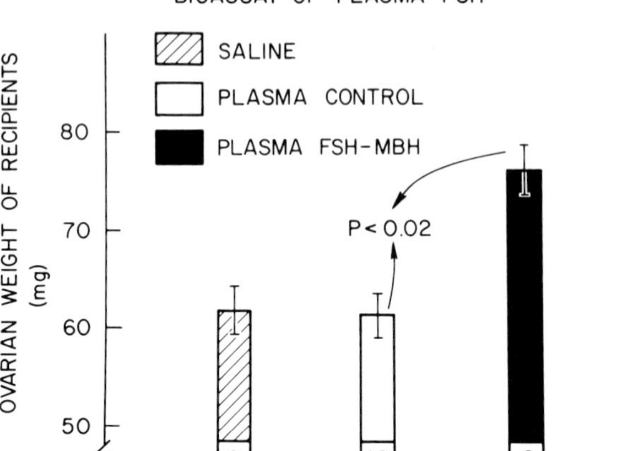

FIG. 26. Determination of plasma FSH by the ovarian augmentation method in 36-day-old prepubertal rats. Twenty donor rats received an FSH implant in the medial basal hypothalamus (MBH) at 32 days of age; 32 control animals had no implants, or had FSH implants outside the MBH. Pooled plasma from the experimental and control groups were bioassayed in 16 (control) or 8 (experimental) recipient rats; 9 recipients received only 3 ml of saline solution. Columns represent mean values ±SE. From Ramirez, 1971; reproduced with permission of the editor.

The implantation was done at 32 days of age and the animals killed at 36 days of age; the plasma from the different groups was pooled, and the FSH was determined by using the bioassay method of Steelman & Pohley. Figure 27 illustrates the difficulty of the problem of maturation. This is a recent experiment done in collaboration with Dr. C. H. Sawyer, in which we implanted FSH in prepubertal rats at 30 days of age and killed the animals at 36 days of age. We took one ovary at 30 days of age and the other 6 days later and looked for compensatory hypertrophy. We repeated this in adult animals (200 g body weight). FSH in the prepubertal rats has a clearcut stimulatory action on compensatory ovarian hypertrophy. On the contrary, in the adult animal this effect was reversed and it was negative. These results could be one explanation why we are finding this plasma FSH difference between female and male immature animals.

DR. FOSTER. Some of our observations, during a longitudinal investigation of the development of the hypothalamic-hypophyseal-gonadal system in the immature rhesus monkey, are that LH concentrations, as measured by our RIA, are fairly stable in the lactating female. However, concentrations of LH in the circulation exhibit marked fluctuations in both male and female infant monkeys throughout the first 4 months after birth; these levels are not so low as the basal levels (400 to 600 ng/ml) observed in the mother but in many cases are as high (1300 to 2600 ng/ml) as the midcycle surges found in the

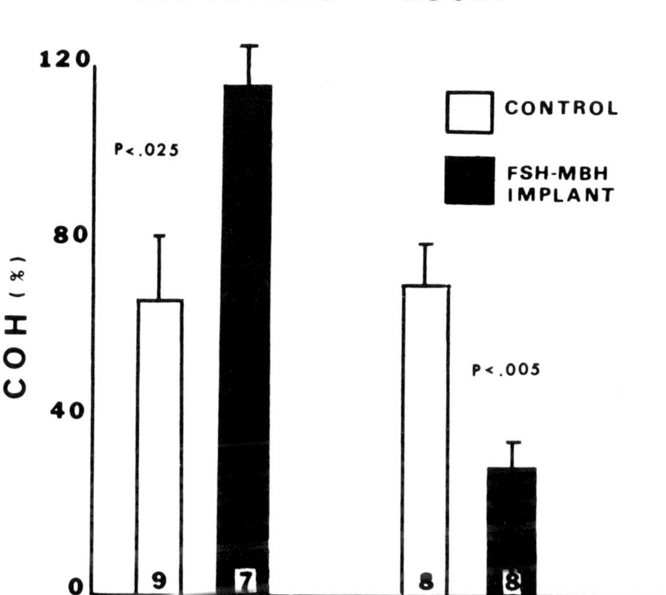

FIG. 27. Effect of medial basal hypothalamic implants of FSH (FSH-MBH) on compensatory ovarian hypertrophy (COH) of prepubertal and adult rats. Each 30-day-old rat received an injection with a 27-gauge needle, the tip of which contained ovine FSH diluted in cocoa butter (1:1). Each adult animal weighing 200 g received an injection with a 25-gauge needle with ovine FSH diluted in cocoa butter (1:1). All animals were killed 6 days after unilateral ovariectomy and implantation. Columns are means ±SE. Numbers inside columns indicate number of animals used. From Ramirez & Sawyer, unpublished.

adult female. Although concentrations of serum LH during infancy tend to be higher in the female, when compared with the male, the difference is not statistically significant. This is different in the rat (Goldman, Grazia, Kamberi, & Porter, 1971) and the lamb (Fostor, Lemons, Jaffe, and Niswender, 1972), in which the elevated levels of gonadotropin shortly after birth occur only in the female. At 4 to 6 months of age LH in the circulation of the infant monkey appears to decrease and become stabilized at levels that are comparable with those seen in the adult. We have performed a preliminary experiment in which infant monkeys (2 males and 2 females) were castrated within the first month of life, during the period when both sexes have high levels of gonadotropins. If a castration response should exist at this early age, one would expect the elevated levels of gonadotropins either to be maintained or to increase further. However, the pituitary seems to be running on its own because, after removal of the gonads, the pattern of LH in the circulation of the castrated infants follows the same time-course in that it decreases in a manner similar to that in intact infants of both sexes. Replacement therapy—and this is very limited data on only 4 animals—performed by giving an implant of estradiol-17β indicates that we cannot knock the levels of LH down. So, we may have a peculiar situation very early in the life of the monkey as compared with the sheep, in that the monkey may not be able to respond either to negative feedback, as suggested by our preliminary studies, or to positive feedback as indicated by Dr. Dierschke. The difference between the two species in this regard is probably due to the state of physiological maturity attained during the first 1 to 2 years of life.

DR. GRUMBACH.   FSH and LH?

DR. FOSTER.   I am measuring only LH and not FSH.

DR. GRUMBACH.   Thank you, Dr. Foster. The point you raise about the sex specificity of the LH surge and the fact that the LH surge is modified in the testosterone-sterilized female rat is significant. However, at present, there is no evidence that the estrogen-induced LH surge in the female primate is sex-specific. Apart from clinical evidence which supports the contention that it is not, the data reported here by Dr. Kulin and some unpublished studies in our laboratory suggest that under the appropriate conditions estradiol can induce a rise in serum LH in the male. It would seem that the rodent differs significantly from man in the regulation of LH: in the primate androgen in the fetal or neonatal period does not appear to prevent the differentiation of the positive feedback mechanism, as evidenced by the capacity of estrogen to evoke an LH surge.

DR. SWERDLOFF.   Positive feedback is complicated to study because of the associated negative feedback that we are trying to separate. When we look at positive feedback and try to compare immature and mature females of any species, we should look at a broad dose range and at various times. Dr. Dierschke, do you have any information on what a dose range of response was like in primates with regard to estradiol benzoate administration?

DR. DIERSCHKE.   In the immature females we injected estradiol benzoate in doses of 7, 42, and 694 μg/kg; none of these regimens evoked a positive feedback response. The lowest dose was also ineffective when administered to adult females during the follicular phase of the menstrual cycle, whereas larger amounts of estradiol, effecting increments in plasma estradiol concentrations of 100 pg/ml or more for 36 to 42 hours, uniformly elicited LH surges in adult animals (Yamaji, Dierschke, Hotchkiss, Bhattacharya, Surve, & Knobil, 1971; Karsch, Weick, Butler, Dierschke, Krey, Weiss, Hotchkiss, Yamaji, & Knobil, 1972). In regard to the male there is little evidence for the existence of a positive feedback system for gonadotropin secretion which responds to estrogen in males of any species. We agree that intact male monkeys, whether immature or adult, will not release LH when challenged with 42 or 694 μg/kg estradiol. In another experimental approach, however, which utilized adult castrated males, we suppressed the chronically elevated plasma concentrations of LH to levels consistent with those observed in intact animals by the use of estrogen-containing implants and then superimposed an injection of 42 μg/kg estradiol benzoate. The resultant LH surges were identical with those that occurred in adult ovariectomized females treated in a similar manner (Karsch et al, in press).

Dr. Grumbach.   In the castrate males did the LH surge which followed exhibition of estrogen exceed the high basal gonadotropin levels in these animals?

Dr. Dierschke.   The maximal LH surge levels exceeded the basal gonadectomized levels.

Dr. Steele.   Some experiments which illustrate in a longitudinal study the negative feedback effects of estrogen on gonadotropin secretion in the immature rat were conduced in conjunction with Dr. Judith Weisz. The standard was provided by Dr. Reichert and the antiserum by Drs. Niswender and Midgley. The overall approach was to interrupt the hypothalamic-pituitary-gonadal axis by ovariectomy and substitute, for the ovary, a constant source of estradiol in the form of a constant infusion. The animals were ovariectomized at 19 days of age, and catheters were inserted a week later. The infusion was interrupted for a period of about 10 minutes each day while blood was withdrawn for plasma LH determinations. The day following the initiation of estradiol infusion the LH levels were at concentrations found in castrates. Within 72 hours after the initiation of the infusion, the gonadotropin levels were suppressed to intact adult values. In the animals in which the catheters remained patent for a week or more vaginal opening was induced by the infused estradiol. In some of these animals vaginal opening was followed by a rise in plasma LH concentration even though the dose of estradiol was adjusted for increases in body weight and maintained throughout the experiment. In the adult rats which were castrated following puberty this same dose was no longer effective, and doses 4 times the dose which was effective in suppressing plasma LH in immature rats were required to suppress LH values to intact levels in the adult rats. We interpret these findings as evidence that a decrease in negative feedback sensitivity occurs at the approximate time at which intact littermates experience their first ovulation. The doses utilized in this study were considered physiological since, in these rats, the vagina opened at approximately the same age as in intact littermates, and the vagina was not fully cornified. We then carried these experiments further because studies by Ramirez and Sawyer (1965) have shown that estradiol promotes precocious puberty. If a decrease in sensitivity of the negative feedback system is important to the process of sexual maturation, stimuli that promote precocious puberty should also promote an earlier occurrence of the change in negative feedback sensitivity. If immature rats are infused with double the minimal dose of estradiol effective in suppressing serum LH in the ovariectomized prepubertal rat to values found in the intact adult, then by day 3 of infusion LH concentrations are suppressed. Immediately thereafter there is a rise in gonadotropin secretion, and from then on the LH values fluctuate between intact and castrate levels of LH. We interpret this finding to be indicative that estrogen can promote not only an earlier onset of the decrease in negative feedback sensitivity but also precocious puberty. Therefore the decrease in negative feedback sensitivity, as well as the onset of puberty, probably occurs as a result of estrogen stimulation. These data help to explain the discrepancy between results in monkeys and humans, compared with those in the rat with respect to positive feedback. As the immature rat approaches puberty estrogen will mature the feedback system so that the observed positive feedback is in response to a stimulus applied to a mature hypothalamic-pituitary-gonadal system, whereas in the monkey and human the estradiol given prior to puberty is given to an immature animal and is not sufficient to mature the hypothalamic-pituitary-gonadal axis. Positive feedback, in response to estradiol administration in the immature rat, is found only around the age at which the animal normally becomes sexually mature (Ying & Greep, 1971). Perhaps, if larger doses of estradiol administered for longer periods of time were given to monkeys or infants, one might see a positive feedback effect.

DR. DONOVAN.   I would like to urge caution in equating estradiol with the estrogen produced by the infant ovary of the rat. Donovan and O'Keefe (1966) were able to show that the ovarian product causing growth of the uterus during infancy was not destroyed in the liver, although estradiol was metabolized by that organ. Hence it seems unlikely that estradiol is responsible for all the estrogenic effects of the infantile ovary.

DR. VAN WYK.   Clinical observations indicate that exposure to androgens as well as to estrogens tends to advance the onset of true puberty. This is very clearly seen in the case of masculinizing adrenal tumors in either sex. If the bone age has been sufficiently advanced by the tumor, true isosexual development will occur precociously when the tumor is removed. Similarly, this sometimes happens following treatment with exogenous androgenic steroids. Some years ago Wilkins and Cara (1954) showed that, following the institution of cortisone treatment in virilizing adrenal hyperplasia, rapid testicular maturation occurred precociously in boys and menstruation precociously in girls if the bone age were sufficiently advanced. Such observations may be pertinent when trying to explain why the female normally has an earlier puberty and also is more prone to sexual precocity than the male. At all ages during childhood the skeletal age is more advanced in the female than in the male. It is my guess that this sexual difference will ultimately be found attributable to the priming effect of the sex steroids elaborated by the prepubescent ovary and testis, respectively. Throughout the prepubescent period the testes histologically undergo very little development and probably secrete only small quantities of biologically active steroids. On the contrary, throughout childhood ovaries undergo significant follicular development and involution. This cellular activity is in all probability accompanied by the secretion of small but significant quantities of biologically active estrogens (Potter, 1963). Ramirez and Sawyer (1965) have shown that exposure to estrogens accelerates the onset of true puberty in the rat. Thus the difference between the two sexes in the timing of puberty (as with other aspects of sex differentiation) is ultimately determined by whether the primitive gonad differentiates as a testis or an ovary.

Dr. Frasier.   A couple of points may be related: (1) the maturational changes that occur during puberty may be discontinuous rather than continuous. In collaboration with Drs. Odell and Horton we followed a group of boys for 4 years. Samples were obtained as frequently as every month and no less frequently than every 6 months. We found that in stages 2 and 3 of puberty there were wide fluctuations in the plasma concentrations of FSH, LH, and testosterone. While increased quantities of (presumed) releasing factors, gonadotropins, and testosterone are produced at one time during early puberty, the levels may return to the prepubertal range and rise again. Although the trend was, as shown in Dr. Faiman's longitudinal data, ever upward and onward, the rise in gonadotropin and testosterone concentration is discontinuous over time. (2) Gonadal steroids may amplify the maturational changes in the hypothalamus. We studied a patient with congenital virilizing adrenal hyperplasia from the time he was first treated at age 6. Bone age was advanced to 13 years. Prior to therapy plasma testosterone concentration was 350 ng/ml and LH and FSH were suppressed. Seventy-two hours after beginning hydrocortisone therapy, the plasma testosterone concentration was 20 ng/100 ml. By the end of 1 week LH and FSH concentrations were in the range observed in normal adult males. Four months after beginning treatment the testes began to enlarge, the plasma testosterone concentration rose to the range for midpuberty, and gonadotropin concentrations were also in the midpubertal range. It would appear that chronic exposure of the hypothalamus to elevated concentrations of sex steroids (testosterone is the only one we measured) resulted in precocious maturation of the hypothalamus, with the result that true precocious puberty was observed when sex steroid production was depressed. Although this clinical situation is unphysiologic, these observations suggest that the discontinuous elaboration of plasma testosterone observed in early male puberty may contribute to hypothalamic maturation.

Dr. Resko.   This is interesting because a delayed puberty occurs if female rhesus monkeys are exposed to androgen prenatally (Goy & Resko, 1972). The female offspring of pregnant rhesus monkeys treated with approximately 10 mg testosterone propionate from day 40 to 80 of pregnancy reached menarche at 1150 days (median) compared with 904 days in untreated controls. In this species it appears that prenatal androgen has something to do with the timing of the onset of puberty; this agrees with the fact that males have a delayed puberty compared with females.

Dr. Paulsen.   Dr. Lawson Wilkins showed that bone age rather than somatic changes correlates more closely with degree of pubertal maturation, particularly with regard to treating congenital adrenal cortical hyperplasia with steroid suppression. This observation also holds true when we treat males who have idopathic delayed puberty with hCG or testosterone. In other words, somatic changes may have progressed to the point at which the patient could be classified as being in stage 2 while bone age lags behind and the response to clomiphene administration remains prepubertal, i.e., "suppressive" rather than "stimulatory."

DR. FRASIER.   Although the onset of puberty correlates well with epiphyseal maturation (bone age), the epiphyses are not producing gonadotropin releasing factor. Bone age reflects only the physiological age of that organ. The physiological age of the hypothalamus is the determining factor in the onset of puberty. Prolonged exposure to sex steroids in our patient may have advanced hypothalamic age and bone age concurrently.

DR. GRUMBACH.   There are two issues here: one is the mechanism and the second is the age of onset of puberty. The timing correlates with bone age. This is well illustrated by the relation between bone age and menarche. We are interested in testing the hypothesis that the pubertal-type LH response to LRF correlates well with bone age. Perhaps Dr. Tanner would comment on factors affecting the time of onset of puberty.

DR. TANNER.   We have recent data in which we relate the events of breast development, pubic-hair development, and bone age, and theer is much independence among them. You are absolutely right in implying that bone age is the one most closely related to menarche. Menarche, surprisingly, is not related to breast development.

REFERENCES

Donovan, B. T. & O'Keefe, M. C. (1966). Liver and feedback action of ovarian hormones in the immature rat. *J. Endocrinol.* **34,** 469–478.

Donovan, B. T., O'Keefe, M. C., & O'Keefe, H. T. (1967). Intrasplenic implants of oestradiol and uterine growth in infantile and pubertal rats. *J. Endocrinol.* **37,** 93–98.

Foster, D. L., Lemons, J. A., Jaffe, R. B., and Niswender, G. D. (1972). *Fourth International Congress of Endocrinology,* Washington, D.C., 1972, p. 101 (Abstract).

Goldman, B. D., Grazia, Y. R., Kamberi, I. A., & Porter, J. C. (1971). Serum gonadotropin concentrations in intact and castrated neonatal rats. *Endocrinology* **85,** 133–143.

Goy, R. W. & Resko, J. A. (1972). Gonadal hormones and behavior of normal and pseudohermaphroditic nonhuman female primates. *Rec. Progr. Hormone Res.* **28,** 707–733.

Kaplan, S. L., Grumbach, M. M., & Shepard, T. H. (1972). Ontogenesis of human retal hormones. I. Growth hormone and insulin. *J. Clin. Invest.* **51,** 3080–3093.

Karsch, F. J., Dierschke, D. J., & Knobil, E. (1972). Sexual differentiation of pituitary function. Apparent difference between primates and rodents. *Science.* In press.

Karsch, F. J., Weick, R. F., Butler, W. R., Dierschke, D. J., Krey, L. C., Weiss, G.,

Hotchkiss, J., Yamaji, T., & Knobil, E. (1972). Induced LH surges in the rhesus monkey: strength-duration characteristics of the estrogen stimulus. *Endocrinology*. In press.

Liu, N., Grumbach, M. M., de Napoli, R. A., & Morishima, A. (1965). Prevalence of encephalographic abnormalities in idiopathic precocious puberty and premature pubarche: Bearing on pathogenesis and neuroendocrine regulation of puberty. *J. Clin. Endocrinol,* **25**, 1296–1308.

Potter, E. (1963). The ovary in infancy and childhood. In *The Ovary,* (H. G. Grady & D. E. Smith, Eds.), Williams & Wilkins, Baltimore, pp. 11–23.

Ramirez, V. D. (1971). Sex and the brain. In *Steroid Hormones and Brain Function,* (C. H. Sawyer, Ed.), U. of California Press, Berkeley, California.

Ramirez, V. D. & Sawyer, C. H. (1965). Advancement of puberty in the female rat by estrogen. *Endocrinology* **76**, 1158–1169.

Wilkins, L. & Cara, J. (1954). Further studies on the treatment of congenital adrenal hyperplasia with cortisone. V. Effects of cortisone therapy on testicular development. *J. Clin. Endocrinol.* **14**, 287.

Yamaji, T., Dierschke, D. J., Hotchkiss, J., Bhattacharya, A. N., Surve, A. N., & Knobil, E. (1971). Estrogen induction of LH release in the rhesus monkey. *Endocrinology* **89**, 1034–1041.

Ying, S-Y. & Greep, R. O. (1971). Effect of age of rat and dose of a single injection of estradiol benzoate (EB) on ovulation and the facilitation of ovulation by progesterone (P). *Endocrinology* **89**, 785–791.

7.

Extrahypothalamic Influences on Gonadotropin Regulation

R. A. GORSKI

One can suggest that the science of neuroendocrinology has reached its adolescent stage. Fron an infancy during which the participation of the brain in the regulation of the pituitary-gonadal axis was hardly realized neuroendocrinology has passed through the stage in its development when hypothalamic mechanisms were thought to be paramount. As it reaches maturity we recognize that the hypothalamus may represent little more than the final step or two in a complex network of control mechanisms. The

Abbreviations

DLF	Dorsal longitudinal fasciculus
EB	Estradiol benzoate
LH	Luteinizing hormone
MBH	Medial basal hypothalamus
MCHT	Medial cortico-hypothalamic tract
MFB	Medial forebrain bundle
GTH	Gonadotropic hormone
HPC	Hippocampus
POA	Preoptic area
ST	Stria terminalis
VAFP	Ventral Amygdalo-fugal Pathway
VTA	Ventral tegmental area

problems that must be faced to elucidate the extrahypothalamic control of gonadotropin secretion are recognized, but we do not yet quite know how to handle the matter. We shall consider several experimental approaches which have already provided some insight into the extrahypothalamic control of pituitary function. The focus will be on the rat in an attempt to avoid the confusion that possible species differences might impose on the formation of general concepts; anatomical and functional complexity, however, make formation of a general concept difficult.

THE HYPOTHALAMIC CONTROL OF GONADOTROPIC HORMONE (GTH) SECRETION

Any concept of the extrahypothalamic regulation of GTH secretion must take into account the probable mechanisms of hypothalamic control which presumably are altered by extrahypothalamic structures. The hypothalamus of the female rat exerts a dual control over GTH secretion, Fig. 1; for re-

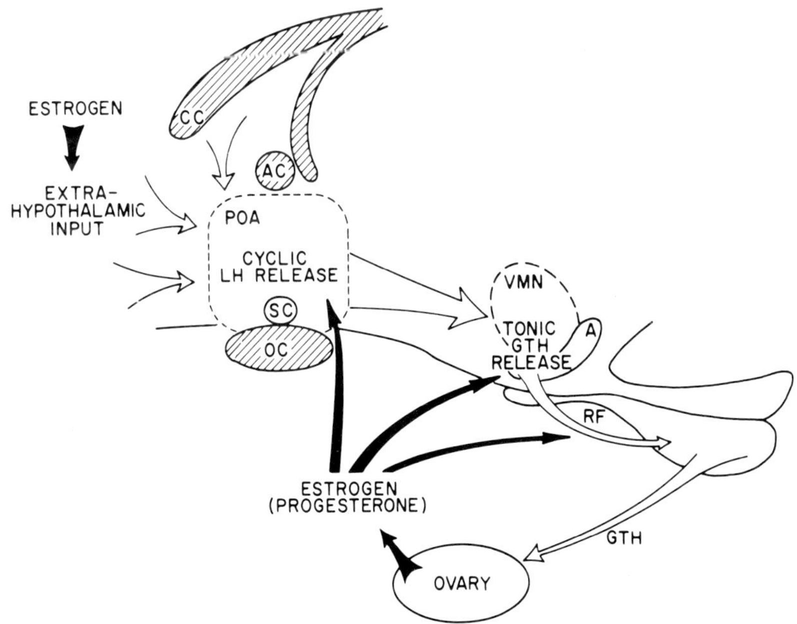

FIG. 1. The localization of the hypothalamic control of the secretion of LH in the normal female rat as projected on a schematic midsagittal view of the hypothalamus. A, arcuate nucleus; AC, anterior commissure; CC, corpus callosum; OC, optic chiasm; POA, preoptic area; SC, suprachiasmatic nucleus; VMN, ventromedial nucleus; and RF, releasing factor. Black arrows represent possible feedback action of ovarian steroids. Reprinted with permission from Gorski (1971).

views see Flerkó, 1966; Barraclough, 1967; Everett, 1969; Gorski, 1971).

The arcuate nucleus appears to be responsible for regulating the tonic secretion of GTH, whereas the preoptic-anterior hypothalamic area is indispensable for the phasic secretion of GTH responsible for ovulation. In the male rat the tonic GTH regulating system may be adequate for normal testicular function, and, in any case, the mechanisms for the phasic regulation of GTH are absent, apparently because of exposure of the brain to androgen during a specific period during development. The use of an ingeniously simple device, the Halász knife, has confirmed the general validity of this concept of hypothalamic function (Halász & Gorski, 1967; Halász, 1969). The effect of partial deafferentation of the medial basal hypothalamus (MBH) (Halász & Gorski, 1967), however, confirmed an earlier study of Everett (1964) which indicated that the neural substrate for ovulation occupied a rather diffuse area of the septo-preoptic-anterior hypothalamic area.

This observation questions the discrete localization of a cyclic release system for GTH, as depicted in Fig. 1. With the discovery that steroid receptor neurons are not restricted to the hypothalamus (Pfaff, 1968; Anderson & Greenwald, 1969; Stumpf, 1971), and the early accounts that limbic structures may influence GTH secretion, it became clear that ovulation is subject to extrahypothalamic control and that gonadal steroids may act on these extrahypothalamic structures. Spontaneous ovulation can occur, however, after neural afferents that reach the preoptic area (POA) are severed (Köves & Halász, 1970; Kaasjager, Woodbury, van Dieten, & van Rees, 1971). The fact that mortality was very high raises some doubt about the significance of this observation. Although the histological localization of these cuts was carefully checked in surviving animals, one cannot exclude the possibility that in the remaining 10 per cent of the total number the functional pathways were, because of biological variation, sufficiently displaced from the typical animal that survival and spontaneous ovulation were possible. There is an additional criticism of these studies. Although deafferentation experiments demonstrated that input into the hypothalamus from posterior is unimportant (Halász & Gorski, 1967), these pathways were intact after anterior deafferentation of the POA. It may be that critical afferent input is still able to reach the POA or MBH in these animals. Exclusive of these possible reservations, the studies suggest that the POA can autonomously support ovulation.

Recent evidence indicates that in the rat a direct retino-hypothalamic projection to the POA exists (Moore, Karapas, & Lenn, 1971) and is considered to be a site of the facilitative feedback of estrogen (Smith & Davidson, 1968). Thus the POA can apparently receive and may integrate two important environmental factors, photoperiod and plasma steroid titers.

This makes the hypothesis that the POA can initiate ovulation even more reasonable. However, does the possibility that the POA can autonomously control ovulation indicate that it normally does so? The purpose of this chapter is to review the experimental data that suggest that the answer to this question is no.

EXTRAHYPOTHALAMIC CONTROL OF GTH SECRETION IN THE ADULT RAT

The technique of stimulation has been used most effectively to demonstrate that several neural sites certainly have the potential to influence GTH secretion in the rat. It must be emphasized, however, that the nature of an exogenous stimulus can be a critical variable. As Everett and Radford (1961) demonstrated, electrical stimuli applied through a steel electrode can deposit iron which acts as an irritative stimulus for a period more prolonged than the actual application of current. On the other hand, the appropriate selection of parameters of stimulation can produce an electrochemical or a purely electrical stimulus (Terasawa & Sawyer, 1969).

On the basis of stimulation studies the amygdala appears to be facilitatory for GTH release. Bunn and Everett (1957) induced ovulation in conscious rats in which persistent estrous had been induced by constant exposure to light by stimulating the amygdala at currents just less than those that would induce convulsions. In similarly prepared animals Velasco & Taleisnik (1969a) found that electrochemical stimulation of the medial amygdala would induce ovulation unless the stria terminalis (ST), a main efferent pathway from the amygdala to the hypothalamus, was transected (Table 1). Carbachol infusion into either the medial or lateral amygdala was also effective; even though convulsions were induced, chemical stimulation of the basolateral complex of the amygdala did not induce ovulation if the ST was transected. Following transection of the ventral amygdalofugal pathway (VAFP) from the lateral amygdala to the hypothalamus, carbachol stimulation of the basolateral complex still induced ovulation. Electrochemical stimulation of the medial amygdala also induced ovulation in cycling rats in which spontaneous ovulation was blocked by atropine or reserpine and induced an increase in plasma LH in ovariectomized animals in which GTH secretion was suppressed by estrogen treatment. The specificity of these responses to stimulation should be questioned, however. Carbachol infusion was accompanied by convulsions, and it is possible that large parameter electrochemical stimulation induced seizure activity. Although apparently transmitted via the ST, such seizure activity could activate the MBH nonspecifically. Fortunately lesion studies in general support these observations as specific.

TABLE 1.   Ovulation induced by electrochemical or chemical stimulation of the amygdala of persistent estrous rats in continuous light[a]

Type of stimulation	Site of stimulation	Efferent pathways	Incidence of ovulation	
			Number ovulated per number stimulated	Per cent
Electrochemical	Medial nucleus	Intact	10/14	71
	Medial nucleus	ST, damaged[b]	0/8	0
	Medial nucleus	ST, transected	0/9	0
	Basolateral complex	Intact	2/12	17
Chemical (Carbachol)	Medial nucleus	Intact	9/11	82
	Basolateral complex	Intact	8/11	73
	Basolateral complex	ST, transected	0/7	0
	Basolateral complex	VAFP, transected	5/8	63

[a] Data from Velasco & Taleisnik, 1969a
[b] By electrode tract.

Similar parameters of electrochemical stimulation have been applied to the hippocampus (HPC) but with opposite results (Velasco & Taleisnik, 1969b). When applied just before the critical period for LH release in the proestrous rat or just before the activation of the amygdala or POA in persistent-estrous rats at parameters normally effective in inducing ovulation, stimulation of the ventral HPC blocked spontaneous and induced ovulation, respectively (Table 2). Although electrochemical stimulation of both the dorsal and ventral HPC was effective in suppressing LH release, that of the latter was more effective. Ventral HPC stimulation also blocked the phasic release of LH facilitated by progesterone injection in proestrous rats and the tonic secretion of LH in the ovariectomized rat, provided that a small amount of estradiol benzoate (EB) had been administered, apparently to sensitize the brain. This seemingly minor proviso is actually an important observation. Although a massive tissue-destroying stimulus is applied, the immediate hormonal environment is critical for some component of the neuroendocrine response. Without the injection of EB, these authors would have concluded that HPC stimulation cannot suppress the tonic secretion of LH.

Transection of the medial corticohypothalamic tract (MCHT), a direct pathway between the HPC and the MBH, markedly reduced the effective-

TABLE 2. Effect of electrochemical stimulation of the hippocampus (HPC) on spontaneous (A) or induced (B) ovulation[a]

| | | Incidence of ovulation | |
| | | | |
Site of stimulation	Medial cortico-hypothalamic tract	Number ovulated per number stimulated	Per cent
A. Stimulated at 12 to 12:45 pm on day of proestrus:			
Sham-ventral HPC	Intact	6/6	100
Ventral HPC	Intact	5/24	21
Ventral HPC	Transected	7/10	70
Ventral HPC	Physiological block by picrotoxin	10/12	83
Dorsal HPC	Intact	6/10	60

B. Stimulated in persistent-estrous rats under constant light 5 minutes before hypothalamic or amygdaloid stimulation:

Site of ovulation-inducing stimulation	Ventral hippocampal stimulation		
Medial amygdaloid nucleus.	No	10/14	71
Medial amygdaloid nucleus	Yes	1/6	17
Preoptic area	No	6/7	86
Preoptic area	Yes	3/10	30

[a] Data from Velasco & Taleisnik, 1969b

ness of stimulation of the HPC in suppressing spontaneous ovulation (Velasco & Taleisnik, 1969b). Further support for the view that the HPC can inhibit LH secretions comes from the observation that picrotoxin, an agent that blocks inhibitory synapses, also blocks the inhibition of ovulation by stimulation of the HPC (Table 2). The inhibitory influence on LH secretion of ventral HPC input via the MCHT has been confirmed by Gallo, Johnson, Goldman, Whitmoyer, and Sawyer, 1971.

Carrer and Taleisnik (1970; 1972) demonstrated both the diversity of the extrahypothalamic structures capable of influencing GTH secretion, at least on electrochemical activation and, importantly, the extreme complexity of the possible interrelation between these structures and the hypothalamus. In a remarkable series of experiments these investigators mapped the mesencephalon with respect to its potential influence on GTH secretion. Electrochemical stimulation of the medial raphe nuclei, the periaqueductal gray of the rostral midbrain or, most effectively, of the ventral tegmental area (VTA) extending from the caudal border of the mammillary body just rostral to the interpeduncular nucleus blocked spontaneous ovulation when applied just before the proestrus critical period (Table 3A; Carrer & Taleisnik, 1970). That the inhibition of ovulation was not the result of lesions produced by the electrochemical stimulation was established by the finding that cathodal lesions of the VTA did not interfere with ovulation. The electrochemical stimulation which blocked ovulation also inhibited the phasic release of LH facilitated by progesterone injection in either the spontaneously proestrous rat or the ovariectomized animal in which GTH secretion was first suppressed with EB. For the actual sites of stimulation, both positive and negative, the reader should consult the original papers.

In an extension of this study Carrer and Taleisnik (1972) analyzed the probable pathways by which electrochemical stimulation of these areas can inhibit GTH release (Table 3B). Stimulation of the dorsal longitudinal fasciculus (DLF), a pathway interconnecting the medial hypothalamus and

TABLE 3. Effect of mesencephalic electrochemical stimulation in proestrous rats on spontaneous ovulation[a]

	Incidence of ovulation	
Site of stimulation	Number ovulated per number stimulated	Per cent
A.		
Ventral tegmental area	10/27	37
Medial raphe nucleus	10/25	40
Periaqueductal gray	12/23	51
Lateral reticular formation	15/16	94
Dorsal tegmentum	8/10	80
Superior colliculus	17/18	94
B.		
Dorsal longitudinal fasciculus		
caudal	2/14	14
rostral	0/5	0
Medial forebrain bundle		
at level of hypothalamus	6/23	26
at level of preoptic area	18/18	100
Premammillary area	9/10	90
Superior colliculus	15/15	100
None	15/15	100

[a] Data from Carrer & Taleisnik, 1970 (A), 1972 (B).

the central gray, or of the medial forebrain bundle (MFB) caudal to the POA also blocked spontaneous ovulation. (The MFB is an extensive pathway interconnecting olfactory systems, hypothalamus, and the midbrain.) The DLF and MFB represent, at least in part, the pathways by which electrochemical stimulation of the VTA inhibits ovulation, since transection of these pathways blocked the inhibitory effect of VTA stimulation (Table 4). The fact that the inhibitory effect of VTA stimulation was also blocked by transection of the MCHT indicates that the HPC may play a role in this response.

The inhibition of ovulation produced by direct electrochemical stimulation of the DLF, however, was not prevented by transection of the MFB or the MCHT, nor did DLF or MCHT transection prevent the inhibition of ovulation induced by stimulation of the MFB at the level of the posterior

TABLE 4.   Effect of transecting neural pathways to the hypothalamus on the inhibition of spontaneous ovulation induced by electrochemical stimulation of the proestrous rat[a]

		Incidence of ovulation	
Site of stimulation	Transected pathways	Number ovulated per number stimulated	Per cent
Ventral tegmental area		16/40	40
	Dorsal longitudinal fasciculus	16/19	84
	Medial forebrain bundle	11/12	92
	Medial corticohypothalamic tract	6/6	100
	Stria terminalis	5/14	35
Dorsal longitudinal fasciculus		2/14	14
	Medial forebrain bundle	2/6	33
	Medial corticohypothalamic tract	1/6	16
Medial forebrain bundle		6/23	26
	Dorsal longitudinal fasciculus	4/7	57
	Medial corticohypothalamic tract	1/6	16
	Both dorsal longitudinal fasciculus and medial corticohypothalamic tract	5/5	100

[a] Data from Carrer & Taleisnik, 1972.

hypothalamus. Interestingly, when *both* the DLF and MCHT were transected, MFB stimulation was without effect on ovulation. According to these investigators, the MFB represents a pathway by which the midbrain and HPC are related, yet each has a more direct route to the basal hypothalamus, the DLF and MCHT, respectively.

These results illustrate one of the difficulties in interpreting the results of stimulation experiments. Although the same parameters were used for stimulus, the effect of stimulating the VTA, but not the DLF, was prevented by transection of either the MFB or MCHT. Carrer and Taleisnik (1972) suggest that this difference could be the result of a difference in cell density between the loosely organized VTA and the more compact fiber system, the DLF. In addition to the anatomical geometry and connectivity of the region stimulated, the results presumably vary with the intensity, frequency, and duration of stimulation, the depth of anesthesia and the immediate hormonal environment.

Carrer and Taleisnik (1970) also stimulated the dorsal mesencephalic tegmentum, lateral and inferior to the central gray, but found no *inhibition* of spontaneous ovulation. However, when this region (but not the VTA) was stimulated electrochemically in the persistent-estrous rat under constant illumination, ovulation was *induced*. Furthermore, such stimulation produced a rapid but brief rise in plasma LH in gonadectomized animals in which GTH secretion was suppressed by EB. Thus the midbrain can inhibit or facilitate GTH release, depending on the site stimulated.

These authors call attention to the possibility that the sites of electrochemical stimulation of the midbrain which inhibit or facilitate GTH release correlate in general with the localization of serotoninergic and noradrenergic neurons, respectively. It must be emphasized that the monoamines may play a critical role in the regulation of neuroendocrine function (for review see Fuxe & Hökfelt, 1970; Coppola, 1971; Kordon, 1971; Wurtman, 1971a). Labhsetwar (1971), for example, proposed that antagonistic serotoninergic and catecholaminergic systems participate in the regulation of ovulation. It has been clearly demonstrated that the midbrain gives rise to anatomically complex ascending monoaminergic pathways (Anden, Dahlstrom, Fuxe, Larsson, Olson, & Ungerstedt, 1966; Ungerstedt, 1971). Figure 2 illustrates the ascending noradrenergic pathway as an example. Although alterations in the aminergic input to the basal hypothalamus may be the mechanism by which stimulation of extrahypothalamic structures modify GTH secretion, further discussion of this topic is beyond the scope of this chapter.

The cerebral cortex may also participate in the regulation of GTH secretion since the injection of hypertonic saline into the cortex induces a release of LH as measured by ovarian ascorbic acid depletion in the

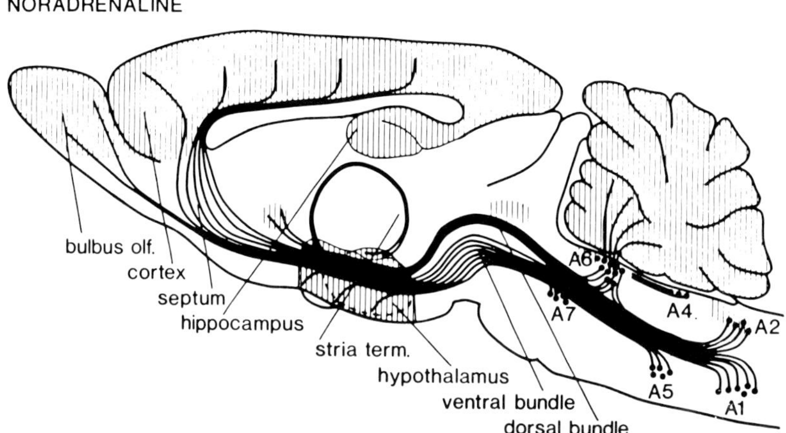

FIG. 2. Sagittal projection of the ascending noradrenergic pathways in the rat brain. The striped areas indicate the major nerve terminal areas. Reprinted with permission from Ungerstedt (1971).

same animal (Taleisnik, Caligaris, & de Olmos, 1962). Whether the release of LH was induced by cortical stimulation or by suppression of cortical activity by the phenomenon of spreading depression is unknown. If the latter is true, one could consider that the effect of saline injection represents a functional lesion of the cortex.

Other experiments however, show more clearly that lesions of extra-hypothalamic structures alter GTH secretion. Lawton and Sawyer (1970) reported that the cortical nucleus of the amygdala is inhibitory to LH secretion, for its destruction in ovariectomized rats increases plasma LH levels significantly above those of ovariectomized controls. Although this observation conflicts with the stimulatory effect of the amygdala described, it could be that during the production of the lesion iron was deposited and stimulated LH release. Lawton and Sawyer, however, indicated that sham procedures which damaged the ST produced a similar increase in LH secretion and question that the irritative stimulus of iron deposition can persist for weeks. Eleftheriou, Church, Zolovick, Norman, and Pattison (1969) reported that electrocoagulation of the basolateral amygdala also led to an increased secretion of LH in male rats. On the other hand, Smith and Lawton (1972) have shown that discrete lesions of the cortical nucleus of the amygdala or of the ST, which do not alter ovulation or vaginal cycles, completely inhibit ovarian compensatory hypertrophy.

The potential role of the amygdala and the HPC in the regulation of ovulation has been further clarified by studies in which these structures have been effectively "lesioned" by transection of their efferent pathways to the hypothalamus (Table 5). Transection of the ST, anterior deafferentation, or electrocoagulation of the medial amygdala by means of a platinum electrode inhibited ovulation, although transection of the MCHT on the morning of proestrus did not interfere with ovulation (Velasco & Taleisnik, 1971). This inhibition was only temporary, and all rats except those with the anterior deafferentation resumed normal ovulatory cycles. Halász and Gorski (1967) observed that a small anterior deafferentation would block ovulation acutely but not chronically and interpreted these results in terms of transient trauma to intact components of the POA. The results of ST transection indicate that the abrupt interruption of potentially facilitative stimuli from the amygdala also prevents ovulation. The POA system, however, has the ability to adjust by some mechanism so that input via the ST is no longer essential for ovulation.

Velasco and Taleisnik (1971) also studied the ability of gonadal steroids to induce ovulation in spontaneously ovulating rats with long-term transection of the ST. In 4-day cycling rats the cycle was extended to 5 days by an injection of progesterone on the first day of diestrus; when 20 μg EB was injected on the second day of the artificial cycle, ovulation was induced 1 day earlier, even though the ST was cut (Table 6). Thus for EB-induced ovulation input from the amygdala is not necessary. Although

TABLE 5.   Effect on spontaneous ovulation immediately (acute) or more than one month (chronic) after transection of limbic-hypothalamic connections or destruction of the medial amygdala nucleus[a]

| | Incidence of ovulation | | | |
| | Acute | | Chronic | |
Treatment	Number ovulated per number stimulated	Per cent	Number ovulated per number stimulated	Per cent
None	9/10	90	—	—
Anterior deafferentation	0/6	0	0/6	0
Preoptic roof section	0/6	0	8/10	80
Medial corticohypothalamic tract section	6/7	86	6/6	100
Stria terminalis section	0/19	0	16/19	84
Medial amygdaloid lesions	0/7	0	—	—
Control lesions	33/37	89	19/20	95

[a] Data from Velasco and Taleisnik, 1971.

TABLE 6.   Effect of transection of limbic-hypothalamic connections on the induction of ovulation by gonadal steroids during an artificial 5-day cycle[a]

Steroid used to induce ovulation	Preparation	Incidence of ovulation	
		Number ovulated per number injected	Per cent
Estradiol benzoate	Intact	6/8	75
	Stria terminalis cut	5/6	83
Progesterone	Intact	9/10	90
	Stria terminalis cut	3/11	27
	Stria cut plus picrotoxin	6/8	75
	Stria cut plus preoptic roof section	6/8	75

[a] Data from Velasco and Taleisnik, 1971

a second injection of progesterone on the third day of diestrus also induced precocious ovulation (Everett, 1961), progesterone was not effective in animals with the transected ST. The lack of ovulation in these animals is apparently due to the unbalanced inhibitory influence of the HPC, since progesterone can induce ovulation in similar animals if the fornix is also transected (preoptic roof section) or if the animals are injected with picrotoxin (Velasco & Taleisnik, 1971). The results of these experiments, therefore, are consistent with the view that the amygdala and the HPC transmit facilitative and inhibitory inputs to the hypothalamus which may normally counterbalance one another.

The close interrelationship between extrahypothalamic structures and hypothalamic GTH function has also been documented by recording experiments. Terasawa and Timiras (1968a) measured the local seizure threshold for the dorsal HPC and amygdala throughout the estrous cycle. The seizure threshold for the HPC decreased between the mornings of proestrus and estrus, whereas that of the lateral amygdala showed a reciprocal change (Fig. 3). The seizure threshold of the medial amygdala, however, decreased markedly just before the morning of proestrus.

We have already reviewed the experimental evidence that demonstrates that limbic structures modulate GTH secretion; these data suggest that gonadal hormones in turn modulate the excitability of these structures, although cause and effect relationships have yet to be determined. If limbic structures play an important role in the regulation of GTH secretion, it is reasonable to predict that they will be directly or indirectly "informed" of the stage of the estrous cycle. Finally, Kawakami and Kubo (1971) have

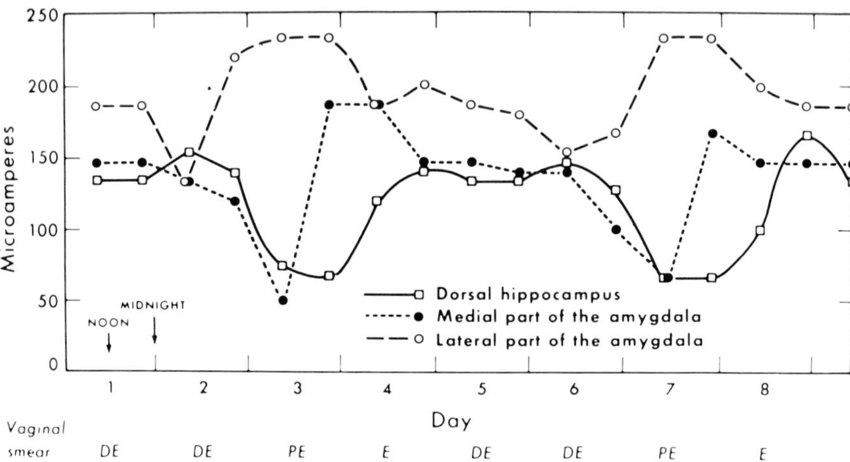

FIG. 3. Comparison of localized seizure threshold curves for 3 portions of the limbic system during 2 consecutive estrous cycles. Data from the hippocampus and lateral amygdala from one rat; data for medial amygdala from another rat. DE, diestrus; PE, proestrus; E, estrus. Reprinted with permission from Terasawa & Timiras (1968a).

demonstrated the existence of complex and reciprocal interrelations of the amygdala, HPC, and midbrain on the electrical activity of single hypothalamic neurons.

In summary, complex neural pathways, which have been demonstrated anatomically, electrophysiologically, and functionally, interconnect various extrahypothalamic structures. On the basis of stimulation studies in the adult the amygdala appears to exert a facilitative influence on the phasic and tonic secretion of LH, whereas the HPC appears to be inhibitory. In the midbrain stimulation studies reveal the existence of both inhibitory (VTA, DLF, MFB) and facilitative (dorsal tegmentum) areas and pathways. Lesions of the cortical or basolateral nuclei of the amygdala increase the tonic secretion of LH, and the former also inhibit ovarian compensatory hypertrophy. On the other hand, lesions of the amygdala and HPC have not been observed to influence spontaneous ovulation in the long term, whereas destruction of the amygdala or transection of the ST does block ovulation acutely.

These results support the general view that the many areas that influence GTH secretion act by modulating GTH controlling mechanisms within the POA or basal hypothalamus. In the adult rat these extrahypothalamic structures represent a complex and highly interrelated series of facilitative and inhibitory influences which may be considered as a system of checks and balances to ensure the normal and appropriate regulation of reproductive endocrinology. It is also clear that extrahypothalamic structures influence the regulation of sexual behavior as well; for example, we have obtained evidence that the cerebral cortex exerts a tonic inhibitory influence on female sexual behavior (Clemens, Wallen, & Gorski. 1967) and also that progesterone may act within the mesencephalon to facilitate this behavior (Ross, Claybough, Clemens, & Gorski, 1971).

EXTRAHYPOTHALAMIC STRUCTURES AND PUBERTY

The fact that various extrahypothalamic structures exert opposing but appropriately balanced influences on the control of GTH release in the adult raises a germane question. Do these modulating influences play an important role in the inhibition of gonadal function before puberty or in the actual pubertal process? Although experimental data are limited, it is likely that extrahypothalamic neural structures do play such a role.

We reported that complete deafferentation of the basal hypothalamus, or anterior deafferentation, leads to precocious ovarian development and vaginal opening (Ramaley & Gorski, 1967). Although precocious ovulation is not produced, the surgical procedure itself prevents ovulation and suggests that the basal hypothalamus without its extrahypothalamic neural input reaches functional maturity early. Other studies indicate that the amygdala may specifically inhibit GTH secretion in the prepubertal rat, an inhibition which would be eliminated abruptly by deafferentation.

Although the amygdala in the adult rat facilitates ovulation, electrolytic lesions of the medial amygdala induce true precocious puberty (Elwers & Critchlow, 1960). This effect is not caused by irritation of surviving amygdaloid tissue by iron deposits, since stimulation of the corticomedial amygdala for 6 hours a day effectively delays vaginal opening (Bar-Sela & Critchlow, 1966). Similarly, destruction of the amygdala and pyriform cortex by suction results in the precocious appearance of the adult patterns of running activity in both male and female rats but does not alter postpubertal gonadal weight (Riss, Burstein, & Johnson, 1963). In regard to the possible role of the amygdala in puberty, it has been observed recently that the age at the time of surgery may be a critical variable. Lesions of the medial amygdala produced in the neonatal female rat markedly delay, rather than advance, vaginal opening (Relkin, 1971a). Although this appears to contradict the previous experiments, stimulation of the amygdala, while producing the lesion in the neonatal period, may profoundly delay the pubertal process independent of the actual destruction of the amygdala. Relkin (1971b) also reported a sex difference in the amygdala in the prepubertal rat because its destruction did not alter descent of the testes.

In the adult rat the evidence suggests that the HPC exerts an inhibitory influence on GTH secretion, but in the prepubertal rat the function of the HPC is less clear. Kling (1964) produced surprisingly large lesions merely by inserting a needle into the brain of the infant rat. Severe destruction of the dorsal HPC did not affect vaginal opening or ovarian weight, an observation that is not consistent with the inhibitory role of the HPC in the adult. A further suggestion that the HPC of the prepubertal rat may have a different function is the report of Riss et al (1963), who found that destruction of the HPC by suction applied at 1 week of age depressed gonadal weight and reduced running activity near the time of normal puberty in both males and females. Although these observations on running activity were not studied in relation to vaginal opening or gonadal histology, they also are not consistent with an inhibitory function of the HPC in the prepubertal rat.

Recently Kawakami and Terasawa (1972) subjected rats to electrical stimulation of various brain sites and measured both pituitary and plasma FSH and LH by RIA. Immediately after stimulation of the dorsal HPC of the 27-day-old rat both pituitary and plasma FSH increased, but no significant change in FSH was produced by stimulation of the medial amygdala. When the same stimulus was repeated in other animals for 3 consecutive days, HPC stimulation decreased pituitary FSH and did not change plasma FSH, whereas stimulation of the amygdala increased plasma FSH. These investigators reasoned that the increase in FSH secretion produced by the initial stimulation might have evoked estrogen secretion which in turn hastened sexual maturation (Ramirez & Sawyer, 1965). They reported that electrical stimulation of the HPC on day 27 advanced vaginal opening by 4 to 6 days; therefore they administered 2.5 μg EB to 26-day-old rats and on the initial stimulation of the HPC two days later failed to observe an increase in plasma FSH. No changes in serum LH were observed.

Although the significance of a very rapid and brief secretion (plasma FSH levels were not significantly different from control 30 minutes after HPC stimulation) is open to question, the confirmation of these experiments would support the interesting possibility that the nature of the influence of the amygdala and HPC on GTH secretion would reverse rather abruptly at puberty. Kawakami and Terasawa (1972) suggest that maturation of an HPC system which facilitates FSH secretion in the prepubertal rat leads to ovarian development and increased estrogen secretion. Under the influence of estrogen the amygdala would attain its adult role of facilitating GTH release, whereas the HPC would lose its stimulatory function. Terasawa and Timiras (1968b) reported that the threshold current necessary to induce local seizures in the medial amygdala and dorsal HPC changes in the immature rat with age. Amygdaloid threshold fell just before puberty, perhaps because of the action of endogenous estrogen; unfortunately, no clear change in HPC threshold could be detected, although there was a slight decrease at 30 days, well before puberty.

Because Kawakami and Terasawa (1972) did not demonstrate an increase in GTH secretion after stimulation of the amygdala of the prepubertal rat, their experiment is still consistent with the concept that the amygdala is predominantly inhibitory before puberty. If puberty does involve a reversal in the nature of the limbic influence on GTH secretion, it is not necessary to postulate a complete reversal of function. Although considerable experimental evidence indicates that the amygdala facilitates GTH release in the adult rat, the observations of Lawton and Sawyer (1970) and Eleftheriou et al (1969) demonstrate that the amygdala can still suppress GTH secretion in the adult. Sawyer (1972) has postulated the existence of two functional pools of neurons in the adult amygdala. The pubertal process may involve merely a change in the *predominant* functional role of the amygdala and/or the HPC.

THE PINEAL GLAND AND GTH SECRETION

So far this discussion has considered only the neural centers outside the hypothalamus which may influence GTH secretion and puberty. However, there is one additional major extrahypothalamic influence on gonadal function—the pineal gland. Because the literature on this gland is extensive, the reader is referred to several reviews that clearly establish the pineal as an important gland in endocrine physiology (Reiter & Fraschini, 1969; Wurtman, 1971b; Reiter, 1972a). For the present discussion the role of the pineal is reviewed very briefly in terms that have been applied to neural extrahypothalamic systems which influence GTH secretion, again in the rat.

The functional pathways of neural extrahypothalamic structures are complex and probably not fully described, yet are discrete neuroanatomical systems. Although the afferent pathway to the pineal is also discrete, the influence of the pineal on endocrine function is mediated by hormonal substances and is therefore diffuse. The afferent pathway to the pineal has been clearly, although not completely, defined. Visual input from the retina passes via the inferior accessory optic tract through the MFB to the rostral midbrain (Moore, Heller, Bhatnager, Wurtman, & Axelrod, 1968). From this region neural information is transmitted by still unknown pathways to the preganglionic neurons of the thoracic outflow of the sympathetic component of the autonomic nervous system, from which postganglionic fibers reach blood vessels of the meninges and ultimately the pineal

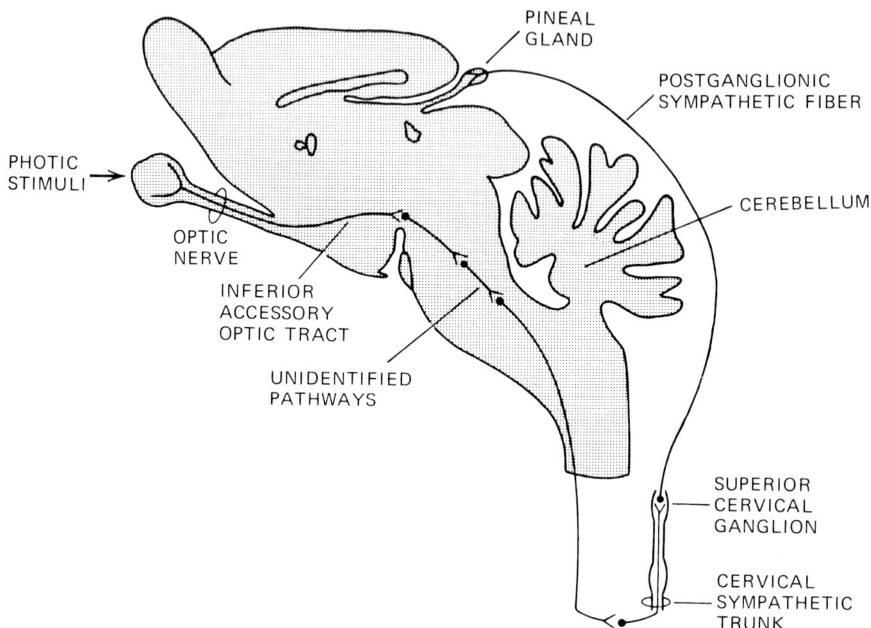

FIG. 4.   Neural afferent input from the retina to the pineal gland. See text for
discussion. Reprinted with permission from Reiter & Fraschini (1969).

(Fig. 4). Superior cervical ganglionectomy, which denervates the pineal,
is functionally comparable to pinealectomy (Moore & Rapport, 1971).
The unknown mesencephalic components of this circuitous path to the
pineal may prove to be significant for its function. Because the pineal
appears to be an additional regulatory influence on GTH secretion, it is
reasonable to predict that the neural extrahypothalamic systems which
modulate pituitary activity also modify pineal activity. No experiments
are known to have demonstrated a direct effect of amygdala or HPC
manipulation on pineal function, although, for example, if such influences
exist they may act at the level of the mesencephalic component of the
afferent pathway to the pineal.

The function of this pathway appears to be the modification of enzyme
activity within the gland so that its production and release of various
factors is altered. Although the precise identity of the active pineal factors
is not clearly established (Moszkowska, Kordon & Ebels, 1971) the compound *N*-acetyl-5-methoxytryptamine (melatonin) has been extensively
studied as a prototype of the pineal hormones. The site of action of melatonin is still under investigation. If one assumes that melatonin is secreted
into the blood, it could be delivered to the gonads, the pituitary, and at

least to some areas of the brain. It is also possible that melatonin is secreted directly into the cerebrospinal fluid, by which route it could reach effective sites in the brain at rather high concentration. Fraschini, Mess, and Martini (1968) reported that the implantation of crystalline melatonin or fragments of pineal tissue into the median eminence or lateral midbrain (but not into the pituitary) significantly reduced pituitary LH content in castrated male rats. Although this supports the view that melatonin acts centrally and, although the orientation of the present discussion is toward central mechanisms that regulate GTH secretion, the reader is cautioned to remember that in the experiments that follow the precise site of action of pineal factors is not established.

Two experimental techniques which have been used to elucidate the neural control of GTH secretion have counterparts applicable to study of the pineal. Pinealectomy may be considered equivalent to, if not more specific than, the electrolytic destruction of neural tissue. The production of lesions in neural tissue may stimulate adjacent tissues and destroy the neurons arising in as well as merely passing through the lesion. Removal of the circumscribed pineal is complete, and sham procedures can readily identify nonspecific responses to trauma. Nervous tissue can be activated by electrical, electrochemical. or chemical stimulation. The pineal gland may be stimulated physiologically by exposing an animal to short photoperiods. The effects of activation of the pineal may be approached by administering pineal extracts or purified factors, including melatonin. Although the influence of pineal substances in the electrical activity of the brain might be expected to yield valuable data, this approach has apparently not been used, nor has the possible feedback regulation of the pineal gland been investigated.

In the hamster the physiological role of the pineal has been defined most clearly. The male hamster exhibits a marked seasonal variation in testicular development, and during the winter months, when the photoperiod is short, the testes undergo marked atrophy unless the animals are pinealectomized (Czyba, Girod, & Durand, 1964; Reiter, 1972b). Although the role of the pineal gland has been studied extensively in hamsters exposed to an artificial ultrashort photoperiod (1 hour light/day) or after blinding (see Reiter, 1972a), the above demonstration of an important influence of the pineal under natural lighting appears to justify this approach. As Reiter (1972a) has stated, exposure of such a nocturnal animal as the rat to ultrashort days, under which circumstances the inhibitory influence of the pineal becomes evident, may more closely approach the physiological situation than maintaining the animal on an artificially long day in the laboratory. Reiter also has proposed that housing rats continually under constant, long photoperiod illumination actually may produce a "physiological pinealectomy". Such a concept could certainly help to explain the controversial history of pineal experimental physiology.

In rats housed under routine laboratory conditions, pinealectomy increases the incidence of vaginal estrus (Chu, Wurtman, & Axelrod, 1964); however, the physiological significance of this observation is difficult to assess because the vaginal smear is not a reliable estimate of the state of ovarian function under all circumstances. In the adult male rat pinealectomy increases the weights of the seminal vesicles and prostate (Fraschini et al, 1968), and pituitary LH content increases to postcastration levels. Certain conditions potentiate the influence of the pineal, perhaps by rendering neuroendocrine regulatory mechanisms more sensitive to the pineal hormones. Neonatal androgenization of both the male (Reiter, Sorrentino, Hoffman, & Rubin, 1968) and female rat (Reiter, 1969) renders these animals particularly sensitive to the pineal; thus blinding these rats at weaning markedly suppresses gonadal function as measured by gonadal and seminal vesicle or uterine weight at 2 to 3 months of age (Table 7). Pinealectomy essentially prevents this effect of blinding. Reiter and his

TABLE 7.   Per cent decrease in reproductive tissue weight induced by blinding in control or androgenized, intact, or pinealectomized rats[a]

	Number of rats	Gonadal weight (mg)	Per cent decrease	Seminal Vesicle[b] or uterine weight	Per cent decrease
A. *Males*					
None	9	3018±88	—	382±28	—
Blind	8	2552±89	15	294±30	23
Androgenized	9	2195±114	—	278±33	—
Androgenized, blind	10	740±170	66	39±31	86
Androgenized, blind, plus pinealectomy	8	2126±125	3	259±34	7
Androgenized, blind, plus ganglionectomy	10	2198±96	0	276±31	0
B. *Females*					
None	15	59.8±5.2	—	312±15	—
Blind	12	48.6±8.5	19	272±20	13
Androgenized	10	35.4±3.2	—	308±24	—
Androgenized, blind	14	25.4±4.5	28	175±24	43
Androgenized, blind, plus pinealectomy	13	33.5±3.6	5	301±22	2

[a] Data from Reiter, et al, 1968 (males) and Reiter, 1969 (females).
[b] Plus coagulating gland.

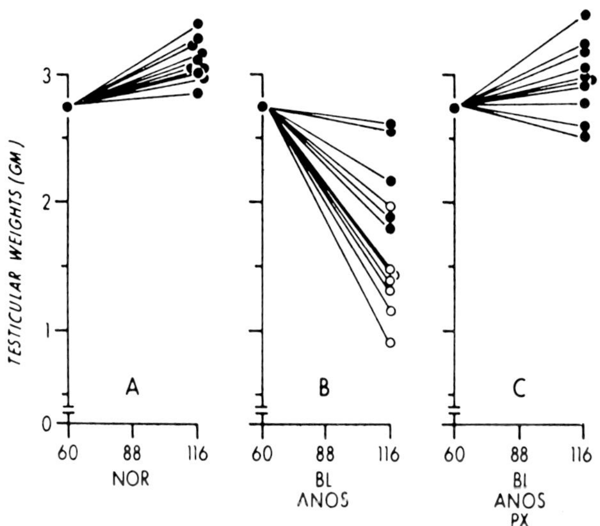

FIG. 5. Testicular weight of animals that were untreated (A), blinded (BL), and anosmic (ANOS) (B), or blinded, anosmic, and pinealectomized (PX) (C). Animals were sacrificed 8 weeks after surgery was performed at 60 days of age. The single point on each vertical axis represents the mean weight of the testes from control rats killed at 60 days. All other points indicate the testicular weights of individual animals. Solid circles designate testes that exhibited normal spermatogenic activity; open circles designate testes that showed degenerative changes of the germinal epithelia. Reprinted with permission from Reiter (1972).

colleagues have also shown that double sensory deprivation also renders the immature rat more responsive to the pineal (Fig. 5). Photic and olfactory sensory deprivation, produced by optic enucleation and olfactory bulbectomy at weaning, markedly inhibit testicular development unless the rats are also pinealectomized (Reiter, Klein, & Donofrio, 1969).

Although these experiments demonstrate that the pineal gland exerts a dramatic effect on gonadal function under specific conditions, they do not elucidate the possible mechanisms nor the site of this interaction. Moszkowska et al (1971) reviewed several experiments which together suggest one possible mechanism for the effect of pinealectomy. Because systemic or intracerebral injection of serotonin inhibits GTH secretion and the hypothalamic content of serotonin of 30-day-old female rats was reduced by more than 50 per cent by pinealectomy at 10 days of age, these investigators suggest that pinealectomy may alter serotonin turnover in the hypothalamus. The resulting decrease in hypothalamic serotonin, which can inhibit GTH activity, may be a mechanism by which pinealectomy alleviates GTH suppression.

The prepubertal state may be another condition in which the rat is sensitive to the pineal, as judged by the many reports that pinealectomy leads to precocious sexual maturation in both the male (Thieblot & Blaise, 1963; Roth, 1965) and the female (Kitay, 1954; Simonnet, Thieblot, Melik, & Segal, 1954; Wurtman, Altschule, and Holmgren, 1959; Kincl & Benagiano, 1967; Motta, Fraschini, & Martini, 1967; Relkin 1971a). Wurtman, Axelrod, and Chu (1963) also reported that treatment with melatonin, but not with serotonin, delayed puberty. In contrast, pinealectomy of the 3-day-old female rat did not alter ovarian development or vaginal opening (Wragg, 1967). Finally, Baum (1968) reported that pinealectomy produced a transient acceleration of the appearance of mounting behavior in male rats housed in darkness.

CONCLUSION

Although the hypothalamus is ultimately responsible for the regulation of GTH activity, many regions of the brain can modify hypothalamic function in the adult. Experimental evidence suggests that the cortex, amygdala, HPC, and diverse areas of the mesencephalon have the potential to alter GTH secretion (Fig. 6). These areas may represent a system of checks and balances that ensures that GTH secretion is appropriate to both ex-

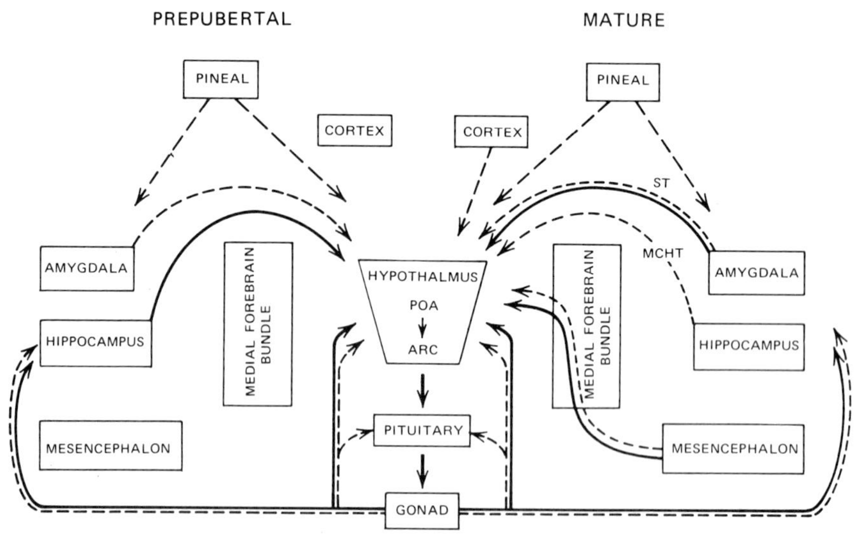

FIG. 6. Highly schematic diagram of the extrahypothalamic influences on the hypothalamic regulation of gonadotropin secretion in the prepubertal (*left*) and mature (*right*) rat. Solid lines designate facilitation; broken lines designate inhibitory influences. ARC, arcuate nucleus; MCHT, medial corticohypothalamic tract; POA, preoptic area; ST, stria terminalis.

ternal and internal environments. The influences of those limited areas, which have also been studied in the prepubertal rat, appear to be opposite in direction.

As a highly speculative hypothesis, it may be proposed that puberty involves, or perhaps is caused by, a maturation of extrahypothalamic structures and possibly a reversal of their predominant function. Fig. 6 emphasizes that the experimental support for the hypothesis is incomplete. The extrahypothalamic regulation of hypothalamic function is mediated not only by complex but by discrete neuroanatomical pathways, for the pineal gland also exerts a potentially important effect on reproductive activity by means of the production and release of pineal hormones. It is interesting that the nature of the pineal influence appears to be inhibitory both in the immature and the adult. It is possible, however, that the significance of pineal factors changes with the development and maturation of the brain. It has been demonstrated clearly that the responsiveness of the reproductive system to the pineal can be markedly altered, for example, neonatal androgenization or olfactory bulbectomy dramatically increase the effectiveness of the pineal in suppressing gonadal function when the animals are also blinded. It remains to be determined whether the prepubertal state is also a condition in which pineal influences are particularly important. One consequence of the existence of a complex system of facilitative and inhibitory structures which can alter GTH secretion is that rather subtle but inappropriate changes in one or more of its components can lead to significant alterations in gonadal function or in the normal functional maturation of the entire system. Thus abnormal changes in any one of its components may disturb the functional balance of this complex system and either retard or facilitate puberty. However, elucidation of the role of extrahypothalamic structures in the pubertal process must await the complete identification of the structures in this system as well as the clarification of their functional and anatomical interaction with one another and with the hypothalamus.

REFERENCES

Anden, N. E., Dahlstrom, A., Fuxe, K., Larsson, K., Olson, L., & Ungerstedt, U. (1966). Ascending monoamine neurons to the telencephalon and diencephalon. *Acta Physiol. Scand.* **67**, 313–326.

Anderson, C. H. & Greenwald, G. S. (1969). Autoradiographic analysis of estradiol uptake in the brain and pituitary of the female rat. *Endocrinology* **85**, 1160–1165.

Barraclough, C. A. (1967). Modifications in reproductive function after exposure to hormones during the prenatal and early postnatal period. In *Neuroendocrinology*, L. Martini & W. F. Ganong, Eds., Vol. 2, Academic, New York, pp. 61–99.

Bar-Sela, M. E. & Critchlow, V. (1966). Delayed puberty following electrical stimulation of amygdala in female rats. *Amer. J. Physiol.* **211**, 1103–1107.

Baum, M. J. (1968). Pineal gland: influence on development of copulation in male rats. *Science* **162**, 586–587.

Bunn, J. P. & Everett, J. W. (1957). Ovulation in persistent-estrous rats after electrical stimulation of the brain. *Proc. Soc. Exptl. Biol. Med.* **96**, 369–371.

Carrer, H. F. & Taleisnik, S. (1970). Effects of mesencephalic stimulation on the release of gonadotropins. *J. Endocrinol.* **48**, 527–539.

Carrer, H. F. & Taleisnik, S. (1972). Neural pathways associated with the mesencephalic inhibitory influence on gonadotropin secretion. *Brain Res.* **38**, 279–298.

Chu, E. W., Wurtman, R. J., & Axelrod, J. (1964). An inhibitory effect of melatonin on the estrous phase of the estrous cycle of the rodent. *Endocrinology* **75**, 238–242.

Clemens, L. G., Wallen, K., & Gorski, R. A. (1967). Mating behavior: facilitation in the female rat following cortical application of postassium chloride. *Science* **157**, 1208–1209.

Coppola, J. A. (1971). Brain catecholamines and gonadotropin secretion. In *Frontiers in Neuroendocrinology, 1971,* L. Martini & W. F. Ganong, Eds., Oxford University Press, London, pp. 129–144.

Czyba, J. C., Girod, C., & Durand, N. (1964). Sur l'antagonism épiphysohypophysaire et les variations saisonnières de la spermatogenèse chez le hamster d'ore (Mesocricetus auratus). *C.R.Soc. Biol. (Paris)* **158**, 742–745.

Eleftheriou, B. E., Church, R. L., Zolovick, A. J., Norman, R. L., & Pattison, M. L. (1969). Effects of amygdaloid lesions on regional brain RNA base ratios. *J. Endocrinol.* **45**, 207–214.

Elwers, M. & Critchlow, V. (1960). Precocious ovarian stimulation following hypothalamic and amygdaloid lesions in rats. *Amer. J. Physiol.* **198**, 381–385.

Everett, J. W. (1961). The mammalian female reproductive cycle and its controlling mechanisms. In *Sex and Internal Secretions,* W. C. Young, Ed., Williams & Wilkins, Baltimore, pp. 497–555.

Everett, J. W. (1964). Preoptic stimulative lesions and ovulation in the rat: "thresholds" and LH-release time in late diestrus and proestrus. In *Major Problems in Neuroendocrinology.* E. Bajusz & G. Jasmin, Eds., Karger, Basel, pp. 346–366.

Everett, J. W. (1969). Neuroendocrine aspects of mammalian reproduction. *Ann. Rev. Physiol.* **31**, 383–416.

Everett, J. W. & Radford, H. M. (1961). Irritative deposits from stainless steel electrodes in the preoptic rat brain causing release of pituitary gonadotropin. *Proc. Soc. Exptl. Biol. Med.* **108**, 604–609.

Flerkó, B. (1966). Control of gonadotropin secretion in the female. In *Neuroendocrinology,* L. Martini & W. F. Ganong, Eds., Vol. 1, Academic, New York, pp. 613–668.

Fraschini, F., Mess B., & Martini, L. (1968). Pineal gland, melatonin and the control of luteinizing hormone secretion. *Endocrinology* **82**, 919–924.

Fuxe, F. & Hökfelt, T. (1970). Central monoaminergic systems and hypothalamic function. In *The Hypothalamus,* L. Martini, M. Motta, & F. Fraschini, Eds., pp. 123–152.

Gallo, R. V., Johnson, J. H., Goldman, B. D., Whitmoyer, D. I., & Sawyer, C. H. (1971). Effects of electrochemical stimulation of the ventral hippocampus on hypothalamic electrical activity and pituitary gonadotropin secretion in female rats. *Endocrinology* **89**, 704–713.

Gorski, R. A. (1971). Gonadal hormones and the perinatal development of neuro-endocrine function. In *Frontiers in Neuroendocrinology, 1971*, L. Martini & W. F. Ganong, Eds. Oxford University Press, London, pp. 237–290.

Halász, B. (1969). The endocrine effects of isolation of the hypothalamus from the rest of the brain. In *Frontiers in Neuroendocrinology, 1969*, W. F. Ganong & L. Martini, Eds., Oxford University Press, New York, pp. 307–342.

Halász, B. & Gorski, R. A. (1967). Gonadotrophic hormone secretion in female rats after partial or total interruption of neural afferents to the medial basal hypo-thalamus. *Endocrinology* **80**, 608–622.

Kaasjager, W. A., Woodbury, D. M., van Dieten, J. A. M. J., & van Rees, G. P. (1971). The role played by the preoptic region and the hypothalamus in spon-taneous ovulation and ovulation induced by progestrone. *Neuroendocrinology* **7**, 54–64.

Kawakami, M. & Kubo, K. (1971). Neuro-correlate of limbic-hypothalamic-pituitary-gonadal axis in the rat: Change in limbic-hypothalamic unit activity induced by vaginal and electrical stimulation. *Neuroendocrinology* **7**, 65–89.

Kawakami, M. & Terasawa, E. (1972). Electrical stimulation of the brain on gonad-otropin secretion in the female prepubertal rat. *Endocrinol. Jap.* In press.

Kincl, F. A. & Benagiano, G. (1967). The failure of the pineal gland removal in neonatal animals to influence reproduction. *Acta Endocrinol.* **54**, 189–192.

Kitay, J. I. (1954). Effects of pinealectomy on ovary weight in immature rats. *Endo-crinology* **54**, 114–116.

Kling, A. (1964). Effects of rhinencephalic lesions on endocrine and somatic develop-ment in the rat. *Amer. J. Physiol.* **206**, 1395–1400.

Kordon, C. (1971). Involvement of catecholamines and indolamines in the control of pituitary gonadotropin release. *J. Neurovisceral Relat. Suppl.* **10**, 41–50.

Köves, K. & Halász, B. (1970). Location of the neural structures triggering ovulation in the rat. *Neuroendocrinology* **6**, 180–193.

Labhsetwar, A. P. (1971). Effects of serotonin on spontaneous ovulation: A theory for the dual hypothalamic control of ovulation. *Acta Endocrinol.* **68**, 334–344.

Lawton, I. E. & Sawyer, C. H. (1970). Role of amygdala in regulating LH secretion in the adult female rat. *Amer. J. Physiol.* **218**, 622–626.

Moore, R. Y., Heller, A., Bhatnager, R. K., Wurtman, R. J., & Axelrod, J. (1968). Central control of the pineal gland: Visual pathways. *Arch. Neurol.* **18**, 208–218.

Moore, R. Y., Karapas, F., & Lenn, N. J. (1971). A retino-hypothalamic projection in the rat. *Anat. Rec.* **169**, 382.

Moore, R. Y. & Rapport, R. L. (1971). Pineal and gonadal function in the rat follow-ing cervical sympathectomy. *Neuroendocrinology* **7**, 361–374.

Moszkowska, A., Kordon, C., & Ebels, I. (1971). Biochemical fractions and mech-anisms involved in the pineal modulation of pituitary gonadotropin release. In *The Pineal Gland*, G. E. W. Wolstenholme & J. Knight, Eds., Churchill, London. pp. 241–258.

Motta, M., Fraschini, F., & Martini, L. (1967). Endocrine effects of pineal gland and of melatonin. *Proc. Soc. Exptl. Biol. Med.* **126**, 431–435.

Pfaff, D. W. (1968). Uptake of ^{3}H-estradiol by the female rat brain. An autoradio-graphic study. *Endocrinology* **82**, 1149–1155.

Ramaley, J. A. & Gorski, R. A. (1967). The effect of hypothalamic deafferentation upon puberty in the female rat. *Acta Endocrinol.* **56**, 661–674.

Ramirez, V. D. & Sawyer, C. H. (1965). Advancement of puberty in the female rat by estrogen. *Endocrinology* **76**, 1158–1168.

Reiter, R. J. (1969). Stratified squamous metaplasia of the uterine epithelium in early androgen-treated rats and its inhibition by light deprivation. *Anat. Rec.* **164**, 479–488.

Reiter, R. J. (1972a). Role of the pineal in reproduction. In *Reproductive Biology*, H. Balin & S. Glasser, Eds., Excerpta Medica, Amsterdam, pp. 71–114.

Reiter, R. J. (1972b). Pineal control of a seasonal reproductive rhythm in male golden hamsters exposed to natural daylight and temperature. *Endocrinology*. In Press.

Reiter, R. J. & Fraschini, F. (1969). Endocrine aspects of the mammalian pineal gland, a review. *Neuroendocrinology* **5**, 219–255.

Reiter, R. J., Klein, D. C., & Donofrio, R. J. (1969). Preliminary observations on the reproductive effects of the pineal gland in blinded, anosmic male rats. *J. Reprod. Fertil.* **19**, 563–565.

Reiter, R. J., Sorrentino, S. D., Hoffman, J. C., & Rubin, P. H. (1968). Pineal, neural and photic control of reproductive organ size in early androgen-treated male rats. *Neuroendocrinology* **3**, 246–255.

Relkin, R. (1971a). Relative efficacy of pinealectomy, hypothalamic and amygdaloid lesions in advancing puberty. *Endocrinology* **88**, 415–418.

Relkin, R. (1971b). Absence of alteration in puberal onset in male rats following amygdaloid lesioning. *Endocrinology* **88**, 1272–1274.

Riss, W., Burstein, S. D., & Johnson, R. W. (1963). Hippocampal or pyriform lobe damage in infancy and endocrine development of rats. *Amer. J. Physiol.* **204**, 861–866.

Ross, J., Claybaugh, C., Clemens, L. G., & Gorski, R. A. (1971). Short latency induction of estrous behavior with intracerebral gonadal hormones in ovariectomized rats. *Endocrinology* **89**, 32–38.

Roth, W. D. (1965). Metabolic and morphologic studies on the rat pineal organ during puberty. *Progr. Brain Res.* **10**, 552–563.

Sawyer, C. H. (1972). Functions of the amygdala related to the feedback actions of gonadal steroid hormones. In *The Neurobiology of the Amygdala*, B. E. Eleftheriou, Ed., Plenum, New York, pp. 745–762.

Simonnet, H., Thieblot, L., Melik, T., & Segal, V. (1954). Nouvelles preuves de l'endocrinie epiphysaire. *Acta Endocrinol.* **17**, 402–413.

Smith, E. R. & Davidson, J. M. (1968). Role of estrogen in the cerebral control of puberty in female rats. *Endocrinology* **82**, 100–108.

Smith, S. W. & Lawton, I. E. (1972). Involvement of the amygdala in the ovarian compensatory hypertrophy response. *Neuroendocrinology* **9**, 228–234.

Stumpf, W. E. (1971). Hypophysiotropic neurons in the periventricular brain: Topography of estradiol concentrating neurons. In *Steroid Hormones and Brain Function*, C. H. Sawyer & R. A. Gorski, Eds., UCLA Forum in Medical Sciences, Los Angeles, California, pp. 215–226.

Taleisnik, S., Caligaris, L., & deOlmos, J. (1962). Luteinizing hormone release by cerebral cortex stimulation in rats. *Amer. J. Physiol.* **203**, 1109–1112.

Terasawa, E. & Sawyer, C. H. (1969). Electrical and electrochemical stimulation of the hypothalamo-adenohypophysial system with stainless steel electrodes. *Endocrinology* **84**, 918–925.

Terasawa, E. & Timiras, P. S. (1968a). Electrical activity during the estrous cycle of the rat: Cyclic changes in limbic structures. *Endocrinology* **83**, 207–216.

Terasawa, E. & Timiras, P. S. (1968b). Electrophysiological study of the limbic system in the rat at onset of puberty. *Amer. J. Physiol.* **215**, 1462–1467.

Thieblot, L. & Blaise, S. (1963). Influence de la glande pineale sur les gonades. *Annal. d'Endocrinol.* **24**, 270–286.

Ungerstedt, U. (1971). Stereotaxic mapping of the monamine pathways in the rat brain. *Acta Physiol. Scand. Suppl.* **367**, 1–48.

Velasco, M. E. & Taleisnik, S. (1969a). Release of gonadotropins induced by amygdaloid stimulation in the rat. *Endocrinology* **84**, 132–139.

Velasco, M. E. & Taleisnik, S. (1969b). Effect of hippocampal stimulation on the release of gonadotropin. *Endocrinology* **85**, 1154–1159.

Velasco, M. E. & Taleisnik, S. (1971). Effects of the interruption of amygdaloid and hippocampal afferents to the medial hypothalamus on gonadotrophin release. *J. Endocrinol.* **51**, 41–55.

Wragg, L. E. (1967). Effects of pinealectomy in the newborn female rat. *Amer. J. Anat.* **120**, 391–402.

Wurtman, R. J. (1971a). Brain monoamines and endocrine function. *Neurosci. Res. Progr. Bull.* **9**, 172–297.

Wurtman, R. J. (1971b). Summary of symposium. In *The Pineal Gland*, G. E. Wolstenholme & J. Knight, Eds , Churchill, London, pp. 379–389.

Wurtman, R. J., Altschule, M. D., & Holmgren, U. (1959). Effects of pinealectomy and of a bovine pineal extract in rats. *Amer. J. Physiol.* **197**, 108–110.

Wurtman, R. J., Axelrod, J., & Chu, E. W. (1963). Melatonin, a pineal substance: Effect on the rat ovary. *Science* **141**, 277–278.

DISCUSSION

DR. ROSS.   Suppose we define puberty as the acquisition of reproductive capability, for females meaning ovulation and for males meaning spermatogenesis adequate to fertilize the female. Has precocious puberty, thus defined, ever been shown to occur as a consequence of an extrahypothalamic lesion?

DR. GORSKI.   In the experiment of Elwers and Critchlow (1960) in which the amygdala was lesioned true precocious puberty was observed in the sense that ovulation, regular cycles, and even pregnancy occurred. But to my knowledge most of the other experiments have not gone that far. In many of the experiments with the pineal gland, for example, the end point has been precocious vaginal opening or a precocious increase in gonadal weight. In many cases the histology of the gonad is not described, so one does not know if functional puberty occurred. In our experiment with Ramaley the procedure by which we produced precocious puberty (deafferentation) by its nature prevents ovulation. I do not agree, however, that because these animals did not ovulate they never really reached puberty.

DR. BOGDANOVE.   I have for some time despaired of using the rat as a model for human precocious puberty. If a female rat normally has its first ovulation around 34 or 35 days and you do something up in the brain and get the animal to ovulate at 29 days, you have advanced that first ovulation by 5 or 6 days, about the length of one cycle. How can you say whether the next ovulation was a consequence of the lesion or merely a sign of normal puberty? Can you be sure that what you have produced is really advancement of puberty and not simply an extra first ovulation which happened a little time before first ovulation would normally occur (but which has not prevented the first ovulation from occurring on schedule, even if it is now the second ovulation)?

DR. GORSKI.   Actually I think I would support it to a degree. This morning the question arose: how do hypothalamic lesions induce precocious puberty? Given the Ramirez and Sawyer (1965) observation that small amounts of estrogen lead to precocious puberty, in some cases lesioning the hypothalamus may actually excite the brain, cause the secretion of gonadotropin, and, in turn, increase steroid production. If by some arbitrary method we induce one ovulation, it, of course, is accompanied by gonadotropin and presumably steroid secretion. The latter may then cause maturation of the brain. My position is that precocious puberty may follow induced ovulation because of the hormonal pattern, but the original experimental manipulation of the brain may be directly concerned only with ovulation. However, I do want to defend the rat as a model system. This morning considerable stress was placed on the hypothalamic control of gonadotropin secretion. There is strong evidence to suggest that the hypothalamus is a way-station, perhaps, between the pineal and reproductive activity but certainly between extrahypothalamic structures and the pituitary. Because the problem is so complex and because a great deal is known about the rat, I favor it as a model system, although certainly it may have its peculiarities.

DR. ODELL.   You confined your remarks to the rat, with a single exception, the hamster. Isn't it also correct that you confined your remarks mostly to the female rat of necessity? The experiments you described were done in the female, for the most part, because it is easier to talk about ovulation alteration in cyclic activity and to quantify changes in ovulation. Do you think it is safe to generalize the conclusions to both sexes, even in the rat, based on the data you have presented?

DR. GORSKI.   Although this may promote general disagreement, I would like to consider the possibility that puberty may, in fact, be a maturation of the tonic system of gonadotropin control. In the female ovulation may simply be a corollary of the resultant increased secretion of estrogen. The cyclic gonadotropin-regulating system may be mature well before puberty, and once estrogen reaches the right level it can trigger ovulation. If this is true, then puberty in the male can be considered to be identical to puberty in the female and can be defined as the attainment of adult tonic gonadotropin levels. It happens that in the female we have the convenient parameters of vaginal opening or ovulation to signal puberty but not necessarily to define it mechanistically. Thus, conceptually, it is safe to use the female, at least as a model, for puberty, but certainly with the realization that the male may, in fact, be different.

DR. DAVIDSON.   Dr. Bogdanove asked if it can be called puberty when one induces ovulation. When you perform various ovulation-inducing treatments before puberty, e.g., giving small doses of estrogen, why do rats often begin to cycle? Once you start it moving, the rock continues to roll down the hill; thereafter you have a normal reproductive organism. This may be related to the phenomenon D. C. Johnson reported a few years ago, in which testosterone given to female rats produced cyclic FSH release over a period of days.

DR. RAMIREZ.   Dr. Advis in our laboratory has produced lesions of the hypothalamus of the rat like those reported by Donovan to induce precocious puberty. We have also induced precocious puberty by a lesion at 16 days. We made sequential measurements of plasma gonadotropin levels in these animals and could not detect any significant changes. We have done only one determination on the blood, killing the animals at intervals of 5 days after we started the lesion. So there are differences in animals, and the complexity of the experiment does not allow us to rule out the possibility of some changes in gonadotropin; but certainly there is no dramatic change in the plasma gonadotropins determined by radioimmunoassay. But we still have the earlier onset of puberty.

DR. GANONG. Very early lesions lead, after some time, to precocious puberty in the rat, with a series of cycles following thereafter. Also, hypothalamic disease in the human can lead to a puberty which is normal except that it occurs at the age of 2 years, and Dr. Grumbach tells us it can occur as early as 3 months. Dr. Bloch and I were unable to confirm that lesions of the amygdala cause precocious puberty.

DR. REITER. In reference to what Dr. Odell was saying, it is our experience that the pineal gland is equally important in the male and the female in terms of its regulatory influence on reproduction (Reiter & Fraschini, 1969). Heretofore there has been a misconception that the pineal has a more important role in the female; there is one experimental situation in which pinealectomized rats have litters earlier than nonpinealectomized control rats (Reiter, 1972a). Dr. Gorski has already alluded to the apparent absence of an effect of pinealectomy on reproduction in some experiments. Many of these studies have been done under the following circumstances. Various parameters of reproductive physiology were studied in pinealectomized animals, and comparisons were made with sham-operated control animals. All animals were characteristically kept under long daily photoperiods (14 to 16 hours light/day). In this situation, in essence, both groups of animals are pinealectomized: one group having had the pineal surgically removed, and the other having had the pineal effect negated by long photoperiods. Thus one should not expect any appreciable differences between the 2 groups. It is unwise to use nocturnal animals in long photoperiods to check the effects of the pineal or pinealectomy.

DR. GORSKI. If you are going to say that keeping animals in the laboratory condition artificially suppresses the pineal, I should ask Dr. Everett if putting a female rat in 14-hour periods of light imposes an artificial critical period for ovulation. Have you studied rats in natural lighting environment?

DR. EVERETT. Only the difference; I compared 12 and 12 against 14 and 10 and found no difference.

DR. STEINBERGER. We are discussing extrahypothalamic influences on puberty, and I do not understand to what investigators refer when they say puberty, particularly in a male rat. Let us define puberty. Even with the female rat it is difficult. In the male rat, I have a suspicion that puberty starts around the fourth day of life. Puberty simply indicates the first appearance of pubic hair, and we have taken it and used it as scientific term. We should be very careful when we discuss puberty, particularly if we are going to look at the extrahypothalamic effects on its onset.

DR. GORSKI. I agree with you, but the shortage of time has prevented me from describing in detail the experiments I have mentioned. In the male rat the descent of the testes, the onset of male sexual behavior, the onset of a spurt in running activity, and a change in gonadotropin secretion have all been used to define puberty. Perhaps we should use the same criterion for both the male and female, if we could ignore ovulation and vaginal opening; i.e., some sort of maturation of pituitary or gonadal secretory activity.

DR. MCCORMACK.   With regard to the time of the "critical period" for LH secretion in photoperiods shorter than 14 hours, I have determined the time of ovulation, which follows the critical period by 12 hours, in rats in which precocious puberty had been induced with pregnant mare's serum gonadotropin (PMS). Experimental groups were exposed to either 10-hour daily photoperiods or continuous darkness (DD). The time of ovulation was the same in these 2 groups of rats as in controls exposed to a 14-hour daily photoperiod. So, although long photoperiods may indeed inhibit pineal function, the fact that the time of ovulation is not shifted by "exposure" to DD (wherein the pineal should be functioning maximally) argues against pineal involvement in the timing of the LH surge. Furthermore, I have shown in PMS-treated rats exposed to DD, and Alleva, Waleski, and Alleva (1970) have shown in adult rats exposed to 12-hour daily photoperiods, that pinealectomy does not alter the time of ovulation.

DR. TANNER.   Going back to the definition of puberty about which you are having some problems, a lot of the people working on rats don't use bone age, which has been established for the rat quite well and which has a parallel situation in the human. This can be done very straightforwardly, and without killing the animal.

DR. REITER.   Studies to date have generally indicated that the pineal gland is not particularly important for the timing of LH release associated with ovulation, nor does it seem to influence the time at which ova are shed. One of its primary roles is determining periods of reproductive dormancy and activity on an annual basis (Reiter, 1972b).

DR. FRISCH.   How does pinealectomy affect food intake or does it?

DR. REITER.   There is little indication that it affects food consumption, but it may modify water intake (de Vries & Kappers, 1971).

DR. FISHER.   Roger, you reviewed a lot of data suggesting extrahypothalamic input on this pubertal system, but it looked as if you had resolved that the amygdala and the pineal are the predominant extrahypothalamic influences on puberty. You deleted the mesencephalon as having any effect. Do you think it is that simple?

DR. GORSKI.   No. The cortex, mesencephalon, amygdala, hippocampus, and the pineal have all been implicated in the control of gonadotropin secretion in the adult. In the immature rat, however, the only extrahypothalamic systems that have been studied are the hippocampus, amygdala, and pineal. I would be surprised if this were a complete list, for either the adult or the prepubertal animal.

DR. FAIMAN.   I wonder about Kallmann's syndrome and if the neurophysiologists have any explanation for the association of hypogonadotropic hypogonadism with anosmia.

DR. REITER.   I can not shed any light on that particular syndrome. Anosmia is, however, a strong potentiating factor for sensitizing the brain to the anti-gonadotropic influence of the pineal gland (Reiter & Sorrentino, Jr., 1971). Hypogonadism associated with anosmia may well involve the pineal gland.

DR. SCHWARTZ.   Our criterion of puberty in the male rat has been the appearance of sperm at the end of the penis; it works rather well on both rats and the hamster. In the rat, for example, there is a pretty reliable appearance between 55 and 65 days, the time that FSH and LH start dropping in the pituitary and when fertility occurs. Recently this has been confirmed in the hamster, too. This is later than in the female, I suspect, not because there has been a central maturational delay but simply because of the length of time it takes to go through the steps to get sperm, in contrast to the steps required to get viable follicles that are ready to ovulate.

REFERENCES

Alleva, J. J., Waleski, M. V., & Alleva, F. R. (1970). The Zeitgeber for ovulation in rats: non-participation of the pineal gland. *Life Sci. I,* **9**, 241–246.

de Vries, R. A. C. & Kappers, J. A. (1971). Influence of the pineal gland on the neurosecretory activity of the supra-optic hypothalamic nucleus in the male rat. *Neuroendocrinology* **8**, 359–366.

Ramirez, V. D. & Sawyer, C. H. (1965). Advancement of puberty in the female rat by estrogen. *Endocrinology* **76**, 1158–1168.

Reiter, R. J. (1972a). Effects of the pineal gland on reproduction, organ growth and fertility in dual sensory deprived female rats. *Endocrinol. Exp. (Bratisl)* **6**, 3–10.

Reiter, R. J. (1972b). Evidence for refractoriness of the pituitary-gonadal axis to the pineal gland in golden hamsters and its possible implications in annual reproductive rhythms. *Anat. Rec.* **173**, 365–372.

Reiter, R. J. & Fraschini, F. (1969). Endocrine aspects of the mammalian pineal gland, a review. *Neuroendocrinology* **5**, 219–225.

Reiter, R. J. & Sorrentino, Jr., S. (1971). Factors influential in determining the gonad-inhibiting activity of the pineal gland, in Ciba Foundation **Symposium:** *The Pineal Gland,* G. E. W. Wolstenholme & J. Knight, Eds., C. Livingstone, Edinburgh, pp. 329–344.

8.

The Central Nervous System and Precocious Puberty

N. D. BARNES, M. D. CLOUTIER, and A. B. HAYLES

The rare occurrence of extremely precocious sexual maturation has attracted attention since very early times. Reports from the ancient world include those of Craterus, from the third century B.C., who described an individual who was "child, youth, old man, begat a child, and died, all within seven years," and of Pliny, who recorded a clear case of neurogenic precocity, "the son of Euthymenes grew to 4 feet 6 inches in his third year, he walked slowly, was dull of sense, became sexually quite mature, had a bass voice, and was carried off by a sudden attack of paralysis when he turned three." In 1766 Von Haller, in his book *Elementa Physiologiae Corporis Humani*, collected reports of 13 boys and 5 girls with sexual precocity, including the famous Anna Mummenthaler who menstruated from 2 years, gave birth to a stillborn child at 9 years, went through the menopause at 52 years, and died at 75 years of age. The unfortunate children afflicted with this condition in the seventeenth, eigh-

---

Abbreviations

FSH	Follicle stimulating hormone
GH	Growth hormone
TSH	Thyroid stimulating hormone

teenth, and nineteenth centuries were regarded as freaks of nature, exhibited in public, made to do heavy work because of their strength, and sometimes segregated from other children (Thamdrup, 1961).

In more recent years a large number of cases have been reported. Seckel (1946) reviewed 772 published cases of precocious sexual development, 591 girls and 181 boys. Series in which the cases have been examined personally and reported fully include those of Jolly (1955), Thamdrup (1961), Wilkins, (1965), and Sigurjonsdottir and Hayles (1968). We shall review, largely from the work of these authors, the clinical aspects of those forms of sexual precocity that are mediated by organic or functional derangements of the central nervous system.

CLINICAL CLASSIFICATION

Puberty represents the period of sexual transition from the immaturity of childhood to the maturity of adult life. A strict biologic definition of sexual maturity requires the production of viable gametes and attainment of full reproductive potential. These considerations are clearly of little value in formulating a working definition of puberty for clinical use, and we have chosen to regard as "true" or "complete" puberty those changes that together indicate (except in the very rare cases of ectopic gonadotropin production) that the hypothalamic-pituitary-gonadal axis is active, e. g., growth acceleration, maturation of the external genital organs and the testes in the male, development of secondary sex characteristics or the presence of cyclic uterine bleeding in females. "Incomplete" puberty, in contrast, represents only the development of secondary sex characteristics, usually either breasts or pubic hair, which may result from a number of causes, including intrinsic lesions of the gonads or adrenals independent of stimulation by the central nervous system. A clinical classification of precocious sexual development, based on these concepts, is presented in Table 1.

The definition of precocity is equally arbitrary, for the age of sexual maturation shows considerable normal variation and is also affected by numerous racial, genetic, and environmental factors (Zacharias & Wurtman, 1969). However, we have conformed to the practice of most recent authors, except Jolly (1955) (who set a limit of 10 years in both sexes), by considering sexual development before the age of 8 years in girls and 10 years in boys to be abnormal.

Complete precocious puberty may be divided into two major forms— idiopathic and neurogenic. Table 2 indicates the incidence and sex distribution of these two forms in those series that summarize the total experience of a single investigator or endocrine unit. Although such com-

TABLE 1.   Classification of isosexual precocious puberty

A. *Complete, true*

    1.   Idiopathic, constitutional, or cryptogenic

        a.   sporadic
        b.   familial

    2.   Neurogenic, cerebral lesions (see Table 3)
    3.   McCune-Albright syndrome
    4.   Juvenile hypothyroidism with precocious puberty, "hormonal overlap" syndrome
    5.   Silver's syndrome

B. *Extra-pituitary gonadotropins*

    1.   Gonadotropin-secreting tumors
    2.   Exogenous gonadotropin administration

C. *Incomplete*

    1.   Premature pubarche
        a.   sporadic
        b.   neurogenic

    2.   Premature thelarche
    3.   Adrenal lesions

        a.   congenital adrenal hyperplasia
        b.   Cushing's syndrome, adrenal hyperplasia
        c.   tumors

    4.   Testicular tumors
    5.   Ovarian tumors
    6.   Iatrogenic (androgen or estrogen administration)

TABLE 2.   Distribution of idiopathic and neurogenic precocious puberty

Series	Idiopathic		Neurogenic	
	M	F	M	F
Jolly (1955)	3	31	4	5
Thamdrup (1961)	4	34	7	11
Wilkins (1965)	13	67	10	5
Sigurjonsdottir & Hayles (1968)	8	54	16	16

prehensive surveys are more representative of the true incidence than collected case reports, the practice of such individuals and institutions tends to be biased toward the more difficult and complex problems. Thamdrup (1961) includes a number of mental institutions, so that he is likely to show a preponderance of neurogenic cases.

Idiopathic Precocious Puberty

The idiopathic, constitutional, or cryptogenic form of precocious puberty is by far the most common, constituting 66 per cent of the cases (Table 2). By definition, such cases should have no demonstrable lesion of the central nervous system, yet the changes of puberty are presumed to be mediated by premature activation of the central components of the hypothalamic-pituitary-gonadal axis. However, although precocious development may be the first or only sign of a lesion in the hypothalamic area, especially a hamartoma, full investigation is seldom undertaken in the absence of other findings because such lesions rarely are amenable to treatment. Thus, some "idiopathic" cases later prove to have been misclassified. It is reassuring to find that subsequent development of neurologic problems is rare, even with prolonged observation. Occasional examples have been reported (Gesell, Thoms, Hartman, & Thompson, 1939; Wolman and Balmforth, 1963; Hung, Milhorat, Nelson, & August, 1971), and we have encountered three:

Case 1 was a boy who had an enlarged penis at birth. Pubic hair developed at 5 years and 3 months; at that time clinical (and full neurologic) examination revealed no other abnormality, but at 7 years, 9 months, he developed diabetes insipidus and headaches 6 months later. When he was investigated further at 9 years, 9 months, a pineal tumor was demonstrated. The tumor was subtotally removed and a Torkildsen shunt was inserted, but he died at the age of 14 years and 2 months.

Case 2 was a boy who at the age of 6 years developed headaches for which no cause was found and which resolved spontaneously. He underwent rapid sexual maturation at 9 years, and re-examination shortly thereafter again revealed no other abnormality. However, at 16 years, 6 months he developed temporal lobe seizures. Although he has made good progress on anticonvulsant medication, it seems likely that his precocity had a neurogenic basis.

Case 3 was a boy who had the onset of rapid growth and sexual maturation at the age of 2½ years. No cause for his precocity was found at 4 and 6 years of age. At 11 years of age he developed headaches and at 12 a calcified mass in the hypothalamic area and erosion of the clinoids were noted. The funduscopic examination at this time was normal. Surgical exploration disclosed a large tumor of the optic radiation extending into the hypothalamus. The tumor could not be removed, but a biopsy was obtained. The pathologic diagnosis was glioma of the optic nerve.

Previously unsuspected organic central nervous system lesions have also been discovered occasionally at autopsy (Driggs & Spatz, 1939; Bauer, 1954); since no autopsy reports on patients with idiopathic precocious puberty are available, the true incidence of organic lesions remains uncertain. Liu, Grumbach, de Napoli, and Morishima (1965), however, found a high incidence of nonspecific electroencephalographic abnormalities in children with idiopathic precocious puberty. Money (1969) demonstrated a significantly elevated verbal IQ in children with this disorder.

The prognosis is generally good; the only problem in most of these children is their moderately short adult height resulting from early epiphyseal fusion. Sexual and reproductive function is normal, and these patients do not undergo premature menopause or senility.

There is a remarkable preponderance of females in all large series of cases of idiopathic precocious puberty but no clue to the reason for increased susceptibility to this presumably functional neuroendocrine disturbance. It has been shown that the presence of testicular tissue at a critical period in fetal or neonatal life suppresses the cyclic female pattern of gonadotropin release and imprints on the hypothalamus the relatively constant patterns that characterize the male (Harris & Naftolin, 1970). Therefore, gonadotropin release in the male is free of the influence of the hypothalamic "clock" which might be vulnerable to functional derangement. Girls who have precocious puberty generally have normal cycles, however.

Idiopathic precocious puberty also provides graphic demonstration of the fact that the anterior pituitary and gonads are capable of responding and maturing in a normal manner long before puberty generally occurs. The youngest recorded cases have shown clear evidence of sexual maturation at birth and have proceeded to full maturation at an early age (Wilkins, 1965). Seckel (1946) found records of 18 pregnancies between the ages of 5 and 10 years, the youngest being the famous Lina Medina of Peru who at the age of 5 years and 7 months was delivered by Cesarean section of a 6½-pound boy.

The changes of precocious puberty frequently follow the same sequence and occupy a similar period of time as the changes of normal puberty, but the pattern can vary considerably, especially in girls. In our series uterine bleeding was the first sign of sexual maturation in 5 patients and occurred simultaneously with the growth of pubic hair and breast development in 2 more; in 3 the growth of pubic hair preceded breast development. These aberrations of the usual orderly sequence of events in puberty not only give rise to some diagnostic difficulty but also suggest the possibility that subtle derangements in control by the central nervous system may be present.

Another interesting aspect of idiopathic precocious puberty is rare familial occurrence. In contrast to the sporadic cases, this phenomenon has been reported more frequently in males; in some families, the males of several generations have been affected. Generally, the condition has been inherited as a sex-linked autosomal dominant trait, transmitted only from affected male to affected male. Other patterns of inheritance have been described, however, and there is probably genetic heterogeneity within this group (Rimoin & Schimke, 1971). We have observed 2 brothers from a large pedigree with familial male precocity. Although it is a common observation that female relatives of such patients may have somewhat early development, it is surprising that few instances of familial precocious puberty involving females have been reported. In one case, a brother and sister (Beas, Zurbrügg, Leibow, Patton, & Gardner, 1962) and, in another, a girl and her paternal grandmother (Wilkins, 1965) were affected. We have encountered a family in which 2 sisters showed this disorder, one of whom later developed signs suggestive of the Stein-Leventhal syndrome.

The fact that idiopathic precocious puberty in boys may occur as a familial disorder, inherited as a Mendelian trait, suggests that premature activation of the hypothalamic-pituitary-gonadal axis can result from the influence of a single mutant gene.

Recent studies have shown that the hormonal changes associated with precocious puberty are, like the somatic changes, consistent with premature activation of the normal mechanisms governing puberty (Penny, Guyda, Baghdassarian, Johanson, & Blizzard, 1970) and have begun to delineate the changes in sensitivity of the gonadal-hypothalamic feedback mechanisms which regulate the secretion of gonadotropins (Kulin, Grumbach, & Kaplan, 1972). The onset of puberty in girls generally correlates well with the attainment of a certain "critical weight" (Frisch & Revelle, 1971); however, the factors that initiate these changes remain obscure.

Spontaneous remission of the changes rarely, if ever, occurs. No really effective treatment is available, but medroxyprogesterone acetate, a progestin without clinically detectable estrogenic or androgenic properties, has been used widely to control the changes of idiopathic precocious puberty. It is presumed to work by suppressing pituitary gonadotropin secretion, but a reduction of urinary gonadotropin levels has not been observed in all patients (Rifkind, Kulin, Cargille, Rayford, & Ross, 1969). Unfortunately, although its use usually results in reduction of breast size and cessation of menses in girls and suppression of erections and spermatogenesis and prevention of further genital growth in boys, bone-age advancement cannot be arrested even with doses large enough to cause Cushingoid changes and pituitary-adrenal suppression (Richman, Underwood, French, & Van Wyk, 1971).

Studies with a new antigonadotropic agent, an ethinyl testosterone analogue (Danazol), have been reported (Sherins, Gandy, Thorslund, & Paulsen, 1971). Preliminary clinical observations in precocious puberty suggest that this compound may hold considerable therapeutic promise (Greenblatt, Dmowski, Mahesh, & Scholer, 1971).

Neurogenic Precocious Puberty

Precocious puberty can occur in association with lesions of the central nervous system in the hypothalamic region. In contrast to the idiopathic form, which is much more common in girls, precocious puberty due to structural neurologic lesions seems to occur slightly more frequently in boys. Therefore, boys with precocious puberty are far more likely than girls to have a demonstrable lesion.

The variety of documented neurologic lesions which have been associated with precocious puberty is presented in Table 3. It is evident that expanding and destructive and possibly merely distorting lesions may produce a similar effect. The site of the lesion in the hypothalamic area is more critical than the type of lesion. Exact localization is often impossible because widespread neurologic damage may be present. Among 60 cases of hypothalamic disease reviewed by Bauer (1954) the majority of those with precocious or delayed puberty had destruction of much of the hypothalamus at the time of death. When, however, it has been possible to localize a relatively discrete lesion, it is evident that the critical area of the hypothalamus lies posterior to the median eminence and includes the tuber cinereum, the mammillary bodies and the floor of the posterior part of the third ventricle. Lesions of the pineal gland, especially in boys, may also be associated with precocity. Similar lesions in the anterior hypothalamus generally result in delayed development or hypogonadism (Bauer, 1954). Intrinsic pituitary lesions are also usually associated with delayed maturation; an intact pituitary gonadotropin function is an essential prerequisite for true puberty. Thus, most neurologic lesions can cause precocious puberty by interfering with structures that normally exert an inhibitory effect on the release of gonadotropin.

Some of the neurologic lesions are of particular interest. More than 30 patients with precocious puberty, approximately three quarters of whom were boys, have been reported to have hyperplastic malformations at the base of the hypothalamus formed from neural tissue of normal appearance and called hamartomas or gangliocytomas (Schmidt, Hallervorden, &

TABLE 3.   Neurogenic lesions associated with precocious puberty

A. *Neoplasms*	**B. *Infections***
1. Hypothalamus	1. Meningitis
astrocytoma	tuberculous
neurofibroma	other
ependymoma	2. Encephalitis
craniopharyngioma	epidemic
ganglioneuroma	measles
ganglioglioma	3. Toxoplasmosis
infundibuloma	4. Syphilis
cyst of third ventricle	**C. *Inherited disease***
2. Tuber cinereum and mammillary bodies	1. Neurofibromatosis
	2. Tuberous sclerosis
hamartoma	**D. *Developmental defects***
3. Pineal	1. Aqueduct stenosis
	2. Congenital cerebral defect
teratoma	3. Porencephalic cyst
pinealoma	4. Microcephaly
chorioepithelioma	5. Craniostenosis
4. Optic nerve	**E. *Trauma***
	1. Birth
glioma	2. Accidental
5. Other	**F. *Sturge-Weber syndrome***
	G. *Diffuse encephalopathy*
cerebellar astrocytoma	
cerebral astrocytoma	**H. *Idiopathic epilepsy***

Spatz, 1958). These malformations form a pedunculated mass generally about 5 to 10 mm in diameter, but sometimes considerably larger, which is attached to the pial surface of the posterior region of the tuber cinereum or near the mammillary bodies and occupies the interpeduncular space. Histologically, it resembles the gray matter of the tuberal region and is characterized by no excess of glial tissue, many small nerve cells, small groups of larger nerve cells comparable to those of the tuberomammillary complex, and nerve fibers some of which are myelinated. Fiber tracts connected to the hypothalamus have been demonstrated, and occasionally the nerve cells and fibers contain a neurosecretory substance (Wolman & Balmforth, 1963). Similar malformations have been discovered as an incidental finding at autopsy in patients without evidence of precocious puberty, but it may be significant that no connection with the hypothalamus was demonstrated. When specifically sought, minute "hamartomatous" nodular malformations of this region were found in 21 per cent of 121 brains examined consecutively (Sherwin, Grassi, & Sommers, 1962). In most cases precocious puberty in association with hamartomatous malformations has occurred at a very young age and may be preceded or followed by other problems caused by pressure on surrounding structures. Most patients have died young, but long survival has been recorded (Wolman & Balmforth, 1963). Generally, these lesions have been considered inoperable, but successful removal has been reported (Northfield & Russell, 1967). The mechanism by which these intriguing tumors may cause precocious puberty is unknown. They may act to overcome normal gonadotropin-inhibiting impulses either by suppressing the hypothetical inhibitory center in the tuber cinereum or by directly exciting the neurosecretory fibers which elaborate gonadotropin releasing factor. They might also have an intrinsic neurosecretory function and produce a gonadotropin releasing factor.

Richter (1951) distinguished two types of hamartoma, nondestructive and destructive, but the latter may be better classified as a ganglioglioma. These congenital tumors arise in the floor of the third ventricle and may replace the entire region of the tuber and mammillary bodies. Histologically, they consist of astrocytes but also contain nerve cells and fibers which seem to be an integral part of the tumor (Sheehan, 1969). The pattern of precocious puberty is similar to that caused by true hamartomas and the patients usually die in childhood.

The influence of the pineal gland on sexual maturation, both normal and abnormal, remains a matter of controversy. Pineal tumors in children are rare, but approximately 30 per cent of the patients, almost exclusively boys, have shown precocious sexual development. Kitay and Altschule (1954) reviewed 160 cases of pineal tumor in children under 16 years of age, 130 boys and 30 girls, of whom 43 (all boys) showed precocious sexual development.

Two major hypotheses have been advanced to account for the association of pineal tumors with precocious puberty. One proposes that precocity occurs from loss of the gonadotropin-inhibiting effect of one or more pineal hormones, and the other that it is a direct result of hypothalamic damage in a manner analogous to the effect of other tumors in this area. The latter hypothesis has been favored by most recent authors (Wilkins, 1965; Reichlin, 1968). There is, however, a considerable body of evidence that suggests a more specific role for the pineal (Wurtman, 1968); (1) precocity can occur with hypoplasia of the pineal (8 of 9 cases quoted by Kitay and Altschule, 1954); (2) the size of the tumor seems to be unrelated to its endocrine effects; (3) tumors may be associated not only with precocity but also with delayed puberty or hypogonadism; (even though difficulties in histologic classification have plagued the field, most authorities agree that precocity more frequently accompanies nonparenchymatous tumors and that hypogonadism is associated with parenchymatous tumors); (4) experimental evidence in mammals demonstrates that pineal secretions are antigonadotropic; recent studies in rats suggest that melatonin and 5-hydroxytryptophol suppress secretion of LH and that serotonin and 5-methoxytryptophol suppress secretion of FSH (Fraschini, Collu, & Martini, 1971).

Parenchymatous pinealomas may show temporary response to external irradiation and chemotherapy, but the only hope of cure is by surgery. Encouraging results of surgical removal have been reported from Japan (Suzuki & Iwabuchi, 1965).

In general, it is not possible to correlate the character, sequence, or timing of pubertal changes with a particular neurologic lesion. However, some clues may be derived from the method of presentation. Very early onset of pubertal changes without other evidence of neurologic deficit suggests the presence of a hamartoma or ganglioglioma of the tuber cinereum. More frequently, the type of lesion can be inferred from associated somatic or neurologic abnormalities, such as the manifestations of neurofibromatosis or tuberous sclerosis, and the characteristic syndromes of aqueductal stenosis or an expanding lesion in the pineal region.

Aberrations of the normal sequence of puberty occur in neurogenic as well as in idiopathic precocious puberty, especially in girls. We observed uterine bleeding as the first manifestation of puberty in 3 of 16 girls with neurogenic precocious puberty, and growth of pubic hair preceded breast development in 3.

Treatment of tumors by irradiation or surgery is sometimes possible, and occasionally other neurologic lesions may be remediable, e.g., by cerebrospinal fluid diversion, in aqueductal stenosis. Occasionally, such measures have been followed by slight but definite regression of the signs of precocity (Horrax, 1936; Dietz et al, 1953; Northfield & Russell, 1967).

In 1963 we observed a boy, 6 years, 4 months old, with a 2-month history of rapid growth and sexual development. His penis and testes enlarged, pubic hair appeared, and his voice deepened. During the course of our study he developed progressive neurologic findings. A pneumoencephalogram disclosed slight dilatation of the ventricles and enlargement of the mammillary bodies. The consulting neurosurgeon considered surgical exploration unwarranted. Roentgen therapy was administered; the neurologic signs regressed rapidly and there was an arrest of sexual maturation. At age 14 he had another growth spurt and further sexual maturation.

Premature Pubarche

Premature pubarche or adrenarche, the isolated growth of sexual hair, is another form of precocious sexual development that may be neurogenically determined. It occurs more frequently and earlier in girls than in boys and is generally accompanied by a moderate increase in the rate of growth and skeletal maturation but without a generalized excess of body hair, clitoral enlargement, or other evidence of virilization or precocity. These patients eventually mature at a normal age. Thamdrup (1961) described 17 patients who were discovered in institutions for the mentally defective, of whom 12 showed evidence of severe organic brain lesions. Seven of 29 children described by Silverman, Migeon, Rosemberg, and Wilkins (1952) also showed evidence of mental retardation, but other authors note the association with cerebral lesions to be infrequent (Ferrier, Shepard, & Smith, 1961; Sigurjonsdottir & Hayles, 1968). In contrast to complete precocious puberty, this condition tends to be associated with widespread diffuse central nervous system disease without specific localization to the hypothalamus or other areas. Recent studies have demonstrated excess secretion of adrenal androgens which can be suppressed by the administration of dexamethasone (Conly, Sandberg, & Cleveland, 1967; Rosenfield, 1971).

McCune-Albright Syndrome

Precocious puberty is a characteristic feature of this syndrome, in which there is an association with polyostotic fibrous dysplasia of bone and areas of cutaneous pigmentation. The syndrome occurs almost exclusively in girls, and there is no recorded genetic component. The sequence of pubertal changes is frequently deranged and vaginal bleeding may precede other signs of maturation by several years (Benedict, 1962). It has been suggested that the precocious development may occur as a result of pressure on the hypothalamus due to sclerosis of the base of the skull, but sexual maturation has occurred before skull changes could be demonstrated. Other endocrine abnormalities can also occur in this syndrome, notably hyperthyroidism. It has been suggested that the endocrine manifestations may represent a widespread failure of neuroendocrine control, with inappropriate secretion of one or more of the releasing factors (Hall & Warrick, 1972).

Silver's Syndrome

The association of precocious puberty with this syndrome is also of interest. Typically, children with this condition are of low birth weight for the period of gestation and later have small stature, with retarded bone age, craniofacial disproportion, asymmetry, clinodactyly, normal genitalia, and increased gonadotropin levels. Some undergo precocious maturation, presumably because of increased gonadotropin production. The cause of the disorder is unknown (Silver, 1964).

Sexual Precocity with Primary Hypothyroidism

The sexual precocity which sometimes accompanies primary hypothyroidism in the prepubertal child has been called the "hormonal overlap" syndrome. A number of clinical features (Hayles & Cloutier, 1972) as well as direct measurements of gonadotropin levels (Costin, Kogut, Kershnar, & Turkington, 1972) suggest that the precocity is caused by gonadotropin secretion. This secretion is presumably mediated through the hypothalamus, and it may be supposed that in some way activation of thyrotropin releasing factor and thyroid stimulating hormone "overlap" to produce excessive gonadotropin secretion. In this condition, also, there is dissociation of the pubertal changes; in particular, sexual hair growth is delayed and scanty.

SUMMARY AND CONCLUSIONS

In a homogeneous population under similar environmental conditions the sequence and timing of the changes of puberty are fairly constant, occurring approximately 2 years earlier in girls than in boys and following an orderly progression with each feature showing a standard deviation in timing of approximately 1 year (Tanner, 1969). The onset of puberty normally correlates well with attainment of a critical weight, but the signal, the manner in which it is sensed by the nervous system, and the central limb of the mechanism that initiates and maintains the changes of puberty remain obscure. In some children a process of maturation that may be indistinguishable clinically from normal puberty occurs several years before the normal age of puberty. Such children may attain full maturity, as judged by all criteria including reproductive potential. This indicates that the hypothalamic-pituitary-gonadal axis, and presumably its central connections, is capable of an adult type of response from an early age. In most of these children the changes occur in the absence of a demonstrated lesion in the central nervous system. Therefore this idiopathic form of precocious puberty has been considered a functional neurological problem. Rarely, the condition occurs as a familial trait which can be inherited in a simple Mendelian fashion. It is an interesting and unexplained fact that girls develop this problem much more frequently than boys, yet among the familial cases boys are more frequently affected than girls.

A wide variety of expanding and destructive lesions affecting the hypothalamic area can cause an identical process of maturation. Although these lesions are often diffuse, precocity can also result from small localized malformations in the region of the tuber cinereum and mammillary bodies. The pituitary must be intact for sexual maturation to occur, and intrinsic lesions of the pituitary and also of the anterior hypothalamus can cause delayed puberty. Tumors that destroy the pineal gland are associated with precocity, whereas parenchymatous pinealomas are more frequently associated with delayed maturation.

These observations suggest that the pituitary is stimulated by a center in the anterior hypothalamus and is inhibited by a center in the posterior hypothalamus. The destructive nature of many of the lesions in the posterior hypothalamus which cause precocity suggests that neuronal damage and loss cause precocity; it also indicates that this region is concerned with inhibiting gonadotropin release (Donovan & van der Werff ten Bosch, 1965). Occasionally treatment can lead to regression of the changes, which suggests that the neuronal damage may sometimes be reversible. The fact that destruction of pineal parenchymatous tissue also leads to precocity indicates that this gland can also provide an overriding inhibitory influence on gonadotropin secretion. Significant alterations of the sequence of pubertal changes occur in both idiopathic and neurogenic precocious puberty and are the rule in the McCune-Albright syndrome and the "hormonal overlap" syndrome of juvenile hypothyroidism. Thus, assuming that the end organs are normally responsive, it seems probable that subtle abnormalities of central control are present. The occurrence of premature growth of sexual hair without other manifestations of puberty, followed by normal puberty at a normal time, suggests that pubarche may be initiated by a separate mechanism. Then neurogenic cases of premature pubarche indicate that this mechanism is likely to be central but do not enable us to localize the site.

Thus study of the clinical disorders associated with precocious sexual development may provide many clues to a better understanding of the physiology of normal sexual maturation and the pathogenesis of its derangements in man.

REFERENCES

Bauer, H. G. (1954). Endocrine and other clinical manifestations of hypothalamic disease: a survey of 60 cases, with autopsies. *J. Clin. Endocrinol.* **14**, 13–31.

Beas, F., Zurbrügg, R. P., Leibow, S. G., Patton, R. G., & Gardner, L. I. (1962). Familial male sexual precocity: report of the eleventh kindred found, with observations on blood group linkage and urinary C_{19}-steroid excretion. *J. Clin. Endocrinol.* **22**, 1095–1102.

Benedict, P. H. (1962). Endocrine features in Albright's syndrome (fibrous dysplasia of bone). *Metabolism* **11**, 30–45.

Conly, P. W., Sandberg, D. H., & Cleveland, W. W. (1967). Steroid metabolism in premature pubarche and virilizing adrenal hyperplasia. *J. Pediat.* **71**, 506–511.

Costin, G., Kogut, M. D., Kershnar, A. K., & Turkington, R. W. (1972). Plasma prolactin levels in juvenile hypothyroidism and precocious puberty. *Pediat. Res.* **6**, 351.

Diez, L. F., Staffieri, J. J., & Celoria, J. E. (1953). Pubertad precoz en un niño de tres meses por tumor del tercer ventriculo. *Medicinia* (Buenos Aires) **13**, 116–123.

Donovan, B. T. & van der Werff ten Bosch, J. J. (1965). *Physiology of Puberty,* Williams & Wilkins, Baltimore.

Driggs, M. & Spatz, H. (1939). Pubertas praecox bei einer hyperplastischen miszbildung des Tuber cinereum. *Virch. Arch. Path. Anat. Physiol.* **305**, 567–592.

Ferrier, P., Shepard, II, T. H., & Smith, E. K. (1961). Growth disturbances and values for hormone excretion in various forms of precocious sexual development. *Pediatrics* **28**, 258–275.

Fraschini, F., Collu, R., & Martini, L. (1971). Mechanisms of inhibitory action of pineal principles on gonadotropin secretion. In *The Pineal Gland*, G. E. Wolstenholme & J. Knight, Eds., Churchill, Livingstone, Edinburgh, pp. 259–278.

Frisch, R. E. & Revelle, R. (1971). Height and weight at menarche and a hypothesis of menarche. *Arch. Dis. Child.* **46**, 695–701.

Gesell, A., Thoms, H., Hartman, F. G., & Thompson, H. (1939). Mental and physical growth in pubertas praecox: report of 15 years' study of a case. *Arch. Neurol. Psychiat.* **41**, 755–772.

Greenblatt, R. B., Dmowski, W. P., Mahesh, V. B., & Scholer, H. F. L. (1971). Clinical studies with an antigonadotropin-Danazol. *Fertil. Steril.* **22**, 102–112.

Hall, R. & Warrick, C. (1972). Hypersecretion of hypothalamic releasing hormones: a possible explanation of the endocrine manifestations of polyostotic fibrous dysplasia (Albright's syndrome). *Lancet* **1**, 1313–1316.

Harris, G. W. & Naftolin, F. (1970). The hypothalamus and control of ovulation. *Brit. Med. Bull.* **26**, 3–9.

Hayles, A. B. & Cloutier, M. D. (1972). Clinical hypothyroidism in the young—a second look. *Med. Clin. N. Amer.* **56**, 871–884.

Horrax, G. (1936). Further observations on tumor of the pineal body. *Arch. Neurol. Psychiat.* **35**, 215–228.

Hung, W., Milhorat, T. H., Nelson, K. B., & August, G. P. (1971). Sexual precocity as the only sign of a brain tumor in a 9-year-old boy. *Amer. J. Dis. Child.* **121**, 524–527.

Jolly, H. (1955). *Sexual Precocity*, Thomas, Springfield, Ill.

Kitay, J. I. & Altschule, M. D. (1954). *The Pineal Gland: Review of the Physiologic Literature.* Harvard University Press, Cambridge, Mass.

Kulin, H. E., Grumbach, M. M., & Kaplan, S. E. (1972). Gonadal-hypothalamic interaction in prepubertal and pubertal man: effect of clomiphene citrate on urinary follicle-stimulating hormone and luteinizing hormone and plasma testosterone. *Pediat. Res.* **6**, 162–171.

Liu, N., Grumbach, M. M., de Napoli, R. A., & Morishima, A. (1965). Prevalence of electroencephalographic abnormalities in idiopathic precocious puberty and premature pubarche: bearing on pathogenesis and neuroendocrine regulation of puberty. *J. Clin. Endocrinol.* **25**, 1296–1308.

Money, J. (1969). Psychologic aspects of endocrine and genetic disease in children. In *Endocrine and Genetic Disease of Childhood*, L. I. Gardner, Ed., Saunders, Phildaelphia, pp. 1004–1014.

Northfield, D. W. C. & Russell, D. S. (1967). Pubertas praecox due to hypothalamic hamartoma: report of two cases surviving surgical removal of the tumour. *J. Neurol. Neurosurg. Psychiat.* **30**, 166–173.

Penny, R., Guyda, H. J., Baghdassarian, A., Johanson, A. J., & Blizzard, R. M. (1970). Correlation of serum follicular stimulating hormone (FSH) and luteinizing hormone (LH) as measured by radioimmunoassay in disorders of sexual development. *J. Clin. Invest.* **49**, 1847–1852.

Reichlin, S. (1968). Neuroendocrinology. In *Textbook of Endocrinology*, R. H. Williams, Ed., Saunders, Philadelphia, pp. 967–1016.

Richman, R. A., Underwood, L. E., French, F. S., & Van Wyk, J. J. (1971). Adverse effects of large doses of medroxyprogesterone (MPA) in idiopathic isosexual precocity. *J. Pediat.* **79**, 963–971.

Richter, R. B. (1951). True hamartoma of the hypothalamus associated with pubertas praecox. *J. Neuropath. Exptl. Neurol.* **10**, 368–383.

Rifkind, A. B., Kulin, H. E., Cargille, C. M., Rayford, P. C., & Ross, G. T. (1969). Suppression of urinary excretion of luteinizing hormone (LH) and follicle stimulating hormone (FSH) by medroxyprogesterone acetate. *J. Clin. Endocrinol.* **29**, 506–513.

Rimoin, D. L. & Schimke, R. N. (1971). *Genetic Disorders of the Endocrine Glands*, Mosby, St. Louis.

Rosenfield, R. L. (1971). Plasma 17-ketosteroids and 17-beta hydroxysteroids in girls with premature development of sexual hair. *J. Pediat.* **79**, 260–266.

Schmidt, E., Hallervorden, J., & Spatz, H. (1958). Die Entstehung der Hamartome am Hypothalamus mit und ohne Pubertas praecox. *Dtsch. Z. Nervenheilk.* **177**, 235–262.

Seckel, H. P. G. (1946). Precocious sexual development in children. *Med. Clin. N. Amer.* 183–209.

Sheehan, H. L. (1969). Neurohypophysis and hypothalamus. In *Endocrine Pathology*, J. M. B. Bloodworth, Jr., Ed., Williams & Wilkins, Baltimore, pp. 12–74.

Sherins, R. J., Gandy, H. M., Thorslund, T. W., & Paulsen, C. A. (1971). Pituitary and testicular function studies. I. Experience with a new gonadal inhibitor, 17α-pregn-4-en-20-o-(2, 3-d) isoxazol-17-ol (Danazol). *J. Clin. Endocrinol.* **32**, 522–531.

Sherwin, R. P., Grassi, J. E., & Sommers, S. C. (1962). Hamartomatous malformation of the posterolateral hypothalamus. *Lab. Invest.* **11**, 89–97.

Sigurjonsdottir, T. J. & Hayles, A. B. (1968). Premature pubarche. *Clin. Pediat.* **7**, 29–33.

Silver, H. K. (1964). Asymmetry, short stature, and variations in sexual development: a syndrome of congenital malformations. *Amer. J. Dis. Child.* **107**, 495–515.

Silverman, S. H., Migeon, C., Rosemberg, E., & Wilkins, L. (1952). Precocious growth of sexual hair without other secondary sexual development: "premature pubarche," a constitutional variation of adolescence. *Pediatrics* **10**, 426–432.

Suzuki, J. & Iwabuchi, T. (1965). Surgical removal of pineal tumors (pinealomas and teratomas): experience in a series of 19 cases. *J. Neurosurg.* **23**, 565–571.

Tanner, J. M. (1969). Growth and endocrinology of the adolescent. In *Endocrine and Genetic Diseases of Childhood*, L. I. Gardner, Ed., Saunders, Philadelphia, pp. 19–60.

Thamdrup, E. (1961). *Precocious Sexual Development: A Clinical Study of 100 Children,* Thomas, Springfield, Ill.

Wilkins, L. (1965). *The Diagnosis and Treatment of Endocrine Disorders in Childhood and Adolescence,* 3rd ed., Thomas, Springfield, Ill.

Wolman, L. & Balmforth (1963). Precocious puberty due to a hypothalamic hamartoma in a patient surviving to late middle age. *J. Neurol. Neurosurg. Psychiat.* **26**, 275–280.

Wurtman, R. J. (1968). The pineal gland. In *Endocrine Pathology,* J. M. B. Bloodworth, Jr., Ed., Williams & Wilkins, Baltimore.

Zacharias, L. & Wurtman, R. J. (1969). Age at menarche: genetic and environmental influences. *New Eng. J. Med.* **280**, 868–875.

DISCUSSION

Dr. Root. Are there data concerning production rates of gonadotropins in patients with primary hypothyroidism and sexual precocity? Might elevated gondotropin levels in these patients reflect nonspecific cross reactivity with the glycoprotein TSH? It is difficult to conceive that the pituitary cannot distinguish between the need for TSH and that for gonadotropins. Inasmuch as the gonads of hypothyroid rats are quite sensitive to gonadotropins (Wallach, 1968), might this not also be true in man? The role of prolactin, whose secretion is also increased by thyrotropin releasing hormone, must also be elucidated, because prolactin may induce sexual precocity in rats (Clemens, Minaguchi, Storey, Voogt, & Meites (1969).

Dr. Van Wyk. In the dozen years that have elapsed since Dr. Grumbach and I described these patients a few aspects have become clear. In 1960 we could only infer that there was some type of overlap, but we did not know whether this was a molecular or cellular overlay or whether it occurred at the hypothalamic or at the pituitary level. It is now clear that TRH also stimulates the release of prolactin. Turkington has confirmed that these patients with long-standing hypothyroidism and inappropriate sexual precocity have very high prolactin levels in their serum. Although this satisfactorily explains the galactorrhea of these patients, it is still not apparent why the girls with this syndrome menstruate and why boys have testicular enlargement in the face of retarded bone age and absence of sexual hair. Most observers have been unable to show any elevation of urinary gonadotropins by the old unsatisfactory bioassay method; I do not know of any studies in which the plasma gonadotropin levels have been measured by radioimmunoassay. Such studies might be difficult to interpret, since the A chains of TSH and the gonadotropins are identical, and most antisera cross-react. Because of this molecular similarity, it would not be difficult to imagine that in a situation in which there is extreme overproduction of TSH, there might very well be elaboration of excessive quantities of gonadotropins. It is likewise possible that TSH itself have some intrinsic gonadotropin activity; if it is given in high enough dosage, it might overlap by interacting with gonadotropin release or stimulating the gonads directly. In summary, the mechanism of the lactation in these patients is now clear, the sexual precocity is not.

Dr. Grumbach. The patients with the syndrome of hypothyroidism, sexual precocity, and, in affected girls, galactorrhea may exhibit several poorly understood clinical findings about which Dr. Van Wyk and I have had many lively discussions; for example, the testes are enlarged in boys with this syndrome and in girls ovarian cysts are not uncommon. Indeed, a large ovarian cyst may be present, as in the first patient that Jud Van Wyk and I studied. This raises the question: Is there a relation between the high concentration of serum prolactin and gonadal function in this syndrome, especially a possible effect on the action of gonadotropins on gonadal steroidogenesis? The obstetricians are well aware that ovulation and menstruation are rare in women who breast-feed for the first few months postpartum. Tyson, Friesen, and Anderson (1972) suggested that there may be a relation between the failure to ovulate and the secretion of prolactin in lactating women. Stated in another way: Does prolactin in the human being diminish gonadal responsiveness to gonadotropin, especially in relation to gonadal steroidogenesis? This possibility will, no doubt, seem apocryphal to the animal experimentalist, especially those studying rodents. However, such an effect may explain, in part, the peculiar form of precocious sexual development that children with this syndrome manifest; for example, the lack of, or poorly developed, sexual hair, despite large ovaries or testes and, in girls, breast development and uterine bleeding. Is the high concentration of prolactin inhibiting gonadal steroidogenesis to a degree sufficient to promote increased gonadotropin secretion and leading to gonadal enlargement or is the elevated prolactin modifying the steroidogenic action of the gonadotropins, the latter being secreted at pubertal levels by a different mechanism? Clearly, we have much to learn about the effect of prolactin on gonadal function and on gonadotropin secretion in man.

DR. DAVIDSON.   Apropos of prolactin, Clemens et al (1969) demonstrated that prolactin precipitates precocious puberty in rats, and this has since been confirmed a number of times.

DR. ODELL. We have seen three patients with pinealomas over the last few years in whom precocious puberty was caused by tumor elaboration of gonadotropin; concentrations were outside the physiological range but less than that which would be detected by tests for pregnancy. The neoplasms were all pineal teratomas. Considering only pinealomas and precocious puberty, is tumor production of gonadotropin common or uncommon?

DR. HAYLES.   I think it is uncommon. I did not get into the problem of the teratomas of the pineal. Teratomas may rarely be gonadotropin producing.

DR. ODELL.   Both you and Dr. Gorski have reviewed that anterior hypothalamic lesions in the female rat cause precocious puberty; such lesions do not cause precocious puberty in the human. Are you aware of any anatomic data that explain that difference?

DR. GORSKI.   The rat is not the human. However, Dr. Hayles mentioned one male patient who had signs of precocious puberty. After treatment there was a remission of these signs, and then he went into normal puberty. The question is, how pubertal was he in the first place? In other words, can a person enter puberty twice?

Dr. Hayles.   He is an extremely interesting patient. There are not many such patients described. This boy has clear evidence of precocious puberty, with frequent erections, sexual hair growth, and rapid growth of the penis and testes. After radiotherapy there was cessation of sexual maturation, and he had only an occasional erection. Sex hair did not develop further. He remained stable, and I wondered if his testes would grow when he got to the age of puberty. He returned recently; his testes have grown, and he has had a growth spurt. He is now normal in height, is sexually well developed, has erections and ejaculations, and has no significant neurologic deficit. I cannot say that he had a regression in sexual development, but he certainly had a cessation of rapidly progressing sexual development. In the patients described by Northfield and Russell there was rapid regression in muscle development, but we do not know whether their patients re-entered puberty or continued later into puberty. I expect it is more accurate to say that puberty was arrested, but the very fact that arrest can occur disturbs me in my understanding of what happens in the hypothalamus.

Dr. McCann.   Dr. Grumbach stated that in patients with hypothyroidism and high prolactin levels prolactin may be suppressing the action of gonadotropin and alluded to amenorrhea of lactating women as an example of that. My suggestion is that the amenorrhea of lactating women is due to suppression of release of gonadotropin as a result of the suckling stimulus rather than any effect of the prolactin in blocking gonadotropin action at the ovarian level. We showed that suckling suppressed LH release in the rat (McCann, Crowes, & Taleisnik, 1961)). I would like Dr. Grumbach to tell us more about this inhibitory effect of prolactin on the action of gonadotropin, if indeed it exists.

Dr. Grumbach.   There is evidence in lactating women that the amenorrhea is not related to diminished gonadotropin secretion, as pointed out by Dr. James Bradbury and his group some 10 years ago. On the other hand, Tyson found that in lactating women the vaginal smear shows a poor estrogenic effect. These observations could be explained either by diminished estrogen secretion by the gonad or by decreased end-organ responsiveness to estrogen. This problem should be clarified when studies are available of sex steroid and gonadotropin secretion in patients with high prolactin levels who are restudied when the prolactin concentration is suppressed. Again, there may be important species differences in the effect of prolactin on gonadal function.

Dr. Faiman.   We have had occasion to look at a small number of postpartum women (Reyes, Winter, & Faiman, 1972), and it appears that FSH levels are low in all subjects for 10 days to 2 weeks after delivery, following which there is recovery of FSH levels to normal. However, the recovery of suppressed estradiol levels following this FSH increment appears to be intimately related to whether they are lactating or not lactating and also correlates well with prolactin levels. Those who are lactating and have higher prolactin levels have delayed recovery of estradiol levels. In addition, Zarate, Canales, Soria, Ruiz, and MacGregor (1972) gave human postmenopausal gonadotropin to a group of lactating women and showed impaired ovarian responsiveness.

DR. ROSS.   The pigeon provides a classical example of altered gonadal function in relation to pituitary prolactin secretion. In this species both males and females produce crop milk and the gonads of both sexes undergo profound atrophy during this period of crop-milk production.

DR. HAYLES.   I precede the era of birth control. Years ago there were schoolyards full of children who were not supposed to be there because their mothers were lactating!

DR. REITER.   In the past calcification of the human pineal generally was taken to mean that the organ was atrophic. This is probably incorrect. The activity of several enzymes in the pineal remain active throughout life (Wurtman, Axelrod, & Barchas, 1964). In fact, the reverse may be true, i.e., pineal calcification may mean increased activity. In 4 recent cases of hypogonadotropic hypogonadism associated with anosmia the one noticeable feature was obvious pineal calcification (Tagatz, Failkow, Smith, & Spadoni, 1970). The pineal may have induced gonadal regression in these individuals (Berg & Klein, 1971). In another case of sexual infantilism in a 10-year-old boy, reported by Moreau and Cohen (1965), the only aberrant feature, besides the delayed genital development, was a hypercalcified pineal. It may be worthwhile to look at the degree of pineal calcification and gonadotropin levels in humans; I do not feel a calcified pineal is nonfunctional.

DR. JOB.   Figure 1 shows data on central precocious puberty observed in 7 patients aged 2 to 9 years (3 boys and 2 girls, 2 tumoral and 5 apparently idiopathic) and in 2 cases of premature thelarche. The children with precocious puberty (Nos. 1 to 7) have never had elevated basal levels of gonadotropins but all have had peak levels of FSH and/or LH over the normal prepubertal range. The 2 girls with isolated premature thelarche (Nos. 8 and 9) have surprisingly high FSH reserve, and one patient (No. 9) also has an elevated LH reserve.

DR. FISHER.   Dr. Hayles's statistics of a male-to-female ratio of 6:1 in cases of precocious puberty are of interest in that the incidence of delayed adolescence is much higher in males than females; rarely is there delayed adolescence in a female. This is germane to Dr. Odell's question about whether there is some male-female difference in extrahypothalamic influence on the hypothalamus prepubertally. The other comment has to do with the 60 or 70 per cent of Dr. Hayles's patients who were considered to have precocious puberty, i.e., those in whom discrete CNS lesions could not be found. Dr. Grumbach has published that 80 per cent of the females in his study group had abnormal electroencephalograms. It is often difficult to tell which patients are neurogenic and which idiopathic; sometimes it takes a while, and the gray area is often very wide. When you look carefully at these females, you can sometimes find signs of what pediatricians now loosely call minimal brain dysfunction or even mild mental retardation, often noticed when affected

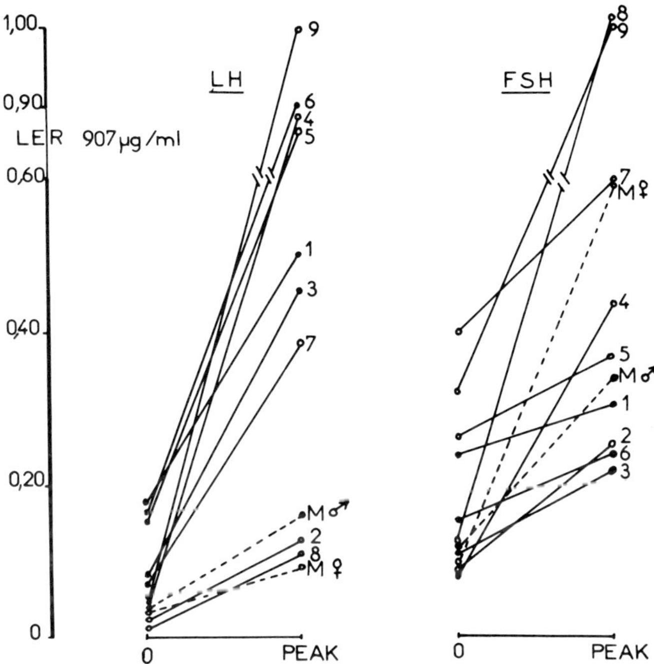

FIG. 1.   Mean basal levels and peak levels of LH and FSH after LH-RH (0.1 mg) in 7 cases of precocious puberty and 2 cases of premature thelarche (M: mean of prepubertal controls; see text.).

children get far enough along in school. You might find incoordination or some other subtle manifestations, including special sensory disorders. Thus I wonder if any of these are collated in your series of idiopathic patients. Do you think this is really so?

DR. HAYLES.   There is no question that some patients have subtle, nonprogressive neurologic abnormalities. Whether or not these abnormalities are a part of, due to, or coincidental with changes of puberty, I do not know. The problem is much more important in the male because of the high incidence of demonstrable organic lesions of serious consequence. Although we cannot often satisfactorily treat these patients, the earlier we identify them, the more likely it is that something can be done for them.

DR. BEJAR.   It is true about the electroencephalographic abnormality. I do not entirely agree with the soft neurological findings. In most of the "idiopathic precocities" we do not find any neurological abnormality, and intelligence appears to be normal. Another phenomenon in the small girl is the development of breasts, one or two menstrual periods, and then regression of all the signs of puberty. I have seen two such cases, with elevation of gonadotropin.

DR. HAYLES.   Most such small children will be found to have ingested grandmother's estrogen or mother's birth control pills.

DR. BEJAR.   I cannot deny such a possibility, but we were careful in taking the histories; the parents denied the possibility of drug ingestion. I do not understand this phenomenon, but it is striking that the gonadotropins in the urine were elevated.

DR. HAYLES.   We have been unable to measure gonadotropin in the urine of these children. We frequently find synthetic estrogens in their urine.

DR. BLIZZARD.   We cannot confirm electroencephalographic changes in sexual precocity. Dr. Money ought to say something about whether these girls with sexual precocity have any evidence of neurological disease; he has examined more of these girls than anyone else.

DR. MONEY.   Over the years we have seen one or two precocious girls who obviously had a severe degree of clumsiness and motor incoordination, but they are very much the minority in the group as a whole. In an actual survey of these patients a suprising number of them have above average or superior level IQ, so much so that part of the case management is to have the children accelerated at school. Acceleration reduces the amount of time they have to spend with a disparity between their physique age and chronological age, with their social age drifting somewhere in between. Acceleration speeds them into mixing with the social group of teenagers of similar physique age, sometimes 2 years earlier (Money & Alexander, 1967; Money & Meredith, 1967; Money & Neill, 1967; Money & Walker, 1971). In brief, we do not really have any evidence of signs of soft neurological or minimal brain damage in sexually precocious girls.

DR. GANONG.   Dr. Hayles, you said that someone had removed hamartomas and gotten a regression of puberty. The point is very important because these are very small benign tumors; if they are removed, and the disease regresses, this is strong evidence that they are still irritative and not destructive in terms of their effects on gonadotropin secretion.

DR. HAYLES.   I know of only 2 patients who have had hamartomas removed; 1 had extreme muscular development which regressed within 3 weeks. However, I do not want to leave the impression that the patient returned to normal; he simply had a cessation of pubertal development.

DR. WINTER.   We have examined gonadal steroids and gonadotropins in children with idiopathic sexual precocity. Serum levels of testosterone are distinctly elevated above the normal range. Similar elevations of serum estradiol are found in girls with precocious puberty. We were therefore initially surprised to find that not all of these children had elevated serum gonadotropin concentrations; 4 of 8 boys had serum LH levels below the male upper normal range, whereas 2 of 9 girls had levels within the female range for age. Several of these patients have shown normal LH and FSH levels on repeated daytime testing. Initially we thought that this might represent increased gonadal sensitivity to gonadotropin stimulation, but now I wonder whether they are perhaps showing nocturnal sleep-associated bursts of gonadotropin release. Has anyone examined LH and FSH during sleep in similar patients?

DR. BOYAR.   We studied 3 patients with idiopathic precocious puberty and advanced bone age at 20-minute intervals for 24 hours, as in our reported normal studies. In precocious puberty some patients had normal prepubertal concentrations of LH and FSH during waking hours; however, at night, there was episodic secretion of LH and FSH similar to that found during normal puberty. Idiopathic precocious puberty, then, is the early activation of the normal pubertal process. There is no hypersecretion at night; the patterns are the same as they are in early pubertal patients.

DR. ROSS.   This is another way in which precocious puberty and puberty at the expected age are similar.

DR. ROSENFIELD.   Dr. Davidson suggested that when normal pubertal processes are initiated the progress of puberty is as inexorable as a rock rolling downhill after a push. Experience with cases of sexual precocity, as in the McCune-Albright syndrome, indicates that puberty may progress to the point of menarche, yet feminization may regress subsequently. Menarche in such cases may represent overflow or withdrawal bleeding and ovulation, the "point of no return" in puberty. But this remains to be proved. The syndrome of precocious adrenarche seems to me to result from a maturational change in the adrenal biosynthetic response to ACTH (Rosenfield, 1971). The factors responsible for this change are not well understood, but it seems that adrenarche does not necessarily result from increased pituitary activity. I would like to ask Dr. McCann where dopamine fits in. Does its administration consistently release gonadotropins in the rat? We (Porter, Rosenfield, & Lawrence, 1972) and others have reported that when you give L-dopa to prepubertal children you do not get gonadotropin release, though GH is discharged.

DR. McCANN.   There is considerable evidence for an adrenergic link in the gonadotropin control system. Some evidence points to dopamine as a transmitter to stimulate GRF release. Other evidence points to a role for norepinephrine in the preovulatory release of gonadotropins (McCann et al, 1972). The Swedish workers, Ufute and Hokfelt, even claim that dopamine has an inhibitory role. The response to dopamine probably depends on the hormonal background and is augmented by estrogen. This important point may explain the fact that you did not get any response to L-dopa, which has presumably been taken up by the hypothalamus and converted to dopamine and norephinephrine in the brains of these children; for example, Schneider's experiments in our laboratory produced no significant response in ovariectomized animals when dopamine was put in the third ventricle and no significant response on the first day of diestrus. We got a response on diestrus day 2 and the best response was on the morning of the proestrus, indicating that estrogen predisposes to this response. Our more recent work suggests that probably norepinephrine is involved in the ovulatory surge of gonadotropins rather than dopamine.

DR. JAFFE.   In the intact human I am not sure that one should expect to get a gonadotropic response; although Lebovitz showed that one could stimulate GH in the adult with L-dopa, we and others have demonstrated that you can suppress prolactin with L-dopa. One cannot stimulate gonadotropins with the comparable doses that stimulate growth hormone or suppress prolactin in the adult human female.

DR. KULIN.   There is good evidence that the hormonal changes which accompany puberty in the human last many years. There appears to be a slow, steady increase in gonadotropins which takes place during the years before the precipitous rise that occurs during puberty. This pattern of events may be contrasted to the rapid onset of sexual maturation which may take place in some very young children with precocious puberty. Certain irritative stimuli in the region of the hypothalamus seem capable of influencing a "switch-type" mechanism, suddenly turning on the whole process. I have trouble reconciling these 2 types of maturational pattern.

REFERENCES

Berg, G. R. & Klein, D. C. (1971). Non-cartesian pineal function. *New Eng. J. Med.* **284**, 332.

Clemens, J. A., Minaguchi, H., Storey, R., Voogt, J. L., & Meites, J. (1969). Induction of precocious puberty in female rats by prolactin. *Neuroendocrinology* **4**, 150–157.

McCann, S. M., Graves, T., & Taleisnik, S. (1961). Effect of lactation on plasma LH. *Endocrinology* **68**, 873–875.

Money, J. & Alexander, D. (1967). Eroticism and sexual function in developmental anorchia and hyporchia with pubertal failure. *J. Sex Res.* **3**, 31–47.

Money, J. & Meredith, T. (1967). Elevated verbal IQ and idiopathic precocious sexual maturation. *Pediat. Res.* **1**, 59–65.

Money, J. & Neill, J. (1967). Precocious puberty, IQ and school acceleration. *Clin. Ped.* **6**, 277–280.

Money, J. & Walker, P. A. (1971). Psychosexual development, maternalism, non-promiscuity, and body image in 15 females with precocious puberty. *Arch. Sex Behav.* **1**, 45–60.

Moreau, M. H. & Cohen, A. L. (1965). Calcification precoz de la glandula pineal e hipogenitalismo (un caso). *Rev. Asoc. Med. Argent.* **79**, 226–229.

Porter, B. A., Rosenfield, R. L., & Lawrence, A. M. (1972). L-dopa stimulation of growth hormone (GH) release in children and its significance. *Pediat. Res.* **6**, 350.

Reyes, G., Winter, J. S. D., & Faiman, C. (1972). Pituitary ovarian interrelationships during the puerperium. *Amer. J. Ob. Gyn.* **114**, 589–595.

Rosenfield, R. L. (1971). Plasma 17-ketosteroids and 17-beta hydroxysteroids in girls with premature development of sexual hair. *J. Pediat.* **79**, 260–266.

Tagatz, G., Failkow, P. J., Smith, D., & Spadoni, L. (1970). Hypogonadotropic hypogonadism associated with anosmia in the female. *New Eng. J. Med.* **283**, 1326–1329.

Tyson, J. E., Friesen, H. J., & Anderson, M. S. (1972). Human lactational and ovarian response to endogenous prolactin release. *Science* **177**, 897–890.

Wallach, E. E. (1968). Female isosexual pseudoprecocious puberty. *Clin. Ob. Gyn.* **11**, 795–815.

Wurtman, R. J., Axelrod, J., & Barchas, J. D. (1964). Age and enzyme activity in the human pineal. *J. Clin. Endocrinol.* **24**, 299–300.

Zarate, A., Canales, E. S., Soria, J., Ruiz, F., & MacGregor, C. (1972). Ovarian refractoriness during lactation in women: Effect of gonadotropin stimulation. *Amer. J. Ob. Gyn.* **112**, 1130–1132.

9.

Delayed Sexual Maturation, with Special Emphasis on the Occurrence of the Syndrome in the Male

H. E. KULIN and E. O. REITER

We have used the standards of Marshall and Tanner (1969; 1970) to define the late-maturing boy or girl. Ninety-five per cent of American girls have their first episode of vaginal bleeding by age 15 and 98 per cent have breast budding (which may be compared to the first increase in testicular size in boys) by age 13. If the Marshall and Tanner standards are applied to American boys (which cannot be done for girls because of the earlier age of menarche in most United States studies compared with the English subjects of Marshall and Tanner), then pubertal delay (>2.5 SD beyond

---

Abbreviations

FSH	Follicle stimulating hormone
GH	Growth hormone
hCG	Human chorionic gonadotropin
hMG	Human menopausal gonadotropin
LH	Luteinizing hormone
LH-RH	Luteinizing hormone-releasing hormone
TP	Testosterone propionate

the mean) is present if the testes have not started to enlarge by age 14. These British workers (1970) state, however, that they have observed "several boys who went through a perfectly normal puberty, beginning after they were 15." This is not surprising, for marked pubertal delay is found far more frequently in boys than in girls. Genitalia of adult size are reached within 4½ years from the onset of pubertal development in 98 per cent of the male population. The time between breast budding and menarche encompasses a similar period for 98 per cent of girls. Marshall and Tanner (1969; 1970) state that in neither girls nor boys is the time taken to pass through the various pubertal stages related to the age of onset. Frisch and Revelle (1971) found that early- and late-maturing girls differ by approximately 8 months from the initiation of the growth spurt to menarche. Comparable figures are not available for boys, but it would be of interest to know the duration of puberty in the "several boys" whom Marshall & Tanner (1970) stated had the onset of increased testicular size after age 15.

CLINICAL SYNDROMES

Delayed puberty may result from intrinsic gonadal disease or from lack of adequate gonadotropin stimulation; some patients may have relative deficiencies of both gonadal and pituitary hormones (Bardin, Ross, Rifkind, Cargille, & Lipsett, 1969). Primary gonadal diseases, such as anorchia or gonadal dysgenesis, may be detected even before the age of puberty, since elevated gonadotropins can be measured in both urine and blood (Kulin, Rifkind, Ross, & Odell, 1967; Penny, Guyda, Baghdassarian, Johanson, & Blizzard, 1970; Winter & Faiman, 1972). Phenotypic girls with chromosomal disorders have been studied most extensively (Penny et al, 1970); elevated levels of blood follicle stimulating hormone (FSH) can correctly delineate the gonadal status of most such individuals at an early age. Boys with Klinefelter's syndrome have not yet been similarly evaluated, although the associated elevation in gonadotropins found in adult men with this disorder becomes manifest at the usual age of pubertal onset or earlier.

Much more puzzling and difficult to diagnose at the time of expected puberty are the clinical syndromes associated with absolute or relative hypogonadotropism. For unknown reasons these conditions occur far more frequently in the male. This finding is as enigmatic as the increased incidence of idiopathic precocious puberty in the female. Basically there are 3 hypogonadotropic syndromes: (1) *gonadotropin deficiency*, which may accompany a lack of other pituitary tropic hormones, whether the cause is a tumor invading the sella turcica or hypothalamus or an unknown neural lesion; (2) *isolated gonadotropin deficiency,* which may take place in either the male (more commonly) or female; genetic factors are also involved in some; and a defect in the ability to smell is an associated finding (Santen & Paulsen, 1973a,b); (3) *physiologic delayed adolescence* is a relatively common clinical disorder which must be differentiated from true gonadotropin deficiency. Unfortunately distinguishing features of these last 2 conditions are frequently absent and all too commonly time alone must be relied on to ensure the diagnosis.

PHYSIOLOGY

Some of the recent concepts in the physiology of normal human puberty may shed light on the syndromes of delayed adolescence and hypogonadotropism. Are there differences in the physiology of sexual maturation of males compared with females that might explain why delayed puberty of the physiologic variety is so much more common in boys?

The presence of gonadotropins in blood and urine of prepubertal children has been firmly established (Kulin & Reiter, 1973). Although Faiman and Winter have reported at this conference that significantly greater fluctuations in the levels of serum FSH and LH occur in girls in the first 2 years of life, during the remainder of childhood these hormones are present in similar amounts for both sexes. Negative feedback to sex steroid hormones is established at an early age in both sexes (Laron & Zilka, 1969; Penny et al, 1970; Winter & Faiman, 1972). Also, in both male and female a change in sensitivity of the hypothalamic-pituitary axis to negative feedback by estrogen accompanies the rise in gonadotropins that takes place during puberty. (Kulin, Grumbach, & Kaplan, 1969; 1972; Kelch, Grumbach, & Kaplan, 1972). It is not known when this change begins in each sex and how much it antedates the onset of physical manifestations of puberty. Available data indicate that gonadotropins rise continuously during childhood, with an abrupt elevation just before and during sexual maturation (Kulin & Reiter, 1973).

Santen, Leonard, Sherins, Gandy, and Paulsen (1971) have shown that men with idiopathic isolated hypogonadotropism may exhibit a gonadotropic response to clomiphene citrate similar to that produced by the drug in immature children. FSH and LH are depressed, rather than stimulated, by clomiphene, seemingly as a result of its weakly estrogenic action combined with a highly sensitive estrogen receptor apparatus in the hypothalamus of such individuals. Santen and his colleagues (1971) also suggest that some cases of the syndrome of hypogonadotropic hypogonadism may result from a maturational arrest of the mechanisms which cause FSH and LH to rise at the appropriate time rather than from a prepubertal deficiency of these hormones.

An important event in sexual maturation in the female is the development of positive gonadotropin feedback to estrogen. This phenomenon, now thought to be integral to the normal midcycle ovulatory LH surge, appears to be a relatively late pubertal event. It becomes manifest only after the change in negative feedback sensitivity is well advanced (Kulin et al, 1972; Reiter, Kulin, & Hamwood, 1973).

The human male also displays positive feedback to estrogen administration; this also may be a maturational event (Kulin & Reiter, in preparation). Figure 1 shows the results of LH and steroid determinations from 4 normal men who were given 15 μg/Kg of 17 β-estradiol intramuscularly for 5 days. Following initial suppression of LH and testosterone, these hormones increased toward baseline levels in the presence of elevated estradiol concentrations. We administered similar doses of estrogen to 10 pre- or early pubertal boys without such positive feedback effects. Unfortunately 3 mature men given estradiol did not exhibit an LH rise after suppression, so that the ability to demonstrate the phenomenon does not seem invariable in the intact adult male. The presence of endogenous testosterone may play a role, as Yamaji, Dierschke, Hotchkiss, Bhattacharya, Surve, and Knobil (1971) have been able to elicit an LH rise with estrogen in castrate but not in intact adult male rhesus monkeys.

Estrogen-induced LH stimulation does not appear to be clinically useful as a maturational marker in the normal male. A rise in gonadotropin following clomiphene may serve as such a marker (Kulin et al, 1972), although the mechanism of action of that drug still remains unclear. A derangement in positive feedback maturation may be a factor in delayed menarche in the female, but there is no reason to postulate a similar defect for delayed puberty in the male.

DIAGNOSIS

Gonadotropin deficiency, when combined with a lack of other tropic hormones from the pituitary gland, may be assessed in the prepubertal child by the measurement of serum LH. Penny et al (1972) studied a group of hypopituitary subjects and showed that serum LH concentration below the normal range for prepubertal patients is suggestive of a deficiency in that gonadotropin. Such hormone measurements, however, approach the limits of sensitivity of the RIA for LH, and we acknowledge the limited usefulness of such measurements for diagnosis in a given patient.

It is also important to realize that although children with isolated growth

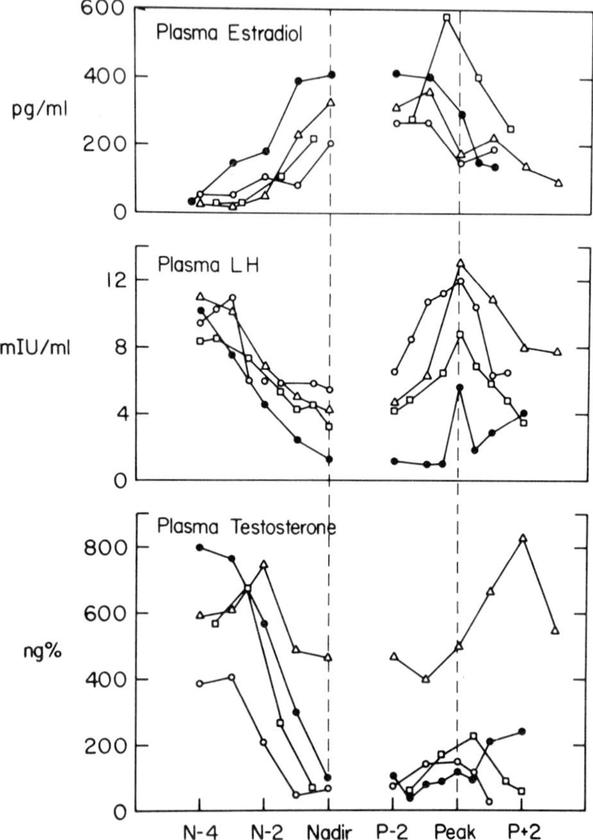

FIG. 1. The effect on plasma LH (Odell, Rayford, & Ross, 1967); testosterone (Dufau, Catt, Tsuruhara, & Ryan, 1972); and estradiol (Loriaux, Ruder, & Lipsett, 1971) in 4 normal adult men who were given 17β-estradiol in a daily dose of 15 μg/Kg for 5 days. The values for each patient have been aligned on the basis of the LH peak and nadir. $N-4 = 4$ days before the nadir, $P+2 = 2$ days after the peak, etc.

hormone deficiency will eventually attain puberty almost all exhibit delayed pubertal maturation. Growth seems to be a requirement for normal puberty to ensue (Frisch & Revelle, 1971), so that individuals deficient in growth hormone will mature but at a much slower rate.

Isolated hypogonadotropism may be associated with a number of non-endocrine problems, such as defects in smell, ataxia, or genetic factors (Rimoin & Schimke, 1971; Santen & Paulsen, 1973a). A primary gonadal defect may also be present (Bardin et al, 1970; Zachman, 1972), usually associated with cryptorchidism. Isolated gonadotropin deficiency may also exist without these associated disorders; in some patients with a partial lack of FSH and/or LH signs of an apparently normal puberty may actually begin. In such instances the diagnostic possibilities in the boy of adolescent age may be narrowed quickly either to physiologic delayed adolescence or to true isolated hypogonadotropic hypogonadism. Only the unsatisfactory approach of "wait and see" will definitely distinguish between these two syndromes. Are there any other means that might prove effective in differential diagnosis? The patterns of gonadotropin change may be helpful diagnostically but the patterns of physical change may be less so.

The Patterns of Physical Changes in Physiologic Delayed Adolescence

The pattern of physical changes in boys with physiologic delayed adolescence is not well defined, particularly in those who experience the onset of puberty between 13 and 15 years. Some may exhibit relatively rapid maturational changes once the process has started, but others remain a diagnostic dilemma despite careful attention to family history, bone age, and somatic growth. We recently studied 3 individuals with this condition who demonstrated just how long the normal pubertal process may take.

R. H. (Fig. 2) was first admitted to the Clinical Center at the National Institutes of Health at 14-5/12 years with complaints of sexual infantilism. At that time he was of normal stature; he had no pubic hair; his testes measured 2.5 × 1.5 cm bilaterally, and his bone age was 14 years. Plasma FSH and LH ranged between 4 and 7 mIU/ml and plasma testosterone 105 ng/100 ml. After a 1-week course of clomiphene there was no change in serum gonadotropins but testosterone decreased to 50 ng/100 ml, after which 4000 U hCG were given for 4 days and plasma testosterone rose to 600 ng/100 ml.

This patient has been followed frequently in 8 hospitalizations over a period of 6 years. He is pictured (Fig. 2) at the time of his first and seventh admissions, at ages 14-5/12 and 19-7/12, respectively. At the time of the seventh hospitalization his testes measured 4.0 × 2.5 cm, plasma testosterone was 400 ng/100 ml, and motile sperm were found on analysis of semen. Testing with clomiphene at age 15-1/2 resulted in nonstimulatory gonadotropin response, but at age 18 a third clomiphene test resulted in a prompt two- to three-fold rise in serum FSH, LH, and testosterone. R. H. took more than 5 years to attain adult (or genital stage 4) sexual maturation after a delayed start.

Two brothers, R. M. and J. M., were also studied over the last 2 years. These boys were both normal but they exhibited, as did several other family members, certain aspects of physiologic delayed adolescence. They are shown in Fig. 3 with some of their endocrine data, at ages 19 (J. M.) and 15 (R. M.). When R. M. was first seen at age 13-5/12, his testes measured

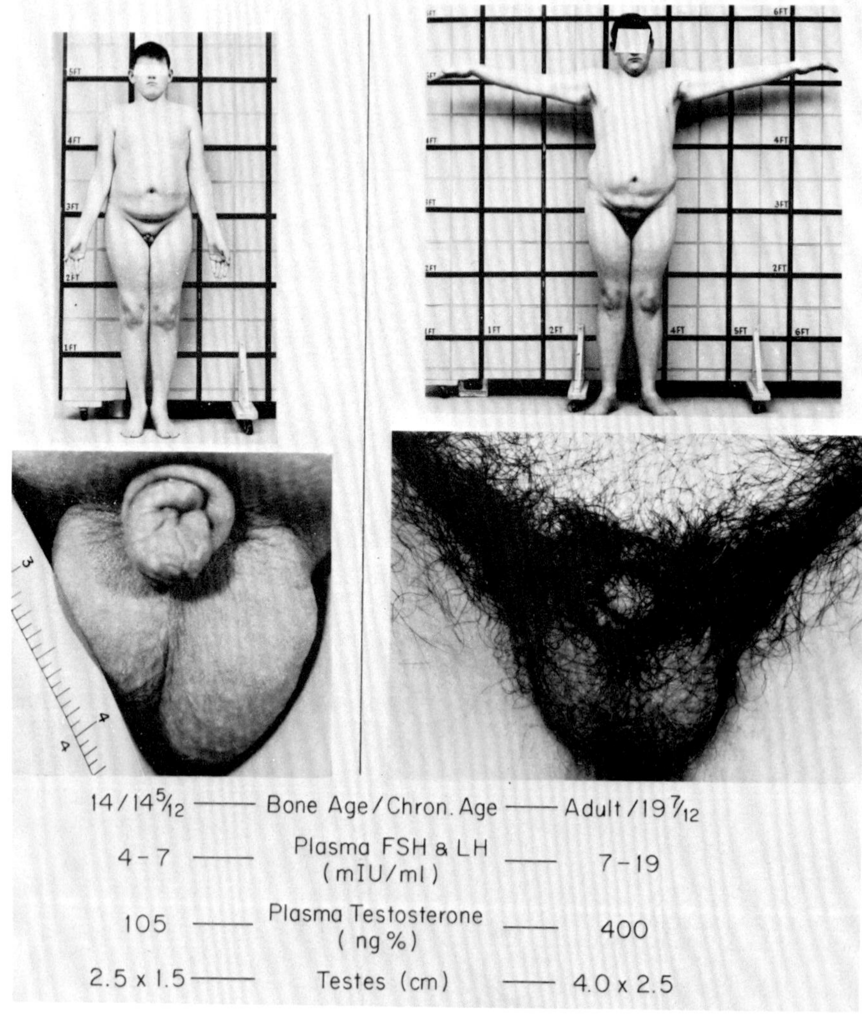

FIG. 2.   Patient R. H. with constitutional delay in puberty. Plasma gonadotropins were measured by radioimmunoassay (Odell et al, 1967) and testosterone by a radio-ligand technique (Dufau et al, 1972).

3.1 × 1.6 cm. Unfortunately, we do not have serial photographs for each of the brothers, but it is likely that their pubertal patterns will be similar, particularly with such a clear family history of late sexual development. R. M. displays a Marshall and Tanner (1970) genital stage 3 and J. M., the older sibling, is at stage 4 or possibly 5. The span of 4-8/12 years between the brothers suggests a duration of puberty considerably in excess

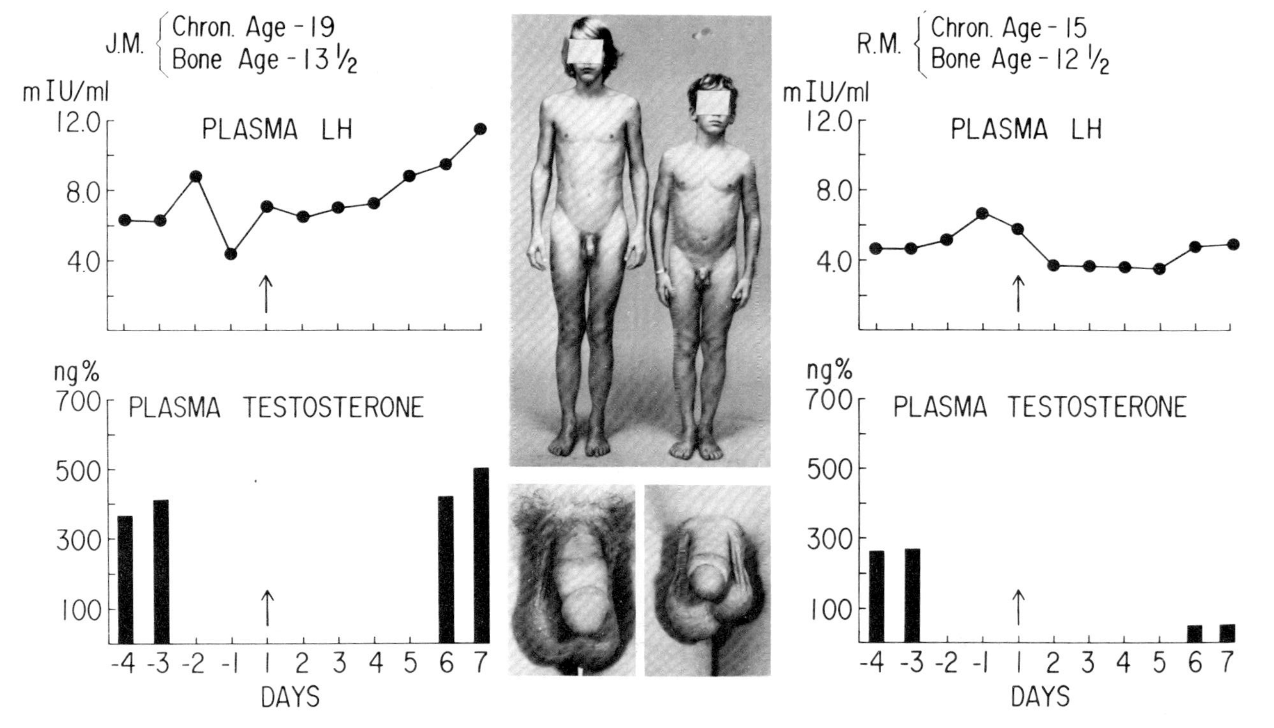

FIG. 3. Two brothers, R. M. and J. M., with constitutional delay in puberty. Note the differences in the response to clomiphene in the 2 boys.

of the 4.7 years required for full genital development by 98 per cent of the normal boys studied by Marshall and Tanner (1970).

It is of interest to note that 4 boys with isolated growth hormone deficiency reported by Penny et al (1972) took 2.9, 4.3, 4.6, and 2.5 years from early to late stages of sexual development. All had the onset of puberty at about age 15 or even later; the delay was caused, presumably, by a deficit of growth hormone. Nevertheless, they progressed through sexual maturation at a rate close to the normal range.

Though based on a small number of patients, we should like to suggest that some boys with physiologic delayed adolescence progress through the changes of sexual maturation at an abnormally slow rate. In them the hypothalamic clock might move more slowly than normal, though differences in end-organ responsiveness could be playing a primary role in their delayed development. Thus the patterns of physical change in some patients with delayed adolescence may have little diagnostic import. The patterns of gonadotropin change, however, may provide more useful information.

The Patterns of FSH and LH Changes in Physiologic Delayed Adolescence and in Hypogonadotropic Hypogonadism

Unfortunately large numbers of patients have not been studied longitudinally in order to gain some insight into the precise patterns of change in gonadotropins and in steroids during normal pubescence.

M. S. and R. G. (Fig. 4) were referred to us at ages 13-8/12 and 13-2/12, respectively, for evaluation of pubertal delay. Both boys were short and in the very earliest stages of sexual development. The testes measured 2.3 × 1.3 cm in M.S. and 2.6 × 1.6 cm in R. G.; growth hormone levels were normal. After their initial hospitalization they were readmitted between 5 and 8 months for repeat determinations of gonadotropins and testosterone, at which time the photographs in Fig. 4 were taken. Though plasma FSH, LH, and testosterone remained close to, or below, the limits of assay sensitivity in this interval, urinary FSH excretion, as determined in 4 to 5 individual 24-hour specimens, increased by threefold in both boys, which is significant ($p < 0.01$). The urinary FSH increments were accompanied by only minimal physical changes. These patients are now progressing through an apparently normal puberty.

Figure 5 shows a boy (C. S.) who was studied in collaboration with Drs. Melvin Grumbach and Selna Kaplan (Kulin et al, 1972). He was admitted to the University of California-San Francisco Medical Center at the age of 15-2/12 for evaluation of delayed adolescence. His testes then measured 2.2 × 1.4 cm and there was no pubic hair. He was studied 8 and 16 months later. On all 3 occasions he received a 1-week course of clomiphene. In just 8 months FSH excretion almost tripled and LH rose from

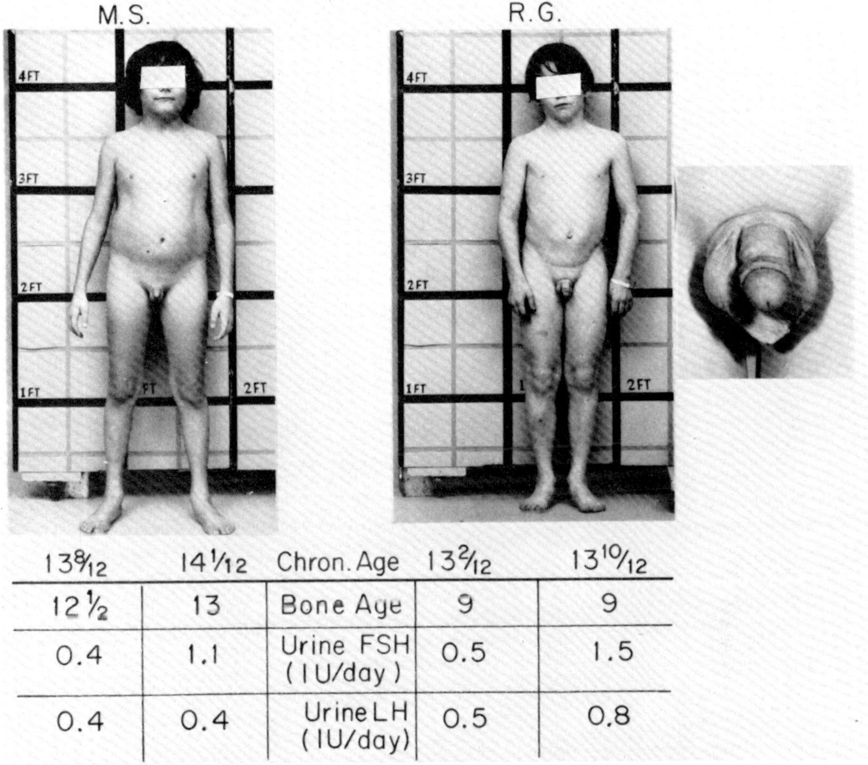

13 8/12	14 1/12	Chron. Age	13 2/12	13 10/12
12 1/2	13	Bone Age	9	9
0.4	1.1	Urine FSH (I U/day)	0.5	1.5
0.4	0.4	Urine LH (I U/day)	0.5	0.8

FIG. 4. Patients M. S. and R. G., with constitutional delay in puberty. Urinary FSH increased significantly in both boys over a 5 to 8 month interval while plasma gonadotropins (not shown) changed negligibly. All samples (4 to 5 at each age) were run in the same assay.

undetectable levels into the pubertal range. In the same period there were negligible changes in plasma gonadotropins and only very small increments in testicular size.

These 3 boys (Figs. 4 and 5), each with a relatively late onset of puberty, displayed a marked rise in urinary FSH once the process had started. In contrast is L. M., who is shown (Fig. 6) at age 19, shortly after his initial referral for evaluation of delayed puberty. At that time the left testis measured 1.7 × 1.2 cm and only a few strands of dark pubic hair were present. Sequential gonadotropin studies were performed every 6 months over a 2-year period (Table 1). No significant increments were determined by the RIA of multiple blood and urine samples; both FSH and LH levels were just detectable and remained in the prepubertal range. Tests with clomiphene were performed on 3 different occasions and gonadotropins

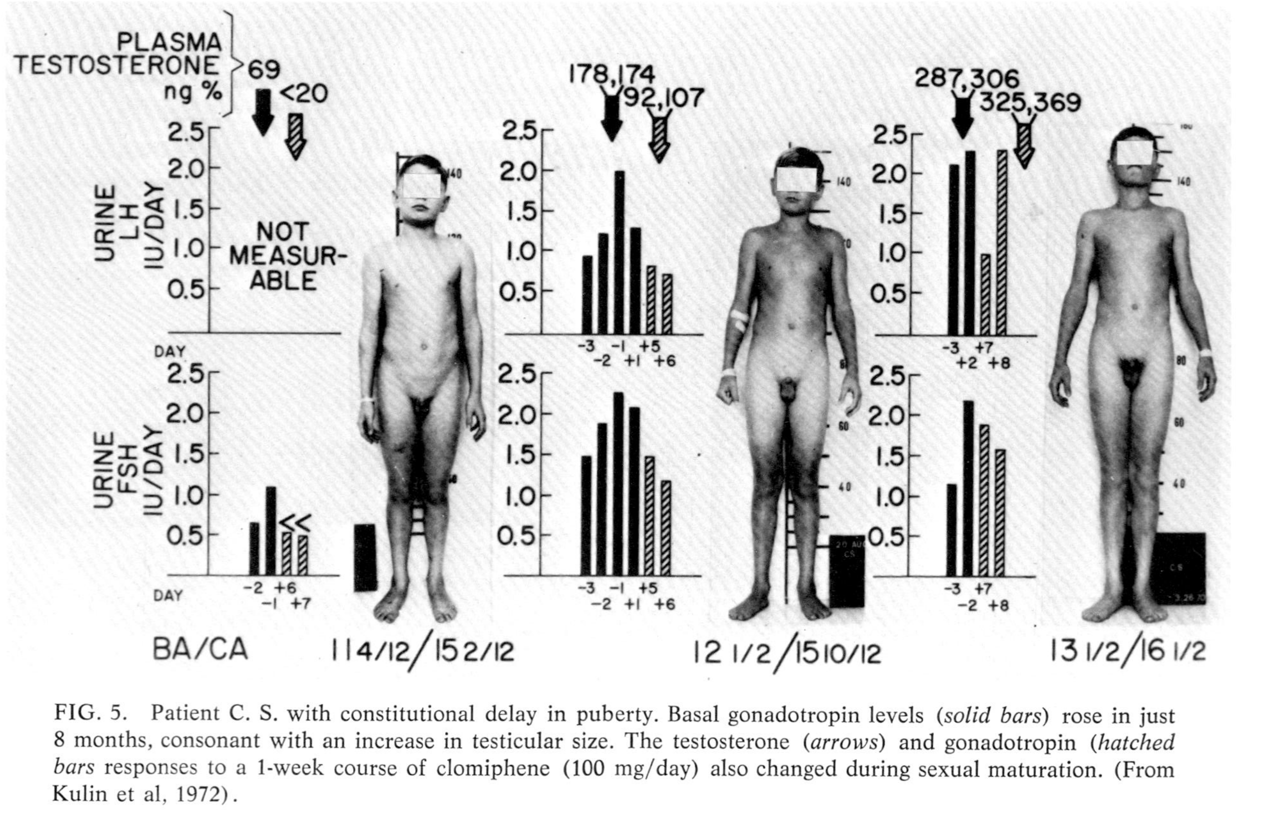

FIG. 5.   Patient C. S. with constitutional delay in puberty. Basal gonadotropin levels (*solid bars*) rose in just 8 months, consonant with an increase in testicular size. The testosterone (*arrows*) and gonadotropin (*hatched bars* responses to a 1-week course of clomiphene (100 mg/day) also changed during sexual maturation. (From Kulin et al, 1972).

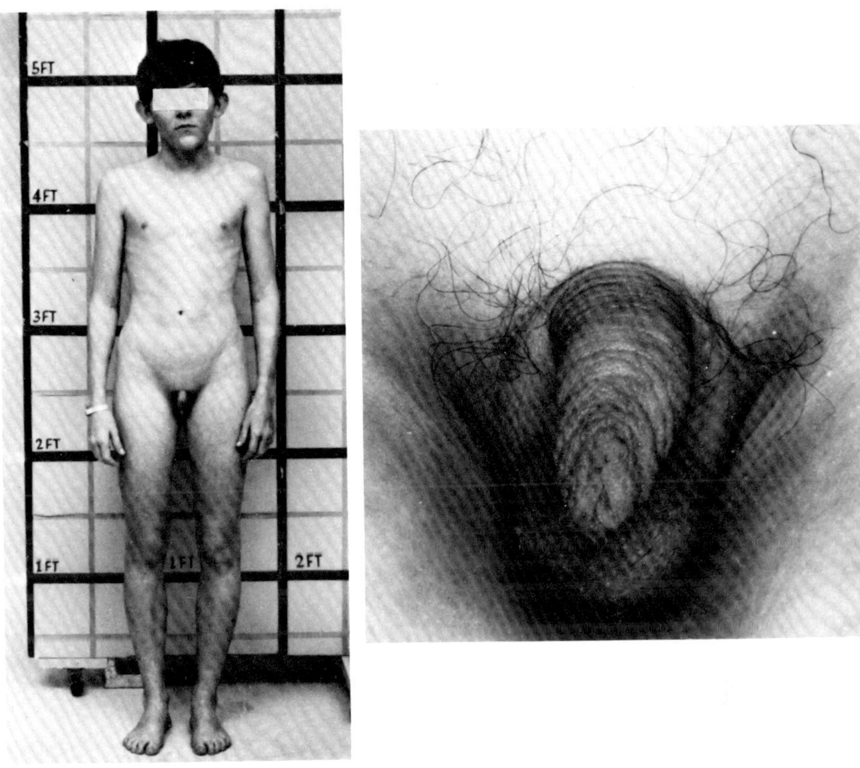

FIG. 6.   L. M., at age 19, a patient with isolated hypogonadotropic hypogonadism, a normal sense of smell, and unilateral cryptorchidism.

TABLE 1.   Sequential gonadotropin studies[a] in patient L. M. (Fig. 6)

Chronological/Bone age (years)	Plasma[b]		Urine[c] FSH
	LH	FSH	
18½ / 14	2.6±0.1	1.3±0.1	0.4±0.1
19 / 14	2.7±0.2	1.4±0.2	0.8±0.1
19½ / 14½	2.6±0.0	1.3±0.1	0.3±0.0
20 / —	2.5±0.1	1.5±0.2	0.4±0.1

[a] Three to 5 individual specimens examined at each interval.

[b] $\overline{X}$±SE in mIU/ml 2nd IRP/hMG.

[c] $\overline{X}$±SE in IU/day 2nd IRP/hMG.

failed to rise on each. Basal testosterone levels were less than 25 ng/100 ml but rose to more than 300 ng/100 ml after 10 weeks of hCG treatment.

It is reassuring when a rise in gonadotropin levels takes place with increasing age over a relatively short time. In addition, these hormonal increments may be detected more readily by the RIA of urinary concentrates than by blood measurements (Reiter et al, 1973; Kulin & Reiter, 1973). Conversely, the lack of change in FSH or LH over many months in a boy of pubertal age with no secondary sexual characteristics, or with slow attainment, is a strong indicator of true hormone deficiency.

Not to oversimplify the situation, the studies obtained on another patient (T. S.) must be reviewed. T. S. is shown in Fig. 7 at age 23, at which time

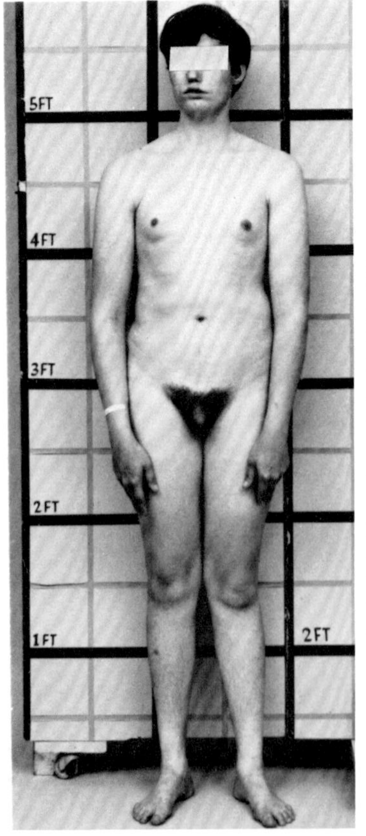

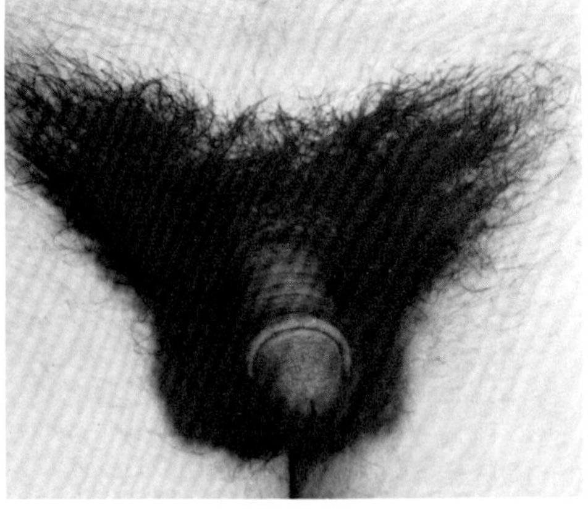

FIG. 7.   T. S., a patient with partial hypogonadotropism and Möbius syndrome, at age 23.

his bone age was that of an adult. He also had Möbius' syndrome, with paralysis of cranial nerves III, IV, VI, and VII, and has been reported by Olsen, Bardin, Walsh, and Engel (1970). Between the ages of 19-1/2 and 22 he received fluoxymesterone (Halotestin), 5 mg twice daily, and since then has been receiving injections of 200 mg testosterone enanthate every 3 weeks.

Results of gonadotropin studies performed while off therapy for a suitable length of time, at ages 22 and 23, are shown in Table 2. FSH excretion increased significantly ($p < 0.01$) from prepubertal levels and, despite androgen treatment, testicular size enlarged from 2.0 × 2.9 cm to 2.1 × 3.5 cm. LH has remained low. Clomiphene administered at age 22 resulted in no increase in gonadotropins in blood or urine.

This man may have the form of partial hypogonadotropism which constitutes the fertile eunuch syndrome (Faiman, Hoffman, Ryan & Albert, 1968). Though no data on sperm production are presently available, urinary FSH is in the pubertal range and LH is low. Of particular interest is the onset of the rise of FSH at age 22. Perhaps T. S. will continue to have further increments in gonadotropins, though we think it unlikely.

We wish to emphasize the wide ranges in the patterns of physical and hormonal events that take place in these syndromes. A broad spectrum extends from the boy with varying degrees of physiologic delayed adolescence to the fertile eunuch and finally to the more profoundly hypogonadotropic individual. Such patients display great variability in physical characteristics, in the absolute amounts of hormone present, and in the timing of mechanisms in the central nervous system which account for the pubertal increment in gonadotropins. Nevertheless, we suggest that the longitudinal study of excretion of gonadotropin may provide important clues to the eventual maturational status of any patient in whom the outcome is unclear. There is certainly evidence that once FHS begins to rise abruptly marked changes can take place over a relatively short time.

TABLE 2.   Sequential gonadotropin studies in patient T. S. (Fig. 7)

Chronological/Bone Age (years)	Plasma[a]		Urine[b]	
	LH	FSH	LH	FSH
22/16-17	2.6±0.1	2.1±0.1	—	0.4±0.0
23/Adult	3.1±0.0	2.3±0.2	0.6±0.0	1.6±0.2

[a] $\overline{X}$±SE in MIU/ml 2nd IRP/hMG; 3 to 8 individual specimens examined at each interval.

[b] $\overline{X}$±SE in IU/day, 2nd IRP/hMG; 4 to 6 individual specimens examined at each interval.

Other Diagnostic Tests

Other means of distinguishing physiologic delayed adolescence from hypogonadotropic hypogonadism are, in particular, the response to clomiphene citrate (Kulin et al, 1972). Patients with hypogonadotropic hypogonadism will not show a rise in gonadotropins after ingestion of the drug, although normal individuals will demonstrate an increment in FSH and/or LH by mid-puberty. Thus for purposes of reassurance about the continued development of normal puberty repeated testing with clomiphene is useful. The 2 brothers with delayed adolescence (Fig. 3) are good examples of this phenomenon. Unfortunately there is still no clear indication when a stimulatory response can be expected. We have never seen a rise in gonadotropin after clomiphene ingestion with basal testosterone levels of less than 300 ng/100 ml. In fact, we have tested 2 boys with suppressive type gonadotropin responses whose basal testosterone measurements were between 200 and 300 ng/100 ml.

We are all waiting to see whether releasing hormones (RH) might provide diagnostic information. There is every reason to believe that hypogonadotropic hypogonadism is a hypothalamic disease (Gauthier, 1960), so that such patients might be expected to have an elevated LH following an injection of LH-RF. The studies of Weinstein and Reitz (1973, and unpublished observations), who administered LH-RF to 2 hypogonadotropic men, bear out this expectation. However, similar results were not obtained by Job, Garnier, Chaussain, Binet, Canlorbe, Rivaille, and Milhaud (1972) in Paris. These French workers found a poor FSH and LH response in 5 patients with isolated hypogonadotropism, compared to normal prepubertal children and adults, or to 3 boys with physiologic delayed adolescence. Obviously, more normal and abnormal subjects need to be tested before any definite conclusions can be drawn. As Roth, Kelch, Kaplan, and Grumbach (1972) have suggested, the amount and duration of endogenous LH-RF exposure may influence responsiveness to the acute test situation.

The testosterone response to short-term hCG administration may also serve to identify some patients with isolated hypogonadotropism (Bardin et al, 1969; Zachmann, 1972), but again a much wider experience with this test is necessary before conclusions can be made.

TREATMENT

Because problems in rational treatment result from difficulties in the differential diagnosis of the syndromes of delayed puberty in the male, we should like to comment on certain aspects. Procrastination is a poor means of dealing with some of these patients. Under any circumstances adolescence is a trying period, and the boy of pubertal age is entitled to secondary sexual characteristics at an appropriate time.

Short-term treatment with either hCG or testosterone should be considered in any boy with potentially functional testes who has reached the age of 14 years without *significant* sexual maturation and who has prepubertal levels of gonadotropin. Such treatment should, of course, be considered only after a careful clinical and laboratory evaluation. If indicated, we suggest repeated 2- to 3-month courses of therapy followed by withdrawal of drugs for 6 to 8 months, a period that is frequently sufficient to detect spontaneous progression of puberty.

There is no firm evidence to date that either mode of treatment, i.e., hCG or testosterone, results in any permanent damage to the prepubertal or early pubertal gonad. Furthermore, Kaplan, Moshang, Bernstein, Parks, and Bongiovanni (1973) have shown that final height is not affected by such a regimen. Cost and convenience clearly favor a long-acting preparation of testosterone, though there may be some advantage in the Leydig cell stimulation provided by hCG; i.e., the use of hCG may stimulate the interstitial cells so that they are readier to take over when endogenous gonadotropins do increase.

The safety of hCG has been questioned since Maddock and Nelson (1952) suggested that tubular damage might result from the drug, possibly by means of FSH suppression. We have shown that 4 daily injections of 4000 IU of hCG will in fact suppress FSH (Table 3), probably because of an increase in production of estrogen from the testes (Reiter, Kulin, & Loriaux, 1972). In this acute setting the degree of suppression of urinary FSH in 6 normal adult men was at about one-third of baseline levels, a significant change (<0.01) in each subject.

Peritubular fibrosis, basement membrane hyalinization, and disturbances of spermatogenesis occur in postpubertal men who have been hypophysectomized (Mancini, Seigur, & Perez Lloret, 1968) and in men with choriocarcinoma (Mark & Hedinger, 1965); both situations provide a low FSH

TABLE 3. Urinary FSH in normal men following hCG administration for 4 days

Patient	1	2	3	4	5	6
Control[a]	5.0±0.5	3.6±0.4	4.9±0.5	17.4±1.8	8.6±0.4	9.3±0.9
hCG[b]	2.9±0.3	0.8±0.3	1.4±0.0	4.1±0.5	1.4±0.3	3.3±0.8

[a] $\overline{X}$±SE (IU 2nd IRP hMG/day) of 4 to 6 samples.
[b] $\overline{X}$±SE for last day of hCG course plus 2 subsequent 24-hour samples.

milieu. The extent or duration of deficiency of FSH or the maturational status of the testes may all be factors that produce changes in tubular histology. Men with choriocarcinoma, for instance, have the lowest levels of urinary FSH of any patient group, less than 1/100 of the normal adult male measurements in some cases (Reiter & Kulin, 1971).

The extensive work of Bergada (1970), who studied a large number of prepubertal and pubertal boys given short-term therapy with hCG for cryptorchidism, would indicate that hCG does not have a harmful effect on testes that have not attained adult development. Despite FSH suppression in a patient given hCG, the rise in intratesticular testosterone may produce tubular growth, even during drug administration. An increase in testicular size can be expected with the use of hCG alone, a finding not usually present with replacement testosterone administration.

SUMMARY

The age range is wide at which sexual maturation may take place. There may be some boys who take longer than normal to attain adult-size genitalia. Boys of pubertal age with isolated hypogonadotropic hypogonadism without associated defects of smell or without a family history of the disorder are those who are most difficult to differentiate from patients with physiologic delayed adolescence. True hypogonadotropism has a variety of manifestations, which extend from a profound decrease in FSH and LH to only mild degrees of hormone deficiency.

It has not been established whether the cause of the hypogonadotropic conditions is located in the hypothalamus or the pituitary gland or in both sites. There may be a true deficiency of releasing factors or a defect in the mechanism that causes gonadotropins to rise. The pattern of gonadotropic changes may allow the physician to detect patients who are likely to progress through complete puberty, though too few subjects have been studied longitudinally to make a conclusive statement. There is a need for further work in this area.

Clomiphene is the only marker of normal pubertal progression presently known; but a stimulatory gonadotropic response to this drug occurs only around the time of midpuberty. Patients with true hypogonadotropic hypogonadism will not show an increase in their levels of FSH and LH with clomiphene.

Because of problems in diagnosis, a short-term trial treatment with hCG or testosterone should be considered in any boy who is approaching the age of 14, does not have *significant* pubertal development, but has normal prepubertal-size testes and prepubertal levels of gonadotropins.

ACKNOWLEDGMENT

We wish to thank Dr. Griff T. Ross for many stimulating discussions concerning the subject of delayed adolescence and for his kind review of the manuscript. This work was done at the National Institute of Child Health and Human Development, Reproduction Research Branch, National Insitutes of Health, Bethesda, Maryland 20014.

REFERENCES

Bardin, C. W., Ross, G. T., Rifkind, A. B., Cargille, C. M., & Lipsett, M. B. (1969). Studies of the pituitary-Leydig cell axis in young men with hypogonadotropic hypogonadism and hyposmia: Comparison with normal men, prepubertal boys, and hypopituitary patients. *J. Clin. Invest.* **48**, 2046–2056.

Bergada, C. (1970). Effect of gonadotropins on the prepubertal testis. In *The Human Testis,* E. Rosemberg & C. A. Paulsen, Eds., Plenum, New York, pp. 393–403.

Dufau, M., Catt, K. J., Tsuruhara, T., & Ryan, D. (1972). Radioimmunoassay of plasma testosterone. *Clin. Chim. Acta.* **37**, 109–116.

Faiman, C., Hoffman, D. L., Ryan, R. J., & Albert, A. (1968). The "fertile eunuch" syndrome: Demonstration of isolated luteinizing hormone deficiency by radio-immunoassay technique. *Mayo Clin. Proc.* **43**, 661–667.

Frisch, R. E. & Revelle, R. (1971). Height and weight at menarche and a hypothesis of menarche. *Arch. Dis. Child.* **46**, 695–701.

Gauthier, G. (1960). La dysplasia olfacto-genitale. *Acta Neuroveget.* **21**, 345–393.

Job, J. C., Garnier, R. E., Chaussain, J. L., Binet, E., Canlorbe, P., Rivaille, P., & Milhaud, G. (1972). L'hormone de liberation de la luteostimuline (LH-RH). *Presse Med.* **1**, 1633–1636.

Kaplan, J. G., Moshang, Jr., T., Bernstein, R., Parks, J. S., & Bongiovanni, A. M. (1973). Constitutional delay of growth and development: Effects of treatment with androgens. *J. Pediat.* **82**, 38-41.

Kelch, R. P., Grumbach, M. M., & Kaplan, S. L. (1972). Studies in the mechanisms of puberty in man. In *Gonadotropins,* B. Saxena, H. Gandy & F. Beling, Eds. Wiley, New York, pp. 524–534.

Kulin, H. E., Rifkind, A. B., Ross, G. T., & Odell, W. D. (1967). Total gonadotropin activity in the urine of prepuberal children. *J. Clin. Endocrinol.* **27**, 1123–1128.

Kulin, H. E., Grumbach, M. M., & Kaplan, S. L. (1969). Changing sensitivity of the pubertal gonadal hypothalamic feedback mechanism in man. *Science* **166**, 1012–1013.

Kulin, H. E., Grumbach. M. M., & Kaplan, S. L. (1972). Gonadal hypothalamic inter-actions in prepubertal and pubertal man: Effects of clomiphene citrate on urinary follicle stimulating hormone and luteinizing hormone and plasma testosterone. *Pediat. Res.* **6**, 162–171.

Kulin, H. E. & Reiter, E. O. (1973). Gonadotropins during childhood and adolescence: a review. *Pediatrics* **51**, 260–271.

Laron, Z. & Zilka, E. (1969). Compensatory hypertrophy of testicle in unilateral cryptorchidism. *J. Clin. Endocrinol.* **29**, 1409–1413.

Loriaux, D. L., Ruder, H. J., & Lipsett, M. B. (1971). Measurement of estrone sulfate in plasma. *Steroids* **18**, 463–472.

Maddock, W. O. & Nelson, W. O. (1952). Effects of chorionic gonadotropins in adult men: Increased estrogen and 17-ketosteroid excretion, gynecomastia, Leydig cell stimulation and seminiferous tubule damage. *J. Clin. Endocrinol.* **12**, 985–1014.

Mancini, R. E., Seiguer, A. C., & Perez Lloret, A. (1968). Effect of gonadotropins on the testes of hypophysectomized patients. In *Gonadotropins,* E. Rosemberg, Ed., Geron-X, Los Angeles, Calif., pp. 503–511.

Mark, G. J. & Hedinger, C. (1965). Changes in remaining tumor-free testicular tissue in cases of seminoma and teratoma. *Virch. Arch. Path. Anat.* **340**, 84–92.

Marshall, W. A. & Tanner, J. M. (1969). Variations in pattern of pubertal changes in girls. *Arch. Dis. Child.* **44**, 291–303.

Marshall, W. A. & Tanner, J. M. (1970). Variations in the pattern of pubertal changes in boys. *Arch. Dis. Child.* **45**, 13–23.

Odell, W. D., Rayford, P. L., & Ross, G. T. (1967). Simplified, partially automated method for radioimmunoassay of human thyroid-stimulating, growth, luteinizing, and follicle stimulating hormones. *J. Lab. Clin. Med.* **70**, 973–980.

Olsen, W. H., Bardin, C. W., Walsh, G. O., & Engle, W. K. (1970). Moebius Syndrome, *Neurology* **20**, 1002–1008.

Penny, R., Guyda, H. J., Baghdassarian, A., Johanson, A. J., & Blizzard, R. M. (1970). Correlation of serum follicular stimulating hormone (FSH) and luteinizing hormone (LH) as measured by radioimmunoassay in disorders of sexual development. *J. Clin. Invest.* **49**, 1847–1852.

Penny, R., Foley, Jr., T. P., & Blizzard, R. M. (1972). Serum follicular-stimulating hormone and luteinizing hormone as measured by radioimmunoassay correlated with sexual development in hypopituitary subjects. *J. Clin. Invest.* **51**, 74–80.

Reiter, E. O. & Kulin, H. E. (1971). Suppressed follicle stimulating hormone in men with chorionic gonadotropin secreting testicular tumors. *J. Clin. Endocrinol.* **33**, 957–961.

Reiter, E. O., Kulin, H. E., & Loriaux, D. L. (1972). FSH suppression during short term hCG administration: A gonadally mediated process. *J. Clin. Endocrinol.* **34**, 1080–1084.

Reiter, E. O., Kulin, H. E., & Hamwood, S. M. (1973). Preparation of urine containing small amounts of FSH and LH for radioimmunoassay: Comparison of the kaolin-acetone and acetone extraction techniques. *J. Clin. Endocrinol.* **36**, 661–665.

Rimoin, D. L. & Shimke, R. N. (1971). *Genetic Disorders of The Endocrine Glands,* Mosby, St. Louis, Chapter 2.

Roth, J. C., Kelch, R. P., Kaplan, S. L., & Grumbach, M. M. (1972). FSH and LH in response to luteinizing hormone releasing factor in prepubertal and pubertal children, adult males and patients with hypogonadotropic and hypergonadotropic hypogonadism. *J. Clin. Endocrinol.* **35**, 926–930.

Santen, R. J., Leonard. J. M., Sherins, R. J., Gandy, H. M., & Paulsen, C. A. (1971). Short- and long-term effects of clomiphene citrate in the pituitary-testicular axis. *J. Clin. Endocrinol.* **33**, 970–979.

Santen, R. J. & Paulsen. C. A. (1973a). Hypogonadotrophic eunuchoidism I: Clinical study of the mode of inheritance. *J. Clin. Endocrinol.* **36**, 47–54.

Santen, R. J. & Paulsen, C. A. (1973b). Hypogonadotropic eunuchoidism II. Gonadal responsiveness to exogenous gonadotropins, *J. Clin. Endocrinol.* **36**, 55–63.

Weinstein, R. L. & Reitz, R. E. (1974). Pituitary-testicular responsiveness in male hypogonadotropic hypogonadism, I. Biochemical observations. In press.

Winter, J. S. D. & Faiman, C. (1972). Serum gonadotropin concentrations in agonadal children and adults. *J. Clin. Endocrinol.* **35**, 561–564.

Yamaji, T., Dierschke, D. J., Hotchkiss, J., Bhattacharya, A. N., Surve, A. H., & Knobil, E. (1971). Estrogen induction of LH release in the rhesus monkey. *Endocrinology* **89**, 1034–1041.

Zachman, M. (1972). Evaluation of testicular endocrine function before and in puberty. *Acta Endocrinol. Suppl.* **164**, 1–94.

DISCUSSION

DR. STEINBERGER. Dr. Kulin, you mentioned that at the age of 14 there is an increase in testicular size. Now, from our measurements of testes of developing boys, we found that there is a gradual increase in size which then becomes more acute. This is important because it means that there is no sudden throw of a switch to make the testes start growing when they have not been growing up to that point. Did you do an experiment in which testosterone was given and in spite of that there was an increase in testicular size?

DR. KULIN. I was referring to a patient with partial gonadotropin deficiency who received testosterone treatment and, despite the steroid replacement, still exhibited increasing testicular size.

DR. STEINBERGER. I do not know whether it is despite. Then you made an important point that administration of testosterone and hCG to immature boys will not cause damage late in life, and you equated that to the fact that the testes may be damaged when there are low levels of FSH. Is that correct?

DR. KULIN. FSH deficiency has been proposed as a possible cause of tubular damage. There are several examples of germinal cell changes which occur in the presence of low FSH. A cause and effect relationship has not been proven.

DR. STEINBERGER. We should also clarify the point that we do not have much evidence that administration of testosterone or hCG in early life is totally innocuous; we do not have good data in older men and, secondly, what does "damage" mean. Just because the male happens to produce sperm, and may even be fertile, does not mean he does not have damaged testicles. He may have grossly damaged testicles and still produce sufficient sperm to fertilize. Animals will remain fertile and will show quite good testicular morphology after treatment with testosterone or hCG or estrogen early in life, but spermatogenesis will not be completely normal.

DR. KULIN. I appreciate your words of caution and voice them myself. Would you go so far as to say you would remain so cautious about testosterone or hCG therapy that you would not use such treatment in a boy of 14 or 15 who was not showing any pubertal changes? This is an important point to establish.

DR. STEINBERGER. The important thing to establish is whether we should not be worried that every physician is giving hCG to boys who come to the office because their mothers are concerned that the boys have not developed yet. This is what I was bringing out

DR. KULIN.   Would you rather use testosterone?

DR. STEINBERGER.   No.

DR. KULIN.   In other words, you would rather wait. This is a reasonable course taken by many physicians. But, because of the diagnostic difficulties, I think we should consider replacement therapy at an earlier rather than later age.

DR. STEINBERGER.   No. I am not suggesting you wait. I suggest these patients be worked up carefully and that we do not give a blanket approval of indiscriminate treatment with hCG or testosterone during puberty.

DR. KULIN.   A thorough evaluation and individualization of treatment is, of course, extremely important.

DR. JOB.   It is difficult to know if a patient with delayed puberty is pathologic or not. Testing with LH-RH may be useful, as mentioned earlier in the conference. Figure 8 shows data obtained with an LH-RH test in 9 nonpubertal hypopituitary dwarves (8 idiopathic and 1 with a craniopharyngioma) versus

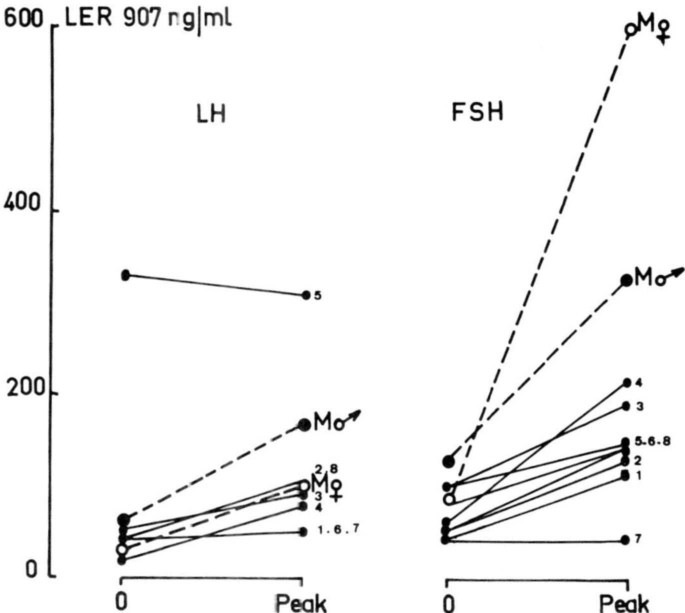

FIG. 8.   Mean basal and peak levels of LH and FSH after LH-RH (0.1 mg) in 9 hypopituitary dwarves (M = mean of prepubertal controls).

the mean of prepubertal controls. Two patients with isolated GH deficiency and one with GH + ACTH deficiency (Nos. 1, 3, and 8) are in the normal or low-normal range, although patient 8 has an isolated LH response. Other patients had multiple deficiencies and can be regarded as gonadotropin-deficient, although two were only 8 and 11 years old. Ten patients clinically diagnosed as having delayed adolescence demonstrated gonadotropic pituitary reserve in the normal prepubertal range, low peaks of FSH in two males being similar to those observed in some normal boys (Fig. 9). So, the LH-RH test may help to differentiate delayed adolescence from pituitary gonadotropic deficiency. In Fig. 10 are data related to 8 cases of isolated hypogonadotropic hypogonadism, aged 15 to 21 years. Patients Nos. 1 to 6 were anosmic, Nos. 7 and 8 were not. Three patients (Nos. 1, 6, and 7) had no significant reserve of both gonadotropins, but the others had a LH and/or FSH peak in the normal or low-normal range. Would higher doses of LH-RH have more effect in nonresponders? Or does normal response mean primary hypothalamic failure and absence of response primary pituitary defect? I am not yet sure that the LH-RH test can distinguish in all cases between simple delayed adolescence and actual hypogonadotropism.

DR. FAIMAN.   The levels of LH seem to be inordinately high in some individuals whom you say have hypogonadotropic hypogonadism. The LH values,

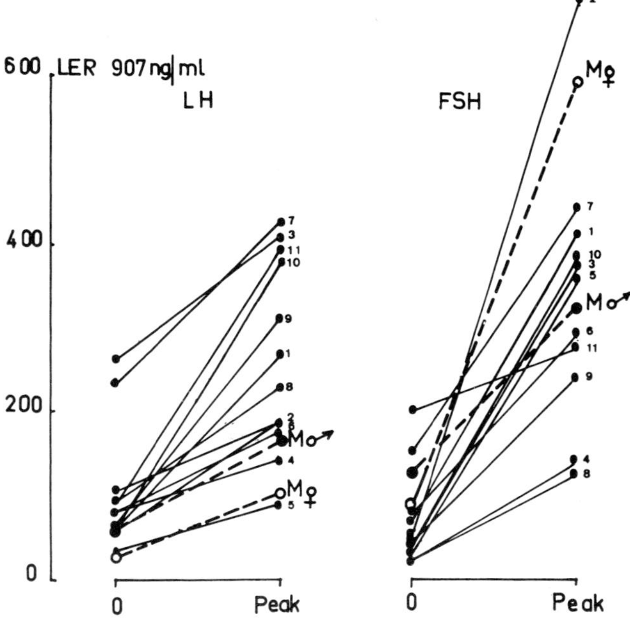

FIG. 9.   Mean basal and peak levels of LH and FSH after LH-RH (0.1 mg) in 10 cases of simple delayed adolescence (M = mean of prepubertal controls).

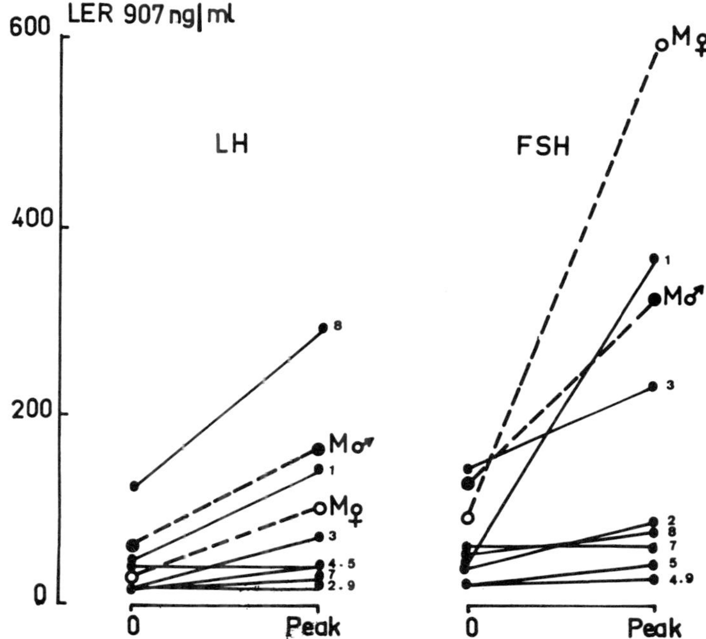

FIG. 10.   Mean basal and peak levels of LH and FSH after LH-RH (0.1 mg) in 8 cases of hypogonadotropic hypogonadism (M = mean of prepubertal controls).

as I recollect, go up to 20 μg/100 ml; these are in the adult castrate range for our assay system.

DR. JOB.   Yes, 20 μg/100 ml of LER-907 in one patient.

DR. FAIMAN.   And what is the castrate range in your system?

DR. JOB.   The scale for castrates is tenfold higher.

DR. TANNER.   This diagnosis in not entirely characteristic of the male. Many girls also suffer from late puberty. A visiting lady endocrinologist who ran an adolescent clinic had nearly as many delayed girls in her clinic as I had delayed boys in mine. We should not forget the cultural impact of this, especially since we are talking about doing something that I would fairly violently disagree with, i.e., inducing puberty in all boys who have not got there by 14. It has been said to have been done routinely once in certain Italian towns. I would like to draw your attention to two things: (1) the possibility of measuring bone age and its usefulness, very surprisingly, has not been mentioned; (2) rather than use the diagnosis of so-called delayed puberty we talk about delayed growth, because all cases are already delayed in their growth a long time before puberty. It is *not* the case that they go along perfectly normally and then one fine day puberty does not occur. Figure 11 shows a typical case, with breast and pubic hair stages and the bone age which

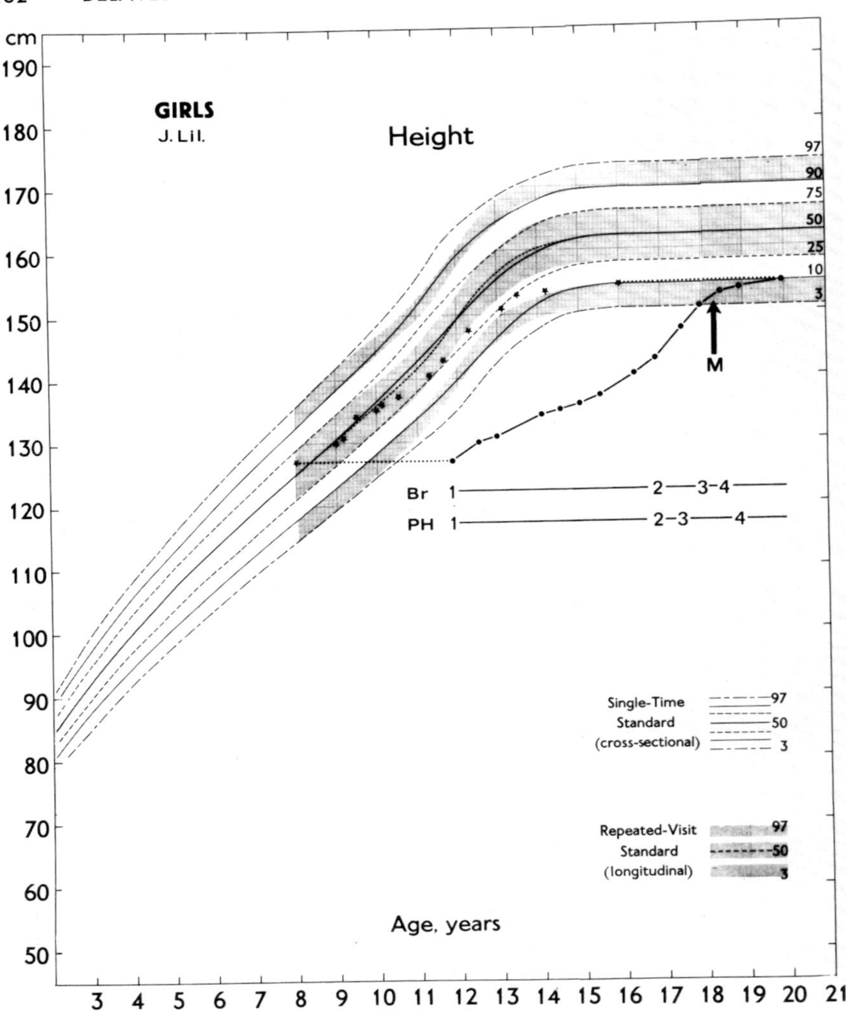

FIG. 11.   Case history of delayed adolescence in a girl of pubertal age. (M = menarche; Br = breasts; PH = pubic hair).

is grossly delayed. The stages through which she went not only were normal but developed normally. Figure 12 shows the velocity of the growth and the spurt and the position of menarche in relation to it. The breast and pubic hair stages were all perfectly normally placed; they were not prolonged in any way. She also went through a normal adolescence. It is all very well to treat your boys either with hCG or testosterone, but you should not do that unless you are quite certain that you are not going to cause some short grown-ups;

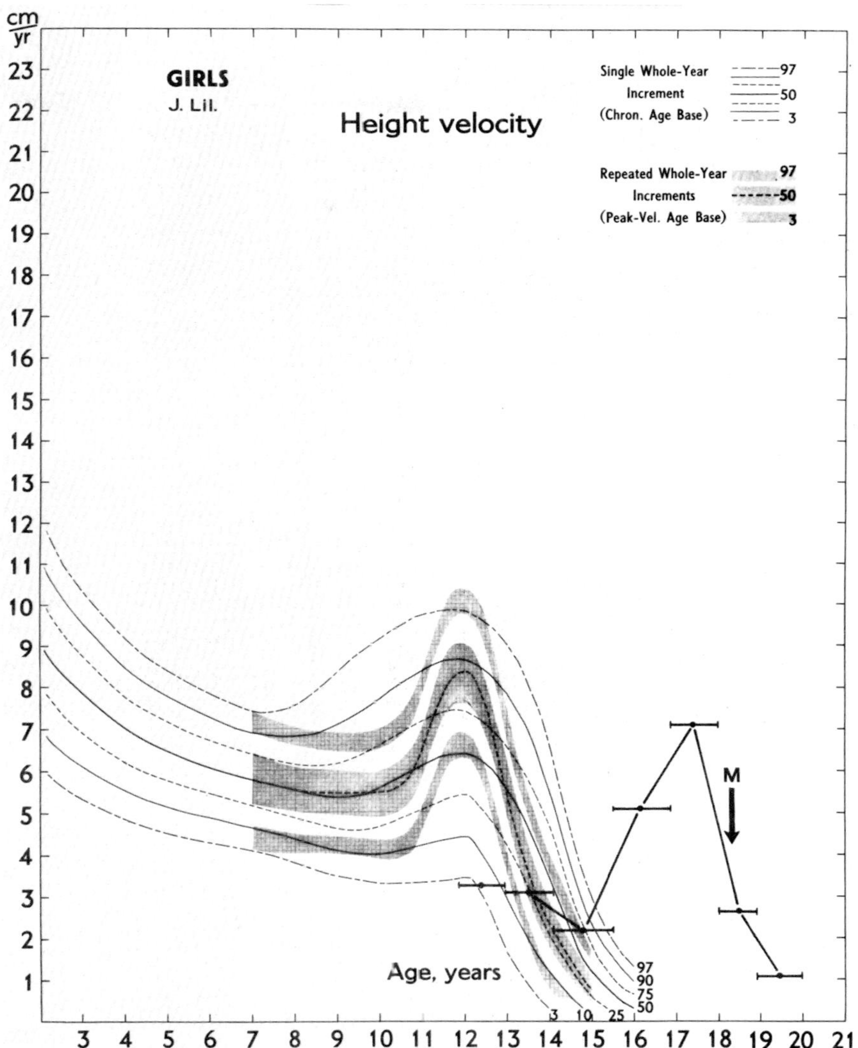

FIG. 12.   Velocity of growth in case shown in Fig. 11.

most people feel that you often do just that. A little bit of psychotherapy and social support is best for these kids while they are waiting to do what is really normal. It is not too good for a hospital serving a big mass of people to think about 2 standard deviations, because there are several thousand children in London who are 2 standard deviations below the mean stature for age (and it seems to me they all come to my clinic). There are, after all, people who are normal but who are 3 standard deviations below the mean normal, or 3.5, and hospitals specifically sample them.

DR. KULIN.   Bone age as well as childhood patterns of growth are certainly important diagnostic bits of information. Unfortunately many boys who present with delayed adolescence come to the physician for the first time at age 14 or 15, and retrospective data are not available. All information at hand should be utilized before making a decision to treat. My point is only that there remains a significant number of adolescent boys about whom we are puzzled. They should receive the benefit of our doubt in the form of treatment at a relatively early rather than later age.

DR. MONEY.   I stand somewhere in the middle in this debate about whether to treat or not to treat delayed puberty hormonally. One really does have to individualize each case in making the decision. We sometimes work with very short people who have a delayed bone age and try to sustain them psychologically while they are waiting, untreated. We try to help them to make a decision as to whether they are going to trade off some years of maturity of physique for some extra inches in stature, or vice versa. I am not dogmatic about this issue, since there are some children for whom a little maturity in physique is more important than anything else, provided they are not going to be excessively dwarfed. It is very difficult for some youngsters to be caught in that no-man's-land between their chronological age and their physique age, trying to keep up their social age, their academic age, their personality age, and their psychosexual age, in conformity with their chronological age. You simply cannot achieve that in adolescence if you look like a kid, because other adolescents will not accord adolescent status to you. An estimation of the diagnosis and prognosis is extraordinarily important. There is a persistent problem, as far as I am concerned, and which is far from solved. I am still involved, along with the people who work with me, in making a survey of 200 or so cases of delayed puberty that I have known and followed over the last 20 years (Bobrow, Money, & Lewis, 1971; Lewis, Money, & Bobrow, 1973; Money, 1970; Money & Alexander, 1967; Money & Wolff, 1973). We have had extraordinarily good luck with long term follow-up. We managed to find out when patients became well-developed, whether they had married, whether they had children of their own, etc. As a result of all the information assembled I am convinced that we simply do not know all the categories of delayed puberty and their prognoses. Therefore it is currently impossible to make blanket generalizations about whether or not to treat and when. I would like to mention specifically Kallmann's syndrome, which can open up a Pandora's box. With regard to the sense of smell, by the logic of associative thinking involved, I am reminded that Vandenbergh, Drickamer, and Colby (1972) published data on the onset of puberty in female mice. The onset of puberty was substantially accelerated by putting the smell of a male in the cage. Not even the male! Only the smell of his urine. I am further reminded that McClintock (1971) at Harvard found the menstrual cycling of girls at Radcliffe tended to synchronize as they lived together in the same dormitory. There is a word we have not mentioned in this conference so far: pheromones. We really had better not only mention it, but start thinking about it if we are going to deal with puberty. Michael (1972) in London has now demonstrated in the rhesus monkey that there is a pheromonal influence on sexual behavior. The vaginal odor at ovulation attracts the male. Proof that one pheromone exists in a primate allows the possibility of another, perhaps related to the timing of pubertal onset. We have found that patients with Kallmann's syndrome tend, along with some other hypogonadotropic males, to have great difficulty in falling in love. That is another term that we haven't mentioned so far in this conference. Yet I would like to remind you that one of the essential aspects of puberty is that the visual image takes on a new importance with regard to erotic affection, and there is this fascinating and extraordinary phenomenon of falling in love, which we all leave alone as if it were a red hot stone when it comes to scientific discussion. It is high time somebody took it seriously, especially since there is at least a chance of relating it scientifically to pair-bonding and mate preference in animals. Love is not so outside the scope of scientific study as poets have sometimes thought it to be. The problem of falling in love for some of the hypogonadotropic people relates to the general issue of whether you treat or not, because some of the people with delayed puberty do have associated psychosexual and psychosocial difficulties. Yet, if you think that giving some treatment to initiate puberty will resolve the problems of their social development, in some instances you will be in for a bitter disappointment. I have had that disappointment. One sometimes has to deal with two aspects: maturation of physique and of behavior. It is because the very deficit that creates gonadotropin deficiency also does something else up there in the hypothalamus; i.e., one has deficiency also with regard to sexual behavior, erotic behavior, and falling in love.

DR. WINTER.   We have also been concerned with techniques by which one could differentiate simple delayed adolescence from hypogonadotropic hypogonadism, hopefully by age 14 or 15. Serum testosterone concentrations in boys with delayed puberty do not begin to rise above the prepubertal or hypopituitary range until signs of puberty are imminent. Serum gonadotropin measurements are more discriminatory. It is reassuring to find serum LH concentrations in the pubertal range; however, many boys with delayed adolescence will not show such levels of LH until after age 14. While an elevated LH value signals spontaneous puberty, the clear differentiation from hypogonadotropic values is always difficult and impossible before age 14. Therefore we need some form of stimulation test to determine which boy's pituitary is capable of normal gonadotropin production. Our experience with cis-clomiphene has been interesting but disappointing: boys with delayed adolescence do not demonstrate a rise in serum LH, FSH, testosterone, or estradiol until they are in puberty stage 4 with serum testosterone levels in excess of 200 ng/100 ml and obvious secondary sexual characteristics. Newer tests, such as determination of sleep-associated LH secretion or response to LH-releasing hormone, may effectively make this discrimination at an earlier age.

Dr. Grumbach.   Our group has found the LRF test of LH reserve to be especially useful in this regard. It is pubertal in constitutional delayed adolescence but is usually low or inappropriate for the stage of maturation in hypogonadotropic hypogonadism.

Dr. Ojeda.   In Dr. McCann's laboratory we found a decrease in sensitivity to the inhibitory effect of testosterone during development in the male rat. The rats were castrated at several ages—15, 26, 56, and 86 days—and immediately afterward were treated with different doses of testosterone propionate (TP) on the basis of 100 g of body weight once daily for 20 days. TP treatment in 28-day-old rats decreased serum LH and FSH significantly, even at a dose of 100 μg; larger doses produced a further decrease in serum gonadotropins. Sham-operated levels were obtained with 25 to 40 μg; 80 μg produced lower levels. At 58 days of age 10 μg of TP was no longer effective; this lack of effect of TP is particularly clear for FSH. Even with a dose of 125 μg of TP, serum FSH was not decreased to sham-operated levels. In Dr. Ramirez's laboratory we tested the ability of estradiol benzoate to prevent the postcastration rise in plasma gonadotropins and found a relative lack of effectiveness during the first 15 days of life; this was followed by a highly sensitive period between 20 and 35 days of age. At puberty estrogen was again unable to prevent the postcastration rise of LH and FSH. Figure 13 illustrates the results. Animals were castrated at intervals of 5 days and estradiol benzoate treatment was administered for 4 days, starting immediately after ovariectomy [0.05 μg/day (100g body weight)]. In view of these results we suggest that estrogen negative feedback during the first days of life is not operating to the same extent as in the adult or prepubertal animals.

Dr. Swerdloff. We have heard some discussion about the difference in the models used for studying negative feedback of gonadal steroids; we would agree that differences in models are important considerations in evaluating feedback data. Dr. Patrick Walsh and I have evaluated the effect of duration of castration on feedback inhibition by testosterone in the adult male rat. Feedback inhibition of FSH secretion by testosterone administration is blunted in the 5-day castrate animal when compared with the acutely castrated animal. We have not found any similar differences between the chronically and acutely castrated rats with regard to LH.

Dr. Rosenfield.   What we perceive as a change in hypothalamic-pituitary sensitivity may result from maturation of the neuroendocrine axis to the point at which the gonadotropin response to a given level of a sex hormone is determined by other influences, including time. Several factors that may affect gonadotropin release have not been discussed at these conferences; for ex-example, adrenal (Rosenfield, 1972) and pineal secretions. In addition, the possibility that FSH secretion is influenced by a specific seminiferous tubule product (van Thiel, Sherins, Myers, & de Vita, 1972) has not been considered in studies of the mechanisms controlling the onset of puberty. Perhaps neither model is ideal; when we look at suppressive effects in the male at different

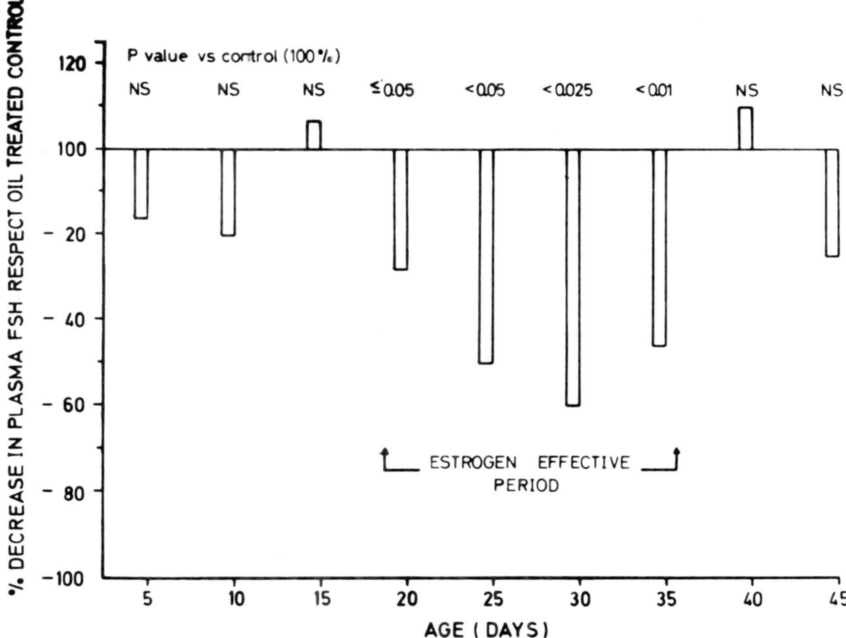

FIG. 13.   Ability of estradiol benzoate to prevent postcastration rise in FSH in young female rats of various ages (per cent decrease in plasma FSH with respect to oil-treated controls versus age in days).

ages, we ought to be looking at dose-response in the intact animal. We are currently accumulating that data. In the female rat interpretation of data on negative and positive feedback of LH and FSH after estrogen administration is more difficult. If we wished to separate these opposite effects, it would be helpful to administer a broad range of steroid doses and to measure serum gonadotropins at a number of time intervals. Even then the data would be difficult to interpret; for instance, administration of a given dose of estradiol may suppress LH on day 2 through 4 of treatment, then stimulate LH release on day 5. The effect you see depends on when you look.

DR. PAULSEN.   I should like to address myself to several points. First, the administration of hCG does not damage the testis of patients with delayed puberty who receive this therapeutic agent. Turner, Nelson, and Zanartu conducted a 10-year follow-up on 153 patients to evaluate this point and con-cluded that there was no damage. Second, testicular damage has been observed by our group in examining serial testicular biopsy specimens after administration of hCG to patients with hypogonadotropic eunuchoidism. Third, the clomiphene stimulation test has uncovered an important pathophysiologic point. Santen and his group (1971) studied the response to clomiphene administration in a number of normal men and in patients with pituitary disorders. *Before clomiphene* 1 such patient exhibited full spermatogenesis by testicular biopsy, 85 million sperm in 0.25 ml ejaculate, low plasma testosterone levels, but normal serum and urine FSH. Despite the normal basal FSH levels, clomiphene administration *failed* to stimulate FSH or LH secretion. The final point concerns our inability to separate the patient with delayed puberty prospectively from the patient who has hypogonadotropic eunuchoidism and *no* genetic marker such as anosmia. Dr. Boyar has some interesting data on this point.

DR. GRUMBACH.   The differentiation of delayed adolescence and hypogonadotropic hypogonadism is difficult and in some cases impossible at present. This is not surprising, for hypogonadotropic hypogonadism encompasses a spectrum of severe FSH and LH deficiency, on the one hand, and partial gonadotropin deficiency on the other. We have already mentioned that determination of the excretion of urinary FSH and LH is often more useful than measurement of plasma LH; in general, there is less overlap between the prepubertal and pubertal values even though the daily excretion of LH may vary significantly. In addition to studies with clomiphene, which were discussed by Dr. Kulin, there is the prospect that the LRF test will be of use clinically in the differential diagnosis but not in all cases. In the group of patients who had isolated gonadotropin deficiency, or gonadotropin deficiency in association with hypopituitary dwarfism, in whom our group studied the FSH and LH response to LRF, we found a spectrum of responses. Some patients had virtually no rise in the concentration of serum FSH and LH, whereas in others the response was within the range for normal adult males. We suspect that those patients who had a rise in neither serum FSH nor LH have severe gonadotropin deficiency and may never exhibit full sexual maturation spontaneously.

DR. BOYAR.   We had the opportunity to study 6 untreated patients with hypogonadotropic hypogonadism, 5 of whom were between the ages of 18 and 24; 5 had skeletal abnormalities, and 2 had anosmia. One 16-year-old with anosmia and a delayed bone age was felt to have hypogonadotropic hypogonadism on clinical grounds. Is there any way to separate the "normal" boy with delayed puberty from the patient with hypogonadotropic hypogonadism? Endocrine evaluation showed normal TSH, PBI, and metyrapone tests, but subnormal sleep-associated growth hormone release in 4 patients tested. Plasma testosterone was between 0.01-0.06 μg/100 ml. Acute hCG stimulation (5000 units daily x 4 days) showed that the 6 patients fell into 2 groups: 1 patient with a subnormal incremental rise of plasma testosterone similar to the previous report of Bardin et al, the other 3 with a normal increase in plasma testosterone of 0.24 to 0.79 μg/100 ml similar to what has been repored for "normal" boys with delayed puberty. A blunted acute testosterone rise after hCG may be an indication of hypogonadotropic hypogonadism. Long-term treatment with hCG resulted in the achievement of normal adult male plasma testosterone concentrations in all 6 patients. So this defect, although blunted acutely, becomes normal with continued hCG stimulation. All these patients have also developed normal secondary sexual characteristics after prolonged hCG administration. When we measured isolated plasma samples of LH and FSH, we found no significant difference between normal prepubertal children and patients with hypogonadotropic hypogonadism. This fits with the theory that this disorder results from a defect in the initiation of the normal pubertal process rather than a defect in gonadotropic synthesis. When we studied the 24-hour, 20 minute interval plasma concentrations in 3 of the patients with hypogonadotropic hypogonadism and in 3 "normal" boys with delayed puberty, we found that the 2 boys with delayed puberty had sleep-associated episodic secretion of LH which resulted in higher mean LH concentrations during sleep than during wakefulness. In the 3 hypogonadotropic patients studied the plasma LH and FSH levels were relatively constant over the 24-hour period. There was no significant episodic secretion of LH during sleep. So we believe that one possible way of definitively distinguishing delayed puberty from hypogonadotropic hypogonadism is the demonstration of the LH sleep-associated pubertal program. If we demonstrate sleep-associated LH secretion, we reassure the patient and his family that the normal pubertal process has started and that normal puberty will occur. The first 2 subjects with delayed puberty who showed episodic LH secretion during sleep have since developed normally. Thus, this test, although difficult to perform routinely, may provide a way of finally separating these two disorders.

DR. SIZONENKO.   We studied some patients with hypogonadotropic hypogonadism in whom we found FSH to be low and LH normal. We treated them with testosterone and hCG, but we did not find a good answer. Probably there was an end-organ problem, too. Dr. Kulin, I was surprised that you did not speak of anabolic steroids, because in delayed puberty you have the problem of a clock that is not at the right time. If you give an anabolic steroid, you advance bone age and growth, and you probably set the clock at the right time.

DR. KULIN.   This is part of the reason for using short term therapy; it may well speed up "the clock."

DR. ROSS.   Measurements of gonadotropins in fractional urine collections, the first morning void, particularly, might enable us to determine if pituitary gonadotropin secretion of the sort Dr. Boyar described is occurring at night and may provide a satisfactory alternative to collecting blood samples at night.

DR. MOSHANG.   We have just completed a retrospective study of children treated with androgens at the Children's Hospital of Philadelphia. We also recommend individualized criteria for therapy and therefore had an equal number of treated and untreated children who had reached their final height. We found no statistical differences in final heights between the treated and the control groups. The treated children were mostly treated for 4 to 6 months with 20 mg/day of methyltestosterone; some received a second or even a third course of therapy.

REFERENCES

Bardin, C. W., Ross, G. T., Rifkind, A. B., Cargille, C. M., & Lipsett, M. B. (1969). Studies of pituitary Leydig cell axis in young men with hypogonadotropic hypogonadism and hyposmia: comparison with normal men, prepubertal boys, and hypopituitary patients. *J. Clin. Invest.* **48**, 2046–2057.

Bobrow, N. A., Money, J., & Lewis, V. G. (1971). Delayed puberty, eroticism, and sense of smell: a psychological study of hypogonadotropism, osmotic and anosmotic (Kallmann's syndrome). *Arch. Sex. Behav.* **1**, 329–344.

Lewis, V. G., Money, J., & Bobrow, N. A. (1971). Psychologic study of boys with short stature, retarded osseous growth, and normal age of pubertal onset. *Adolescence.* In Press.

McClintock, M. K. (1971). Menstrual synchrony and suppression. *Nature* **229**, 244–245.

Michael, R. P. (1972). Determinants of primate reproductive behaviour. *Acta Endocr. Suppl.* **166**, 322–361.

Money, J. (1970). Hormonal and genetic extremes at puberty, In *The Psychopathology of Adolescence*, J. Zubin & A. M. Freedman, Eds., Grune & Stratton, New York.

Money, J. & Alexander, D. (1966). Psychosexual development and absence of homosexuality in males with precocious puberty. *J. Nerv. Ment. Dis.* **148**, 111–123.

Money, J. & Alexander, D. (1967). Eroticism and sexual function in developmental anorchia and hyporchia with pubertal failure. *J. Sex Res.* **3**, 31–47.

Money, J. & Neill, J. (1967). Precocious puberty, IQ and school acceleration. *Clin. Ped.* **6**, 277–280.

Money, J. & Walker, P. A. (1971). Psychosexual development, maternalism, non-promiscuity, and body image in 15 females with precocious puberty. *Arch. Sex. Behav.* **1**, 45–60.

Money, J. & Wolff, G. (1973). Late puberty, retarded growth and reversible hyposomatotropinism (psychosocial dwarfism). *Adolescence.* In press.

Rosenfield, R. L. (1972). Role of androgens in growth and development of fetus, child and adolescent. *Adv. Pediat.* **19**, 171–213.

Santen, R. J., Leonard, J. M., Sherins, R. J., Gandy, H. M., & Paulsen, C. A. (1971). Short- and long-term effects of clomiphene citrate on the pituitary-testicular axis. *J. Clin. Endocrinol.* **33**, 970–979.

Vandenberg, J. G., Drickamer, L. C.. & Colby, D. R. (1972). Social and dietary factors in the sexual maturation of female mice, *J. Reprod. Fertil.* **28**, 397–405.

van Theil, D. H., Sherins, R. J., Myers, Jr., G. H., & deVita, V. T., Jr. (1972). Evidence for a specific seminiferous tubular factor affecting follicle-stimulating hormone secretion in man. *J. Clin. Invest.* **51**, 1009–1020.

10.

Ontogeny of Estrogen and Androgen Receptors

A. J. EISENFELD

Estrogen and androgen accumulation and binding have been demonstrated in some target organs that are highly specific with respect to organ and steroid. There is circumstantial evidence consistent with the possibility that the binding proteins in target organs are the drug receptors; i.e., the biologic effects of the steroids may be due to the interaction of the steroids with the binding proteins in target organs. At least theoretically, however, binding in tissues could serve other functions—for example, as a local storage mechanism or even to inactivate the hormone. To identify the binding proteins as the receptors it is necessary to produce specific effects by adding the steroid-binding protein complex to a system that is not responsive to the steroid alone.

It is currently thought that the onset of puberty may be due, at least in part, to altered feedback control by estrogens or androgens at the hypothalamus or other brain regions. In the female two changes may be occurring with puberty: (1) negative feedback control on FSH secretion by estrogens may be decreased; (2) increased estrogen secretion may be re-

---

Abbreviations

DHT	Dihydrotestosterone
mRNA	Messenger RNA

sponsible for an ovulatory surge of secretion of LH in the mature female. This positive feedback control by estrogens on gonadotropin secretion may appear first at puberty. Thus it is appropriate to describe the estrogen and androgen receptor mechanisms, to examine the available information for changes at puberty and, in particular, to emphasize the information concerning the binding systems in the hypothalamus and other portions of the brain.

Ontogeny has been studied at an early stage, but the information currently available is fragmentary. To place these data in context, the evidence for estrogen and androgen binding in mammalian brain and pituitary is reviewed, and related information concerning the interactions in peripheral target organs is presented. For more complete discussions of the binding mechanisms and the proposed mechanisms of action of the sex steroids the reader is referred to reviews of estrogens (Jensen & DeSombre, 1972; Means & O'Malley, 1972) and androgens (Williams-Ashman & Reddi, 1972; Wilson & Gloyna, 1970; Baulieu, Alberga, Jung, Lebeau, Mercier-Bodard, Milgrom, Raynaud, Raynaud-Jammet, Rochefort, Truong, & Robel, 1971).

ESTROGENS

Extraction of Radioactivity After Systemic Administration

In an experimental approach to receptor characterization it was observed that, after systemic administration of tracer doses of radioactive estrogens of high specific activity, higher concentrations were found in the uterus than in plasma (Glascock & Hoekstra, 1959; Jensen & Jacobson, 1962). Such studies in other organs of the rat are illustrated in Fig. 1. One hour after intravenous administration of ^{3}H-17β-estradiol in the anterior pituitary of male and female rats concentration was about 100 times greater than in plasma (Eisenfeld & Axelrod, 1965; 1966). Also, the anterior pituitary retained high levels of radioactivity for as long as 16 hours after administration (Attramadal, 1964). It was more difficult to demonstrate concentration of estradiol in the hypothalamus. One hour after intravenous administration of 0.1 μg/100 g the levels in the brain were much lower than in either pituitary or uterus. However, the concentration of unconjugated estradiol in the hypothalamus was twice that found in the cerebrum and 4 times that in plasma (Eisenfeld & Axelrod, 1966). (Unless otherwise specified, the hypothalamic section includes the medial preoptic region and the pituitary stalk with pars tuberalis.) The difference between hypothalamus and cerebrum is found to be due to longer retention in the hypothalamus (Eisenfeld, 1967a; McGuire & Lisk, 1968). This retention is not higher because of a difference in initial delivery via

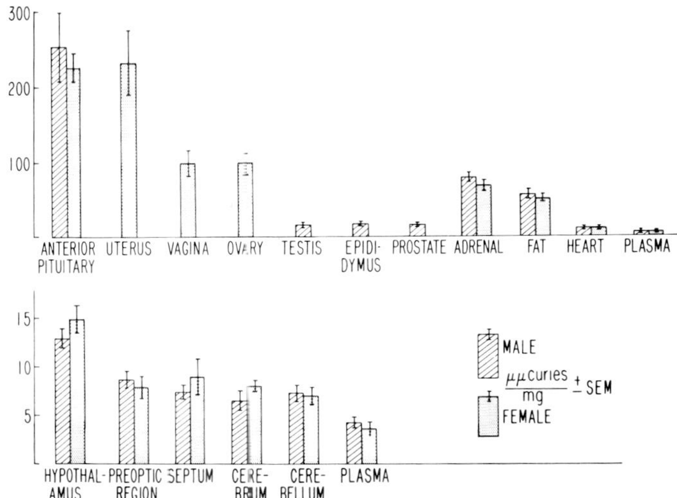

FIG. 1.   Distribution of ³H-estradiol in male and female rats. ³H-estradiol (0.1 μg/ 100 g, 38 Ci/mM) was injected intravenously and the tissues removed 1 hour later. The tissues were homogenized in water and unconjugated radioactivity extracted into toluene and measured. Reproduced from Eisenfeld & Axelrod (1966) by permission of the publisher.

the bloodstream; at 2 minutes after intravenous administration the concentration in the hypothalamus is equal to that of the cerebrum and exceeds that of plasma (Eisenfeld, 1967a, b).

Digital computer analysis of the kinetics of distribution is consistent with the concept that there are 2 hypothalamic pools of estradiol—one attached to a limited concentration of binding molecules, and a nonspecific second in which concentration of estradiol parallels that of plasma (Eisenfeld, 1967a). The concentration of estradiol in the hypothalamic nonspecific pool is approximated by the concentration of radioactivity measured in the cerebrum. Thus the concentration of estradiol, which behaves as if attached to binding molecules (bound pool), in the hypothalamus can be estimated by subtraction of the cerebral from the hypothalamic concentration. With a slight increase in estradiol dosage (in the 0.1 to 2 μg/100 g range) its accumulation in the anterior pituitary, bound hypothalamic pool, and uterus approaches limiting values (Eisenfeld & Axelrod, 1965). This accumulation is specific. Prior administration of estriol, estrone, or diethylstilbestrol (a nonsteroidal synthetic estrogen with high potency) reduces the concentration of radioactive estradiol in the hypothalamus, anterior pituitary, and uterus, whereas even large doses of testosterone, progesterone or its derivatives, or hydrocortisone do not (Eisenfeld &

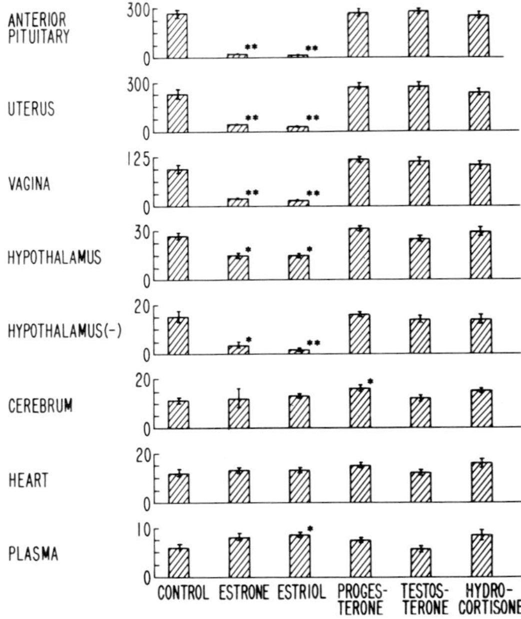

FIG. 2. Effect of steroid hormones on the distribution of ^{3}H-estradiol. ^{3}H-estradiol (0.1 μg/100 g, 38 Ci/mM) was injected intravenously 30 seconds after 25 μg/100 g of nonradioactive estrone or estriol or 1 mg/100 g of progestrone, testosterone, or hydrocortisone. Subtraction of the cerebral concentration from the hypothalamic concentration is expressed by the symbol (I). Results are expressed as μμc/mg ± SE; *$p < .05$, **$p < .001$ compared with control concentrations. Reproduced from Eisenfeld & Axelrod (1966) by permission of the publisher.

Axelrod, 1966; 1967; Figs. 2 and 3). Clomiphene, a fertility drug in women and a partial estrogen agonist, reduces estradiol accumulation in the hypothalamus (Eisenfeld & Axelrod, 1967) as well as in the pituitary and uterus (Roy, Mahesh, & Greenblatt, 1964; Eisenfeld & Axelrod, 1967; Fig. 3). Studies with such drugs as dimethylstilbestrol or U11100 (1-(2-(p-(3,4 dihydro-6-methoxy-2-phenyl-1-naphthyl) phenoxy) ethyl)-pyrrolidine hydrochloride) provide strong support for the concept that the retention of ^{3}H-estradiol in organs concerned with reproduction represents interaction with receptors. These drugs, which antagonize some of the effects of coadministered estradiol, reduce estradiol accumulation in hypothalamus and pituitary (Eisenfeld & Axelrod, 1967) and uterus (Jensen, Jacobson, Flesher, Saha, Gupta, Smith, Colucci, Shiplacoff, Neumann, DeSombre, & Jungblut, 1966; Fig. 4).

In the hypothalamus the region of the median eminence has the highest concentration of ^{3}H-estradiol, the anterior hypothalamus has the next high-

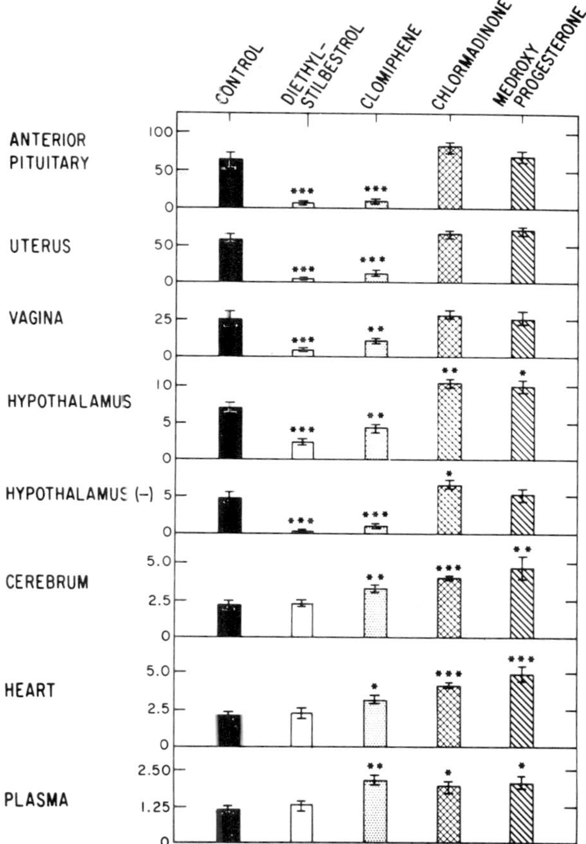

FIG. 3.   Effect of drugs on the distribution of ^{3}H-estradiol. Diethylstilbestrol (25 μg/100 g), clomiphene (5 mg/100 g), chlormadinone acetate (1 mg/100 g), or medroxyprogesterone acetate (1 mg/100 g) were injected intravenously 30 seconds before 0.1 μg ^{3}H-estradiol/100 g (9.7 Ci/mM). Tissues were analyzed for ^{3}H-estradiol concentrations 1 hour later. Results are expressed as $\mu\mu$c/mg $\pm$ SE; $*P < 0.05$, $**P < 0.01$, $***P < 0.001$ compared with concentrations in the controls. Reproduced from Eisenfeld & Axelrod (1967) by permission of the publisher.

est (Kato & Villee, 1967). The ratio of radioactivity in the middle or anterior hypothalamus to that in cerebrum increases with time after injection (Kato & Villee, 1967; McGuire & Lisk, 1969a). Chronic administration of clomiphene or acute administration of 10 μg of 17β-estradiol (but not the weak estrogen 17 α-estradiol) reduces this accumulation in the anterior and middle hypothalamus (Kato, Kobayashi, & Villee, 1968; Kato & Villee, 1967).

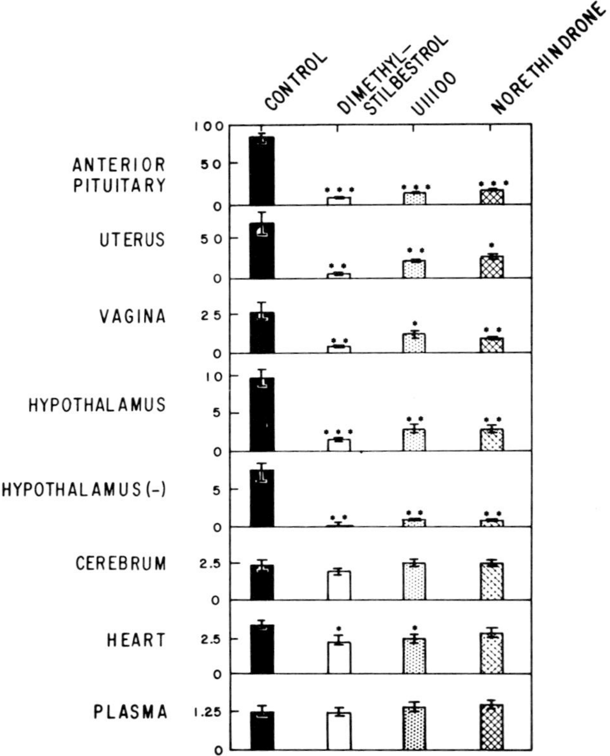

FIG. 4. Distribution of ³H-estradiol after administration of dimethylstilbestrol, U11100, or norethindrone. Dimethylstilbestrol (100 μg/100 g), U11100 (1 mg/100 g) or norethindrone (800 μg/100 g), was administered by tail vein 30 seconds before 0.1 μg ³H-estradiol/100 g (9.7 Ci/mM). The concentration of ³H-estradiol in tissues 1 hour later is indicated as μμc/mg ± SE. *$p < .05$, **$p < .01$, ***$p < .001$, compared with control concentrations. Reproduced from Eisenfeld & Axelrod (1967) by permission of the publisher.

Differential centrifugation has shown that some of the radioactivity in the hypothalamus and in the anterior pituitary is retained in the nuclear fraction. One hour after in vivo administration more than 50 per cent of the radioactivity from the hypothalamus and anterior pituitary is found in the 600 x g crude nuclear pellet after homogenization and centrifugation (Eisenfeld, 1967b). Highly purified nuclei contain 40 per cent of the estradiol from the hypothalamus (Zigmond & McEwen, 1970). The nuclear radioactivity per milligram of protein is 13 times that of the whole homogenate for the hypothalamus; the corresponding figure for the cerebrum is 0.8. ³H-estradiol concentration in this highly purified nuclear fraction is reduced by low doses of 17β-estradiol but not by high doses of testosterone. The accumulation of radioactivity in the nuclear pellet is abolished almost completely by 1 mg of unlabeled estradiol, whereas in the whole tissue it is reduced to 35 per cent of control. Also, nuclear retention in the anterior hypothalamus and pituitary is depressed by chronic administration of clomiphene (Mowles, Ashkenazy, Mix, & Shepard, 1971).

The highest concentration of estrogen among brain regions of the rhesus monkey is found near the arcuate nucleus of the hypothalamus. High concentrations are found in the anterior pituitary, all portions of the uterus and fallopian tubes, the vaginal epithelium, and the adrenal cortex (Eisenfeld, Gardner, & van Wagenen, 1971; and unpublished material).

In the human estradiol concentrates in the endometrium, myometrium, and vaginal epithelium relative to plasma (Brush, Taylor, & King, 1967). No localization studies of the human brain or pituitary have been reported except for one in a 15-week-old fetus (Davis, Wiener, Jacobson, & Jensen, 1963).

Autoradiographic Studies

A second approach to the study of the interaction of labeled estrogens with organs in vivo is by autoradiography. The usual autoradiographic techniques were modified in order to reduce the loss of estrogens into solvents and movement within the cells. Frozen unfixed and unembedded sections dipped into photographic emulsion showed the hypothalamus to have a high concentration of silver grains in some neurons after local implantation of ^{14}C-diethylstilbestrol diacetate (Michael, 1962). After systemic administration of ^{3}H-hexestrol the grain counts were higher in the anterior pituitary than in uterine glands and 8 to 80 times greater in the region of the midline hypothalamus and lateral septum of the limbic system than in the lateral hypothalamus, cerebral cortex, cerebellum, caudate, or cervical cord (Michael, 1965a). Furthermore, after systemic administration some neurons in the hypothalamus accumulated radioactivity (Michael, 1965b).

In dry mount autoradiography tissue sections are freeze-dried and applied to a dry emulsion (Stumpf, 1968a). With this technique labeled neurons are found in the nucleus arcuatus, the pars lateralis of the nucleus ventromedialis, the anterior portion of the nucleus paraventricularis with its outgrowth of nucleus paraventricularis parvicellularis, in a group of cells ventral to the magnacellular portion of nucleus paraventricularis, and in the nucleus preopticus medialis, nucleus preopticus suprachiasmatis, and nucleus interstitialis striae terminalis. Labeled neurons are also found in the nucleus accumbens, nucleus septi lateralis, nucleus triangularis septi and the organon subfornicale. This radioactivity is concentrated in the nuclear subcellular fraction. The distribution pattern of labeled neurons is identical to regions of termination of the stria terminalis which originate in the nuclei of the amygdala (Stumpf, 1968a). Unlabeled regions include the following nuclei: supraopticus; suprachiasmatis; ventromedialis (pars ventralis, centralis, dorsalis, and medialis); dorsomedialis; hypothalamicus lateralis; hypothalamicus posterior; and mammillaris. In general, this localization in the hypothalamic and preoptic neurons has been confirmed by using either frozen sections melted onto slides covered with emulsion (Anderson & Greenwald, 1969) or freeze-dried sections fixed with osmium vapor, epon-embedded, and coated with stripping film (Attramadal, 1970a). The only differences have been the failure to find labeled neurons in the nucleus triangularis septi and in the organon subfornicale (Anderson & Greenwald, 1969). The grain count is reduced in the preoptic area and ventromedial arcuate nucleus region by pretreatment with 2 μg of estradiol or 2.5 mg of progesterone 1 hour before the ^{3}H-estradiol.

A different hypothalamic localization has been described in the only report of autoradiography on a primate. Twelve hours after intramuscular administration of ^{3}H-estradiol to a monkey the hypothalamus was sectioned by freezing microtomy and examined by autoradiography. Silver grains were found in an area of specialized ependymal cells (situated anteriolaterally in the tuber cinereum and distinguished by having long processes that extend to the region of the pars tuberalis); grains were not concentrated elsewhere (Anand-Kumar & Knowles, 1967).

The amygdala also has extensive labeling of neurons after ^{3}H-estradiol administration. Localization has been described in nuclei medialis (Anderson & Greenwald, 1969; Stumpf, 1972), corticalis, basalis, and the pars anterior (Stumpf, 1972).

In the anterior pituitary radioactive grains are concentrated in the nuclei of acidophils, basophils, and chromophobes (Stumpf, 1968b; Attramadal, 1970b). These grains are reduced by pretreatment with estradiol but not significantly by progesterone (Anderson & Greenwald, 1969).

In the periphery ^{3}H-estradiol localizes in the nuclei of epithelial and connective tissue and muscle cells of the uterus, oviduct, and vagina, granulosa cells in the ovary (Stumpf, 1969), and epithelial cells in the breast (Sander & Attramadal, 1968).

Macromolecular Interactions

Estrogens attach to protein-containing macromolecules prepared from the supernatant fraction of the uterus (Toft & Gorski, 1966). In solutions of low ionic strength the estrogen-binding macromolecules have sedimentation coefficients of approximately 8 to 9.5S with ultracentrifugation in sucrose gradients (Toft & Gorski, 1966; Jensen, Suzuki, Numata, Smith, & DeSombre, 1969). These uterine-binding molecules have high specificity for estrogens (Korenman, 1969) and have sulfhydryl groups that are important for the estrogen binding (Jensen, Hurst, DeSombre, & Jungblut, 1967). The current concept is that the initial interaction of estradiol with a protein in the uterus occurs in the cytoplasm. In a temperature-dependent process, the entire estradiol-cytoplasmic-protein complex enters the nucleus (Jensen, Suzuki, Kawashima, Stumpf, Jungblut, & DeSombre, 1968) and attaches to chromatin (Maurer & Chalkley, 1967; Shyamala & Gorski, 1969). (Alternatively, the estradiol may be transferred from the cytoplasmic protein to a different nuclear protein.) This concept is based on the observation that cytoplasmic-binding molecules appear to be required in order to demonstrate subsequent macromolecular binding in the nucleus (Jensen, Numata, Smith, Suzuki, Brecher, & DeSombre, 1969a; Shyamala & Gorski, 1969).

Estrogen-binding macromolecules are also present in supernatant fractions from the hypothalamus and pituitary. Tissues from chronically ovariectomized rats were homogenized by Tris HCl containing 0.0015 M EDTA, the supernatant fraction obtained by ultracentrifugation, and low concentrations of ^{3}H-estradiol mixed with the supernatant fractions. After incubation, radioactivity associated with macromolecules was separated from unbound estradiol by the use of small polyacrylamide gel filtration columns at room temperature (Eisenfeld, 1969). Average values in dpm/mg protein in the macromolecular fraction were uterus 18,000, anterior pituitary, 11,000, hypothalamus, 1500, cerebrum, 300, cerebellum, 250, heart, 200, and plasma, 50 (Eisenfeld, 1970). The radioactivity in the macromolecular fraction from the hypothalamus and anterior pituitary chromatographs was identical to that of authentic estradiol. Approximately equal concentrations of estrogen-binding macromolecules are found in the anterior and middle hypothalamus (Eisenfeld, unpublished).

The equilibrium dissociation constant for the binding has been determined by incubating various concentrations of ^{3}H-estradiol with the supernatant fractions. The K_D is 2×10^{-10} M for the hypothalamus, anterior pituitary, and uterus at 4°C and indicates a high affinity (Eisenfeld, 1972a). Steroid specificity for these estrogen-binding macromolecules has been examined by mixing various nonradioactive steroids with ^{3}H-estradiol before adding the tissue supernatant fraction (Eisenfeld, 1970; 1972b). Nonradioactive estradiol (10^{-7} M) markedly reduces ^{3}H-estradiol concentrations, whereas progesterone or testosterone (10^{-5} M) does not (Fig. 5).

Two estrogens in common use in oral contraceptives are 17α-ethinyl estradiol and mestranol (3-methoxy-17α-ethinyl estradiol), each tablet containing 50 to 125 μg of one of them; 17α-ethinyl estradiol appears to bind well to the hypothalamic and anterior pituitary estrogen-binding macromolecules. In contrast, high concentrations of mestranol compete poorly

(Fig. 5), which suggests that mestranol must be metabolized in the body to form 17α-ethinyl estradiol in order to be involved in the inhibition of ovulation (Eisenfeld, 1972b).

Macromolecular binding may also occur in vivo. Rats in one group were

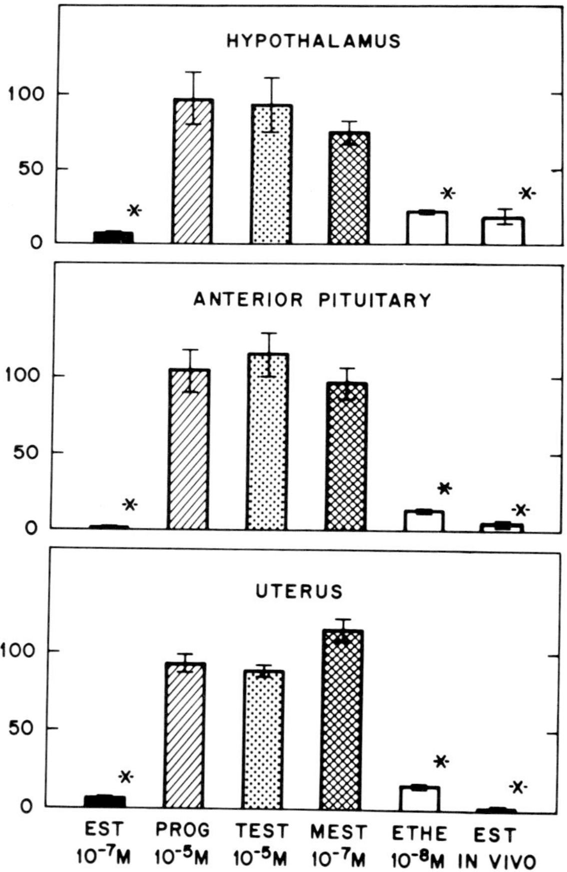

FIG. 5. ³H-estradiol was mixed with estradiol (est), progestrone (prog), testosterone (test), and mestranol (mest) or 17α-ethinyl-estradiol (ethe) or their vehicle (5μl ethanol), and 0.2 ml of tissue supernatant fractions were added. One group of animals was pretreated with estradiol 10 μg/100 g 75 minutes before removing their organs (est in vivo). The final concentration of ³H-estradiol was 2 × 10⁻⁹ M (48Ci/ mM); the final concentrations of the drugs are indicated in the graph. After 1 hour in ice with estradiol, progesterone, testosterone, or estrogen in vivo or 24 hours with mestranol or 17α-ethinyl-estradiol macromolecular-bound ³H-estradiol was measured by gel filtration. The results are expressed as the percentage of respective controls ± SE. *p < .05 compared with control concentrations. Reproduced from Eisefeld (1972b), by permission of the publisher.

pretreated with nonradioactive estradiol before their organs were removed (Fig. 5). When ^{3}H-estradiol was mixed with the supernatant fraction of hypothalamus and anterior pituitary, the radioactivity in the macromolecular fraction from these pretreated animals was less than 20 per cent of that found in control animals (Eisenfeld, 1970).

In order to characterize, in part, the chemical composition of the binding molecules supernatant fractions were incubated with ^{3}H-estradiol in the presence of various degradative enzymes (Eisenfeld, 1970). Binding in the hypothalamus and pituitary was markedly reduced by chymotrypsin (Fig. 6), which indicates that the binding molecules contain protein. In contrast, binding in the hypothalamus and pituitary was not reduced by DNase or RNase. Parachloromercuriphenylsulfonate, a reagent that reacts with free sulfhydryl groups, reduced macromolecular binding in hypothalamus and anterior pituitary.

Some radioactive estradiol will sediment at about 9.5S after in vitro incubation of the supernatant fraction from the bovine anterior pituitary, median eminence, and possibly the anterior and posterior hypothalamus, but not from the cerebral cortex. No binding of ^{3}H-progesterone or ^{3}H-testosterone is found (Kahwanago, Heinrich, & Herrmann, 1969). Incubation with high concentrations of clomiphene or p-chloromercuriphenylsulfonate reduces 9S binding to approximately 50 per cent of control in the anterior hypothalamus, 20 per cent in the median eminence plus pars tuberalis, and 10 per cent in the anterior pituitary (Kahwanago, Heinrich, & Herrmann, 1970).

The pituitary supernatant fraction binds about 30 per cent more ^{3}H-estradiol than the uterus in the 8S region after ultracentrifugation (Jensen et al, 1969b). After incubation of ^{3}H-estradiol with the hypothalamic supernatant there is a discrete peak of bound radioactivity fractionated by polyacrylamide gel electrophoresis (Phuong, Sauer, & Rapoport 1972).

Several in vitro binding properties of the hypothalamic and anterior pituitary supernatant fractions are thus similar to those of the uterus. In addition, there is a parallel between the properties of in vitro macromolecular binding and in vivo accumulation in the hypothalamus and anterior pituitary as well as the same relative concentration among organs, a finite capacity, and a high specificity for estrogens.

In the in vitro studies low concentrations of radioactivity have been found in the macromolecular fraction by using the supernatant fractions of such organs as the cerebrum, cerebellum, or heart, which are not known to be affected directly by estrogens. The radioactivity is decreased about half by 10^{-7} M estradiol, chymotrypsin, or p-chloromercuriphenylsulfonate (Eisenfeld, 1970). The possibility is, therefore, that the difference between hypothalamus, pituitary, and uterus, and such organs as the cerebrum and heart, with respect to supernatant-binding macromolecules, is not qualita-

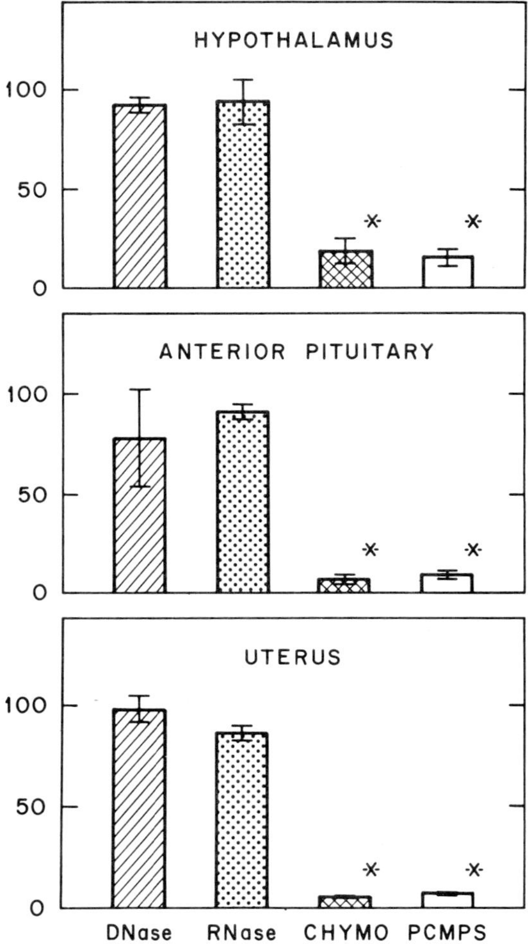

FIG. 6. Supernatant fractions were shaken at 24°C with 2×10^{-9} M ^{3}H-estradiol and 250 μg/ml of deoxyribonuclease (DNase), ribonuclease (RNase), or chymotrypsin (CHYMO). In another experiment sodium p-chloromercuriphenylsulfonate (PCMPS) (1×10^{-3} M) was added to the supernatant in ice one-half hour before adding ^{3}H-estradiol. Macromolecular-bound estradiol was measured 1 hour after the addition of ^{3}H-estradiol. The results show the mean $\pm$ SE expressed as the percentage of respective controls. *$p < .01$. Reproduced from Eisenfeld, 1972b by permission of the publisher.

tive but quantitative. The hypothalamus has at least a tenfold, and the anterior pituitary a sixtyfold, higher concentration of specific binding macromolecules than either cerebrum or cerebellum.

In the hypothalamus the capacity for estrogen binding seems to be concentrated in highly selective groups of neurons; axons with myelin sheaths and glia, which constitute the bulk of the hypothalamus, do not appear to concentrate estradiol highly. In contrast, most cells in the anterior pituitary and uterus do concentrate estradiol. When this difference is taken into consideration, the number of estradiol-binding molecules per cell in those neurons in the hypothalamus that do concentrate estradiol may be in the same range as that in anterior pituitary or uterus.

Although the initial interaction of estrogen in the hypothalamus and anterior pituitary appears to be with cytoplasmic proteins, the ultimate cellular locus in vivo is predominantly nuclear, as shown by differential centrifugation or autoradiography. Nuclear retention of estradiol has now been shown after in vitro incubation of tissue fragments of hypothalamus and anterior pituitary. After incubation of pieces of tissue with ^{3}H-estradiol retention of the estradiol in purified nuclei is 4 times greater in hypothalamus than in cerebellum. The nuclear accumulation of radioactive estradiol is reduced by estradiol but not by cortisol, testosterone, or progesterone (Chader & Villee, 1970). Homogenates of anterior pituitary incubated with ^{3}H-estradiol have eightfold higher nuclear uptake than liver; this accumulation of radioactivity in nuclei is not observed with incubation of anterior pituitary homogenates with ^{3}H-corticosterone, ^{3}H-progesterone, or ^{3}H-testosterone (Leavitt, Friend, & Robinson, 1969).

Some evidence also shows that cytoplasmic binding may be required for nuclear uptake in the hypothalamus and pituitary. If isolated nuclei are incubated with ^{3}H-estradiol in buffer, the nuclear retention of radioactivity is low in both hypothalamus and cerebellum. If the supernatant and nuclear fractions are mixed with ^{3}H-estradiol in vitro and the nuclei then reisolated, the nuclear retention in hypothalamus is increased to about 3 times that in cerebellum (Chader & Villee, 1970). If anterior pituitary nuclei are incubated with ^{3}H-estradiol in either pituitary supernatant fractions or buffer, the nuclear pellet contains a fivefold higher concentration of radioactivity from the samples suspended in the supernatant fraction in relation to those suspended in buffer (Leavitt et al, 1969).

After in vivo administration, most of the radioactivity in the nuclear fraction of the pituitary is macromolecular-bound. The sedimentation coefficients of the binding macromolecules from the pituitary and hypothalamus may be different from those of the uterus. The binding of the supernatant fraction from anterior pituitary is 4S in low salt-containing gradients, and the nuclear fractions of both the anterior pituitary and the hypothalamus contain 7S binding (Mowles et al, 1971).

The nucleus may also contribute target-organ-specific components involved in the nuclear retention of the estradiol-cytoplasmic-protein complex. The following results suggest that the chromatin from target organs differs from that of nontarget organs in its acceptor capability. Estradiol reacted with the supernatant fraction of the uterus to form a cytoplasmic complex, which was then added to chromatin from different tissues. There was 2 to 5 times more binding to chromatin from the uterus than from spleen, liver, lung, or kidney (Steggles, Spelsberg, Glaser, & O'Malley, 1971).

The only normal human tissue source in which the estradiol binding macromolecules have been partly characterized is the supernatant fraction from the uterus. Characteristics seem to be similar to those previously found in the uterus of the rat (Wyss, Karznia, Heinrichs, & Herrmann, 1968; Martin, 1972; Makler & Eisenfeld, 1971).

The current sequence of events for the interaction of estrogens with uterine macromolecules is summarized in Fig. 7. The estradiol attaches to a cytoplasmic protein. The complex undergoes a conformational change, either before or after crossing the nuclear membrane, then attaches to an acceptor protein on chromatin.

Mechanisms of Action

Changes in response to a hormone at different ages could be the result of a modification of the receptor-hormone interaction or of the metabolic events triggered by the hormone-receptor complex. We shall describe some

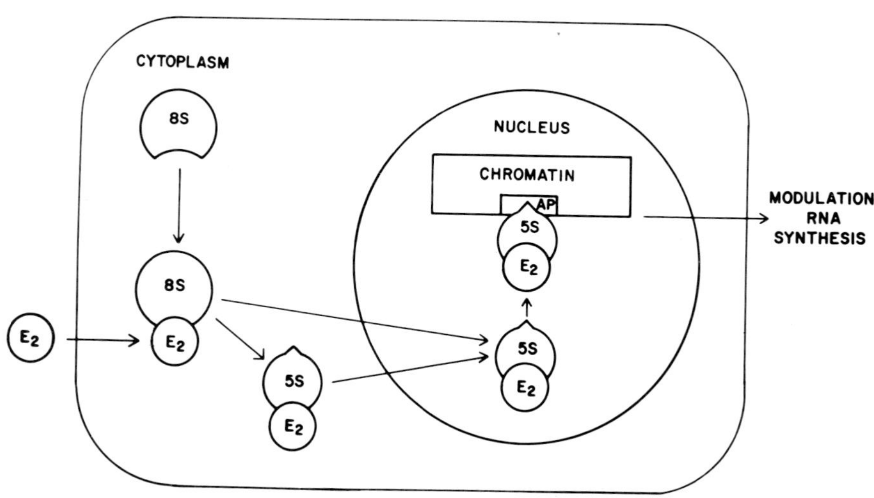

FIG. 7. Schematic drawing representing the initial steps in the interaction of estradiol with the uterus. Estradiol (E_2) attaches to an 8S binding protein in the cytoplasm. The complex crosses the nuclear membrane either before or after conformational change of the protein to 5S. The complex attaches to acceptor proteins (AP) on chromatin and modulates RNA synthesis.

of the early changes in cellular metabolism that may represent the initial responses to the hormone.

Almost all information concerning early estrogen responses in mammalian systems has been obtained from the uterus. It is not known at what step tissue differentiation is expressed. The ultimate cellular modifications promoted by the sex steroids are quite different in the brain when compared with peripheral reproductive organs. Estradiol promotes uterine growth and secretion, vaginal epithelium cornification, and pituitary hypertrophy and acts at the hypothalamic level to influence neuronal function. The early steps in the sequence of action could, however, be similar if different mRNAs were produced in the various tissues or if tissue differentiation were expressed at a later point.

The ultimate nuclear localization of most of the radioactive estradiol and its association with chromatin suggests an early effect of estrogens on the transcription process. Within 1 hour after administration of estradiol there was an increase in radioactive RNA synthesis from ^{3}H-uridine given shortly before animal sacrifice (Knowler & Smellie, 1971). The predominant form of RNA synthesized with short pulses of ^{3}H-uridine is of high molecular weight and is thought to contain portions with mRNA activity.

There is some evidence for the early synthesis of RNA in the subsequent synthesis of selective proteins. Within 30 minutes after in vivo or in vitro administration estradiol increases the incorporation of amino acid into one protein fraction, separated by gel electrophoresis (Barnes & Gorski, 1970), which can be blocked by administration of high concentrations of actinomycin D and which suggests that RNA must first be synthesized. This induced protein fraction synthesis can also be blocked by administration of α-amanitine (Wira & Baulieu, 1972). Alpha amanitine is thought to inhibit RNA polymerase which is not associated with nucleoli and which may be involved in the synthesis of mRNA.

Other evidence suggests a direct effect of estradiol on the nucleolus. After incubation of calf endometrium with radioactive estradiol 19 per cent of the bound estradiol was sedimented with the nucleoli; however, nucleolar localization was not higher than other nuclear regions of the uterus by autoradiography (Stumpf, 1969). Some of the radioactive estradiol could be extracted from the nucleolus as a 14S complex that has both RNA polymerase activity and, after dissociation, a ^{3}H-E$_2$ 5S complex. The nucleolar RNA polymerase activity was greater from estrogen-treated than from control-calf endometrium. When nucleolar RNA polymerase was partially purified with phosphocellulose column chromatography, addition of either the ^{3}H-E$_2$ cytoplasmic 5S or the ^{3}H-E$_2$ nucleolar 5S complex increased the activity of this RNA polymerase preparation (Arnaud, Beziat, Borgna, Guilleux, & Mousseran-Canet, 1971).

The main function of the nucleolus is thought to be synthesis of ribosomal RNA; an increased rate of ribosomal synthesis is not observed until 1 to 2 hours after administration of estradiol in the rat.

Another relatively early change may involve histones and proteins associated with the histones. Within 1 hour increased synthesis of an acidic protein is associated with the arginine-rich histone fraction after extraction from the uterus (Barker, 1971). A related finding is that 1 hour after addition of estradiol the ratio of arginine-rich histone to DNA decreases to 73 per cent of control. These are both changes that may increase DNA-directed RNA synthesis. In vitro addition of histones to uterine chromatin reduces the template activity; if chromatin-extracted acidic proteins are also added, the template activity is restored (Teng & Hamilton, 1969).

To summarize, there appears to be an early increase in heterodispersed RNA synthesis. One line of evidence that demonstrates RNA dependence for early synthesis of an induced protein fraction suggests that the synthesis of specific messenger RNAs may be the initial metabolic change. An alternative proposal involves a direct interaction of the estrogen-cytoplasmic-protein-binding complex with the nucleolus to associate with and modify the activity of RNA polymerase. Other work suggests that early changes may increase acidic proteins associated with histones and reduce the histone concentration on chromatin.

Although not an early event, there is now direct evidence that a steroid hormone can increase the synthesis of a specific mRNA. RNA from various sources was tested for its ability to direct the synthesis of ovalbumin in the rabbit reticulocyte-ribosomal protein-synthesizing system (Rosenfield, Comstock, Means, & O'Malley, 1972). RNA obtained from hen oviduct (but not from liver) led to ovalbumin synthesis. Chick oviduct RNA synthesized ovalbumin only after the chicks had been pretreated with estrogens. Animals at different stages of development can also differ potentially with respect to later cellular events, several steps removed from the original receptor-estrogen interaction.

In the hypothalamus and in other brain regions the estrogen effects are probably expressed as changes in synthesis or discharge of various neurotransmitters or as the synthesis or discharge of releasing factors. In the pituitary estrogens could function to modulate synthesis or secretion of the anterior pituitary hormones. The sequence of events between binding of the estrogen and the ultimate effect on neurotransmitters, releasing factors, and pituitary hormones is unknown.

Ontogeny

Almost all the information concerning the ontogeny of the estrogen binding system has been obtained in studies on the rat. Evidence for the presence of the accumulation system in the uterus is found early in life. At day 22 of fetal life there is nuclear concentration of radioactivity in all cell types of the oviduct and (in primitive germ cells of the ovary) after hypophysectomy (Nakai, Sakamoto, Kigawa, & Shigematsu, 1972). Postnatally, radioactive estradiol concentration is higher in the uterus than in all other organs studied from day 5 (Presl, Rohling, Horsky, & Herzman, 1970). The concentration of uterine estradiol-binding macromolecule increases fourfold between days 1 and 10 and then is relatively constant through day 22. The increase in concentration is not controlled by ovarian estrogen secretion, for it also occurs in castrates (Clark & Gorski, 1970). Some estradiol is bound to uterine chromatin in the calf (Maurer & Chalkley, 1967) and in the adult castrate rat (Hamilton, 1968).

Plasma levels of radioactivity remain high in rats less than 10 days old, and a concentration in the pituitary relative to plasma is not observed before this time (Kato Sugimara, & Kobiyashi, 1971a; Alvarez & Ramirez, 1970). The pituitary concentration of radioactivity, however, is much higher than that in brain regions as early as day 3 to 5 (Kato et al, 1971a; Presl et al, 1970; Wocley, Holinka, & Timiras, 1969).

There is little difference in the accumulation of radioactivity in the anterior pituitary, uterus, or ovary of prepubescent or adult female rats (Eisenfeld & Axelrod, 1966; Presl et al, 1970; Kato et al, 1971a). The t½ of estrogen retention in the anterior pituitary, as well as the autoradiographic localization in all cell types, is similar in adult males and females; in both sexes administration of nonradioactve estradiol (but not testosterone) decreases the radioactive accumulation (Attramadal & Aakvaag, 1970; Attramadal, 1970b). The only available data concerning distribution in the immature human describes the radioactivity in fetal tissues after administration of radioactive estradiol to the mother before abortion. These studies were performed at about 15 weeks gestation, and the radioactivity was administered 2 hours before the operation. Its concentration was greater in the pituitary than in the fetal blood, but in contrast it was not greater in the uterus or ovary than in the blood and the level in the brain was very low (Davis et al, 1963).

There are few studies that compare the early biochemical responses to estradiol of the immature with the mature uterus. Both the 22-day-old and the mature uterus respond by increased synthesis of the induced protein fraction (Barnes & Gorski, 1970). There is an early increase in rapidly labeled RNA synthesis in the uterus of 18-to-22-day-old (Knowler & Smellie, 1971) and mature castrates (Hamilton, 1968). The time course of an increased content of RNA and protein is similar in the uterus of 24-day-old (Billing, Barbiroli, & Smellie, 1969) and mature castrates (Aizawa & Mueller, 1961).

In contrast to the presumed early development of the binding system in the uterus and in the anterior pituitary there is suggestive evidence that the system in the hypothalamus may not be fully developed in very young rats. In one study starting at day 5 a concentration of radioactivity in the median eminence or anterior hypothalamus calculated as the ratio to cerebral cortex concentration was not observed until day 20 to 30 (Presl et al, 1970). The interpretation of in vivo distribution studies earlier than day 20, however, was complicated by high levels of radioactivity retained in the plasma. One factor for the persistence of high levels of radioactivity in plasma is probably the presence of an estrogen-specific binding protein in plasma (Nunez, Savu, Engelmann, Benassayag, Crepy, & Jayle, 1971; Raynaud, Mercier-Bodard, & Baulieu, 1971). This binding protein has high affinity (K_D 10^{-9} M) and at 5 days high capacity (75 μM). The concentration of the protein decreases with increasing maturation; at 20 days it is 4 μM; by 30 days the protein is not observable. Not only are plasma levels high, but all tissue levels, including brain regions, are high in the very young. This suggests that metabolism and excretion of the estrogens are also poorly developed. The microsomal enzyme system in liver, responsible for hydroxylating drugs and steroids (including estradiol), is not fully developed until 30 days of age (Kato, Vassanelli, Frontino, & Chiesara, 1964). The glucuronidation system for some steroids has a very low activity in the newborn (Driscoll & Hsia, 1958). In 4- and 15-day-old rats most of the radioactivity in tissues is extractable into toluene and chromatographed similarly to authentic estradiol (Wooley et al, 1969). In an interpretation of the data the physiologic significance of the ratio of the concentration in hypothalamic regions to that in cortex was unclear. The kinetics of distribution have not been reported for the very young after administration of low doses of ^{3}H-estradiol. Perhaps a better estimate of a bound pool might be obtained by considering the difference between concentrations measured in the hypothalamus and cerebrum. When the data are recalculated as this difference, selective concentration is present in the median eminence by day 10, but again it seems to be absent in the anterior hypothalamus until day 15 to 20 (Presl et al, 1970).

In another study the ratio of total radioactivity in the median eminence to cortex 4 hours after administration was 1.6 at day 3, 1.5 at day 12, and 6.4 at day 25 (Kato et al, 1971a). The concentration of radioactivity in the anterior hypothalamus relative to cortex increased from 1.0 at day 3, 1.1 at day 12, to 4.9 at day 25. Recalculation of these data as the difference between hypothalamic region and cortex suggests that the accumulation system is present in the median eminence at day 3 but not in the anterior hypothalamus until day 12 or 25. Another approach compares the accumulation of estradiol in vitro of basal hypothalamus (representing predominantly the region around the median eminence) and cortex. The toluene-extractable radioactivity is higher in the basal hypothalamus than in cortex at all ages in the female from 20 days of gestation throughout adulthood (Kulin & Reiter, 1972).

Hypothalamic 8.5S binding has been described after in vitro addition of ^{3}H-estradiol to the supernatant fractions of day 21 or older rats. It is very low at 7 days and at day 14; at both days there is binding that sediments about 4S (Kato, Atsumi & Inaba, 1971b). There is insufficient information to tell whether this 4S binding is contamination with, or similar to, the plasma-binding protein found at these ages.

So far there are no experimental findings to indicate a substantial change in the estradiol accumulation system in the hypothalamic or preoptic region immediately before puberty. Accumulation in vivo does not differ substantially in pre- or postpubescent females in the hypothalamus or preoptic regions (Eisenfeld & Axelrod, 1966; Presl et al, 1970; Kato et al, 1971a). The localization of estradiol-concentrating neurons is the same in the hypothalamic-preoptic regions of immature females (day 25 or 29), immature males (day 24), and ovariectomized mature females (Stumpf, 1968b). Other regions of the brain have not been compared by auto-radiography before or after puberty; 8.5S supernatant macromolecular hypothalamic binding decreases shortly before vaginal opening to 67 per cent of that found at day 28, then increases after the onset of puberty (Kato et al, 1971b). The accumulation of radioactivity is slightly higher in the nuclear subcellular fraction of the anterior hypothalamus of 28-day-old females than in that of mature females (Vertes & King, 1972).

In mature rats (Fig. 1) there is little difference in hypothalamic or preoptic levels between males and females (Eisenfeld & Axelrod, 1966; McEwen & Pfaff, 1970; McGuire & Lisk, 1969a). In an autoradiographic study of the anterior and medial basal parts of the hypothalamus essentially similar localizations are found in adult males or females and the results are not influenced by castration (Attramadal, 1970a).

Neonatal Androgenization. Administration of androgen in the neonatal period sterilizes females so that they cannot ovulate when mature; this sterilization is due to modifications in the regulation of gonadotropins by the brain (Harris & Levine, 1965). These androgenized females may fail to develop positive feedback control by estrogens; the distribution of ^{3}H-estradiol in them has been compared with that in normal females with conflicting results. Reports describe a partial decrease in accumulation of estrogens in the anterior hypothalamus, middle hypothalamus, pituitary, and uterus, with no change in the posterior hypothalamus or cortex (Flerko, Mess, & Illei-Donhoffer, 1969), a decrease in pituitary concentration but not in portions of the hypothalamus (McGuire & Lisk, 1969b), and a slight decrease in the hypothalamus but not in the preoptic region or pituitary (McEwen & Pfaff, 1970). Another study describes a decrease in anterior and middle hypothalamus and uterus, with no decrease in anterior pituitary, median eminence, or several other brain regions (Tuohimaa & Johansson, 1971). Neonatal administration of estrogens also produces sterilization of females, with a syndrome similar to neonatal androgenization. The estrogen-treated group, however, has lower accumulation in all portions of the hypothalamus, the pituitary, and the uterus (McGuire & Lisk, 1969b).

After in vivo administration of androgen accumulation of ^{3}H-estradiol in the 700 x g pellet of the anterior pituitary and possibly the anterior hypothalamus is decreased in neonatally androgenized females (Vertes & King, 1972). By autoradiography neonatally androgenized females have one-half the normal number of labeled cells in the preoptic and ventro-medial-arcuate regions and a significant decrease in grain concentration in the pituitary (Anderson & Greenwald, 1969).

From information obtained by various neuroendocrine techniques the anterior hypothalamic-preoptic region is clearly involved in promoting ovulation. Most of the data indicate that estrogen accumulation in this portion of the brain is lower in neonatally androgenized females, possibly because of their inability to ovulate. However, because normal female and male accumulation in this region does not appear to be different, this may not be the normal mechanism of sexual differentiation, or it may be an exaggeration of the normal.

The current information concerning the ontogeny of the estrogen system in the female rat brain can be summarized. The specific accumulation system in the median eminence appears to be present at least in part shortly after birth but may be more fully developed in the prepubescent rat. In contrast, the anterior hypothalamic binding system may not develop until day 12 to 20. So far no dramatic changes have been observed around the time of vaginal opening (used here as an index of puberty). The possible late full development of the binding system in the median eminence might be correlated with the increased sensitivity of the prepubescent female rat (in relation to very young females) to negative feedback control of gonadotropin secretion by estrogens (Ojeda & Ramirez, 1972). Furthermore, the late appearance of a binding system for estradiol in the anterior hypothalamus might correlate with the earliest stage at which estrogens will produce an ovulatory surge of LH secretion (positive feedback). The information currently available does not demonstrate a difference between males and females in the accumulation of ^{3}H-estradiol in the hypothalamus or preoptic regions. Rather, it suggests that neonatally androgenized females have lower accumulation of ^{3}H-estradiol in portions of the hypothalamus than normal females, which might contribute to their inability to ovulate.

ANDROGENS

Extraction of Radioactivity After Systemic Administration

Unlike estradiol, which is retained in its target organs unmetabolized, radioactive testosterone is converted in part to DHT, a specific metabolite. DHT represents a major proportion of the radioactivity in the prostate, seminal vesicle, and preputial gland shortly after intravenous administration of ^{3}H-testosterone. Some DHT is found in the blood and kidney but none in heart, lung, levator ani muscle, liver, gut, or testis (Bruchovsky & Wilson, 1968a). The metabolic step involves a reduction of the double bound at C4 in the A ring, and the hydrogen added at carbon 5 is oriented in the alpha direction. Reductase activity is present in the peripheral target organs; the enzyme utilizes NADPH as the hydrogen source. This reduction can occur in the anterior pituitary and hypothalamus; radioactivity with the chromatographic mobility of DHT has been found in both sites (Stern & Eisenfeld, 1971). Slices of pituitary and hypothalamus are capable of converting testosterone into DHT (Massa, Stupnicka, Kniewald, & Martini, 1972). Unmetabolized ^{3}H-testosterone is also concentrated in the seminal vesicle (Stern & Eisenfeld, 1969) and in the anterior pituitary in relation to levels in plasma (Resko, Goy, & Phoenix, 1967; Stern & Eisenfeld, 1971). In the ring dove (Stern, 1972) and guinea pig (Resko et al, 1967), but not in the rat, there is a concentration gradient of testosterone in hypothalamus in relation to plasma. In ring dove and rat the concentration of DHT is higher in the hypothalamus than in plasma (Stern, 1972); Stern & Eisenfeld, 1971). The concentration of testosterone and DHT in seminal vesicle, anterior pituitary, and hypothalamus in relation to plasma is decreased by previous administration of nonradioactive testosterone, progesterone, or cyproterone, an androgen antagonist (Stern & Eisenfeld, 1971).

After systemic administration of ^{3}H-testosterone DHT and some testosterone can be found concentrated in prostatic nuclei and chromatin (Bruchovsky & Wilson, 1968b; Rennie & Bruchovsky, 1972). In the hypothalamus of the ring dove the nuclear concentration of radioactivity per microgram of protein is 14 times higher than in cerebrum 1 hour after systemic administration of ^{3}H-testosterone (Zigmond, Stern, & McEwen, 1972).

Autoradiography. By using dry mount autoradiography after administration of ^{3}H-testosterone radioactivity localizes in nuclei of epithelial cells of the prostate and seminal vesicles (Sar, Laio, & Stumpf, 1970). In the anterior pituitary ^{3}H-testosterone is concentrated only in nuclei of basophils (Sar & Stumpf, 1972). In the male castrate brain radioactivity is concentrated in the nuclei of selective neurons. The regions that concentrate the androgen overlap or are identical, in part, to those described for estradiol localization in the hypothalamus, preoptic-septal-paraolfactory region, and amygdala. In addition, radioactivity also localizes in neurons of the dentate gyrus, hippocampus, and periventricular nucleus of the hypothalamus (Stumpf, 1971).

Macromolecular Interactions

Androgens attach to prostatic macromolecules in vivo and in vitro. In the castrate androgens bind to 8 to 10S (Mainwaring, 1969; Baulieu, Alberga, Jung, Lebeau, Mercier-Bodard, Milgrom, Raynaud, Raynaud-Jammet, Rochefort, Truong, & Robel, 1971) or 6S (Hansson, Tveter, Unhjem, & Djoseland, 1972) proteins from the prostatic supernatant fraction; DHT has a slightly better affinity than testosterone (Jung & Baulieu, 1971; Cole & Eisenfeld, unpublished). The binding has been described as 3S in non-castrate prostatic supernatant fractions (Fang, Anderson, & Liao, 1969).

There may be several different binding systems for androgens in target organs. In the epidydimis the supernatant binding may be 4S in low salt in contrast to 6S for the prostate (Hansson et al, 1972). In the supernatant fraction of the levator ani muscle 1 nM ^{3}H-testosterone binds in the 8 to 10S region, whereas 1 nM ^{3}H-DHT binds in the 4 to 5S region (Jung & Baulieu, 1971).

Following intracarotid administration of ^{3}H-testosterone to intact or to castrate male rats or the addition of ^{3}H-testosterone to homogenates or tissue sections, some radioactivity in the supernatant is bound to macromolecules (Samparez, Thieulant, & Jouan, 1969). Low doses of testosterone (but not DHT) decrease the radioactivity slightly in the macromolecular fraction after incubation of the anterior pituitary cytosols with ^{3}H-testosterone. If the cytosols are incubated at 25° C with ^{3}H-testosterone, the bound radioactivity is testosterone and an unidentified metabolite different from DHT and androstenedione (Jouan, Samparez, Thieulant, & Mercier, 1972). Future studies of androgen macromolecular binding in brain should be directed toward evaluating the possibility of differences in the receptor mechanisms between brain and periphery. Furthermore, there is a possibility of differences in the brain between the androgen mechanisms responsible for negative feedback control of gonadotropins, male sexual behavior, and androgen-directed male-female differentiation of the brain.

The molecular basis of action of the antiandrogen in male sexual accessory glands seems to be due to its capability to compete for supernatant-binding macromolecules (Stern & Eisenfeld, 1969). If the cytoplasmic binding is required for nuclear binding, the prevention of the cytoplasmic binding of androgens by cyproterone could then be responsible for the failure of androgen-binding macromolecules to appear in the nucleus (Fang & Liao, 1969; 1971). Involvement of the cytoplasmic-bound androgens (rather than free androgens) in the eventual nuclear accumulation is indicated by the following pulse chase experiment: a pulse of ^{3}H-testosterone is administered intravenously and followed 10 minutes later by a large dose of nonradioactive testosterone, at a time when the macromolecular binding of androgens is higher in the prostatic cytoplasm than nucleus. At 30 and 60 minutes after radioactive administration the nuclear binding has increased and the concentration is 4 times higher than in the supernatant fraction (Rennie & Bruchovsky, 1972).

After in vivo administration of testosterone most of the macromolecular-bound radioactivity in prostatic nuclei is DHT. Some testosterone is also bound to macromolecules in the nucleus (Bruchovsky & Wilson, 1968b; Rennie and Bruchovsky, 1972). Proteolytic enzymes but not nucleases destroy the nuclear macromolecular binding so that the binding macromolecule contains protein (Bruchovsky & Wilson, 1968b). The sedimentation coefficient of the bound androgens from the prostatic nuclei is 3S (Fang et al, 1969; Baulieu et al, 1971; Hansson et al, 1972).

Although the nucleus binds free androgens poorly, it may also contain target-organ-specific components involved in the nuclear retention of the supernatant-bound androgens. ^{3}H-DHT has been mixed with prostatic supernatant to form a protein complex; nuclei are then added. After reisolation of the nuclei the 3S-bound DHT is at least tenfold higher in the nuclei from the prostate than from liver, brain, thymus, or diaphragm (Fang & Liao, 1971). Nuclear retention may be due in part to the attachment of the cytoplasmic protein-androgen to chromatin. By utilizing prostatic supernatant with bound ^{3}H-DHT mixed with chromatin from various tissues the binding to chromatin is 3 times higher from prostate or testis than from liver, spleen, or lung (Steggles et al, 1971).

Mechanisms of Action

One of the earliest changes in a male sexual accessory gland is an increase in RNA synthesis, which occurs within minutes of androgen administration (Wicks & Kenney, 1964). The multiplicity of androgen-induced early changes in accessory sexual glands can be found in the review by Williams-Ashman and Reddi (1972). So far no studies directly implicate the binding proteins in an androgen response and almost no information exists concerning early metabolic changes in the anterior pituitary or brain regions after androgen administration.

DHT may be responsible for some of the effects of testosterone, and other effects may be due to other metabolites. The addition of high concentrations of testosterone to organ cultures of prostate promotes epithelial cell hyperplasia and an increase in cell height and secretion. High concentrations of DHT provoke greater epithelial cell hyperplasia than testosterone but do not increase cell height or secretion (Baulieu, Lasnitzki, & Robel, 1968). Chronic treatment with DHT produces almost twice the prostatic growth in rats as equivalent amounts of testosterone; the prostates also have more fibrosis and lower acinar height than the testosterone-treated rats. Unlike testosterone, DHT administration does not restore male sexual behavior to castrate male guinea pigs, even though both testosterone and DHT have negative gonadotropin feedback activity (Feder, 1971). DHT administration to neonatal females does not produce the neonatally androgenized syndrome (Whalen & Luttge, 1971).

Thus there are suggestions of differences in the androgen receptor mechanisms between the periphery and the brain and in the brain between the mechanims for regulation of gonadotropins, male sexual behavior, and differentiation of the brain in the male pattern.

It has been proposed that testosterone produces male sexual behavior and neonatal androgenization by being metabolized in brain cells to form estrogens (Ryan, Naftolin, Reddy, Flores, & Petro, 1972). Testosterone or androstenedione can be converted in part by human fetal or other hypothalamic homogenates to estrogens. DHT, which cannot be aromatized to estrogens, does not restore male sexual behavior or produce neonatal androgenization. Estradiol is potent in restoring male sexual behavior (Pfaff, 1970) and in producing a syndrome resembling neonatal androgenization (Harris & Levine, 1965). In addition, estradiol reduces radioactivity in some brain regions after ^{3}H-testosterone administration; 1 mg of estradiol, a high dose, partially decreased the radioactivity after systemic ^{3}H-testosterone in the preoptic region, septum, olfactory bulb, and pituitary but not in other brain regions, including the hypothalamus and amygdala. However, accumulation of ^{3}H-estradiol in brain regions after systemic administration of ^{3}H-testosterone has not been described.

An alternative proposal is that the brain has an androgen receptor mechanism that is responsible for male sexual behavior with binding properties similar to those found in the prostate, but the relative agonistic and antagonistic capabilities of various drugs, once attached, are different. Cyproterone (Block & Davidson, 1971) and estrogens (Pfaff, 1970) are antagonists of androgen effects in male accessory glands but do not antagonize androgen-directed male sexual behavior; instead they mimic testosterone. Cyproterone is thought to be devoid of other endocrine properties (Neumann, von Berswordt-Wallrabe, Elger, Steinbeck, Hahn, & Kramer, 1970). It reduces radioactivity with the chromatographic mobility of testosterone and DHT in the hypothalamus, pituitary, and seminal vesicle after systemic administration of ³H-testosterone (Stern & Eisenfeld, 1971). In the prostate estrogens in high dose prevent cytosol and nuclear binding of ³H-testosterone and ³H-DHT in vitro (Cole & Eisenfeld, unpublished). This would suggest that DHT may attach but not lead to male sex behavior, whereas testosterone, cyproterone, or estrogen will.

Studies with cyproterone acetate (which has both antiandrogenic and progestational activity) suggest a difference between the mechanism for male sexual behavior and androgen-directed differentiation of the brain. Cyproterone acetate as well as testosterone can restore male sexual behavior to adult male castrates (Bloch & Davidson, 1971). However, administration of cyproterone acetate to pregnant rats converts androgen-directed differentiation of the pattern of gonadotropin regulation to a female pattern in the male offspring (Neumann et al, 1970).

Ontogeny

Androgen-binding macromolecules are present in high concentrations as early as day 20 in the rat prostatic and seminal vesicle supernatant fractions. The apparent concentration decreases abruptly, starting at about day 40. The decrease in supernatant binding about day 40 may be due to the endogenous androgens secreted in increasing amounts by the maturing testis and already occupying the binding macromolecules. Either the endogenous androgens cannot be displaced from the binding macromolecules in the supernatant fractions under the in vitro conditions or the supernatant-binding macromolecules are no longer present in the fraction (Cole & Eisenfeld, unpublished). Some of the supernatant-binding macromolecules after attachment of endogenous androgens may have moved into the nucleus. Consistent with this possibility radioactive androgens will bind to macromolecules prepared from isolated nuclei of mature rats but not from immature or castrate rats (Baulieu et al, 1971). Binding studies on peripheral tissues have not been described at earlier ages. Most of the early changes have been studied after androgen administration in the accessory sexual glands in the adult castrate rat. In one study of 3-week-old rats the rapid incorporation of radioactive cytidine into RNA was increased in the ventral prostate, seminal vesicle, and liver but not in the thymus 2 hours after administration of testosterone (Fujii & Villee, 1968). Immature male rats require higher doses of testosterone propionate to stimulate prostatic growth and histologic development (Hooker, 1942; Ojeda & Ramirez, 1972).

High reductase activity is found in the genital tubercle at day 17 of rabbit fetal life. This precedes demonstrable sexual differentiation of the genital tubercle and the major surge of testosterone secretion by 2 to 4 days. In contrast, little enzymatic activity for the conversion of testosterone to DHT is found in the Wolffian or Müllerian ducts until sexual differentiation is advanced to the stage of obvious gender identification (Wilson & Lasnitzki, 1971).

There is some limited information concerning androgen accumulation in the brain and pituitary at various ages. In 3- to 8-day-old female rats the concentration of radioactivity extractable into an organic solvent is higher in the pituitary than in blood at 5 and 15 minutes but not at 60 minutes after intraperitoneal injection of ^{3}H-testosterone. At 2 to 5 days the concentration in the hypothalamus is equal to that in cerebrum and lower than that in the spleen. The levels in the medial preoptic region are similar to those in the medial basal hypothalamus (Alvarez & Ramirez, 1970). After systemic administration of radioactive testosterone radioactivity has been extracted from tissue into methylene chloride. The concentration of radioactivity is higher in the pituitary, hypothalamus, preoptic area, and septum than in other brain regions. Similar patterns of accumulaton are observed in 11- and 38-day-old males, adult males that had been castrated neonatally or in adulthood, and adult females ovariectomized when adult or treated in the neonatal period with testosterone propionate. Unlike all other groups, the 11-day-old males had a relatively high accumulation in the olfactory bulb. The percentage of the radioactivity that is unmetabolized testosterone differs among the various groups, but the percentage of testosterone in each group of animals did not differ between the brain regions specified and other brain regions (McEwen, Pfaff, & Zigmond, 1970). The conversion of testosterone to DHT by tissue slices has been studied from day 7, when the activity is highest in the anterior pituitary, basal hypothalamus, cerebral cortex, and amygdala of the male. Activity decreases approximately to one-half at day 14, then remains relatively constant from 21 to 60 days (Massa et al, 1972). The autoradiographic study after administration of ^{3}H-testosterone does not indicate whether differences in brain localization are found between the immature and mature male castrate (Stumpf, 1971).

The pattern of development of androgen binding in the very young brain requires further investigation. There is no evidence at present of a change in the male androgen brain-binding pattern at puberty.

Testicular Feminization

Experimentally, androgen-directed tissue differentiation can be modified by the administration of the antiandrogen cyproterone acetate to pregnant animals. The male offspring have a vagina, no male ducts, accessory glands in some animal species, and the potential to develop large breasts. Cyproterone produces nearly the same changes. Administration of cyproterone acetate to pregnant rats produces a female pattern of gonadotropin regulation in the male offspring. These males have estrus cycles, as evidenced by periodic cornification of the vaginal epithelium, and can ovulate as shown by the development of corpora lutea in transplanted ovaries. They also have a characteristic female behavior pattern; they respond to mounting attempts by normal males with lordosis. Unlike normal males, they will act as a foster parent to care for the young and retrieve them when they escape from the nest (Neumann et al, 1970).

Testicular feminization, with many similarities to that produced by the antiandrogen administration, occurs as a genetic disorder transmitted on the X chromosome from mother to the male offspring. It is thought that some defect in the androgen receptor system is responsible for the failure of androgen-directed differentiation of the male accessory glands and genitalia and for subsequent unresponsiveness to androgen administration.

In human XY males with this syndrome the secretion of androgens, at least in later life, appears to be normal or increased. The plasma LH is elevated in the presence of normal or elevated plasma androgens which indicates impaired sensitivity to the negative feedback effect (Tremblay, Foley, Corvol, Park, Kowarski, Blizzard, Jones, & Migeon, 1972). Patients with testicular feminization do not respond normally to administration of testosterone or DHT with respect to anabolic effects, as reflected by changes in urinary excretion of nitrogen, phosphorus, or citric acid (Strickland & French, 1969).

There are two rodent models of this syndrome that have X-linked inheritance of males with female genitalia: the Stanley-Grumbeck rat strain and the testicular-feminized mouse strain. These models have been used to study the syndrome, but the defect has not yet been clearly and consistently pinpointed. The prostate and seminal vesicles do not develop in these pseudohermaphrodites, which thus necessitates the study of androgen distribution in other normally androgen-responsive organs.

The preputial gland of the testicular-feminized Stanley-Grumbeck rat is unresponsive to administration of testosterone or DHT. After intravenous administration of ^{3}H-testosterone the nuclear accumulation of radioactivity in the preputial gland at 30 and 60 minutes is the same in normal male castrates as in the pseudohermaphrodites. However, most of the radioactivity in the nuclei from normals is DHT, whereas the nuclei of the pseudohermaphrodite has little DHT and the most predominant steroid is testosterone (Bullock & Bardin, 1970). The kidney hypertrophies in normal animals to which androgen has been administered. After intravenous administration of ^{3}H-testosterone the cytoplasmic radioactivity in the kidney is similar in the testicular-feminized rat and in male castrates. The pseudohermaphrodites have only 10 to 30 per cent of the normal amount of radioactivity in the nucleus; the nuclear radioactivity in the normal is 80 per cent testosterone, whereas in the pseudohermaphrodite there is very little (Ritzen, Nayfeh, French, & Aronin, 1972).

There has been one report that the kidney of the testicular-feminized male pseudohermaphrodite mouse had a diminished concentration of supernatant-binding macromolecule (Gehring, Tompkins, & Ohno, 1971). Another group has detected macromolecular binding by sucrose gradient centrifugation in the kidney supernatant fraction of normal males, females, and pseudohermaphrodites and has found similar concentrations of testosterone and DHT in the kidney supernatant of all 3 groups. The nuclear radioactivity (predominantly testosterone) is 10 to 25 times lower in the pseudohermaphrodite than in normal male or female kidney (Bullock, Bardin, & Ohno, 1971). The submandibular glands of these pseudohermaphroditic mice have deficient androgen-mediated synthesis of several proteins. The concentration of 3S supernatant DHT-binding protein is the same in male or female castrates as in pseudohermaphrodites. It is unclear if the initial defect in testicular feminization is in cytoplasmic or nuclear binding. Ultimate nuclear binding does appear deficient.

SUMMARY

Estrogens

There is evidence of specific accumulation of estradiol in selective organs, including the uterus, anterior pituitary, and hypothalamus. Localization is found in all cell types of the uterus and anterior pituitary and in neurons of specific brain loci. The selective localization is due predominantly to the presence of supernatant-binding proteins in the uterus, anterior pituitary, and hypothalamus. The estrogen is thought to interact first with the protein in the cytoplasm; then the entire complex crosses the nuclear membrane and localizes in the nucleus. In the uterus the complex attaches to chromatin and may modulate the synthesis of RNA. Another level of specificity may be that the chromatin of target organs contains acceptor sites for the cytoplasmic protein-estrogen complex. No information is currently available concerning binding systems in the human pituitary and brain.

Ontogeny has been studied only in the rat. The accumulation system appears to be present, at least in part, in the uterus and pituitary at the earliest times studied at birth. In contrast, the binding system may not be fully developed in the median eminence until day 20 and may not appear in the anterior hypothalamus until sometime between days 12 and 20. The development of the binding system in the median eminence might be correlated with increased sensitivity of the prepubescent female to negative feedback by estrogens and the appearance of the anterior hypothalamic accumulation to the development of positive feedback. Some data suggest that estrogen interaction may be deficient in portions of the hypothalamus of neonatally androgenized females. There is no evidence of a major change in the hypothalamic preoptic region at the time of vaginal opening, and no substantial differences have been described in the binding pattern of ^{3}H-estradiol in brains of prepubescent or mature females and males.

Although estradiol is thought to act in its target organs without metabolism, some androgen effects of testosterone are dependent on the formation of DHT, a specific metabolite. This metabolite is found in the male accessory sexual glands, pituitary, and hypothalamus. Testosterone is also concentrated in the pituitary and in some animals in the hypothalamus. Administration of DHT to adult male castrates will inhibit gonadotropins, but unlike testosterone DHT does not restore male sexual behavior or produce neonatal androgenization. There is evidence of an initial cytoplasmic interaction with a binding protein, transfer of the complex to the nucleus, and attachment to the chromatin of the prostate. Cyproterone may antagonize androgens by competitively preventing the attachment of the androgen to the cytoplasmic protein. After administration of ^{3}H-testosterone autoradiography indicates concentration of radioactivity in the nucleus of neurons in specific loci of the hypothalamus and limbic system and in basophils of the anterior pituitary. Ultimate nuclear binding appears defective in testicular feminization, an androgen-unresponsive genetic disorder.

The distribution of radioactivity after systemic administration of ^{3}H-testosterone is not very different in brain regions of males from day 11 on. The relative developmental roles of testosterone, DHT, and other metabolites in the pituitary and brain remain to be established.

ACKNOWLEDGMENT

This work was supported by Contract 70-2258 and Grant CA-10748, National Institutes of Health, Bethesda, Maryland.

REFERENCES

Aizawa, V. & Mueller, G. C. (1961). The effect in vivo and in vitro of estrogens on lipid synthesis in the rat uterus. *J. Biol Chem.* **236**, 381–386.

Alvarez, E. O. & Ramirez. V. D. (1970). Distribution curves of ^{3}H-testosterone and ^{3}H-estradiol in neonatal female rats. *Neuroendocrinology* **6**, 349–360.

Anand-Kumar, T. C. & Knowles, F. (1967). A system linking the third ventricle with the pars tuberalis of the Rhesus monkey. *Nature* **215**, 54–55.

Anderson, C. H. & Greenwald, G. S. (1969). Autoradiographic analysis of estradiol uptake in the brain and pituitary of the female rat. *Endocrinology* **85**, 1160–1165.

Arnaud, M., Beziat, Y., Borgna, J. L., Guilleux, J. C., & Mousseron-Canet (1971). Le recepteur de l'oestradiol, l'amp cyclique, et la RNA polymerase nucleolaire dans l'uterus de génisse. Stimulation de la biosynthèse RNA in vitro. *Biochim. Biophys. Acta* **254**, 241–254.

Attramadal, A. (1964). Distribution and site of action of oestradiol in the brain and pituitary gland of the rat following intramuscular administration. *Proc. 2nd Intl Cong. Endocrinology, Part I, Excerpta Medical Foundation, Amsterdam.*

Attramadal, A. (1970a). Localization of oestradiol in the hypothalamus. *Z. Zellforsch* **104**, 572–581.

Attramadal, A. (1970b). A cellular localization of ^{3}H-oestradiol in the hypophysis. An autoradiographic study in male and female rats. *Z. Zellforsch* **104**, 597–614.

Attramadal, A. & Aakvaag, A. (1970). The uptake of ^{3}H-oestradiol by the anterior hypophysis and hypothalamus of male and female rats. *Z. Zellforsch* **104**, 582–596.

Barker, K. L. (1971). Estrogen-induced synthesis of histones and a specific non-histone protein in the uterus. *Biochemistry* **10**, 284–291.

Barnes, A. & Gorski, J. (1970). Estrogen induced protein. Time course of synthesis. *Biochemistry* **9**, 1899–1904.

Baulieu, E. E., Alberga, A., Jung, I., Lebeau, M. C., Mercier-Bodard, C., Milgrom, E., Raynaud, J. P., Raynaud-Jammet, C. Rochefort, H., Truong, H., & Robel, P. (1971). Metabolism and protein binding on sex steroids in target organs: an approach to the mechanism of hormone action. *Rec. Progr. Hormone Res.* **27**, 351–420.

Baulieu, E. E., Lasnitzki, I., & Robel, P. (1968). Metabolism of testosterone and action of metabolites on prostate glands grown in organ culture. *Nature* **219**, 1155–1156.

Billing, R. J., Barbiroli, B., & Smellie, R. M. S. (1969). The mode of action of estradiol II. The synthesis of RNA. *Biochim. Biophys. Acta* **190**, 60–65.

Bloch, G. J. Davidson, J. M. (1971). Behavioral and somatic responses to the antiandrogen cyproterone. *Hormones & Behav.* **2**, 11–25.

Bruchovsky, N. & Wilson, J. D. (1968a). The conversion of testosterone to 5α-androstan-17β-ol-3-one by rat prostate in vivo and in vitro. *J. Biol. Chem.* **243**, 2012–2021.

Bruchovsky, N. & Wilson, J. D. (1968b). The intranuclear binding of testosterone and 5α-androstan-17β-ol-one by rat prostate. *J. Biol. Chem.* **243**, 5933–5960.

Brush, M. G., Taylor, R. W., & King, R. J. B. (1967). The uptake of (6,7-^{3}H) oestradiol by the normal human female reproductive tract. *J. Endocrinol.* **39**, 599–607.

Bullock, L. P. & Bardin, C. W. (1970). Decreased dihydrotestosterone retention by preputial gland nuclei from the androgen insensitive pseudohermaphrodite rat. *J. Clin. Endocrinol.* **31**, 113–115.

Bullock, L. P., Bardin, C. W., & Ohno, S. (1971). The androgen insensitive mouse: absence of intranuclear androgen retention in the kidney. *Biochem. Biophys. Res. Comm.* **44**, 1537–1543.

Chader, G. J. & Villee, C. A. (1970). Uptake of oestradiol by the rabbit hypothalamus. *Biochem. J.* **118**, 93–97.

Ciaccio, L. A. & Lisk, R. D. (1972). Effect of hormone priming on retention of ³H-oestradiol by males and females. *Nature New Biol.* **236**, 82–83.

Clark, J. H. & Gorski, J. (1970) Ontogeny of the estrogen receptor during early uterine development. *Science* **169**, 76–78.

Davis, M. E., Wiener, M., Jacobson, H. I., & Jensen, E. V. (1963). Estradiol metabolism in pregnant and non-pregnant women. *Amer. J. Ob. Gyn.* **87**, 979–989.

Driscoll, S. G. & Hsia, D. Y. (1958). The development of enzyme systems during early infancy. *Pediatrics* **22**, 785–845

Eisenfeld, A. J. (1967a). Computer analysis of the distribution of ³H-estradiol. *Biochim. Biophys. Acta,* **136**, 498–507.

Eisenfeld, A. J. (1967b). Estradiol binding sites in the hypothalamus. *Fed. Proc.* **26**, 365.

Eisenfeld, A. J. (1969). Hypothalamic estradiol-binding macromolecules. *Nature* **224**, 1202–1203.

Eisenfeld, A. J. (1970). ³H-estradiol: In vitro binding to macromolecules from the rat hypothalamus, pituitary and uterus. *Endocrinology* **86**, 1313–1318.

Eisenfeld, A. J. (1972a). Estrogens in oral contraceptives: difference in binding affinities in vitro. *5th Intl. Congr. Pharmacol.* p. 62.

Eisenfeld, A. J. (1972b). Interaction of estrogens, progestational agents and androgens with brain and pituitary and their role in the control of ovulation. *Neuropharmacology,* **11**, 113–142.

Eisenfeld, A. J. & Axelrod, J. (1965). Selectivity of estrogen distribution in tissue. *J. Pharmacol. Exptl. Therap.* **150**, 469–475.

Eisenfeld, A. J. & Axelrod, J. (1966). Effect of steroid hormones, ovariectomy, estrogen pretreatment, sex and immaturity on the distribution of ³H-estradiol. *Endocrinology* **79**, 38–42.

Eisenfeld, A. J. & Axelrod, J. (1967). Evidence for estradiol binding sites in the hypothalamus. *Biochem. Pharmacol.* **16**, 1781–1785.

Eisenfeld, A. J. & Axelrod J. (1966). Effect on steroid hormones, ovariectomy, estrogen pretreatment, sex and immaturity on the distribution of ³H-estradiol. *Endocrinology* **79**, 38–42.

Eisenfeld, A. J., Gardner. W. U. & van Wagenen, G. (1971). Radioactive estradiol accumulation in endometriosis of the Rhesus monkey. *Amer. J. Ob. Gyn.* **109**, 124–130.

Fang, S., Anderson, K. M., & Liao, S. (1969). Receptor proteins for androgens. *J. Biol. Chem.* **244**, 6584–6595.

Fang, S. & Liao, S. (1969). Antagonistic action of anti-androgens on the formation of a specific dihydrotestosterone-receptor protein complex in rat ventral prostate. *Molec. Pharmacol.* **5**, 428–431.

Fang, S. & Liao, S. (1971). Androgen receptors. *J. Biol. Chem.* **246**, 16–24.

Feder, H. (1971). The comparative actions of testosterone propionate and 5α-androstan-17β-ol-3-one propionate on the reproductive behavior, physiology and morphology of male rats. *J. Endocrinol.* **41**, 241–252.

Flerko, B., Mess, B., & Illei-Donhoffer, A. (1969). On the mechanism of androgen sterilization. *Neuroendocrinology* **4**, 164–169.

Fujii, T. & Villee, C. A. (1968). Effect of testosterone on ribonucleic acid metabolism in the prostate, seminal vesicle, liver and thymus of immature rats. *Endocrinology* **82**, 463–467.

Gehring, U., Tompkins, G. M., and Ohno, S. (1971). Effect of the androgen-insensitivity mutation on a cytoplasmic receptor for dihydrotestosterone. *Nature New Biol.* **232**, 106–107.

Glascock, R. F. & Hoekstra, W. G. (1959). Selective accumulation of tritium-labeled hexoestrol by the reproductive organs of immature female goats and sheep. *Biochem. J.* **72**, 673–682.

Hamilton, T. H. (1968). Control by estrogen of genetic transcription and translation. *Science* **161**, 649–661.

Hansson, V., Tveter, K. J., Unhjem, O., & Djoseland, O. (1972). Studies of the interaction between androgen and macromolecules in male accessory sex organs of rat and man. *J. Steroid Biochem.* **3**, 427–439.

Harris, G. W. & Levine, S. (1965). Sexual differentiation of the brain and its experimental control. *Physiology* **181**, 379–400.

Hooker, C. W. (1942). Pubertal increase in responsiveness to androgen in the male rat. *Endocrinology* **30**, 77–84.

Jensen, E. V. & DeSombre, E. R. (1972). Estrogens and progestins. *Biochem. Actions of Hormones* **2**, 215–255.

Jensen, E. V., Hurst, D. J., DeSombre, E. R., & Jungblut, P. W. (1967). Sulfhydryl groups and estradiol-receptor interaction. *Science* **158**, 385–387.

Jensen, E. V. & Jacobson, H. I. (1962). Basic guides to the mechanism of estrogen action. *Rec. Progr. Hormone Res.* **18**, 387–414.

Jensen, E. V., Jacobson H. I., Flesher, J. W., Saha, N. N., Gupta, G. N., Smith, S., Colucci, V., Shiplacoff, D., Neumann H. G., DeSombre, E. R., & Jungblut, P. W. (1966). Estrogen receptors in target tissues In *Steroid Dynamics*, G. Pincus, T. Nakao, & J. F. Tait, Eds. Academic, New York, pp. 133–157.

Jensen, E. V., Numata, M., Smith, S., Suzuki, T., Brecher, P. I., & DeSombre, E. R. (1969a). Estrogen-receptor interaction in target tissues. *Develop. Biol. Suppl.* **3**, 151–171.

Jensen, E. V., Suzuki, T., Kawashima, T., Stumpf, W., Jungblut, P. W., & DeSombre, E. R. (1968). A two-step mechanism for the interactions of estradiol with rat uterus. *Proc. Natl. Acad. Sci.* **59**, 632–638.

Jensen, E. V., Suzuki, T., Numata, M., Smith, S., & DeSombre, E. R. (1969b). Estrogen binding substances of target tissues. *Steroids* **13**, 417–427.

Jouan, P., Samparez, S., Thieulant, M-L., & Mercier, L. (1972). Etude de recepteur cytoplasmique de la (1,2-³H) testostérone dans l'hypophyse antérieure et l'hypothalamus du rat. *J. Steroid Biochem.* **2**, 223–236.

Jung, I. & Baulieu, E. E. (1971). Neo-nuclear androgen receptor in rat ventral prostate. *Biochimie* **53**, 807–817.

Kahwanago, I., Heinrich, W. L., & Herrmann, W. L. (1969). Isolation of oestradiol "receptors" from bovine hypothalamus and anterior pituitary gland. *Nature* **223**, 313–314.

Kahwanago, I., Heinrichs, W. L., & Herrmann, W. L. (1970). Estradiol "receptors" in hypothalamus and anterior pituitary gland: inhibition of estradiol binding by SH-group blocking agents and clomiphene citrate. *Endocrinology* **86**, 1319–1326.

Kato, J., Atsumi, Y., & Inaba, M. (1971b). Development of estrogen receptors in the rat hypothalamus. *J. Biochem.* **70**, 1051–1053.

Kato, J., Kobayashi, T., & Villee, C. A. (1968). Effect of clomiphene on the uptake of estradiol by the anterior hypothalamus and hypophysis. *Endocrinology* **82**, 1049–1052.

Kato, J., Sugimara, N., & Kobayashi, T. (1971a). Changing patterns of the uptake of estradiol by the anterior hypothalamus, the median eminence, and the hypophysis in the developing rat. In *Hormones in Development*, M. Hamburgh, E. J. W. Barrington Eds. Appleton, Century, Crofts, New York, pp. 689–703.

Kato, R., Vassanelli, P., Frontino, G., & Chiesara, E. (1964). Variation in the activity of liver microsomal drug-metabolizing enzymes in rats in relation to the age. *Biochem. Pharmacol.* **13**, 1037–1051.

Kato, J. & Villee, C. A. (1967). Factors affecting uptake of estradiol-6,7-^{3}H by the hypophysis and hypothalamus. *Endocrinology* **80**, 1133–1138.

Knowler, J. T. & Smellie, R. M. S. (1971). Synthesis of ribonucleic acid in immature rat uterus responding to oestradiol-17β. *Biochem. J.* **125**, 605–614.

Korenman, S. G. (1969). Comparative binding affinity of estrogens and its relation to estrogenic potency. *Steroids* **13**, 163–177.

Kulin, H. E. & Reiter, E. O. (1972). Ontogeny of the in vitro uptake of tritiated estradiol by the hypothalamus of the female rat. *Endocrinology* **90**, 1371–1374.

Leavitt, W. W., Friend, J. P., & Robinson, J. A. (1969). Estradiol: Specific binding by pituitary nuclear fraction in vitro. *Science* **165**, 496–498.

McEwen, B. S. & Pfaff, D. W. (1970). Factors influencing sex hormone uptake by rat brain regions. I. Effects of neonatal treatment, hypophysectomy, and competing steroid on estradiol uptake. *Brain Res.* **21**, 1–16.

McEwen, B. S., Pfaff, D. W., & Zigmond, R. E. (1970). Factors influencing sex hormone uptake by rat brain regions II. Effects of neonatal treatment and hypophysectomy on testosterone uptake. *Brain Res.* **21**, 17–28.

McGuire, J. L. & Lisk, R. D. (1968). Estrogen receptors in the intact rat. *Proc. Natl. Acad. Sci.* **61**, 497–503.

McGuire, J. L. & Lisk, R. D. (1969a). Localization of estrogen receptors in the rat hypothalamus. *Neuroendocrinology* **4**, 289–295.

McGuire, J. L. & Lisk, R. D. (1969b). Oestrogen receptors in androgen or oestrogen sterilized female rats. *Nature* **221**, 1068–1069.

Mainwaring, W. I. P. (1969). A soluble androgen receptor in the cytoplasm of rat prostate. *J. Endocrinol.* **45**, 531–541.

Makler, A. & Eisenfeld, A. J. (1971). Human endometrium: ^{3}H-estradiol binding *in vitro. Fed. Proc.* **30**, 361.

Martin, J. E. (1972). Estrogen receptors in the human uterus: Characterization by sucrose gradient centrifugation. *Endocrinology* **91**, 594–596.

Massa, R., Stupnicka, E., Kniewald, Z., & Martini, L. (1972). The transformation of testosterone into dihydrotestosterone by the brain and anterior pituitary, *J. Steroid Biochem.* **3**, 385–399.

Maurer, H. & Chalkley, G. R. (1967). Some properties of a nuclear binding site of estradiol. *J. Molec. Biol.* **27**, 431–441.

Means, A. R. & O'Malley, B. W. (1972). Mechanism of estrogen action: Early transcriptional and translational events. *Metabolism* **21**, 357–370.

Michael, R. P. (1962). Estrogen-sensitive neurons and sexual behavior in female cats. *Science* **136**, 322–323.

Michael, R. P. (1965a). Selective accumulation of estrogens in the neural and genital tissues of the cat. *Hormonal Steroids* **2**, 469–481.

Michael, R. P. (1965b). Oestrogens in the central nervous system. *Brit. Med. Bull.* **21**, 87–90.

Mowles, T. F., Ashkanazy, B., Mix, Jr., E., & Shepard, H. (1971). Hypothalamic and hypophyseal estradiol-binding complexes. *Endocrinology* **89**, 484–491.

Nakai, T., Sakamoto, S., Kigawa, T., & Shigematsu, A. (1972). Nuclear concentration of ^{3}H-estradiol in target tissues of a fetal rat demonstrated by dry mount autoradiography. *Endocrinol. Jap.* **19**, 47–52.

Neumann, F., von Berswordt-Wallrabe, R., Elger, W., Steinbeck, H., Hahn, J. D., & Kramer, M. (1970). Aspects of androgen-dependent events as studied by anti-androgens. *Rec. Progr. Hormone Res.* **26**, 337–404.

Nunez, E., Savu, L., Engelmann, F., Benassayag, C., Crepy, O., & Jayle, M. F. (1971). Origine embryonnaire de la protéine sérique fixant l'oestrone et l'oestradiol chez la ratte impubere. *C. R. Acad. Sci. (D) (Paris)* **273**, 242–245.

Ojeda, S. R. & Ramirez, V. D. (1972). Short term steroid treatment on plasma LH and FSH in castrated rats from birth to puberty. *4th Intl. Congr. Endocrinol.* (abstract).

Pfaff, D. (1970). Nature of sex hormones effect on rat sex behavior. *J. Compar. Physiol. Psychol.* **73**, 349–358.

Phuong, N. T., Sauer, G., & Rapoport, S. (1972). Evidence for a specific estradiol receptor in the rat hypothalamus. *Acta Biol. Med. Germ.* **28**, 379–381.

Presl, J., Rohling, S., Horsky, J., & Herzman, J. (1970). Changes in uptake of ^{3}H-estradiol by the female rat brain and pituitary from birth to sexual maturity. *Endocrinology* **86**, 899–902.

Raynaud, J-P., Mercier-Bodard, C., & Baulieu, E. E. (1971). Rat estradiol binding plasma protein. *Steroids* **18**, 767–788.

Rennie, P. & Bruchovsky, N. (1972). In vitro and in vivo studies of the functional significance of androgen receptors in rat prostate. *J. Biol. Chem.* **247**, 1546–1554.

Resko, J. A., Goy, R. W., & Phoenix, C. H. (1967). Uptake and distribution of exogenous testosterone 1,2-^{3}H in neural and genital tissues of the castrate guinea pig. *Endocrinology* **80**, 490–498.

Ritzen, E. M., Nayfeh, S. N., French, F. S., & Aronin, P. A. (1972). Deficient nuclear uptake of testosterone in the androgen insensitive (Stanley-Grumbeck) pseudohermaphrodite male rat. *Endocrinology* **91**, 116–124.

Rosenfeld, G. C., Comstock, J. P., Means, A. R., & O'Malley, B. W. (1972). Estrogen-induced synthesis of ovalbumin messenger RNA and its translation in a cell free system. *Biochem. Biophys. Res. Comm.* **46**, 1695–1703.

Roy, S., Mahesh, V. B., & Greenblatt, R. B. (1964). Effects of clomiphene on the physiology of reproduction in the rat. *Acta Endocrinol.* **47**, 669–675.

Ryan, K. J., Naftolin, F., Reddy, V. Flores, F., & Petro, Z. (1972). Estrogen formation in the brain. *Amer. J. Ob. Gyn.* **114**, 454–460.

Samparez, S., Thieulant, M-L., & Jouan, P. (1969). Mise en evidence d'une association macromoléculaire de la testostérone 1-2-3H dans l'hypophyse antérieure et l'hypothalamus du rat normal et castré. *C.R. Acad. Sci. (D) (Paris)* **268**, 2965–2967.

Sander, S. & Attramadal, A. (1968). An autoradiographic study of oestradiol incorporation in the breast tissue of female rats. *Acta Endocrinol.* **58**, 235–242.

Sar, M., Laio, S., & Stumpf, W. E. (1970). Nuclear concentraton of androgens in rat seminal vesicles and prostate demonstrated by dry-mount autoradiography. *Endocrinology* **86**, 1008–1010.

Sar, M. & Stumpf, W. E. (1972). Cellular and subcellular androgen localization in the anterior pituitary. *4th Intl. Congr. Endocrinol.* Abstract #247.

Shyamala, G. & Gorski, J. (1969). Estrogen receptors in rat uterus. *J. Biol. Chem.* **244**, 1097–1103.

Steggles, A. W., Spelsberg, T. C., Glaser, S, R., & O'Malley, B. W. (1971). Soluble complexes between steroid hormones and target-tissue receptors bind specifically to target-tissue chromatin. *Proc. Natl. Acad. Sci.* **68**, 1479–1482.

Stern, J. M. (1972). Androgen accumulation in hypothalamus and anterior pituitary of male ring doves; influence of steroid hormones. *Gen. Compar. Endocrinol.* **18**, 439–449.

Stern, J. M. & Eisenfeld. A. J. (1969). Androgen accumulation and binding to macromolecules in seminal vesicles: inhibition by cyproterone. *Science* **166**, 233–235.

Stern, J. M. & Eisenfeld, A. J. (1971). Distribution and metabolism of ^{3}H-testosterone in castrated male rats; effects of cyproterone, progesterone and unlabeled testosterone. *Endocrinology* **88**, 1117–1125.

Strickland, A. L. & French, F. S. (1969). Absence of response to dihydrotestosterone in the syndrome of testicular feminization. *J. Clin. Endocrinol.* **29**, 1284–1286.

Stumpf, W. E. (1968a). Estradiol-concentrating neurons: Topography in the hypothalamus by dry mount autoradiography. *Science* **162**, 1001–1003.

Stumpf, W. E. (1968b). Cellular and subcellular ^{3}H-estradiol localization in the pituitary by autoradiography. *Z. Zellforsch.* **92**, 23–33.

Stumpf, W. E. (1969). Nuclear concentration of ^{3}H-estradiol in target tissues. Dry mount autoradiography of vagina, oviduct, ovary, testis, mammary tumor, liver and adrenal. *Endocrinology* **85**, 31–37.

Stumpf, W. E. (1971). Autoradiographic techniques and the localization of estrogen, androgen and glucocorticoid in the pituitary and brain. *Amer. Zool.* **11**, 725–739.

Stumpf, W. E. (1972). Estrogen, androgen, and glucocorticosteroid concentrating neurons in the amygdala, studied by dry autoradiography. *Adv. Behav. Biol.* **2**, 763–774.

Teng, C-S. & Hamilton. T H. (1969). Role of chromatin in estrogen action in the uterus. II. Hormone-induced synthesis of nonhistone acidic proteins which restore histone-inhibited DNA-dependent RNA synthesis. *Proc. Natl. Acad. Sci.* **63**, 465–472.

Toft, D. & Gorski. J. (1966). A receptor molecule for estrogens: Isolation from the rat uterus and preliminary characterization. *Proc. Natl. Acad. Sci.* **55**, 1574–1581.

Tremblay, R. R., Foley, T. P., Corvo, P., Park, I-J., Kowarski, A., Blizzard, R. M., Jones, H. W., & Migeon, C. J. (1972). Plasma concentration of testosterone, dihydrotestosterone, testosterone-oestradiol binding globulin, and pituitary gonadotrophins in the syndrome of male pseudo-hermaphroditism with testicular feminization. *Acta Endocrinol.* **70**, 331–341.

Tuohimaa, P. & Johansonn, R. (1971). Decreased estradiol binding in the uterus and anterior hypothalamus of androgenized female rats. *Endocrinology* **88**, 1159–1164.

Vertes, M. & King, R. J. B. (1972). Mechanism of oestradiol binding in rat hypothalamus: Effect of androgenization. *J. Endocrinol.* **51**, 271–282.

Whalen, R. E. & Luttge, W. G. (1971). Perinatal administration of dihydrotestosterone to female rats and the development of reproductive function. *Endocrinology* **89**, 1320–1322.

Wicks, W. D. & Kenney, F. T. (1964). RNA synthesis in rat seminal vesicles: stimulation by testosterone. *Science* **144**, 1346–1347.

Williams-Ashman, H. G. & Reddi, A. H. (1972). Androgenic regulation of tissue growth and function. *Biochem. Actions Hormones* **2**, 257–294.

Wilson, J. D. & Gloyna, R. E. (1970). Intranuclear metabolism of testosterone in the accessory organs of reproduction. *Rec. Progr. Hormone Res.* **26**, 309–336.

Wilson, J. D. & Lasnitzki, I. (1971). Dihydrotestosterone formation in fetal tissues of the rabbit and rat. *Endocrinology* **89**, 659–668.

Wira, C. R. & Baulieu, E. E. (1972). Response ribonucleique precole de l'uterus à l'oestradiol, in vivo et in vitro, *C.R. Acad. Sci. (D) (Paris)* **274**, 73–76.

Wooley, D. E., Holinka, C. F., & Timiras, P. S. (1969). Changes in ^{3}H-estradiol distribution with development in the rat. *Endocrinology* **84**, 157–161.

Wyss, R. H., Karznia, R., Heinrichs, W. L., & Herrmann, W. L. (1968). Inhibition of uterine receptor binding of estradiol by antiestrogens (Clomiphene and CL-868). *J. Clin. Endocrinol.* **28**, 1824–1828.

Zigmond, R. E. & McEwen, B. S. (1970). Selective retention of oestradiol by cell nuclei in specific brain regions of the ovariectomized rat. *J. Neurochem.* **17**, 889–899.

Zigmond, R. E., Stern, J. M., & McEwen, B. S. (1972). Retention of radioactivity in cell nuclei in the hypothalamus of the ring dove after injection of 3H-testosterone. *Gen. Comp. Endocrinol.* **18**, 450–453.

DISCUSSION

DR. JAFFE.   Dr. Eisenfeld, could you tell us the amount of radioactivity in microcuries for the experiments you described with estradiol and testosterone? In the seminal vesicle and the other target tissue you were talking about picocuries per milligram; in the slide that showed the hypothalamus the scale ran 2 to 10 dpm/mg, which in terms of counts is not really very many. Therefore I wondered how much you put in and what significance you attach to that amount of accumulation.

DR. EISENFELD.   In the in vivo studies of estrogen and androgen distribution we injected 0.1 μg/100 g intravenously. The slide from the androgen study (Stern & Eisenfeld, 1971) illustrates that after ^{3}H-testosterone administration there is radioactivity with the chromatographic mobility of DHT in the hypothalamus and pituitary. The hypothalamic level is 5.5 dpm/mg (weight 50 mg) and the anterior pituitary 46 dpm/mg (weight 10 mg). A very small percentage of the administered radioactivity is retained in target organs, including the hypothalamus and anterior pituitary. The accumulation pattern of ^{3}H-estradiol has been replicated many times. The in vivo androgen distribution studies involved identification of radioactivity of tissues from 15 control rats, each extracted and chromatographed separately. Although the counts are low, the pattern is reproducible between animals.

DR. JAFFE.   How much is that in terms of microcuries?

DR. EISENFELD.   0.1 μg/100 g steroid with a specific activity of 40Ci/mM is 15 μC/100 g.

DR. RAMALEY.   A few years ago Flerko and Mess (1968) reported that estrogen uptake was lower than normal in tissues from animals that had been sterilized with androgens early in life. Have you any information on uptake of steroids by the brain of androgen-sterilized females?

DR. EISENFELD.   Although different laboratories have various results, there may be decreased estrogen accumulation in target organs of neonatally androgenized females. This includes the hypothalamus and anterior pituitary. Because the accumulation pattern in the hypothalamus of normal males and females appears to be similar, however, the neonatal androgenization modification may be an exaggeration of, or different from, the normal differentiation process. McGargon and Weiss found very little difference in the anterior hypothalamus with neonatal androgen, but they did find a big decrease in the neonatal estrogen. There may be a slight decrease in the hypothalamus with neonatal androgenization, but it is very difficult to be sure and it is very difficult to know the meaning of a slight reduction in the accumulation of estradiol. The system appears to operate with a relatively large excess of binding protein in the cytoplasm. Thus it is not clear what the small difference in the concentration would mean. Another possibility is that this may represent a falling out of cells in the hypothalamus with neonatal androgenization. The concentration may be more not because there are fewer binding molecules in all cells to take it up but perhaps because there are fewer cells. Anderson has looked at neonatally-androgenized animals by audioradiography and has also found some reduction in the hypothalamus.

DR. KULIN.   Dr. Edward Reiter and I have recently published a report (1972) on the ontogeny of estradiol uptake in the neonatal female rat. Our experiments indicate that as early as 3 or 4 days of age there is preferential estrogen uptake in the basal parts of the hypothalamus. The male rat also displays a similar pattern of steroid uptake within the first week of life (unpublished data). Further work in our laboratory indicates that preferential uptake of estradiol by the anterior hypothalamus takes place later in the female rat, perhaps not until 20 or 21 days of age. Neonatal androgenization induced by the injection of testosterone in the first 2 days of life causes a reduction in estradiol uptake by both basal and anterior hypothalamic areas, beginning at ages at which the respective centers become avid for estrogen. Seemingly, the neonatal exposure to androgens can influence estrogen receptors at a variety of stages in the development of binding sites.

DR. EISENFELD.   Your in vitro studies suggest that estrogen binding may be present in some portions of the hypothalamus within the first few days of life.

DR. BOGDANOVE.   Kingsley and Bogdanove (1971) implanted 3 different androgens into the anterior pituitary; the criterion of androgen action was primarily a marked elevation of the intrapituitary FSH/LH ratio (which is a specific response to androgen). All 3 androgens (testosterone propionate, DHT benzoate, and 7α-methyl-19-nortestosterone acetate) were effective. The "superandrogen" (the 7α-methyl compound) was about 10 times as potent in the pituitary as the other 2, which were about equally potent. My question is brought to focus by the findings of others that DHT may not affect neural processes that do respond to testosterone (or at least those neural processes involved in sexual behavior), whereas testosterone may not be able to influence peripheral organs (such as the prostate) until it has been converted to DHT. Since all 3 androgens were directly effective when implanted within the pituitary, have we enough information to answer the question whether metabolic conversion may be a necessary condition for the direct effects of some androgens on the pituitary gonadotropins? Could DHT and 7α-methyl-19-nortestosterone have been converted to testosterone, or could the 2 unreduced steroids have both undergone 5α reduction? Can we yet infer that pituitary androgen receptors (unlike both brain and prostate receptors) are ambivalent, capable of reacting to reduced DHT or unreduced (testosterone, 7α-methyl-19-nortestosterone) androgenic molecules?

DR. EISENFELD.   The presence of DHT in the anterior pituitary and hypothalamus after systemic administration of ^{3}H-testosterone and in vitro studies indicates that these tissues can convert testosterone to DHT; DHT and 7α-methyl-19-nortestosterone are not known to be converted to testosterone. I am not aware of studies that can tell us whether the C4 double bond of 7α-methyl-19-nortestosterone can be reduced by pituitary tissue to the 5α-derivative. The work of Liao indicated that 7α-methyl-19-nortestosterone binds to a protein fraction of ventral prostate better than DHT under in vitro conditions in which the unsaturated bond at C4 is not reduced, so that this compound possibly could act without reduction.

DR. RAMIREZ.   We have to be careful when we talk about the ability of the pituitary of the neonatal rat to take up the estradiol in vitro or in vivo. The in vivo pituitary of a 5-day-old rat cannot take up and cannot retain tritiated estradiol (Alvarez & Ramirez, 1970). If you incubate it in vitro there is a definite uptake. The presence of the sex protein mentioned by you that disappeared after 20 days of age is quite interesting. The 5-day-old rat treated with a single injection of tritiated estradiol had very high levels of blood radioactivity, but the pituitary did not take up the radioactivity. In contrast, the uterus of the same 5-day-old rat took up the estradiol and was capable of concentrating it above blood level 4 or 5 times. So here we have the same animal, the same condition, but two types of "receptor" causing different uptakes. Could you comment?

DR. EISENFELD.   The presence of a plasma-binding protein for estradiol in the very young rat complicates the interpretation of the ratio of radioactivity in a tissue to that in plasma. The binding system in the anterior pituitary is at least present in part within a few days of birth, because most studies indicate that the concentration of radioactivity is much higher in pituitary than in many other organs.

DR. WEISZ.   When showing the uptake data for testosterone, you were only counting organic solvent-extractable radioactivity. That may be misleading, particularly for testosterone. We have attemped to identify and quantify metabolites of testosterone in brain. The findings were disheartening because there is clearly a rapid metabolism of testosterone, and a large number of metabolites accumulate in brain both in vivo and in vitro. These metabolites, which are recognized potential mediators of testosterone action and residual testosterone, represent only a small proportion of the total radioactivity. Small amounts of testosterone are left; DHT is there, as is 3α-5α-androstenediol; also a minute amount of estradiol. However, the bulk of the radioactivity is present, especially after an injection of testosterone in vivo, in the form of unknown metabolites which may be very large in number. We will have to identify specific molecular events within neurons, which can then be linked to specific actions of the androgen before any statement can be made about the importance of the metabolites and the accumulation of radioactivity per milligram tissue.

DR. SNIPES.   In our incubations of testosterone with various areas of the rat brain we can account for most of the radioactivity by adding up testosterone, androstenedione, and DHT. How much of each different steroid you have after incubation may depend on your incubation condition (Shore & Snipes, 1971).

DR. EISENFELD.   Elucidation of the androgen system in the brain is complicated by the extensive metabolism of the androgens. All identification of radioactivity must be considered tentative until confirmed by chromatography in several systems, recrystallization to constant specific activity, and synthesis of derivatives. The work of other laboratories on the ontogeny of the androgen system must be considered only as a first approach.

DR. RODGERS.   Dr. McCann showed that testosterone was high between days 1 and 5. Has anyone looked for binding in male brains before day 11?

DR. RAMIREZ.   When comparing the distribution of testosterone and estradiol in 5-day-old rats, we could not find any particular curve in the testosterone distribution that would tell us that there was some hypothalamic preferential uptake; it looked only like distribution of the radioactivity throughout the tissue but not like any special uptake. When we extracted the tissue and used thin-layer chromatography to try to identify what was there, we found some compounds that were not testosterone. Maybe the sensitivity of the method was not enough to detect testosterone, even though we found some other compounds.

DR. JACOBSEN.   Regarding your comment on the lack of incorporation of radioactive mestranol into uterine cytosol in vitro, some time ago we also showed that, like all estrogens, when injected in radioactive form into rats, it does deliver a substantial charge of radioactivity to the rat uterus. But when this radioactivity is isolated and analyzed for its chemical nature we found that it is not mestranol; it was demethylated and is 17α-estradiol.

DR. EISENFELD.   With respect to studies with radioactive mestranol it has been shown that the metabolite ethinyl estradiol is retained by the uterus. However, the estrogenic component of the oral contraceptive acts at the hypothalamus or anterior pituitary, not the uterus, to inhibit ovulation. Our studies show that mestranol binds poorly and ethinyl estradiol avidly to hypothalamic and pituitary macromolecules and suggest that mestranol must be concentrated to ethinyl estradiol for antifertility activity.

DR. DAVIDSON.   Dr. Eisenfeld's remarks about DHT action on the brain were based on the failure to stimulate sexual behavor in male rats with DHT. This has been demonstrated in at least 4 laboratories, including our own. On the other hand, it is true that DHT is at least as effective as testosterone, if not more so, in inhibiting gonadotropin secretion. Phyllis Johnston, in our laboratory, has looked at the effect of crystalline DHT implantaton in the brain and pituitary to circumvent the possibility that systemically administered steroid may have difficulty reaching the relevant brain cells. When you implant the crystalline DHT in the brain, it has only a slight effect in stimulating sexual behavior in the castrated male rat. On the other hand, DHT implants in the medial basal hypothalamus are at least as effective as testosterone implants in inhibiting the reproductive system, whereas similar implants in the pituitary are ineffective.

DR. ARIMURA.   Dr. Kato lent me 3 slides which supplement those shown by Dr. Eisenfeld. Figure 8 shows the radioactive estrogen taken up in vitro by the hypothalamic tissue from female rats of various ages. The peaks show the radio-activities of the fractions of the sucrose density gradient with sedimentation coefficient of 8, which represent estrogen receptors of the hypothalamus. There is a considerable increase in the peak at 21 days of age when the feedback mechanism of gonadotropin secretion is known to start operating. Figure 9 indicates that the available estrogen receptors decrease at 35 days of age, just before the vaginal opening. Figure 10 shows the difference of the hypothalamic estrogen receptor of 38-day-old female rats with and without the vaginal opening, the former having greater numbers of receptors. Dr. Kato also reported

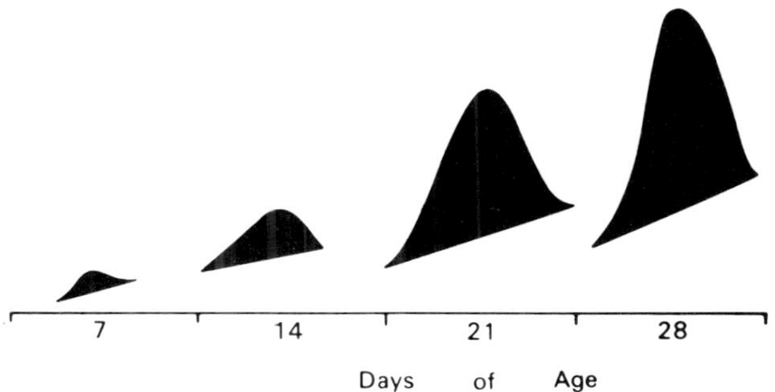

FIG. 8.   Relative amounts of radioactive estrogen taken up in vitro by hypothalamic tissue of female rats during the first postnatal month. Peaks indicate radioactivities of sucrose density gradient with sedimentation coefficients of 8.

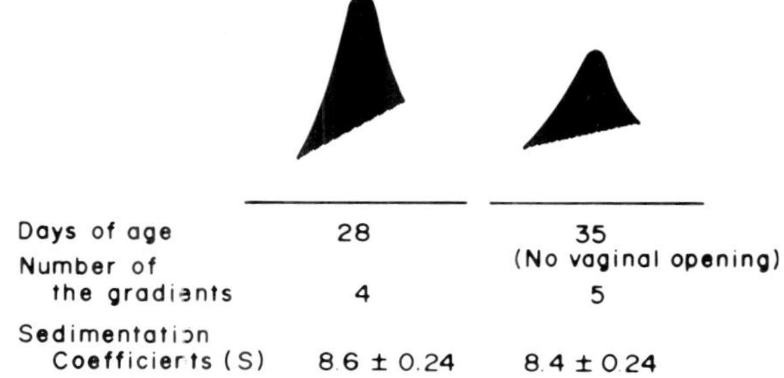

	28	35 (No vaginal opening)
Days of age	28	35
Number of the gradients	4	5
Sedimentation Coefficients (S)	8.6 ± 0.24	8.4 ± 0.24

FIG. 9.   Relative amounts of radioactive estrogen taken up in vitro by hypothalamic tissue of 28- and 35-day-old female rats. Peaks indicate radioactivity of 8S bands on sucrose density gradient.

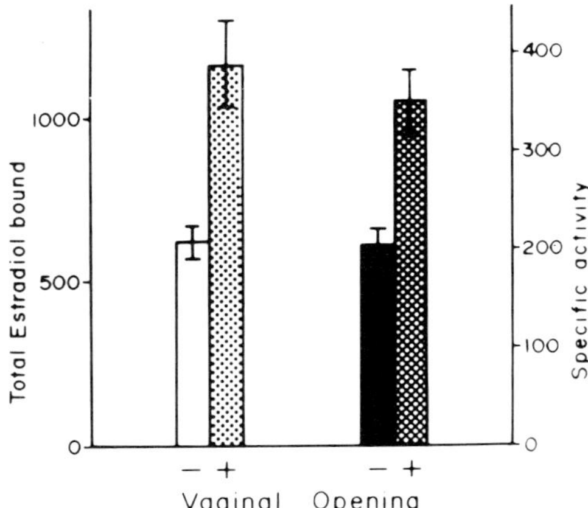

FIG. 10. Total amounts and specific activities of estriol bound to hypothalamic estrogen receptors in 38-day-old female rats. With (+) and without (−) vaginal opening.

that in the cycling female rats the amount of available hypothalamic estrogen receptors was smallest at proestrus than at any other stages of estrous cycle.

DR. EISENFELD. Dr. Kato's work indicates an increase in binding in the 8S peak of the hypothalamus between 7 and 21 days and a slight reduction in the ^{3}H-estradiol binding before vaginal opening; this might reflect decreased synthesis of the binding protein or increased levels of endogenous estrogens.

REFERENCES

Alvarez, E. O. & Ramirez, V. D. (1970). Distribution curves of ^{3}H-testosterone and ^{3}H-estradiol in neonatal female rats. *Neuroendocrinology* **6**, 349–360.

Davis, M. E., Wiener, M., Jacobson, H. I., & Jensen, E. V. (1963). Estradiol metabolism in pregnant and non-pregnant women. *Amer. J. Ob. Gyn.* **87**, 979–991.

Flerko, B. & Mess, B. (1968). Reduced oestradiol-binding capacity of androgen sterilized rats. *Acta Physiol. Hung.* **33**, 111–113.

Kingsley, T. R. & Bogdanove, E. M. (1971). Direct androgen-pituitary feedback. *Fed. Proc.* **30**, 253.

Kulin, H. & Reiter, E. O. (1972). Ontogeny of the *in vitro* uptake of tritiated estradiol by the hypothalamus of the female rat. *Endocrinology* **90**, 1371–1374.

Shore, L. S. & Snipes, C. A. (1971). Metabolism of testosterone in vitro by hypothalamus and other areas of rat brain. *Fed. Proc.* **30**, 363.

Stern, J. M. & Eisenfeld, A. (1971). Distribution and metabolism of ^{3}H-testosterone in castrated male rats. Effects of cyproterone, progesterone and unlabeled testosterone. *Endocrinology* **88**, 1117–1126.

11.

The Role of the Gonads in Sexual Maturation

W. D. ODELL and R. S. SWERDLOFF

Consideration of the CNS-pituitary-gonadal system (Fig. 1) reveals several possible etiologies for the process of sexual maturation (Table 1). Kulin, Rifkind, Ross, and Odell (1967); Odell and Ross (1966); and Odell, Ross, and Rayford (1967) reported the presence of biologically active and immunoreactive LH in blood and urine of prepubertal children. These findings led us to review existing data in rats and to apply the then-current theory for rats to children. According to that hypothesis, (1) a sensitive dynamic feedback exists between the hypothalamic-pituitary and gonadal units before puberty, and (2) a decrease in sensitivity of this feedback system is the likely cause of sexual maturation. However, we have come to

---

Abbreviations

CNS	Central nervous system
FSH	Follicle stimulating hormone
hCG	Human chorionic gonadotropin
LH	Luteinizing hormone
LRH	Luteinizing hormone releasing hormone
RIA	Radioimmunoassay

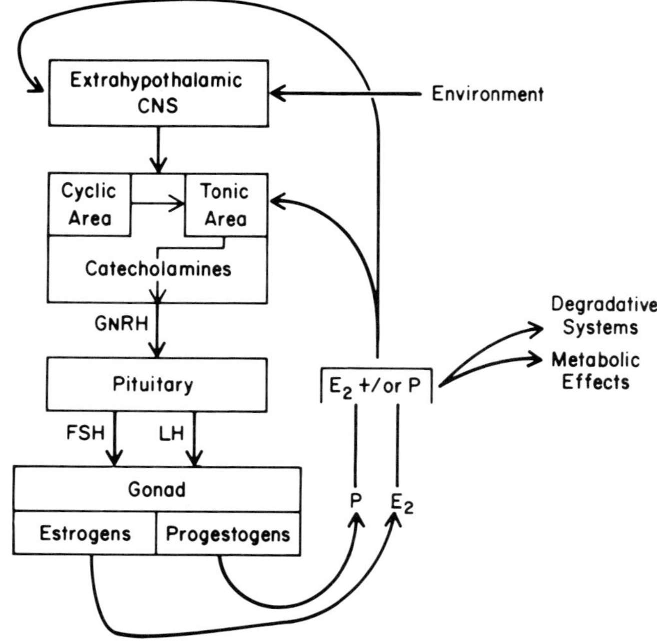

FIG. 1.   Schematic presentation of central nervous system—pituitary-gonadal interrelations in the female. Modification by deletion of functional activity in the "cyclic area" and substituting "estrogen plus androgen" for "estrogens plus progestogens" would also apply to the male. Although catecholamine transmission is involved in the female and presumably also in the male, experimental data to support this are meager.

TABLE 1.   Possible etiologies of sexual maturation

I.   Extrahypothalamic-central nervous system areas
   A.   Increasing extrahypothalamic-central nervous system stimulation of hypothalamic centers governing LH and/or FSH secretion.
   B.   Decreasing extrahypothalamic-central nervous system inhibition of hypothalamic centers governing LH and/or FSH secretion.
   C.   Decreasing sensitivity to gonadal steroid feedback suppressive effects.

II.   Hypothalamic areas
   A.   Increasing hypothalamic stimulation of LH and/or FSH secretion ("maturation process").
   B.   Decreasing feedback sensitivity to gonadal steroid feedback suppressive effects.

III.   Pituitary
   A.   Increasing LH and/or FSH secretion to constant LRH stimulation.

IV.   Gonads
   A.   Increasing response to LH and/or FSH stimulation.

V.   Sex accessory organs
   A.   Increasing sensitivity to gonadal steroid stimulation.

---

question whether this is the major cause of sexual maturation. If this were the cause, one would expect to find (1) increasing LH and FSH concentrations during sexual maturation (the postulated decreasing sensitivity to feedback suppression of LH and FSH should result in such increases), and (2) that a direct determination of the threshold dose of gonadal steroids required for feedback suppression should reveal that a higher dose is required after rather than before sexual maturation. We have attempted to obtain these data in rats, cattle, and humans.

Most experimental data supporting the changing sensitivity concept originally came from studies in rats, usually in parabiotic animals. Kallas (1929) used parabiotic sexually immature rats (postweanling but with prevaginal opening and estrus) and demonstrated that castration of one partner increased ovarian weight in the other. This study (considerably ahead of its time in general acceptance) showed that a dynamic feedback existed in sexually immature animals.

Byrnes and Meyer (1951) used the same design in postweanling parabiotic rats to confirm these findings and showed that a dose of estrogen administered to the castrate animal could be small enough to produce no increase in uterine weight but could still cause inhibition of gonadotropin secretion in the intact partner (as shown by prevention of stimulation of ovarian weight (Table 2). They concluded that a sensitive feedback system occurred before sexual maturation in rats and that the dose of estrogen required for inhibition of gonadotropin secretion was less than that required for stimulation of uterine growth. Note that both studies (Kallas, 1929; Byrnes & Meyer, 1951) were performed in females, that the effect on ovarian weight was primarily (but not exclusively) related to FSH action, and that no direct comparison was made with feedback by identical doses of estradiol in adults.

Johnson (1966) joined hypophysectomized to intact immature animals and demonstrated effects of gonadotropin in the hypophysectomized partner, thus indicating that the noncastrate immature animal did secrete LH and/or FSH. Wiesner (1932) showed that castration of rats before sexual maturation resulted in decreases in sex accessory tissue weight and indicated that steroids were being secreted by the prepubertal gonad. Ramirez and McCann (1965) attempted to determine the dose of testosterone required to suppress LH concentrations in castrate rats before puberty, compared with the suppression dose after sexual maturation. They found that a dose 3 to 4 times greater was required after maturation. In these studies LH was quantified by use of the ovarian ascorbic acid depletion assay.

In humans a variety of studies demonstrate the changes in LH and FSH that occur in groups of boys and girls during sexual maturation (Burr, Sizonenko, Kaplan, & Grumbach, 1970; Guyda, Johanson, Migeon, &

TABLE 2.   Effects of estradiol on gonadotropin secretion in parabiotic immature rats[a,b]

Group	Treatment	Dose (μg/day)	Number (pairs)	Ovarian weight (mg)	Uterine weight (mg)
Intact-intact	None (noncastrated controls)	0	5	17	...
Castrate-intact	None	0	23	160	52
Castrate-intact	Estradiol to castrate	0.0032	2	146	47
		0.0065	2	122	60
		0.0065	1	15	43
		0.009	2	16	45
		0.012	3	25	51
		0.020	3	20	65
		0.025	3	25	135
		0.050	2	29	168

[a] Modified from Byrnes & Meyer (1951)

[b] Immature female rats were joined in parabiotic union; the ovaries averaged 17 mg. When one partner was castrated, the ovarian weight increased from increased gonadotropin secretion and averaged 160 mg. Varying doses of estradiol were administered to the castrate partner. Inhibition of pituitary gonadotropin secretion, without stimulation of uterine weight, occurred when doses of 0.0065 to 0.020 μg/day of estradiol were administered. Lower doses failed to inhibit pituitary secretion; higher doses inhibited pituitary secretion but also stimulated uterine weight. Intact-intact here means immature female rat joined by parabiosis to another immature female rat; castrate-intact means castrate immature female rat joined by parabiosis to intact immature female rat.

Blizzard, 1969; Penny, Guyda, Baghdassarian, Johanson, & Blizzard, 1970; Raiti, Johanson, Light, Migeon, & Blizzard, 1969; Sizonenko, Burr, Kaplan, & Grumbach, 1970; Wieland, Yen, & Pohlman, 1970; Yen & Vivic, 1970). All have shown small incremental increases in average LH and FSH with changing states of maturation which are significantly different when calculated as SE, but with great overlap in individuals. All investigators agree that such progressive increases in LH and FSH occur with sexual maturation in children. It is not known whether they cause increasing gonadal steroid production or whether increasing gonadal steroid production may not in fact (via *positive feedback*) produce them. Several studies on feedback sensitivity in children have been reported; Kulin, Grumbach, and Kaplan (1969; 1972) observed that clomiphene, a drug which stimulates LH and FSH secretion in adults, suppressed LH and FSH secretion in children in doses approximately 1:100th of that used for stimulation in adults. These stimulation versus suppression effects are currently difficult for us to interpret. Kelch, Grumbach, and Kaplan (1972) administered ethinyl estradiol to a small group of children at different stages of puberty. Unfortunately the number of subjects was too small for critical analysis.

We (Odell, Hescox, & Kiddy, 1970) observed that cattle during sexual maturation showed no change in average LH between 15 days and 12 months of age, the usual age of sexual maturation (Fig. 2). These studies also showed that castration of male and female cattle as young as 1 to 4 months of age produced increases in concentrations of serum LH that were indistinguishable from those in adult cattle (Fig. 3). Castration of rats at 10 days of age produced marked increases in serum LH in males and females (Fig. 4). The response in adult females was less than in the immature and the adult males had a similar response (Swerdloff, Walsh, Jacobs, & Odell, 1971; 1974). In contrast, Kelch et al (1972) and Penny et al (1970) have shown in children that in the absence of functioning gonads LH is not significantly increased, whereas FSH is increased modestly but not to the concentrations found in adults.

When we observed the changes in serum LH and FSH in rats undergoing sexual maturation (between 10 days of age and sexual maturation), we were surprised to find that between weaning and the first estrus cycle in females FSH fell instead of rising, whereas LH did not change (as in cattle) (Walsh, Swerdloff, & Odell, 1973; Swerdloff et al, 1974). In males (Swerdloff et al, 1971; 1972) FSH fell but LH increased slightly (as LH does in the human).

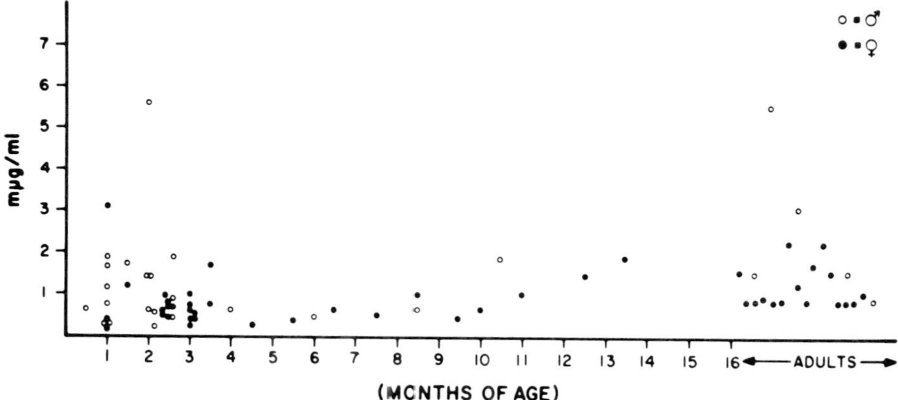

FIG. 2.   Scattergram of LH in cattle during sexual maturation. The onset of estrus in these cattle occurs at about 12 months. Each sample was taken from a single animal and all samples were quantified in a single assay. No significant difference existed before and after maturation. From Odell et al (1970).

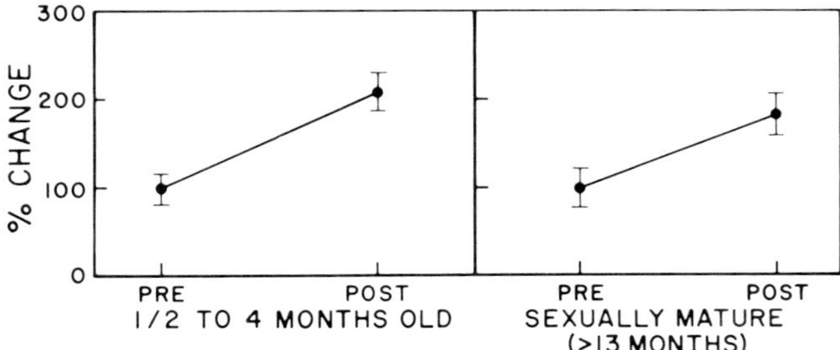

FIG. 3.   Effects of castration on serum LH in sexually immature and sexually mature cattle. The data in the immature animals consist of 10 consecutive daily samples before and 10 consecutive daily samples immediately after castration in 11 animals (7 males and 4 females). The data after sexual maturation consist of single samples obtained from sexually mature animals and single samples obtained at random times (longer than 5 days) after castration. Males and females did not differ in this small number of animals, and the data were pooled.

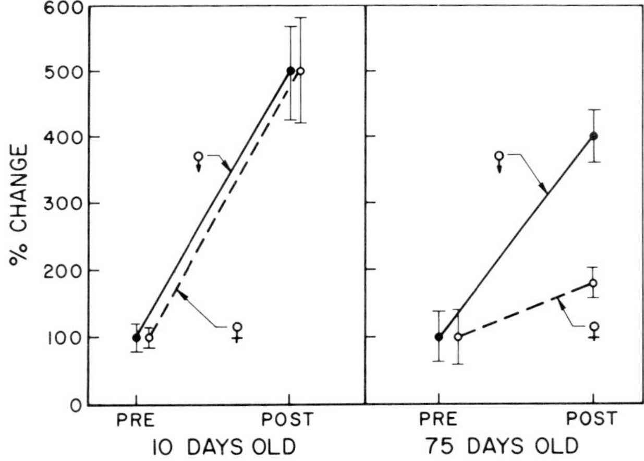

FIG. 4.   The effects of castration on serum LH in rats. Each group contains 10 animals among the 10-day-old rats; each group contained 6 animals among the sexually mature animals. Samples were obtained 5 days after castration in both groups.

Our studies suggested that since FSH (and LH in females) was not increasing during sexual maturation increasing feedback sensitivity was not likely to be present and that, alternatively, the studies in rats were being done at a time after the changes initiating sexual maturation had occurred. This would be an interesting possibility, for, classically, the weanling rat with relatively small sex accessory organs had been considered a sexually immature animal. Figure 5 shows the changes in LH and FSH that occur between 10 days of age and sexual maturity. These studies in rats are particularly important because previous studies on this animal formed the basis for the theory of decreasing feedback sensitivity as a cause of sexual maturation.

We also attempted to make direct assessment of feedback sensitivity for suppression by gonadal steroids (Odell & Swerdloff, 1974). Figures 6 and 7 give these data for the male and female castrate rat at 10, 21, and at 75 days of age after sexual maturation. In the male no significant differences could be observed in feedback sensitivity for LH (Fig. 8*a*) suppression; in the female (Fig. 8*b*) the presence of positive feedback with small doses of estrogen, superimposed on negative feedback at higher doses, makes interpretation of inhibitory sensitivity difficult. In both sexes slightly smaller doses of gonadal steroids suppressed FSH in the 10-day-old animal than were required in the 20-day-old immature or sexually immature animal. It is interesting that the slope of suppression of FSH in the female appeared to be different at 10 than at 21 and 75 days (Odell & Swerdloff, 1974).

Each of the possible explanations of sexual maturation listed in Table 1, with the exceptions of categories IV and V, would be associated with increasing FSH and/or LH concentration and/or a change in feedback sensitivity. Because both the female rat and cow had no changes in LH and because both the male and female rat also had a fall in FSH (observations not explainable on the basis of increasing sensitivity), we initiated studies to assess the possbility of occurrence of either increasing gonadal response to LH and/or FSH stimulation or increasing stimulation of sex accessory organs by gonadal steroids.

RESPONSE OF SEX ACCESSORY ORGANS TO
ANDROGEN AND ESTROGEN STIMULATION

We first determined whether any differences in sensitivity to androgen (in males) or to estrogen (in females) stimulated the development of sex accessory organs. Groups of 10-, 21-, and 75-day-old-male and female rats were castrated. Five days after surgery varying doses of testosterone propionate were administered to the male rats and ethinyl estradiol to the female rats. Steroids were dissolved in safflower oil and administered subcutaneously every day to a group of ten 10-day-old or six 21- and six 75-day-old animals. After 5 days of treatment all animals were sacrificed under ether anesthesia. Ventral prostrates and uteri were weighed. Since the baseline uterine and prostatic weights and the absolute weight increments attained with maximal steroid stimuation varied greatly at the different ages

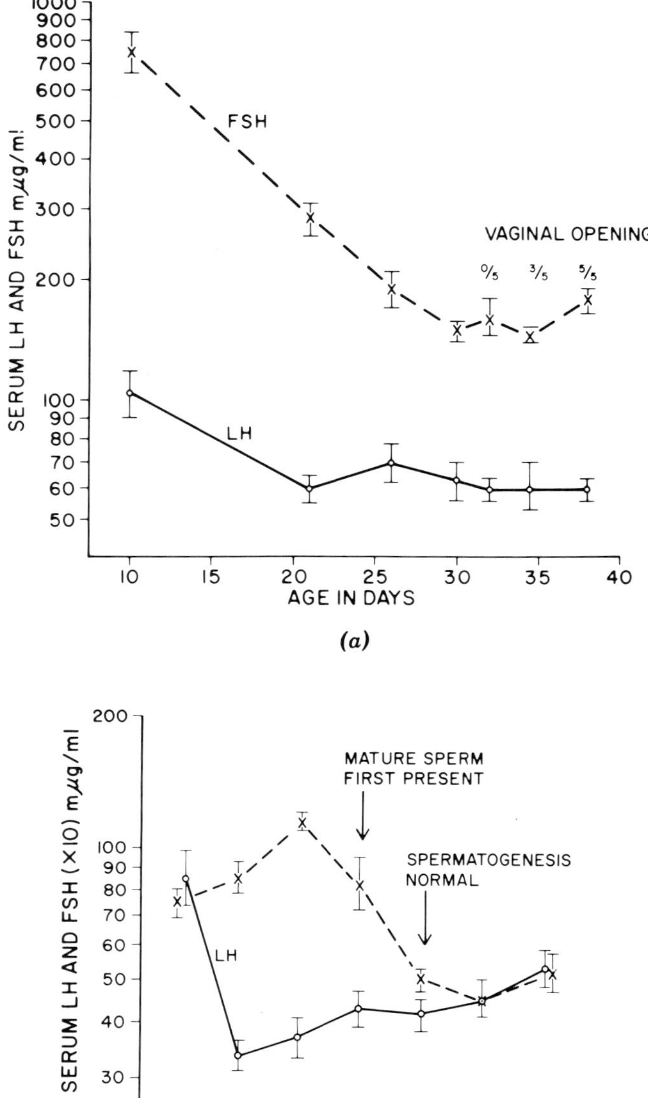

FIG. 5. Changes in serum LH and FSH concentrations in female (a) and male (b) rats between 10 days of age and sexual maturation. Each group of 10-day-old animals consisted of 10 animals; the older group contained 6 animals each. Mean and SE are shown. From Swerdloff, Jacobs, & Odell, 1974.

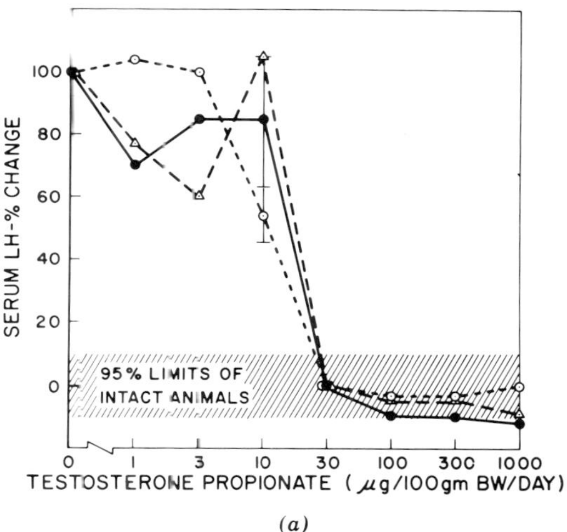

(a)

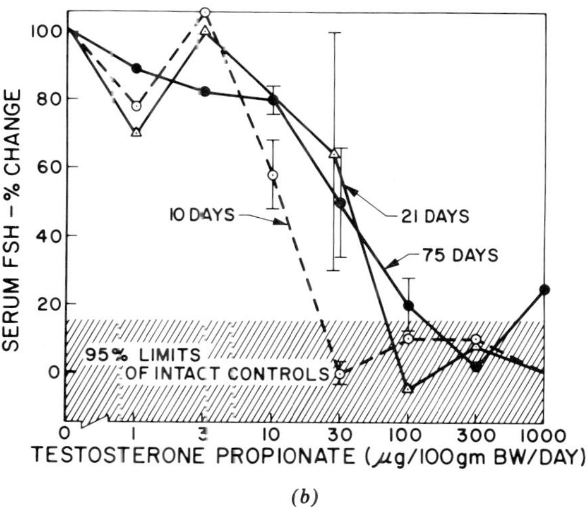

(b)

FIG. 6. Suppression of serum LH (a) and FSH (b) with varying doses of testosterone propionate in male rats at 10, 21, and 75 days of age. Groups of animals at 10, 21, and 75 days of age were castrated. Five days later testosterone propionate in doses shown was administered subcutaneously in oil for 5 days. ⊙ = 10-day-old, △ = 21-day-old, ● = 75-day old animals. Brackets indicate SE.

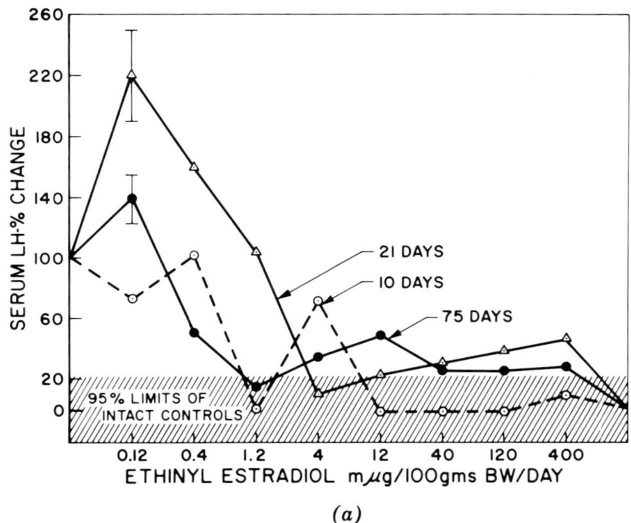

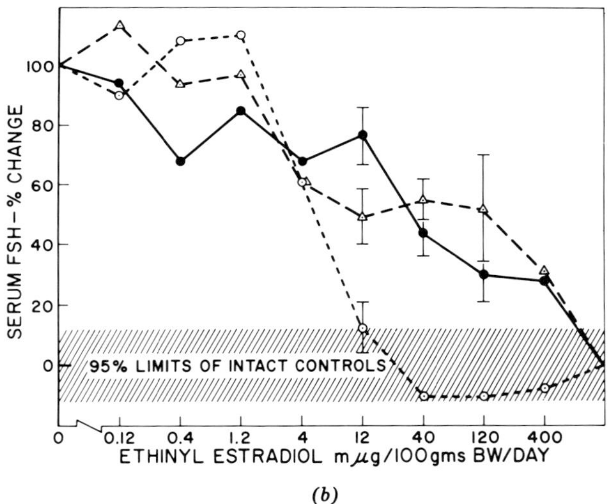

FIG. 7. Suppression of serum LH (a) and FSH (b) in female rats at 10, 21, and 75 days of age. Groups of animals were castrated at 10, 21, and 75 days of age. Five days later ethinyl estradiol was administered in oil subcutaneously for 3 days. Note that low doses of estradiol exerted a positive feedback or stimulatory action in the 21- and 75-day-old animals making suppression difficult to interpret. Symbols are the same as in 6a and b. From Walsh, Swerdloff, and Odell (1973).

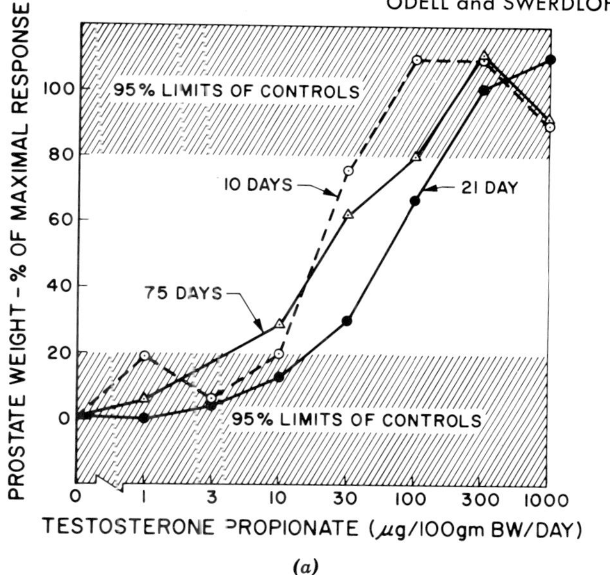

(a)

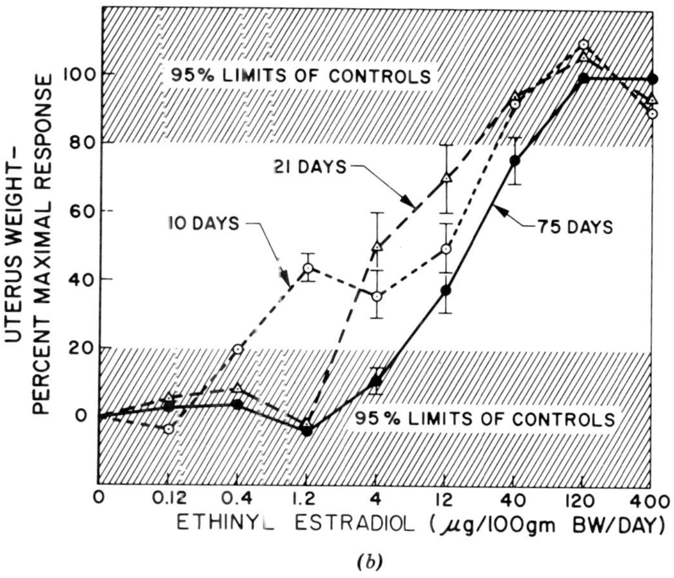

(b)

FIG. 8. Response of uterine weight to varying doses of ethinyl estradiol in female rats and of prostatic weight to testosterone propionate in male rats before and after sexual maturation. For the male (a) the response of 10- and 75-day-old animals was similar, whereas the response of the 21-day-olds showed a slight shift to the right. For the female (b) the 10- and 21-day-olds responded similarly, but the 75-day-old response was shifted slightly to the right.

studied, results were calculated as a percentage of maximal possible response. Results (Fig. 8*a-b*) indicate that no large differences in sensitivity appeared to exist, although the 75-day-old female and the 21-day-old male responded slightly less well. We concluded that it is unlikely that sexual maturation is caused by differences in sensitivity to steroid effects.

GONADAL SENSITIVITY TO LH AND FSH STIMULATION OF STEROID PRODUCTION

Hypophysectomized Male Rat

We used the previous data as background to indicate the necessity of examining gonadal LH/FSH sensitivty, prostatic weight as an indicator of testosterone secretion, and uterine weight as an indicator of estrogen production (Odell, Swerdloff, Jacobs, & Hescox, 1973). Figure 9 shows the increase in prostatic weight in response to NIH-LH-B7 given over a period of 5 days to the immature male rat hypophysectomized 24 hours before the onset of the study. Prostatic weight increased progressively with increased LH dosage. In contrast, when the same LH preparation was administered 5 days after hypophysectomy, there was no response even when doses up to 400 μg/100 g body weight were used. Figure 10 shows this failure of response in the immature 21-day-old male rat; but after 5 days a good response to this LH preparation is seen in the sexually mature animal.

In contrast to the lack of response to LH, the 5-day hypophysectomized immature male rat responds well to FSH (Fig. 11). Testicular tubular

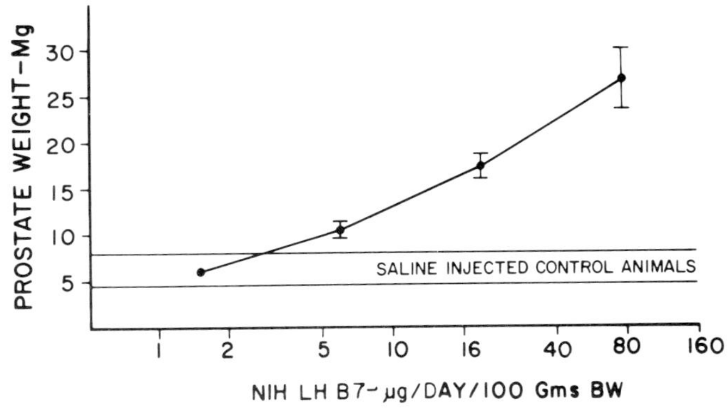

FIG. 9. Increase in prostatic weight in response to NIH-LH-B7 in the male rat hypophysectomized within 24 hours of the study. Brackets enclose SE. From Odell et al (1973).

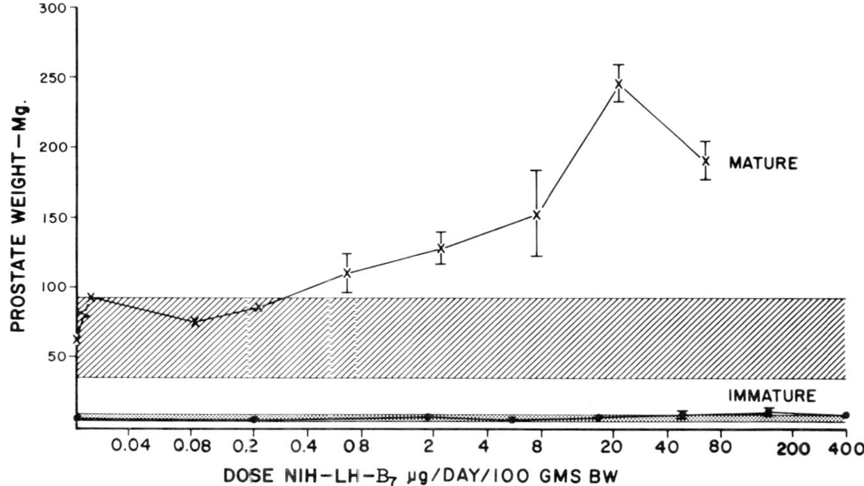

FIG. 10. Effects of NIH-LH-B7 on protastic weight in the 21-day-old and the sexually mature male rat subjected to hypophysectomy 5 days before the onset of treatment. The shaded area encloses the 95 per cent limits of prostate weight in saline-treated controls and the brackets enclose SE. From Odell et al (1973).

regression, the main determinant of testicular weight, does not show profound changes 5 days after hypophysectomy in the adult, for testicular weight is not a good indicator of response in the sexually mature male. These data show, however, that in the immature male the response to FSH was good in contrast to the failure of response to LH.

Because the immature animal responded well to FSH but not to LH, we asked whether FSH pretreatment would restore the ability of the testis to respond to LH. Table 3 shows that when groups of rats received a constant dose of 70 µg/day (100 g) body weight of LH after varying periods of pretreatment with FSH the response to LH was noted to increase progressively with duration of FSH pretreatment.

These studies may be summarized as follows. The immature male rat 5 days after hypophysectomy showed no significant response of Leydig cells to doses up to 400 µg/100 g body weight of this LH preparation. However, responsiveness could be restored by prolonged pretreatment with FSH. In essence, FSH induced a responsiveness to LH sensitivity.

Other data also support the contention that in the male a synergistic action of LH and FSH exist. Lostroh (1969) has shown that restoration

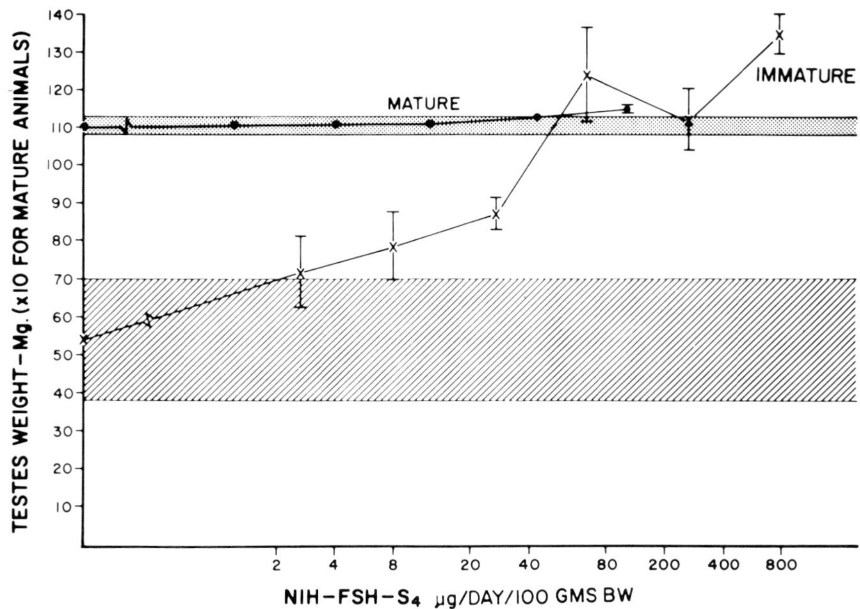

FIG. 11. Effects of NIH-FSH-S4 on testicular weight in the 21-day-old and in the sexually mature male rat. The shaded areas enclose the 95 per cent limits of saline-treated controls. In contrast to the failure of LH to produce an effect in the 5-day hypophysectomized male FSH readily produced a response. Odell et al (1973).

TABLE 3.[a] Prostatic weight response to LH[b] in rats receiving pretreatment with FSH[c] for varying times

| Treatment | Duration of treatment | | |
	10 days	25 days	30 days
Saline	5.3±0.3	5.2±0.2	4.7±0.4
LH	6.6±0.3	5.6±0.4	4.9±0.3
FSH	6.8±0.4	6.7±0.4	6.2±0.4
FSH & LH	7.2±0.2	8.5±0.6	13.5±2.4

From Odell, Swerdloff, Jacobs, & Hescox (1973).

[a] The format of this study was to administer FSH for varying periods of time (10, 25, and 30 days) and to combine FSH with LH during the last 5 days of treatment.

[b] LH—20 µg/day last 5 days of study.

[c] FSH—60 µg/day for periods indicated.

of spermatogenesis, once complete regression had occurred after hypophysectomy, required the synergistic action of both LH and FSH; this
action also required several weeks of treatment. Johnson & Ewing (1971),
in the isolated perfused rabbit testis, showed that LH alone produced only
a small increment in testosterone production, but a profound increase in
testosterone production occurred when FSH was added to the same
amount of LH.

We postulate (Odell et al. 1973) that a major factor in sexual maturation in the male rat may be a time-related FSH induction of sensitivity to
LH which requires several weeks. Hypophysectomy in immature animals
returned the testis to a "base-line, non-FSH-affected state," and varying
times of pretreatment with FSH produced a progressive return of LH sensitivity. In essence, a time-related response existed for the ability of FSH
to restore LH sensitivity to the testis. The time intervals were sufficiently
long to permit speculation that this phenomenon may be the major factor
in maturation in the rat. The high FSH concentration found at very young
ages (10 to 20 days) would be consistent with an important action of FSH
not later required. Our data and that of Lostroh (1969) taken together
indicate that a similar time-related induction, requiring both hormones,
may be necessary for development of spermatogenesis. Table 4 shows
testicular weight from the same animals as in Table 3 and indicates a
progressive ability of FSH to increase testicular weight and a profound
synergistic action of LH and FSH.

Intact Male Rat

We next studied intact male rats (Odell & Swerdloff, 1973) by making direct
measurements of blood androgen production in response to treatment with
LH. In preliminary studies a response to LH was observed to be maximal
at approximately 1 hour. Therefore we administered a given dose of LH
intraperitoneally to a group of ten 10-day-old or six 21-day- and six 75-

TABLE 4.   Testicular weight response to LH[a] in rats receiving pretreatment
with FSH for varying times

Treatment	Duration of treatment		
	10 days	25 days	30 days
Saline	134± 6.3	135± 5.8	115± 3.8
LH	168± 6.2	142± 7.2	141± 2.8
FSH	371±21.2	409±61.3	535±102
FSH and LH	381±10.6	565±92.8	853±145

From Odell et al (1973).

[a] LH and FSH doses and duration of treatment as in Table 3.

day-old animals. One hour later the animals were sacrificed by decapitation and blood was obtained for testosterone assay. A range of LH doses was administered to include those below the minimal effective dose and those above the maximal effective dose. Testosterone was determined by RIA; we used an antiserum produced in our laboratory.

The results of these studies are presented in Table 5. Note that in 10-day-old animals the serum testosterone increased to just over 200 per cent, even at doses of 30 μg/100 g body weight (day). In 21-day-old animals it increased to 633 per cent at doses of only 3.0 μg and the response was 760 per cent at 30 μg doses. The response to 30 μg was 277 per cent at 10 days, 760 percent at 21 days, and 2260 percent at 41 days of age.

Hypophysectomized Female Rat

Similar studies were performed in 5-day-old hypophysectomized female rats. Figure 12 shows the effects of varying doses of NIH-LH-B7 on their uterine weight. As in the male, doses up to 400 μg/100 g body weight (day) failed to elicit a response in the weanling rat, but relatively small doses ($<$3 μg) elicited a response in the sexually mature animal. NIH-FSH-S4 (which had extremely little effect on development of prostatic weight in males) produced a marked increase in uterine weight (Fig. 13). This indicated that induction of gonadal production of steroids was controlled differently in the two sexes. Precocious sexual maturation has often been produced by a variety of central nervous system alterations, such as exposure to constant light and anterior hypothalamic lesions in the female rat but to our knowledge has not been reported in the male. Also, precocious puberty in humans is usually a "functional" disturbance in girls,

TABLE 5.   Per cent change in serum testosterone

Days of age	10	21	41	62
		Per cent increase over controls		
Dose of LH[a] μg/100 g BW (day)				
0.3	99[b]	132± 9	100	277±136
1.0	151	132± 18	130± 14	150± 41
3.0	174	633±139	200± 62	237± 47
10.0	190	612± 73	631± 233	1038±384
30.0	277	760± 98	2260±1175	1583± 95

[a] NIH-LH-B5.

[b] For the 10-day animals blood from groups of 10 animals were pooled. The 10-day values are the average of 2 such groups (total 20 animals). Thus no SE is given.

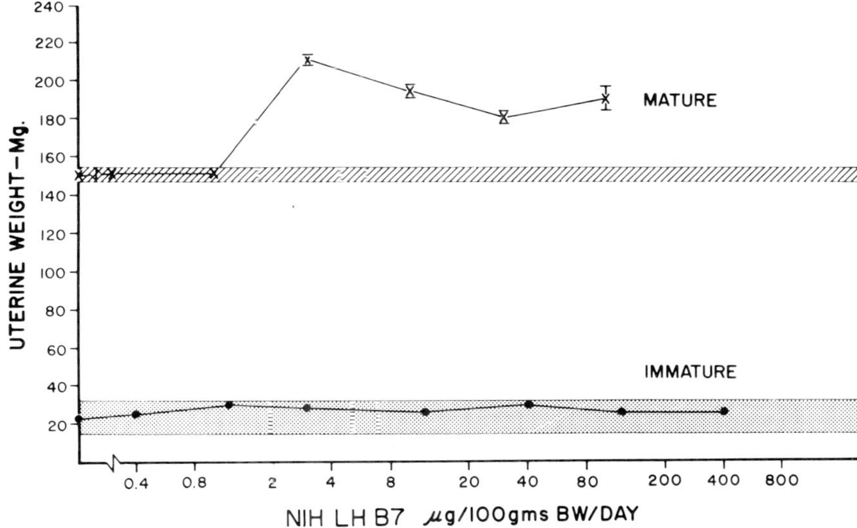

FIG. 12   Effects of NIH-LH-B7 on uterine weight in the 5-day hypophysectomized 21-day-old and sexually mature female rat. Shaded areas enclose the 95 per cent limits of saline injected controls. Brackets enclose SE. From Odell & Swerdloff, in preparation.

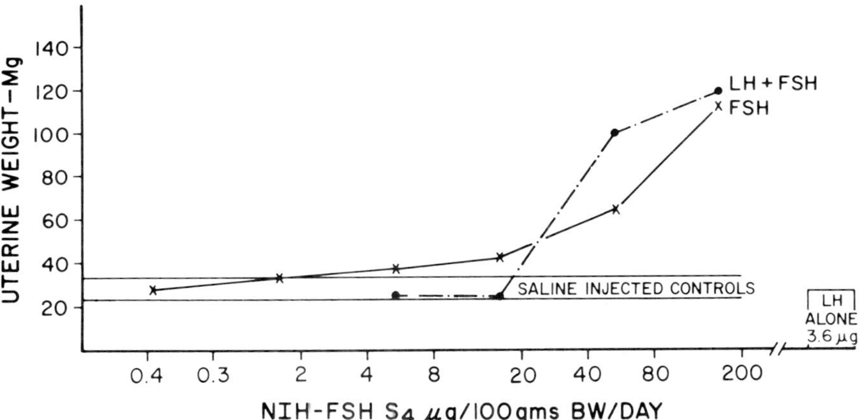

FIG. 13.   Effects of NIH-FSH-S4 on uterine weight in the 5-day hypophysectomized, sexually immature female rat. Shaded areas enclose the 95 per cent limits of saline-injected controls; brackets enclose SE. All animals were hypophysectomized at 21 days of age and treatment was initiated 5 days later: X describes groups of animals that received FSH alone in the doses indicated; ● depicts animals that received 3.6 μg/100 g body weight/day NIH-LH-B7, plus FSH in the doses indicated. (This dose produced a maximal response in mature animals.) The box to the right shows that no response to LH given alone in this dose was observed, nor were there additive or synergistic effects of FSH on LH action. From Odell & Swerdloff, in preparation.

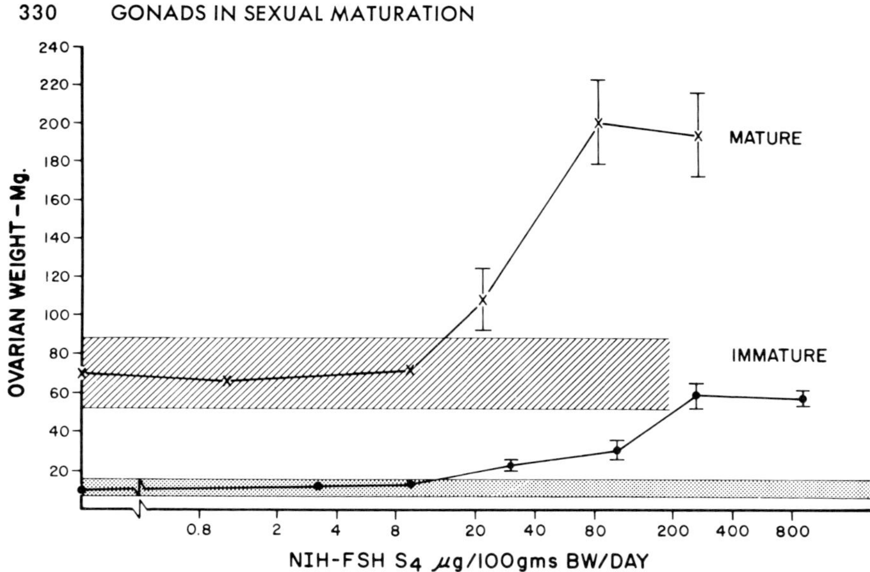

FIG. 14. The ovarian weight response to NIH-FSH-S4 in sexually immature (21-day-old) and sexually mature (75-day-old) 5-day-hypophysectomized female rats. Note the similar minimal effective dose in both age groups. From Odell & Swerdloff, in preparation.

whereas in boys it is most commonly produced by mass lesions, often CNS neoplasms.

The ovarian weight response in 21-day-old and sexually mature female rats is shown in Fig. 14. No differences were observed between the 2 groups.

SUMMARY

We concluded the following about rats: (1) the testis in the total absence of FSH effects will not produce androgens in response to LH stimulation; (2) the LH-unresponsive testis may be made responsive by prolonged administration of FSH; (3) a time-response relationship exists for the testis and constant doses of LH produce progressively greater effects related to duration of FSH pretreatment; (4) these effects (1 to 3) may explain sexual maturation in the male rat; (5) the ovary in the total absence of FSH effects will not produce estrogens in response to LH stimulation, but FSH alone will stimulate estrogen production; (6) sexual maturation in the female may be controlled differently than in the male.

It is not known whether gonadal responsiveness to LH stimulation is a factor in sexual maturation in the human, for comparable studies have not been performed. It is known that the testis and the ovary in children do respond to exogenous or to tumor-produced gonadotropin. However, relative sensitivities to such stimulation have not been determined for adults and children. Winter and Faiman (1971) reported that FSH concentrations in girls 0 to 2 years old were higher than in girls 4 to 9 years. They also reported that FSH and LH fell progressively in girls between 0 and 8 years of age. No similar data for boys were presented but those for girls provide intriguing support for our hypothesis.

REFERENCES

Burr, I. M., Sizoneko, P. C., Kaplan, S. L., & Grumbach, M. M. (1970). Hormonal changes in puberty I: correlation of serum luteinizing hormone and follicle stimulating hormone with stages of puberty, testicular size, and bone age in normal boys. *Pediat. Res.* **4**, 25–35.

Byrnes, W. W. & Meyer, R. K. (1951). The inhibition of gonadotrophic hormone secretion by physiological doses of estrogen. *Endocrinology* **48**, 133–136.

Guyda, H. J., Johanson, A. J., Migeon, C., & Blizzard, R. M. (1969). Determination of serum luteinizing hormone (SLH) by radioimmunoassay in disorders of adolescent sexual development. *Pediat. Res.* **3**, 538–544.

Johnson, B. H. & Ewing, L. L. (1971). Follicle-stimulating hormone and the regulation of testosterone secretion in rabbit testes. *Science* **173**, 635–637.

Johnson, D. C. (1966). The use of non-castrate parabiotic rats for evaluation of plasma gonadotrophins. *Acta Endocrinol.* **51**, 269–280.

Kallas, H. (1929). Puberte precoce par paraboise. *C.R.Soc.Biol. (Paris)* **100**, 979-980.

Kelch, R. P., Grumbach, M. M., & Kaplan, S. L. (1972). Studies on the mechanism of puberty in man. In *Gonadotropins*, B. B. Saxena, C. G. Beling, & H. M. Gandy, Eds., Wiley, New York, pp. 524.

Kulin, H. E., Grumbach, M. M., & Kaplan, S. L. (1969). Changing sensitivity of the pubertal gonadal hypothalamic feedback mechanism in man. *Science* **166**, 1012–1013.

Kulin, H. E., Grumbach, M. M., & Kaplan, S. L. (1972). Gonadal-hypothalamic interaction in prepubertal and puberal man: effect of clomiphene citrate on urinary follicle-stimulating hormone and luteinizing hormone and plasma testosterone. *Pediat. Res.* **6**, 162–171.

Kulin, H. E., Rifkind, A. B., Ross, G. T., & Odell, W. D. (1967). Total gonadotropin activity in the urine of prepubertal children. *Clin. Endocrinol.* **27**, 1123-1128.

Lostroh, A. J. (1969). Regulation by FSH and ICSH (LH) of reproductive function in the immature male rat. *Endocrinology* **85**, 438–445.

Odell, W. D., Hescox, M. A., & Kiddy, C. A. (1970). Studies of hypothalamic-pituitary-gonadal interrelations in prepubertal cattle. In *Gonadotrophins and Ovarion Development*, W. R. Butt, A. C. Crooke, & M. Ryle, Eds., Livingstone, Edinburgh, pp. 371–385.

Odell, W. D. & Ross, G. T. (1966). Some aspects of the physiology of human luteinizing hormone as determined by radioimmunoassay. *J. Clin. Invest.* **45**, 1052.

Odell, W. D., Ross, G. T., & Rayford, P. L. (1967). Radioimmunoassay for luteinizing hormone in human plasma or serum: physiologic studies. *J. Clin. Invest.* **46**, 248–255.

Odell, W. D. & Swerdloff, R. S. (1974). The gonadal sensitivity to LH and FSH in female rats during sexual maturation. In preparation.

Odell, W. D. & Swerdloff, R. S. (1973). FSH modulation of sensitivity to LH-stimulation of testosterone secretion: role in sexual maturation. *Program of the Endocrine Soc.,* p. A-95 (abstract).

Odell, W. D., Swerdloff, R. S., Jacobs, H. S. & Hescox, M. A. (1973). FSH induction of LH sensitivity: one cause of sexual maturation in the male rat. *Endocrinology,* **92,** 160–165.

Penny, R. Guyda, H. J., Baghdassarian, A., Johanson, A. J., & Blizzard, R. M. (1970). Correlation of serum follicular stimulating hormone (FSH) and luteinizing hormone (LH) as measured by radioimmunoassay and disorders of sexual development. *J. Clin. Invest.* **49,** 1847–1852.

Raiti, S., Johanson, A., Light, C., Migeon, C. J., & Blizzard, R. M. (1969). Measurement of immunologically reactive follicle-stimulating hormone in serum of normal male children and adults. *Metabolism* **18,** 234–240.

Ramirez, V. D. & McCann, S. M. (1965). Inhibitory effect of testosterone on luteinizing hormone secetion in immature and adult rats. *Endocrinology* **76,** 412–417.

Sizonenko, P. C., Burr, I. M., Kaplan, S. L., & Grumbach, M. M. (1970). Hormonal changes in puberty. II. Correlation of serum luteinizing hormone and follicle stimulating hormone with stages of puberty and bone age in normal girls. *Pediat. Res.* **4,** 36–45.

Swerdloff, R. S., Jacobs, H. J. & Odell, W. R. (1972). Hypothalamic-pituitary-gonadal interrelationships in the rat during sexual maturation. In *Gonadotropins,* B. B. Saxena, C. G. Beling & H. M. Gandy, Eds. Wiley, New York, pp. 546–561.

Swerdloff, R. S., Jacobs, H. J., & Odell, W. D. (1974). Hypothalamic pituitary axis during sexual maturation in the female rat. In preparation.

Swerdloff, R. S., Walsh, P. C., Jacobs, H. S., & Odell, W. D. (1971). Serum LH and FSH during sexual maturation in the male rat: effect of castration and cryptorchidism. *Endocrinology* **88,** 120–128.

Walsh, P. C., Swerdloff, R. S., & Odell, W. D. (1973). Feedback control of FSH in the male: role of estrogen. *Acta Endocrinol.* **74,** 449–460.

Wieland, R. G., Yen, S. S. C., & Pohlman, C. (1970). Serum testosterone levels and testosterone binding affinity in prepubertal and adolescent males; correlation with gonadotropins. *Amer. J. Med. Sci.* **259,** 358–360.

Wiesner, B. P. (1932). Effects of early oophorectomy in rats. *J. Physiol.* **75,** 39P (abstract.)

Wiesner, B. P. (1932). Post-natal development of the genital organs in the albino rat with discussion of a new theory of sexual differentiation. *J. Brit. Ob. Gyn. Br. Comm.* **41,** 867–922.

Winter, J. S. D., & Faiman, C. (1971). Pituitary-gonadal axis in the female child during infancy and at puberty. *Pediat. Res.* **5,** 401 (abstract).

Yen, S. S. C., Vicic, W. J., & Kearchner, D. V. (1969). Gonadotropin levels in puberty: I. Serum luteinizing hormone. *J. Clin. Endocrinol.* **29,** 382–385.

Yen, S. S. C. & Vicic, W. J. (1970). Serum follicle-stimulating hormone levels in puberty. *Amer. J. Ob. Gyn.* **106,** 134-137.

DISCUSSION

Dr. BLOCH.   How is FSH really working in the testes? How is FSH working on the tubule? Maybe Dr. Steinberger could make some comment on that. Also what is the relationship between FSH and the Leydig cell? Why, in our experiments, don't we see a very marked change in LH levels around the time of puberty in rats? Maybe FSH is primarily responsible for testicular maturation in rats at the time of puberty. Dr. Odell's observation about positive changes with estrogen is similar to the results seen in males. Three different groups of male rats, 10, 40, and 70 days old, respectively, were castrated and subsequently injected with graded doses of testosterone propionate. They were injected daily for 10 days, then killed for determination of serum LH levels. With low doses of testosterone propionate there was a positive effect on levels of LH about twice as high as castrate levels in pubertal 40-day-old animals killed at 50 days, as well as in the adult rats. These results are similar to those reported by Dr. Odell in the female. With that type of injection and that kind of timing there were clear differences in the negative feedback information. The 20-day-old rats had normal levels of LH with injections of 12 μg/100 g body weight testosterone propionate; the pubertal and adult rats required somewhere between 50 and 100 μg to suppress LH back to intact levels. Perhaps the main difference is that we started injections on the day of castration and injected for 10 days.

Dr. ODELL.   At the moment we do not know what FSH is doing to the testes. One can hypothesize, of course, that there actually is a change in receptor formation for LH in the Leydig cell.

Dr. SIZONENKO.   We have been studying hCG response in cryptorchidism and in hypopituitarism. Testosterone and plasma FSH concentrations are represented in Fig. 15 before the injection of hCG. There is a correlation between the FSH levels and the basal testosterone levels. Three days after the injection of 5000 IU/m^2 hCG the testosterone response correlated with the FSH levels on day 0 (Fig. 16). We found no correlation between day 0 testosterone and basal LH, nor between the testosterone response to hCG and basal LH. The second study on hypopituitarism was performed with Drs. Rappaport and Dray from Paris. In some cases of hypopituitarism there is only a slight response of testosterone to hCG. Among 14 hypopituitary patients whose bone age was above 13 years, 4 responded markedly to hCG after 10 days (Fig. 17). The FSH levels were between 2.2 and 6.9 mU/ml. In the middle group (4 cases who had low basal levels of testosterone but who demonstrated a good response to hCG)

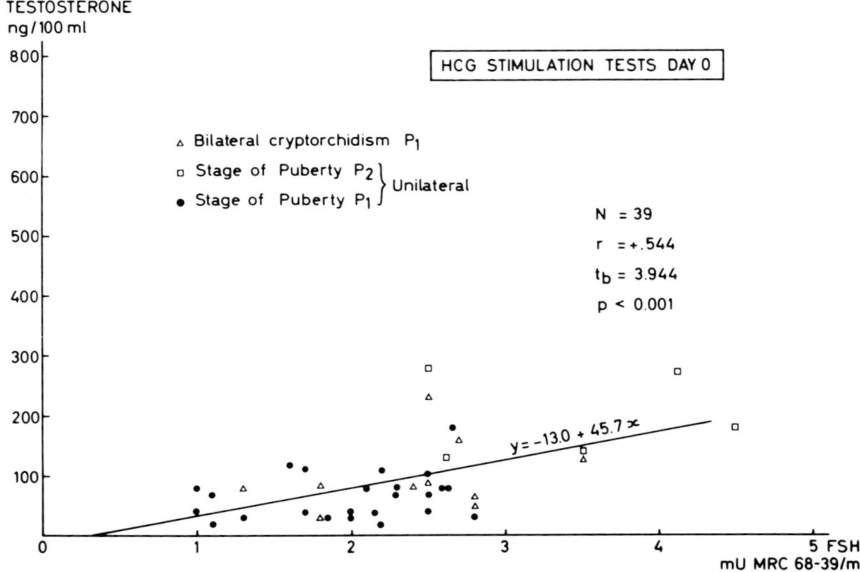

FIG. 15.   Correlation of plasma testosterone and FSH levels on day 0, before the injection of hCG.

the FSH levels were between 1.3 and 3.8 mU/ml. The last 6 cases had low basal levels of testosterone and 10 days afterward still had the same low levels. The FSH levels were between 0.5 and 1.2 mU/ml. There was no correlation with the LH values. We studied 10 more cases of hypopituitarism (Fig. 18), altogether 24, and found a good correlation between the testosterone response to hCG and the basal concentrations of plasma FSH. No such correlation was observed with the LH. This strongly suggests that FSH plays an important mediating role in the secretion of testosterone in humans.

DR. ODELL.   There is one other publication that also bears on this hypothesis: Johnson and Ewing (1971) perfused the rabbit testes in vivo and showed that LH alone increases testosterone production to one level of maximal response, but when they added FSH to the LH there was a prompt and much greater increase in androgen production.

DR. VAN WYK.   Drs. Nayfeh, Baggett, French, Coffey, and Strickland in our laboratory have reported a series of observations on the maturation of steroidogenesis in the rat. They observed that if testes from a prepubescent rat (between 20 and 40 days) are incubated with labeled precursors, such as progesterone or cholesterol, virtually no testosterone is found in the incubation at the end of 3 hours. Under similar conditions, using testes from the newborn period or after maturity, considerable amounts of the precursor are recovered as testosterone.

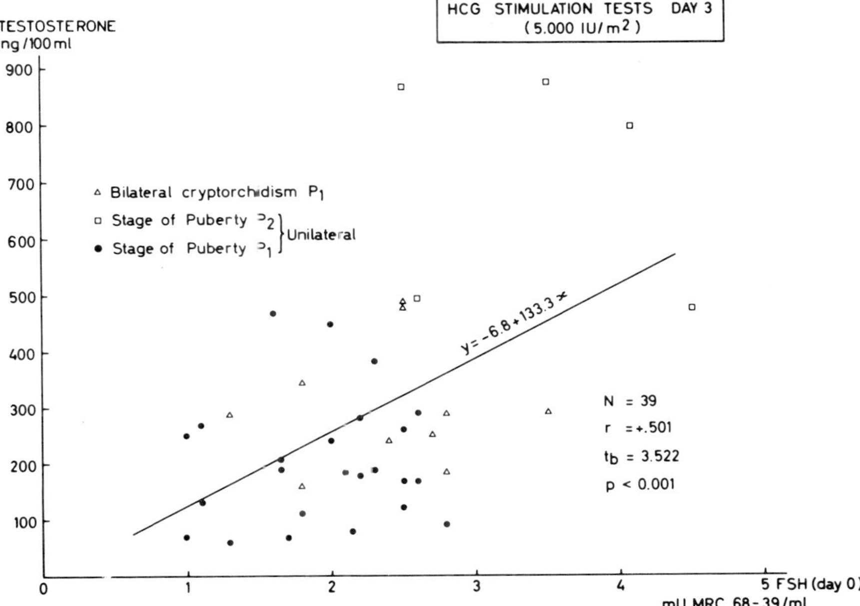

FIG. 16. Correlation of plasma testosterone concentrations on day 3 (after the administration of hCG) and the basal (day 0) FSH levels.

These prepubescent testes are not metabolically inert, however, since they metabolize fully as much labeled precursor as the mature testes. Analysis of the incubation mixture reveals large quantities of androstenediol. If the incubation period is shortened to 15 minutes, however, it is possible to find traces of testosterone. If, in addition, one puts in a trap with unlabeled testosterone, it is possible to demonstrate that the production of testosterone is almost as vigorous during the prepubescent period as in the adult. The failure of secretion, therefore, is due to a very active reductase in the immature testis. Thus male adolescence might be viewed as the loss of 5α-reductase activity. Similar data have been obtained by Dr. Steinberger and by some workers in Japan; these collective observations fit well with what you have been saying. Whether the loss of reductase activity at puberty is brought about by stimulation with gonadotropic hormones has not been studied in our laboratory. It would fit your hypothesis very nicely if it could be shown that the loss of this reductase is related to a rise in FSH superimposed on already substantial LH levels.

Dr. Odell.   That would be an attractive alternative mode of FSH action. One would expect under those circumstances, though, to see Leydig cell hypertrophy in response to the LH stimulation in the kinds of animals we are treating. So far we do not see that.

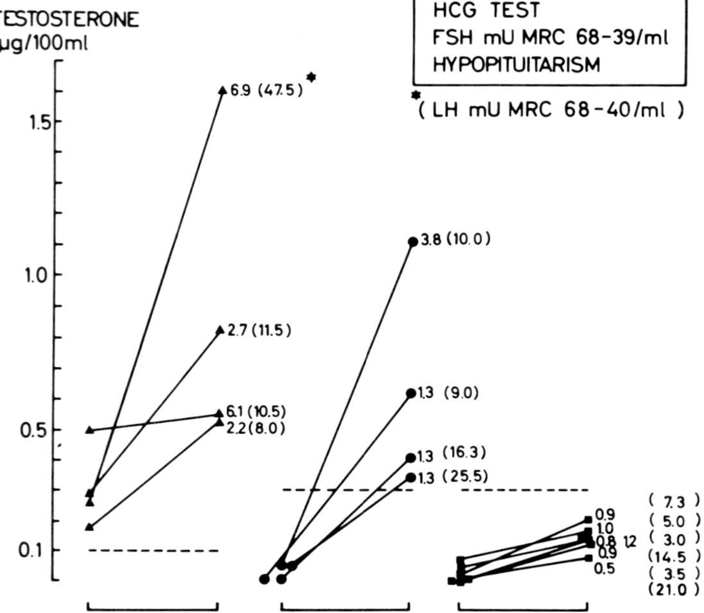

FIG. 17.   Testosterone responses to hCG stimulation in 14 boys with hypopituitarism and bone age of more than 13 years. Plasma FSH concentrations were plotted without brackets. Plasma LH values are enclosed in brackets.

DR. VAN WYK.   I don't know what cells are carrying out steroidogenesis in the prepubescent rat testis because there are no visibly differentiated Leydig cells. Before I was aware of these observations I thought that fully differentiated Leydig cells were needed in order to have steroidogenesis. Obviously this is wrong.

DR. ODELL.   Perhaps steroidogenesis could be going on somewhere else at this period of time.

DR. STEINBERGER.   I do not think that the testicle is a reservoir of testosterone and that if you add LH it opens up the faucet and lets testosterone flow. For the last 6 years or so we have studied the changes in the androgen pathways in the developing testis. From day 1 to 20 there is a marked drop in the capacity of the testis to convert the precursors to testosterone. As mentioned by Dr. Van Wyk, the testis is not quiescent by any means. As a matter of fact, it metabolizes various precursors avidly. But the major metabolites are a group of 5α-reduced androgens, one being testosterone, the other 5α-androstenediol. Initially the ratio of androstenediol to testosterone is greater than 1; as maturation progresses it reverses, which supports the old data of Linder in the bull, who showed that the ratio of androstenediol to testosterone in cattle is reversed. If you look at mature animals with gonadotropins, what happens to the path-

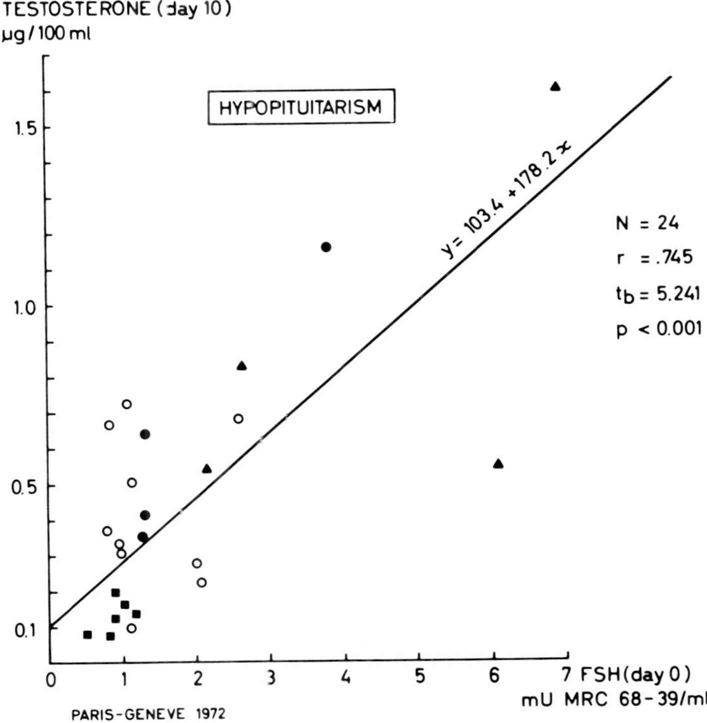

FIG. 18. Correlation of plasma testosterone concentrations observed on day 10 and basal (day 0) plasma FSH levels in 24 hypopituitary boys. Closed signs refer to the 14 subjects presented in Fig. 17; open circles to the 10 other patients.

ways? First of all, in the newborn control the testis converts about half the precursors to testosterone; this pattern is similar to that found in the adult— almost indistinguishable. In a 20-day-old testis, on the other hand, very little testosterone is formed, and the major metabolite is 5α-androstenediol. If the animal is treated from day 10 with hCG, there still is no accumulation of testosterone. (Incidentally, these animals show marked hypertrophy of the Leydig cells; as a matter of fact, at 20 days the testicle is almost like a Leydig cell gland.) Evidently changes in the enzymes must be under some control that is not gonadotropin control. Maybe inborn inscribed information dictates that the testis has to undergo a certain form of maturation before it will respond to gonadotropin.

DR. ODELL.   What was the gonadotropin you used?

DR. STEINBERGER.   It was hCG; we did not try FSH.

DR. WINTER.   Boys in whom the only sign of puberty is early testicular en- largement (presumably FSH-mediated) show a greater serum testosterone rise following short-term hCG stimulation than prepubertal boys (Winter, Taraska, & Faiman, 1972). This would support Dr. Odell's thesis of increasing gonadal sensitivity to gonadotropin stimulation as a feature of normal puberty. We cannot, however, conclude that the initiation of puberty results solely from such a mechanism. We know that FSH and LH levels rise during human puberty. Furthermore, we have observed that even agonadal children demonstrate a significant elevation in serum FSH and LH levels around age 12. This is proof that at least part of the mechanism for the initiation of puberty can operate in the absence of a functioning gonad.

DR. ODELL.   There is something else going on in the human but it does not strictly bear on the rat data. We have heard that the response to castration in the human between the years, say, 2 to 10 is different prepubertally than it is postpubertally; yet those differences do not exist in most of the animal models that have been studied. So it is almost as if there were the insertion of some new aspect for a period of time in the human in which the tonic control is altered. There is no such counterpart in any animal life that I know.

DR. WEISZ.   In the female as well as in the male, underlying what we call "responsiveness," there must be a sequence of maturational changes involving cellular differentiation. These in turn must involve changes in the biochemical machinery. As far as the rat ovary is concerned there are no biochemcial data comparable to what we have on the male testis. However, if we look at the morphological changes that the rat ovary undergoes between day 1 and puberty, it is quite clear that when you stimulate 10-, 20-, or 30-day-old ovaries, you are really dealing with quite different tissues. At 10 days of age only the interstitial tissue looks steroidogenic. By 20 days there are follicles, including the theca interna that look steroidogenic, though histochemically they differ somewhat from the follicles of the mature rat. By 30 days the ovary looks very much more like that of a mature animal except, of course, that it lacks corpora lutea. Therefore just to talk in terms of responsiveness is a first step. We will have to define the underlying morphological and biochemical maturational changes and the way that our interference (shoving in hormones at the wrong time and in the wrong amounts) modifies the course of differentiation.

DR. GAY.   It seemed to me, Dr. Odell, that the effective dose for your FSH injections was about 200 μg, whereas the effective dose for LH was somewhere between 1 and 10 μg. If your preparations, like the NIH preparations, have a 1 or 2 per cent contamination of LH in the FSH, it follows that 200 μg of FSH may contain as much as 4 μg of LH. Have you any data to suggest that the LH contamination of the FSH was not an important stimulus for the testes?

DR. ODELL.   There is LH contamination of the NIH-FSH preparation to a small degree, but any doses of FSH that we could administer to the male did not stimulate testosterone production, which indicates that LH was unimportant in that context. Now that doesn't mean that if we gave 10 times as much we would not detect it in the intact animal, but it wasn't effective under the conditions of our studies.

DR. SNIPES.   It seems that the guinea pig uses a much simpler method of changing the production of testosterone by shifting the steady-state equilibrium between androstenedione and testosterone. This can be demonstrated by incubating minces of testes with androstenedione or testosterone (Figs. 19 and 20). The equilibrium lies far toward testosterone in the adult and at the weaker androstenedione in the immature animal (Becker & Snipes, 1968).

DR. SCHWARTZ.   I am pleased to see a link up between the high FSH value and the potentiality of gonadal response to FSH. We have been puzzled by our inability in adult animals to alter gonadal structure or function with anti-FSH-serum, whereas we could easily do so with anti-LH-serum. We predicted that this would be so because in a mature animal FSH has already done what it is going to do with the most mature gametes and it would take a long time afterward to demonstrate a lack. We carried out an experiment ranging over the ages of your experiment but using a rather different technique. Everything confirms that FSH is important in both males and females during this prepubertal age.

DR. DAVIDSON.   What, in your opinion, causes the high FSH levels in early prepubertal life in the male? Do you think, perhaps, that there is a differential feedback sensitivity situation then, opposite to the one we have been discussing, in the sense that the pituitary is less sensitive at that time to feedback effects, at least from the point of view of FSH?

DR. ODELL.   We do not know whether it is a change in sensitivity or, alternatively, a system that is operating maximally without feedback suppression and that becomes "engaged" later.

DR. JOHNSON.   I wanted to make a point of the fact that these measurements of FSH and LH give only mean values. Obviously, the mean concentration can be modified by amplitude or frequency modulation of periodic gonadotropin output. We already know that if you take away the gonads the frequency of pulsations of gonadotropins increases; this raises the mean level. If you give a steroid you may lower the frequency and therefore lower the mean. The high level in the prepubertal animal would imply a high frequency of discharge of gonadotropin. If you give a steroid, for example, you reduce the mean level and produce 1 cyclic daily surge of FSH for 4 days. This does nothing to puberty. If you give 2 injections of testosterone 48 hours apart then you get 8 days of 1 cycle per day of FSH release and puberty will be advanced. If you give estradiol, you get a 48-hour periodicity in FSH release; this for 4 times will also advance puberty but you will have lowered the mean concentration of FSH. If you put diurnally active animals into constant light, you also lengthen periodicity; this leads to advanced puberty. If you put them into constant darkness, this shortens periodicity and delays the onset of puberty. One could make a case for the concept that lengthening the periodicity of gonatropic discharge is the basis for the onset of puberty.

DR. ODELL.   You must mean that these studies were done in females with testosterone and estradiol, not in males?

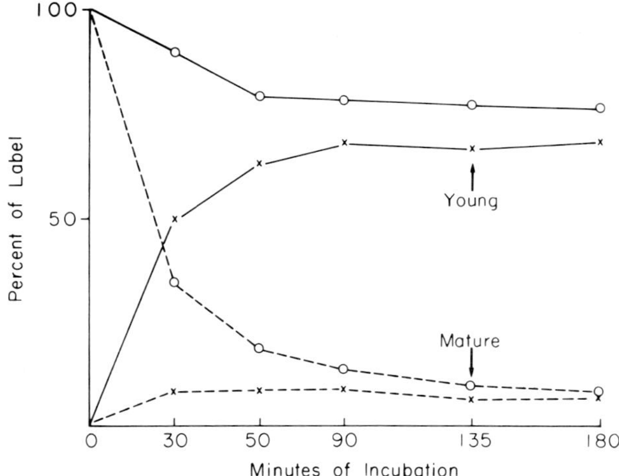

FIG. 19. Percentage of label in androstenedione after incubation of minces of guinea-pig testes with ^{14}C–androstenedione (o) or ^{14}C–testosterone (x) for several intervals. All points are means of incubation of two lots of minces of testes. From Becker & Snipes, 1968.

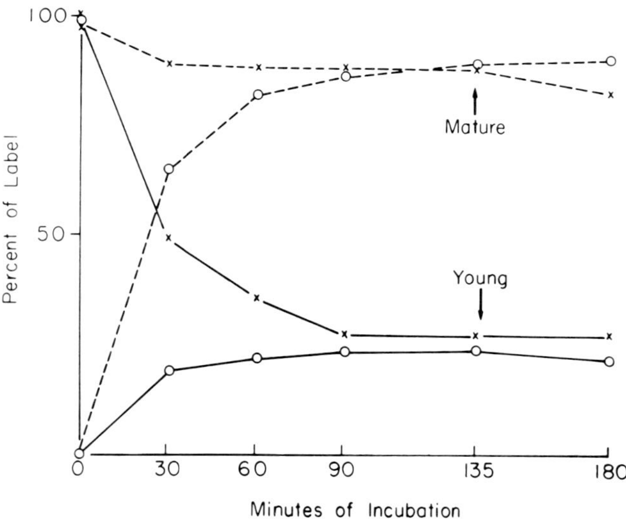

FIG. 20. Percentage of label in testosterone after incubation of minces of guinea-pig testes with ^{14}C–androstenedione (o) or ^{14}C–testosterone (x) for several intervals. All points are means of incubation of two lots of minces of testes. From Becker & Snipes, 1968.

Dr. Johnson.   That is right, but you could come to the same conclusion with a male, because if you see a fall in FSH as testosterone appears it could also be due to a frequency modulation; a reduction in the frequency is therefore a reduction in the mean concentration.

Dr. Goldman.   Several years ago Dr. R. K. Meyer and I carried out some experiments in which we administered continuous intravenous infusion of gonadotropin preparations to immature (primarily female) rats, both intact and hypophysectomized. When we infused an FSH preparation (NIH-FSH-S3) similar to the one you used, we observed increases in ovarian weight. We obtained these increases with much smaller doses of FSH by intravenous infusion, compared with twice daily injections. However, we felt very strongly, from looking at the results, that the amount of LH contamination was a limiting factor in stimulating ovarian growth. This is not to say that the FSH is not also essential; we felt that the LH needed to be there. In interpreting your data it might be interesting to see what would happen if you used FSH preparations that had different amounts of LH contamination. I think that LH as well as FSH probably will enter into the picture in ovarian growth in the prepubertal animals.

Dr. Kulin.   With the limited methodology we have available, the tendency for all of us is to jump for joy when we see a rise in some hormone at the time of puberty. The most obvious example is the increase in FSH, which now seems to be clearly associated with the first change in testicular size. We should be more cautious. In the human there is plenty of FSH around in the prepubertal period. An LH rise, even though we do not see it, may well be the first physiologically significant hormonal increment that acts to increase intratesticular testosterone.

Dr. Odell.   We are not denying that FSH is circulating in the human or the rat before puberty. That may be why intact animals respond to LH in the first place. We postulate that without any FSH they might not respond to LH at all.

REFERENCES

Becker, W. G. & Snipes, C. A. (1968). Shift with age in steady-state concentrations of androstenedione and testosterone in incubations of guinea-pig testis. *Biochem. J.* **107**, 35–41.

Johnson, B. H. & Ewing, L. L. (1971). Follicle-stimulating hormone and testosterone in rabbit testes. *Science* **173**, 635–637.

Shore, L. S. & Snipes, C. A. (1971). Metabolism of testosterone in vitro by hypothalamus and other areas of a rat brain. *Fed. Proc.* **30**, 363.

Winter, J. S. D., Tarasaka, S., & Faiman, C. (1972). The hormonal response to HCG stimulation in male children and adolescents, *J. Clin. Endocrinol.* **34**, 348–354.

12.

The Interrelationship of Steroids, Growth Hormone, and Other Hormones on Pubertal Growth

R. M. BLIZZARD, R. G. THOMPSON, A. BAGHDASSARIAN,
A. KOWARSKI, C. J. MIGEON, and A. RODRIGUEZ

The growth spurt of the adolescent has been well described by several
observers, including Tanner (1962) and Gallagher (1966). The characteristically greater growth spurt of males has been attributed to testosterone,
a growth-promoting hormone which contrasts with growth-inhibiting estrogen. The mechanism by which testosterone acts and its interrelationship
with the production and action of GH has been studied extensively in
animals but not in humans. This chapter presents preliminary data concerning this interrelationship, relates them to the onset of puberty, compares the findings in humans with those reported in animals, and considers
the observations concerning thyroxine, FSH, and cortisol production

---

Abbreviations

FSH	Follicle stimulating hormone
GH	Growth hormone
GHPR	Growth hormone production rate
hGH	Human growth hormone
ICGH	Integrated concentration growth hormone
MCR	Metabolic clearance rate

reported by others in relation to normal and abnormal adolescent development.

METHODS

Thirty-seven adult women between 23 and 62 years of age and 16 adult men between 31 and 71 years of age volunteered for this study on GH production. Ten women were receiving oral contraceptives and five were postmenopausal. All volunteers were in good health and receiving no medication except for the contraceptives. Five adult women volunteered to return for repeat studies after receiving prednisone 20 mg t.i.d. for 6 days before and during repeat testing. Five more returned while receiving prednisone 60 mg in 1 dose every other day. These women had studies of GH production on two consecutive days, initially on the day when prednisone was taken, and the following day when no medication was given.

Seventeen normal boys between 7 and 16 years of age and 10 normal girls between 8 and 13 years of age had GH integrated concentrations determined. X-rays were taken on all subjects for skeletal maturation, and all boys had plasma testosterone determined. Five more boys with a diagnosis of constitutional delay of growth and adolescence were studied to evaluate the role of GH in this diagnosis. The one boy who was treated with testosterone had studies before and after testosterone. Three documented GH-deficient patients also were studied, two 9- and 14-year-old boys, and the 32-year-old, GH-deficient mother of the 14-year-old GH-deficient boy.

The insignificant excretion of immunoreactive GH in urine described by Bala and Beck (1971) has prevented the application of this method to the measurement of the GH production rate. Tait's (1963) constant intravenous infusion method has been used by Cameron, Burger, Catt, and Daig (1969), Taylor, Finster, and Mintz (1969), and MacGillivray, Frohman, and Doe (1970) to determine the metabolic clearance rate (MCR) of GH. Although the 24-hour rate of production of GH can be determined if both the MCR and the mean 24-hour concentration of GH are known, the rapid fluctuation of GH in plasma makes the use of a single determination of GH meaningless for the calculation of its production. Frequent collections of samples for GH determination over short periods of time, as used by Taylor et al (1969) and MacGillivray et al (1970), will approximate its production only over that time and does not necessarily represent accurate production over a 24-hour period.

We used the recently developed constant withdrawal pump of Kowarski, Thompson, Migeon, and Blizzard (1971) to determine the integrated concentrations of growth hormone (ICGH) over a 24-hour period. The samples were assayed for GH by the double antibody technique described by Schalch and Parker (1964). The GH standard (GH HS 1394*), which was used for all determinations, has growth activity of 2.0 IU/mg.

The production rate of GH can be determined if the ICGH and the MCR of GH are known. The MCR, utilizing ^{131}I-hGH, was determined by the method described by Kowarski et al (1971). The validity of this technique was demonstrated by showing that the MCR of GH is not different from labeled GH, that it does not alter with changing concentrations of GH, and changes only minimally with normal ambulation. Taylor et al (1969) demonstrated that the MCR of GH has no diurnal variation. The production rate was calculated by multiplying the MCR in milliliters per minute by the ICGH in nanograms per milliliter to give the production rate in nanograms per minute. The actual amount of GH produced during each withdrawal period was then calculated by multiplying the MCR by ICGH by the time of collection.

To evaluate the effect of testosterone on pubertal growth when GH and gonadotropin deficiency was present 13 male patients (11 with idiopathic hypopituitarism and 2 with organic hypopituitarism which had resulted from removal of craniopharyngiomas) received orally 10 to 30 mg methyltestosterone per day or 200 to 300 mg of testosterone enanthate intramuscularly every 3 to 4 weeks until epiphyseal fusion was obtained. Skeletal maturation was assessed by the Wilkins (1965) method. None of the patients received GH; however, thyroxine and cortisol were administered in physiologic replacement doses when indicated.

The effect of GH on growth in a hypothyroid child was determined by administering 2.5 mg of Wilhelmi GH daily for 6 months to a 9.5-year-old girl with acquired hypothyroidism. Thyroxine was not given during that period, although it was administered after GH was discontinued. Testosterone determinations were made by the method described by Tremblay, Beitins, Kowarski, and Migeon (1970).

RESULTS

The mean 24-hour ICGH's in normal adults are shown in Fig. 1. The mean in premenopausal females of 3.0 ng/ml ± 1.6 (SD) is significantly lower ($p<0.005$) than the mean of 6.6 ± 2.9 for women taking oral contraceptives. The mean for postmenopausal females of 1.5 ± 0.75 is significantly lower ($p<0.05$) than that of premenopausal females on no medication. Normal males (age 30 to 50) also had significantly lower ($p<0.01$) ICGH (mean 1.8 ± 1.0) than the premenopausal females who were not taking birth control pills.

Growth hormone production rates (GHPR) show similar differences

* Prepared by Dr. Alfred Wilhelmi for the National Pituitary Agency.

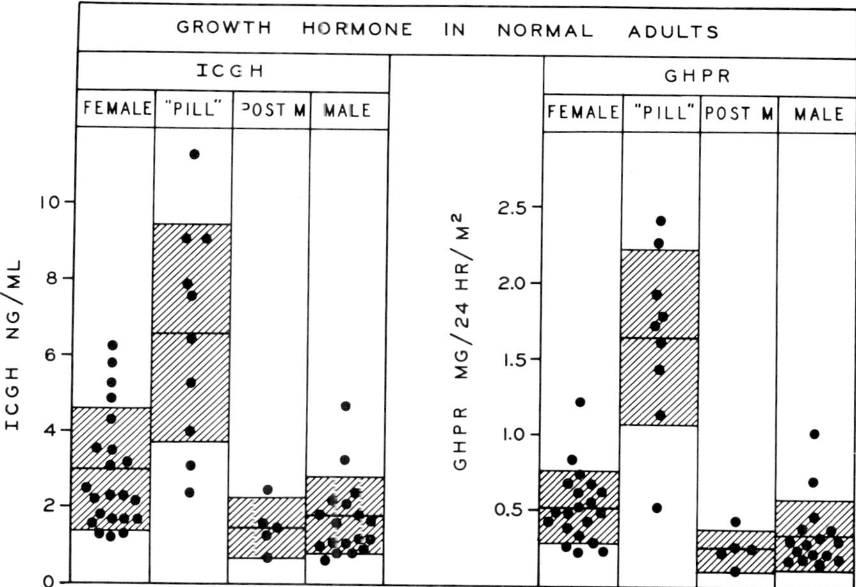

FIG. 1. The ICGH and GHPR in the 4 groups of normal adults: premenopausal females on no medication (female); women taking oral contraceptives (pill); postmenopausal females (post-M); and normal males (30 to 50 years of age). The shaded areas represent mean ± 1 SD.

among the 4 groups of adults in Fig. 1. Premenopausal females on no medication have a mean of 0.52 mg/24 hr (M²) ±0.24 (SD), significantly lower ($p<0.005$) than the mean of 1.65 ±0.58 for the women on oral contraceptives, and significantly higher than the mean of 0.26 ±0.12 ($p<0.025$) for postmenopausal females and the mean of 0.35 ±0.23 ($p<0.025$) for adult males.

The effect of two dose schedules of prednisone on the MCR, the ICGH, and the GHPR are expressed as percentage changes when patients received two different schedules of prednisone (Fig. 2). Prednisone in a dose of 20 mg t.i.d. for 7 days resulted in a decrease of ICGH from a mean of 5.75 ng/ml to 2.5 ($p<0.05$) and a decrease of GHPR from 2.1 to 0.74 mg/24 hr ($p<0.025$). Prednisone in a single 60 mg dose given every other day results in less consistent reduction of GH production. The mean ICGH of 3.1 ng/ml on the day following prednisone was significantly lower ($p<0.025$) than the control of 4 9 ng/ml, whereas the mean of 3.9 ng/ml for the day of prednisone was not statistically different. The mean GHPR's for the 3 collection periods (control 1.45, day of prednisone 1.28, and day of no medication 0.7 mg/24 hr) are not statistically different, although a trend toward decreased production is evident.

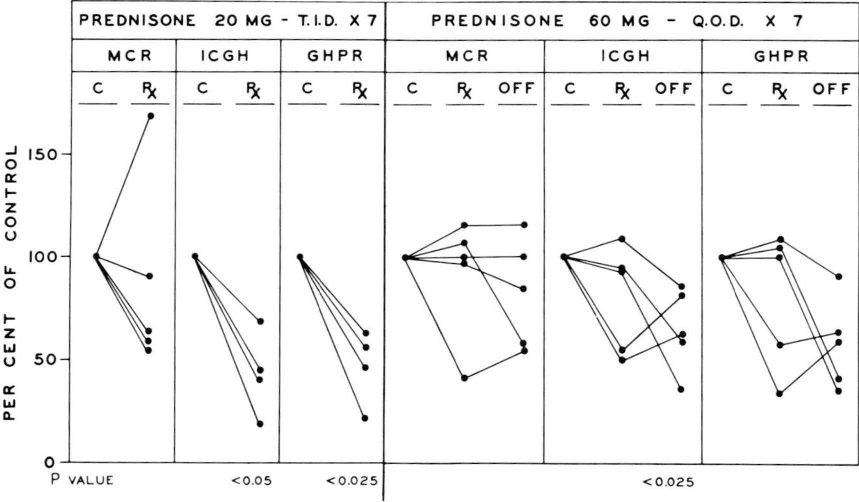

FIG. 2.   The effect of 2 different dose schedules of prednisone on MCR, ICGH, and GHPR. Control studies (C) are plotted as 100 per cent and values from days of medication (Rx) and the day after the q. o. d. dose (OFF) are shown as per cent ages of the control values. P values are shown only when statistically different from control.

Seventeen normal boys, 7 to 16 years old, had a mean ICGH of 5.6 ng/ml ± 3.6 (SD) which was significantly higher ($p<0.005$) than the mean of 1.8 ± 1.0 for adult males (Fig. 3). The ICGH did not consistently change with age (Fig. 3) or stage of sexual development (Fig. 4). The mean ICGH for prepubertal boys of 5.3 ng/ml is not significantly different ($p>0.3$) from the mean of 6.2 ng/ml for boys in Tanner's (1962) stages 2-4. The ICGH did not correlate with the increasing levels of plasma testosterone observed in normal pubertal progression (Fig. 4). Metabolic clearance rates were not done in all these boys, which means that production rates were available in only 12 boys. The prepubertal and pubertal boys had a mean GHPR of 0.89 mg/24 hr/M^2 ± 0.49, which is higher ($p<0.005$) than the mean of 0.35 ± 0.23 in adult males.

Ten prepubertal and pubertal girls, ages 8 to 13, had a mean ICGH of 4.7 ng/ml ± 1.9 (SD), which is higher ($p<0.025$) than the mean of 3.0 ± 1.6 for premenopausal females not receiving oral contraceptives. The 5 girls in stage 1 had a mean ICGH of 4.4 ng/ml, whereas the 5 in stages 2-4 had a mean ICGH of 5.0 (Fig. 5). Production rates of GH are available on only 7 girls. The mean GHPR in these girls of 0.51 mg/24 hr/M^2 ± 0.30 (SD) is almost identical to the GHPR of 0.52 ± 0.24 for the adult females not receiving oral contraceptives.

Five boys with diagnoses of constitutional delay of growth and adoles-

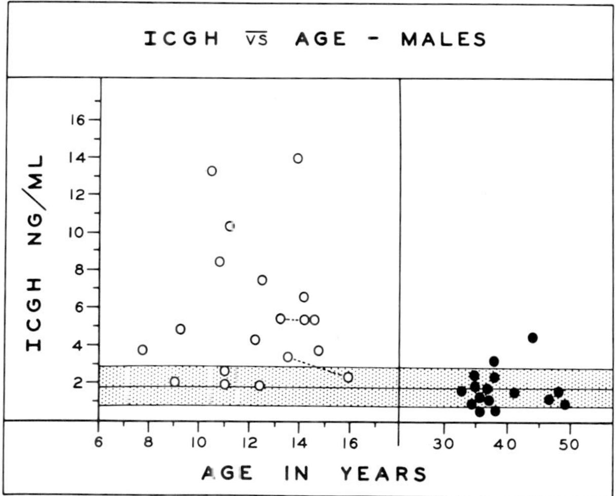

FIG. 3. Integrated concentrations of GH in preadolescent and adolescent males compared with adult males. Dashed lines connect sequential studies. The shaded area represents the mean ± 1 SD for adult males.

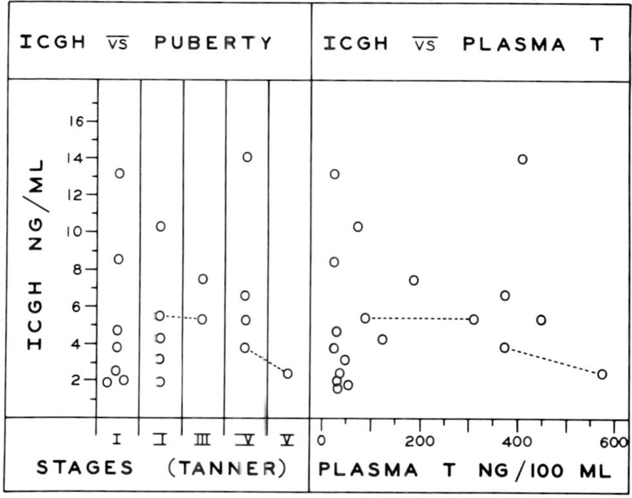

FIG. 4. Comparison of the ICGH to stage of puberty and plasma testosterone (T). Dashed lines connect sequential studies.

cence had a mean ICGH of 5 2 ng/ml; one had an ICGH of 1.4 ng/ml which is markedly lower than normal boys of comparable age. His GH status has not been re-evaluated, but re-examination revealed a growth of 3.8 in. in the subsequent 14 months.

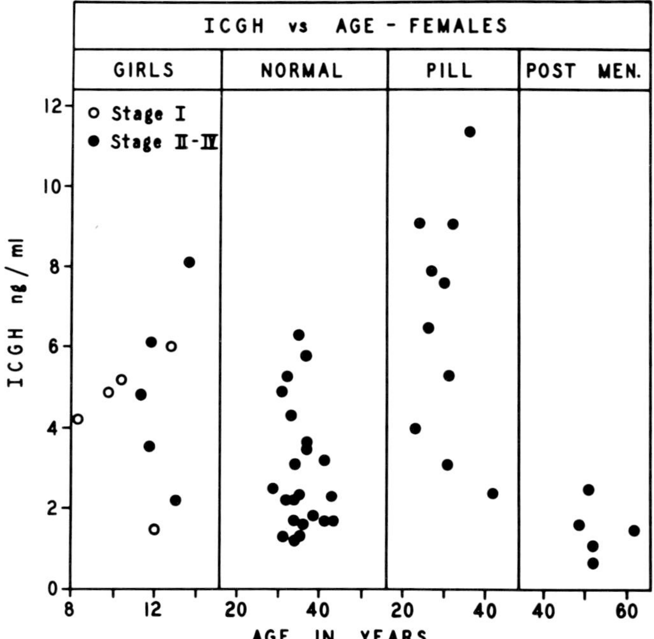

FIG. 5. The ICGH in 5 prepubertal (stage 1) and 5 pubertal (stages 2 to 4) girls compared with premenopausal women on no medicine (normal), women taking oral contraceptives (pill), and postmenopausal females (postmen).

To evaluate the effect of testosterone on the ICGH one 14-year-old boy with constitutional delay received 200 mg of testosterone enanthate every 4 weeks for 6 months. The ICGH was 4.4 ng/ml for 24 hours pretreatment and 5.1 ng/ml 5 days after the last injection (while also receiving methyl testosterone 30 mg/day to ensure increased testosterone levels).

Three patients with documented GH deficiency had determinations of ICGH for 24 hours; the 2 boys (9 and 14 years of age) had values of 0.7 and 1.1 ng/ml compared with a mean of 5.6 for normal boys of comparable age. The 32-year-old mother of the 14-year-old boy with GH deficiency failed to respond to arginine- or insulin-induced hypoglycemia with a significant increase in concentration of plasma GH. Her ICGH was 1.0 ng/ml which compares with a mean of 3.0 ng/ml for adult females of menstrual age who were not taking oral contraceptives.

The total growth during testosterone treatment in the 13 males with GH and gonadotropin deficiency is shown in Fig. 6. Although the increase in height was usually inversely related to the bone age at the initiation of therapy, there was considerable variation in response to testosterone.

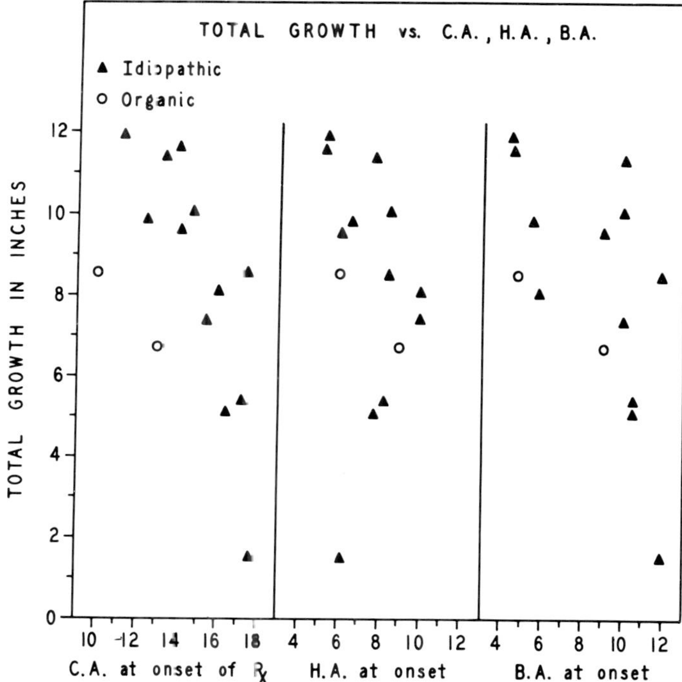

FIG. 6. Total growth observed during testosterone therapy in boys with GH and gonadotropin deficiency. The growth is plotted against chronological age (CA), height age (HA) and bone age (BA) at the time testosterone was started.

The ultimate height of these patients did not correlate well with the initial bone age (Fig. 7). The increase in growth rate was almost invariably achieved at the expense of rapid advancement of bone age (Fig. 8).

The 9.5-year-old girl with severe hypothyroidism, whom we studied ($T_4 = 0.2$ μg/ml), had grown only 1.5 in. in the 2 years before diagnosis. Despite a dose of 2.5 mg Wilhelmi GH daily (without thyroid replacement), which was given for a period of 6 months to evaluate the effect of exogenous GH on growth when serum thyroxine levels are abnormally low, no growth occurred. Appropriate thyroid replacement resulted in a growth of 3.75 in. in the first 6 months.

DISCUSSION

The inability to make accurate measurement of the production rate of GH has limited the understanding of the role played by GH at puberty. GH response to various stimulation tests has resulted in conflicting results

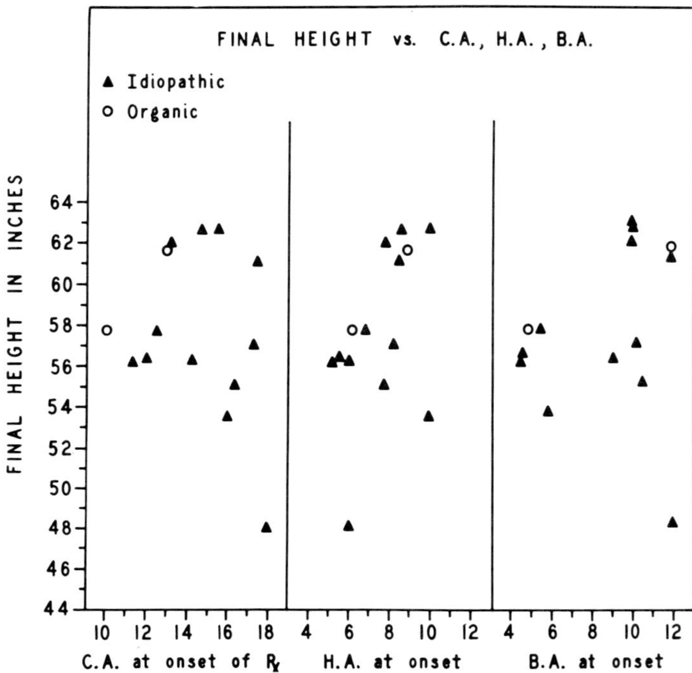

FIG. 7. Final height achieved after testosterone therapy in boys with GH and gonadotropin deficiency. Final height is plotted against chronological age (CA), height age (HA), and bone age (BA) at the initiation of testosterone treatment.

(Table 1). Frasier, Hilburn, and Smith (1970) observed significantly greater GH responses to insulin-induced hypoglycemia in adolescent subjects compared with preadolescent controls; males and females had comparable results. This is in contrast to the observations of Sperling, Kenny, and Drash (1970), who found increased GH release to arginine infusion in pubertal girls but no difference in the responses of pubertal boys and prepubertal children. This inconsistency is not surprising in view of the well-recognized negative response in some normal controls to the various stimulation tests. Penny, Blizzard, and Davis (1969) found that only 33 of 52 nonhypopituitary patients had positive GH response to both arginine and insulin; 9 responded only to arginine, and 10 responded only to insulin. These findings demonstrate the need for a test which can accurately measure the true production rate of GH over an extended period.

In our present study prepubertal and pubertal males had increased integrated concentrations of GH (Fig. 3) and GH production rates when compared with adult males. Earlier studies prompted conjecture that increased

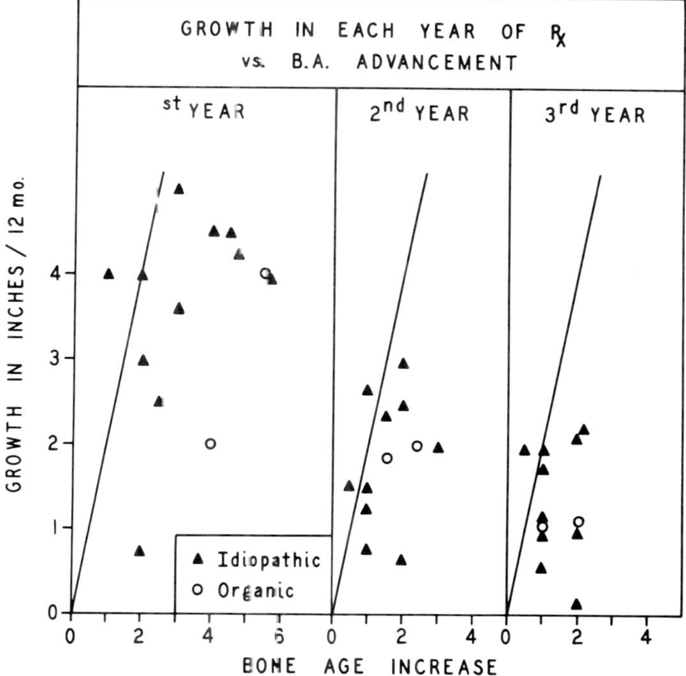

FIG. 8. Height increase during each year of testosterone treatment plotted against the advancement in bone age during the same period. The diagonal line represents growth of 2 inches for each year of bone age advancement.

ICGH would parallel the testosterone level and the stage of puberty. Illig and Prader (1970) found increased GH response to stimulation tests after exogenous testosterone therapy. Martin, Clark, and Conner (1968) reported similar increases in 3 patients with constitutional delayed growth who were stimulated with insulin after treatment with exogenous testosterone or hCG or after spontaneous entry into puberty. Penny and Blizzard (1972) found normalization of GH response after spontaneous puberty in 3 males who originally presented with apparent GH deficiency.

The concept that testosterone stimulates release of GH is not supported by our current data, for the prepubertal boys in our series had elevated ICGH before any increase in plasma testosterone or pubertal changes. There was an absence of correlation of ICGH with either stage of pubertal development or plasma testosterone (Fig. 4). Because these studies were obtained without the use of such exogenous stimuli as arginine or insulin-induced hypoglycemia, there may be a possibility that testosterone increases the response when these stimuli are administered.

The similarity in ICGH between prepubertal and pubertal males is in

TABLE 1. Growth hormone response to various stimulation tests

	Insulin-induced				Arginine-induced			
	Preadolescent		Adolescent		Preadolescent		Adolescent	
	Male	Female	Male	Female	Male	Female	Male	Female
Frasier et al (1970)	Same		<	Same				
Sperling et al (1970)					(	→ same ←	)	<

	Insulin		Arginine		
	Pre-	Post-	Pre-	Post-	
Illig & Prader (1970)					
Test	<		Not done		
Martin et al (1968)					3 patients with constitutional delayed growth and adolescence
Test hCG, or spontaneous puberty	<		Not done		
Penny et al (1969, 1972)					3 patients with apparent GH deficiency
Spontaneous puberty	<		<		

conflict with the observations of Finkelstein, Boyar, Roffwarg, Kream, and Hellman (in press), who obtained blood samples for GH every 20 minutes in 4 prepubertal males and 10 pubertal children (4 males and 6 females). Significantly lower GH production was found in prepubertal than in pubertal children in contrast to our findings of comparable ICGH in the 2 groups. The 2 studies differed significantly in format in that the patients studied by Finkelstein et al remained at bed rest except for bathroom privileges, whereas our patients were allowed to ambulate freely. Roth, Glick, Yalow, and Berson (1963), Hanson (1970), and others have documented the stimulating effect of exercise on GH release. The difference in activity between the 2 groups might explain the discrepancy between the 2 studies.

The preliminary observation that boys with constitutional delay of growth and adolescence have an ICGH comparable to normally statured boys of similar age indicates that GH plays little, if any, role in this entity. Most boys with this diagnosis release normal amounts of GH to stimulation tests. These tests did not, however, exclude the possibility that less GH was produced during normal activity by patients with constitutional delay in growth. Our results in 4 of 5 such cases do not seem to confirm this possibility, an observation which lends credence to the hypothesis that the increased plasma testosterone levels seen during puberty are directly responsible for the rapid linear growth that occurs in boys. The increased growth rate during treatment with testosterone for 6 months in the patient with constitutional delayed growth and sexual development is compatible with this hypothesis. This increased growth rate occurred despite an insignificant change in ICGH from 4.4 ng/ml before therapy to 5.1 ng/ml at the completion of his testosterone treatment.

A direct effect of testosterone on growth without an increased production of GH is strongly suggested by the data presented in Figs. 6 to 8. Testosterone increased the growth rates significantly in all patients with idiopathic and organic hypopituitarism. Several who were tested for immunoreactive GH after they had been virilized by exogenous testosterone produced insignificant amounts. The possibility cannot be eliminated that testosterone generated somatomedin production or in some way made the very small amounts of immunoreactive GH more effective. Normal growth has been observed in some organic hypopituitary patients without measurable immunoreactive GH.

Such a direct effect of testosterone on growth is in conflict with the observations in rats (Simpson, Marks, Becks, & Evans, 1944; Simpson, Asling, & Evans, 1950). Although testosterone stimulated growth in normal rats, in the absence of the pituitary there was no significant increase in weight or length when the animals were injected with testosterone.

Some augmentation of the effects of GH by testosterone has been reported, however, in hypophysectomized rats when both compounds are given together. From these results it has been inferred that the growth-promoting effects of testosterone in normal animals are due to stimulation of the pituitary to produce GH or to the synergistic action with GH. The action of testosterone in the human and rat may be different; it is possible that testosterone releases GH in the rat but not the human, or it may be that testosterone and GH act synergistically in both species.

The results of GH production obtained in the 4 groups of normal adults document the stimulatory effect of estrogen on the levels of immunoreactive GH. Premenopausal females have significantly higher integrated concentrations and production rates of GH than postmenopausal females and adult males. Women who take oral contraceptives have significantly higher GH concentrations and production rates than age-matched women who are not receiving them. Although estrogen stimulation has been consistently reported (Frantz & Rabkin, 1964) to increase the fasting levels of immunoreactive GH and the levels observed in the serum following arginine and insulin stimulation, estrogen is inhibitory to the peripheral action of GH. Schwartz, Wiedemann, Simon, and Schiffer (1969), who administered GH to 3 osteoporotic males and then GH plus estradiol, found that the positive nitrogen retention, hypercalciuria, and hydroxyprolinuria observed with GH administration were reversed when estrogen was given simultaneously. Wiedemann and Schwartz (1972) subsequently demonstrated that estrogen suppressed somatomedin (sulfation factor) in 4 acromegalic patients without changing the levels of immunoreactive GH. The somatomedin levels in 3 hypopituitary patients rose significantly while they were receiving GH but fell when estrogen was given simultaneously. The stimulated production of immunoreactive GH resulting from estrogen administration may be caused by peripheral inhibition of GH action rather than direct stimulation by estrogen on the hypothalamus or the pituitary; i.e., the increase in immunoreactive GH with estrogen stimulation may be the result of a negative feedback rather than a positive stimulation by estrogen itself.

A peripheral inhibitory effect of estrogen on growth has been reported in castrated female rats, which grow more rapidly than noncastrated rats. Also normal female rats receiving GH grow less rapidly than castrated female rats receiving the same dosage of GH (Simpson et al, 1950).

The effect of estrogen on release of GH does not explain the observations that prepubertal and pubertal girls have the same integrated concentrations of GH as normal females of menstrual age. The 5 prepubertal girls with no clinical evidence of estrogenization had an ICGH of 4.4 ng/ml, which was elevated when compared with other groups with similar low estrogen levels such as the postmenopausal females with a mean ICGH of 1.5 ng/ml and adult males with a mean ICGH of 1.8 ng/ml. Girls younger than 8 years have not been studied, therefore we cannot comment on variations in GH in younger children.

These data on prepubertal males and prepubertal females who have no demonstrable estrogen effect indicate that immunoreactive GH is produced in larger amounts in children than in adult males and in larger relative amounts in children than in adult females; estrogen production in adult females causes the release of immunoreactive GH by indirect or direct means. The high levels of ICGH found in prepubertal and pubertal males and females fall subsequently to a greater extent in males than females. The mechanism that decreases the production rate of GH in adults not under the influence of estrogen is not yet known.

Although the fact that corticosteroids inhibit normal growth has been established, the mechanism of this inhibition has been controversial. Frantz and Rabkin (1964), Friedman and Strang (1966), and Hartog, Gaafar, and Fraser (1964) found a decreased GH response to insulin-induced hypoglycemia after administration of prednisone to adults, in contrast to the observations of Morris, Jorgenson and Jenkins (1968) in which no inhibition of insulin-induced GH release was found in children receiving various doses of prednisone. Nakagawa, Horiuchi and Mashime (1969) also reported divergent results between two different stimulation tests while the patients were receiving corticosteroids; there was no suppression of arginine-induced GH release, whereas insulin-induced GH release was suppressed. Our results (Fig. 2) without the use of artificial stimuli, indicate that prednisone significantly reduces GH production (GHPR) when given in doses of 20 mg t. i. d.

The improved growth described by Sadeghi-Nejad and Senior (1969) in patients treated with prednisone in a single dose every 48 hours instead of steroids given daily in divided doses has not been explained. Three of the 5 women studied before and during a regimen of alternate-day prednisone had little change in ICGH and no change in GH production on the day of prednisone (Fig. 2). Although the decrease in GHPR with prednisone given every other day is less consistent than when it is given in divided doses, another possible explanation for the decreased growth retardation with this regimen is that the inhibition of the peripheral actions of GH (described by Soyka & Crawford, 1965) may also be less marked during part of the 48 hours between prednisone doses.

Although the interrelationship of pharmacological doses of glucocorticoids to GH has been delineated, there is no evidence that cortisol production changes with adolescent sexual development (Migeon, Green, & Eckert, 1963) or that testosterone, estrogen, or GH affects the production of glucocorticoids. Also, reportedly, there is no change in serum thyroxine levels (Dreyer & Man, 1962). Hung, Gancayo, and Heald (1965) demonstrated that the thyroxine level and half-life of obese adolescents are comparable to nonobese adolescents at the same stage of sexual development.

Although there is no apparent thyroxine-gonadotropin interrelationship in the child with normal adolescent development, the production of gonadotropins is sometimes enhanced by thyroxine deficiency. In the syndrome of sexual precocity and hypothyroidism (Sadeghi-Nejad & Senior, 1971) the relatively insensitive urinary gonadotropin assay produced no positive results when the urine of these children was tested. However, VanGelderen (1962) and Silver (1958) found significant levels of gonadotropins in 2 of these children. Sadeghi-Nejad and Senior (1971) reported serum LH values that were greater than those observed in prepubertal girls, and Laron, Karp, and Dolberg (1970) reported an FSH level in the normal adult range obtained from the serum of a 6-year-old boy with sexual precocity and hypothyroidism. Thus, the interrelationship of thyroxine and pituitary function probably can contribute to abnormal adolescent development.

Thyroxine deficiency can also affect GH production and action. In the hypothyroid human, there is diminished GH release secondary to arginine and insulin stimulation (Brauman & Corvilain, 1968; MacGillivray, Aceto, & Frohman, 1968). In the rat, the pituitary content of GH and the acidophils, which are believed to be responsible for GH production, are decreased (Levey & Roberts, 1958; Asling & Evans, 1956). The administration of GH to thyroidectomized or thyroidectomized-hypophysectomized rats stimulates growth, but the dosage required to treat hypophysectomized animals is 25 times greater (Simpson et al, 1950). We report the only comparable study in the prepubertal human with primary hypothyroidism in whom no growth was observed while she received 2.5 mg of hGH daily for 6 months.

SUMMARY AND CONCLUSIONS

Prepubertal and adolescent children of both sexes have significantly greater integrated concentrations of immunoreactive GH (boys, 5.6 ng/ml; girls, 4.7 ng/ml) than adult males 30 to 50 years of age (1.8 ng/ml). Preliminary data suggest that there is actually a decrease in ICGH with age in both sexes, whereas the reduction in GHPR observed in females does not occur until menopause; the mechanism of this decrease with age is unexplained.

The adolescent growth spurt is independent of increasing ICGH, for prepubertal males and females have levels comparable to adolescent children of all stages of sex development. The growth spurt of adolescent males is probably attributable to the action of testosterone alone or synergistically with GH. Growth hormone-deficient patients who receive testosterone grow significantly, in contrast to hypophysectomized rats that are given testosterone but do not grow at all. The human differs from the rat, possibly because small amounts of GH act as substrate or because testosterone acts independently. The growth spurt of the adolescent female may be attributable to adrenal androgens and is probably less than that of the male because these androgens are less potent growth-promoting agents than testosterone and because estrogen inhibits growth (as demonstrated in both rat and human).

There is no change in thyroxine production during normal adolescence. A deficiency of thyroxine may, however, occasionally induce precocious adolescence because of the increased production of or sensitivity to gonadotropin. The observation of gonadotropin determinations which are advanced for age in 4 such patients suggests that increased gonadotropin production may be the correct explanation. Thyroxine deficiency can also lead to growth retardation. There is evidence of decreased GH release in the human stimulated with arginine and insulin as well as in the pituitaries of hypothyroid rats. Growth hormone will not substitute for thyroxine as a growth promoting agent, since 2.5 mg of hGH given daily over 4 months to a hypothyroid child did not increase the height. This is consistent with data reported for rats.

Also, cortisol production is apparently not altered during normal adolescent development; however, excessive cortisol production decreases GH production and inhibits its action peripherally.

Further investigation concerning the adolescent growth spurt is indicated because the observations of some investigators are not in agreement with the observations we report. Some studies suggest increasing GH production with adolescence, which could be related to serum testosterone concentrations. In addition, the role of somatomedin in relation to the hormonal changes observed during adolescence, and the mechanism by which GH appears to diminish with age in adulthood, need to be investigated.

ACKNOWLEDGMENT

This work was supported by Grants HD-01852, RO1HD-06284, and 5-NO1-RR-0052 from the National Institutes of Health.

REFERENCES

Asling, C. W. & Evans, H. M. (1956). Anterior pituitary regulation of skeletal development. In *The Biochemistry and Physiology of Bone* G.H. Bourne, Ed. Academic, New York, p. 671.

Bala, R. M. & Beck, J. C. (1971). Human growth hormone in urine. *J. Clin. Endocrinol.* **33**, 799-806.

Brauman, H. & Corvilain, J. (1968). Growth hormone response to hypoglycemia in myxoedema. *J. Clin. Endocrinol.* **28**, 301–304.

Cameron, D. P., Burger, H. G., Catt. K. J., & Daig, A. (1969). Metabolic clearance rate of radioiodinated human growth hormone in man. *J. Clin. Invest.* **48**, 1600–1608.

Dreyer, D. J. & Man, E. B. (1962). Thyroxin binding proteins and butanol extractable iodine in sera of adolescent males. *J. Clin. Endocrinol.* **22**, 31–37.

Finkelstein, J. W., Boyar, R. M., Roffwarg, H. P., Kream J., & Hellman, L. Age-related change in the twenty-four hour spontaneous secretion of growth hormone. In press.

Frantz, A. G. & Rabkin, M. T. (1964). Human growth hormone, clinical measurement, response to hypoglycemia, and suppression by corticosteroids. *New Eng. J. Med.* **271**, 1375–1381.

Frasier, S. D., Hilburn, J. M., & Smith, F. G. (1970). Effect of adolescence on the serum growth hormone response to hypoglycemia. *J. Pediat.* **77**, 465–467.

Friedman, M. & Strang, L. B. (1966). Effect of long term corticosteroids and corticotropin on the growth of children. *Lancet* **2**, 568–572.

Gallagher, J. R. (1966). *Medical Care of the Adolescent,* Meredith, New York.

Hanson, A.P. (1970). Abnormal serum growth hormone response to exercise in juvenile diabetics. *J. Clin. Invest.* **49**, 1467-1478.

Hartog, M., Gaafar, M. A., & Fraser, R. (1964). Effects of corticosteroids on serum growth hormone. *Lancet* **2**, 376-378.

Hung, W., Gancayo, G. P., & Heald, F. P. (1965). Thyroxine metabolism in obese adolescent males. *Pediatrics* **36**, 877-881.

Illig, R. & Prader, A. (1970). Effect of testosterone on growth hormone secretion in patients with anorchia and delayed puberty. *J. Clin. Endocrinol.* **30**, 615–618.

Kowarski, A., Thompson, R. G., Migeon, C. J., & Blizzard, R. M. (1971). Determination of integrated plasma concentrations and true secretion rates of human growth hormone. *J. Clin. Endocrinol.* **32**, 356–360.

Laron, L., Karp, M., & Dolberg, L. (1970). Juvenile hypothyroidism with testicular enlargement. *Acta Paediat. Scand.* **59**, 317–322.

Levy, H. A. & Roberts, S. (1958). Paper electrophoretic studies on pituitary extracts from normal and thyroidectomized rats. *Endocrinology* **63**, 629–641.

MacGillivray, M. H., Aceto, Jr., T. & Frohman, L. A. (1968). Plasma growth hormone responses and growth retardation of hypothyroidism. *Amer. J. Dis. Child.* **115**, 173–176.

MacGillivray, M. H., Frohman, L. A., & Doe, J. (1970). Metabolic clearance and production rates of human growth hormone in subjects with normal and abnormal growth. *J. Clin. Endocrinol.* **30**, 632–638.

Martin, L. G., Clark, J. W., & Connor, T. B. (1968). Growth hormone secretion enhanced by androgens. *J. Clin. Endocrinol.* **28**, 425–428.

Migeon, C. J., Green, O. C., & Eckert, J. P. (1963). Studies of adrenocortical function in obesity. *Metabolism* **12**, 718–739.

Morris, H. G., Jorgensen, J. R., & Jenkins, S. A. (1968). Plasma growth hormone concentration in corticosteroid-treated children. *J. Clin. Invest.* **47**, 427–435.

Nakagawa, K., Horiuchi, Y., & Mashime, K. (1969). Responses of plasma growth hormone and corticosteroids to insulin and arginine with or without prior administration of dexamethasone. *J. Clin. Endocrinol.* **29**, 35–40.

Penny, R. & Blizzard, R. M. (1972). The possible influence of puberty on the release of growth hormone in three males with apparent isolated growth hormone deficiency. *J. Clin. Endocrinol.* **34**, 82–84.

Penny, R. Blizzard, R. M., & Davis, W. T. (1969). Sequential arginine and insulin tolerance tests on the same day. *J. Clin. Endocrinol.* **29**, 1499–1501.

Roth, J., Glick, S. M., Yalow, R. S., & Berson, S. A. (1963). Secretion of human growth hormone: physiologic and experimental modification. *Metabolism* **12**, 577–579.

Sadeghi-Nejad, A. & Senior, B. (1969). Adrenal function, growth, and insulin in patients treated with corticoids on alternate days. *Pediatrics* **43**, 277–283.

Sadeghi-Nejad, A. & Senior, B. (1971). Sexual precocity: an unusual complication of propylthiouracil therapy. *J. Pediat.* **79**, 833–837.

Schalch, D. S. & Parker, M. L. (1964). A sensitive double antibody immunoassay for human growth hormone in plasma. *Nature* **203**, 1141–1142.

Schwartz, E., Wiedemann, E., Simon, S., & Schiffer, M. (1969). Estrogenic antagonism of metabolic effects of administered growth hormone. *J. Clin. Endocrinol.* **29**, 1176–1181.

Silver, H. K. (1968). Juvenile hypothyroidism with precocious sexual development. *J. Clin. Endocrinol.* **18**, 886–891.

Simpson, M. E., Asling, C. W., & Evans, H. M. (1950). Some endocrine influences on skeletal growth and differentiation. *Yale J. Biol. Med.* **23**, 1–27.

Simpson, M. E., Marks, W., Becks, H., & Evans, H. M. (1944). Effect of testosterone propionate on the body weight and skeletal system of hypophysectomized rats. *Endocrinology,* **35**, 309–316.

Soyka, L. F. & Crawford, J. D. (1965). Antagonism by cortisone of the linear growth induced in hypopituitary patients and hypophysectomized rats by human growth hormone. *J. Clin. Endocrinol.* **25**, 469–475.

Sperling, M. A., Kenny, F. M., & Drash, A. L. (1970). Arginine-induced growth hormone responses in children: effect of age and puberty. *J. Pediat.* **77**, 462–465.

Tait, J. F. (1963). Review. The use of isotopic steroids for the measurement of production rate *in vivo. J. Clin. Endocrinol.* **23**, 1285-1297.

Tanner, J. M. (1962). *Growth at Adolescence,* Blackwell, Oxford.

Taylor A. L., Finster, J. L., & Mintz, D. H. (1969). Metabolic clearance and production rates of human growth hormone. *J. Clin. Invest.* **48**, 2349–2358.

Tremblay, R. R., Beitins, I. Z., Kowarski, A., & Migeon, C. J. (1970). Measurement of plasma dihydrotestosterone by competitive protein-binding analysis. *Steroids* **16**, 29–40.

VanGelderen, H. H. (1962). Precocious menstruation in hypothyroidism. *Arch. Dis. Childh.* **37**, 337–339.

Wiedemann, E. & Schwartz, E. (1972). Suppression of growth hormone-dependent human serum sulfation factor by estrogen. *J. Clin. Endocrinol.* **34**, 51–58.

Wilkins, L. (1965). *The Diagnosis and Treatment of Endocrine Disorders in Childhood and Adolescence.* Thomas, Springfield, Ill.

DISCUSSION

DR. ROSENFIELD. The dose, type of estrogen, and route of administration seem to be important determinants of estrogen effects. This has not been taken into consideration in the animal studies of estrogen action. On the basis of our studies I suspect that physiological doses of estrogen do actually stimulate growth. The second reason I think that estrogen may be important for growth is that we don't see growth spurts in normal children undergoing isolated adrenarche; for example, there is a group of boys with delayed gonadarche who develop scrotal hair in association with free testosterone levels in the low adult female range (distinctly above the prepubertal level). They don't have a growth spurt. So I don't think early adrenarchal androgens are present in a great enough concentration to induce the growth spurt. The growth spurt in females is probably related to estrogenization.

DR. BLIZZARD. You raised a most interesting question, one that has to be scrutinized in greater detail. It is possible that the estrogens induce androgen production by the adrenal and the androgens are responsible for the growth spurt. With respect to estrogens inhibiting growth in the rat, it was demonstrated a long time ago that female immature rats grow at a slower rate than male immature rats. If one takes out the ovaries, the growth rate in the females then increases. These data were interpreted as indicative that at least something in the ovary, presumably small amounts of estrogen, was accounting for the difference in growth rates between the two sexes.

DR. FINKELSTEIN. We have used a somewhat different technique to study the secretion rate of GH over a 24-hour period. Our technique utilizes intermittent blood sampling, in which a sample of blood is taken every 20 minutes around the clock for a 24-hour period. From this a curve is constructed which shows the peaks and valleys that Dr. Blizzard graphically illustrated, from which, using an equation developed by Drs. Hellman and Gallagher for the calculation of the secretion rate of cortisol, we have calculated the secretion rate of GH in a group of completely normal prepubertal and pubertal individuals. In Fig. 9 GH concentration is represented in relation to clock time and the sleep period. We have found that prepubertal patients characteristically have no detectable secretion of GH during the waking hours. Immediately on falling asleep there is a distinct release of GH and usually several episodes of GH secretion during the sleep period. There does not seem to be any distinct correlation with a particular stage of sleep in this group of individuals, although

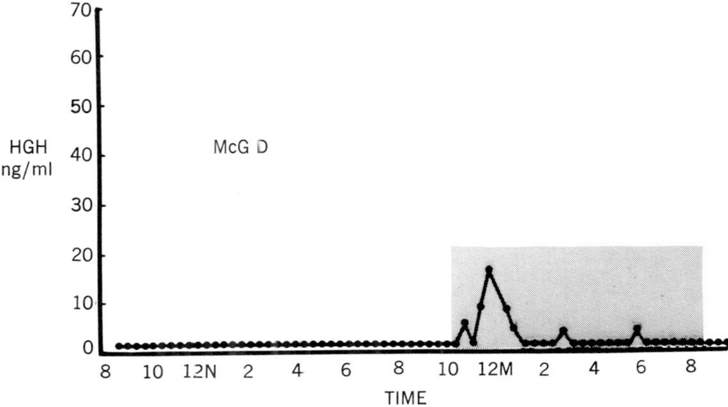

FIG. 9.   Variation during a 24-hour period in levels of GH in serum of prepubertal individuals.

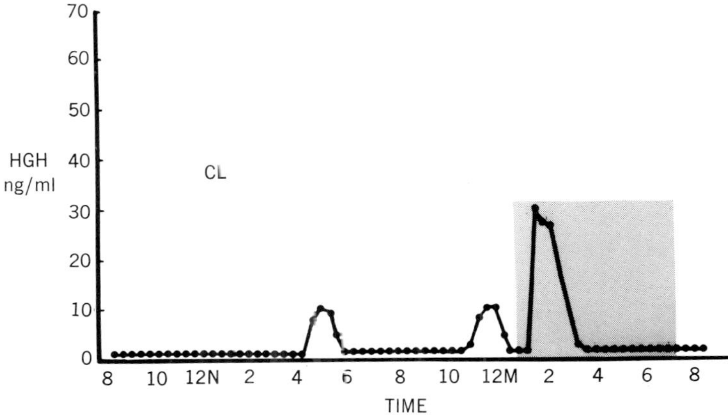

FIG. 10.   Variation during a 24-hour period in levels of GH in serum in early puberty.

the first release usually accompanies stage 3 to 4 sleep. On awakening GH secretion seems to cease, and these concentrations are usually under 2 ng/ml. The average secretion of GH over this period has been about 93 μg/day. In the early pubertal individual (Fig. 10) you begin to see some secretion of GH during waking hours. There is still marked augmentation of GH secretion during sleep. Figure 11 charts data from a patient in advanced puberty who showed marked increase in GH secretion; there is considerable secretion of GH during waking hours and again, augmented release during the sleep period. In this individual there happens to be coincident secretion of GH and cortisol in the first episode during sleep, so that the physiological release of cortisol during this time does not inhibit the normal release of GH. The mean concentration

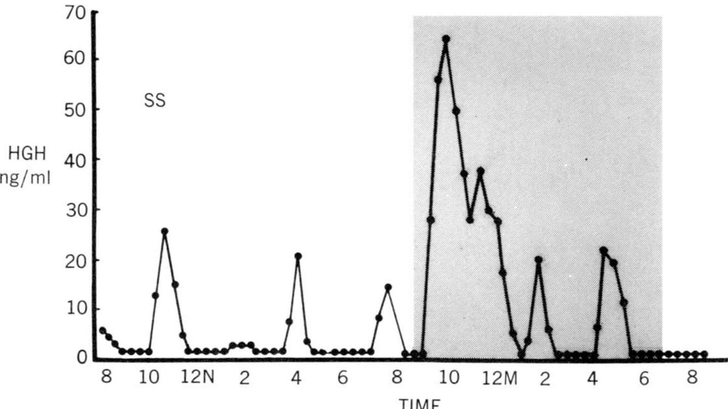

FIG. 11.   Variation during a 24-hour period in levels of GH in serum in advanced puberty.

and secretion rate of GH in our adolescent group is 500 μg/24 hours, which is significantly different from that of the prepubertal group. In addition to that, many of our patients have had a redetermination of the LH and FSH concentrations in puberty and have been found to have marked elevations of both gonadotropins. As Dr. Blizzard indicated, this whole subject is not closed. Perhaps the problem may lie in the fact that our patients who were prepubertal were also a bit older (the youngest was around 8 years old); perhaps younger individuals need to be studied. Gotlin, who studied a few younger individuals, reported findings similar to ours.

DR. BLIZZARD.   It is very possible that immunoreactive GH concentrations may go up at the time of prepuberty or puberty, but this increase does not appear to be related to the testosterone per se. We agree that younger patients need to be studied.

DR. TANNER.   We have a small series of patients to whom we have given testosterone as well as GH at a time when adolescence should have occurred but was not doing so because of a lack of gonadotropins. We divided the year into 4 quarters and in the first quarter gave GH and testosterone enanthate, 250 mg/2 weeks; in the second quarter testosterone only, in the third quarter, both drugs, and in the fourth quarter, testosterone. So you have GH-testosterone; testosterone only. The growth rates in these quarters, on the average in these few patients, were (1) 9 cm/yr (testosterone-GH); (2) 6 cm/yr (testosterone only); (3) 8 cm/yr (testosterone-GH); and (4) 5 cm/yr (testosterone only). These data bear out very much what you were saying. Testosterone does work in the human in the absence of GH, but it seems that the two hormones simply add up in effect. In the curve of adolescent-growth velocity you have a baseline that presumably is under GH control, and on top of it there is the testosterone. It should not surprise anyone that testosterone doesn't work exactly in the same way and do the same thing in the rat as it does in the human because the biological fact is that secondary sex characteristics in the rat are not quite the same as in the human.

DR. MACGILLIVRAY.   Some of the differences in the results observed in the human and animal studies may be attributable to the dissimilarities in the experimental models. It is probably unwise to assume that the hypophysectomized rat is endocrinologically equivalent to the child with idiopathic hypopituitarism. Patients with idiopathic hypopituitarism may represent a broad spectrum in which some children have absence and others have milder deficiencies of GH. If this is true, then patients who grew 4 in./yr may have had some pituitary reserves of GH which were potentiated by the androgen treatment. In order to evaulate the effects of androgens in the absence of GH, it is probably necessary to do the study in the hypophysectomized human in whom a total absence of plasma GH and negligible linear growth are present. Your results are quite dissimilar to our findings in 12 idiopathic hypopituitary children who received 6 months of GH followed by 6 months of GH plus androgen. The doses of GH and androgen were standardized on the basis of body weight throughout the study. During the period of combined hormone treatment the growth rates were significantly greater than during treatment with GH alone. We concluded that linear growth and weight gain were enhanced by the synergistic interaction of androgen and GH. Reports from Drs. Prader and Sobel indicate that androgen treatment in hypopituitary patients failed to give the expected increases in linear growth or improvements in sexual maturation. Did your group of hypopituitary patients manifest generous sexual hair growth, penile enlargement, and improved muscular development? I am concerned that final heights of 54 in. resulted from this form of treatment. I wonder whether we are dealing with the same population of children.

DR. BLIZZARD.   We gave two alternative explanations: one is that testosterone did it alone and the other is that testosterone acted synergistically with GH. No patients classified as idiopathic hypopituitary who are growing an inch a year are totally hypopituitary. They must be making small amounts of hormone even if we do not measure it.

DR. WINTER.   I should like to describe an experiment of nature that may bear on the question of GH-gonadotropin and GH-androgen interaction. A boy in whom we diagnosed GH and TSH deficiency at age 2 (ACTH function was normal) was treated with thyroxine immediately and with GH at age 3. When first seen he had small testes and a microphallus, but at age 4 to 5 he began to show rising levels of serum gonadotropins and testosterone and growth of the testes and phallus. This suggests that the administration of hGH (which was shown to contain insignificant amounts of FSH and LH) permitted the appearance of sexual precocity. We presume a common hypothalamic lesion underlies both the GH and TSH lack and the FSH and LH overproduction. The second surprising thing about this boy is that in spite of elevated serum testosterone concentrations for several years he has no sexual hair. Possibly this reflects some degree of GH lack, since he is receiving only 6 mg hGH weekly for only 6 months of each year. Finally, although his sexual precocity has resulted in a marked advance in his rate of bone maturation, there has been no apparent improvement in his growth velocity, whether he is on or off the GH injections.

Dr. Grumbach.   Dr. Winter, have you any prolactin data on this child?

Dr. Winter.   They ranged from 5.8 to 7.0 ng/ml, using the Friesen standard.

Dr. MacGillivray.   I wonder if this child has somatomedin deficiency. We have one 18-year-old patient who is 52 in. adult height, fully sexually developed, and who is now pregnant. This is a very pretty young lady whom we have followed for the last 6 years. She had absolutely no GH response on the stimulation tests and when treated with GH did not grow. Unfortunately we did not have a sulfaction factor measurement.

Dr. Winter.   Our child has GH deficiency: the levels of GH were negligible, and the response to exogenous GH was satisfactory in that he grew more than a centimeter per month while receiving the hormone.

Dr. Raiti.   I would like to speak about synergism between androgens and GH. We have used oxandrolone, a weak androgen, as a growth stimulant. We compared its growth-stimulating effects with those of hGH. We used one hormone, then the other drug, and then the two combined. We found no synergism when oxandrolone was used with GH. However, we found that no matter which of these was used first growth was always best in the first year of therapy. We also had to take into account that when hGH therapy was stopped we found inhibition of growth when compared with pretherapy growth rates. This inhibition was not found after oxandrolone was stopped. In other words, after oxandrolone, the patients grew at the rate at which they were growing before therapy, whereas when GH was stopped there was a definite fall-off in growth rate.

Dr. Grumbach.   What has emerged from this discussion is the interrelationship between the anabolic effects of GH and testosterone. As Dr. Blizzard pointed out, estrogen, acting directly or indirectly, appears to have an effect on growth at adolescence. It is of interest that Dr. Ernest Schwartz has shown that pharmacologic doses of estrogen may inhibit somatomedin generation and, in the adult, exhibit anti-GH metabolic effects.

Dr. Root.   While we are discussing the interactions of hormones, it may be of interest to note that clinical grade hGH inhibits thyrotropin releasing hormone (TRH) and induces secretion of thyroid-stimulating hormone (TSH) in patients with and without hyposomatotropism (Root, Snyder, Rezvani, George, & Utiger, 1973). Whether this effect is due to hGH, to its prolactin content, or to some other factor has not been elucidated. MacLeod, Bass, Buxton, and Benson (1966) and MacLeod, DeWitt, and Smith (1968) demonstrated decreased thyroid function and pituitary TSH content in rats bearing GH-prolactin-secreting tumors but not in animals with pure GH-secreting neoplasms. He concluded that prolactin was the agent responsible for suppression of the pituitary-thyroid axis. Because TRH stimulates the secretion of prolactin as well as that of TSH, it seems that the regulation of this system is becoming increasingly complex.

DR. CHEEK.   We can put a lot of store in absolute amounts and concentrations, but the whole business of puberty in adolescence may be the responsiveness of the tissues to hormones and their rate of secretion. A second point is that if you have patients with real GH deficiency, and you inject GH, then stop, then start for periods, body composition changes. As shown by Dr. Novak, exhibition of the hormone causes fat stores to decrease; and, on cessation of treatment, fatty tissue increases once again. You must take this into account when talking about giving or not giving GH.

DR. MOSHANG.   I would like to comment on the interrelationship of GH and testosterone in terms of the peripheral responsiveness of target organs. I have studied the metabolism of testosterone by the rat prostate in vitro. In normal intact rats the prostate forms dihydrotestosterone (DHT) at an increasing rate until the rate of formation of DHT reaches a steady state and plateaus with increasing concentrations of substrate (testosterone). The rate of formation of DHT by the prostate from hypophysectomized rats is markedly inhibited by increased substrate concentrations. When the hypophysectomized rat is treated with GH, the substrate inhibition of formation of DHT persists. Therefore the lack of pituitary factors does affect the metabolism of testosterone at the target organ, but GH is not the deficient pituitary factor.

DR. BOGDANOVE.   I would like to seek clarification on one point. Dr. Finkelstein, you showed very high levels of GH in your subjects during late puberty and coincident with this, very high levels of cortisol in one. There seemed to be no evidence of a diurnal rhythm of cortisol. Could this reflect a stress situation to which the changes in GH might be attributed?

DR. FINKELSTEIN.   This is an important point because there has been a report in which it was suggested that these procedures may be extraordinarily stressful to some patients. We have been careful in choosing our patients and whenever possible, have used volunteers and staff members at the hospital for the normal controls. We have also used some volunteers from Boy Scout troops, none of whom were related to any of our patients. I should like to point out that the cortisol pattern in this individual is a bit unusual. Usually, during this period, one sees extremely low concentrations of cortisol and the peak often occurs late. In this patient we found the reverse. There was a low concentration of cortisol during sleep, and this 12-year-old boy, in the middle of his adolescent growth spurt, was not, as far as we could tell, doing very well. Also, although he had lots of episodes of secretion of corticoids during the day, this condition was not inconsistent with all the other patients we have studied. They all show a period, somewhere within 24 hours, of negligible secretion of corticoids; we have calculated their secretory rates and they are well within the normal limits for adults.

DR. RAMALEY.   Did not Dr. Blizzard say that the cortisol production rate does not change during adolescence? Yet it looked to me that there were fewer and lower amplitude spurts of cortisol before puberty. I have seen changes in corticosterone levels in the rat at puberty (Ramaley, 1972).

Dr. Finkelstein.   We have demonstrated no difference in cortisol production rates by this or any other technique.

Dr. Tanner.   There is no evidence of actual synergism, only of additive actions of testosterone and GH.

Dr. Frasier.   Dr. Blizzard carefully dissociated himself from discussing the possible role of GH in initiation of puberty. Individuals with isolated GH deficiency have a late but relatively normal puberty. Dr. Grumbach has reported, and many of us have observed, that pubertal development may begin for the first time when GH therapy is instituted in the child with isolated GH deficiency.

Dr. Grumbach.   We have observed on many occasions that GH treatment of patients with isolated GH deficiency who have a bone age of more than 11 to 12 years is followed by the onset of signs of puberty over the next few months to 1 to 2 years. This is in contrast to the mean age of puberty in untreated boys (19 to 20 years) and girls (about 17 years), as reported by Rimoin.

Dr. Faiman.   Dr. Blizzard, I wonder about the reproducibility of your technique as well as that of Dr. Finkelstein. In addition, could you clarify the effect of prednisone on the MCR of GH. In 4 of 5 subjects you showed a diminution in clearance and in one there was a substantial increment.

Dr. Blizzard.   MCR fell off in 4 of the 5 patients receiving cortisol, which was surprising. It did go up in the fifth. I do not know whether that was an error, a difference in the patient, or what. In respect to reproducibility, we have gone back and measured production rates in 8 or 10 of the women to find out whether we could get the same results at different times. Some of these measurements were made at 6-month and others at 4-month intervals. Those data indicate that the production rate over a 24-hour period is similar from time to time.

Dr. Finkelstein.   We have done only 1 patient several times and his nocturnal peak responses were quite similar. Other workers have also reported that the pattern is fairly reproducible from night to night. In addition, we have studied (and have tried to use this technique whenever we can) 2 dissimilar patients in the same room, at the same time, who were experiencing the same kind of stimuli; i.e., we do a pubertal and prepubertal subject at the same time and their patterns are vastly different.

REFERENCES

MacLeod, R. M., Bass, M. B., Buxton, E. P., Dent, J. N., & Benson, D. G. (1966). Suppression of thyroid function by pituitary tumor. *Endocrinology* **78**, 267-277.

MacLeod, R. M., DeWitt, G. W., & Smith, M. C. (1968). Suppression of pituitary gland hormone content by pituitary tumor hormone. *Endocrinology* **82**, 889-895.

Ramaley, J. A. (1972). Changes in daily serum corticosterone values in maturing male and female rats. *Steroids* **20**, 185–197.

Root, A. W., Snyder, P. J., Rezvani, I., George, A. M. D., & Utiger, R. D. (1973). Inhibition of thyrotropin-releasing hormone-mediated secretion of thyrotropin by human growth hormone. *J. Clin. Endocrinol.* **36**, 103–106.

13.

Follicular Maturation

N. B. SCHWARTZ, C. H. ANDERSON, L. G. NEQUIN, and C. A. ELY

Induction of follicular maturation in its totality can be thought of as all of that input and those processes that intervene between the time of formation of primordial follicles and when a given group of follicles is capable of secreting steroid and responding to a surge of gonadotropin by ovulation and luteinization. Primordial follicles follow several time-trajectories that result in a variety of fates, only one of which is "maturation" in this definition.

A complete understanding of follicular maturation must ultimately include an understanding of the following questions. (1) In prenatal or neonatal life what initiates the association of "granulosa cells" with the oocyte while it is in meiotic prophase? (2) What determines the stochastic or nonstochastic differences among follicles that determine the temporal sequencing of the recruitment of follicles into growth phases throughout the life span of the ovary? (3) What initiates and controls the growth and atresia of follicles before puberty? (4) Why do not follicles go through the total maturational process before puberty? (5) What factors control the

---

Abbreviations

FSH	Follicle stimulating hormone
hCG	Human chorionic gonadotropin
hMG	Human menopausal gonadotropin
LH	Luteinizing hormone
NRS	Normal rabbit serum
PMSG	Pregnant mare serum gonadotropin

maturation of follicles during adult cycles and during prolonged luteal phases such as pregnancy? (6) Is the atresia of the adult cycle caused by similar factors as the atresia that occurs prepubertally? (7) What regulates the number of mature follicles that ovulate in a given species? (8) What is the mechanism by which superovulation can be induced? (9) What is the nature of the (two-way) communication between oocyte and surrounding follicle cells? (10) Has atresia a function or is it a redundant mechanism by which more follicles are brought toward maturation than will eventually mature, as a "fail-safe" mechanism? Although we are unable to review all these questions, much less answer them, we shall cover briefly some of the extrinsic and intrinsic (ovarian) factors implicated in the total process and present some preliminary data on the role of one such extrinsic factor—the gonadotropins—in follicular maturation during early postnatal life in the rat.

NATURAL HISTORY OF FOLLICLES

In most mammalian species, the process of germ cell division (mitosis) is complete before or shortly after birth, and the oocytes remain in an arrested or diapause stage (diplotene stage of meiosis) (Baker, 1972; Mauleon, 1969) until the oocyte dies in atresia or until meiosis is again resumed following a gonadotropic surge or removal of the oocyte from the follicle (Donahue, 1972; Hoffmann & Schwartz, 1972).

When meiosis is arrested (called the dictyate stage in the rat and mouse), the oocyte is contained within a single layer of cells; this microorgan is called a primordial follicle and initiates the postnatal history of follicles. The entire population of follicles within an ovary can be divided at any given time into two groups—nonproliferating and proliferating; the first group constitutes the pool from which the second group is derived (Pedersen, 1972). Once a follicle enters the proliferating pool, as evidenced by an increase in numbers of granulosa cells surrounding the oocyte, it must proceed to maturation and ovulation or it degenerates by atresia.

In a number of species, even in very early neonatal life, follicles are growing and becoming atretic (Pedersen, 1972; Mauleon, 1969; Baker, 1972; Zamboni, 1972); thus the total pool size of oocytes declines steadily as the animal ages. The major difference between the neonatal and the mature animal with respect to follicle maturation is that the largest and most mature follicles are not seen prepubertally.

The oocyte and follicle populations decline throughout the lifespan of the ovary. During neonatal life atresia or degeneration appears to take place from follicles of intermediate size, but in the cycling animal atresia seems to take place from medium and large follicles (Pedersen, 1972). "Wastage" of oocytes and follicles is characteristic throughout life, for, even during fertile cycles, more follicles begin to grow than normally ovulate (except when a superovulatory stimulus is superimposed) (Hoffmann & Schwartz, 1972). During prolonged luteal phases, such as pregnancy, fewer follicles may grow, but follicle depletion proceeds nevertheless (Pedersen, 1972).

During the estrous cycles of adult rats and mice differential follicle counts may be seen at different stages, particularly in the largest follicle sizes (Pedersen, 1970). By flash labeling with thymidine-^{3}H Pedersen (1970) and Peters and Levy (1966) demonstrated that 16 to 20 days are required for growth from the primary follicular size to the maximal "mature" size capable of ovulation. Anderson and Schwartz (unpublished observations) have also estimated that the small follicles in the adult rat which take up labeled thymidine in one cycle will not ovulate for four cycles.

FACTORS RESPONSIBLE FOR FOLLICULAR MATURATION AND ATRESIA

Pituitary Gonadotropic Hormones

The fundamental role of gonadotropic hormones in follicular maturation is clear in the prepubertal and adult animal. Within a few days hypophysectomy causes a loss of ovarian follicles in the medium- or large-size range ("proliferating") (Hisaw, 1947; Mauleon, 1969; Schwartz & McCormack, 1972). Furthermore, hypophysectomy also retards the total loss of oocytes from the ovary, even after irradiation; the latter effect of hypophysectomy can be reversed by PMSG treatment (Jones & Krohn, 1961; Beaumont, 1969). From the information taken from hypophysectomized animals that some combination of FSH and LH can induce maturation of follicles or superovulation it is clear that pituitary hormones are responsible in some way for bringing follicles from the nonproliferating to the proliferating compartment, thus leading to atresia or maturation (Schwartz & McCormack, 1972; Mauleon, 1969; Lostroh & Johnson, 1966; Hisaw, 1947; Goldenberg, Reiter, Vaitukaitis, & Ross, 1972a, b). Thymectomy at 3 days in the mouse causes loss of follicles even in the presence of the pituitary; subsequent hypophysectomy further damages interstitial development (Nishizuka & Sakakura, 1971).

Granting the role of the pituitary in follicular maturation, as shown in extreme conditions of hypophysectomy and exogenous hormone treatment, what causes the maturation of follicles during cycles or during persistent estrous or diestrous conditions? Both FSH and LH are present in the serum of a number of species during the "follicular" phase, although not at very high levels; nor is it necessary that these levels change appreciably during the cycle to have follicular maturation (Hoffmann & Schwartz, 1972). Antiserum injection or hypophysectomy in rats close to the time of induced or spontaneous ovulation can cause atresia or nonresponsivity to hCG in the largest set of follicles (Sasamoto & Kennan, 1972; Schwartz & Ely, 1970). Thus proliferating follicles are continuously dependent on the presence of FSH and LH, but there is no clear indication that they need increasing amounts of the hormones to exhibit maturation.

The role of the pituitary gonadotropic hormones in follicle growth and atresia in neonatal animals is not so clear. In rodents or other species the ovary is said to be independent of pituitary hormones during the period from birth to a few days before weaning (Hertz, 1963; Hertz & Hisaw, 1934). If this is so, it would have to be concluded that the proliferating small follicles and the growth in ovaries and sex accessory tissue in the first few weeks of life in rats and mice are not dependent on FSH or LH. Examination of this hypothesis leads one, however, to at least a reasonable degree of doubt.

First of all, the ovaries (and uterus) of rats from 6 to 14 days *do* grow in response to exogenous equine gonadotropin (Price & Ortiz, 1944); ovaries of 15-day-old rats increase in weight with hCG injection (Shiino & Rennels, 1967). Follicular development per se is not so stimulated as ovarian weight, however. Ovaries from newborn rats show growth and development when transplanted into the eyes of castrated recipients (Dunham, Watts, & Adair, 1941); by day 15 there is clear ovarian responsiveness to FSH and LH (Ryle, 1971).

Serum levels of FSH and LH in very young female rats are surprisingly high in the first 15 days of life and then fall (Goldman, Grazia, Kamberi, & Porter, 1971; Kragt & Dahlgren, 1972; Ojeda & Ramirez, 1972). It is not yet known whether the ovaries are sensitive *at these times* to *these high levels* because no comparison has been made of serum levels achieved with effective exogenous doses. However, gonadotropin levels in the pituitary and serum can respond to bilateral ovariectomy very early: pituitary gonadotropin (nonspecific) can rise by day 15 (Clark, 1935), and pituitary FSH can fall by day 15 (Baker & Kragt, 1969). Ovariectomy in female pups during the first 10 days of life either raises or does not alter (after 24 hours) the already high values of serum LH and FSH (Goldman, Grazia, Kamberi, & Porter, 1971); estradiol appears to lower serum FSH in intact 6-day-old rat pups, but it is difficult to assess this in serum LH because of the preoperative variability in this hormone (Goldman & Gorski, 1971). It has been claimed that hemiovariectomy at birth induces contralateral hypertrophy at day 10 (Dunlap, Preis, & Gerall, 1972). Ojeda and Ramirez (1972) and Baker and Kragt (1969) maintain that it does not.

With respect to a different but related issue, i.e., whether sex accessory organ growth during the neonatal phase is steroid-dependent, uterine weight is responsive to exogenous estradiol by 10 days (Price & Ortiz, 1944) and is reduced below control (10-day) levels in pups castrated at birth (Plagge, 1956; Baker & Kragt, 1969).

In rodents between the approximate age of weaning (18 to 21 days) and the time of puberty (near 40 days) there is clear responsivity of gonads to FSH and LH, a definite response of gonadotropic hormone secretion rate to gonadectomy, obvious dependence of accessory sex tissue on estradiol, and the possibility of endogenous LH release leading to fertile ovulation (Donovan & van der Werff ten Bosch, 1965). Gonadotropic hormone levels in blood are at low adult values (Ojeda & Ramirez, 1972; Kragt & Dahlgren, 1972), and pituitary levels are generally higher than the usual values seen in adults (Baker & Kragt, 1969; Kragt & Ganong, 1968; Dupon & Schwartz, 1971). The ovarian augmentation assay for FSH performed during this period has demonstrated that hCG or estradiol treatment enhances FSH uptake by the ovary and leads to follicular maturation and to increased ovarian weight (Goldenberg et al, 1972a,b).

During this juvenile period, when all parts of the system seem to "go," puberty does not take place (Donovan & van der Werff ten Bosch, 1965). Earlier data indicated higher negative feedback sensitivity in the prepubertal rat, perhaps because of a lower set point so that less estrogen could suppress the pituitary secretion. Recent evidence of Swerdloff, Jacobs, and Odell (1972) suggests that this may not be the whole explanation but that *relative* gonadal insensitivity to FSH and LH may exist in 21-day-old female rats. In "systems" parlance this would imply a lower ovarian transducer function in immature rats; what process might take place during the ensuing few weeks to increase this sensitivity is unknown, but increase in gonadotropin receptor sites could be a partial mechanism (Goldenberg et al, 1972a,b).

Steroid Hormones

Estradiol can enhance the response of the ovary (increase in weight and follicular development) to gonadotropic hormones (Hisaw, 1947). Recent observations in the weaning rat (Goldenberg et al, 1972a) suggest that estrogen acts at least in part by increasing FSH uptake by the ovary. Data indicate that ovaries are needed for uterine growth even in the very immature rat (about 10 days). Because estradiol secretion itself is presumably a function of gonadotropic hormone secretion, there is a possibility of a *positive* feedback relationship, the self-limiting safety factors in this potential runaway system are the negative feedback of estrogen on FSH secretion and the eventual ovulation or atresia of follicles (Schwartz, 1969).

More recent work with progesterone suggests that this steroid hormone may play a local role in the final stages of follicular maturation (Schwartz & McCormack, 1972; Schuetz, 1972). Amphibian follicles in vitro can be made to exhibit germinal vesicle breakdown (reinitiation of meiosis) by progesterone or LH; LH seems to be more successful than the steroid in causing ovulation (Schuetz, 1972). Schuetz intimates that LH acts on the follicle wall to release progesterone as an intermediary in these events. Furthermore, progesterone can induce final follicular maturation in oocytes still contained within the follicle. Estrogenic substances may inhibit these effects of LH in vitro (Schuetz, 1972).

The Oocyte. Maturation of the oocyte has been defined as a series of events in the period between the onset of arrested meiosis (first division) and the formation of the first polar body which initiates a second stage of arrest before fertilization (Donahue, 1972). In most species this oocyte *maturational* process occurs within the follicle as a result of a gonadotropin surge which also induces ovulation. The oocyte and cells of the cumulus are connected by projections across the zona pellucida (Zamboni, 1972) and provide a communications pathway. The ability of the oocyte to respond to pituitary hormones appears to be dependent on the state of the follicle surrounding it (Baker & Neal, 1972). Suboptimal gonadotropin, however, can result in oocyte maturation in *mature* follicles without ovulation; oocyte maturation (and ovulation) can also occur (but less frequently) in follicles that are not completely matured (Donahue, 1972; Baker & Neal, 1972).

Conversely, the oocyte exerts control over the follicle. The early development of follicles occurs around oocytes; moreover, atresia is generally first detectable in the oocyte (Baker, 1972; Zamboni, 1972). Removal of the oocyte from a follicle leads to luteal transformation of the cells of the follicle (Nalbandov, 1972). The suboptimal gonadotropin levels that can lead to oocyte maturation without ovulation (entrapped oocyte) can also cause luteinization with an entrapped oocyte (Nalbandov, 1972; Schwartz & Ely, 1970), which is an indication that the luteinization may be the indirect result of alteration of the oocyte.

These data suggest a two-way communication between oocyte and follicle cells that is just beginning to be explored.

Gonadotropins acting on the follicle during maturation may require the presence of a normal (diapausal) oocyte, and once normal follicular maturation has taken place the surge of LH which triggers ovulation, oocyte maturation, and luteinization may funnel into a common site of action. The postulated pathway (Schuetz, 1972) is via steroid secretion by follicular cells; action of steroids on a common pathway through the oocyte would serve as a synchronizing mechanism for completion of the first meiosis, ovulation, and luteinization.

Local Factors Within the Ovary.   The ultimate puzzle of follicular maturation concerns the process by which regular attrition in numbers of primordial follicles occurs in all phases of reproductive life, even when complete maturation is not taking place. It seems unlikely that the sequencing of follicle (and oocyte) entrance into proliferating pools (thence to inevitable loss) is *programmed* into the follicles from the time that mitosis stops. If there is no predetermination, then what is happening?

If it is suspected that a given primordial follicle had the same probability of remaining in the nonproliferating pool as every other follicle, perhaps the process that transforms it into the trajectory of proliferation would be purely stochastic. In the absence of pituitary hormones one may imagine a probability that determines a given follicle's movement associated with each follicle at each moment of time (perhaps because of stochastic differences in local metabolic rate). The role of FSH and LH would then be to raise the general level of "activation" in the total pool of nonproliferating follicles so that it would become more probable that some could move to the next size within a given time. This theory may or may not be heuristic, but it does seem to fit in with the adaptive significance of a sequential and continuous provision of oocytes in a slow and orderly fashion throughout the reproductive lifespan rather than in an explosive manner. Viewed this way, atresia, which seems a waste, simply represents the cost of a constant supply of oocytes nearing maturation when the opportunity for fertilization occurs.

PRELIMINARY STUDIES ON THE ROLE OF FSH AND LH DURING THE IMMATURE PHASE OF OVARIAN DEVELOPMENT IN THE RAT

Our review of the literature regarding the effects of FSH and LH on follicular maturation in the first 18 days of life in the rat revealed some doubt that the onset of follicular proliferation at that time requires pituitary hormones. Use of antisera to specific gonadotropins has been a useful technique in the examination of the roles played by gonadotropins in adult animals (Schwartz & Ely, 1970; Schwartz, Krone, & Talley, 1973) and has been applied to the question of the infant rat.

Three kinds of experiments that make use of antisera have been conducted in immature rats or mice. Antiserum to LH (cross reacting with FSH) could modify phallic development and behavior in males when administered on days 1, 3, and 5, apparently by blocking androgen secretion (Goldman et al, 1972). Kupperman, Meyer, and Finerty (1942) gave rather large doses of nonspecific gonadotropin antiserum to rats from days 10 to 19 of life and saw premature vaginal opening and ovarian hypertrophy, presumably by eliciting hypersecretion of gonadotropins by the recipient's pituitary. Eshkol and Lunenfeld (1972) treated mice from birth with daily injections of an antiserum to rat gonadotropins, and in some mice, superimposed treatment with FSH or hMG. A partial arrest in follicular development was seen with antiserum alone (the controls had a group of larger follicles at 7 and 14 days). FSH and hMG injection restored some of the changes toward normal. These studies indicate that antiserum can cause changes early in gonadal life and suggest that the high serum gonadotropin values seen in immature rats may be functional.

We reinvestigated this point in the following experiment. Litters from Sprague-Dawley rats on day 5 were adjusted to 8 pups (4 of each sex— the results obtained on males are not reported at this time) and 4 treatment groups were formed: (1) pups handled daily from days 5 through 15; (2) normal rabbit serum (0.3 ml) injected from day 5 to day 15; (3) 0.03 ml antiserum to ovine LH injected on days 5 to 15 (antiserum potency of this daily amount is equivalent to 3000 ng LH); (4) 0.06 ml antiserum to ovine FSH (anti-FSH potency = 37,000 ng). Each amount was diluted to a volume of 0.1 ml for subcutaneous injection. The 11 injections administered were made at 0900 to 1000 hours daily. On day 15 one-half of the groups were autopsied; some rats received 0.5 μCi/g ^{3}H-thymidine 2 hours before autopsy at 1400 to 1500 hours. The serum and pituitary were collected for LH and FSH measurement by radioimmunoassay and the ovaries, adrenals and uteri were weighed. Ovaries were prepared for serial section with hematoxylin and eosin stain or for autoradiography; in those ovaries in which ^{3}H-thymidine was incorporated into DNA determination was made by scintillation counter. The remainder of each group of rats was used for determination of the time of vaginal opening. Some were autopsied at 49 days; others were permitted to undergo pregnancy tests after 90 days of age.

Data on organ weight on day 15 are noted in Table 1. Uterine weights were significantly heavier in the treated groups than in the controls. At this time serum LH data are not available; FSH data and pituitary LH content are given in Table 2. As expected, the serum values of FSH are high in the controls. Except for 1 animal treated with antiserum to LH (which showed serum FSH of 300 ng/ml) FSH values were considerably higher in this group than in the controls (1000 to 2850 ng/ml). In rats treated with antiserum to FSH (the last injection was given 5 hours before serum collection) no free FSH was detectable and 100 per cent binding of the iodinated rat FSH was seen in the assay. Pituitary FSH contents did not differ significantly between groups; the large standard errors resulted from a bimodal distribution of values within each group (10 to 26 μg/pituitary versus 40 to 65 μg/pituitary). Pituitary LH contents also did not differ among groups (Table 1). Our control serum FSH values were lower than those reported by others for 10 to 15-day-old female rats (Ojeda & Ramirez,

TABLE 1.   Female rat organ weight data at autopsy on day 15

Treatment[a]	No.	Body weight (g)	Ovary (mg)	Uterus (mg)
Handling	9	32.0 ±0.4	7.67 ±0.46	18.99 ±1.58
Normal rabbit serum	9	31.7 ±0.5	9.07 ±0.69	17.50 ±0.94
Antiserum to FSH	8	30.0 ±1.5	8.59 ±0.84	23.29 ±1.38
Antiserum to LH	9	33.3 ±0.7	9.98 ±0.68	20.29 ±1.21

Mean±SE.

[a] Days 5 through 15.

t-tests.   No differences between handling and normal rabbit serum (NRS) controls in any variable. Antiserum to FSH: ovarian weight not different from NRS; uterine weight different from NRS ($p < 0.005$). Antiserum to LH: ovary weight not different from NRS, body weight and uterine weight borderline different from NRS ($p < 10, > .05$).

TABLE 2.   Female rat pituitary gonadotropin data at day 15

Treatment	Pituitary weight (mg)	Serum FSH (ng/ml)	Pituitary FSH (μg/pit.)	Pituitary LH (μg/pit.)
Handling	1.12 ±.08 (9)[b]	693 ±47 (3)	25.7 ±8.3 (4)	0.98 ±.18 (4)
Normal rabbit serum	1.39 ±.06 (9)	654 ±71 (4)	35.2 ±10.6 (5)	0.78 ±.20 (5)
Antiserum to FSH	1.42 ±.07 (9)	117%[a] ±10 (4)	34.8 ±7.5 (5)	1.07 ±.11 (5)
Antiserum to LH	1.51 ±0.12 (8)	1313 ±543 (4)	39.7 ±10.1 (5)	1.02 ±.19 (5)

Mean±SE.

(N)

[a] Binding of FSH-^{131}I was in excess of 100%.

FSH standard—FSH-RP-1.

LH standard—NIH-LH-S14.

[b] Numbers in parentheses = number of animals studied.

1972; Goldman et al, 1971; Kragt & Dahlgren, 1972); they were higher than in adult females, except during the proestrous surge. Developmental differences between strains or experiments could account for the lower values in our controls. Pituitary FSH and LH contents (Table 2) are in the same general range observed earlier in rats around 15 days of age (Dupon & Schwartz, 1971; Baker & Kragt, 1969; Kragt & Ganong, 1968; Lisk, 1968; Matsuyama, Weisz, & Lloyd, 1966).

Ovarian histology at day 15 revealed normal follicular growth in all groups and equivalent thymidine labeling of granulosa cells (total thymidine uptake in DNA was also not different among groups). Interstitial cell development, particularly in the anti-LH-serum treated rats (Fig.-1a-d), was deficient in both groups treated with antiserum.

The time of vaginal opening in the treated rats was more variable than in controls but tended to be earlier (Fig. 2). This was not because of faster growth rates, as can be seen by the lower body weights at the time of vaginal opening (Fig. 2) and by the normal weights at 15 and 49 days (Tables 1 and 3). Organ weights on day 49 were not different between groups and vaginal cycling was seen in all rats. Further data are being collected on all these groups and will be reported.

The poor interstitial tissue development observed in our preparations indicates that this part of the ovary may be dependent in some way on both FSH and LH because deprivation of either one is detrimental. The origin of interstitial cells has been studied in the mouse, with indications that in the first 2 weeks of life the interstitial cells are dividing; thereafter, any addition would have to arise from follicular rests (Byskov, Pedersen, & Peters, 1969). Whether the rat is similar in this respect has not been

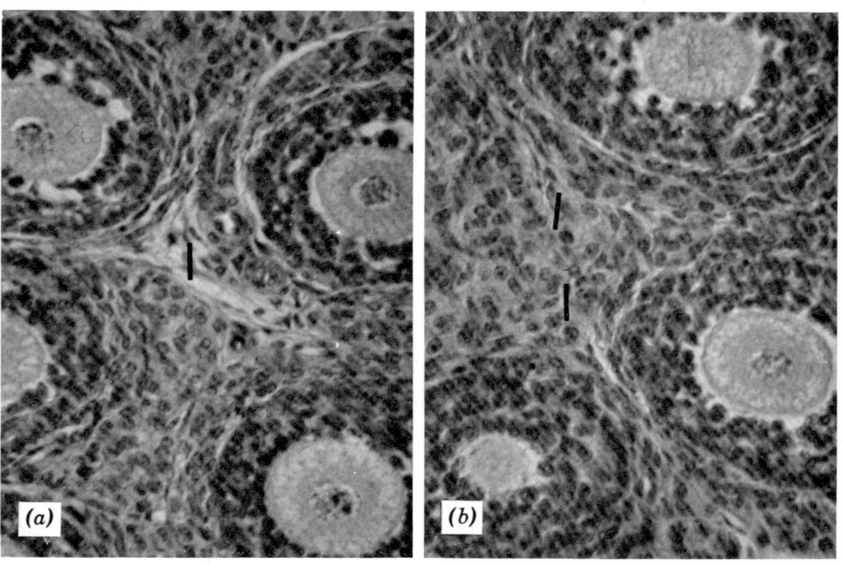

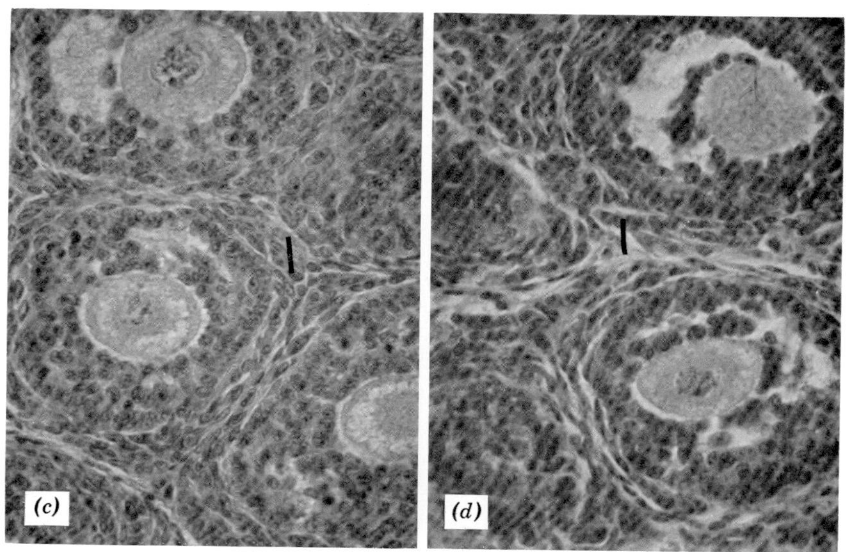

FIG. 1. Ovarian follicular and interstitial tissue development at 15 days of age: (*a*) handled control; (*b*) normal rabbit serum injection; (*c*) antiserum to LH; (d) antiserum to FSH. (450 X).

TABLE 3. Female rat data at autopsy

Treatment[a]	No.	Body weight (g)	Ovary (mg)	Uterus (mg)	%VC[b]
Handling	4	160	78.8	207.0	36.6
		±3	±5.8	±16.5	±4.3
Normal rabbit serum	2	162	69.4	185.6	28.5
		±4	±3.2	±5.7	±0.0
Antiserum to FSH	4	166	74.9	230.2	40.2
		±5	±4.7	±16.4	±3.4
Antiserum to LH	4	168	69.1	226.3	37.4
		±2	±3.1	±20.6	±2.8

$X \pm SE$.

[a] Days 5 through 15.

[b] Per cent VC. Per cent of daily vaginal smears showing only nucleated and/or cornified cells between day of vaginal opening and day 49.

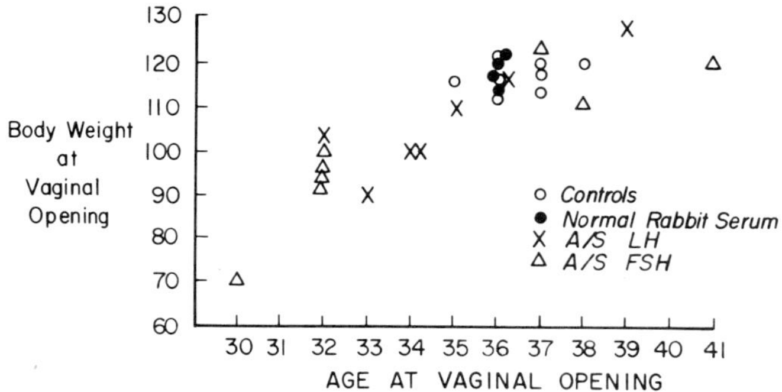

FIG. 2. Body weight on the day of vaginal opening for each pup is plotted as a function of day of age.

determined. On day 15, in all our pups, few interstitial cells were labeled with ^{3}H-thymidine and none of the large differentiated cells exhibited any signs of cell division. In spite of the poor interstitial tissue development, the ovarian weight was normal for the subjects treated with antiserum. Thus we did not find follicular development affected by either antiserum alone, a result similar to that reported by others who used different experimental paradigms (Pedersen, 1970; Eshkol & Lunenfeld, 1972; Price & Ortiz, 1944; Shiino & Rennels, 1967). The larger uteri in the groups treated with antiserum raises a question about the origin of early prepubertal estrogens; as mentioned, ovariectomy at birth results in smaller uteri by day 10 (Plagge, 1956; Baker & Kragt, 1969).

There is a high secretion rate of gonadotropins in rats 5 to 15 days of age (Kragt & Dahlgren, 1972; Goldman et al, 1971; Ojeda & Ramirez, 1972), and removal of ovaries neonatally is detrimental to uterine growth (Plagge, 1956; Baker & Kragt, 1969). Gonadotropin inhibition for some time by antisera tends to bring about an early puberty (Kupperman et al, 1942, and our study), which suggests an induction of higher secretion rates in response to treatment (Table 2). The evidence of increased secretion rates of gonadotropins seen in the present studies may be the result of alterations in a "short feedback circuit" activation in these rats (Ojeda & Ramirez, 1969). The results indicate that the early high levels of gonadotropin secretion are important to normal developmental sequences, including ovarian stromal maturation and setting the control of the onset of puberty.

The follicular maturation in the 15-day-old pups that were deprived of one or the other gonadotropin for 11 days indicates that development of this element of the ovary is probably not dependent on the presence of normal ratios or amounts of FSH and LH during 5 to 15 days of life. That the surviving pups could go through puberty and show apparently normal cycles is preliminary evidence of lack of detrimental effect on ovarian, pituitary, or hypothalamic function.

ACKNOWLEDGMENT

We wish to thank Mr. William L. Talley and Mrs. Brigitte Mann for their technical assistance, the Endocrinology Study Section, Dr. A. F. Parlow for the NIAMDD kit used for FSH assay, and Drs. G. Niswender, A. R. Midgley, and Leo Reichert for the materials used in the 0:0 radioimmunoassay for LH. These experiments were supported by Public Health Service Grants HD-0440, HD-04471, and HD-5865.

REFERENCES

Baker, T. B. (1972). Oogenesis and ovarian development. In *Reproductive Biology*, H. Balin & S. Glasser, Eds., *Excerpta Medica*, Amsterdam, pp. 398–437.

Baker, F. D. & Kragt, C. L. (1969) Maturation of the hypothalamic-pituitary-gonadal negative feedback system. *Endocrinology* **85**, 522–527.

Baker, T. G. & Neal, P. (1972). Gonadotropin-induced maturation of mouse graafian follicles in organ culture. In *Oogenesis*, J. Biggers & A. W. Schuetz, Eds., University Park Press, Baltimore, pp. 377–396.

Beaumont, H. M. (1969). Effects of hormonal environment on the radio-sensitivity of oocytes. In *Radiation Biology of the Fetal and Juvenile Mammal*, M. R. Sikov & D. D. Mahlum, Eds., *U.S. Atomic Energy Commission, Conf. 690501*, pp. 943–954.

Byskov, A. G., Pedersen, T., & Peters, H. (1969). Development of the stroma in the immature mouse ovary. In *Gonadotropins and Ovarian Development*, W. R. Butt, T. Pedersen, & H. Peters, Eds., Williams & Wilkins, Baltimore, pp. 228-231.

Clark, H. M. (1935). A sex difference in the change in potency of the anterior hypophysis following bilateral castration in newborn rats. *Anat. Rec.* **61**, 193–202.

Donahue, R. P. (1972). Relation of oocyte maturation to ovulation in mammals. In *Oogenesis*, J. Biggers & A. W. Schuetz, Eds., University Park Press, Baltimore, pp. 413–438.

Donovan, B. T. & van der Werff ten Bosch, J. J. (1965). *Physiology of Puberty*, Williams & Wilkins, Baltimore.

Dunham, L. J., Watts, R. M., & Adair, F. L. (1941). Development of newborn rat ovaries implanted in the anterior chambers of adult rats' eyes. *Arch. Path.* **32**, 910–927.

Dunlap, J. L., Preis, Jr., L. K., & Gerall, A. A. (1972). Compensatory ovarian hypertrophy as a function of age and neonatal androgenization. *Endocrinology* **90**, 1309–1314.

Dupon, C. & Schwartz, N. B. (1971). Pituitary LH patterns in prepuberal normal and testosterone-sterilized rats. *Neuroendocrinology* **7**, 236–248.

Eshkol, A. & Lunenfeld, B. (1972). Gonadotropic regulation of ovarian development in mice during infancy. In *Gonadotropins*, B. B. Saxena, C. G. Beling, & H. M. Gandy, Eds., Wiley, New York, pp. 335–346.

Goldenberg, R. L., Reiter, E. O., Vaitukaitis, J. L., & Ross, G. T. (1972a) Interaction of FSH and hCG on follicle development in the ovarian augmentation reaction. *Endocrinology* **91**, 533–536.

Goldenberg, R. L., Vaitukaitis, J. L. & Ross, G. T. (1972b) Estrogen and follicle stimulating hormone interactions on follicle growth in rats. *Endocrinology* **90**, 1492–1498.

Goldman, B. D. & Gorski, R. A. (1971). Effects of gonadal steroids in the secretion of LH and FSH in neonatal rats. *Endocrinology* **89**, 112–115.

Goldman, B. D., Grazia, Y. R., Kamberi, I. A., & Porter, J. C. (1971). Serum gonadotropin concentrations in intact and castrated neonatal rats. *Endocrinology* **88**, 771–776.

Goldman, B. D., Quadagno, D. M., Shryne, J., & Gorski, R. A. (1972). Modification of phallus development and sexual behavior in rats treated with gonadotropin antiserum neonatally. *Endocrinology* **90**, 1025–1031.

Hertz, R. (1963). Pituitary independence of the prepubertal development of the ovary of the rat and the rabbit and its pertinence to hypo-ovarianism in women. In *The Ovary*, H. G. Grady & D. E. Smith, Eds. Williams & Wilkins, Baltimore, pp. 120–127.

Hertz, R. & Hisaw, F. L. (1934). Effects of follicle-stimulating and luteinizing pituitary extracts on the ovaries of the infantile and juvenile rabbit. *Amer. J. Physiol.* **108**, 1–13.

Hisaw, F. L. (1947). Development of the Graafian follicle and ovulation. *Physiol. Rev.* **27**, 95–119.

Hoffmann, J. C. & Schwartz, N. B. (1972). Ovulation—basic aspects. In *Reproductive Biology*, H. Balin & S. Glasser, Eds., *Excerpta Medica*, Amsterdam, pp. 438–476.

Jones, E. C. & Krohn, P. L. (1961). Effects of hypophysectomy on age changes in the ovaries of mice. *J. Endocrinol.* **21**, 497–509.

Kragt, C. L. & Dahlgren, J. (1972). Development of neural regulation of follicle stimulation hormone (FSH) secretion. *Neuroendocrinology* **9**, 30–40.

Kragt, C. L. & Ganong, W. F. (1968). Pituitary FSH content in female rats at various ages. *Endocrinology* **82**, 1241–1245.

Kupperman, H. S., Meyer, R. K. & Finerty, J. C. (1942). Precocious gonadal development occurring in immature rats following a short-time treatment with antigonadotropic serum. *Amer. J. Physiol.* **136**, 293–298.

Lisk, R. D. (1968). Luteinizing hormone in the pituitary gland of the albino rat: concentration and content as a function of sex and age. *Neuroendocrinology* **3**, 18–24.

Lostroh, A. J. & Johnson, R. E. (1966). Amounts of interstitial cell stimulatory hormone and follicle stimulating hormone required for follicular development, uterine growth and ovulation in the hypophysectomized rat. *Endocrinology* **79**, 991–996.

Matsuyama, E., Weisz, J. & Lloyd, C. W. (1966). Gonadotrophin content of pituitary glands of testosterone sterilized rats. *Endocrinology* **79**, 261–267.

Mauleon, P. (1969). Oogenesis and folliculogenesis. In *Reproduction Domestic Animals*, 2nd ed., H. H. Cole & P. T. Capps, Eds., Academic, New York, pp. 187–215.

Nalbandov, A. V. (1972). Interaction between oocytes and follicular cells. In *Oogenesis*, J. Biggers & A. W. Schuetz, Eds., University Park Press, Baltimore, pp. 513–522.

Nishizuka, Y. & Sakakura, T. (1971). Effect of combined removal of thymus and pituitary on post-natal ovarian follicular development in the mouse. *Endocrinology* **89**, 902–903.

Ojeda, S. R. & Ramirez, V. D. (1969) Automatic control of LH and FSH secretion by short feedback circuits in immature rats. *Endocrinology* **84**, 786–797.

Ojeda, S. R. & Ramirez, V. D. (1972). Plasma level of LH and FSH in maturing rats; response to hemigonadectomy. *Endocrinology* **90**, 466–472.

Pedersen, T. (1970). Follicle kinetics in the ovary of the cyclic mouse. *Acta Endocrinol.* **64**, 304–323.

Pedersen, T. (1972). Follicle growth in the mouse ovary. In *Oogenesis*, J. D. Biggers & A. W. Schuetz, Eds., University Park Press. Baltimore, pp. 361–376.

Peters, H. & Levy, E. (1966). Cell dynamics of the ovarian cycle. *J. Reprod. Fertil.* **11**, 227–236.

Plagge, J. C. (1956). Effects of prepuberal castration on body and thymus weight in the immature albino rat. *Anat. Rec.* **124**, 101–110.

Price, D. & Ortiz, E. (1944). Relation of age to reactivity in the reproductive system of the rat. *Endocrinology* **34**, 215–239.

Reiter, E. O., Goldenberg, R. L., Vaitukaitis, J. L., & Ross, G. T. (1972). A role for endogenous estrogen in normal ovarian development in the neonatal rat. *Endocrinology*. In press.

Ryle, M. (1971). Time factor in responses to pituitary gonadotrophins by mouse ovaries in vitro. *J. Reprod. Fertil.* **25**, 61–74.

Sasamoto, S. & Kennan, A. L. (1972). Effect of anti-PMS serum on follicular ovulability in hypophysectomized immature female rats pretreated with PMS. *Endocrinology* **91**, 350–354.

Schuetz, A. W. (1972). Hormones and follicular functions. In *Oogenesis*, J. Biggers & A. W. Schuetz, Eds , University Park Press, Baltimore, pp. 479–511.

Schwartz, N. B. (1969). A model for the regulation of ovulation in the rat. *Rec. Progr. Hormone Res.* **25**, 1–55.

Schwartz, N. B. & Ely, C. A. (1970). Comparison of effects of hypophysectomy, antiserum to ovine LH, and ovariectomy on estrogen secretion during the rat estrous cycle. *Endocrinology* **86**, 1420–1435.

Schwartz, N. B., Krone, K., Talley, W. L., & Ely, C. A. (1973). Administration of antiserum to ovine FSH in the female rat: failure to influence immediate events of cycle. *Endocrinology*. In press.

Schwartz, N. B. & McCormack, C. E. (1972). Reproduction: gonadal function and its regulation. *Ann. Rev. Physiol.* **34**, 425–472.

Shiino, A. & Rennels. E. G. (1967). Pituitary follicle stimulating hormone *in vivo* and ovarian development in the infant rat. *Endocrinology* **81**, 1379–1386.

Swerdloff, R. S., Jacobs, H. S., & Odell, W. D. (1972). Hypothalamic-pituitary-gonadal interrelationships in the rat during sexual maturation. In *Gonadotropins*, B. B. Saxena, C. G. Beling, & H. M. Gandy, Eds., Wiley, New York, pp. 546–561.

Zamboni, L. (1972). Comparative studies on the ultrastructure of mammalian oocytes. In *Oogenesis*, J. Biggers & A. W. Schuetz, Eds., University Park Press, Baltimore, pp. 5–45.

DISCUSSION

Dr. Ramirez.   We have found that ovine FSH in the immature female rat has a positive feedback action on pituitary FSH. The implantation of ovine FSH directly in the medial basal hypothalamus can induce an endogenous secretion of FSH in the immature rat. This may not be true in the adult animal (over 200 g) and may explain the high level of plasma FSH that we are finding in the infantile female rat.

Dr. Schwartz.   It is possible that we may have studied the same feedback mechanism inadvertently.

Dr. Weisz.   At 15 days of age the follicles are histochemically still quite unimpressive and there is little thecal differentiation in terms of histochemical characteristics or the electronmicroscopic appearance of the cells around the antral follicles. The interstitial cells of the ovary are plump and full of lipids, $\triangle^5$-3β-hydroxysteroid dehydrogenase, and glucose-6-phosphate dehydrogenase; these are the only steroidogenic cells up to and including this stage of development of the ovary. When testosterone propionate or dehydrotestosterone propionate is injected at 5 days of age, the peaks of FSH and LH found in normal females at around 14 days of age are suppressed and the interstitial cells look flat and contain less lipid and less steroid dehydrogenase activity. Morphologically, the ovaries of such androgen-treated rats look very much like those of the antibody-treated ones shown here. Therefore we think that the gonadotropins are needed for the normal differentiation of the primary interstitial gland tissue. Such morphological, histochemical changes have a biochemical correlate at least in the neonatally androgen-treated rat. In our laboratory Dr. Quattropani has studied the conversion of labeled progesterone to estrone and estradiol in vitro by infantile rat ovaries at different ages between 5 and 14 days of age. Two incubations were carried out at each age, each containing at least 10 ovaries. The tissue substrate ratio was kept constant and the quantification of steroids was made by double isotope dilution technique. There was an impressive conversion of progesterone to estrogens. In terms of per cent conversion, the ovaries of immature rats did much better than ovaries of normal adult rats under identical conditions. The per cent conversion rose after 5 days of age, reached a maximum at 10 days, and then decreased. Injection of 100 μg testosterone propionate caused a marked decrease in both the amounts of estradiol and estrone formed by ovaries of 7- and 10-day-old rats. We were lucky enough to include a group of animals that was injected only with sesame oil on day 5 and were surprised by the marked increase in conversion of progesterone to estradiol and estrone by the ovaries of these animals at 7 days of age. This reinforces what Dr. Schwartz has said: we are dealing with a very labile system.

DR. SCHWARTZ.   We used a sham injection or handled another group of animals as controls, an important part of working with these young animals, as shown by what happened in Dr. Weisz's rats with the sesame oil. Dr. Weisz, you showed maximal in vitro conversion of estradiol at day 10, but by day 15, with a somewhat depleted interstitium, there appeared to be increased estradiol output, at least using the uterine weight as a criterion.

DR. WEISZ.   The most disturbing aspect of Dr. Schwartz's findings is the fact that the uteri of the antibody-treated rats were heavier. What does the histology of the uterus show? Normally one can see evidence of estrogenic stimulation by 15 days of age.

DR. SCHWARTZ.   We did not look. We were doing wet:dry ratios and did not cut out a slice to look at. I am pretty sure this is an estrogenic stimulation, but I have no idea what the endometrium looked like.

DR. WEISZ.   Our findings do not necessarily mean that the ovaries were actually secreting a great deal of estrogens in vivo, although, as I have said before, circulating estradiol and estrone levels are high in immature rats.

DR. SCHWARTZ.   In vivo it is going to be difficult to get at what the ovaries are secreting at this time because of the adrenals.

DR. GANONG.   The situation with the anti-FSH is reminiscent of that reported when you have circulating antibodies to other hormones for a long period; for example, we raised antibodies to circulating renin without producing any apparent renin deficiency (Ganong, Lee, van Brunt, & Biglier, 1965). In animals with these antibodies the renin-secreting cells become huge and hyperplastic and the renal renin content rises. Analogous changes have been reported by others with circulating anti-TSH and anti-insulin antibodies.

DR. STEINBERGER.   In the male one can totally suppress FSH and LH. By giving estrogen or testosterone we have shown that newborn rats have essentially no gonadotropins in the pituitary plasma when we treat them with these two steroids.

DR. FISHER.   We have raised antibody to ovine TSH, T4, and T3, vasopressin, and glucagon in rabbits, and, with one exception, none of the rabbits have clinical hormone deficiency syndromes associated with the high antibody titers. So it is extremely difficult to know what the free circulating hormone levels are; for instance, the T4- and T3-immunized animals are not hypothyroid. One out of 5 of the vasopressin-immunized rabbits manifested clinical diabetes insipidus, but obviously even that is uncommon because 4 out of 5 did not. Also, it is possible that you transiently raise the free hormone concentrations in some circumstances; for example, if you have a high concentration of bound hormone and somehow it becomes disassociated by a change in pH.

DR. SCHWARTZ.   This was done after a lot of work on adult animals in which (with either chronic or acute injections of anti-LH-serum), we were able to abolish anything we wanted to in terms of function. Thus the antiserum does tie up antigen. With the anti-FSH serum we have not been successful in the adult, but this may be because the adult does not need FSH in the same way as the immature animal. Incidentally, this is not the first observation made of this kind in the rat. Kupperman published a fine paper some years ago in which he discussed a much higher amount of a nonspecific antiserum given to young rats. He first showed a suppression, then an enhancement of gonadotropic function. We may not have seen the suppression but only the enhancement, and I do not think we know whether it is a peripheral phenomenon or synergism or a circulating but biologically active antigen-antibody complex.

DR. RODGERS.   Dr. Weisz was using a quantity of testosterone that causes sterilization in the female. I am curious to know whether she tried smaller amounts of testosterone and still obtained a repressed conversion. Is it dose-dependent?

DR. WEISZ.   We have only looked at the effect of smaller doses of testosterone on the histochemistry of the ovary. There is a graded response in terms of the decreased $\triangle^5$-3β-ol steroid dehydrogenase activity and lipid depletion.

DR. GESCHWIND.   Drs. Serra and Sheridan have been doing some experiments in which they injected male rats with antiserum that reacts against both FSH and LH for 10 days. On the eleventh day the testicular weight was reduced, but only slightly; but by the twentieth day, after they had discontinued treatment for 10 days, the testicular weights were significantly higher than those of animals that had received no treatment. In addition, female rats that were treated for 10 days with antiserum showed puberty; they began cycling about 7 or 8 days earlier than normal females. In both the males and females, when we tested the serum in an immunoassay system (serum taken on day 20, 10 days after antibody injections were stopped), there seemed to be evidence of excess circulating antibody, although we were putting it into a tube instead of into an animal. There is the possibility of a rebound effect from the antibody; also, if you deprive the animal of the steroids for several days by the antibody treatment, there might be some sort of a resetting of the hypothalamic gonadostatic action, as suggested by comparing the results of Swerdloff and Odell with others in castrated rats.

DR. SCHWARTZ.   The resetting could have taken place because a reset to a higher level would account for an apparent rise in steroid and gonadotropin.

DR. PAULSEN.   Dr. Schwartz, what range of potency of your antiserum did you administer?

DR. SCHWARTZ.   The daily dose of the anti-LH serum was enough to oppose about 3000 ng of ovine LH on the OAAD assay. The antiserum to FSH was given in a daily dose which, if injected into a Steelman-Pohley recipient in the presence of sheep FSH, would antagonize 37,000 ng.

DR. PAULSEN.   You are referring to S-1 equivalents?

DR. SCHWARTZ.   No, S-3.

DR. PAULSEN.   The reason I raise this point concerns some interesting observations Drs. Maddock, Leach and I made when studying the properties of hog FSH. We administered this preparation to both men and women to evaluate, in part, the relationship between antihormone titers and gonadal function. The potency of the antihormone titers was determined by bioassay in the immature female rat that received both the patient sera in varying quantities and hog FSH. With sera having low antihormone titers, augmentation of the simultaneously administered FSH occurred; on the other hand, sera of high antihormone potency inhibited the biologic effect of the administered FSH, as one would expect.

DR. SCHWARTZ.   What test were you using in the recipient?

DR. PAULSEN.   The ovarian weight and uterine weight.

DR. SCHWARTZ.   In an intact recipient?

DR. PAULSEN.   We administered the antiserum and FSH at different sites to intact immature female rats.

DR. SCHWARTZ.   We have never seen the augmentation. We use a standard Steelman-Pohley system and inject FSH 30 minutes before each combined injection of the FSH and hCG (we give 6 injections over 3 days). We have either seen no effect if the dose is low enough, or we have seen a blocking effect of FSH.

DR. GESCHWIND.   Ahern, Cole, Geschwind, and Itze (1972) reported some results on immunizing sheep with hCG, and I would remind you of the classical responses that were observed. One is a progonadotropic effect, another is a gonadotropic effect, and the third is an antigonadotropic effect. It would seem that you have the whole gamut of these things, Dr. Schwartz.

REFERENCES

Ahern, C., Cole, H. H., Geschwind, I. I., & Itze, L. (1972). Physiological studies on the identity of the gonadotropic and progonadotropic substance(s) in sera of ewes immunized against hCG. *Endocrinology* **90**, 1619–1633.

Ganong, W. F., Lee, T. C., van Brunt, E. E., & Biglieri, E. G. (1965). Aldosterone secretion in dogs immunized with hog renin. *Endocrinology* **76**, 1141–1149.

14.

Maturation of Male Germinal Epithelium

E. STEINBERGER

The fundamental concepts dealing with the kinetics of maturation of the seminiferous epithelium were formulated in the nineteenth century by Von Ebner (1871) and Benda (1887), who suggested that the epithelium in the seminiferous tubules undergoes a constant and progressive development, characterized by formation of more mature and more differentiated cells from young germ cells. Subsequently numerous authors investigated this process and numerous hypotheses were proposed to explain the kinetics of spermatogenesis (Regaud, 1901; Curtis, 1918; Beylot & Baudrimont, 1926; Roosen-Runge & Giesel, 1950).

In the last 25 years an active effort to define the kinetics of spermatogenesis has resulted in the creation of a body of information that allows a relatively clear understanding of the qualitative as well as the quantitative aspects of spermatogenesis. The formation of mature spermatozoa from the *adult* form of immature germ cells, the spermatogonia, has been clarified in great detail for a number of species (reviewed by Steinberger

---

Abbreviations

FSH	Follicle stimulating hormone
hLH	Human luteinizing hormone

& Steinberger, 1969; Clermont, 1972). Several major areas still remain unclear however: (1) the details of the formation of the *adult* form of germ cells from the *fetal* form of germ cells, the gonocytes; (2) the mechanisms by which the stem cell (an adult form of a germ cell) renews itself and concurrently produces progeny that enter the process of spermatogenesis which results in the formation of spermatozoa; (3) the details of the hormonal control of each segment of the spermatogenic process.

For this discussion the entire spermatogenic process is divided into 3 phases (Fig. 1): the fetal, transitional, and adult. In the fetal phase spermatogenesis is characterized by the presence of primordial germ cells (gonocytes) in the seminiferous tubules, which serve as the precursors of primitive type A spermatogonia. In the transitional phase the primitive type A spermatogonia which predominate in this phase of development of the seminiferous epithelium appear in the testes shortly after birth and give rise to the adult germ cells. In the adult phase the germ cells include the entire sequence of germinal epithelial cells from type A spermatogonia to mature spermatozoa.

During their development the gonocytes replicate, differentiate, and ultimately transform into transitional germ cells (the primitive type A spermatogonia). These cells probably also undergo a differentiative process, but no information is available concerning the details. Whether they replicate under normal in vivo conditions has not been determined; however, in vitro studies, have shown that they replicate and may continue to do so for months (Steinberger & Steinberger, 1967). The primitive type A spermatogonia definitely are capable of transforming in vivo to the adult form of germ cells (type A spermatogonia).

The descriptive phase of investigations on the development and kinetics

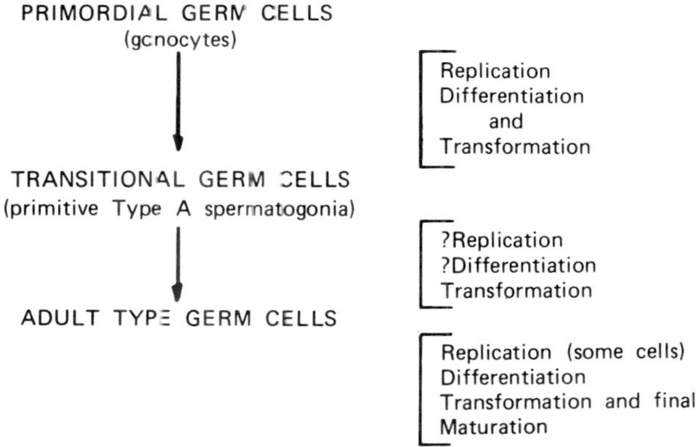

FIG. 1.   Three major phases of germinal cell development.

of the seminiferous epithelium has been essentially completed except for the details of the stem cell renewal and transformation of primitive type A to the adult type A spermatogonia reviewed by Clermont, 1972; Huckins, 1971; Steinberger and Steinberger, 1972. The unanswered questions deal with the hormonal and biochemical mechanisms involved in the control of replication, differentiation, transformation, and final maturation of various types of germ cells.

Figure 2 illustrates the progression of specific germ cell compartments during development. The fetal compartment in the embryonal testis is composed of gonocytes that migrate into the gonadal anlage from the yolk sac and can be detected in the testes of a 14-day-old rat fetus. The gonocytes persist in the testes until about the fourth postnatal day, when they give rise to primitive type A spermatogonia that form the transitional cell compartment. These spermatogonia differentiate into *adult* type germ cells that form 2 compartments, proliferating and differentiating. The proliferating compartment is composed of type A spermatogonia with the capacity to renew themselves and to form the cells of the differentiating compartment. The latter appears about 6 to 7 days postnatally and is composed of cells that differentiate further to form progressively more mature germ cells. Apparently once the germ cells enter the differentiating compartment they are committed to progressive differentiation and result in the formation of mature spermatozoa.

Studies in the 1930s demonstrated clearly that the spermatogenic process is under control of pituitary gonadotropins and androgens (review, Stein-

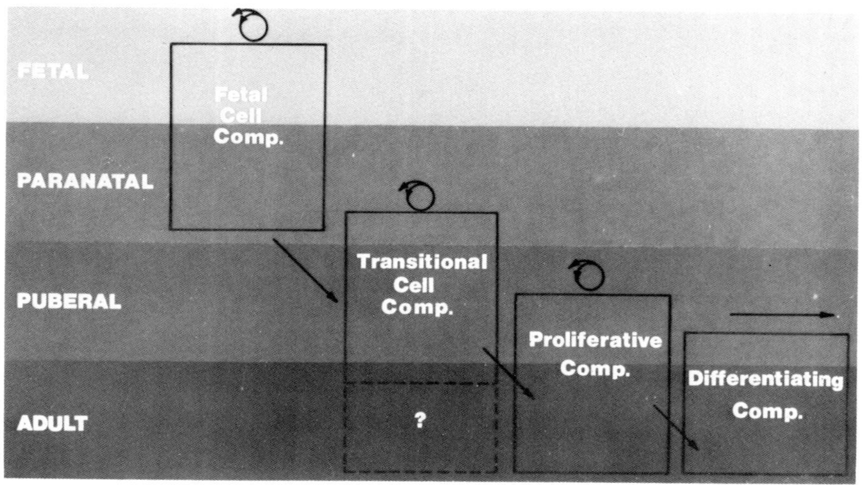

FIG. 2. Normal progression of spermatogenic compartments during development.

berger, 1971). The hormonal requirements for specific segments of spermatogenesis have been a topic of investigation ever since. It is still unclear however, which germ cells or which cellular transformations are under hormonal control. It is also not known which of the gonadotropins or androgens are the active hormones.

Before discussion of the hormonal requirements, I shall attempt to integrate the available information concerning the details of the growth and differentiation of each germ cell compartment, with the rat testis utilized as a mode.

GROWTH AND DIFFERENTIATION OF THE GERM CELL COMPARTMENTS

The Fetal Compartment

Morphologic studies (Beaumont & Mandl, 1963) have shown that between the fourteenth and seventeenth fetal day the gonocytes exhibit intensive mitotic activity, indicating active engagement in the process of replication. After the seventeenth day replication ceases and progressive growth of the gonocytes can be observed for the next 3 to 4 days. Whether the growth of the gonocytes is associated with a process of differentiation cannot yet be stated. There are no direct data suggesting differentiation. Shortly after birth the gonocytes begin to diminish in number. Their diminution is probably the result of their dividing and entering the transitional cell compartment composed of the primitive type A spermatogonia (Fig. 3).

Transitional Cell Compartment

A schematic illustration of the changes occurring shortly after birth in the germ cell population of the rat testes is presented in Fig. 4. During the first 4 days the number of gonocytes diminishes and primitive type A spermatogonia appear; their number increases rapidly until it reaches a maximum between the fourth and fifth day postnatally. At this time the type A spermatogonia of the adult type make their appearance. As they increase in number the primitive type A spermatogonia diminish, and after the seventh or eighth postnatal day only a few remain. The question whether primitive type A spermatogonia persist from this point on into adulthood is unresolved. Information derived from tissue-culture experiments suggests that primitive type A spermatogonia may persist into adulthood because primitive type A spermatogonia can be detected in organ cultures of adult testis after the more differentiated germ cells degenerate (Steinberger & Steinberger, 1967). This observation could be explained by making the assumption that occasional primitive type A spermatogonia do

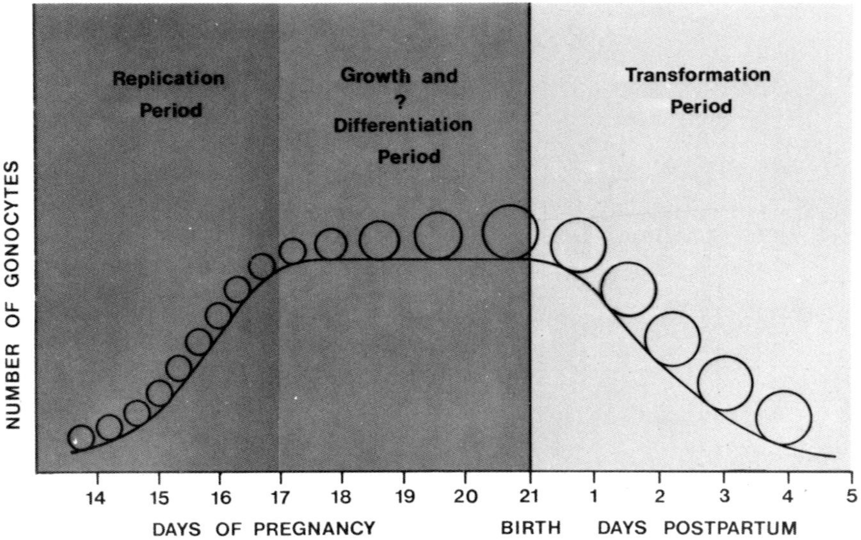

FIG. 3. Development of gonocytes.

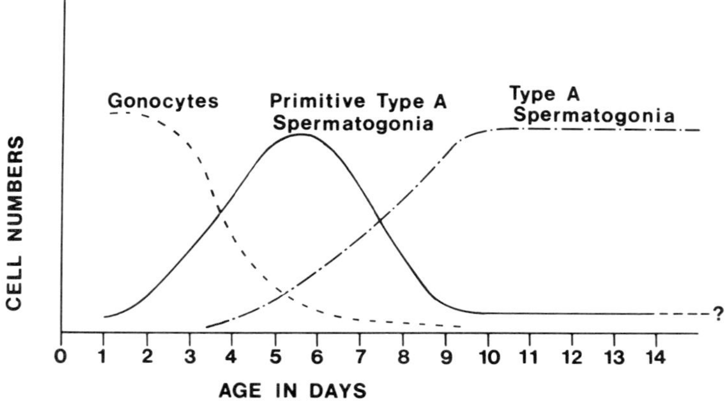

FIG. 4. Schematic illustration of development of germ cells in postnatal testes.

persist in adult testes and under culture conditions become mitotically active. The reason why they are not detected in normal mature testes could be their scarcity. On the other hand, one cannot totally discard the possibility that, under conditions of culture, dedifferentiation of adult type germinal cells (type A spermatogonia ?) to primitive type A spermatogonia may occur.

Adult Germ Cell Compartment

This compartment constitutes cells normally present in adult testes. The continuous supply of germ cells in the "differentiating compartment" is provided, according to the hypothesis suggested by Huckins (1971), by a renewing group of young type A spermatogonia from the "proliferating compartment" (Fig. 5). The kinetics of the "differentiating compartment" involve further replication of young germ cells (type A spermatogonia), differentiation (formation of type B spermatogonia), reduction (meiotic division), and metamorphosis of the round germ cells (spermatids) into highly differentiated motile cells, the spermatozoa (Fig. 5).

HORMONAL REQUIREMENTS

The details of the hormonal requirements for the various phases of the spermatogenic process still remain to be defined. Furthermore, the requirements for initiation of spermatogenesis may differ from those necessary for its maintenance and quantitatively normal spermatogenesis may need a specific hormonal milieu (Steinberger, 1970; Steinberger & Steinberger, 1972). The requirements for maintenance of quantitatively normal spermatogenesis are unknown. Consequently the quantitative aspects of spermatogenesis will not be considered; the primary focus is placed on initiation of the first wave of spermatogenesis in immature testis rather than on its maintenance.

Fetal Compartment

The hormonal requirements for the replication and differentiation of gonocytes for the formation of primitive type A spermatogonia are difficult

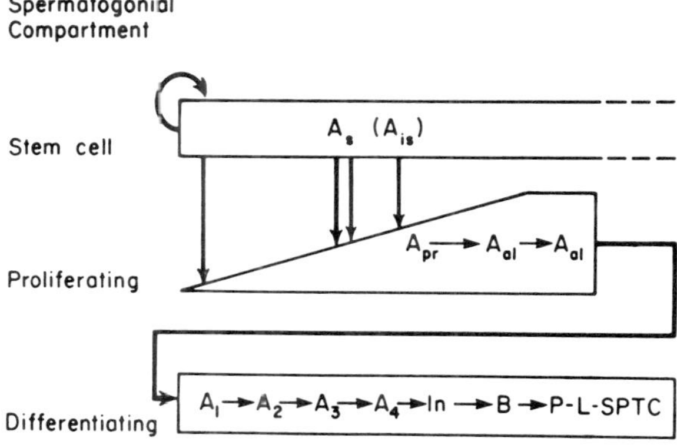

FIG. 5. Proposed model for the renewal and differentiation of spermatogonia in adult rat testes. From Huckins, 1971.

to define because the complexity of the system makes the design of an adequate experimental model difficult. The fetal testes are capable of synthesizing androgen (Noumura, Weisz, & Lloyd, 1966) and probably its secretion. They may also be exposed to fetal pituitary gonadotropins, placental hormones (gonadotropins, lactogens, or steroids), and maternal gonadotropins and gonadal steroids. Under these conditions it is difficult to dissect the possible effect of any one or combination of these hormones. In vivo manipulation of the hormonal level is difficult.

Application of tissue culture techniques has proved to be of distinct advantage in providing a new approach to this problem, but no definite information concerning the hormonal requirements for replication and differentiation of gonocytes has yet come forth. Tissue culture experiments with newborn testes have shown that gonocytes in this stage of development are capable of forming primitive type A spermatogonia in absence of exogenous hormones in the culture medium (Steinberger & Steinberger, 1966). It should be noted, however, that this culture system does not rule out the possibility of an androgen requirement, for explanted fragments of testicular tissue are capable of converting progesterone to testosterone for about 3 days after explantation (Steinberger, Ficher, & Steinberger, 1969). Whether testosterone is actually synthesized de novo and secreted by these cultures is not known. Nevertheless there is a distinct possibility that during the first few days in culture the gonocytes might be exposed to endogenous testosterone. Thus, although the organ culture studies rule out the requirement for gonadotropic hormones, they do not rule out the possibility that testosterone is required for the transformation of gonocytes into primitive type A spermatogonia.

The rat is actually a poor model for the study of hormonal requirements for transformation of gonocytes into primitive type A spermatogonia because this process takes place shortly after birth, when the testes are still producing large amounts of testosterone, and requires only several days for completion. In man, on the other hand, the transformation of gonocytes into primitive type A spermatogonia does not occur until puberty, when the testes again begin to produce androgens. The gonocytes remain for a period of more than 10 years in a testosterone-poor milieu and do not enter the process of transformation until testosterone appears. That testosterone, rather than chronologic age or other factors, is responsible for the initiation of spermatogenesis in human testes was shown recently in a study of a 6-year-old boy who was harboring a testosterone-producing Leydig cell tumor in one testis (Steinberger, 1970).

These observations permit the following conclusions: the hormonal requirements for the process of gonocyte replication are not known; gonadotropins are not essential for the late stages of gonocyte differentiation and for their transformation into primitive type A spermatogonia; testosterone is probably required for transformation of gonocytes into primitive type A spermatogonia, i.e., for initiation of spermatogenesis.

It should be stressed that these processes have been investigated only from a qualitative viewpoint; for optimal quantitative expression of the spermatogenic process other hormonal or nonhormonal factors may be essential.

Transitional Compartment

In vivo experiments with rats, the pituitary gonadotropins of which were blocked with high doses of estradiol since birth, suggest that primitive type A spermatogonia are capable of entering the adult germ-cell compartment in the absence of hormones (Steinberger & Duckett, 1967). Similarly, when testes of four 4-day-old rats containing primitive type A spermatogonia were placed in culture, these cells also entered the adult germ cell compartment and progressed to pachytene spermatocytes in the absence of hormones in the culture medium; however, only one spermatogenetic wave occurred. After a period of time in culture the primitive type A spermatogonia failed to enter the adult germ cell compartment (Steinberger & Steinberger, 1967). It is difficult to ascertain whether this finding indicates a basic deficiency in the culture conditions or whether it suggests that hormones are indeed essential for this step of differentiation. Evidence has been presented that the primitive type A spermatogonia grown in culture for a number of weeks and unable to enter the adult phase of spermatogenesis do so when transplanted into a testis of an adult rat, where they progress to form mature spermatozoa. Furthermore, testicular tissue taken from adult rats and grown in culture to the point at which all germ cells (except for the primitive type A spermatogonia) disappear from the seminiferous tubules when transplanted into adult testes also shows progressive differentiation of primitive type A spermatogonia. These findings clearly indicate that the primitive type A spermatogonia growing in tissue culture in the absence of hormones for a prolonged period of time retain the capacity to enter the adult germ cell compartment when the proper conditions prevail.

Adult Germ Cell Compartment

The hormonal control of the adult germ cells deals with the hormonal requirements for replication and transformation of the type A spermatogenesis in the proliferative compartment and replication transformation and differentiation of germ cells in the differentiative compartment. No publications that are specifically concerned with the hormonal control of the proliferative compartment are available; however, if it is accepted that in hypophysectomized rats all gonadotropins are removed and that the testes produce no androgen, it must be concluded that replication in the proliferative compartment is hormone-independent. The differentiative compartment has been the topic of numerous investigations. Here we are concerned with the progression of type A spermatogonia to spermatozoa. A considerable body of information accumulated from both in vivo and in vitro studies suggests that proliferation of type A spermatogonia, their transformation to type B, formation of primary spermatocytes, and the lengthy meiotic prophase up to diakinesis of pachytene spermatocytes can occur, at least in a qualitative fashion, in the absence of hormones.

In vivo experiments that utilized adult hypophysectomized animals (Nelson & Merckel, 1938; Steinberger & Nelson, 1955; Clermont & Morgentaler, 1955), newborn estrogen-blocked (Steinberger & Duckett, 1965), or young clomiphene-blocked animals (Kalra & Prasad, 1967) support these conclusions. Direct evidence has also been provided by in vitro experiments that employed organ culture techniques. Primitive type A spermatogonia are able to enter the proliferative and differentiating compartments when grown in chemically defined media in the absence of hormones (Steinberger & Steinberger, 1966). The completion of the meiotic division, however, did not occur in these cultures. Furthermore, when late stages of meiotic spermatocytes were explanted, they failed to complete meiotic division. Similarly, when young spermatids were placed in culture, they failed to continue their development and degenerated rapidly.

In animal models with estrogen-blocked pituitary gonadotropins, in which spermatogenesis does not progress beyond pachytene spermatocytes, administration of testosterone permits completion of meiosis and formation of spermatids (Steinberger & Duckett, 1965). The fact that estrogen treatment prevented formation of gonadotropins in these animals has been shown recently by measurement of pituitary and plasma LH and FSH by radioimmunoassay techniques (Steinberger & Chowdhury, unpublished data 1971).

Testosterone appears to be the essential hormone required by spermatocytes for completion of meiotic division; it does not, however, support completion of spermatid development. Treatment of estrogen-blocked animals for several months with testosterone failed to induce formation of mature spermatozoa; the spermatids degenerated at steps 14 to 15 of their development. Administration of gonadotropins with FSH activity permitted the completion of the final steps and the formation of spermatozoa (Steinberger & Duckett, 1967).

SUMMARY AND COMMENT

It has not been demonstrated conclusively that the replication of gonocytes requires hormones, but their transformation into primitive type A spermatogonia probably does take testosterone. Replication of the proliferative compartment may not require hormones, and differentiation of the proliferative compartment to the differentiating compartment is probably hormone-independent. The differentiation of type A spermatogonia all the way through diakinetic pachytene spermatocytes is hormonally independent, but the completion of the meiotic division and formation of spermatids has an absolute requirement for testosterone. Completion of spermatid differentiation is FSH-dependent. Figure 6 presents a tentative hypothesis of hormonal control of spermatogenesis.

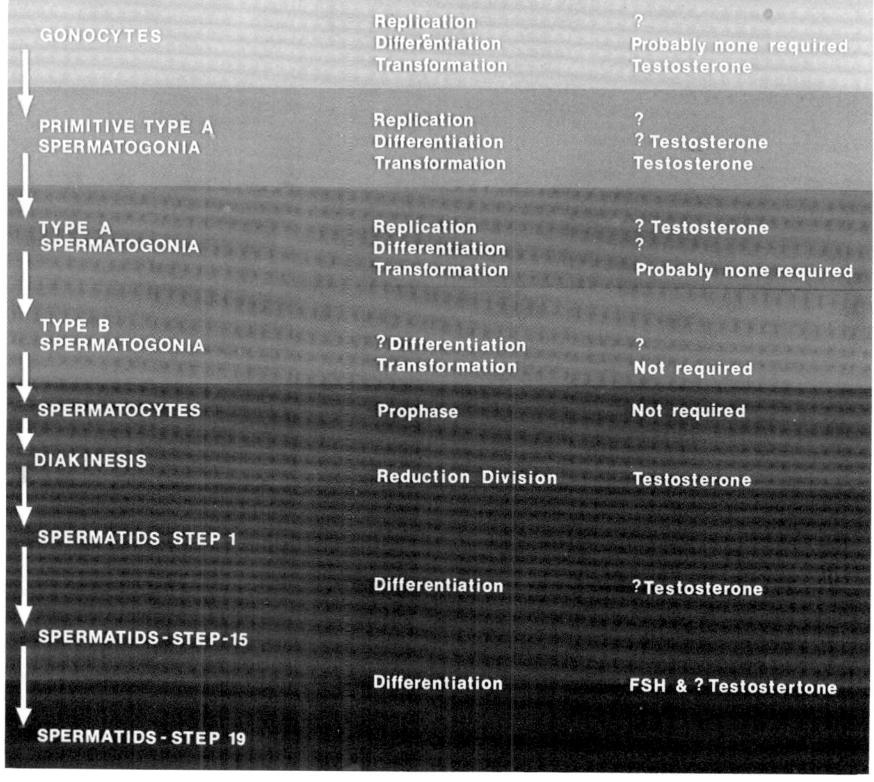

FIG. 6.   Tentative scheme of the hormonal control of initiation of the spermatogenic process.

Studies of patients with Leydig cell tumors of the testes demonstrated that in man spermatogenesis will commence in the presence of high levels of testosterone and will proceed through the meiotic division. In the absence of normal adult levels of gonadotropins, however, the spermatids fail to mature and do not form spermatozoa. These observations indicate that the animal model (rat) may be quite close to the situation encountered in man.

ACKNOWLEDGMENT

This work was supported by U.S. Public Health Service Grant HD 06316 and by a grant from the Ford Foundation.

REFERENCES

Beaumont, H. M. & Mandl, A. M. (1963). A quantitative study of primordial germ cells in the male rat. *J. Embryol. Exptl. Morph.* **11**, 715–740.

Benda, C. (1887). Untersuchungen über den Bau des funktionierenden Samenkanälchens einiger Säugetiere und Folgerungen für die Spermatogenese dieser Wirbelthierklasse. *Arch. Mikr. Anat.* **30**, 49–110.

Beylot, E. M. & Baudrimont, A. (1926). *Cahier de Travaux Partiques d'Histologie.* Vigot Frères, Paris.

Clermont, Y. (1972). Kinetics of spermatogenesis in mammals: Seminiferous epithelium cycle and spermatogonial renewal. *Physiol. Rev.* **52**, 198–236.

Clermont, Y. & Morgentaler, H. (1955). Quantitative study of spermatogenesis in the hypophysectomized rat. *Endocrinology* **57**, 369–382.

Curtis, G. M. (1918). The morphology of the mammalian seminiferous tubule. *Amer. J. Anat.* **24**, 339–394.

Huckins, C. (1971). The spermatogonial stem cell population in adult rats: I. Their morphology, proliferation and maturation. *Anat. Rec.* **169**, 533–557.

Kalra, S. P. & Prasad, M. R. N. (1967). Effect of FSH and testosterone propionate on spermatogenesis in immature rats treated with clomiphene. *Endocrinology* **81**, 965–975.

Nelson, W. O. & Merckel, C. E. (1938). Maintenance of spermatogenesis in hypophysectomized mice with androgenic substances. *Proc. Soc. Exptl. Biol. Med.* **38**, 737–740.

Noumura, T., Weisz, J., & Lloyd, C. W. (1966). In vitro conversion of 7-^{3}H-progesterone to androgens by the rat testis during the second half of fetal life. *Endocrinology* **78**, 245–253.

Regaud, C. (1901). Etude sur la structure des tubes seminifères et sur la spermatogenèse chez les mammifères. *Arch. Anat. Microscop.* **4**, 101–156: 231–380.

Roosen-Runge, E. C. & Giesel, L. O. (1950). Quantitative studies on spermatogenesis in the albino rat. *Amer. J. Anat.* **87**, 1–30.

Steinberger, E. (1970). Discussion of paper by O. Vilar, Histology of the human testis from neonatal period to adolescence. In *The Human Testis*, E. Rosemberg & C. A. Paulsen, Eds., p. 110.

Steinberger, E. (1971). Hormonal control of mammalian spermatogenesis. *Physiol. Rev.* **51**, 1–22.

Steinberger, E. & Duckett, G. E. (1965). The effect of estrogen or testosterone on initiation and maintenance of spermatogenesis in the rat. *Endocrinology* **76**, 1184–1189.

Steinberger, E. & Duckett, G. E. (1967). Hormonal control of spermatogenesis. *J. Reprod. Fertil. Suppl.* **2**, 75–87.

Steinberger, E. & Nelson, W. O. (1955). Effect of hypophysectomy, cryptorchidism, estrogen and androgen upon the level of hyaluronidase in the rat testis. *Endocrinology* **56**, 429–444.

Steinberger, A., Ficher, M., & Steinberger, E. (1969). Bioconversion of progesterone in organ culture of testicular tissue. *Fed. Proc.* **28**, 773 (abstract).

Steinberger, A. & Steinberger, E. (1966). Stimulatory effect of vitamins and glutamine on the differentiation of germ cells in rat testes organ culture grown in chemically defined media. *Exper. Cell Res.* **44**, 429–435.

Steinberger, A. & Steinberger, E. (1967). Factors affecting spermatogenesis in organ cultures of mammalian testes. *J. Reprod. Fertil. Suppl.* **2**, 117–124.

Steinberger, E. & Steinberger, A. (1969). Spermatogenic function of the testes. In *The Gonads*, K. W. McKerns, Ed., Appleton-Century-Crofts, New York, pp. 715–737.

Steinberger, E. & Steinberger, A. (1972). Testis: Basic and clinical aspects. In *Reproductive Biology*, H. Balin & S. Glasser, Eds., Excerpta Medica, Amsterdam, pp. 144–267.

von Ebner, V. (1871). Untersuchungen über den Bau der Samenkanälchen und die Entwicklung der Spermatozoiden bein den Saügethieren und beim Menschem. Rollet's Untersuchungen aus dem Institut f. Physiologie und Histologie in Graz, Leipzig, p. 200.

DISCUSSION

DR. PAULSEN. We have some preliminary data in the human being that bears on your point from steps 15 to 19, relative to the requirement of FSH. In a patient with hypogonadotropic eunuchoidism, whose initial testicular biopsy specimen showed immature gonocytes, we administered human (clinical grade) pituitary LH as the first form of therapy. After 6 months of treatment the repeat testicular biopsy specimen revealed mature spermatids of Sc Sd type. Apparently germ cell maturation proceeded to completeness; administration of FSH was not required. We are continuing these studies in other patients.

DR. ROOT. Might it be possible to include an antiandrogen in the tissue culture medium to define some of the earlier effects of testosterone on spermatogenesis?

DR. STEINBERGER. Yes, obviously, but in culture a hormone has difficulties exerting its activities. I should like to see that done in vivo, except for what I heard today, that an antibody to gonadotropin just induces more gonadotropins. Concerning Dr. Paulsen's comment, the FSH requirement we establish is a definite one in a rat. Whether it is definitely so in a human, I don't know. Interestingly enough, Roberto Mancini presented data on humans who were hypogonadotropic, hypogonadal eunuchs, and hypophysectomized individuals in all of whom he showed that he needed FSH-like activity to complete spermatogenesis.

DR. PAULSEN. Most of Dr. Mancini's experience was based on restoration of spermatogenesis as opposed to initiation, which is an entirely different situation. If the doses of LH he used in the cases in which initiation of spermatogenesis was attempted are carefully examined, the amount of LH was insufficient, at least in terms of the doses we have used.

DR. ODELL. What was the FSH in your patient?

DR. PAULSEN. Undetectable levels by the Steelman and Pohley bioassay. By radioimmunoassay serum FSH was below 200 ng of the LER-907 with batch No. 1 of anti-FSH sera. With this system such a level is below normal for a pubertal or a normal adult male.

DR. SCHWARTZ. If you hypophysectomize a rat and then immediately maintain it on testosterone, are you saying spermatogenesis continues?

DR. STEINBERGER. That is right.

Dr. Schwartz.   Do you mean that at some time in the history of every gamete cell the previously present FSH did something that was necessary and from then on FSH is dispensable?

Dr. Steinberger.   That is right. Our working hypothesis at this moment is that FSH probably induces changes in Sertoli cells. Those changes are essential for the final maturation of the spermatids. Once the change is induced, testosterone will maintain the Sertoli cell. If you remove testosterone and FSH, the Sertoli cell undergoes changes that are ultrastructural, and probably biochemical, and forgets. By giving testosterone you don't make the cell remind itself what to do; but you can give FSH and again induce that piece of information, i.e., that memory in the Sertoli cell. That is a working hypothesis. We have several definite facts. We can maintain spermatogenesis with testosterone in hypophysectomized animals. It is irrefutable. We can, in a gonadotropin-blocked animal, induce reduction division with testosterone or permit it to occur, whichever way you wish. That is another fact. The requirement of FSH in a rat for the first wave of spermatogenesis is a pretty good piece of information.

Dr. Sizonenko.   Figure 7 refers to cryptorchid boys before any sign of puberty who have had bilateral biopsies of the testes. The FSH levels on the vertical axis were correlated with the number of spermatogonia observed. In 11 of 12 cases of bilateral cryptorchidism there were no spermatogonia and FSH levels were high. The mean value of FSH was 2.6 mU/ml MRC 68-39, significantly different from the mean value observed in normal prepubertal

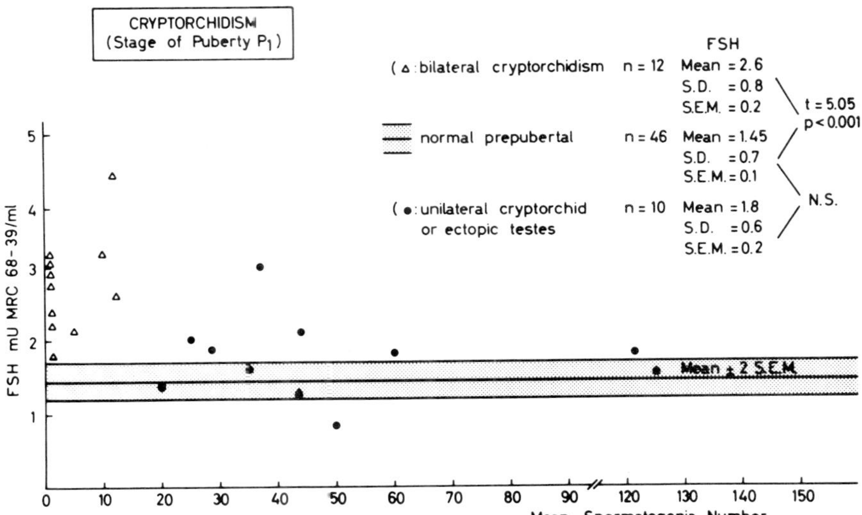

FIG. 7.   Plasma FSH concentrations in prepubertal cryptorchid boys compared with normal prepubertal FSH values in relation to the mean spermatogonial number.

boys whose mean spermatogonia number was 45 and whose plasma FSH was in the normal range. On bilateral biopsies of unilateral cryptorchid or ectopic testes there was a significant number of spermatogonia. Mean FSH level in these cases was normal, 1.8 mU/ml. The data would suggest that there is already an interaction between FSH and spermatogenesis before puberty. Is FSH necessary to go on to the resting stage of spermatogenesis that we see before puberty?

DR. STEINBERGER.   I do not like to think that FSH is essential to the progress of these spermatogonia into spermatogenesis, but I have no evidence for or against. This kind of study is a difficult one. In regard to counting the spermatogonia, are they gonocytes? Are they primitive type A spermatogonia? It makes a difference at which stage you are sampling them. How are they quantified? This is still a major problem. Are you referring to spermatogonia per tubule or per what?

DR. SIZONENKO.   This study was done with Dr. Schindler, who counted the spermatogonia present on twice-50 transverse sections of the tubules on both sides and calculated the mean of the counts. This was done according to the technique of counting spermatogonia (Salle, Hedinger & Nicole, 1968).

DR. STEINBERGER.   This, by itself, is a problem. And when you say spermatogonia to what do you refer?

DR. SIZONENKO.   The spermatogonia could be at any stage before the resting stage.

DR. SWERDLOFF.   Dr. Steinberger, do you think there is any role at all for growth hormone or prolactin in the initiation of spermatogenesis?

DR. STEINBERGER.   When we talk about initiation, do you mean the point at which the germ cells migrate to the gonadal anlage, the point at which the gonocytes divide or form primitive Type A cells, or the point at which these cells end the spermatogenesis?

DR. SWERDLOFF.   By initiation, I mean as differentiated from maintenance of spermatogenesis once it has proceeded to the mature stage.

DR. STEINBERGER.   We have no information on that, only on maintenance in hypophysectomized animals.

DR. DAVIDSON.   You felt that in adult men testosterone was probably involved in maintaining spermatogenesis. Is that based on direct evidence or are you assuming that all actions of LH are via testosterone production?

DR. STEINBERGER.   My primary comment is that in man the initiation of spermatogenesis requires testosterone rather than maintenance; I do not think maintenance can be achieved by testosterone alone.

DR. ODELL.   Can you refer us to the best data on analogous time sequences for the disappearance of gonocytes, the appearance of the primitive type A cells, and the mature type A cells in the human?

DR. STEINBERGER.   There is no good information available. There have been a few attempts to look at this problem, but one of the major points is the broad time period over which humans enter puberty; age alone is of no definite importance. In other words, if you examine the testes of an 11-year-old boy, you may find all kinds of pictures that are not uniform; you cannot say what comes first by using the chronological age of your specimen. You would need a lot of biopsies of normal humans to determine that point.

DR. ODELL.   How late in life do you see gonocytes in the human?

DR. STEINBERGER.   I have seen some all the way through "puberty," maybe even in 13- and 14-year-old boys. However, I do not know when they entered puberty. I have no time frame of reference.

DR. FAIMAN.   Something else puzzles me in relation to the development of spermatogenesis in the male and ovulation in the female. Again the rat may not serve as a useful model, for some of the events that occur neonatally in the rat have probably already occurred in the first trimester in the human. What puzzles me is that from data presented here testosterone levels, at least in the male fetus, are high in the first trimester of pregnancy. We also know that fetuses of both sexes appear to have generous levels of FSH and LH. Why, then, does not spermatogenesis or ovulation occur during fetal life in man?

DR. STEINBERGER.   This is a matter of differentiation in timing. If you could keep those testes in utero in a fetus long enough, you would have a fertile fetus.

DR. ROOT.   In association with Dr. Allen Goldman (Pennsylvania), we investigated the effect of rabbit antiserum against bovine LH administered to pregnant rats between days 15 and 21 of gestation. The mothers demonstrated prolonged periods of anestrus after treatment. The external genitalia of the male fetus were ambiguous, whereas those of the female were normal. In the female offspring of antiserum-treated mothers vaginal opening was significantly earlier, and the estrus cycles of the mature animal were significantly longer than those observed in the female offspring of mothers treated with normal rabbit serum during pregnancy.

DR. JAFFE.   Even though it is tenable that fetal gonadotropins are stimulating the gonads in utero, one can get testosterone formation in the fetal gonad in the absence of gonadotropins. The circulating hCG that is present could be effective. However, the testes were preincubated, which should eliminate at least some of the endogenous hCG.

DR. STEINBERGER.   It strikes me that in regard to spermatogenesis all species have essentially the same developmental pattern in regard to the types of cell and what has to happen sequentially; the only difference between and among the species is that the stages vary in length, and there are breaks and pauses

between stages in different species that may be related to environmental, eco-
logic, and physiological factors which deal with other aspects of gonadotropin
hormonal action, such as the development of secondary sex characteristics and
musculature. If we could study other species and select those appropriate to
each stage of development, we could piece the picture togther.

REFERENCE

Salle, B., Hedinger, C., & Nicole, R. (1968). Significance of testicular biopsies in
cryptorchidism in children. *Acta Endocrinol.* 58, 67–76.

15.

Critical Weight at Menarche, Initiation of the Adolescent Growth Spurt, and Control of Puberty

R. E. FRISCH

The unexpected finding from cross-sectional weight data of Frisch and Revelle (1969a) that the time of fastest weight gain during the adolescent growth spurt occurred at the same mean weight but at differing ages (according to the state of nourishment) prompted us to analyze the adolescent growth spurt by determining the height and weight of each child at each adolescent event from longitudinal growth data. The data for

---

Abbreviations

BGS	Berkeley Guidance Study
BMR	Basal metabolic rate
BW	Body weight
CRC	Child Research Council
HSPH	Harvard School Public Health
LBW	Lean body weight
TW	Total water
PV	Peak velocity

201 girls and 209 boys were collected from 3 comparable studies, the Berkeley Guidance Study (BGS), the Child Research Council Study (CRC), and the Longitudinal Studies of Child Health and Development, the Harvard School of Public Health (HSPH).

We found that the mean weight of girls at the time of initiation of the adolescent growth spurt (30 kg) (Figs. 1, 2, 3) (Frisch & Revelle, 1971a), at the time of peak velocity of weight gain (39 kg) (Frisch & Revelle, 1969b), and at menarche (47 kg) (Figs. 4, 5) (Frisch & Revelle, 1970; 1971b; Frisch, 1972) did not differ for early and late maturing girls. The mean height at each event, however, increased significantly with age (Table 1) (Figs. 2, 4, 6). This finding was also true for boys (Table 2) but at different ages, weights, and heights than those of the girls, except that the latest maturing boys were slightly but significantly heavier at both spurt initiation (Frisch & Revelle, 1971a) and peak velocity (PV) (Frisch & Revelle, 1969b). These results account for the many observations that early maturers have more weight for height than late maturers at spurt intiation and throughout the adolescent spurt, including menarche.

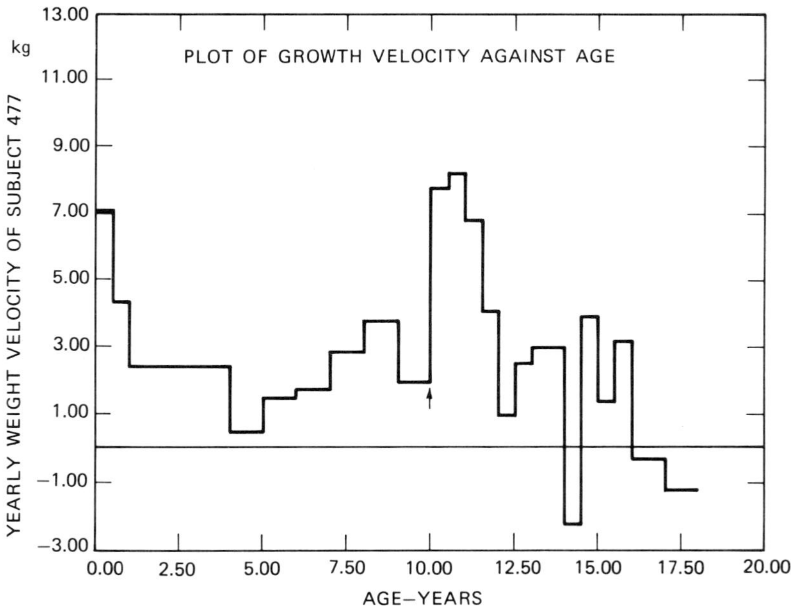

FIG. 1. Computer-plotted yearly weight velocity versus age of a CRC girl showing initiation of weight spurt at age 10. Menarche is at 12.3 years. Such velocity curves were plotted for each child. Frisch & Revelle (1971c), by permission of editor and Wayne State University Press.

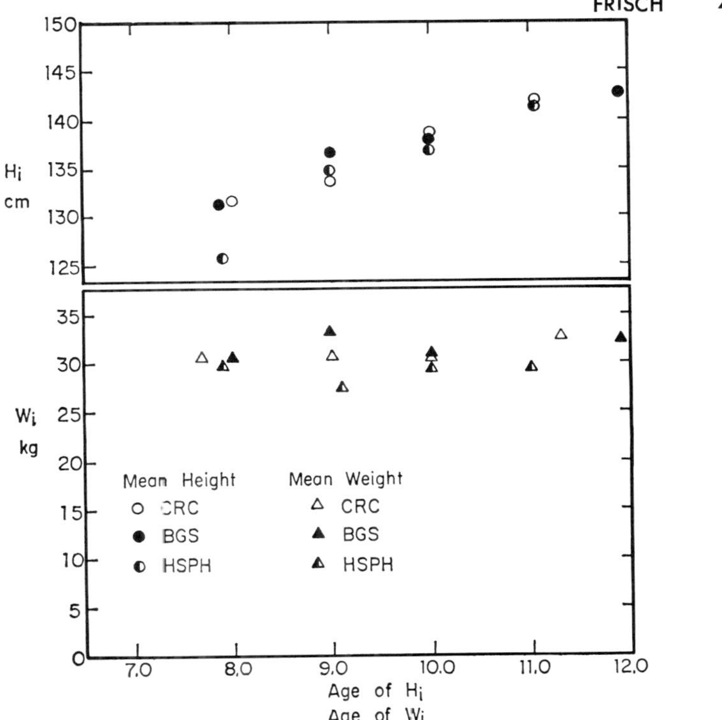

FIG. 2. Mean height at age of initiation (H_i) of the height spurt (age H_i), mean age H_i; and mean weight (W_i) versus mean age of initiation of the weight spurt (age W_i) for girls of CRC, BGS, and HSPH growth studies grouped by mean age of initiation of the height and weight spurt, respectively. Frisch & Revelle (1971c), by permission of the editor and Wayne State University Press.

It was unexpected, however, that three of the major events of human adolescence were each related to an unchanging mean weight.

That puberty is more closely related to weight than to age is well known in other mammals. Data for rats (Widdowson & McCance, 1960; Widdowson, Mavor, & McCance, 1964; McCance, 1962; Kennedy, 1969; Kennedy & Mitra, 1963b), mice (Barnett & Coleman, 1959; Monteiro & Falconer, 1966), pigs (Dickerson, Gresham, & McCance, 1964), and cattle (Crichton, Aitken, & Boyne, 1959; Joubert, 1963) show that sexual maturity, defined by vaginal opening or, more precisely, by the first estrus, is attained at the same mean weight for slow-growing animals as for fast-growing animals but at a significantly later age for those that grow slowly.

Dickerson et al (1964) state that female pigs did not ovulate until they were "approaching the body weight at which ovulation normally occurs." Widdowson and McCance (1960) found that "sexual development (of

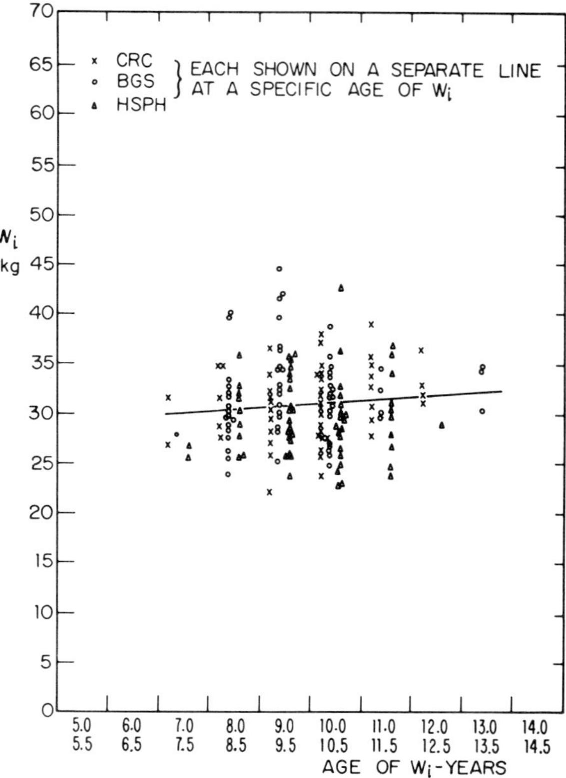

FIG. 3. Weight (W_i) at age of initiation of the weight spurt (age W_i) versus age W_i of girls of CRC, BGS, and HSPH growth studies. Regression line of W_i on age W_i does not differ significantly from zero. Frisch & Revelle (1971c), by permission of the editor and Wayne State University Press.

the rat) was determined primarily by size." Kennedy (1969) says: "Puberty is determined by weight rather than age." Rhesus monkeys treated with androgens gained weight rapidly and had menarche at 1 year instead of the normal age of 2 years but at the weight and length characteristic of 2-year-old animals (van Wagenen, 1949). Thus the relationship between a specific body weight and sexual maturation which we found in humans is a well-known phenomenon in other mammals, including primates.

We propose that there is a direct relation between a critical body weight, representing a critical metabolic rate, and menarche. The mechanism we advance, adapted from that of Kennedy and Mitra (1963b), assumes that the attainment of the critical weight causes a change in

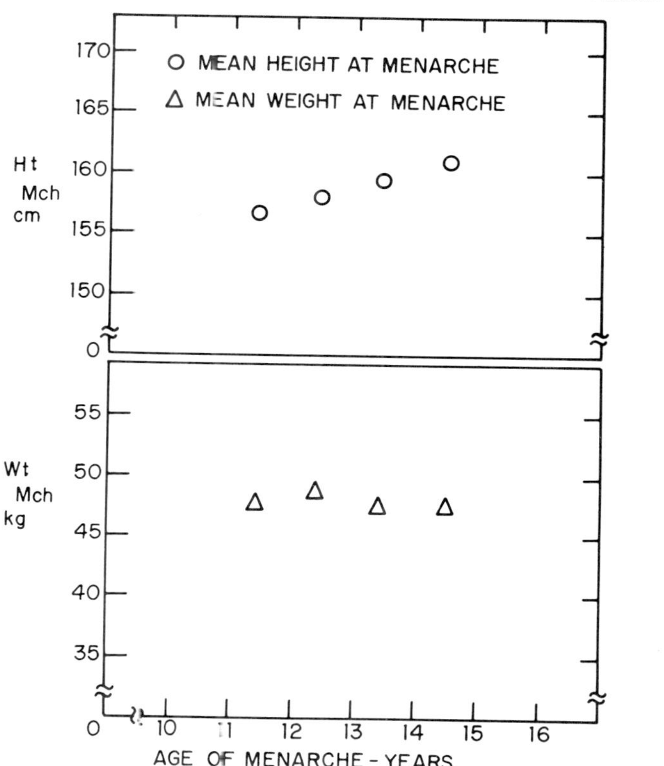

FIG. 4   Mean height at menarche versus mean age at menarche and mean weight at menarche versus mean age at menarche of CRC, BGS, and HSPH girls grouped by age at menarche.

metabolic rate per unit mass (or per unit of surface area) which in turn affects the hypothalamic-ovarian feedback by decreasing the sensitivity of the hypothalamus to estrogen. The feedback is then reset at a level high enough to induce the maturation which results in menarche (Frisch & Revelle, 1970; 1971b). Kulin, Grumbach, and Kaplan (1969, 1972) found evidence of such a change of sensitivity of the hypothalamic "gonadostat" in both girls and boys. Whatever the mechanism, the assumption that a critical weight triggers menarche explains many of the observations associated with early or late onset of menarche.

Earlier menarche is associated with an earlier attainment of critical weight. An important example is the secular trend to an earlier menarche (about 3 or 4 months per decade in Europe) in the last century (Tanner, 1966). Our explanation is simply that children now are bigger sooner;

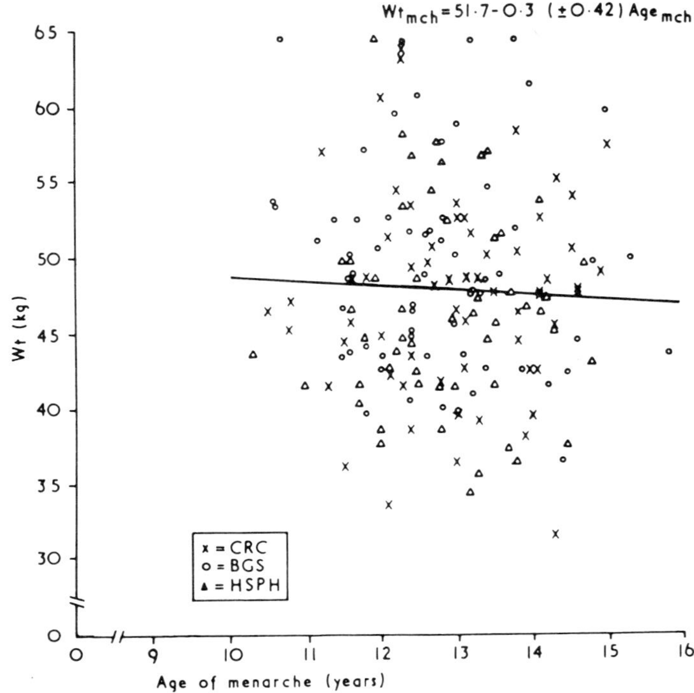

FIG. 5. Weight at menarche (wt$_{mch}$) versus age of menarche (age$_{mch}$) for CRC, BGS, and HSPH girls. Slope of regression line of wt$_{mch}$ on age$_{mch}$ does not differ significantly from zero ($P > 0.50$). Frisch & Revelle (1971), with permission of the editor.

and girls, therefore, reach the mean critical weight, 47 kg, more quickly [the 25th percentile of weight at menarche is 43 kg; the 75th percentile 51.5 kg (Frisch & Revelle, 1971b)]. We hypothesize also that the secular trend should end when the weight of children of successive cohorts remains the same, because of the attainment of maximal nutrition and child care (Frisch & Revelle, 1971b). There is some evidence for our explanation of the secular trend. The mean weight at menarche for Caucasian girls in this decade (Frisch et al 1972; Maresh, 1972; Johnston, Malina, & Galbraith, 1971; van Wieringen, Wafelbakker, Verbrugge, & de Haas, 1971) is the same as the mean weight we found for girls of 3 decades ago (Frisch & Revelle, 1970; 1971b) (Fig. 7). Historically, Boas's (1895) weight data for California girls showed that 46 kg was attained at about 14 years, which is consistent with menarchial ages recorded about 1900 in the United States. Quetelet's growth data (1835) showed that Belgian girls of average social class attained a weight of 46 kg at about age 16½ years, which is consistent with the existing data on age of menarche 150 years

TABLE 1.   Mean age, height, and weight of girls at initiation of the adolescent spurt, peak velocity, menarche, and age 18

Adolescent event	No.	Age of height event (yr)	Age of weight event (yr)	Height[a] (cm)	Weight[b] (kg)
Initiation of spurt (Frisch & Revelle, 1971a)	184	9.5±0.1	9.5±0.1	136.5±0.84	30.6±0.30
Peak velocity (Frisch & Revelle, (1969b)	170	11.3±0.1	12.1±0.1	146.5±0.50	39.3±0.45
Menarche (Frisch & Revelle, 1970, 1971b)	181		12.9±0.1	158.5±0.50	47.8±0.51
Age 18 (Frisch & Revelle, 1970, 1971b)	181		——	165.6±0.48[b]	57.1±0.57[c]

[a] Increases significantly ($p < 0.01$) with increasing age of event.
[b] Does not change significantly with increasing age of event.
[c] Decreases significantly ($p < .02$) with increasing age of event.
±=SE.

TABLE 2.   Mean age (± SE), height, and weight of boys at initiation of the adolescent spurt, peak velocity, and age 18

Adolescent event	No.	Age of height event (yr)	Age of weight event (yr)	Height (cm)	Weight (kg)
Initiation of spurt (Frisch & Revelle, 1971a)	179	11.7±0.1	11.6±0.1	147.3±0.49[a]	36.9±0.36[b]
Peak velocity (Frisch & Revelle, 1969b)	189	14.0±0.1	14.1±0.1	158.3±0.48[b]	47.3±0.52[b]
Age 18 (Frisch & Revelle, 1971a)	179			178.1±0.46[c]	68.2±0.69[d]

[a] Increases significantly ($p < 0.01$) with increasing age of event.
[b] Latest maturers slightly but significantly ($p < 0.01$) heavier than earlier age groups.
[c] Does not change with increasing age of event.
[d] Decreases significantly with increasing age of event.

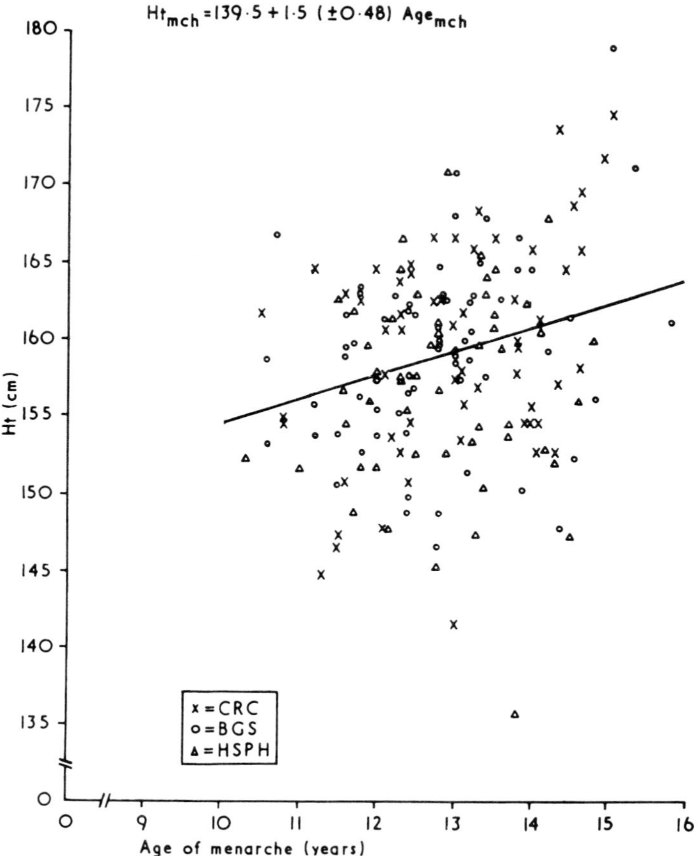

FIG. 6. Height at menarche (ht$_{mch}$) versus age at menarche age$_{mch}$) for CRC, BGS, and HSPH girls. Slope of regression line of ht$_{mch}$ on age$_{mch}$ differs significantly from zero ($P < 0.01$). Frisch & Revelle (1971b), with permission of the editor.

ago (Fig. 7) (Frisch, 1972). Another example of more rapid attainment of the critical weight is the earlier menarche of obese girls (Donovan & van der Werff ten Bosch, 1965; Zacharias, Wurtman & Schatzoff 1970)

Conversely, late menarche is associated with slower pre- or postnatal growth or both, so that the critical weight is reached at a later age. Menarche is also delayed by malnutrition (Dreizen, Spirakis, & Stone, 1967; Frisch & Revelle, 1969a) and altitude (Valšik, Štukovský, & Bernátová, 1963; Valšik, 1965). Twins also have later menarche than singletons of the same population (Tisserand-Perrier, 1953).

In malnutrition the mean weight at menarche of control girls and under-

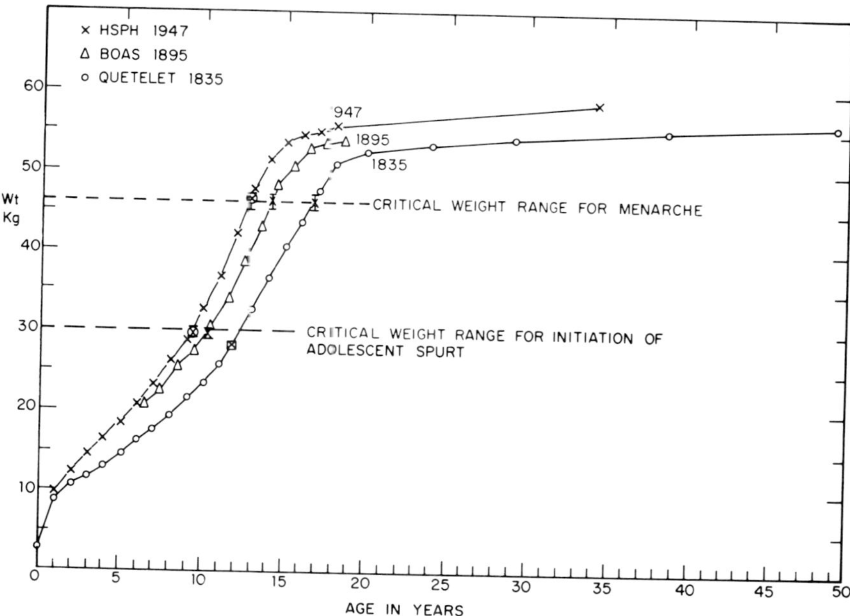

FIG. 7. Weight growth with age of Belgian girls in 1835 (o) (from data of Quetelet 1869), and American girls in 1895 (△), (from data of Boas, 1895), and during 1930–1950, average year of menarche 1947 (×) (from data of Reed & Stuart, 1959), showing age of attainment of the critical weight range for menarche and for the initiation of the adolescent growth spurt: x computed mean ± SE (Frisch & Revelle, 1971a,b). × "Avant la puberté" (before puberty, which seems to mean the time of appearance of secondary sex characteristics and the initiation of the growth spurt) (Quetelet, 1869, p. 90). Frisch (1972a), with permission of the editor and the American Academy of Pediatrics.

nourished girls in Alabama did not differ, although the mean age of menarche of the underfed girls was 2 years later and at a significantly taller height than that of controls (Frisch, 1972) (Fig. 8). Similarly, for the effects of altitude, the well-nourished upper middle-class girls of the CRC study in Denver (altitude 5,280 feet) attained menarche at the same mean weight as comparable California girls (BGS) but at a later age. The birth weights of the Denver girls were significantly lighter than those of the California girls; the Denver girls also grew more slowly until the onset of the adolescent spurt (Frisch et al, 1971a,b).

The initiation of the adolescent spurt may be triggered by a critical weight, which causes a change in critical metabolic rate, whereupon the hypothalamus stimulates the pituitary to increase output of GH (Frisch & Revelle, 1971a). The change to a new metabolic rate may remove an

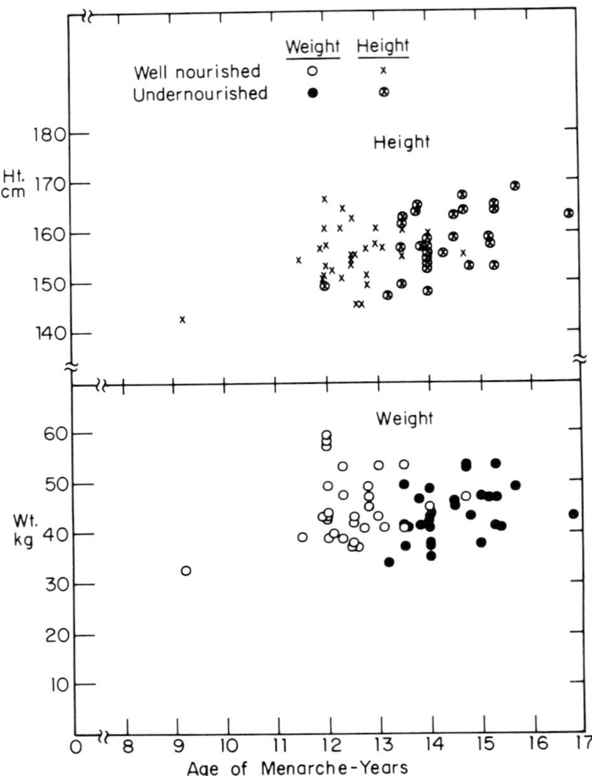

FIG. 8.   Heights and weights versus age at menarche of 30 well-nourished and 30 undernourished girls. Frisch (1972a), with permission of the editor and the American Academy of Pediatrics.

inhibition that increases androgen and estrogen production and, in turn, stimulates the hypothalamic-pituitary axis to increase GH output (Martin, Clark, & Connor, 1968).

METABOLIC SIZE AS A TRIGGER

Evidence from Weight Data

The hypothesis that a critical metabolic size is a trigger for adolescent events is supported by the fact that early- and late-maturing girls gain the same amount of weight from initiation of the spurt to menarche (about 17 kg), even though late maturers grow more slowly than early maturers during the spurt (Frisch & Revelle, 1970, 1971b).

In accord, also, is the finding that, although initiation of the spurt and peak velocity in boys take place at mean weights 6 and 8 kg heavier, respectively, than in girls and 2 years later than those in girls (Tables 1 and 2), each critical weight of boys is equivalent to the same average metabolic rate in calories per kilogram per day (Talbot, 1938) as that of girls at each event (Frisch & Revelle, 1969b; 1971a; 1971b). The consistent weight and time differences between boys and girls at each adolescent event (Tables 1 and 2) suggest that there may be a stage of sexual maturation in boys comparable to menarche in girls which occurs at a weight of about 55 kg and a mean age of 14.9 years (Frisch & Revelle, 1971b).

CORRELATION OF AGE OF GROWTH EVENTS WITH HORMONAL CHANGES

The changes in serum concentrations of LH and FSH found with increasing chronlogy, bone age, or pubertal stage in girls and boys are consistent with the attainment of critical weights at each adolescent event, though the time relationships are approximate, and no cause-and-effect relationship is proved.

A significant rise in FSH concentration and a decrease in the LH/FSH ratio takes place in girls between 9 and 10 years (Sizonenko, Burr, Kaplan, & Grumbach, 1970), the mean age of growth spurt initiation (Frisch & Revelle, 1971a). A second rise in serum FSH occurs between 11 and 12 years (Sizonenko et al, 1970), which is close to the height (11.8 ± 0.1 years) and weight peak (12.1 ± 0.1 years) velocity in girls (Frisch & Revelle, 1969b).

A similar correlation is found between changes in LH and FSH serum concentration in boys (Burr, Sizonenko, Kaplan, & Grumbach, 1970), the age of spurt initiation, 11.6 ± 0.1 years (Frisch & Revelle, 1971a), and age of peak height (14.0 ± 0.1 years) and weight (14.1 ± 0.1 years) velocity (Frisch & Revelle, 1969b).

The first detectable rise in estradiol concentration in girls is between pubertal stages 1 and 2 (Jenner, Kelch, Kaplan, & Grumbach, 1972) at a mean age of about 10.5 years. This is consistent with the appearance of the first secondary sex characteristics, on the average 1 year after the initiation of the growth spurt. 9.5 ± 0.1 years (Frisch & Revelle, 1971a). This supports the idea that the hormonal mechanism initiating the increased growth is different from that which controls the appearance of the secondary sexual characteristics (Tanner, 1969). It also suggests that the changes in growth and thereby in metabolic rate may be necessary for the hormonal changes that cause the appearance of the secondary characteristics. Also, estradiol concentration in girls after pubertal stage 3 (Jenner et al, 1972), which is close to the mean age of peak weight velocity

(12.1 ± 0.1 years, Frisch & Revelle, 1969b) is significantly greater than before that time.

BODY COMPOSITION

Although weight is considered a good measure of metabolic mass in the normal child (Cheek, Graystone, Mellits, & Reba, 1969), total water (TW) and lean body weight (LBW) (TW/0.72) more closely correlate with metabolic rate than body weight (Holliday, Potter, Jarrah, & Bearg, 1967; Keys & Brožek, 1953) because TW and LBW represent the metabolic mass as a first approximation; no correction can yet be made for individual differences in skeletal mass (Forbes, 1962).

Total water was calculated for each girl by using the previously determined height and weight at menarche and at spurt initiation (Frisch & Revelle, 1970; 1971a; 1971b) in the regression equation of Mellits & Cheek (1970): $TW = -10.313 + 0.252$ (wt) and 0.154 (ht), when height $\geqslant$ 110.8 cm.

In accord with the idea of a metabolic mass as a trigger are the following: (1) the variability of calculated TW or LBW is 36 per cent less than that of weight at menarche (Fig. 9); (2) TW (or LBW) does not change

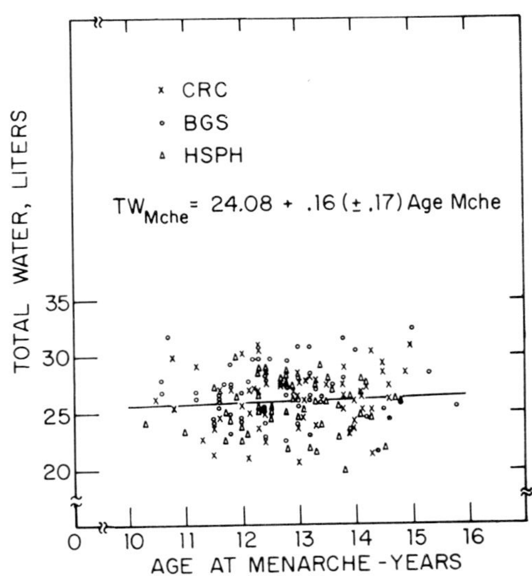

FIG. 9.   TW versus age at menarche for same CRC, GBS, and HSPH girls on the same scale as in Fig. 5. Slope of regression of TW on age_mche does not differ significantly from zero. Reprinted from Frisch, Revelle, and Cook, 1973 by permission of the Wayne State University Press.

significantly with increasing age at menarche (Fig. 9); and (3) girls at
early and late menarche gain about the same amount of TW (8 l) or LBW
(11 kg) and fat (6 kg) from initiation of the spurt to menarche (Fig. 10),
although they grow at different rates. This is a 120 per cent increase in
fat and a 44 per cent increase in LBW, a change in ratio of fat/LBW from
1:5 at spurt initiation to 1:3 at menarche (Frisch, Revelle, & Cook, 1972;
1973).

It is especially significant that the variability of TW as a percentage
of body weight at menarche is 55 per cent less than that of weight at
menarche (Fig. 11). Also 82 per cent of the 169 girls who could be followed from spurt initiation to menarche remained in the same quartiles of
TW/BW from spurt initiation to menarche compared with only 47 per cent
in the same quartiles of weight.

Quartiles of TW/BW are essentially quartiles of fatness. Early maturers
have a lower percentage of TW/BW because they are fatter than late
maturers (Friis-Hansen, 1956; Frisch, Revelle, & Cook, 1972, 1973) (Fig.
11). By using TW/BW quartiles menarche can be predicted from height
and weight of an individual girl at ages 9 through 13 years (Frisch, 1973)

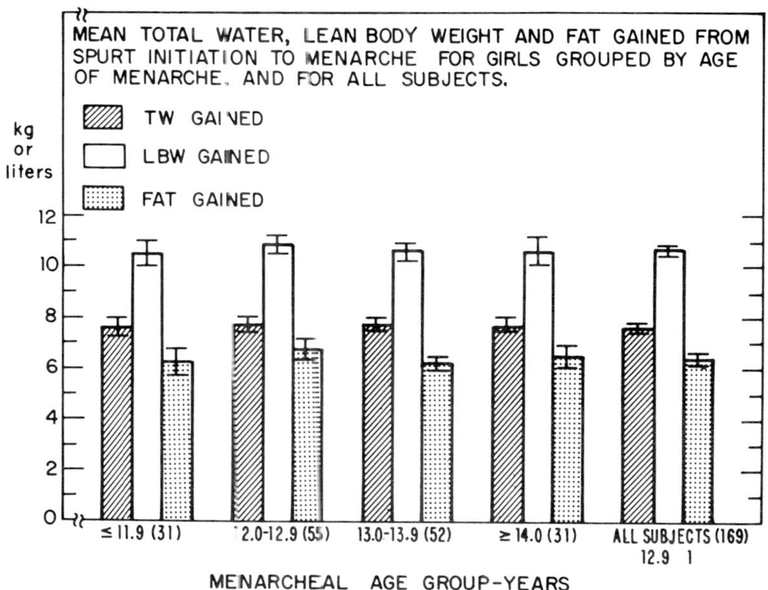

FIG. 10. Mean TW, LBW, and fat gained from spurt initiation to menarche for
girls grouped by age at menarche and for all subjects. Reprinted from Frisch, Revelle,
and Cook, 1973 by permission of the Wayne State University Press.

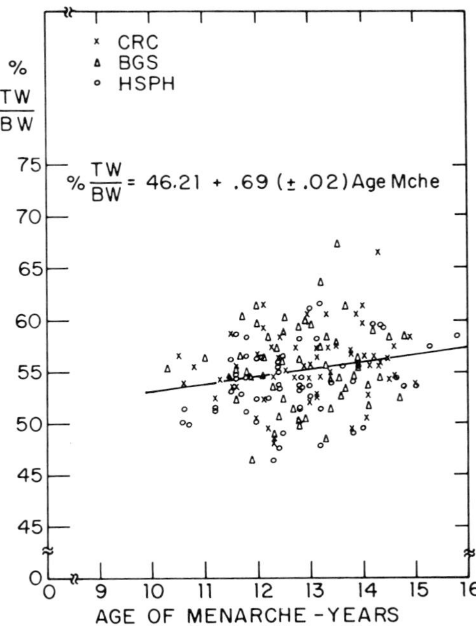

FIG. 11.   Per cent of TW, BW versus age at menarche for CRC, GBS, and HSPH girls. Reprinted from Frisch, Revelle, and Cook, 1973 by permission of the Wayne State University Press.

with a standard error of the estimate about 50 per cent less than that predicted by using pubertal stage. In addition, at menarche the girls at the extremes of the height and weight ranges (Frisch et al, 1971) did not differ significantly in percentage of TW/BW. At all ages of menarche the TW/BW was 56.3 ± 0.5 per cent for the shortest girls who were also lightest in weight (mean height, 147.8 ± 0.7 cm; mean weight, 40.2 ± 0.7 kg). The tallest girls who were also the heaviest in weight (mean height 167.4 ± 0.6 cm; mean weight 51.9 ± 1.0 kg) had a TW/BW of 55.3 ± 0.5 per cent. Thus the very short and light girls whose mean weight seemed to be an exception to the critical weight of about 47 kg (Frisch et al, 1971) were similar to the heaviest and tallest girls in TW/BW per cent (all subjects, 55.1 ± 0.3 per cent). [These very short light girls (14 per cent of total) are still exceptional in that they are less fat at menarche than the taller girls].

During the adolescent spurt the internal organs which contribute the most heat to the basal metabolism (Brožek & Grande, 1955; Holliday, 1971;

Holliday et al, 1967) assume a smaller proportion of the body weight (Holliday et al, 1967). In girls this is mainly because of the large increase in fat (Frisch et al, 1972; 1973). There is therefore a decline in basal metabolic rate (BMR) per kilogram of body weight. The BMR/kg by Talbot's (1938) standards is 35 Cal/kg per day at the mean weight of initiation (30 kg) of the adolescent spurt in girls (Frisch & Revelle, 1971a); at the mean weight (47 kg) of menarche the BMR/kg is 28 Cal/kg per day (Frisch & Revelle, 1970; 1971b). This decrease, as body weight increases, "has the biological advantage of diminishing heat production as the surface to volume ratio decreases" (Holliday et al, 1967).

Two other findings about changes in body fat during the adolescent spurt are of special interest in considering hypothetical mechanisms for the onset of puberty. There is a linear fat increase with increasing LBW for all subjects at menarche and at spurt initiation; at both events fat increases at a

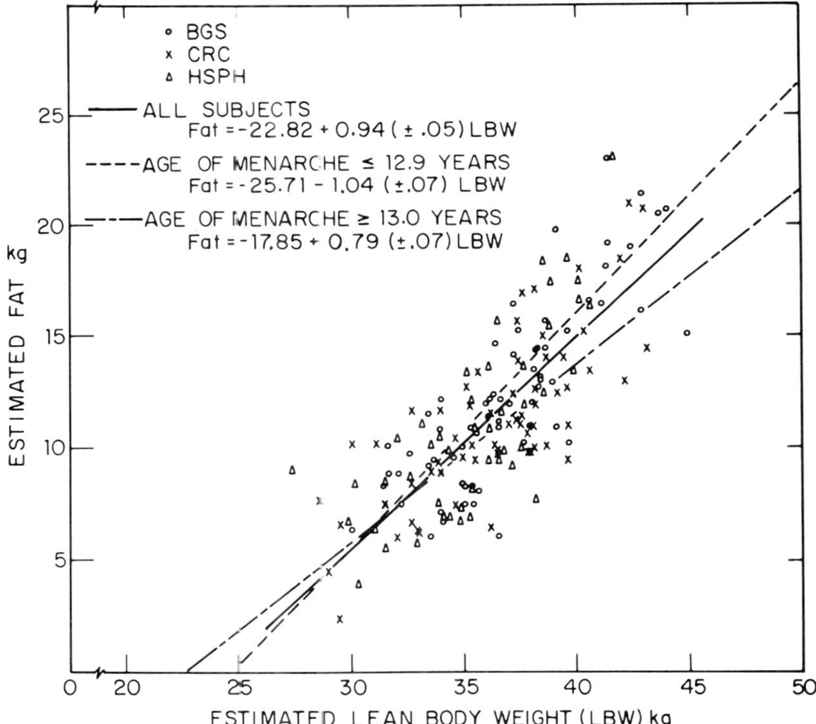

FIG. 12.   Fat versus LBW at menarche for CRC, BGS, and HSPH girls. The slope of the regression for early maturers is significantly greater ($P < 0.01$) than that of the late maturers for LBW. Reprinted from Frisch, Revelle, and Cook, 1973 by permission of the Wayne State University Press.

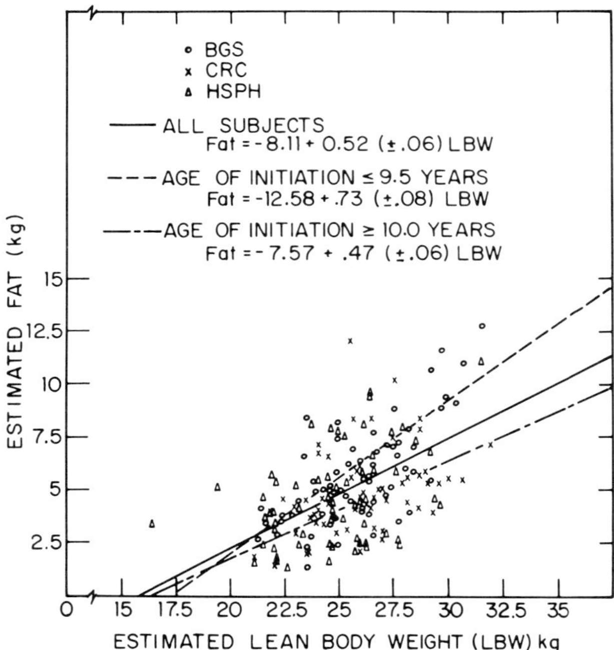

FIG. 13. Fat versus LBW at initiation of the adolescent weight spurt for CRC, GBS, and HSPH girls. The slope of the regression on LBW for early maturers is significantly greater ($P < 0.01$) than for late maturers. Reprinted from Frisch, Revelle, and Cook, 1973 by permission of the Wayne State University Press.

slower rate with increasing LBW in late than in early maturers (Figs. 12 and 13). This explains why late maturers have less fat on the average at each event than do early maturers, although they do not differ in LBW (Frisch et al, 1972, 1973). Widdowson and McCance (1960) also observed this difference in fat gain between fast- and slow-growing rats.

Is this difference in fat deposition between early and late maturers itself a determinant of early and late maturation? It may be that the storage of estrogen in fat depots affects blood levels of estrogen and/or other steroids or their secretion rates. Brown and Strong (1965) found differences in estrogen production and metabolism as a function of body weight, hence, fat. They suggested that estrogen metabolism may be influenced by factors involved in fat metabolism, including thyroid hormones. Another possibility, which does not exclude the others, is that fat concentration is important in regulating energy balance by the hypothalamus (Hervey, 1969; 1971; Kennedy, 1953) and thus may determine the setting of the gonadostat.

The size of the adipose tissue is determined by the number and size of its individual cells. In the rat the cell numbers are determined early in life and early nutritional experiences can determine permanent changes in adipose tissue cellularity (Knittle & Hirsch, 1968; Knittle, 1971; 1972).

If the final number of adipocytes in man is also determined early in life (Hirsch & Knittle, 1970) and there is an interaction between adipose tissue and gonadal hormones or metabolic rate, or both, early or late maturation

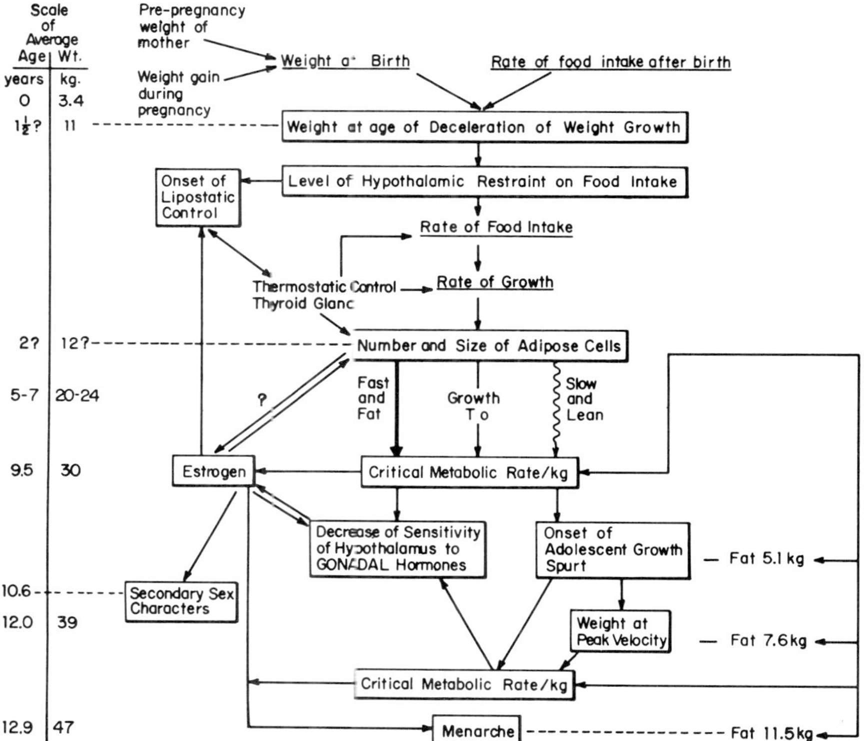

FIG. 14.   Postulated scheme of the relation between body weight, size of adipose tissue, and the control of the onset of puberty for Caucasian girls. Weight at birth is determined by prepregnancy weight of the mother and weight gain during pregnancy. Food intake per kilogram of body weight after birth determines weight at time of deceleration of weight growth (before or about age 2 years in humans), which sets the level of the hypothalamic restraint on food intake and the accompanying onset of lipostatic control. This, at the same age, determines the rate of food intake, which in turn determines rate of growth and number and size of the adipose cells. Rate of growth and number and size of adipose cells determine metabolic rate per kilogram of body weight.

might be determined by differences in fat depots established very early.

Figure 14 shows a hypothetical scheme of determination of human sexual maturation starting at birth (Kennedy, 1953, 1957; Kennedy & Mitra, 1963a,b, for steps 1 to 6, and Widdowson & McCance, 1960). At about age 9½ years in girls [perhaps after the changes of childhood acceleration at average ages 5 to 7 (Frisch & Revelle, 1971a)] a "critical" metabolic rate per kilogram is attained which triggers the adolescent growth spurt and a change in sensitivity of the hypothalamus to estrogen.

The amount of height and weight gained during the adolescent spurt seems to be invariant to rates of growth and independent of previous growth (Frisch & Revelle, 1971b). The second critical metabolic mass (perhaps at two stages—at peak velocity preceding menarche and at menarche) is a signal for a further decrease in sensitivity of the hypothalamus to estrogen, and gonadotropins rise to levels high enough for the ovarian and uterine changes to result in menarche. [A positive hypothalamic-estrogen feedback (Kulin et al, 1972) may be initiated at peak velocity.] Of special interest is the large gain in fat during the interval from peak velocity to menarche (Fig. 14).

SIGNIFICANCE OF THE ADOLESCENT SPURT IN GIRLS

The large increase of fat (120 per cent), gained from spurt initiation to menarche by both early and late maturing girls may have a secondary significance. The mean fat for both early and late maturers at menarche is about 11 kg (Frisch et al, 1972), which is equivalent to 99,000 calories. The number of calories estimated to sustain a pregnancy is 80,000 (FAO, 1957). Adolescent female fat thus may have selective advantage to the species during times of famine. One of the main functions of the adolescent spurt in females may be the storage of this energy to sustain pregnancy and lactation.

With or without causality, the weight dependency of sexual maturation in animals seems important because, by compensating for environmental differences, it regulates species size at sexual maturity and, therefore, at adulthood (Monteiro & Falconer, 1966; Kennedy 1969). The regulation of human female size at sexual maturity by weight dependency of menarche may also have selective advantages for the species, for birth weight is correlated with the prepregnancy weight of the mother (Eastman & Jackson, 1968), and infant survival with birth weight (Frisch, 1972).

REFERENCES

Barnett, S. A. & Coleman, E. M. (1959). Effect of low environmental temperature on the reproductive cycle of female mice. *J. Endocrinol.* **19**, 232–240.

Boas, F. (1895). The growth of first-born children. *Science* **1**, 402–404.

Brown, J. B. & Strong, J. A. (1965). Effect of nutritional status and thyroid function on the metabolism of oestradiol. *J. Endocrinol.* **32**, 107–115.

Brožek, J. & Grande. F. (1955) Body composition and basal metabolism in man: correlation analysis versus physiological approach. *Human Biol.* **27**, 22–31.

Burr, I. M., Sizonenko, P. C., Kaplan, S. L., & Grumbach, M. M. (1970). Hormonal changes in puberty. 1. Correlation of serum hormone and follicle stimulating hormone with stages of puberty, testicular size, and bone age in normal boys. *Pediat. Res.* **4**, 25–35.

Cheek, D. B., Graystone, J. E., Mellits, E. D., & Reba, R. C. (1969). Body composition: anthropometric growth and heat production. In *Adolescent Nutrition and Growth.* F. P. Heald, Ed., Appleton-Century-Crofts, New York, p. 163.

Crichton, J. A., Aitken, J. N., & Boyne, A. W. (1959). Effect of plane of nutrition during rearing on growth, production, reproduction and health of dairy cattle. I. Growth to 24 months. *Animal Product.* **1**, 145–162.

Dickerson, J. W. T., Gresham, G. A., & McCance, R. A. (1964). Effect of undernutrition and rehabilitation on the development of the reproductive organs: pigs. *J. Endocrinol.* **29**, 111–118.

Donovan, B. T. & van der Werff ten Bosch, J. J. (1965). *Physiology of Puberty.* Arnold, London.

Dreizen, S., Spirakis, C. N., & Stone, R. E. (1967). A comparison of skeletal growth and maturation in undernourished and well-nourished girls before and after menarche. *J. Pediat.* **70**, 256–263.

Eastman, N. J. & Jackson, E. (1968). Weight relationships in pregnancy. 1. Bearing of maternal weight gain and prepregnancy weight on birth weight in full-term pregnancies. *Obstet. Gynec. Survey* **23**, 1003–1025.

FAO, Food and Agriculture Organization of the United Nations (1957), *Calorie Requirements.* U.S. Government Printing Office, Washington, D.C.

Forbes, G. B. (1962). Methods for determining composition of the human body. *Pediatrics* **29**, 477–494.

Friis-Hansen, B. J. (1956). Changes in body water compartments during growth. *Acta Paediat. Suppl.* **110**, 1–67.

Frisch, R. E. (1972). Weight at menarche: similarity for well nourished and undernourished girls at differing ages, and evidence for historical constancy. *Pediatrics* **50**, 445–450.

Frisch, R. E. (1973). Age at menarche: a method of prediction from height and weight at ages 9 through 13 years. *Pediatrics,* submitted for publication.

Frisch, R. E. & Revelle, R. (1969a). Variations in body weights and the age of the adolescent growth spurt among Latin American and Asian populations in relation to calorie supplies. *Human Biol.* **41**, 185–212.

Frisch, R. E. & Revelle, R. (1969b). Height and weight of adolescent boys and girls at the time of peak velocity of growth in height and weight: Longitudinal data. *Human Biol.* **41**, 536–559.

Frisch, R. E. & Revelle, R. (1970) Height and weight at menarche and a hypothesis of critical body weights and adolescent events. *Science* **169**, 397–399.

Frisch, R. E. & Revelle, R. (1971a). Height and weight of girls and boys at the time of initiation of the adolescent growth spurt in height and weight and the relationship to menarche. *Human Biol.* **43**, 140–159.

Frisch, R. E. & Revelle, R. (1971b). Height and weight at menarche and a hypothesis of menarche. *Arch. Dis. Childh.* **46**, 695–701.

Frisch, R. E., Revelle, R. & Cook, S. (1971). Height, weight and age at menarche and the "critical weight" hypothesis. *Science* **174**, 1148–1149.

Frisch, R. E., Revelle, R., & Cook, S. (1973). Components of the critical weight at menarche and at initiation of the adolescent spurt: estimated total water, lean body mass and fat. *Human Biol.* **45**, 469–483.

Hervey, G. R. (1969). Regulation of energy balance. *Nature* **222**, 629–631.

Hervey, G. R. (1971). Physiological mechanisms for the regulation of energy balance. *Nutr. Soc. Proc.* **30**, 109–116.

Hirsch, J. & Knittle, J. L. (1970). Cellularity of obese and nonobese human adipose tissue. *Fed. Proc.* **29**, 1516–1521.

Holliday, M. A. (1971). Metabolic rate and organ size during growth from infancy to maturity and during late gestation and early infancy. *Pediatrics* **47**, 169–179.

Holliday, M. A., Potter, D., Jarrah, A., & Bearg, S. (1967). The relation of metabolic rate to body weight and organ size. *Pediat. Res.* **1**, 185–195.

Jenner, M. R., Kelch, R. P., Kaplan, S. L., & Grumbach, M. M. (1972). Hormonal changes in puberty. IV. Plasma estradiol, LH, and FSH in prepubertal children, pubertal females, and in precocious puberty, premature thelarche, hypogonadism, and in a child with a feminizing ovarian tumor. *J. Clin. Endocrinol.* **34**, 521–531.

Johnston, F. E., Malina, R. M., & Galbraith, M. A. (1971). Height, weight and age at menarche and the "critical weight" hypothesis. *Science* **174**, 1147–1148.

Joubert, D. M. (1963). Puberty in female farm animals. *Animal Breeding* **31**, 295–305.

Kennedy, G. C. (1953). Role of depot fat in the hypothalamic control of food intake in the rat. *Proc. Roy. Soc. London* (B) **140**, 578–592.

Kennedy, G. C. (1957). Development with age of hypothalamic restraint upon the appetite of the rat. *J. Endocrinol.* **16**, 9–17.

Kennedy, G. C. (1969). Interactions between feeding behavior and hormones during growth. *Ann. N.Y. Acad. Sci.* **157**, 1049–1061.

Kennedy, G. C. & Mitra, J. (1963a). Hypothalamic control of energy balance and the reproductive cycle in the rat. *J. Physiol.* **166**, 395–406.

Kennedy, G. C. & Mitra, J. (1963b). Body weight and food intake as initiating factors for puberty in the rat. *J. Physiol.* **166**, 408–418.

Keys, A. & Brožek, J. (1953). Body fat in adult man. *Physiol. Rev.* **33**, 245–325.

Knittle, J. L. (1971). Childhood obesity. *Bull. N.Y. Acad. Med.* **47**, 579–589.

Knittle, J. (1972). Maternal diet as a factor in adipose tissue cellularity and metabolism in the young rat. *J. Nutr.* **102**, 427–434.

Knittle, J. L. & Hirsch, J. (1968). Effect of early nutrition on the development of rat epididymal fat pads: cellularity and metabolism. *J. Clin. Invest.* **47**, 2091–2098.

Kulin, H. E., Grumbach, M. M., & Kaplan, S. L. (1969). Changing sensitivity of the pubertal gonadal hypothalamic feedback mechanism in man. *Science* **166**, 1012–1013.

Kulin, H. E., Grumbach, M. M., & Kaplan, S. L. (1972). Gonadal-hypothalamic interaction in prepubertal and pubertal man: effect of clomiphene citrate on urinary follicle-stimulating hormone and luteinizing hormone and plasma testosterone. *Pediat. Res.* **6**, 162–171.

McCance, R. A. (1962). Food, growth, and time. *Lancet* **2**, 671–675.

Maresh, M. M. (1972). A forty-five year investigation for secular changes in physical maturation. *Amer. J. Phys. Arthrop.* **36**, 103–109.

Marshall, W. A. & Tanner, J. M. (1969). Variations in pattern of pubertal changes in girls. *Arch. Dis. Childh.* **44**, 291–303.

Martin, L., Clark, J. W., & Conner, T. (1968). Growth hormone secretion enhanced by androgens. *J. Clin. Endocrinol.* **28**, 425–428.

Mellits, E. D. & Cheek, D. B. (1970). Assessment of body water and fatness from infancy to childhood. *Monogr. Soc. Res. Child Develop.* **35**, 12–26.

Monteiro, L. S. & Falconer, D. S. (1966). Compensatory growth and sexual maturity in mice. *Animal Prod.* **8**, 179–192.

Reed, R. B. & Stuart, H. C. (1959). Patterns of growth in height and weight from birth to eighteen years of age. *Pediatrics* **24**, 904–974.

Sizonenko, P. C., Burr, I. M., Kaplan, S. L., & Grumbach, M. M. (1970). Hormonal changes in puberty. II. Correlation of serum luteinizing hormone and follicle stimulating hormone with stages of puberty and bone age in normal girls. *Pediat. Res.* **4**, 36–45.

Smith, E. R. & Davidson, J. M. (1968). Role of estrogen in the cerebral control of puberty in female rats. *Endocrinology* **82**, 100–108.

Talbot, F. B. (1938). Basal metabolism standards for children. *Amer. J. Dis. Child.* **55**, 455–459.

Tanner, J. M. (1966). Secular trend towards earlier physical maturation. *Tijd. Geneesk.* **44**, 524–539.

Tanner, J. M. (1969). Growth and endocrinology of the adolescent. In *Endocrine and Genetic Diseases of Childhood*, L. I. Gardner, Ed., Saunders, Philadelphia, pp. 19–60.

Tisserand-Perrier, M. (1953). Etude comparative de certains processus de croissance chez les jumeaux. *J. Génét. Hum.* **2**, 87–102.

Valŝik, J. A. (1965). Seasonal rhythm of menarche: a review. *Human Biol.* **37**, 75–90.

Valŝik, J. A., Ŝtukovský, R., & Bernátová, L. (1963). Quelques facteurs géographiques et sociaux ayant une influence sur l'âge de la puberté. *Biotypologie* **24**, 109–123.

van Wagenen, G. (1949). Accelerated growth with sexual precocity in female monkeys receiving testosterone propionate. *Endocrinology* **45**, 544–546.

van Wieringen, J. C., Wafelbakker F., Verbrugge, H. P., & de Haas, H. H. (1971). *Growth Diagrams—1965—Netherlands.* Wolters-Noorhoff, Groningen.

Widdowson, E. M. & McCance, R. A. (1960). Some effects of accelerating growth. I. General somatic development. *Proc. Roy. Soc.* (B) **152**, 188.

Widdowson, E. M., Mavor, W. O., & McCance, R. A. (1964). Effect of undernutrition and rehabilitation on the development of the reproductive organs: rats. *J. Endocrinol.* **29**, 119–126.

Zacharias, L., Wurtman, R., & Schatzoff, M. (1970). Sexual maturation in contemporary American girls. *Amer. J. Ob. Gyn.* **108**, 833–846.

16.

Body Composition, Hormones, Nutrition, and Adolescent Growth

D. B. CHEEK

The growth of the soma in postnatal life does not conform strictly to a sigmoid curve in the primate; indeed, the mathematical expression for weight versus time during growth is the Gompertz type, which represents both additive and multiplicative factors (Laird, 1967). The primate, unlike the rodent, does not rush from weaning into sexual maturation. There is a prolonged resting period, during which adolescence is initiated. The span of adolescence is one of accelerated growth which culminates close to full sexual maturation. In the rodent the steepest point on the sigmoid curve represents sexual maturation in the male or the first estrus in the female (Cheek & Holt, 1963).

In general, this accelerated somatic growth can be divided into 2 aspects, growth of fat and growth of lean tissue. Strong sex differences can be anticipated. At the outset it is important to grasp the fundamental concept

---

Abbreviations

FSH	Follicle stimulating hormone
GH	Growth hormone
LBM	Lean body mass
V_{max}	Maximal somatic growth velocity

of the maturational or biological age index. Various children mature at various ages; sexual maturation may occur at 10 years in one girl or at 13 years in another. Thus, chronological age reflects only the mean maturational age when a large group of children or adolescents is being considered. We have been concerned with methods of determining the biologic age index or the assessment of the anatomical, physiological, and biochemical status during growth and maturation (Cheek, Migeon, & Mellits, 1968; Mellits, Dorst, & Cheek, 1971). Such indices may be reflected by hormonal levels, cell number, bone age or body length. "Height age" has long been appreciated as a better maturational index than chronological age; a combination of body length and bone age (multivariate equation) can be a good predictor of the biological age index (Mellits et al, 1971).

Because adolescence begins with a growth spurt in lean tissue, in the male, we inspected the behavior of body water by mathematical means, for it is a direct index of lean body mass (LBM). The difference between LBM and weight yields body fat. When body water is plotted against body length, a quadratic equation is derived for boys and a similar one for girls (Mellits & Cheek, 1968). Application of the Mellits (1968) breaking-line technique reveals a break at 137 cm for boys (9½ years of age) and at about 113 cm for girls (6 years); the break in the line for girls was not remarkable.

We suggest that this breaking point is meaningful in the male and that it defines the onset of adolescence. The second and upward line for boys

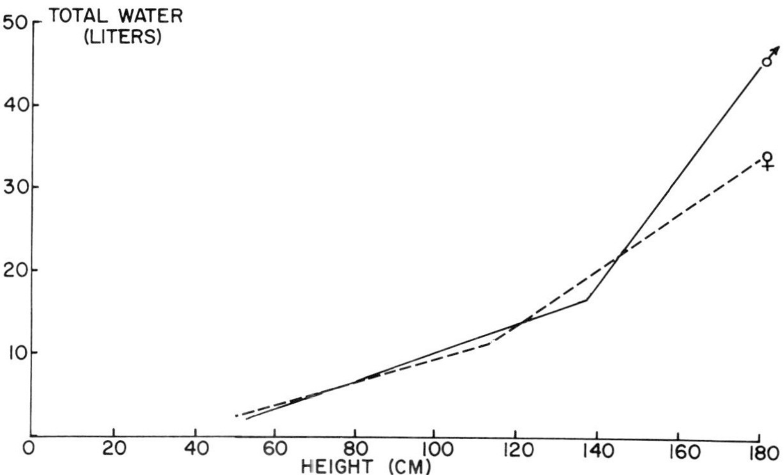

FIG. 1.   The breaking lines, obtained when data points for body water are plotted against body length, are shown for boys and girls. Note the sharp break that occurs for boys at 137 cm.

is steeper than for girls and indicates a more rapid growth of LBM in the male (Fig. 1).

The quadratic equations that describe the relation between body water and length can also be used to predict body fat by plotting it against height age for a normal population (the 50th percentile on the anthropometric grid). The children studied did not distribute differently from a normal population (Drash, Heese, & Brasel, 1968). The plot of body fat against height age (Fig. 2) shows a strong sex difference and a greater growth of fat in the female. At 16 years the boy has 7 kg of fat, the girl 14 kg. The point of maximal growth can be defined by plotting velocity points or the rate of fat deposition per year. Females accelerate their fat deposition in the twelfth year, or when sexual maturation has just been attained, and reach a maximum in the thirteenth year. Males show a peak in their fourteenth year, again when sexual maturation is attained (Fig. 3).

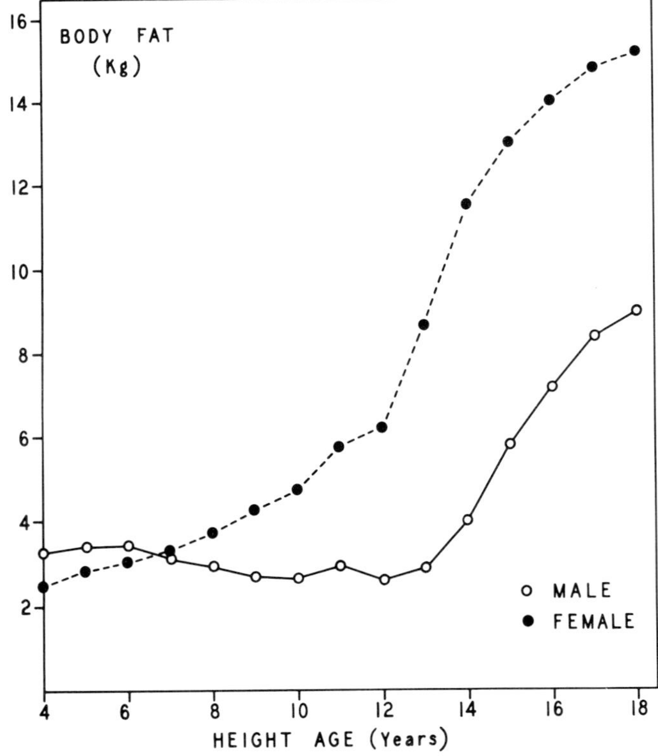

FIG. 2. From our equations that define the relationship of fat to body length it is possible to demonstrate the increasing fatness of boys and girls during the adolescent period.

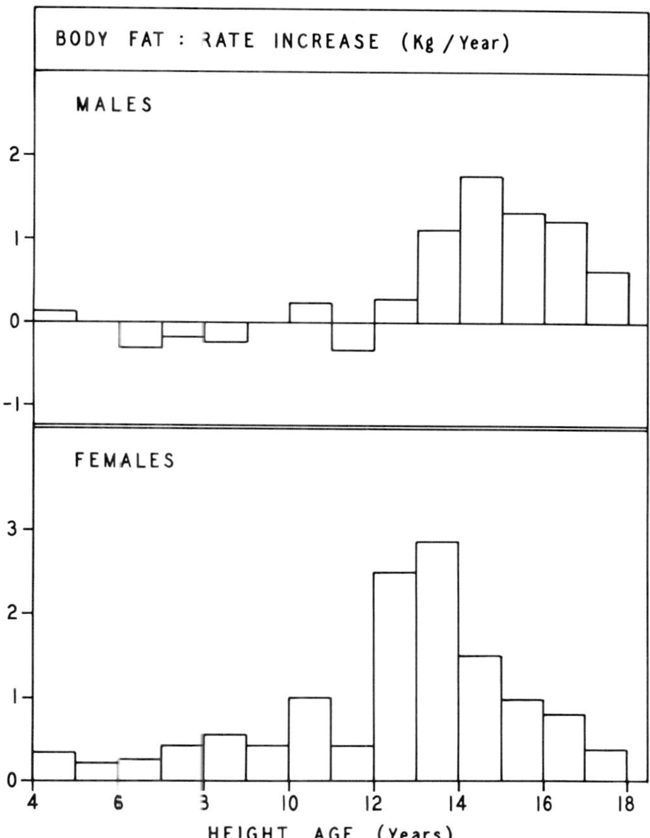

FIG. 3. The rate of gain in body fat is considered against height age. Note the greater and earlier rate of gain for the female.

For boys the growth of lean tissue is characteristic during the adolescent period and attention turns to the cell mass or to metabolically active tissue, such as muscle or visceral tissue.

In earlier work on human growth (Cheek, 1968 a,b), we developed multiple equations for the prediction of lean body components during the growing process, and recently we examined these equations in terms of adolescence; for example, the curves that relate muscle mass to body length can predict the pattern of muscle growth for "height age." We can demonstrate the curves for boys and girls (Fig. 4). The growth of muscle mass is more remarkable in the boy; he doubles his muscle mass during adolescence. Velocity curves (Fig. 5) indicate that the girl reaches her maxi-

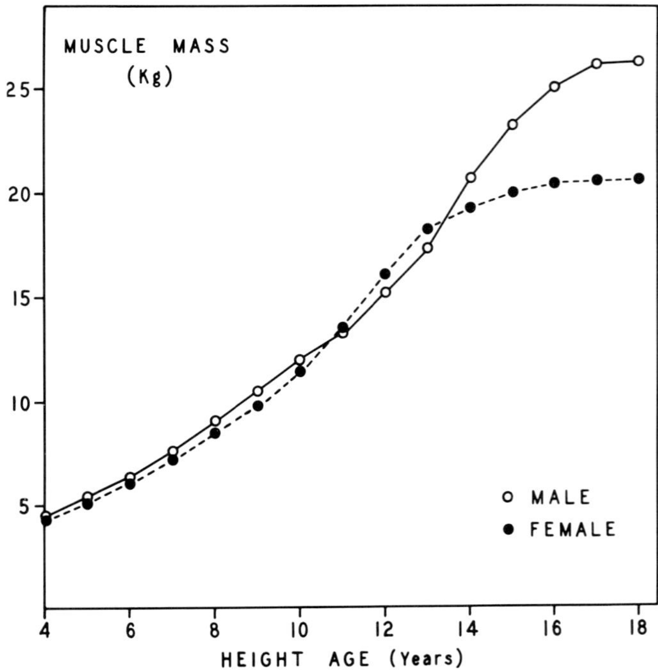

FIG. 4.   Muscle mass (from creatinine excretion) is plotted against height age for boys and girls. Note that muscle mass doubles in boys from 10 to 17 years.

mal muscle growth in the twelfth year, which then slows. In the thirteenth year the rate of growth of muscle is 3 times faster for boys and reaches a maximum in the fourteenth year, with a less remarkable slowing of muscle growth afterward.

Garn (1970) has assessed skeletal mass in large groups of boys and girls by radiological techniques. From his data, in terms of height age, curves are essentially similar to those for muscle growth. The growth of skeletal mass tends to parallel muscle growth (Fig. 6). The boy doubles his skeletal mass.

In girls the rate of increase in skeletal mass (Fig. 7) appears to be maximal and constant from 10 to 14 years (a time when extra fat and lean tissue is deposited) whereas the rate of increase for boys is maximal from 12 to 14 years, again at a period when weight increase is significant.

The inspection of tissue growth against height age emphasizes the sex differences in growth. However, the relationship of lean tissue mass against body length, especially in the boy, may define the onset of adolescence. Boys and girls have a similar height for age until 9 years. We found

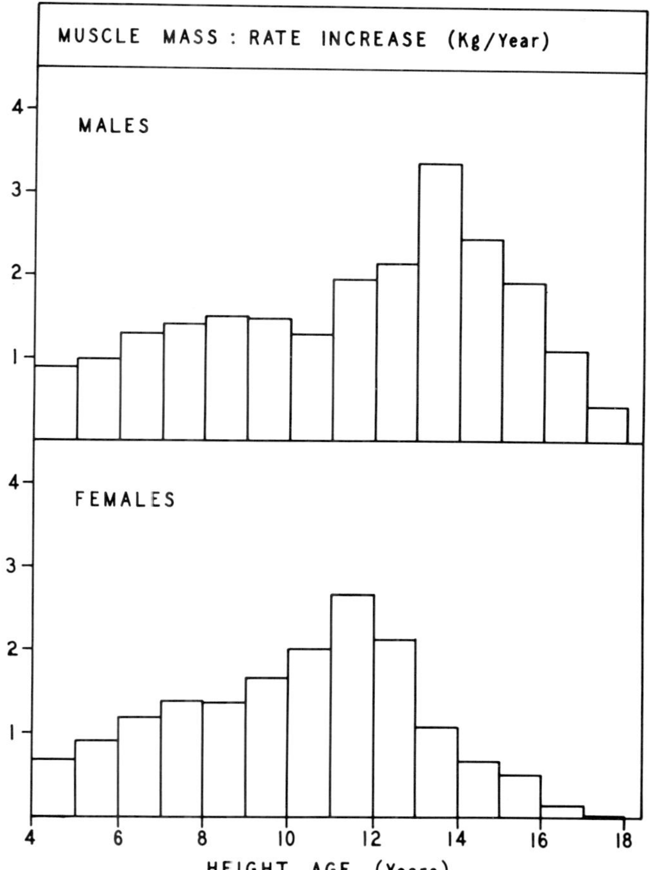

FIG. 5.   The rate of growth of muscle mass is shown for boys and girls.

that if the quadratic equation relating muscle mass, body potassium, intra-cellular mass, and extracellular volume to body length from 5 to 17 years were tested for a breaking point (Cheek, 1968b), it would be found at about 137 cm (9 years). According to the graph (Fig. 8) on skeletal mass versus length, a break is probably present at about the same length (137 cm) for males.

Intracellular water of the body, which is a direct measure of intracellu-lar mass, indicates that there is no sex difference when the points are plotted against body length, except that for boys the curve extends farther and upward (Fig. 9).

Flynn, Woodruff, Clark, and Chase (1972) have plotted data for whole

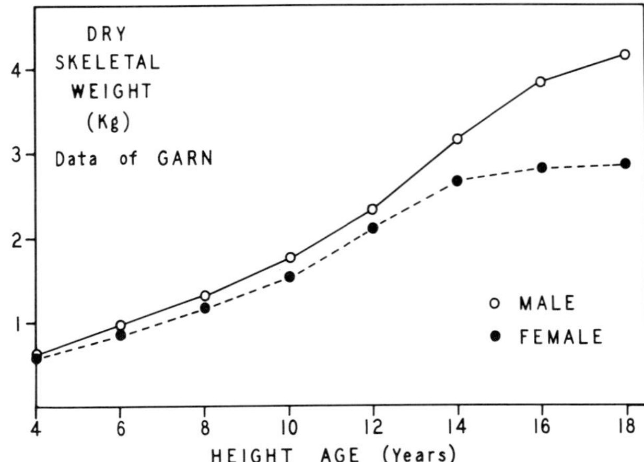

FIG. 6.   Garn's data (1970) show the growth of skeleton versus height age. Clearly the greater gain in body and muscle of the boy is associated with the greater gain in skeletal mass.

body K against body length in a large number of subjects and discarded the quadratic relationship by using a semilog scale for ^{40}K against length. The linear relationships for boys and girls are identical, but surprisingly at 135 cm (9 years) the points plateau for females and do not extend upward. This plateau, beginning at 9 years in the girl, may be fallacious and due to rapid growth of fat; in obesity ^{40}K gives spurious results (Cheek, Schultz, Parra, & Reba, 1970b). The sex difference we found initially between boys and girls, when total water was plotted against total K, is incorrect and probably due to the growth of adipose tissue in the normal girl which acts as a screen for ^{40}K radiation (Reba, Cheek, & Mellits, 1972).

If we inspect cell multiplication in muscle (Fig. 10) or the accumulation of DNA in muscle during growth, we find a strong sex difference. The point of departure for males and females is again 9 years; for boys the data points swing upward and nuclear replication accelerates. We are aware, of course, that a limit has to be reached for both boys and girls. With further data the curve for girls would become quadratic. We have found that the limit for boys is probably close to 3.8×10^{12} nuclei; for girls it must be near 2×10^{12}.

The growth of cytoplasmic mass in muscle also shows a strong sex difference, which is better seen in rats than in humans (Fig. 11). The accretion of protein relative to DNA is faster for the female than for the male, but ultimately the male catches up and may surpass the female, as happens

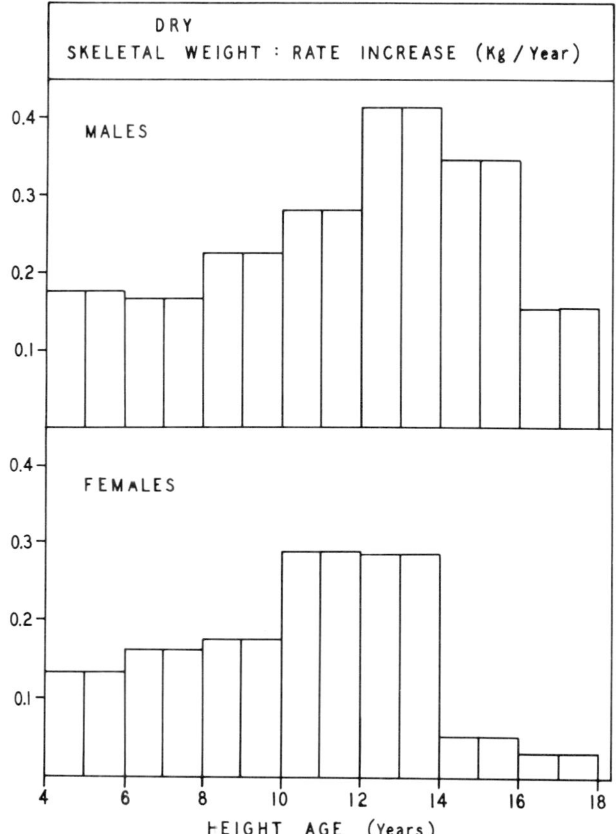

FIG. 7.   When the rate of growth of the skeleton is considered, note the sustained rate for the female 10 to 14 years; for the male a higher rate is reached between 12 and 14 years. These periods represent the time of increasing body weight and the period for maximal muscle growth in boys.

in the rat. The origin of these changes in cell versus organ size or muscle mass is related to genes, hormones, and nutrition. The coincidental sexual maturation of twins leaves little doubt in regard to genetic influence.

That nutrition plays a leading role in the control of adolescence, and sexual maturation can be strongly anticipated by the fact that calorie restriction causes a delay in puberty (Durand, Fauconneau, & Penot, 1967), whereas obese children tend to mature early (Parra, Schultz, Graystone, & Cheek, 1971). Children with protein-calorie restriction tend to have reduced LBM for length, reduced cell number, and reduced protein: DNA ratios in muscle (Cheek, Hill, Cordana, & Graham, 1970a). In the

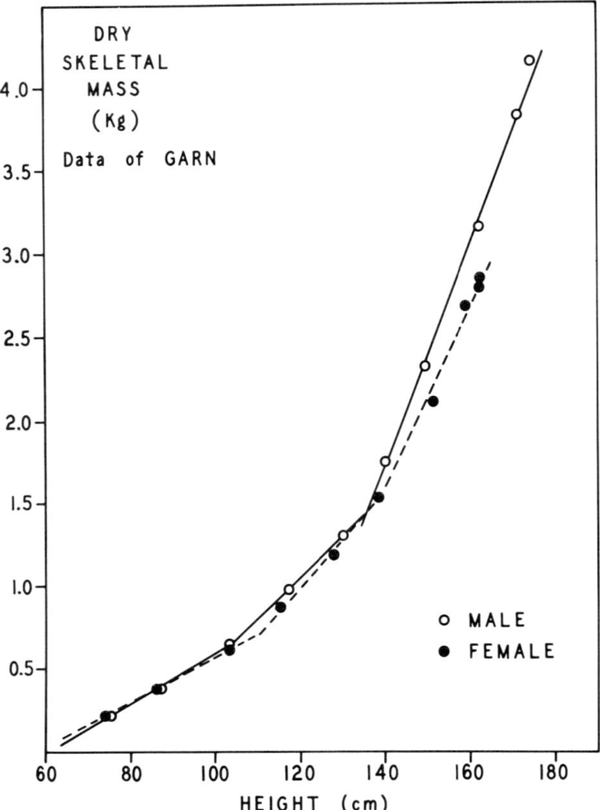

FIG. 8.   When skeletal mass is considered against body length, the rate of growth for the male increases after a length of about 137 cm is reached (Garn, 1970).

experimental animal in which protein intake is sufficient but calories are deficient this produces no reduction in cell cytoplasmic growth, only a slowing of cell multiplication (Hill, Holt, Parra, & Cheek, 1970) and a delay in sexual maturation (Durand et al, 1967). Catch-up growth with sexual maturation is likely to be rapid with refeeding.

Children with advanced maturation have an excess of lean tissue mass, intracellular mass, number of nuclei in muscle (Cheek et al, 1970b), and adipocytes (Knittle & Hirsch, 1968). If these subjects receive surgical treatment, such as ileal bypass which reduces the absorption of substrates, one can demonstrate a loss of all these determinants (Cheek & White, 1972). That a loss of muscle nuclei can occur is not surprising, for it happens in pituitary insufficiency and following cessation of exercise (Cheek,

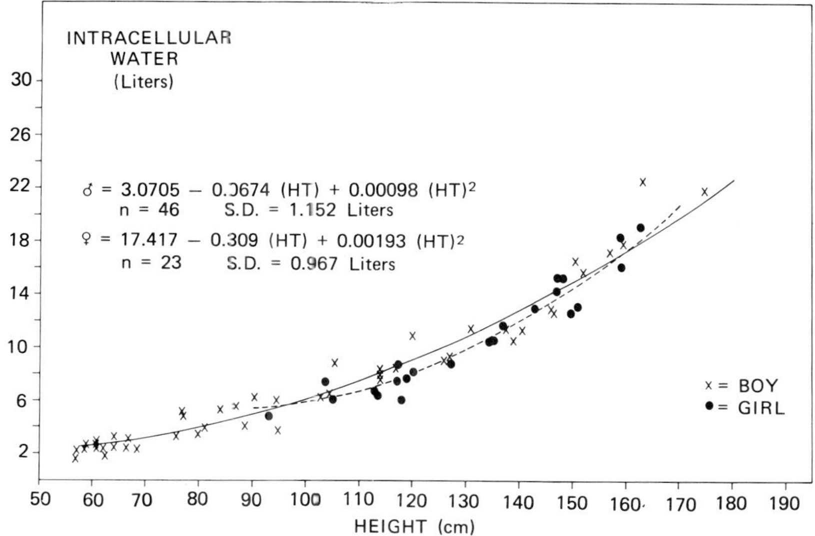

FIG. 9.   Intracellular water (intracellular mass, i.e., muscle and visceral cells) is plotted against body length for boys and girls. Note that the 2 quadratic equations are not different for the sexes; the curve for boys, however, continues farther and upward. Intracellular water was obtained by subtracting the corrected bromide space (a close measure of true extracellular volume) from the total body water (D_2O space).

Holt, Hill, & Talbert, 1971), but a loss of adipocytes is surprising; Knittle and Hirsch (1968) have suspected that adipocyte cell number is fixed.

As boys approach puberty, calorie intake escalates. This information has been reviewed and expanded by Heald (1969). A correlation can be drawn between the increase in LBM, muscle mass, or nuclear number in muscle and the escalation in calorie intake (Cheek, 1968a). Girls show only a slight rise in calorie intake before puberty, as demonstrated in the classical paper by Wait & Roberts (1932).

HORMONES

Insulin and Growth Hormone

Nutrition is vital to growth, and adequate nutrition is mandatory for the proper action of hormones. We have directed major effort toward the study of hormones on muscle, the most extensive tissue of the body, and hypothesized (Cheek & Graystone, 1969; Cheek & Hill, 1970; 1972) that the two major hormones for postnatal growth are insulin and growth hormone

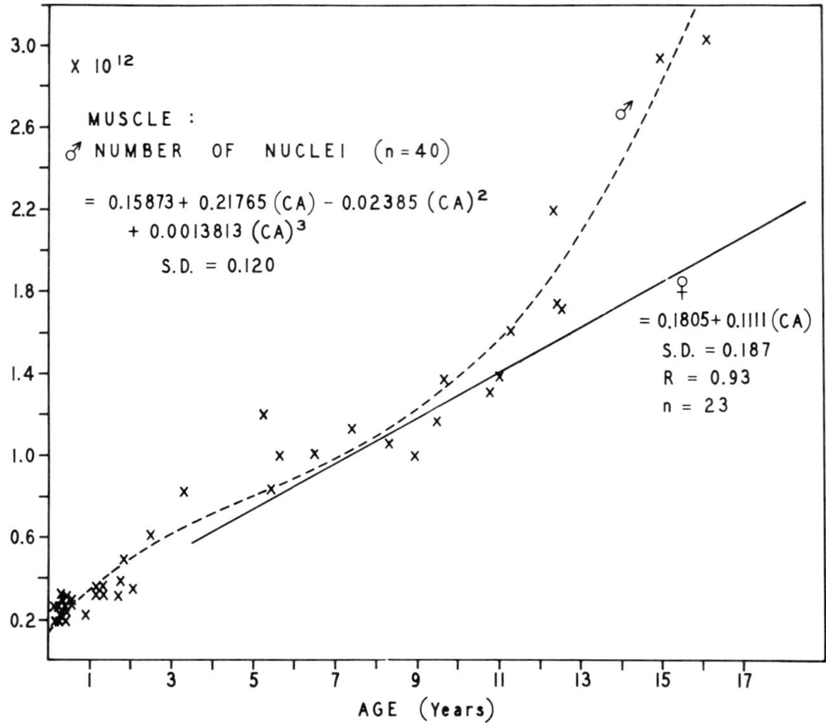

FIG. 10. The number of nuclei in human muscle mass is plotted against age for males (infancy to 17 years), as shown by crosses; for females (4 to 17 years) points are not shown. The relation is cubic for males and linear for females. Increments for males are more remarkable before 2 years and after 9 years (adolescent spurt). There is a fourteenfold increase in the number of nuclei for the postnatal male. Additional information would suggest that this value may reach twentyfold. Thus increments in number of nuclei are more remarkable for the human than for the rat. The sex difference between human males and females is obvious. From Cheek & Graystone, 1969).

(GH). GH is concerned with nuclear replication and insulin with cyto-plasmic growth; the predominant action of one hormone over the other can be gauged by inspection of the nuclear number in the musculature versus the ratio of protein:DNA (Cheek et al, 1971). Thus other hormones may be of secondary importance with respect to childhood and adolescent growth. The evidence can be discussed briefly because it has been reviewed elsewhere (Cheek et al, 1971).

We found (Cheek & Holt, 1963) that the hypophysectomized rat lost nuclei from muscle with the progress of time; the rat rendered hypothyroid

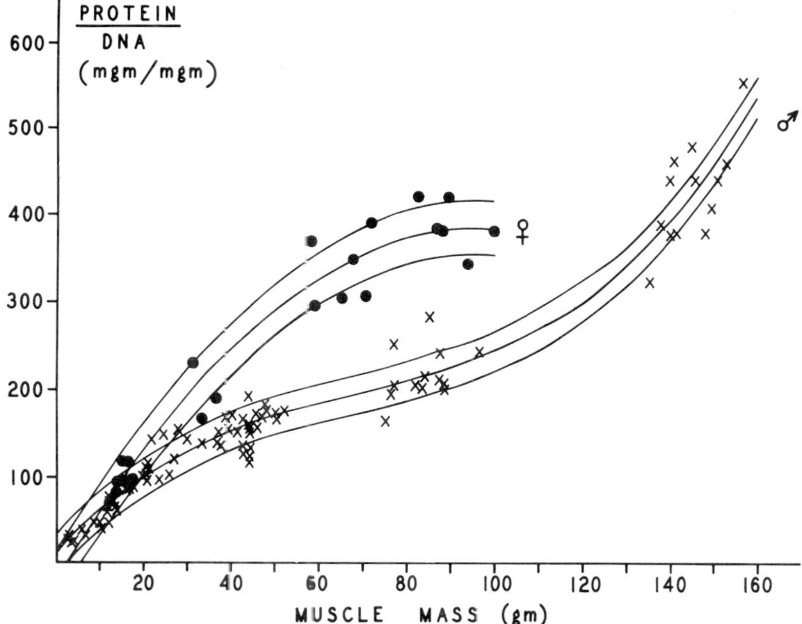

FIG. 11.   The ratio of protein/DNA in muscle tissue is plotted (with SD) against the muscle mass for male and female rats during growth. The relationship is quadratic for females and cubic for males. A sex difference in the growth of muscle cell size is thus revealed. (From Cheek et al, 1971).

failed to gain nuclei in muscle. Because acquired hypothyroidism results in reduced secretion of GH, we suggested that GH per se acts to increase cell number. Injection of GH into hypophysectomized rats or the administration of thyroid hormone to children with acquired hypothyroidism increased the number of nuclei in muscle. The subsequent observations of Daughaday and Reeder (1966) and Beach and Kostyo (1968) were in line with this thinking.

With respect to insulin, the evidence is less clear. Its injection into post-weanling rats causes muscle growth related to an increase of protein relative to DNA (Graystone & Cheek, 1969). However, injection of insulin for an 11-day period into rats 17 days after hypophysectomy produces minimal growth of muscle (Cheek & Graystone, 1959).

We followed the usual procedure of waiting until the hypophysectomized rat had reached a constant weight before treatment. Its gain in weight was thought to be due mainly to fat (Salter & Best, 1953); this is not true, however. Figure 12 shows that muscle mass can almost double after hypo-

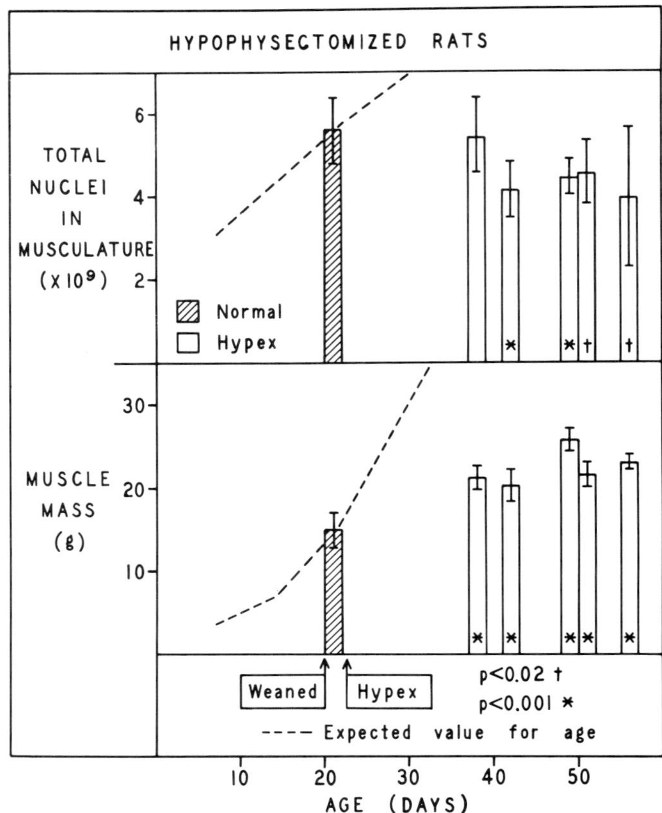

FIG. 12.   Data from groups of rats hypophysectomized at 21 days. The growth that occurs following hypophysectomy is not just related to fat, for muscle mass increases significantly. This increase is not related to an increase of the number of nuclei in muscle; in fact, the DNA content of the musculature declines.

physectomy. The growth is due entirely to a gain in protein relative to DNA and not to a gain in DNA (Fig. 13). Indeed, the hypophysectomized rat has big cells (protein/DNA) for organ size or muscle mass, and we conclude that the growth is due to endogenous insulin, supported by our finding that streptozotocin, an agent that ablates pancreatic cells, inhibits the weight gain of the hypophysectomized rat (Cheek & Hill, 1972).

There is little evidence of predominant action of GH and insulin during adolescence. That calorie-protein intake escalates in the male is in line with the fact that plasma amino acids stimulate hormone secretions. Preadolescent boys have an integrated concentration of GH in plasma (over 24 hours) 4 times the level of the adult male (Thompson, 1972). There is

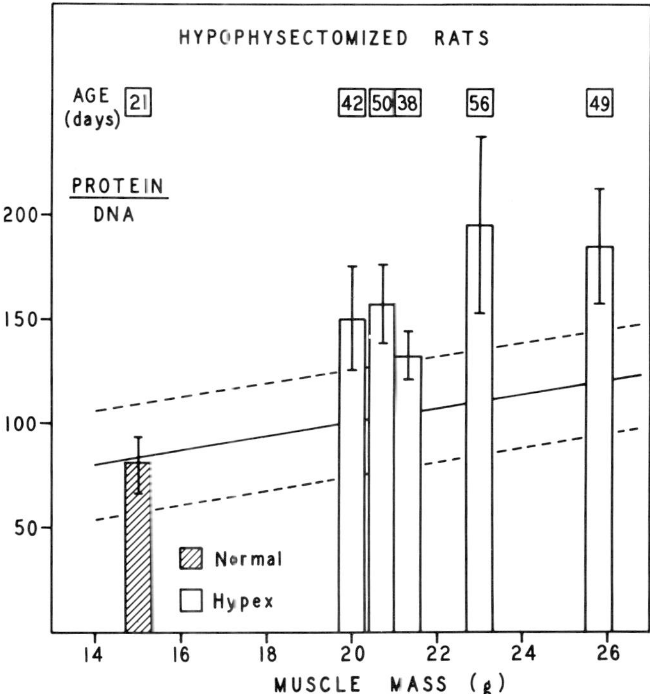

FIG. 13.   From data in Fig. 12, but here the growth of muscle mass following hypophysectomy is related to protein accretion relative to DNA. This may be due to the unopposed action of insulin.

also other evidence that the elevation of testosterone which occurs at 9 to 10 years (Cheek, Brasel, & Graystone, 1968; Frasier, Gafford, & Horton, 1969; August, Grumbach, & Kaplan, 1972) stimulates the production of GH (Illig & Prader, 1970).

The Sex Hormones

Castration of the female rat at weaning causes a pattern of muscle growth similar to that of the male (Cheek et al, 1968). Estrogens inhibit the peripheral action of GH (Wiedemann & Schwartz, 1972; Merrimee & Fineberg, 1971). Androgens stimulate the growth of muscles involved in reproduction and may participate in the protein synthesis in muscle after sexual maturation (Kochakian, 1966). Whether or not androgens do excite GH secretion is unclear, but the pattern of muscle growth for boys and girls separates sharply at 9 years. It is not clear why girls accelerate

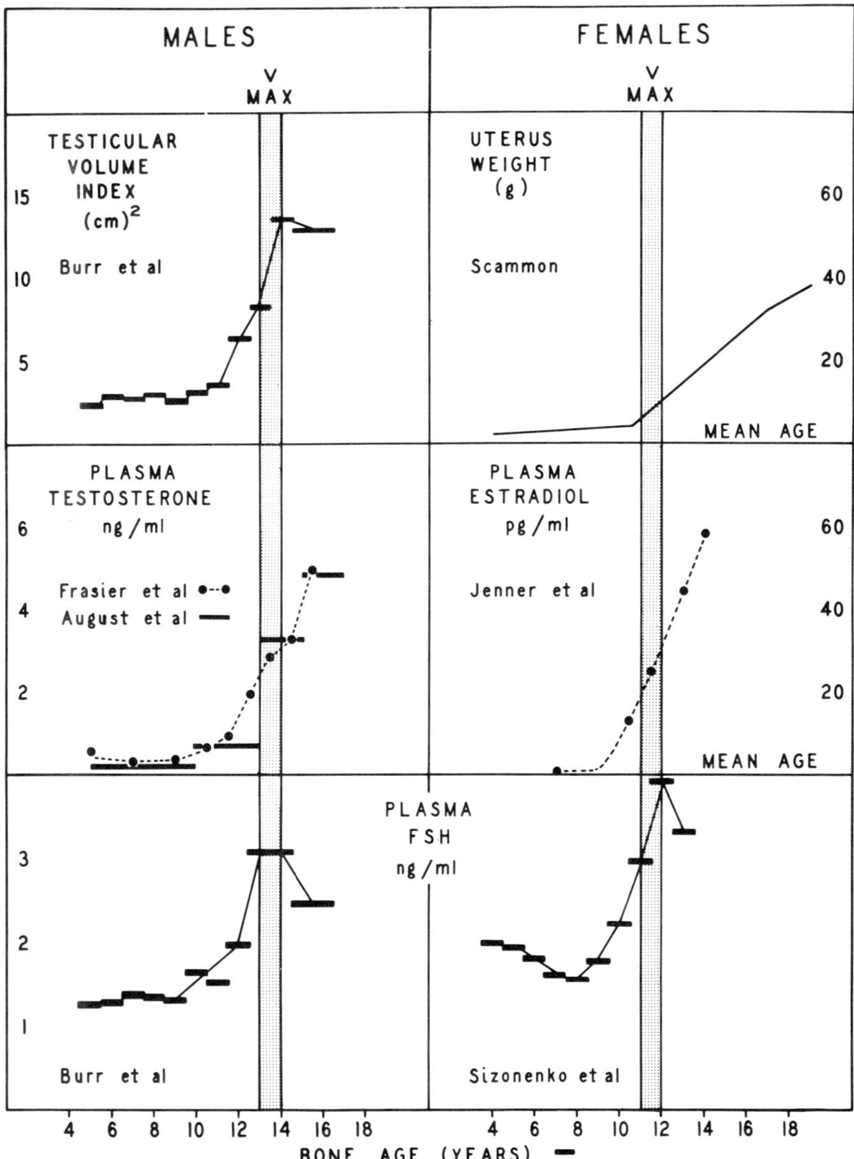

FIG. 14. Changes in the plasma FSH testosterone and testicular volume index for boys during adolescence and changes in plasma estradiol, FSH, and uterine weight for girls. The range of data is shown by the horizontal bars. When possible, bone age (maturational age index) is used on the abscissa. The column V_{max} indicates the point of maximal velocity of somatic growth. The plasma testosterone (boys) and estradiol (girls) increase in concentration from the ninth year. FSH follows this pattern (boys and girls), but when the period of maximal somatic growth is reached FSH concentration decreases. At this point testicular size plateaus but weight of uterus continues.

the accretion of protein relative to DNA in muscle at a faster rate; girls at the tissue level may respond more to insulin than to GH. Insulin may well be involved in the growth of adipose tissue fat during the adolescent period.

Certain information concerning changes in sex hormone production during puberty is summarized in Fig. 14. Changes in testicular volume have been studied by Burr, Sizonenko, Kaplan, and Grumbach (1970). Testicular volume rises appreciably at 10½ years, but FSH is secreted in increasing amounts at 9 years and testosterone secretion rises at the same time. Scammon (1931) demonstrated the increasing growth of the uterus from 10½ years, whereas plasma estradiol (Jenner, Kelch, Kaplan, & Grumbach, 1972) and FSH (Sizonenko, Burr, Kaplan, & Grumbach, 1970) escalate, in terms of secretion at 8 to 9 years. At the time of maximal somatic growth velocity (V_{max}) the FSH reaches its highest value and then subsides.

SUMMARY AND IMPLICATIONS

At about 9 years of age there is a radical departure between boys and girls with respect to growth; presumably the male becomes more responsive to GH at the tissue level. Rapid cell multiplication ensues in muscle, at the epiphyseal plates and to some extent in visceral tissues. Growth of LBM is remarkable and calorie and protein intake escalate accordingly. Fat deposition increases but at a lesser rate. Increased androgen secretion augments cytoplasmic growth in the muscle and may account for continued growth of protein:DNA in the male to about 30 years of age, when testosterone secretion diminishes.

In the female, FSH escalates at 8 years and estradiol at 9. The estrogens restrict the action of GH at the tissue level. The predominating response to insulin leads, we suspect, to a greater growth of adipose tissue and possibly to an accelerated growth of protein:DNA in muscle. Thus the upward growth of lean tissue mass is less remarkable (no break is detected when one inspects growth of lean tissue versus height around 9 years). The growth of muscle is somewhat increased, and skeletal growth follows (as in the male).

It is hypothesized that GH is the major adolescent hormone in the male and insulin the critical adolescent hormone in the female.

ACKNOWLEDGMENT

This work was supported by Grant HD 00 126-08 from the National Institute of Child Health and Human Development, U.S. Public Health Service.

REFERENCES

August, G. P., Grumbach, M. M., & Kaplan, S. L. (1972). Hormonal changes in puberty. III. Correlation of plasma testosterone, LH, FSH, testicular size, and bone age with male pubertal development. *J. Clin. Endocrinol.* **34**, 319–326.

Beach, R. K. & Kostyo, J. L. (1968). Effect of growth hormone on the DNA content of muscles of young hypophysectomized rats. *Endocrinology* **82**, 882–884.

Behar, M. & Guzman, G. (1967). *Malnutrition, Learning and Behavior.* Massachusetts Institute of Technology, Cambridge, Mass.

Burr, I. M., Sizonenko, P. C., Kaplan, S. L., & Grumbach, M. M. (1970). Hormonal changes in puberty. I. Correlation of serum luteinizing hormone and follicle stimulating hormone with stages of puberty, testicular size, and bone age in normal boys. *Pediat. Res.* **4**, 25–35.

Cheek, D. B. (1968a). Cellular growth, hormones, nutrition and time. Borden Award Address, *Pediatrics* **41**, 30–45.

Cheek, D. B. (1968b). *Human Growth,* Lea & Febiger, Philadelphia, pp. 152–158; 171–173; 184–189.

Cheek, D. B., Brasel, J. A., & Graystone, J. E. (1968). Muscle cell growth in rodents: sex difference and the role of hormones. In *Human Growth,* D. B. Cheek, Ed., Lea & Febiger, Philadelphia, pp. 306–324.

Cheek, D. B. & Graystone, J. E. (1969). Action of insulin, growth hormone and epinephrine on cell growth in liver, muscle, and brain of the hypophysectomized rat. *Pediat. Res.* **3**, 77–88.

Cheek, D. B. & Hill, D. E. (1970). Muscle and liver cell growth: role of hormones and nutritional factors. *Fed. Proc.* **29**, 1503–1509.

Cheek, D. B. & Hill, D. E. (1972). Effect of growth hormone on cell and somatic growth. In *Handbook of Physiology,* section 7, *Endocrinology.* In press.

Cheek, D. B., Hill, D. E., Cordano, A., and Graham, G. (1970a). Malnutrition in infancy: changes in muscle and adipose tissue before and after rehabilitation. *Pediat. Res.* **4**, 135–144.

Cheek, D. B. & Holt, A. B. (1963). Growth and body composition of the mouse. *Amer. J. Physiol.* **205**, 913–920.

Cheek, D. B., Holt, A. B., Hill, D. E., & Talbert, J. L. (1971). Skeletal muscle cell mass and growth: the concept of the deoxyribonucleic acid unit. *Pediat. Res.* **5**, 312–328.

Cheek, D. B., Migeon, C. J., & Mellits, E. D. (1968). Concept of biologic age. In *Human Growth,* D. B. Cheek, Ed., Lea & Febiger, Philadelphia, pp. 541–567.

Cheek, D. B., Schultz, R. B., Parra, A., & Reba, R. C. (1970b). Overgrowth of lean and adipose tissues in adolescent obesity. *Pediat. Res.* **4**, 268–279.

Cheek, D. B. & White, J. J. (1972). *Proc. Intl. Congr. Nutr.* Sept. 3–9, Mexico City.

Daughaday, W. H. & Reeder, C. (1966). Synchronous activation of DNA synthesis in hypophysectomized rat cartilage by growth hormone. *J. Lab. Clin. Med.* **68**, 357–368.

Drash, A., Heese, D., & Brasel, J. A. (1968). Clinical material; anthropometric and developmental analysis. In *Human Growth,* D. B. Cheek, Ed., Lea & Febiger, Philadelphia, pp. 60–83.

Durand, G., Fauconneau, G., & Penot, E. (1967). Croissance des tissus du rat et reduction de l'apport energetique de la ration; influence sur la taneru en acides nucleiques. *Ann. Biol. Anim. Biochem. Biophys.* **7**, 145–155.

Flynn, M. A., Woodruff, C., Clark, J., & Chase, G. (1972). Total body potassium in normal children. *Pediat. Res.* **6**, 239–245.

Frasier, S. D., Gafford, F., & Horton, R. (1969). Plasma androgens in childhood and adolescence, *J. Clin. Endocrinol.* **29**, 1404–1408.

Garn, S. M. (1970). *The Earlier Gain and the Later Loss of Cortical Bone in Nutritional Perspective.* Thomas, Springfield, Ill.

Graystone, J. E. & Cheek, D. B. (1969). Effects of reduced caloric intake and increased insulin-induced caloric intake on the cell growth of muscle, liver, and cerebrum and on skeletal collagen in the postweanling rat. *Pediat. Res.* **3**, 66–76.

Heald, F. P. (1969). *Adolescent Nutrition and Growth.* Appleton-Century-Crofts, New York, pp. 17–35.

Hill, D. E., Holt, A. B., Parra, A., & Cheek, D. B. (1970). Influence of protein-calorie versus calorie restriction on the body composition and cellular growth of muscle and liver in weanling rats. *Johns Hopk. M. J.* **127**, 146–165.

Illig, R. & Prader, A. (1970). Effect of testosterone on growth hormone secretion in patients with anorchia and delayed puberty. *J. Clin. Endocrinol.* **30**, 615–618.

Jenner, M. R., Kelch, R. P., Kaplan, S. L., & Grumbach, M. M. (1972). Hormonal changes in puberty. IV. Plasma estradiol, LH, and FSH in prepubertal children, pubertal females, and in precocious puberty, premature thelarche, hypogonadism, and in a child with a feminizing ovarian tumor. *J. Clin. Endocrinol.* **34**, 521–530.

Knittle, J. L. & Hirsch, J. (1968). Effect of early nutrition on the development of rat epididymal fat-pads: cellularity and metabolism. *J. Clin. Invest.* **47**, 2091–2098.

Kochakian, C. D. (1966). *Physiology and Biochemistry of Muscle as a Food,* University of Wisconsin Press, Madison.

Laird, A. K. (1967). Evolution of the human growth curve. *Growth* **31**, 345–355.

Mellits, E. D. (1968). Statistical Methods. In *Human Growth,* D. B. Cheek, Ed., Lea & Febiger, Philadelphia, pp. 33–38.

Mellits, E. D. & Cheek, D. B. (1968). Growth and body water. In *Human Growth,* D. B. Cheek, Ed., Lea & Febiger, Philadelphia, pp. 135–149.

Mellits, E. D., Dorst, J. D., & Cheek, D. B. (1971). Bone age: contribution to the prediction of maturational and biological age. *Physic. Anthrop.* **35**, 381–384.

Merimee, T. J. & Fineberg, S. E. (1971). Studies of the sex based variation of human growth hormone secretion. *J. Clin. Endocrinol.* **33**, 896–902.

Parra, A., Schultz, R. B., Graystone, J. E., & Cheek, D. B. (1971). Correlative studies in obese children concerning body composition and plasma insulin and growth hormone level. *Pediat. Res.* **5** 605–613.

Rabinowitz, D. & Merimee, T. (1968). Peripheral actions and regulation of insulin and growth hormone secretion in intact man. In *Human Growth,* D. B. Cheek, Ed., Lea & Febiger, Philadelphia, pp. 207–220.

Reba, R. C., Cheek, D. B., & Mellits, E. D. (1972). Body composition studies: Growth of intracellular mass and metabolic size and the assessment of maturational age. *Symposium on Nuclear Medicine,* A. E. James, Ed., Johns Hopkins University Press, Baltimore.

Salter, J. & Best, C. H. (1953). Insulin as a growth hormone. *Brit. Med. J.* **2**, 353–356.

Scammon, R. E. (1931). *Proc. 2nd Intl. Congr. on Sex Research,* Oliver & Boyd, London, pp. 118–123.

Sizonenko, P. C., Burr, I. M., Kaplan, S. L., & Grumbach, M. M. (1970). Hormonal changes in puberty. II. Correlation of serum luteinizing hormone and follicle stimulating hormone with stages of puberty and bone age in normal girls. *Pediat. Res.* **4**, 36–45.

Thompson, R. G., Rodriguez, A., Kowarski, A., Migeon, C. J., & Blizzard, R. M. (1972). Integrated concentrations of growth hormone correlated with plasma testosterone and bone age in preadolescent and adolescent males, *J. Clin. Endocrinol.* **35**, 334–337.

Wait, B. & Roberts, J. J. (1932). Studies in food requirements of adolescent girls: energy intake of well-nourished girls 10 to 16 years of age. *Amer. Dietet. A.* **8**, 209–219.

Wiedemann, E. & Schwartz, E. (1972). Suppression of growth hormone-dependent human serum sulfation factor by estrogen. *J. Clin. Endocrinol.* **34**, 51–58.

DISCUSSION

Dr. Forbes.   I have made a compilation of changes in body composition of Rochester children during adolescence. Lean body mass (LBM) was estimated by the ^{40}K method, and body fat is the difference between weight and LBM. We have been careful to calibrate our counter in such a way that we get reasonably good results for children of various body sizes (Forbes, Schultz, Cafarelli, & Amirkhakimi, 1968). Figure 15 is a plot of the LBM: height ratio against age for boys and girls in the age range of 8 to 30 years. During the course of male adolescence LBM increases at a relatively more rapid rate than height, so that this ratio rises rapidly. Changes in the female are much less pronounced (Forbes, In press). Sex differences in body composition are also evident in body fat content. Boys become thinner during late adolescence and girls show an increase in relative fat content. At maturity boys have more LBM (largely muscle) per unit height and girls have more fat per unit weight. LBM bears a linear relationship to height at all ages and in both sexes but, of even more interest, the regression slope of LBM on height changes during adolescence and there is a sex difference (Fig. 16). Not only does the ratio of LBM to height increase as adolescence progresses, but the slope of the regression line does also. The tall 18-year-old male thus has a con-

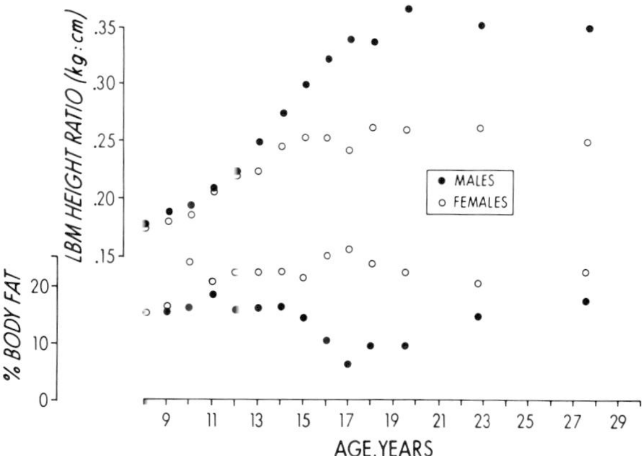

FIG. 15.   LBM: height ratio (kilograms to centimeters) and per cent body fat as a function of age. Reproduced from *Growth,* by permission of the publisher.

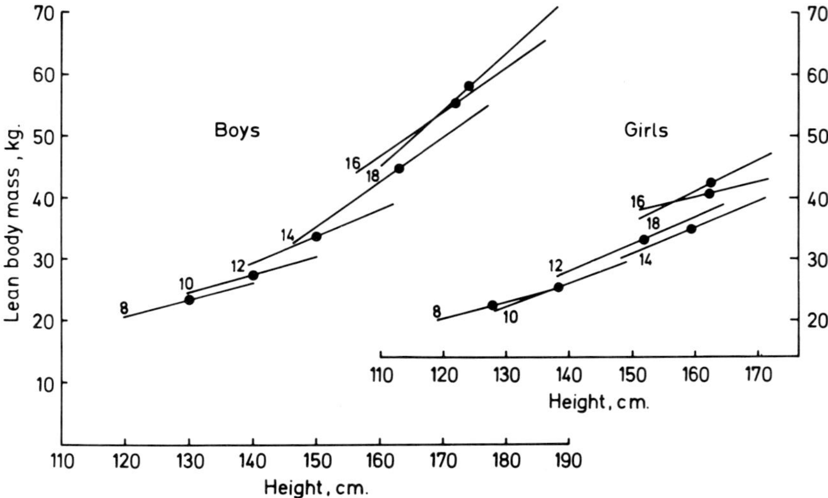

FIG. 16.   Calculated regression lines for LBM versus height for selected ages. Each line embraces the 3rd to 97th height percentiles of the Stuart-Stevenson standards, and the dot is placed at the 50th percentile. Reproduced from *Pediat. Res.* **6**, 35 (1972), by permission of the publishers.

siderable advantage over his shorter age peer with respect to muscle mass. This may be a factor in athletic performance. For the younger boy and girl, however, the influence of height is not nearly so marked (Forbes, 1972). The existence of this relationship between LBM and height permits us to normalize our data to the 50th height percentile and results in a more representative value. Figure 17, which graphs these data, shows a smooth curve drawn among the data points. Maximal values for LBM are reached at an earlier age in the female, but her value is only about 70 per cent that of the male. It is evident that velocity rises to a maximum at an earlier age in girls, but that the peak value is considerably less than that for boys. Figure 18 illustrates mean values for LBM as a function of age for subjects aged 7 to 30 years, including my own data on ^{40}K and data from the literature in which LBM was estimated by densitometry or total body water or indirectly by fat soluble indicators such as radioactive krypton. All of the data have been standardized to the 50th height percentile using the regression slopes as previously published (Forbes, 1972). When this is done, there is a remarkable degree of correspondence among the results of these various methods. The ^{40}K method can yield satisfactory results, provided the instrument is properly calibrated, and it has the advantage of being nontraumatic. Finally, stature must be taken into account when comparing groups of subjects.

DR. FRISCH.   If you use Dr. Forbes' regression equations for LBW on height (Forbes, 1972) and substitute the mean height at menarche, 158.5 cm, in the

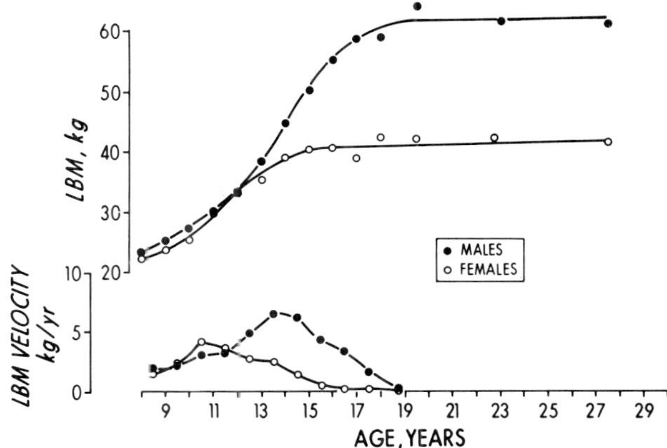

FIG. 17.   LBM values normalized to the 50th height percentile, and calculated LBM velocity (kilograms per year). Reproduced from *Growth* by permission of the publishers.

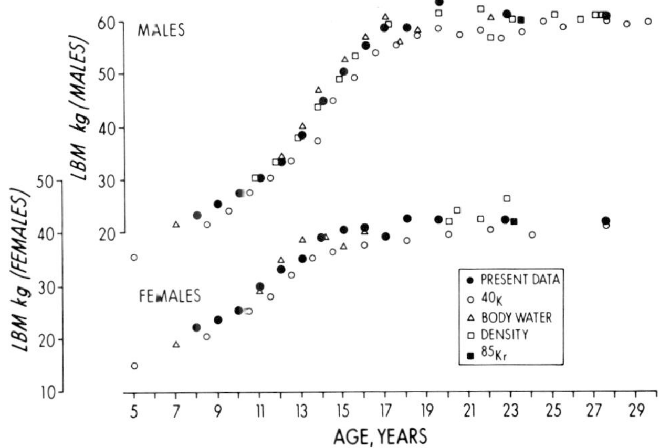

FIG. 18.   LBM as a function of age for boys and girls. Data normalized to the 50th height percentile. Author's data compared with data from the literature. Reproduced from *Growth,* by permission of the publishers.

proper age equation, one gets the same LBW, about 36 kg, as by using Dr. Cheek's equation for total water on height and weight, using height and weight at menarche.

DR. RESKO.   Dr. Cheek, I think you showed that calorie intake decreased in the female at the time of puberty; is that correct?

Dr. Cheek.   That's right.

Dr. Resko.   I wonder if this can be connected in some way to estrogen secretion because in rodents eating behavior decreases when they come into heat. Female rhesus monkeys eat less at the time of midcycle, which can be correlated with the elevated concentrations of estrogen in systemic blood.

Dr. Cheek.   If you look through the nutritional literature you will find a lack of information on calorie and protein intake that is not related to chronological age. Few data relate body length to caloric intake, for example, yet body length is much more meaningful than chronological age.

Dr. Ramirez.   Dr. Advis in our laboratory made thermal lesions in the anterior hypothalamic areas of 16-day-old female rats, and to our surprise the pattern of levels of gonadotropin in the blood of the animals that reached precocious puberty around 32 days of age, induced by the lesions, was not different compared with the normal pattern of control animals (puberty around 38 days). All the animals started at the same average body weight as littermates, but the important fact is that the bilaterally lesioned animals showed a transient body weight gain significantly higher than the controls at 23, 30, and 37 days of age. At the age of 44 days the differences are not significant. The unilateral lesions also induced a significantly higher body weight than found in the control at 30 days. Is it possible that GH could change the sensitivity of the gonad to the same levels of gonadotropins, and could this initiate puberty or does GH do something earlier?

Dr. Ganong.   I do not have an answer. However, these are anterior lesions and they often cause hypothalamic hyperphagia; so, the difference may be an artifact. What about posterior lesions? In Gellert's work and mine the weight of the animals with hypothalamic lesions and precocious puberty was less than that of the controls (Gellert & Ganong, 1960).

Dr. Ramirez.   These lesions did not involve the ventral medial nuclei; they were anterior to it. The main structure destroyed was the anterior hypothalamic region. The people who have worked with hypothalamic lesions have not had this as a possibility to think about.

REFERENCES

Forbes, G. B. (1965). Toward a new dimension in human growth. *Pediatrics* **36**, 825–835.

Forbes, G. B. (1972). Relation of lean body mass to height in children and adolescents. *Pediat. Res.* **6**, 32–37.

Forbes, G. B. (1972). Relation of lean body mass in man. *Growth*. In press.

Forbes, G. B., Schultz, F. Cafarelli, C., & Amirkhakimi, G. H. (1968). Effect of body size on potassium-40 measurement in the whole body counter (tilt-chair technique). *Health Phys* **15**, 435–442.

Gellert, R. J. & Ganong, W. F. (1960). Precocious puberty in rats with hypothalamic lesions. *Acta Endocrinol.* **33**, 569–576.

17.

Sequence and Tempo in the Somatic Changes in Puberty

J. M. TANNER

The somantic changes of puberty constitute the following:

1. A general increase in the growth rate of skeleton, muscles, and viscera, known as the adolescent growth spurt.

2. Sex-specific increases in growth rates, for example, of shoulder and hip width above the general spurt, leading to an enhancement of sexual dimorphism.

3. Changes in body composition caused by an increase in muscle, decrease in fat, and increase in cortical but not medullary bone more pronounced in boys than girls.

4. The development of the reproductive system and secondary sex characteristics.

I deal with these changes in turn but pass fairly rapidly over the simple descriptions of the events themselves, for their details are readily available elsewhere (Tanner, 1962; 1967; 1969; Marshall & Tanner, 1969; 1970).

These problems of sequence and tempo are emphasized:

1. Is the sequence of events the same in all girls and in all boys? If it

---

Abbreviations

HES	(National) Health Examination Survey
PHV	Peak height velocity

varies, what are the normal limits of this variation, and to what is this variation due? Is there perhaps constancy of sequence *within* a given development (e.g., breast development stages); peak velocities of different parts of the body, such as leg and trunk lengths), but inconstancy *between* different areas of development (e.g., skeletal maturation, breast development)?

2. What are the limits to the ages at which somatic changes of puberty occur, i.e., what variations in tempo of growth *before* adolescence can we expect to encounter and what variation of tempo within pubertal developments do we find? Do all boys pass at the same rate from genital stage (G) 2 to 5, for example? If a girl passes rapidly from breast development stage (B) 2 to 5, will she also pass rapidly through her pubic hair stages?

These questions have a certain intrinsic interest, and some have considerable practical importance for the clinician who deals with adolescents.

We should, however, always look beyond the events to their supposed endocrinological causes to the brain, and to the endocrine mechanisms that presumably govern the linkages between them.

THE ADOLESCENT GROWTH SPURT

Figure 1 charts the growth in height of a single individual from the Berkeley Guidance Study (Tuttenham & Snyder, 1954), in which the adolescent spurt is clearly shown. Figure 2 emphasizes in typical velocity curves the difference in the average age at which the peaks of boys and girls are reached and demonstrates the greater amplitude of the spurt in the boys.

A considerable difference exists between these curves of growth in body length in man and the curve of body length (nose to rump) of the rat. Examples of the latter may be found in Hughes & Tanner (1970). The two great growth differences between the human and the rodent (Tanner, 1962, Chapt. 10) are the following:

1. The rat is born very early, at a time corresponding, from most auxological points of view, to about 100 human postmenstrual days.

2. Man has a long period of growth sandwiched in between weaning and puberty, whereas the rat enters puberty shortly after weaning. Thus the problem is not only to determine what may be similar in the control of puberty in the two species but also to explain in endocrinological terms the mechanism of the obvious difference.

As every biologist knows, children differ a great deal in the age at which they begin their adolescent growth spurt and their pubertal changes. In Fig. 3 the height velocity curves of 5 boys are shown with an "average" curve described, quite erroneously, by averaging the 5 according to chro-

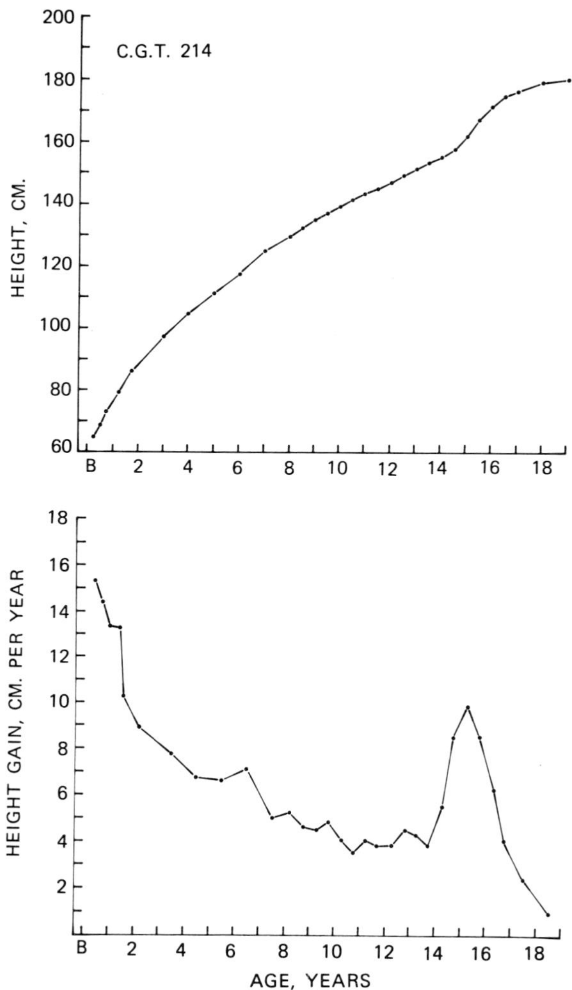

FIG. 1. Growth in height of a single child from the California Guidance Study. Upper = distance (height for age) curve; lower = velocity curve (rate of growth). From Tuttenham & Snyder (1954).

nological age. This methodological error, still sometimes made, has been discussed at length elsewhere (Tanner, 1962). In looking for accelerations over puberty it is invariably misleading to average the values in different children in relation to chronological age. Various methods of allowing for advancement or delay (*tempo of growth*) are in current use; the best one has to be chosen for the particular purpose in hand. When looking for an

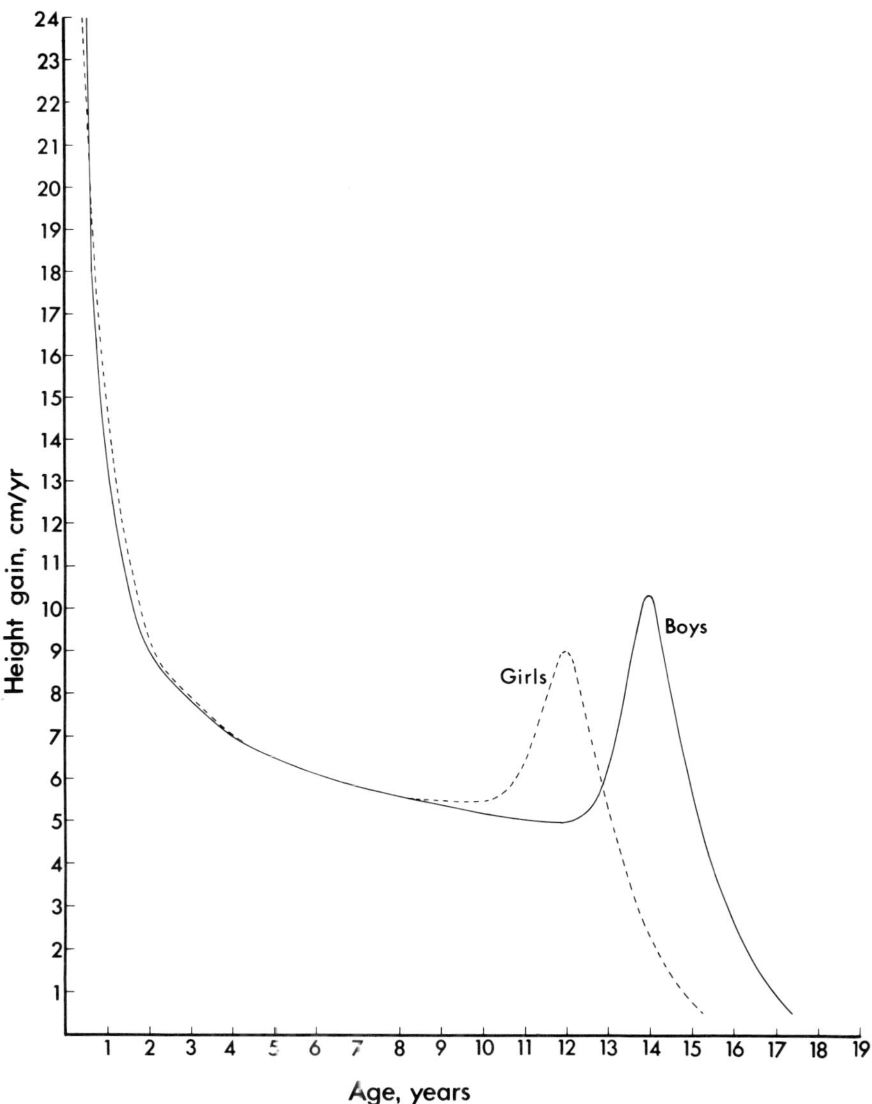

FIG. 2.   "Typical-individual" velocity curves for supine length or height in boys and girls. From Tanner et al (1966).

acceleration in muscle growth, for example, use of a scale of years before and after peak height velocity is appropriate.

Figure 4 shows how early and late developing boys tend to reach the same ultimate height, a necessary fact for the clinician to know. Figure 5

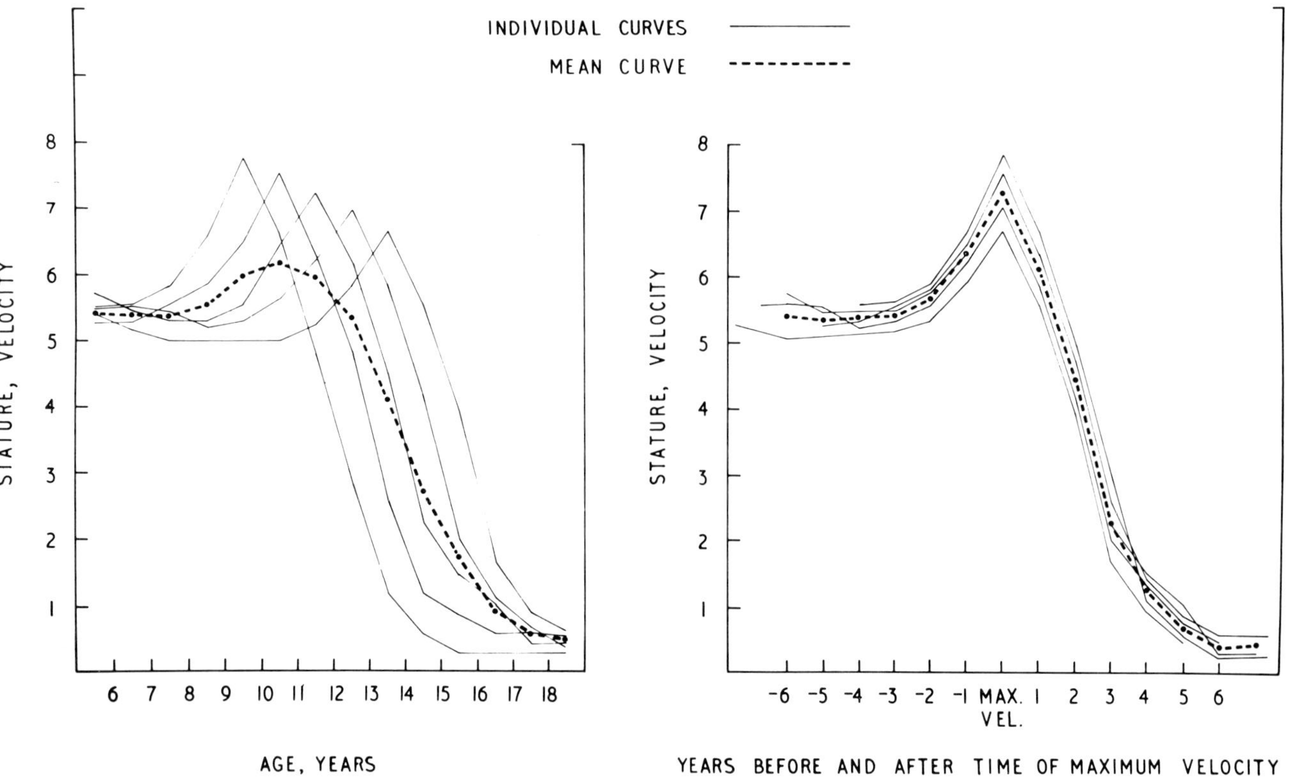

FIG. 3. Height velocity curves of 5 boys, plotted against chronological age (*left*) and age at peak height velocity (*right*). From Tanner (1962).

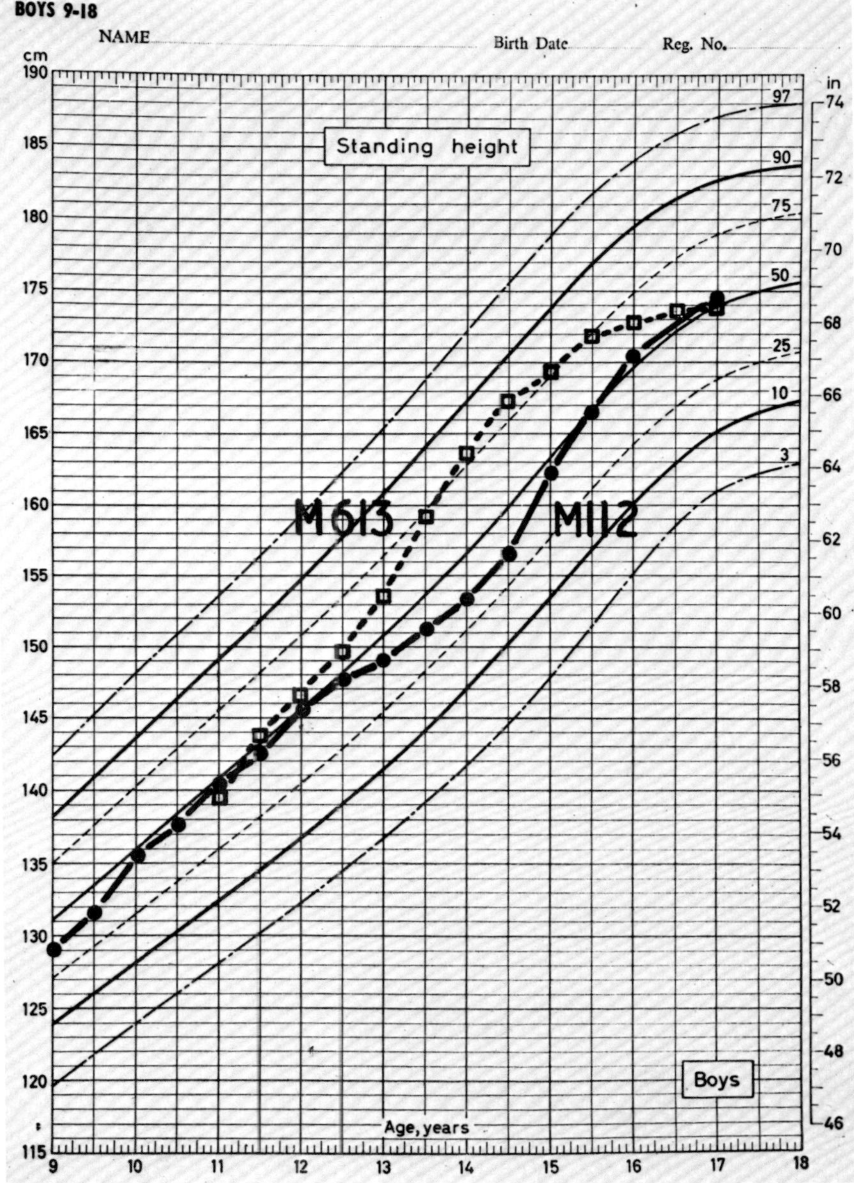

FIG. 4. Height curves during puberty of an early developing boy (M 613) and a late developing boy (M 112). Note both are the same height at the beginning and end of the spurt. From Tanner (1962).

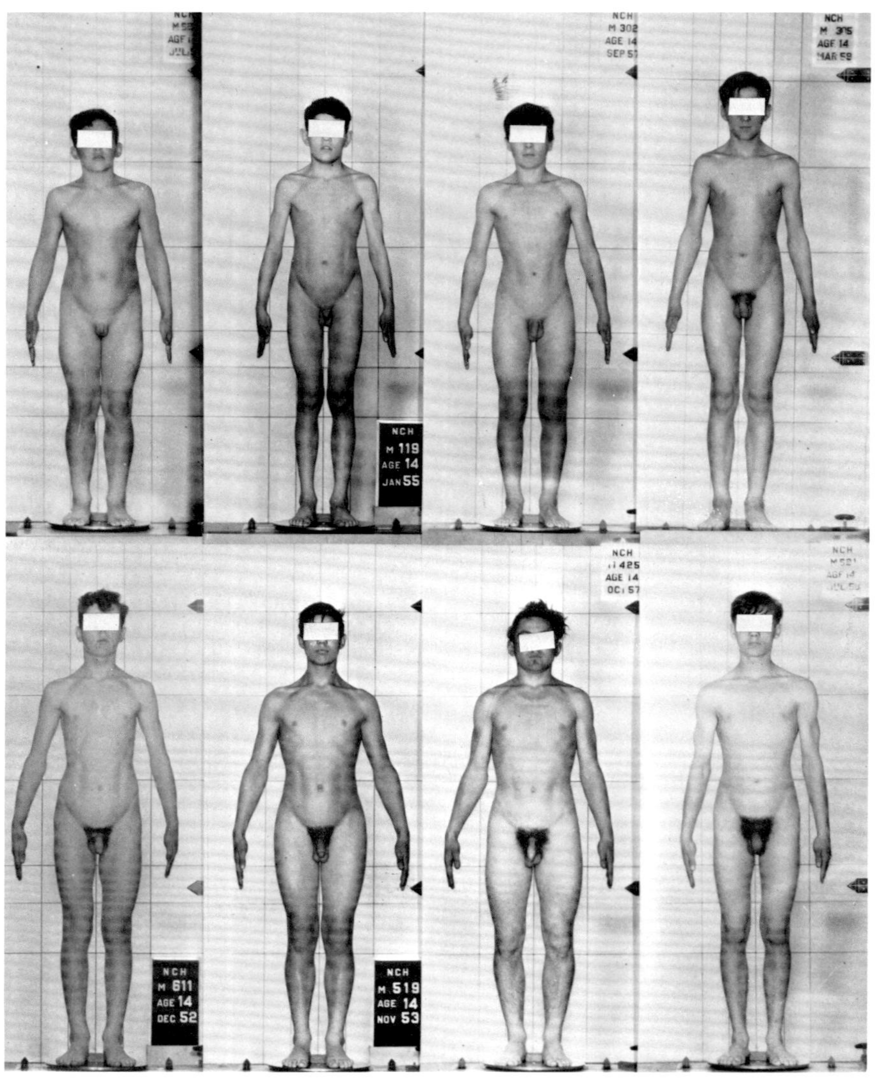

FIG. 5. Eight boys all aged 14.0 years. Note differences in pubertal development. From Tanner (1962).

emphasizes the great difference in ages at the beginning of puberty; all 8 boys are the same chronological age, i.e., 14.0 years. To speak, therefore, of a "boy aged 14" is to be vague to the point of leaving out almost everything that is important about 14-year-old boys. The same is true of talking about 12-year-old girls (or 13-year-old boys or girls, naturally).

Sex Dimorphism

Some body dimensions develop differently in the two sexes, thus completing the sex dimorphism begun in early fetal life. Figure 6 shows the velocity curves of shoulder and hip widths. Note that both are plotted from mixed longitudinal data against age before and after peak height velocity (PHV), not against chronological age. The adolescent spurt is greater in the male in all measurements, except for hip width. In shoulder width the difference in velocity is still greater than in most measurements. This, then, is an example of sex-measurement interaction, something also present in the development of the teeth and bones of the hand and wrist (Tanner, 1962; Tanner, Whitehouse, Healy, Marshall, & Goldstein, 1973).

Changes in Body Composition

Figures 7, 8, and 9 show changes in body composition that occur at puberty. They relate to radiographic measurements of the width of bone, muscle, and fat in the arm, calf, and thigh in a mixed longitudinal study (Tanner, 1968). Again, individual children have been aligned on PHV and the averages then estimated.

Figure 7 shows how the muscle cross section (estimated from measured width by assuming a circular cross section) increases with its peak velocity coinciding, or very nearly coinciding, with PHV.

Figure 8 shows the simultaneous loss of limb fat (negative velocity) which occurs in boys at the same time and which can also be seen in the curves of skinfolds (Tanner & Whitehouse, 1962).

Figure 9 demonstrates the growth in bony cortex (with the absolute amount, not the velocity, plotted), contrasted with the lack of enlargement of the medulla. These illustrations show the large sex difference in muscle and fat growth at adolescence. The development of the cortex of the limb bones is also much more pronounced in boys.

Development of the Reproductive System

Figure 10 is a diagram of the sequence of events in the development of the reproductive system in an average girl and boy. A little mental arithmetic will show that in some boys the penis has finished its growth before it has even started in others. All the children considered in this diagram,

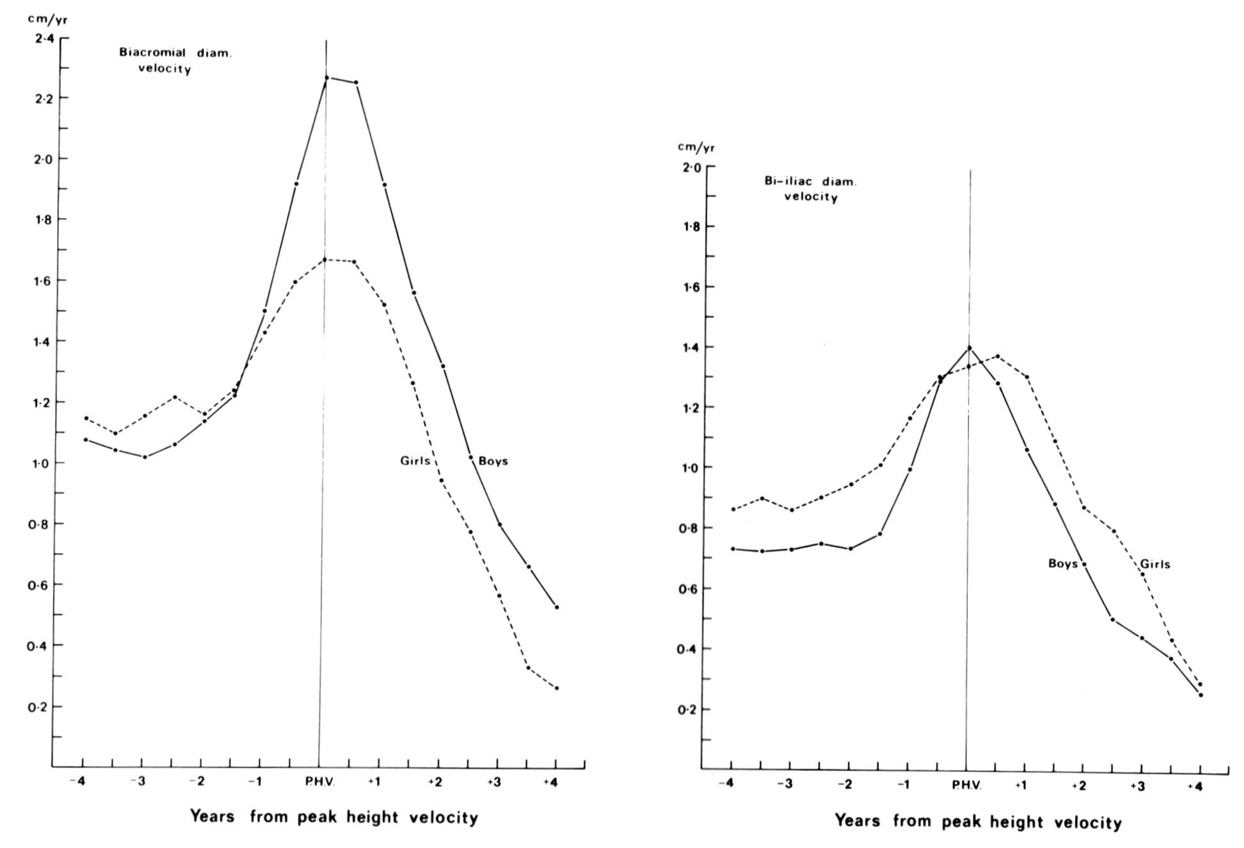

FIG. 6. Adolescent spurt in shoulder width (*left*) and hip width (*right*); longitudinal data plotted against age at peak height velocity (PHV). From Tanner (1969).

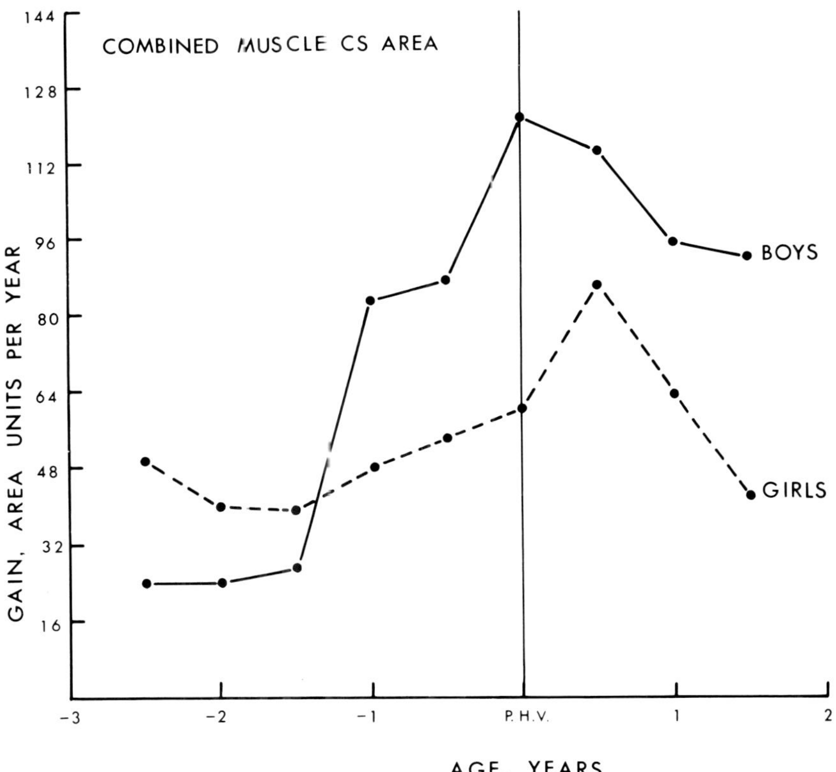

FIG. 7. Rate of growth in cross-sectional area of muscle in arm, calf, and thigh, estimated by radiography. Mixed longitudinal data, plotted against age before or after PHV. From Tanner (1968).

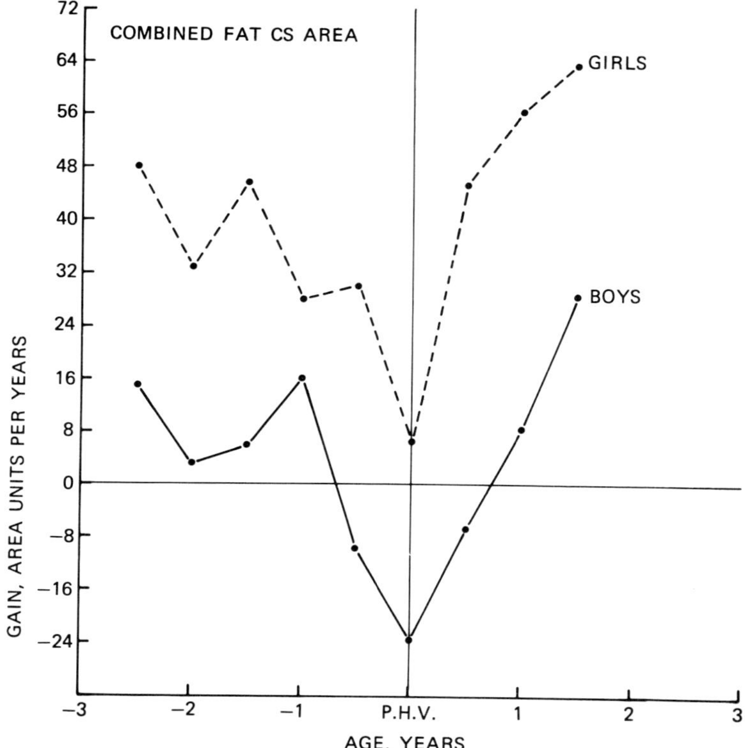

FIG. 8. Rate of growth of subcutaneous fat in arm, calf, and thigh, estimated by radiography on the children in Fig. 7. From Tanner (1968).

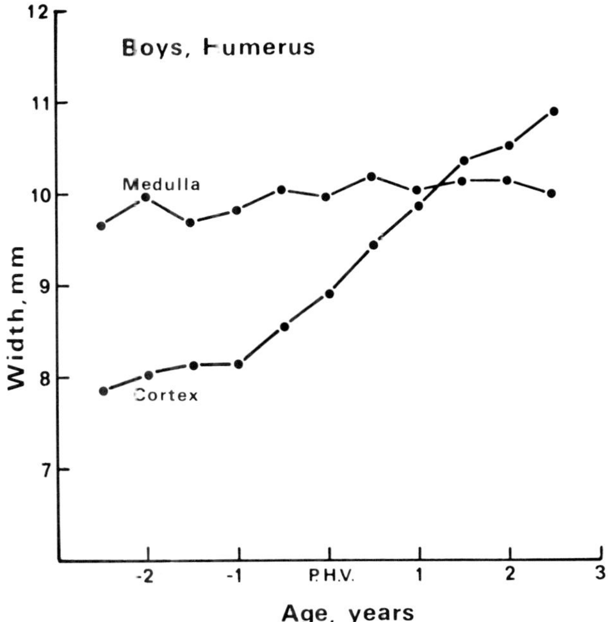

FIG. 9.   Growth of width of cortex of limb bones (arm, calf, and thigh) in boys at puberty. Same subjects as in Figs. 7 and 8 plotted against age before or after PHV. From Tanner (1968).

as in all other figures, are normal and living in the regular school community.

Variation of Pubertal Patterns

Figure 11 shows the relation between 4 series of events, i.e., the height spurt, development of breasts (stages B2 to B5), growth of pubic hair (PH2 to PH5), and menarche, for a girl who was selected as representing the average. Menarche occurs after the height spurt has passed its peak, indeed as deceleration (see lowest line in figure) is at its strongest. B2 occurs in this girl shortly before PHV, PH3 shortly after PHV.

These relationships vary considerably. Figure 12 shows the percentage of boys who reached each stage of pubic hair growth before a given stage of genital development (for definition of stages see Tanner, 1962; 1969). The diagram shows that within G3 boys may be in PH1, 2, 3, or 4 in proportions about 45, 40, 10, and 5 per cent, respectively. Thus the relation between these different series of events is by no means fixed (which is the

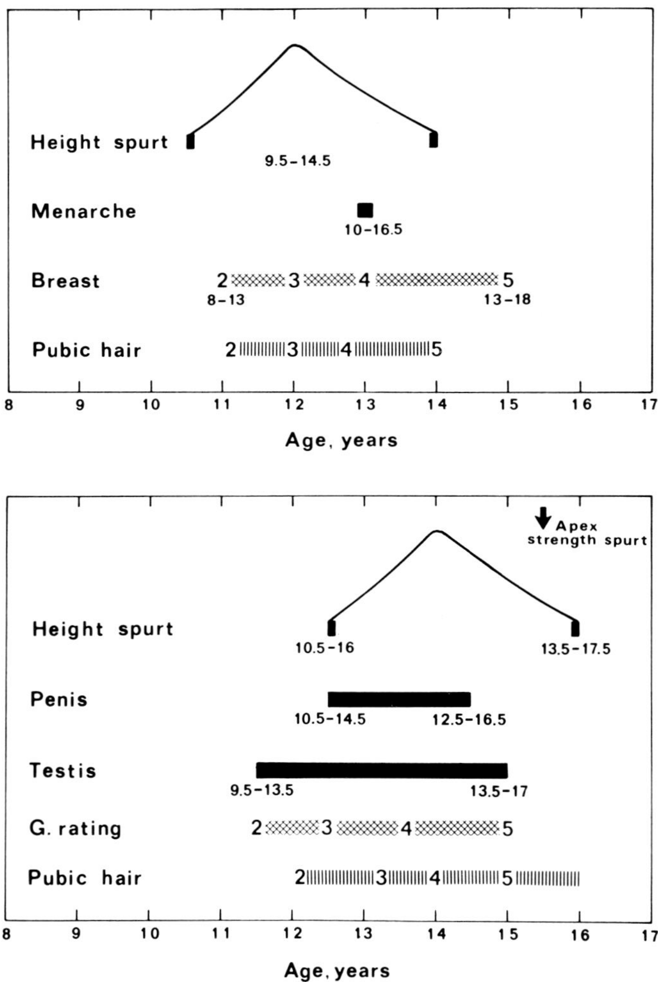

FIG. 10.   Schematic sequence of events at puberty. An average girl (*upper*) and boy (*lower*) are represented. The range of ages within which each event charted may begin and end is given by the figures placed directly below its start and finish. Redrawn from Tanner (1962).

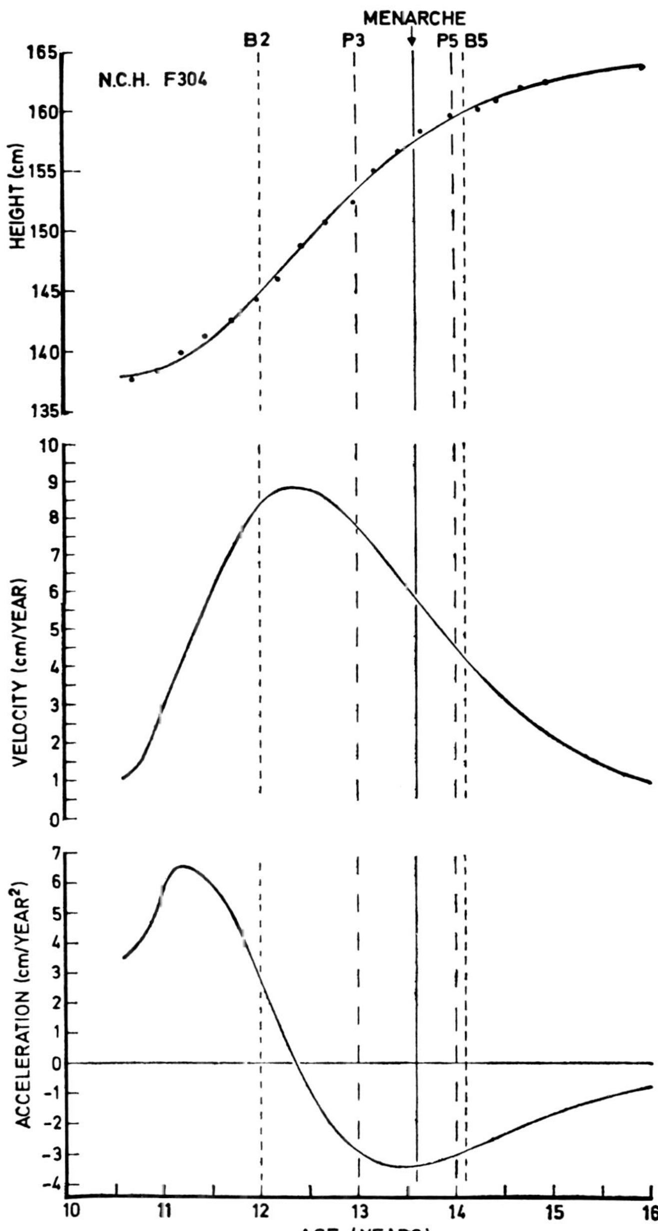

FIG. 11. Height attained, height velocity, and height acceleration curves of a girl at puberty. B2 marks beginning of breast development, B5 adult form. P3 marks intermediate stage of pubic hair development, P5 adult form. From Tanner (1969).

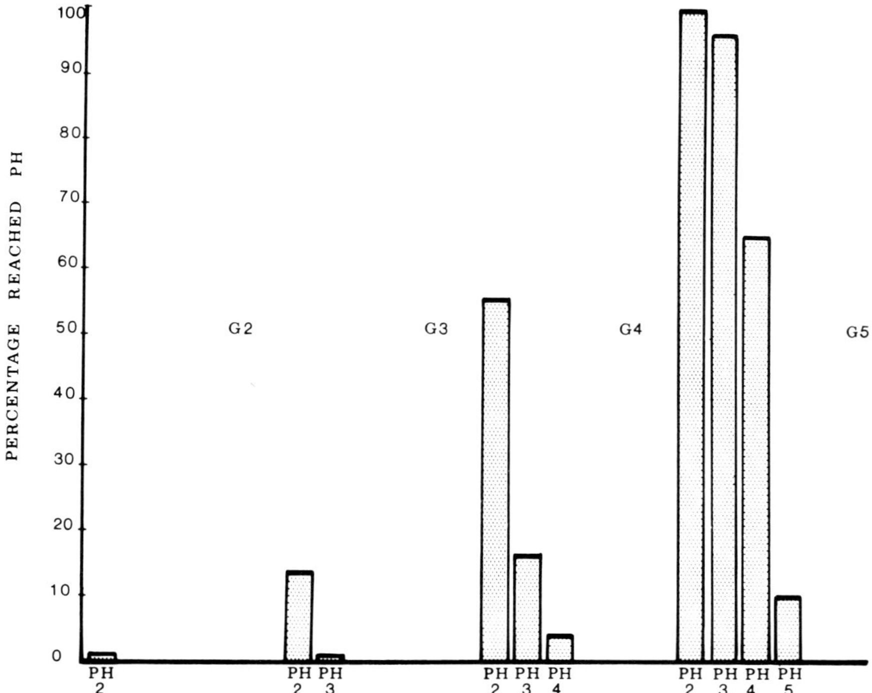

FIG. 12.   Percentage of boys who had reached each stage of pubic hair development (PH) before reaching each stage of genital development. G2, G3, etc., represent the moment of reaching the corresponding genital stages. Thus the histogram between G2 and G3 shows the percentages of boys in genital stage 2 who reached each pubic hair stage before they reached the third genital stage. From Marshall & Tanner (1970).

reason why the steps in puberty should be designated G1, PH1, G2, PH1, G2, PH1, G3, PH2, etc., and not stages II, III, etc.).

The relation of genital development to PHV is closer; only 2 per cent of boys in stage G3 had reached PHV, whereas 76 per cent of the boys in stage G4 had done so. Thus, the majority experienced PHV while at G3 in the genital development; a minority had PHV during the G4 stage.

Figure 13 shows another sort of variation in pubertal development of boys, i.e., the rapidity with which the stages are passed. The average boy takes a little more than a year to go from G2 to G3, but some take as long as 2½ years. The whole of the genital development from beginning to end, on the average, takes 3 years; but, in exceptional though normal boys it may take 5½ years. Note that the most rapidly developing boys pass

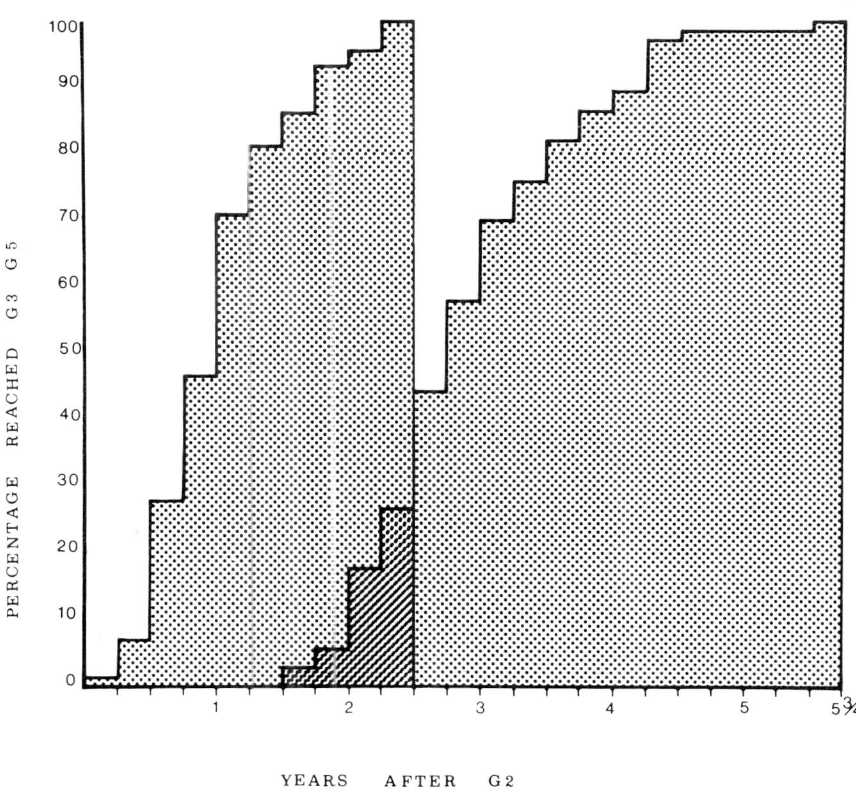

FIG. 13.   Cumulative percentages of boys who had reached G3 (*left hand columns*) and G5 (*right-hand columns*) at given intervals, in years, after reaching G2. From Marshall & Tanner (1970).

from G2 to G5 in less time than the slowest boys take to go from G2 to G3 (the crosshatched area in the diagram).

Figure 14 shows the relation in girls between breast development and menarche and PHV. About 5 per cent experience menarche while still in stage B2, 25 per cent in B3, 60 per cent in B4, and the few remaining in B5. About half the girls reach PHV while in B1 or B2, which is a notable difference from the relation of PHV and genitalia development in boys.

Figure 15 shows the relation of breast and pubic hair stages. Here also considerable variation occurs, so that girls in stage B2 may show any stage of pubic hair development, about 55 per cent being still PH1, 20 per cent PH2, 20 per cent PH3, and 5 per cent PH4 or 5. By the time they reach B4, however, few girls are still in PH1 and by B5, none.

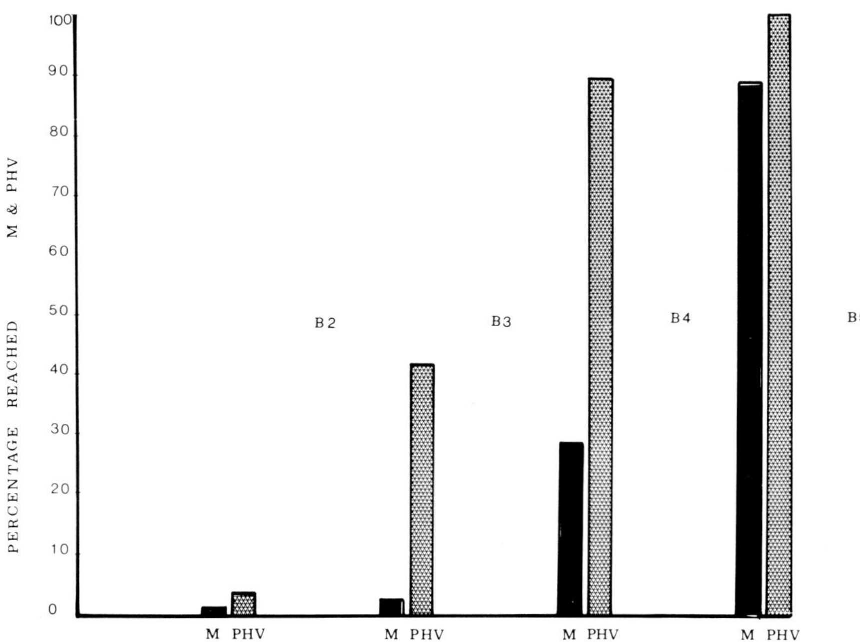

FIG. 14. Percentage of girls who had reached menarche (M) and peak height velocity (PHV) before reaching each successive stage of breast development (B). From Marshall & Tanner (1969).

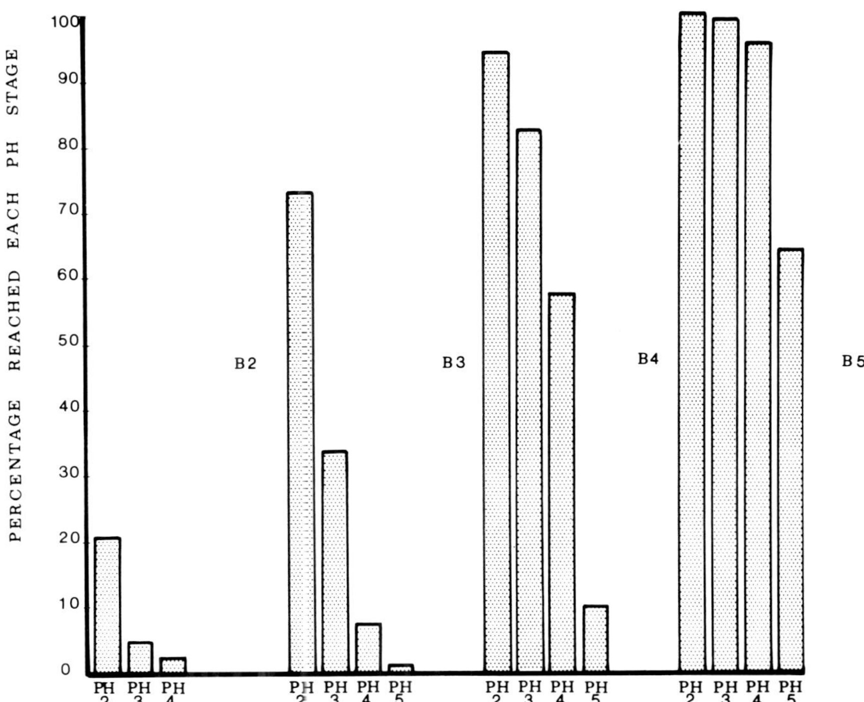

FIG. 15. Percentage of girls who had reached each stage of pubic hair development before reaching each stage of breast development. B2, B3, etc., represent the moments of reaching the corresponding breast stages. Thus the histogram between B2 and B3 shows the percentage of girls in breast stage 2 who reached each pubic hair stage before they reached the third breast stage. From Marshall & Tanner (1969).

Length of Puberty and Age at Puberty

Our data enabled us to examine the question whether children who started puberty early passed rapidly through the stages and those late passed slowly, as had been supposed (Tanner, 1962) largely on statistically invalid grounds. Taking the interval B2 to menarche to represent duration of puberty in girls, we calculated the correlation coefficient between this and the age of the midpoint of this interval (which gives an unbiased statistic (Marshall & Tanner, 1969). The coefficient was not significantly different from zero. In the boys the duration of the G2 to G5 and the PH3 to PH5 intervals were correlated with their ages at midpoints, and again the values were insignificantly different from zero.

We now consider the relation between age and pubertal events, recently examined by Marshall (1973). It has long been said that although men-

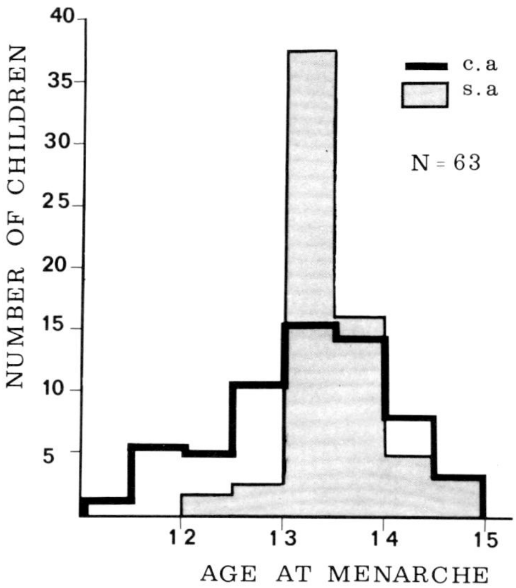

FIG. 16. Variation of chronological (CA) and skeletal (SA) ages at menarche. From Marshall (1973).

arche varies greatly as far as chronological age is concerned it varies much less in terms of skeletal age. Our data show this to be true; the ratio of the variances of chronological age at menarche to skeletal age at menarche is 5.2 ($p<0.001$).

Figure 16 illustrates this point by showing the distribution of chronological and bone ages for the same girls at menarche; the effective range is 10 to 15 for chronological age, but 12 to 14.5 for bone age.

This high association, however, by no means holds for some other events of puberty. Figure 17 shows the distribution for PHV, which is not significantly narrowed, the variance ratio being only 1.3. Figure 18 shows pubic hair; here the distribution is somewhat narrowed, the variance ratio of 1.7 being significant at 5 per cent. Figure 19a gives the ratio for B2 and Fig. 19b for B5, with no narrowing at all in the distribution; both events are no more closely related to bone than to chronological age. It is clear, therefore, that, whatever controls bone age progression exerts a considerable influence over the events culminating in menarche and, to a lesser extent, over pubic hair development. It exerts no control over breast development. We can only suppose that androgens are even more important in the development of the female reproductive system than we thought.

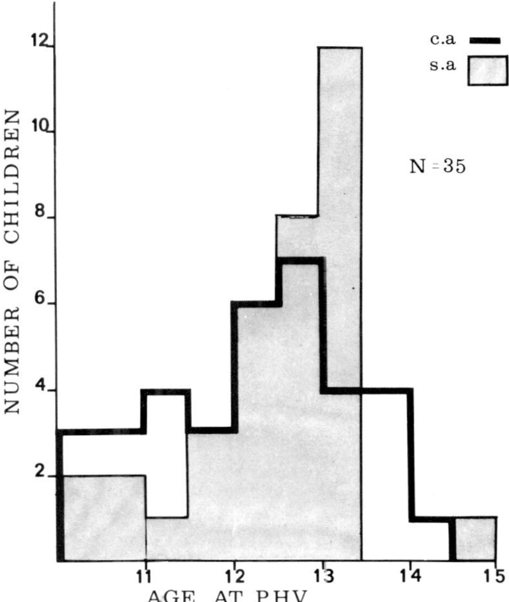

FIG. 17. Variation of chronological (CA) and skeletal (SA) ages at peak height velocity. From Marshall (1973).

To give more specific endocrinological explanations of the events, their sequence and timing, is not within the scope of the present brief summary. Perhaps that is as well, for we have none at present.

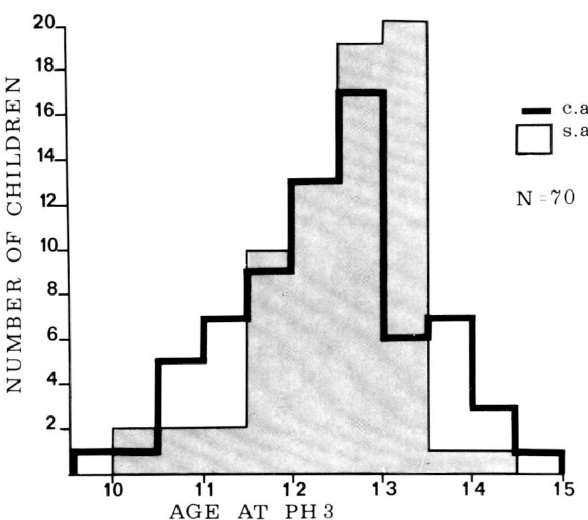

FIG. 18.   Variation of chronological (CA) and skeletal (SA) ages at pubic hair stage 3. From Marshall (1973).

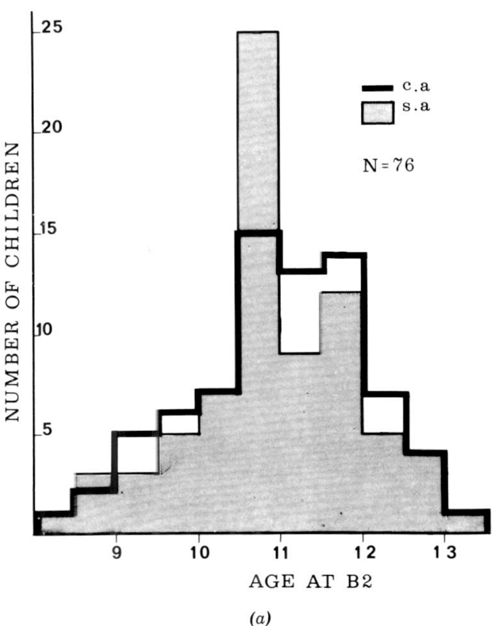

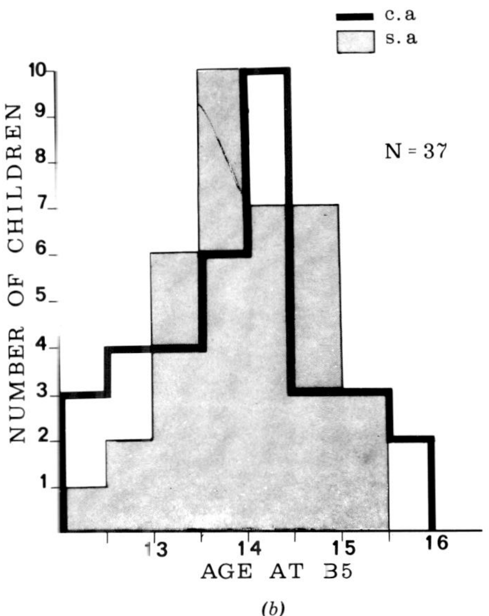

FIG. 19. Variation of chronological (CA) and skeletal (SA) ages at B2 (*a*) and B5 (*b*). From Marshall (1973).

REFERENCES

Huhges, P. C. R. & Tanner, J. M. (1970). A longitudinal study of the growth of the black-hooded rat; method of measurement and rates of growth for skull, limbs, pelvis, nose-rump and tail lengths. *J. Anat.* **106**, 349–370.

Marshall, W. A. (1973). Variation in skeletal maturation at puberty, in normal girls. In press.

Marshall, W. A. & Tanner, J. M. (1969). Variation in the pattern of pubertal changes in girls. *Arch. Dis. Childh.* **44**, 291–303.

Marshall, W. A. & Tanner, J. M. (1970). Variation in the pattern of pubertal changes in boys. *Arch. Dis. Childh.* **45**, 13–23.

Tanner, J. M. (1962). *Growth at Adolescence,* 2nd ed., Blackwell Scientific Publications, Oxford.

Tanner, J. M. (1967). Puberty. In *Advances in Reproductive Physiology,* Vol. II, A. McLaren, Ed., Logos, London.

Tanner, J. M. (1968). Growth of bone, muscle and fat during childhood and adolescence. In *Growth and Development of Mammals,* G. E. Lodge, Ed., Butterworth, London.

Tanner, J. M. (1969). Growth and Endocrinology of the adolescent. In *Endocrine and Genetic Diseases of Childhood,* L. Gardner, Ed., Saunders, Philadelphia.

Tanner, J. M. & Whitehouse, R. H. (1962). Standards for subcutaneous fat in British children. Percentile for thickness of skinfolds over triceps and below scapula. *Brit. Med. J.* **1**, 446–450.

Tanner, J. M., Whitehouse, R. H., Healy, M. J. R., Marshall, W. A., & Goldstein, H. (1973). A revised system (TLII) for estimating skeletal maturity from hand and wrist radiographs, with separate standards for carpals and other bones. In press.

Tanner, J. M. Whitehouse, R. H., & Takaishi, M. (1965). Standards from birth to maturity for height, weight, height velocity, and weight velocity in British children 1965. *Arch. Dis. Childh.* **41**, 454–471; 613–635.

Tuttenham, R. D. & Snyder, M. M. (1954). Physical growth of California boys and girls from birth to eighteen years. *Univ. Calif. Publ. Child Developm.* **1**, 183–364.

DISCUSSION

Dr. Heald. A word of caution about measures of body composition, particularly in the adolescent: all measures of body composition in humans are indirect measures. We really do not know how accurate they are. Ultimate accuracy in their determination by indirect measures can be achieved only by comparison with carcass analysis. Therefore any predictive equations based on unvalidated methods, with unknown degrees of accuracy, further compound the degrees of inaccuracy. I want to caution Dr. Frisch about using some of the predictive equations for body composition in adolescents.

Dr. Van Wyk. Dr. Heald, I understand the technical problems about verifying the analytic methods in humans, but cannot these methods be checked in other species? Why must one depend on human measurements to validate these techniques?

Dr. Heald. Although they have been checked in other animals, I am not familiar with the data.

Dr. Hamill. In our data from the National Health Examination Survey (HES), which we are just starting to publish, the observed findings go along with Dr. Tanner's observations on the diminution of fat increment coincident with the adolescent growth spurt. He observed a great deal of "statistical noise" in cross-sectional data such as ours, due to the difference in phasing of the individually timed growth spurts. Even so, we still demonstrate a sharp diminution in the skinfold's increment. Despite the noise, we can conclude that there is an actual decrement or negative arm fat growth in boys; and as Dr. Tanner showed in girls the increment of fat dips sharply, coincident with the peak height velocity, and it approaches zero. It would fall slightly below zero if it were not for the "statistical noise" caused by the difference of phasing from the cross-sectional data. Our nationally *observed* data definitely support Dr. Tanner's observation on fat accumulation and are quite contrary to Dr. Frisch's predictions. From what we see it looks as if the HES data (which represent all pubescent children in the United States from 1966 to 1970) will put American boys only 1½ years behind the girls, both at peak height and peak weight velocities and other indices, but we do not yet know why. Possibly the secular change toward earlier puberty in the technologically advanced countries in the last century may account for it; the girls' secular increase might have greatly slowed or stopped altogether in the 1950s, but the boys' increase continued, which, of course, would narrow the gap.

DR. BLIZZARD.   The data concerning LH and FSH, which we published quite some time ago, showed that the LH and FSH increased at essentially the same age in males and females, which fits fairly well with Dr. Tanner's data. The onset of the growth spurts differs a great deal. Dr. Tanner indicated that males may have their average growth spurt approximately 18 months after the females. Our LH and FSH data are consistent with these data also, for females reach adult levels of FSH and LH before males.

DR. VAN WYK.   Dr. Frisch, is there a preferred month for menarche, since there is a pronounced variation in the rate of both weight and height increase, depending on the season of the year. I would also like to ask Dr. Tanner how he handles seasonal differences in the rate of growth in the kind of data he is collecting.

DR. FRISCH.   Seasonal variation in age of menarche has been observed, but it is hard to interpret the data. The peak frequency is in winter in cities and towns and in summer in rural areas. Altitude and the age at menarche apparently also affect the seasonal variation (Valsik, 1965).

DR. CHEEK.   The loss of fat in the male at puberty is relative to muscle, and actually there is little change in total fat. We have discussed the relationship between somatic growth and hormones in the initiation of puberty. Dr. Donovan drew attention in his book to the fact that seals apparently have a nonrelationship between sexual maturation and the somatic growth spurt.

DR. FAIMAN.   We should readdress ourselves to the topic of this conference— the control of the onset of puberty. We should remember that correlative findings do not necessarily signify any cause-effect relationship. LBM, depending on whose data you believe, reaches a peak around the age of 30 and then goes downhill inexorably; Dr. Cheek says that this correlated nicely with testosterone production. I have no data directly bearing on testosterone production, but the good news, insofar as unbound serum testosterone is concerned, is that there does not appear to be a decline in the male until around the age of 45.

REFERENCE

Valšik, A. (1965). Seasoned rhythm of menarche, a review. *Human Biol.* **37**, 75–91.

CONCLUDING COMMENTS

Dr. Donovan. Because it is not possible to abstract 12 hours or more of talk in 25 minutes, I shall limit myself to the control mechanisms and to rather personal impressions. One of the problems is the definition of puberty. Dr. Hayles's point is well taken—that we do not test the onset of puberty in human infants by determining whether they are fertile, although we do accept that the ability to reproduce is a fairly valid criterion. In this respect I would take issue with Dr. Dierschke, who defined puberty on the basis of the ability of the hypothalamus to release gonadotropin in response to estrogen. If it is intended to be a general definition, then it certainly does not apply to the sheep, guinea-pig, or rat, in which you can get this effect before puberty occurs normally. Dr. Van Wyk's suggestion, that we should define puberty as the time when pubic hair crinkles, is difficult to apply to creatures such as the gorilla and elephant!

An important point was made by Dr. Weisz and elaborated on by Dr. Schwartz on gonadal structure, when they pointed out that rat ovaries at 10, 20, and 30 days of age are quite different. It is still necessary to distinguish between the responses of the germinal epithelium in the gonad and the endocrine tissue, although the distinction is blurred by the fact that the follicles can themselves produce hormones. The endocrine response of the gonad to trophic stimulation can also change during development. The best-studied example is the change in the ratio of androstenedione to testosterone produced by the testis during sexual maturation.

The question of the refractoriness of the gonads to stimulation is an old one and the subject of some classical work by Price and Ortiz in the early 1940's. It was raised again by Drs. Odell and Swerdloff, who were concerned with the effects of gonadotropins on hormone secretion in hypophysectomized rats. Could the apparent refractoriness be due to inappropriate stimulation? The point made by Odell and Swerdloff, that the insensitivity to LH was removed by the administration of FSH, could be exceedingly important. Perhaps our discussions have paid too little attention to the role of the pituitary gland in sexual development. I should like to have heard more about the hormones (or the hormone cocktail) needed to precipitate sexual development. How much FSH is needed? How much LH? Is prolactin essential?

I remain a bit unhappy about the significance of the high levels of FSH and LH in the blood of prepubertal animals, as assayed immunologically, and should like to be reassured about the biological activity of this material.

When endocrine research was undertaken at the beginning of this century, a lot of work was done in which the ovaries of adults were transplanted to infants of various species. The general conclusion was that the mature ovaries, which were, of course, responsive to gonadotropin, did not show activity in the infant. Why is this if the infant is secreting large amounts of gonadotropin? Perhaps these experiments need to be looked at again.

From some of the remarks made by Dr. Ross it seems that caution is advisable before equating the immunologically assayable hormones of the pituitary with the activity detectable in serum or urine. This is necessary in view of different antigenicities and species-variability. Here lack of knowledge even permits the speculation that the gonadotropins of the infant are not the same as those of the adult. It is possible, though not necessarily likely, that the infant pituitary can form only part of the complete molecule, such as the α-chain, and that gonadal development occurs as the pituitary gains the capacity to add the β-chain to form the adult hormone. The gonadal hormones could operate to favor the synthesis of the complete hormone. Such a mechanism could account for the change in pituitary sensitivity to releasing factors.

It has been implied, on several occasions, that a high secretion of gonadotropin early in life reflects a high output of hypothalamic releasing factor. This point needs to be established; for example, Dr. Grumbach pointed out that the human fetus may produce large amounts of FSH and LH. The serum concentration of FSH in the human fetus reaches a peak at 150 days and then falls as birth approaches. Is a hypothalamic releasing factor involved in the control of FSH secretion at this time?

Dr. Schwartz pointed out that although there are differences in species there is general agreement that in the rat, sheep, monkey, and man there is a high neonatal secretion of gonadotropin, then a fall, followed by a rise as puberty approaches. Now, if this general impression is sustained, attention should be focused on the fall in output of gonadotropins after the neonatal peak, not on the high level of secretion neonatally or at puberty. Analysis of the basis of this inhibition during infancy may be much more revealing than the studies of the mechanisms promoting release of gonadotropins. If the main factor in human puberty is the restraint on the pituitary gland exercised by the hypothalamus, how do we account for the fall in FSH secretion during the latter half of gestation? What removes the inhibition before birth, so that high levels are recorded neonatally? More attempts should be made to account for the differences in the latent period between birth and puberty. What makes the interval so long in primates, shorter in cattle and sheep, and very short in rats, mice, and guinea-pigs? What is the basis of the clock that determines the remarkable consistency in the time of puberty for each species?

This brings me to the brain. What is known of the influence of the hypothalamus and extrahypothalamic structures, so well reviewed by Drs. Davidson and Gorski? Unquestionably the hypothalamus is involved in the control of puberty, for hypothalamic lesions can advance puberty, but, as Dr. Ganong emphasized, the mechanism of action of the lesion is not known. If the process that inhibits secretion of gonadotropins were disturbed, then one would expect that the earlier a lesion were placed the sooner sexual maturation would occur. This is not so. Does the observation of Dr. Ramirez and his colleagues, that lesions in the hypothalamus of rats which advance puberty do not increase secretion of FSH or LH, point to the operation of some hitherto unsuspected factor? Should we look more carefully at changes in the secretion of prolactin, GH, ACTH, or even TSH?

Dr. Gorski pointed out that the activities of the hippocampus and amygdala in the control of secretion of gonadotropin appear to be reversed during infancy. In the adult the amygdala seems to promote release of gonadotropins, whereas in infancy it appears to exert an inhibition. This is a plausible concept until you try to decide what is really meant. At present I cannot think of any other neural mechanism whose activity is reversed in this way. If reversal does occur, where does the change take place? Within the hippocampus, amygdala, or the hypothalamus? Do the neurons in the hypothalamus, on which limbic axons synapse, change their function or do the connections themselves alter?

The locus of action of steroids on the brain has been studied with the aid of labeled hormones, but, as Dr. Eisenfeld stated, such work on the uptake of gonadal steroids has yet to contribute significantly to our understanding of the timing of puberty. This is perhaps not surprising in view of the highly labile and pulsatile nature of pituitary hormone secretion that has been observed in adolescents, chimpanzees, monkeys, and rats. I should like to have heard more on this point from Dr. Johnson. Does a hypothalamic lesion advance puberty by altering the periodicity of the spurts? Does it alter the number or the magnitude of the pulses of gonadotropin?

The lack of a positive feedback action of estrogen in promoting secretion of gonadotropin in the monkey was emphasized by Dr. Dierschke, but what is positive feedback? What do we mean by it? Is it an alteration in the rhythmicity of gonadotropin release or an increase in the amplitude of the spurts? If estrogen is inserted into the hypothalamus of the guinea-pig and left there, secretion of gonadotropin seems to be first increased and then depressed. How is this brought about?

Despite our preoccupation with puberty we should not forget that the hypothalamus controls more than the functions of the ovaries and testes. Besides other endocrine glands, it regulates body weight, body temperature, antidiuretic and oxytocic hormone secretion, food intake, water intake, and a variety of patterns of behavior. Hence it is to be expected that these activities are integrated with one another. This brings me to Dr. Frisch's critical weight hypothesis. There is much evidence that menarche commonly occurs at a critical weight, but it does not necessarily mean that the two are causally related. The events resulting in menarche have been set in motion long before the critical weight is reached. Dr. Blizzard explored the hormonal basis of growth and concluded that the rapid growth near puberty was due to the action of testosterone. Should we therefore reverse Dr. Frisch's concept and say that a critical weight is reached at menarche?

The factors influencing the timing of puberty have been largely ignored in our deliberations. Yet an analysis of the mode of action of exteroceptive factors such as olfaction, vision, and environmental lighting could prove to be illuminating! As Dr. Geschwind pointed out, work on seasonally breeding species is extremely relevant, and I am glad to see that the new methods of hormone assay are being applied to sheep. It would be intriguing if a pulsatile pattern of secretion of gonadotropin were demonstrable outside the breeding season in the ruminant.

Index

D = Discussion

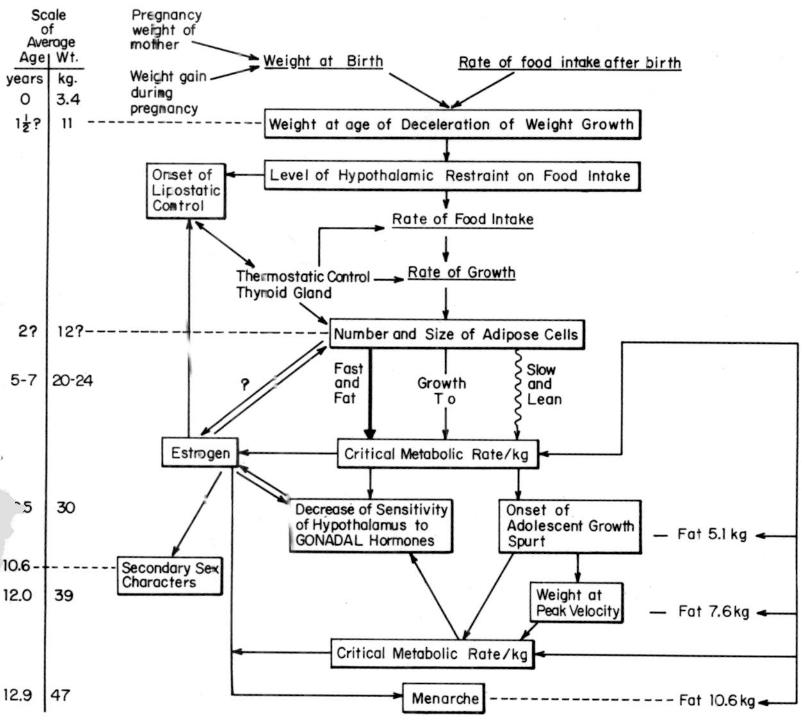

HYPOTHETICAL SCHEME OF THE RELATION BETWEEN BODY WEIGHT, SIZE OF ADIPOSE TISSUE, AND ONSET OF PUBERTY IN CAUCASIAN GIRLS.

Fig. 2

Top

Courtesy of Dr. R.E. Frisch, Critical weight at menarche, from *Control of Onset of Puberty*, M.M. Grumbach, G.D. Grave, and F.E. Mayer (editors) New York, John Wiley & Sons, 1974, pp. 403-423